THE EUROPEAN ALTERNATIVES
An Inquiry into the Policies of the European Community

THE EUROPEAN ALTERNATIVES

An Inquiry into the Policies of the European Community

Edited by

Ghita Ionescu

professor of government
University of Manchester

preface by

Roy Jenkins

president, Commission of the European Communities

SIJTHOFF & NOORDHOFF   1979
Alphen aan den Rijn – The Netherlands

Proceedings of the Conference on "The European Alternatives", jointly organized by the Commission of the European Community, the European Parliament and the Research Committee for European Unification of the International Political Science Association, Brussels, 9–11 June 1977.

ISBN 90 286 0278 X

Printed in the Netherlands.

PREFACE

I think that all of us who are concerned with European integration will find *The European Alternatives* both original and useful.

This book has been published as a result of the conference organized in June 1977 by the Research Committee on European Unification of the International Political Science Association, in collaboration with the European Commission and the European Parliament. The purpose of the conference, and of the two years of research which preceded it, was to study present and possible future policies of the European Community by comparing them with similar policies already carried out at national level by member states. The authors have thus posed the problem of how and whether Community policies can be considered as valid alternatives to national policies. How practicable, effective, and acceptable to public opinion are those which exist? And how should future ones be prepared and presented to the Member States and peoples of the Community?

The European Commission and the European Parliament have always been glad to encourage academic research on European integration, and I applaud an initiative which has brought together political scientists from all over the world. I hope that the present project is only the beginning of cooperation on this subject between practitioners and academics.

The forthcoming direct elections to the European Parliament will provide the first opportunity for the citizens of the Member States to think and act as citizens of the Community. The experience of the first elections will be crucial in the political history of Europe, but its importance will be immeasurably greater if its voters have effective knowledge of the real problems of how to make policy on a European scale.

I wish this book every success.

8 November 1977   President of the European Commission
                                                   Roy Jenkins

CONTENTS

VIII

LIST OF CONTRIBUTORS

Silain Bertoletti: Chief Administrator, Directorate-General for External Relations, Commission of the European Community.

Georges Bublot: Professor, University of Louvain.

Giuseppe Ciavarini-Azzi: Divisional Director, Secretariat-General of the Commission of the European Community.

A. J. Cockerill: Senior Lecturer, University of Salford.

C. A. Colliard: Professor, University of Paris.

Robert De Bauw: Divisional Director, Directorate-General for Energy, CEC.

Guy De Carmoy: Professor, Fondation Nationale de Sciences Politiques, Paris.

Hélène Delorme: Lecturer, Fondation Nationale de Sciences Politiques, Centre d'Etudes et de Recherches Internationales, Paris.

Karl Deutsch: Professor, Harvard University, USA.

Martin Edmonds: Professor, University of Lancaster.

Henri Etienne: Chief Adviser to the Secretariat-General of the Commission of the European Community.

Constantino Friz: Chief Adviser, Directorate-General for Internal Market and Industrial Affairs, CEC.

Pierre Gerbet: Professor, Fondation Nationale de Sciences Politiques, Paris.

Geoffrey L. Goodwin: Professor, London School of Economics.

D. C. Hague: Professor, University of Manchester.

Klaus von Helldorf: Chief Administrator, Directorate-General for Information.

R. Hrbek: Professor, University of Tübingen, Germany.

Ghita Ionescu: Professor, University of Manchester.

B. Küster: Chief Administrator, Directorate General/for Research and Documentation, European Parliament.

David Marquand: formerly Chief Adviser to the Secretariat-General of the Commission of the European Community, Professor, University of Salford.

James B. Mayall: Senior Lecturer, London School of Economics.

François Muller: Divisional Director, European Agricultural Guidance and Guarantee Fund, CEC.

Richard Nobbs: Chief Administrator, Directorate-General for Internal Market and Industrial Affairs, CEC.

Emile Noël: Secretary General of the Commission of the European Community.

Antonio Papisca: Professor, University of Catania, Italy.

John Pinder: Director, Policy Studies Institute, London.
Claude Pleinevaux: Director of special services to the Service of the Environment and Consumer Protection, CEC.
Karlheinz Reichert: Director, Directorate of Coal—Directorate-General for Energy, CEC.
Jean Rey: Former President of the European Commission.
G. K. Roberts: Reader, University of Manchester.
Jonathan Scheele: Administrator, Directorate-General for External Relations, CEC.
Dusan Sidjanski: Professor, University of Geneva, Switzerland.
John Taylor: General Director for Research and Documentation, European Parliament, Luxembourg.
Loukas Tsoukalis: Lecturer, Oxford University.
Roger Williams: Professor, University of Manchester.

INTRODUCTION

by *Emile Noël*

When my friend Ghita Ionescu spoke to me for the first time, early in 1976, about his project for the study of the "European Alternatives", I was at once attracted, even captivated, by the idea.

The meeting of the European Council in Rome had decided, a few weeks before, that the first direct elections to the European Parliament should be held in May/June 1978. But the British Prime Minister had expressed certain reservations. It was therefore even more gratifying that a project, directly linked with the European elections, should originate in the University of Manchester and that the initiative should have been taken before the arrangements for the elections had been finalized.

The success of these elections will depend above all on the awareness shown by the European citizens themselves, who are at the same time the actors and the stake of the future electoral campaign. I do not overestimate the import-ance of the contribution which institutions, by themselves, can make to the preparation and to the activation of the campaign. A spontaneous initiative, emerging, moreover, from academic circles, was all the more to be welcomed since it presaged the political resonance which the elections might achieve.

There is already a considerable number of European voters who see that Communitarian Europe provides both a framework for their own political options, and a broader dimension to these same options. For them, a deeper knowledge of the European mechanisms is one means of rendering their vote more useful and enabling them to influence Community activity more effectively. For those who doubt the Community's ability to produce a valid alternative, either because they distrust the European idea, or because they do not believe the Community to be capable of effective action, or more often than not because of simple ignorance, the "European Alternatives" will offer an opportunity to learn and to reflect on the basis of reliable data.

It is also probable that beyond the debate about ideas, the actual course of the campaign, and especially the extent of electoral participation, will be, in themselves, a test of the Community system. The Community system itself could be more objectively assessed if each citizen could grasp the impact which the election itself and therefore the eventual intervention of an elected Parliament, even with unchanged powers, would have on the functioning of the institutions of the Community. The "European Alternatives" will help one to appreciate what this change could be by examining the functioning of the institutions on the basis of objectively established facts and specific case studies.

It will have been noted that I attach particular importance to the contribution of precise information, which both can be, and has been checked, and on which the political campaign can be based. This approach to problems is characteristic of the British spirit and it is not surprising that such a project should have originated in a British University. On the other hand, the official services of the Community could not, much as they would like to, provide on their own, the basis for this kind of research. The very source of any data offered would make them appear controversial to some elements at least of public opinion. It is in this context that the originality and the usefulness of this project become even more apparent.

The credibility of the whole project has been reinforced by the choice of themes. To see the Community at work, examples were chosen to illustrate successful operations, failures, or attempts to find the right way. From the beginning, the authors involved in the project have stressed that their basic criterion was the feasibility of the policies they were studying. It was necessary to avoid falling into the trap of contrasting an apparently ideal world, represented by the Commission, with the world of the Member States, represented by the Council, seen as embodying the immobilism and the politics of the past. The authors knew only too well that in politics nothing succeeds like success. Failure—and indeed many actions of the Community have failed—might be attributed in some cases to the defects of the system, but in other cases it could be attributed to the mismanagement of some activities, or even to circumstances: the elector will have to work the causes out for himself.

In the preparation of the case studies and the drafting of the conclusions a dialectical procedure has been followed.

The files of the case-studies were prepared by members of the staff of the Community acting in a personal capacity. I would like to thank here those who undertook this task which went beyond their professional obligations. It was most gratifying to see the functionaries of the Community, more often than not those best acquainted with the problems, and therefore, the busiest, offering spontaneously to collaborate with the initiators of the project in order to provide a first, personal, contribution to the success of the European elections.

The basic files produced by the "practitioners" were then examined by the academics, backed up in some special cases by highly qualified experts. Thanks to the vast professional network of the Committee of Research on the Unification of Europe of the International Political Science Association (IPSA) the University world was widely informed of the project. The teams best qualified to do so undertook to examine the files of the case-studies in which they were most interested, thus ensuring that the dialectic was from the very beginning engaged at the highest level of expertise.

The conclusions of each of the case-studies, and subsequently the general conclusions were reached by a process of discussion between the teams of the Community and the teams of the Universities in the presence of eminent political scientists and politicians. I would like to thank them all.

The research project on the "European Alternatives" has been a happy one. In the first place it has been carried out at a brisk pace. Its general lines, initially conceived by Ghita Ionescu, were confirmed a few weeks later at a meeting between members of the IPSA Research Committee of European Unification and a number of high officials of the Community, including my colleagues Hans Nord, General Secretary of the European Parliament, and Professor John Taylor, General Director of Research of the European Parliament. Subsequently the Research Committee on European Unification endorsed the project.

The case-study files were made available to the Universities in the autumn of 1976. Then followed a period of intense exchanges of views and discussions between the Community officials, officials in charge of the case-studies, and the academic rapporteurs and their teams. The separate conclusions were drawn up at a plenary conference on 9–11 June 1977. The general conclusions have been drawn up in a masterly way by Professor Ionescu.

In most cases there were, at first, wide gaps between the initial positions of the authors of the Community files, and the ideas of the academic teams. A long time has passed since the period when academic researchers were mostly interested in the originality and novelty of the specific type of organization embodied by the European Community. The spell has been broken by the passage of time and by failure; political scientists now scrutinize the Community in a spirit of criticism, I would say even of contestation, which pounces on any sign of weakness. Yet, at the end of the discussions on each of the case-studies, gaps between the two sides were noticeably narrowed and, in the majority of cases agreement on a common diagnosis had been reached. At the same time a new type of relationship, deeper and more open, grew up between the European officials and the University teams, contributing a great deal to the remarkable narrowing of the gap between the differing standpoints. I sincerely hope that this first experiment will not remain an isolated case.

Irrespective of individual opinions or preferences, it is highly probable that the institutional system of the Community will not undergo profound changes in the near future. But experience also teaches us that there are considerable possibilities for the modification of the system from within. As I have already mentioned, direct elections to the European Parliament will multiply these possibilities, and this justifies the mobilization of the citizens.

The system of the Community has been and will continue to be based on one pole of initiative represented by the Commission and one pole of acceptance represented by the Member States grouped in the Council. The Commission has moreover the duty to supervise the application of the Treaty and to administer what has been agreed upon, all decisions of the Community being ultimately subject to the scrutiny of the Court of Justice.

A close and careful study of the reports and counter-reports of the project on the European Alternatives gives the impression that the weaknesses and the failures which have been singled out can be attributed in most cases to a lack of "enmeshment" with reality and with public opinion. A more active supervision of policy-making of the Community could therefore lead to a clear improvement of its quality.

As far as the Commission is concerned, its action would gather more momentum if and when the Council and the Committee of Permanent Representatives were faced by a body which would examine problems from other vantage-points than their own. The Commission would find it less difficult to reject the responsibilities it is asked to assume without being given the corresponding powers, and it would also be in a better position to demand the means and the powers which it needs. On the other hand, the Commission would not be so easily forgiven any lack of coherence, or partial viewpoints. Situated within the parallelogram of forces of the future elected Parliament, the Commission would find itself, in this respect, in a position comparable in some ways to that of the government of one of the Member States of the Nine toward its own Parliament.

The studies in this book also cast a new light on one so-called weakness of the European Community namely, that it "does not have a government which governs". If the theme of the research had been "The national alternatives" the failures and disappointments encountered in that field would not have been very different from those encountered in the European field. The national governments, too, would be seen to be engaged, like the institutions of the Community, in a process of permanent negotiations and exposed to political pressures and counter pressures from very different quarters. A government can only seldom command and decide by itself, with due effectiveness. The intrinsic superiority of the European alternative, with its broader dimensions, its more lasting perspectives and its spirit of innovation, should therefore lead it to prevail in the end. This would be even more likely if the European alternative were to enjoy in the future the support which it has missed most until now, namely that of public opinion finding an outlet in a restless and alert Parliament.

Two examples drawn from the present work will help to illustrate both the capacity of the Community system to transform itself, and the speed of its evolution. I will compare here only the situation in June 1977, when the conclusions of the reports and counter-reports were drawn, and the situation in December 1977, as I finish this Introduction.

For methodological purposes, the Economic and Monetary Union, and the March 1971 Resolution of the Council with regard to the Union, were classified in the Research Project among the initiatives which had failed. Yet, only three months after this classification, the public debate has been launched again, on the initiative of Roy Jenkins, President of the Commission, in his Florence speech, which received (even as early as December 1977) the backing or encouragement of the Heads of States or of governments who met in the European Council. The monetary upheaval provoked by the fall of the dollar emphasized with increasing obviousness the need for action. In April 1978 the European Council, on the initiative of the Chancellor Schmidt, endorsed the idea of creating a zone of monetary stability in Europe. At the next session of the Council (Bremen, July 1978) a precise time-table was approved on the basis of a Franco-German working paper, with a view to taking decisions before the end of the year. It is expected that these decisions will be put into effect as from the beginning of 1979. At the same time, the European Council adopted the propositions of a common strategy for economic growth and for employment. Thus the project of Economic and Monetary Union became again a live political reality.

What a spectacular about-turn also, within one year, in the textile policy!

Within just a few months, and in spite of very serious difficulties, the Community, without any dissent, has defined and set up a new external regime, and nobody denies today that the framework of the Community is the most appropriate for effecting the prescribed self-limitations as well as for the transformation of the textile industry. This observation illustrates the fact that the Community does not confine itself to long-term action or to deliberations unrelated to present day problems. The Community, like the Member States, may be called upon to act under the pressure of events—and it has proved that it can do so. If tomorrow elections render it more responsive to the needs of the citizens and to the pressure of public opinion, its institutions can only learn and benefit from such a change. In turn this closer contact with the realities of daily life will be reflected in speedier and more committed Communitarian activity.

In the period of economic and social crisis through which we are now living, is not this the best way to give the European Alternatives more credibility, more power, a wider audience?

AGRICULTURAL POLICY

I. AGRICULTURAL POLICY REPORT

Agricultural Surplus in the European Community, with Specific Reference to Beef, Veal and Dairy Products

by *François Muller*

STRENGTHS AND WEAKNESSES OF THE COMMON AGRICULTURAL POLICY

The CAP, over a short period of years (1962–1970), substituted a set of Community rules for lopsided national controls

This huge task, accomplished in many cases over a very short period compared with the time previously taken to establish the national controls, involved a drastic overhaul of market mechanisms. By introducing common prices, organizing domestic markets with a view to securing minimum prices for farmers, regulating trade across the Community frontier by means of import levies and, concomitantly, export aids known as refunds, the authors of the CAP demonstrated the will to unify European agriculture. Such an approach was the more meritorious in that this economic sector was in many cases the one least open to competition. Not only does the CAP ensure minimum prices for types of farming heavily dependent on trade and industry, as in the case of many raw material producers, but it has promoted the modernization, specialization and increased productivity of farm units. The dismantling of national protectionist barriers has allowed competition to develop over a huge area, thus helping towards the rationalization of certain productions.

It has, however, three weak points:
   a. *A degree of isolation of the CAP from overall economic policies.*
   An economic sector can hardly be fitted into a multinational organization over a prolonged period if in the individual countries it is hedged in by monetary and financial economic policies whose priorities are national. The founders of the CAP counted on the generalized application of European policies in vital economic areas; but this failed to materialize, and the CAP suffers the painful consequences. Increasingly frequent monetary crises endanger the whole system. Not only did "sluice-gates" have to be hurriedly erected to allow goods to pass from one monetary area to another under broadly satisfactory competitive conditions, but the race to uphold or restore market unity triggered off particularly drastic price rises in some Member States. Where these outstripped the climb in production costs, the effect has been to boost production while putting a brake on consumption. In the longer prospect a combination of out-of-step currencies and an attempt to achieve a unified market can create or aggravate certain market disequilibria. For instance, meat production in Ireland and that of tobacco in Italy have been given a boost by devaluation of their "green" currencies, whereas the same phenomenon has inhibited butter consumption in the United Kingdom.

b. *Incompleteness of the CAP in that it is too strictly limited to market policies.*
The structural aspect has not been given sufficient importance, but above all national aids are playing a growing part in the agricultural policies. These aids are on the whole helpful in improving farm structures, enlarging social security and supplementing incomes, but they superimpose predominantly national aims on community targets. While the latter are often achieved, the effects may be contradictory. For instance, stock-raisers are given an incentive, by various forms of aid, to maintain the size of herds, while at the same time the Community urges more slaughtering in order to reduce dairy surpluses.

c. *The hurried installation of market control mechanisms under often unfavourable political and technical conditions.*
After a first phase of installing a market policy, the Community embarked on one of improving it, more especially in respect of market equilibrium. Hence the periodical reviews of the CAP. At the Council's request, the Commission carried out a review exercise whose outcome was a report in 1973 on "adjustments to the CAP"[1] and one in 1975 on "A stocktaking of the CAP".[2] One object of these reviews is precisely to look for improved market equilibrium, which can only be done by far-reaching sectorial analysis. These overall reviews have served to highlight structural surpluses in the dairy produce sector, which prompted the Commission to draw up an action programme in July 1976.

STOCKS, SHORTAGES AND SURPLUSES

It must also be borne in mind that agriculture cannot be kept in being in an industrial society without a minimum of intervention mechanisms, irrespective of the methods adopted, by reason of the specific characteristics of farm economics. The best proof is that all modern States, whether Switzerland, Austria, Sweden, the USA or Canada, have their own market policy. The OECD was the first international organization to compare the various methods used.[3]

Characteristics of laws of supply and demand.

The first reason is that the laws of supply and demand have in the case of agriculture their own characteristics differing in some ways from those for other types of product.

Supply is not so readily controllable as in the case of an industrial product. Despite substantial technological advances, and farmers' greater knowledge and ability to overcome the obstacles they encounter, *climatic conditions* still definitely affected harvests, especially in respect of insolation and rainfall. The complexity of these two natural factors lies not only in their numerical size but also in their duration and season of occurrence. The extreme case is that of a violent hailstorm which may to all intents and purposes ruin a future crop and vintage. Conversely, particularly favourable weather may produce a crop of apples 20% better than average, as in 1975. Sugar is also sensitive to climatic conditions, though these are admittedly less important for other products such as milk and meat. They are the cause of gluts, but also of shortages (sugar in 1973, potatoes in 1976).

Furthermore, *most agricultural products ripen over a period of a few weeks or months,* whereas consumption is spread over the whole year. Hence the need of stockpiling (wheat for bakery purposes, canned fruit). Milk and eggs are among the few steady products, although they follow seasonal cycles.

Lastly, *there are production cycles of several years, varying from one product to another, reminiscent of the biblical "fat kine" and "lean kine".* Man has not yet fully mastered these cycles, whose contributory factors include the inherent nature of the product (it takes two to four years to rear fatstock), climatic conditions (good and bad vintage years) and human behaviour (in times of short supply and high prices, production is stimulated to the point of creating, after a while, temporary surpluses). The cycles are attenuated, or in some cases aggravated by the parameters of up-to-date technology (a drastic speed-up in production at a time of shortages creates in turn a situation of marked surpluses), or politico-economic factors (e.g., a belated slowing down of imports towards the end of a period of shortage tends thereafter to make the ensuing phase of surplus more severe).

There is a certain rigidity of demand, too
Increased consumption tails off at a given level, even if the price is attractive. As standards of living rise, consumption turns towards richer commodities (less bread and potatoes, more meat), more elaborate products (growing proportion of processing costs, or even just packaging, in the cost of manufacture) or more easily assimilated articles. New mental attitudes evolve, or new taboos (butter as a source of cholesterol, according to medical opinion); advertising applies artificial stimuli (brands of margarine). Hence, the authorities have to contend with unforeseen or belatedly observed trends without being able to apply a brake on supply or give a boost to demand.

Hence, a market economy has to have public instruments and procedures enabling very prompt government action to face new situations. There has to be a permanent monitoring of new substitute products of agricultural (maize sugar) or industrial (synthetic petroleum-based meat) origins.

It is no easy matter, then, to achieve complete control of agricultural markets, and unwanted surpluses may occur.

But public opinion only notices the epiphenomenon of a glut in production, to decry or condemn a whole policy. Deep down, it still clings to a sort of notion of the sanctity of food. Older people think back to the privations of wartime, and the young grieve over the prevalence of starvation throughout the world. Historians remind us that we do not have to go back very far in European history to come across famines such as triggered off the French Revolution at the end of the 18th century, and migration to America during the 19th. Do we realize that the last great famine occurred in Ireland in the 1850's and that large numbers perished?

Mountains of scrapped cars and squandered finance are causes of inflation that leave public opinion unmoved, whereas the wilful destruction of surplus fruit is stridently denounced.

It is therefore worthwhile to take a closer look at farm surpluses and possible ways of disposing of them.

To begin with, we cannot talk about surpluses without mentioning *shortages*. Fortunately, farm shortages are rare and are considerably mitigated by the machinery of the CAP. Had there been no high import subsidies for sugar in 1974/75, the situation would have been parlous, especially in Italy and the United Kingdom; without stockpiling when such a product is in abundant supply, and a carry-over to the following crop year, things would be very difficult. Thus, in 1973 200,000 t. of wheat were handed over, by the market intervention authorities in France, Germany and Belgium, to Italy where, especially in parts of the South, there was a famine scare; in 1976 large quantities of powdered milk, and beef and veal, were allocated, as well as wheat.

Let us not forget that with a climate and soils comparable to those of Western Europe, the USSR and East European countries are, for a great many reasons, often on the brink of a shortage.

A clear distinction has to be drawn between *normal stockpiling* in farm cooperatives, industrial and commercial concerns, and in reasonable quantities by the intervention authorities (public, or government recognized private bodies), and the notion of *surpluses*. However, such a distinction is not easily made. Whenever a real surplus arises, normal stocking and surplus supply merge into one another. It is, on the contrary, when there is no surplus, or in the event of a risk of shortfall, that normal stocking should be continued or upgraded. In societies where there are never any surpluses, shortage prevails unless substantial quantities are imported or the financial means for doing so are available, or gifts are donated on humanitarian or political grounds.

One of the problems of organizing world markets is in fact the formation of buffer and market-stabilizing stocks.

Another aspect is that of seasonal stocks. For example, the verdant meadows of springtime mean a rise in output of milk and butter. But in winter, when feeds are less rich the fall in production involves drawing on butter produced in the spring or summer. Seasonal stocking is useful for smoothing consumer supplies.

To sum up, therefore:
– systems of intervention on agricultural markets are a necessity in any modern society;
– a reasonable level of seasonal or permanent stocking is useful for matching supply and demand, and is quite another matter from accumulating surpluses.

It is not easy to define what constitutes a surplus. In the case of an agricultural product, it means anything in excess of a normal stock for a protracted period, involving marketing difficulties or substantial losses. The threshold varies greatly from one product to another, depending on market outlets and technical storage facilities. Thus, as wheat can be stored for a long time with no loss of quality, the quantitative level constituting a surplus is higher than in the case of beef and veal, whose quality is automatically downgraded during cold storage with an inevitable loss of value. There is also some depreciation in the case of butter in cold storage.

In some cases, e.g., fruit and vegetables, conservation in a fresh state is very difficult. Therefore, a surplus does not mean holding undue quantities in storage, but direct retention or destruction at the producer's, as the only means of ensuring an often modest but real profit.

The butter mountains of a few years back, and the more recent ones of milk powder, beef and veal have particularly scandalized public opinion. These two sectors therefore need to be scrutinized, to judge whether such surpluses are unavoidable, a kind of natural calamity, or whether they show up deficiencies of policy and organization that could be remedied.

BEEF AND VEAL: A CYCLICAL OR A STRUCTURAL SURPLUS?

The bovine sector is of particular interest, inasmuch as a surplus arose in 1974, was amplified in 1975 and remained at a high level in 1976. We may therefore inquire into its origins, and whether it is temporary or permanent.

The beef and veal market

The trend in size of herds and output of meat has been as follows:

	No. of livestock (millions)	Meat production (millions of tonnes)
1968	72.76	5.53
1969	72.79	5.5
1970	71.92	5.78
1971	71.81	5.85
1972	74.82	5.29
1973	78.86	5.36
1974	79.33	6.48
1975	77.46	6.6
1976	76.90	6.28
1977	77.05	6.18

To account for this, we should first remember that the average production cycle for bovine meat is about 6 years. The cycles varied from country to country, but the establishment of the Common Market has made them more alike. The cycle varied from a minimum output in 1972/73 to a maximum in 1974/75, and is likely to be at a minimum again in 1978. This is confirmed by production forecasts for 1976 and 1977.

This natural phenomenon was *accentuated for 4 reasons*, fixed agricultural prices, imports, farmers' attitudes and the intervention system.

i. The trend in the guide prices fixed by the Council of Ministers, as an indication for determining market prices, was as shown on p. 8.

7

Harvest year 1968/69	68	UA/100 kg live carcase meat*
1969/70	68	UA/100 kg live carcase meat
1970/71	68	UA/100 kg live carcase meat
1971/72	72	UA/100 kg live carcase meat
1972/73		
(1st stage)	75	UA/100 kg live carcase meat
(2nd stage)	78	UA/100 kg live carcase meat
1973/74	86.2	UA/100 kg live carcase meat
1974/75		
(1st stage)	96.5	UA/100 kg live carcase meat
(2nd stage)	101.33	UA/100 kg live carcase meat
1975/76	109.94	UA/100 kg live carcase meat
1976/77	118.74	UA/100 kg live carcase meat

* One UA = the green unit of account used for the purposes of the CAP, at exchange rates determined by the EEC Council of Ministers.

After three years of stagnation, prices were raised by decision of the Council, with a consequent growth incentive from 1972 on. The rise of 26% in 3 years was intended, quite apart from its function of improving farm incomes, to boost lagging production in the Community.

ii. Imports from third countries underwent a substantial increase during these years of flagging output, 1972 and 1973. They were stimulated, in conditions more favourable to the consumer, by a suspension of customs duty and import levies during the major part of 1973. The net shortfall in imports and exports respectively varied as follows:

	Europe of the Six	*Europe of the Nine*
1968	460,000 tonnes	
1969	630,000 tonnes	
1970	610,000 tonnes	
1971	520,000 tonnes	570,000 tonnes
1972		970,000 tonnes
1973		900,000 tonnes
1974		110,000 tonnes
1975		−90,000 tonnes
1976		+200,000 tonnes

What the figures fail to show is that disagreement among the governments on the advisability of largely suspending imports[4] prevented the Council from taking such action until nearly the end of the first quarter of 1974, whereas the state of the market would have warranted doing so several months earlier. By mid-1973 producer prices were decidedly on the downgrade and by June–August already about 6% below the level for January.

As it only takes a comparatively small quantity to upset the market, unduly high meat imports just when the increased numbers of cattle held out prospects of greater domestic production added to the difficulties recorded in 1974. While a temporary discontinuance of imports may help to restore market equilibrium, the problem is actually merely displaced by creating difficulties for traditional meat exporting countries in the rest of the world, e.g., Latin America. Consequently, because of the Community's traditional open-endedness towards the developing countries, the European governments were very loath to take such action. Nevertheless, it must be remembered that while supply and demand are balanced, numerically, Europe's output is not big enough to satisfy all demands in respect of quality and choice of meats. Therefore imports can never be wholly suspended, a minimum flow has to be maintained possibly by a system of set-off such as the Community introduced.

iii. Then there are the attitudes of the stockmen. Some miscalculated the market trend. Actually average prices varied as follows:

1968	63.97 UA/100 kg live weight
1969	67.84 UA/100 kg live weight
1970	68.81 UA/100 kg live weight
1971	71.55 UA/100 kg live weight
1972	87.58 UA/100 kg live weight
1973	91.68 UA/100 kg live weight
1974	85.29 UA/100 kg live weight
1975	94.68 UA/100 kg live weight

The 1972 and 1973 prices were so high as to give the producers an incentive to keep back cattle ready for slaughtering in the hope of greater profits. When the trend was reversed, they flooded the market, thus causing a collapse of prices.

Although there were signs of an improvement in 1976, the drought occasioned greater deliveries to the slaughterhouses, thus artificially prolonging the period of surplus. On the other hand this might help to show up an inadequacy of production rather sooner than would have been the case in the natural cycle, failing more resolute support measures.

iv. In December 1972, on a request by the French Government, the Commission proposed, and the Council decided, to introduce a permanent system of intervention. This took the place of an optional system and unavoidably increased the numbers of cattle delivered to the intervention agency with a view to securing a minimum income.

The numbers of livestock subject to the various kinds of intervention varied as follows, in equivalent carcase weight:

	As at 31 Dec.	Change during year	
		min.	max.
1973	23,000 tonnes	—	
1974	276,000 tonnes	46,000 tonnes	276,000 tonnes
1975	311,000 tonnes	276,000 tonnes	363,000 tonnes
1976	345,000 tonnes	299,000 tonnes	351,000 tonnes
(forecast)			

The permanent intervention system has little impact in 1973, as the market prices were higher than the intervention price. Intervention only became attractive following a marked drop in market prices.

Originally intervention, meaning the purchase of fully grown livestock, was triggered by any substantial drop in market prices. The method was used to set a weekly market price based on a number of reference markets.

Intervention took place at two levels: when the price was within 98% of the guide price, it remained optional, and when the price fell short of 93% for two weeks running, it became compulsory.

This highly flexible system seldom operates because market prices remained at a high level, so no precise lessons can be learnt from it.

While intervention is still optional when prices are high, compulsory intervention was replaced by a new system, effective from December 1972, whereby farmers could submit livestock to the authority irrespective of market price and be paid 93% of the guide price. The equalization machinery was very favourable for the producer and ran the risk of inducing production with an eye to its operation, or rather cutting out the function performed by the trade by accepting a reduction of about 7%, a fairly small margin. As meat loses value after cold storage, the operation usually cost the EAGGF dearly. It took the Council two years to decide, on a proposal by the Commission, to make intervention less attractive by lowering the intervention price level, to 90% of the guide price. Various other restrictive measures were taken; other more generous ones were temporarily introduced during the summer months of 1976 to aid farmers hard hit by the drought.[5]

An almost three year phase of surplus production is now ending, and from 1977 on there will be a shortfall. However, it will be mainly covered in 1977 by existing stocks and imports from the third world which are likely to expand again in 1978.

The shortfall might be attenuated by permanently diverting the surplus of dairy production capacity to meat production.

Concurrently, use might be made of this respite to draw the lesson to be learnt from permanent intervention. It may be wondered whether, while retaining the function of intervention in promoting the maintenance of production capacity to avoid in the second phase of the production cycle any shortage liable to cause a sudden spurt of consumer prices, the machinery ought not to be overhauled. The existing system "feather-beds" the producer and also tends to neutralize the function of the middleman by allowing the easy way out of handing over livestock to the intervention authorities, at the risk of shortly thereafter making the butcher buy in frozen meat at a sizeable loss to public funds.

Without claiming to be able to solve this tricky problem, we may mention for example the establishment of guarantees differing according to quality of livestock or importance of supplier, a review of the gaps between intervention and guide prices and of market price formation, the charging to the big producer of part of the financial losses, the temporary limitation of deliveries to the intervention authority whenever a surplus occurs. Such limitation might e.g., take the form of a temporary lowering of the intervention price,

10

together with a bonus on livestock withheld to encourage temporary storage "on the hoof".

In 1974/75 the Community seemed somewhat nonplussed by the beef crisis. It was the more hesitant to take action in that there were so many differences in the Member States' traditions, interests and approach to such problems. The British idea of bonuses won wider support, but in the anarchial context of a Europe *à la carte*. No less than 5 kinds of bonus, often answering opposing needs, were introduced for slowing down market supplies or making up for losses of income by supplementing the intervention guarantee, or again for keeping up size of herds to avoid future shortages. Some 700 m or 800 m.UA will have been paid out in $2\frac{1}{2}$ years, from late 1974 to 1977. A thorough review of the scope of bonuses in regulating markets and providing income support would be eminently desirable, with specific reference to the intervention system.

The *conclusions* for the beef and veal sector are therefore:

a. There exists a six-year production cycle, which has to be allowed for;
b. The cycle may be dangerously amplified, in both its production surplus phase and that of shortfall, by the official management of the market and farmers' behaviour;
c. The risk of a cyclical surplus grows greater as the Community draws closer to self-sufficiency, and could easily give rise to a smaller or greater structural surplus;
d. The Community was somewhat at a loss in dealing with the first and sudden occurrence of a sizeable surplus, and failed to take the necessary action in time to regulate the market;
e. The Commission ought to be able to draw the lesson to be learnt from this painful and costly experience, and so obviate unduly high cyclical surpluses or their hardening into structural surpluses; market management policy can be refined by adjusting the modes of intervention and bonus systems as well as by striking an admittedly delicate balance with the dairy product sector.

DAIRY PRODUCE: CAN THE STRUCTURAL SURPLUS BE CHANGED BACK INTO A CYCLICAL ONE?

Few sectors of agriculture have raised such controversy as the dairy sector, especially as there can be no gainsaying now that a structural surplus does exist in it. The odds are against a successful solution in a sector in which Community interrelations are numerous, negotiations difficult and clashes of interest violent. However, a study of the sector can teach valuable lessons about the functioning of the CAP.

The milk market

The outstanding features are a brilliantly successful growth in milk collection, and a gloomy prospect for market sales under the existing CAP.

Increase in milk production
The trend in supplies has been as follows:[6]

1970	74.1 million tonnes
1971	74.9 million tonnes
1972	79.5 million tonnes
1973	80.1 million tonnes
1974	80.8 million tonnes
1975	81.7 million tonnes
1976	83.5 (estimate)

There has been a steady upward movement, particularly steep in 1972, only slightly slowed down by drought in 1976.

The increase in output was not due to greater numbers of dairy herds. While these also follow a pluriannual cycle similar to that for store cattle, the overall trend is for a slight decline in total numbers.

Thus for the nine EEC countries total numbers of dairy cattle were, in 1969 26 m and are currently almost 25 m. But the yield per cow is steadily rising from 3.300 kg in 1969 to over 3.700 kg in 1976, or an average overall increment of 12% and an annual rate of about 1.4%. The highest yields were in the Netherlands, FRG, Denmark and the U.K. (4,000–4,600 kg) and the lowest in the other 5 (2,700–3,600 kg), which would suggest the existence of a fairly big margin for increased productivity in the latter.

The steady increase in yields is partly attributable to improved livestock, more rational use of feedstuffs and above all massive use of highly nutritious compound feeds.

The Community imported 80% of the proteins used for livestock feeding in general, chiefly oilcakes. Thus, 14 mt. of oilcakes were imported in 1974, of which 8.5 mt. of soya cakes.

As it takes about 1 kg of oilcake to produce 2 kg of milk, the price ratio of soya cake to milk is a determining factor in yield per cow. The trend in prices has been as follows:

	Target price for milk (UA/100 kg)	Index	World price soya oilcakes (UA/100 kg)	Index
1970/71	10.3	100	10.2*	100
1971/72	10.9	105.8	12.0	117.6
1972/73	11.77	114.3	25.3	248.0
1973/74	12.42	120.6	15.2	149.0
1974/75	13.41	130.2	12.–	117.6
(phase I)				
(phase II)	14.08	136.7		
1975/76				
(phase I)	14.92	144.9	15.6	152.9
(phase II)	15.59	151.4		

* per annum from 1971 on.

As oilcake imports are duty free under international agreements dating back to the early years of the Common Market, the oilcake/milk price ratio offers an incentive to using this feed for greater milk production. An expenditure sufficient to buy 1 kg of oilcake will sell 2 litres of milk; the benefit derived covers processing costs.

The type of foodstuff, and especially its comparative cost in relation to milk prices, is therefore a determining factor in production growth.

Note too that supplies delivered to the dairy are on the up-grade, from 85% in 1968 to 90% now, as more and more farms discontinue butter and cheese production and direct sales of milk, and compound feeds partially supplant milk used for fattening calves.

So the farmer produces more milk and steps up his deliveries to the dairy cooperative on which he relies for marketing most of his product. Last year's drought, so catastrophic in some regions, did not cause any overall drop in production but only a smaller increase, estimated at about 1.5%.

Limited prospective sales

Milk is consumed in many different forms by both humans and livestock, and to a lesser extent as an industrial raw material. But only about 1/3rd of the milk is consumed directly, the other 2/3rds being consumed in the form of butter, cheese, milk powder and casein.[7]

In fact, direct consumption of milk remains stationary and that of butter has difficulty in contending with competition from margarine, while, in some cases with government support, powder milk consumption remains stationary despite efforts to sell to developing countries; only cheese consumption is showing a little buoyancy.

Thus consumption of liquid skimmed milk for feeding livestock fell from 16.7 mt. in 1960 to 5.8 mt. in 1973. The big drop in sales for that purpose is partly offset by sales of milk powder, but more and more substitute products are coming into use. Hence a growing difficulty in marketing powdered milk because its price is uncompetitive with that of substitutes for it.

Income requirements solely met by uniform prices and the intervention system

As milk gives farmers a regular income, the price is officially fixed by the Council of Ministers at Community level, instead of as formerly by each individual country. But as it is not a product that can be stored, such a price fixing system will only work if indirectly supported. Hence the European market organization includes intervention prices for the two constituents of milk, butter fat and proteins, which mainly serve to produce powdered milk by the drying process.[8] This is why imbalances of supply and demand of dairy produce chiefly take the form of a stockpiling of butter or powdered milk, or both.

Surpluses and various ways of absorbing or obviating them

Unlike those of beef and veal, the European market organization for milk has in its short but chequered history undergone many crises and attempts at finding a solution.

Butter surpluses

i. *Successful absorption in 1968–1970*

In July 1968, the Europe of the Six inaugurated a definitive system of market organization in the dairy sector, which left on its hands an annual over-production of 100–200,000 t. out of a total 1.4 mt. and public stockpiles amounting to 300,000 t. by the end of 1969.

On a proposal by the Commission, the Council boldly agreed to freeze dairy prices for three years (1968–1971), which meant, *inter alia*, a slight decrease in butter production. In addition, beef slaughtering bonuses were introduced to hold down production.

Special measures were taken to dispose of the butter surplus, enabling the public stocks to dwindle to 100,000 t. in 1970 and 150,000 t. in 1971.

But Europe also had luck on its side. Indeed, dairy production decreased in most regions of the world owing to unfavourable climatic conditions, and this facilitated European exports.

Thus, by a combination of deliberate action and some flukes of luck, the first crisis was successfully weathered.

ii. *Contested absorption of surpluses in 1972/73*

After the brake had been applied, production in 1972 rose faster than con-sumption, especially due to a very big increase in yield per cow, as in France, where it went up from 3,050 kg to 3,400 kg in the space of one year. This take-off enabled France to catch up on countries of higher yields, giving rise to a disquieting growth of official EEC stocks, which amounted by the end of the year to 300,000 t. Recovery was also boosted by an understandable official price rise after the three-year freeze. Thus the price of milk went up from 10.3 UA/100 kg to 10.9 in 1971/72 and 11.7u in 1972/73. Finally there was a glut on the world market, as recovery had been practically universal.

In 1973 stocks accumulated even faster because substantial quantities of butter from third countries, notably New Zealand, became "europeanised" when the EEC was enlarged by the accession of 3 new Member States.

It was at this point that a spectacular operation took place whereby 200,000 t. of butter were sold to Russia at considerable financial loss. The operation was mounted by a business consortium, and officially accepted by the Com-mission, with governments' discreet approval: it cleared the market at one stroke, but caused a great outcry from public opinion, accusing the European institutions of selling off butter, to the benefit of non-Community consumers, at the expense of the European taxpayers. This was quite true, but such a large extra tonnage of butter could not have been sold to a European consumer.

Subsequently, the butter market has raised no major problem, thanks to great vigilance on the part of the Community and to the Commission ringing the changes on a wide set of measures such as:
– a very moderate raising of the intervention price so as not to discourage consumption
– various measures for cut-price sales and aid to the consumer,
– export supports, especially food aid to the developing countries,
– slowing down imports.

Nevertheless stocks are tending to rise once more, and might create problems in late 1977 or 1978.

In the case of butter, then, we see on average two years of surplus out of every four, calling for numerous and often costly support measures and absorption aids. The surpluses are apparently cyclical, though to some extent also structural, for even in years of no surplus measures have to be continued to keep stocks from increasing too fast. Thus about 100,000 t. of butter are annually sold off at special prices, the losses being borne by EAGGF.

Milk powder surpluses

The balance sheet at Annex V shows that as far back as 1968/69 there was a substantial stockpile, but the three-year price freeze helped, as in the case of butter, to hold back production. Also sales outlets for livestock improved for a time.

But there were spectacular surges of output, as from 1,360,000 t. for the Nine in 1971 to 1,650,000 t. in 1972 and 1,850,000 t. in 1973.

The increase was partly due to a big rise in intervention prices, thus making milk powder production attractive for the dairy concerns, and substitute products less competitive. The increase was the more dramatic in that that of butter had been held down so as not to discourage consumers, as seen from the following list:

| | Trend in intervention prices | | | |
| | Butter | | Powdered milk | |
	(UA/100 kg)	Index	(UA/100 kg)	Index
1968/69 to 70/71	173.50	100	41.25	100
1971/72	178	102.6	47	113.9
1972/73 (phase I)	180	103.7	54	130.9
(phase II)	186	107.2	—	—
1973/74	176	101.4	66	160.0
1974/75 (phase I)	176	101.4	79	191.5
(phase II)	183.58	105.8	82.74	200.6
1975/76 (phase I)	194.63	112.2	88.7	215.0
(phase II)	209.58	120.8	—	—
1976/77 (phase I)	218.08	125.7	91.37	221.5
(phase II)	223.80	129.0	—	

While the butter intervention price went up by 29% in 6 years, or a rate of 5% per annum, that of milk powder went up by 121.5%, or 20% per annum compared with the phase of frozen prices.

As competitor products were imported free of tariff protection and their prices even declined following the slippage of the dollar, the obvious outlet of use for livestock feeding was handicapped in the case of any quantities in excess of the minimum normally included in such feeds.

Whereas production goes on rising, there was a slight sag in consumption by livestock, owing to the effect of cheaper substitute proteins. Hence stocks climbed steeply from 850,000 t. at the end of 1974 to 1,112,000 t. at the end of 1975. After two butter crises, the Community has another crisis on its hands, this time for milk powder.

Stocks would have risen further in 1976 had not the Community taken the bold step of compelling the foodstuff industries to absorb 400,000 t. of milk powder. Sales were artificially boosted in this manner, but production costs soared, and the farmers had to bear the brunt, because the industrial concerns passed on all or part of the extra cost.

From the standpoint of milk powder alone, the only possible solution can be selling at a heavy loss, or compulsory incorporation of the product, which the European authorities have undertaken not to repeat because of the adverse effect on industry.[9]

At all events this third crisis had the merit of making the Community review the dairy problem as a whole and frame an overall policy.

In quest of an overall policy for eliminating the structural surplus
In July 1976 the Commission proposed a "1977/80 action programme for a gradual establishment of equilibrium on the dairy market". Noting the existence of a structural surplus of milk that will persist or even worsen in years to come, it proposes a set of measures:
– to hold back production by bonuses for non-deliveries of milk and a switch to beef and veal, together with a programme for slaughtering bovines affected by diseases like brucellosis, etc.
– halting investment by suspending national and community aid,
– making the producers bear a share of the cost to the Exchequer of marketing surpluses,
– taxing vegetable fats in order to reduce the imbalance between them and animal fats.
– looking for other sales outlets.

All these are useful measures and constitute for the first time a coherent action programme, but they will be lengthily argued over by all concerned, and the Council will have difficulty in promptly and completely adopting such a programme.[10]

But the market imbalance is so great that it may be wondered whether these measures will in the long run suffice, even if they are all quickly adopted by Council and resolutely applied.

A heavy increase in the cost of compound feeds in respect of their non-milk content might hold back productivity and place pasture-based production in a better position, but it runs counter to the constant trend towards increased output throughout our society. Hence its chances of being adopted are slim, especially as the combined interest of the food industry, third country exporters and farmers making abundant use of compound feeds, holds out small prospect of such a solution.

Another variant would be a fresh price freeze or very low adjustment, but this would possibly have to be supplemented by direct aids to low-income farmers. Such a solution would once again be a big drain on public spending, without any certainty of reequilibrium in the longer term. Price freezes, in agriculture as in industry, are often followed by a phase of quicker pace, in order to catch up lost ground, as has been seen before in the Community's short history.

A third, complementary and more radical solution would be to introduce a high rate of bonus to ensure adequate farm incomes for a switch to meat or other productions. In that case the bonus would have to be the equivalent of about 1 year's income, or at least 550 UA per head of livestock. The cost would be very heavy but would in turn bring substantial savings in Community finance.

In conclusion:

a.   There is a structural surplus of milk, currently involving an annual butter surplus of about 100,000 t. and one of milk powder of 500,000 t.

b.   this imbalance, often regarded as structural, is now acknowledged to be cyclical,

c.   it is the consequence of a policy aimed both to ensure adequate farm incomes by means of a guaranteed price, and to enable massive imports of protein-rich cattle feeds at interesting prices without an EEC import levy,

d.   it can be abolished by stringent measures by the Council on the basis of the Commission's action programme, which is not certain to be able to overcome the problem,

e.   the action should primarily be aimed at milk production, for there would seem to be no chance of spectacular new sales within the near future,

f.   the structural surplus can only revert to a cyclical one after a prolonged period of implementation of various measures.

So the situation is not hopeless, though it calls for clearsightedness, together with some measure of political courage and much perseverance in implementing a programme for restoring market equilibrium.

CONCLUSIONS

1. To ensure a regular supply to the population at large and avoid sharply rising consumer prices, food stocks serve a useful purpose, having regard to the specific characteristics of agricultural production. Not every quantity held in stock is to be regarded as surplus to requirements. A surplus occurs when it can be foreseen that a given amount of stocks cannot be disposed of without considerable loss. This is the way in which cyclical surpluses of beef, and structural surpluses of butter and milk powder, arise.

2. Cyclical surpluses in reasonable quantities are unavoidable unless the agricultural policy is so administered that European production falls decidedly short of demand. In such case any shortfall is made up by suitably varying imports, provided the commodities are available on the world markets. This exposes the consumer to risks of a shortage or of soaring prices, as was the case for sugar in 1973, world-wide. But to opt for a substantial drop in agricultural production would add to the balance of payments difficulties of several European countries, especially as Europe is poor in energy resources and raw materials. Doing without one of the few raw materials it does have, in the form of agricultural produce, would be very ill-advised. Moreover,

17

since it is one of the most favourably situated regions for farming in a world of rapidly increasing population, the option would also be of world importance. Europe's exports of farm products, by way of trade or in the form of gifts, are valuable in a great many respects.

3. These considerations by no means militate against so organizing and administering agricultural policy as to avoid cyclical surpluses turning into structural surpluses. Just think of what the situation would be if there were no Community policy! Living as we have done within a framework of Common Market policy for the past 15 years it is not easy to imagine what it would be like. The juxtaposition of nine separate agricultural policies would probably have led to a lowering of the farmers' standard of living because of the lack of market outlets, an inward-looking agriculture in some regions due to the absence of any competitive spur, and disorder in inter-State trade that would be a source of more serious friction than any the Community has encountered. More severe crises would probably have shaken certain States, for surpluses would have had to contend with more formidable obstacles and world shortages would have created more painful situations.

4. The bigger the unified economic area, the more economically capable of solution the problem of surpluses becomes, if as is the case in the Europe of the Nine the area comprises natural and traditional differences in agricultural production. There are therefore no underlying reasons to warrant the continued existence of some kinds of structural surplus. Rather, these reflect policy. The example of milk is instructive, as to what Europe should avoid for the sake of its reputation, public finance and economic growth. But the possible solutions are not always to be found within the narrow framework of agricultural policy proper. Other policies have to be encompassed, especially commercial policy, in which Europe has traditionally shown great understanding with regard to third world imports even at the cost of additional difficulties in its own agriculture.

What is happening now for milk may be true of fruit and vegetables, wine and olive oil tomorrow, as a result of the European policy of access to and expansion in the Mediterranean countries. Clearly, a mere extension, with no precaution being taken, of 16 existing market organization provisions to Greece, Portugal and Spain could not fail to cause further difficulties and run the risk of further structural surpluses, since the support machinery and level of European prices will, in view of living standards in all three countries, constitute a strong inducement to high output.

5. To combat structural surpluses, particular heed should be taken of instruments, procedures and arbitration arrangements among the contending interests. The instruments applied from the outset to identify prospective trends in production and consumption have to be highly sophisticated. In our type of rapidly evolving society we have to be constantly alive to new developments.

The procedures for monitoring new developments and the measures to be adopted have to be very fast-operating. With a highly sensitive market economy and very rapidly changing technical and commercial trends, the Community has to be able to respond to whatever challenges it may be involuntarily faced with.

Lastly, the arbitration machinery to cope with the divergent economic,

18

commercial, financial, social and political interests should be smooth and efficient, to safeguard the general Community interests. In this context, the election of the European Parliament by universal suffrage should bring a more democratic and more humane dimension to European affairs, as well as help in identifying more precisely where the general interest lies.

Development of the European Parliament should go hand-in-hand with stronger powers for arbitration between divergent interests, whether at Commission or Council level, for unless such powers can be wielded it will be difficult to make any great improvement in sectorial policy or to prosecute vigorously other kinds of policy.

NOTES

1. COM 1850 final of the 31.10.1973.
2. COM (75) 100 of the 26.2.1975.
3. OECD reports.
4. By stopping the issue of import licences.
5. Extending the intervention system to lower-grade storecattle e.g., certain categories of livestock.
6. cf. detailed figures of livestock numbers, production and supplies at Annex II.
7. See Annexes III, IV and V for particulars.
8. Cheese is also obtained, but as there is such variety in its production and marketing possibilities, the Community's intervention has been confined to certain kinds of cheese only.
9. It should be noted that the Court of Justice of the European Communities in its judgments of 5th July 1977 has declared this regulation to be null and void, arguing that "The obligation to purchase at such a disproportionate price constituted a discriminatory distribution of the burden of costs between various agricultural sectors (Granaria BV-V-Hoofdproduktschap voor Akkerbouwprodukten [1975] ECR 1247 at p. 1265).
10. In April 1977 the Council adopted these measures while replacing the proposed tax on vegetable fats by a temporary aid for the consumption of butter (the so called "Christmas butter"). In May 1978 the producers' contribution to the incidental costs of disposal was reduced from 1.5% of the target price for milk to 0.5%. The package of measures including those for disposal at high cost have helped to steady the levels of intervention stocks, without however eliminating even to a small extent the structural surpluses in this sector. In September 1978 the Commission will put forward supplementary proposals in this sector.

Extract from the statement by Mr. HOUDET, Chairman of the
Committee for Agriculture of the European Parliament, on 14 November 1976

On the occasion of the debate on measures to cope with the surplus of dairy
products

"I wish to deprecate some of the attacks on our common agricultural
policy. We are told that the market organization, simply by its price supports,
causes the piling up of mountains of beef, dairy produce and the like, which
cost the EAGGF dearly.

I think it is wrong to lay such a sweeping charge against all agricultural
products. Certainly the CAP is expensive, and it is our duty to explore all
possible economies. But all the same we have to know in what sector to make
the economies in, without infringing Article 39 of the Rome Treaty which
provides not only for producers' earnings but also regular supplies to the
consumer at reasonable prices.

What are being called 'mountains' often constitute buffer stocks, for
staving off shortages in a particular year, that cost the EAGGF and the
consumer more than it takes to absorb certain cyclical surpluses. Let us not
forget the crises in the supply of cereals and sugar in 1973, caused by speculative pressure on world prices.

Nor should it be forgotten that the lack of any market organization for
potatoes is at the root of the current breakdown of supplies.

While it is relatively easy to trim industrial production to market requirements, the case is not the same for agricultural produce dependent on
climatic conditions unpredictable at the start of the season, and on total
hours of sunshine.

But, like a good many of you, I realize that the dairy surpluses have assumed
a structural character that calls for emergency measures, and that they may
be aptly called 'mountains'. Hence the need to take action, with all speed."

ANNEX II

Livestock Numbers, Production and Supply of Milk to Dairies in the Enlarged Community (1973–1976)

	Year	D	F	I	NL	B	L	EUR 6	UK	IRL	DK	EUR 9
1. Dairy cows (1000 head) Dec. prev. year	1973	5,466	7,402	3,256	1,998	974	68	19,164	3,482	1,182	1,130	24,958
	1974	5,486	7,683	3,051	2,171	1,018	72	19,481	3,545	1,389	1,154	25,569
	1975	5,393	7,751	2,927	2,215	997	73	19,356	3,387	1,344	1,130	25,217
	1976	5,402	7,590	2,883	2,196	980	70	19,121	3,249	1,300	1,106	24,776
2. Other cows (1000 head) Dec. prev. year	1973	100	2,279	763	—	66	2	3,210	1,546	680	49	5,485
	1974	153	2,478	796	—	66	6	3,499	1,824	684	49	6,056
	1975	157	2,456	772	—	67	6	3,458	1,955	690	96	6,199
	1976	140	2,613	744	—	72	6	3,575	1,834	563	96	6,068
3. Total cows (1000 head) Dec. prev. year	1973	5,566	9,681	4,019	1,998	1,040	70	22,374	5,028	1,862	1,179	30,443
	1974	5,639	10,161	3,847	2,171	1,084	78	22,980	5,369	2,073	1,203	31,625
	1975	5,550	10,207	3,699	2,215	1,064	79	22,814	5,342	2,034	1,226	31,416
	1976	5,542	10,203	3,627	2,196	1,052	76	22,696	5,083	1,863	1,202	30,844
4. Milk production of dairy cows (1000 T)	1973	21,266	24,850	9,350	9,358	3,611	239	68,674	14,316	3,566	4,729	91,285
	1974	21,508	24,900	8,826	9,915	3,709	251	69,109	13,913	3,436	4,818	91,276
	1975	21,604	24,855	8,689	10,217	3,621	248	69,234	13,856	3,699	4,918	91,707
	1976											93,000

(continued)

ANNEX II (*cont.*)

	Year	D	F	I	NL	B	L	EUR 6	UK	IRL	DK	EUR 9
5. Milk production of other cows (1000 T)	1973	192	4,441	400	—	125	4	5,162	2,168	850	93	8,273
	1974	291	4,570	551	—	142	11	5,548	2,374	855	93	8,870
	1975	298	4,831	484	—	142	11	5,766	2,384	862	182	9,194
	1976											9,000
6. Total milk production (1000 T)	1973	21,458	29,291	9,750	9,358	3,736	243	73,836	16,484	4,416	4,822	99,558
	1974	21,799	29,470	9,377	9,915	3,834	262	74,657	16,287	4,291	4,911	100,146
	1975	21,902	29,686	9,173	10,217	3,763	259	75,000	16,240	4,561	5,100	100,901
	1976											102,000
7. Yield dairy cows (kg/head)	1973	3,891	3,357	2,872	4,684	3,707	3,515	3,583	4,111	3,017	4,185	3,658
	1974	3,921	3,241	2,893	4,567	3,643	3,486	3,548	3,925	2,474	4,175	3,570
	1975	4,006	3,207	2,969	4,613	3,632	3,397	3,577	4,091	2,752	4,352	3,637
	1976											3,754
8. Supplies to dairies (1000 T)	1973	18,812	21,094	7,067	8,850	2,712	224	58,761	13,700	3,148	4,538	80,147
	1974	19,076	21,137	7,142	9,386	2,815	239	59,794	13,298	3,062	4,611	80,765
	1975	19,366	21,285	6,822	9,864	2,775	236	60,348	13,315	3,296	4,718	81,678
	1976											83,500

ANNEX III

Production, External Trade and Consumption in the Enlarged Community, for Principal Dairy Products (1973–1976)

Product	Production	Imports	Exports	Available for Consumption
Whole Milk Powder				
1973	365	4	205	164
1974	345	—	192	153
1975 E	360	—	197	163
1976 E	370	—	200	170
Skimmed Milk Powder				
1973	1,851	6	266	1,591
1974	1,826	—	313	1,513
1975 E	1,976	20	129	1,867
1976 E	2,060	—	350	1,710
Condensed Milk				
1973	1,416	—	408	1,008
1974	1,433	—	429	1,004
1975 E	1,386	—	378	1,008
1976 E	1,400	—	400	1,000
Butter				
1973	1,735	150	410	1,475
1974	1,661	132	162	1,631
1974 E	1,715	120	92	1,743
1976 E	1,750	120	130	
Cheese				
1973	2,672	112	154	2,630
1974	2,878	80	185	2,773
1975 E	3,031	96	139	2,988
1976 E	3,080	100	150	3,030
Casein				
1973	56	26	12	70
1974	59	22	79	62
1975 E	44	17	9	52
1976 E	55	15	10	60

E = estimate

ANNEX IV

Balance Sheet of Butter

	EUR "6"					EUR "9"			
	1968	1969	1970	1971	1972	1973	1974	1975	1976
1. Stocks on 1/1	168	299	302	131	106	393	230	147	164
2. Production	1,403	1,349	1,298	1,230	1,378	1,735	1,661	1,715	1,750
3. Imports	5	7	3	5	3	150	132	120	120
4. Consumption of which:	1,171	1,248	1,273	1,064	1,105	1,638	1,714	1,726	1,640
– market price	1,150	1,192	1,161	1,049	1,070	1,518	1,573	1,608	1,530
– at greatly reduced prices	21	56	112	15	35	120	141	118	110
5. Exports	106	105	199	196	79	410	162	92	130
of which: commercial	106	89	138	182	56	306	130	60	75
– food aid	—	—	14	14	16	18	32	32	55
– special action	—	16	47	—	7	86	—	—	—
6. Stocks on 31/12	299	302	131	106	303	230	147	164	264
of which:									
– public	—	—	—	—	—	—	—	71	160
– private	—	—	—	—	—	—	—	93	104

Balance Sheet of Skimmed Milk Powder

	EUR "6"					EUR "9"			
	1968	1969	1970	1971	1972	1973	1974	1975	1976
1. Stocks on 1/1	104	238	361	92	22	349	466	580	1,150
of which									
– public	—	—	—	—	—	149	166	365	1,112
– private	—	—	—	—	—	200	300	215	38
2. Production	1,318	1,215	1,191	1,140	1,357	1,851	1,826	1,976	2,060
3. Imports	21	21	11	4	1	6	—	20	—
4. Consumption of which:	963	1,022	1,237	1,073	1,238	1,474	1,399	1,297	1,750
– human	110	110	110	110	110	276	256	250	250
– livestock	853	882	1,042	963	1,128	1,198	1,143	1,047	1,100
– pigs and poultry	—	30	85	—	—	—	—	—	400
5. Exports of which:	242	91	234	141	93	266	313	129	350
– comm.	242	91	209	94	37	220	266	77	200
– food aid	—	—	25	47	56	46	47	52	150
6. Stocks on 31/12 of which	238	361	92	22	49	466	580	1,150	1,110
– public	—	—	—	—	—	166	365	1,112	1,070
– private	—	—	—	—	—	300	215	38	40

II. AGRICULTURAL POLICY COUNTER-REPORT

General Problems of Equilibrium in the Beef and Dairy Markets within the European Economic Community

by *Georges Bublot*

For several years now massive expenditure from the European Agricultural Guidance and Guarantee Fund has been required to support the market in milk products and beef and veal; this problem is constantly occupying the minds of those responsible for the common agricultural policy.

In 1974 and 1975 expenditure by the EAGGF amounted to 2,400 million UA for milk and 1,300 million UA for beef, that is, 30.3% and 16.7% respectively of the total guarantee expenditure from the EAGGF.

The situation has shown little improvement since then. Under the combined influence of technical progress and the restructuring of farms and dairies, stocks of skimmed milk powder have accumulated and totalled 1,100,000 tonnes on 31 December 1976, i.e., 54% of production in 1976, while butter stocks amounted to 250,000 tonnes by 31 December 1976, i.e., 14% of production in 1976.[1]

In this situation the Community authorities—Commission and Council—are faced with two problems: (1) in the short-term, that of arranging for the disposal of existing stocks at minimum cost and (2) in the medium-term, that of preventing the recurrence of similar surpluses or, at the other extreme, the development of shortages; this necessitates measures which, short of achieving a balance on the markets, will at least prevent the development of too flagrant an imbalance. The attainment of these objectives requires flexible machinery which can adapt to temporary shortages or occasional surpluses.

The disposal of existing stocks is a relatively simple problem entailing a choice between various possible solutions based on the present market situation.

Our purpose here is mainly to examine closely those measures by which market equilibrium might be achieved in the medium-term, setting out: (1) the difficulties and obstacles, (2) the types of equilibrium required, and (3) a survey of possible solutions. We shall end with some general conclusions.

DIFFICULTIES AND EXIGENCIES

The precarious nature of market equilibrium

The reason for this is to be found in the particular features of supply and demand for milk products and beef and veal. However varied and flexible the intervention machinery might be, temporary surpluses and shortages cannot easily be avoided. As soon as a balance is established on the market, any variation in production or modification of demand following an unforeseen event, whether climatic, economic or political, will tend to lead to an increase in stocks and affect prices all the more sharply because of the inelasticity and apparent instability of demand. This fact also explains the growing instability observed on the world markets during recent years.

This extreme sensitivity to disequilibrium has been noted during the last few years in the case of milk products: with consumption stagnant the growth of production has added to stocks which have increased at an enormous rate: stocks of skimmed milk powder rose from 349,800 tonnes in January 1975 to 1,385,300 tonnes in August 1976, while butter stocks increased from 68,200 tonnes in January 1975 to 423,100 tonnes in August 1976.

The complex interdependence of the products

The ways in which these products interrelate are very complex and cannot be easily predicted, varying considerably according to the particular economic situation. At production level, for instance, bovine products can be substituted for other products, but the principal ones—milk and meat—can each be substituted for the other, influencing many factors as a result. With regard to consumption, there are even more ways in which products can compete with one another, for example butter with margarine and butter with cheese, unskimmed milk with butter (in human consumption), or skimmed milk powder with vegetable proteins and liquid skimmed milk with other foodstuffs (in animal feed).

The conflicting nature of possible solutions

The measures taken to ensure market balance have to satisfy mutually irreconcilable requirements: to ensure that international commitments are honoured, guarantee an adequate income for farmers, keep the social cost of market support as low as possible, and safeguard supplies to consumers at reasonable prices.

The impact of the various solutions differs from group to group. Any decision to lower producer prices transfers the cost of rationalization onto the producers themselves and is felt all the more keenly as a modification in prices leads in the short term to a variation in incomes which is all the more substantial as the proportion of the selling-price accounted for by costs paid (real expenditure) is high. The real burden of any measure that leads to an increase in the retail prices of foodstuffs is borne by the consumers of these products and indirectly by the consumers of competing products. Any measure which necessitates Community intervention is supported indirectly by the consumer of products subject to a levy or customs duty, or by the taxpayers of the Member States insofar as Community resources are derived from the contributions of the Member States.

The task of reconciling these conflicting demands is all the more delicate as the main groups concerned, except for the consumers, are putting considerable pressure on the Community decision-making authorities. The farmers are demanding remunerative prices for milk, which involves fixing high intervention prices for butter and skimmed milk powder; this will make it even more difficult to sell these products, especially as many substitutes are available at a lower price. In addition, the dairies hope to step up production in order to pay for the investments in rationalization measures to which they have recently agreed. On the other hand, firms in the animal feed sector, faced with keen competition, have to obtain their raw materials at the lowest possible price.

The result of these conflicting constraints is that, within the existing structures, the decisions taken will necessarily be compromise solutions making for an acceptable distribution of the burden of costs between the groups concerned.

The social aspects of the problem and the political nature of the decisions taken

Bovine products are certainly the most "social" of agricultural products because cattle-farming is a traditional activity of the smallest farms often situated in the least favoured regions of the Community (hill and mountain areas).

This fact is particularly significant at a time when, for various reasons, changes are taking place in social values, reflected particularly in the establishment of institutions (social security . . .), statutory devices (redistribution of wealth through taxation . . .), or infrastructures (public ownership, collective facilities . . .) all of which increase the solidarity among members of the communities (regions, countries . . .).

The result is that the problems are being increasingly felt in social terms and as a corollary less in economic terms. The decisions, which are essentially of a political nature, cannot in future be dissociated from their social implications.

If the economists are not inevitably and constantly in the uncomfortable position of having all their recommendations rejected on political and social grounds, it must be admitted that much of their expertise goes into solving secondary problems: rationalization of production, forecasts and projections, econometric studies, calculation of the comparative cost of alternative solutions, day-to-day management of the markets . . . .

The scale of the market and technicality of Community regulations

The bulky and perishable nature of milk may be one reason for the lack of transparency in the milk market (at least for unprocessed milk) and the difficulty of establishing an effective system of competition between the dairies. Moreover, conditions in which milk and beef and veal are produced in the Community are extremely varied; similarly the pattern of consumption reflects very different habits according to country, region and population density . . .

Besides, if realistic solutions are to be found, it is necessary not only to understand the basic mechanisms of supply and demand, but also to be acquainted with numerous local situations, the way in which the markets function as well as the statutory provisions governing them. However, it is difficult to survey the whole of the Community market precisely because it is so vast, while it is not at all easy to penetrate the maze of regulations on milk because of their number—several hundred—and the technical nature of the texts.

THE TYPES OF EQUILIBRIUM REQUIRED

Equilibrium of the market in milk and milk products

Milk production in the Europe of the Nine rose by 4% between 1970 and 1976, mainly as a result of the increase in the milk yield due to technical improvements, the actual number of milk cows having decreased by 9% in the same period.

The proportion of non-skimmed milk in the total quantity of milk produced (human consumption, feed for calves, whole milk powder . . .) is about 40% and shows little sign of changing; correspondingly, skimmed milk powder constitutes 60% of the milk produced and this proportion, too, is relatively stable.

However, over the past few years there have been fundamental changes in the method of treating milk. Traditionally this was done on the farms and led to the production of butter, sold on the local market, and liquid skimmed milk, used in animal feeding stuffs (calves, pigs) and, incidentally, to the production of skimmed milk cheese. In this situation there was obviously no surplus. But over the years the dairies have collected more and more of the milk produced, from 75% in 1968 to 90% in 1976, mainly under the combined influence of the following factors:

1. structural changes on the farms, consisting of increases in the size of the herds of cattle, increasing rationalization and specialization;

2. incentives offered to farmers to supply milk, particularly by the dairies, with their newly installed modern equipment for collecting milk and manufacturing skimmed milk powder;

3. developments in the price policy: the principal feature here has been the considerable rise in the intervention price for skimmed milk powder (122% between 1970/71 and 1976/77), making its use less and less competitive in relation to alternative sources of protein.[2]

Furthermore, the quantity of butter obtained from a given quantity of whole milk is equal to only about half the quantity of powder obtained from the skimmed milk product from the same original volume of whole milk.[3]

All these factors taken together are sufficient to explain the marked difference in production trends between 1970 and 1976: the increase is most pronounced for skimmed milk powder, moderate for butter and least pronounced in the case of whole milk (Table I).

TABLE 1.   *Development of EEC production of whole milk, butter and skimmed milk powder, 1970 to 1976*

	Whole milk		Butter		Skimmed milk powder	
	1000 metric t.	1970 = 100	1000 metric t.	1970 = 100	1000 metric t.	1970 = 100
1970	89,302	100	1,457	100	1,374	100
1971	87,466	97.9	1,416	97.2	1,358	98.8
1972	91,436	102.4	1,615	110.8	1,651	120.2
1973	91,285	102.2	1,735	119.1	1,851	134.7
1974	91,276	102.2	1,661	114.0	1,826	132.9
1975	91,707	102.7	1,715	117.7	1,976	143.8
1976	93,000	104.1	1,750	120.1	2,060	149.9

Source: SOEC Statistical Publications

The rise in the price of skimmed milk powder has encouraged its production by the dairies and incidentally the supply of milk to the dairies. But it has led to a gradual accumulation of stocks which are becoming all the more difficult to dispose of as the price of competitive products is generally much lower. This situation raises the difficult problem of the equilibrium of the market in skimmed milk powder, which is closely linked to the equilibrium of the butter market on account of the inter-play between the intervention prices of these two products in determining the target price for milk.

The joint equilibrium of the markets in milk and in beef and veal

The production of milk and of beef and veal is generally combined on farms breeding dual-purpose cattle. At present only some 20% of cows are bred for purposes other than milk production of which the production of meat is the only one of real importance. But all other cows, that is 80%, are used to produce both milk and meat in varying proportions. In the breeding of dairy cows, meat production can at a pinch be regarded as a byproduct of the production of milk, although all the animals—culled cows, heifers not needed to improve the stock and young animals—are ultimately intended for slaughter and the meat produced may represent quite a large proportion of the total sales. Meat production does not give rise to the production of any milk where it involves strictly meat breeds or nurse cows, but the production of milk is otherwise always valued in farms with dual-purpose breeds, even those mainly involved in meat production.

Besides, the production of milk and the production of meat are inter-changeable. From the same production factors it is possible to obtain varying quantities of each, more especially because both come from cows and the type of resources required for each are very similar (premises, land, professional skills . . .) except for the labour factor which decreases in inverse proportion to the volume of meat production.

If these features are common to both types of production, there are nevertheless fundamental differences between them. Whereas the markets are periodically flooded with surplus milk production, there has only once been a slight excess of beef and veal in 1975, the only year when there was a net export of 90,000 tonnes of beef and veal. For the years from 1970 to 1974 support expenditure for the market in beef and veal amounted to 393.2 million UA, i.e., 8.1% only of support expenditure for milk products. Furthermore, the effect of demand on incomes and prices is more elastic in the case of beef and veal than for milk products.

Finally, while it is only too likely that technical progress will produce new surpluses of milk products, such a situation is unlikely in the case of beef and veal, at least in the immediate future (1977 and 1978), because the cycle in the number of milk cows will probably reach its lowest level during those years.

In view of the present situation and future prospects ways must be sought in which milk production might be reduced and beef production increased, without this entailing any change in the overall volume of resources allocated to bovine production.

Equilibrium between milk and meat production and the other forms of agricultural production

Finally, if and when the production of milk and of beef and veal move into surplus—possibly after 1980—it will be necessary to take measures to reduce the number of cows, to allocate fewer resources to bovine production and thereby prevent structural market imbalances.

A SURVEY OF POSSIBLE SOLUTIONS

The surpluses of milk products (butter, skimmed milk powder . . .) are due to excessive dairy production, but this is never too high in its initial form. Part of the milk produced is consumed in its natural form: there is never any shortage of drinking milk since it only has to be taken from the milk produced. Similarly any milk not in fact consumed is transformed into various products (butter, cheese, powdered milk, casein . . .); it is only with these that surpluses may arise. All these products contain either milk fat or protein.

An exhaustive list of measures required to ensure the equilibrium of the markets would need to take into account all possible combinations of the following situations: (1) a surplus or shortage of beef and veal, (2) a surplus or shortage of milk fats and (3) a surplus or shortage of milk proteins. If we rule out the possibility of a shortage of milk fat or of milk protein neither of which has occurred in recent years or is likely to occur in future, the eight possibilities mentioned are most likely to produce the following two situations:

1. a shortage of beef and veal and a surplus of milk products;

2. a general surplus of all bovine products. Because of the present state of the market, however, it is necessary to consider measures by which to reduce the amount of skimmed milk powder produced from a given volume of milk and, more generally to establish an equilibrium on the markets in milk fat and meat proteins.

Equilibrium of the market in the constituents of milk: fat and protein

The most serious imbalances at present are on the markets in milk products where there are large surpluses. We shall first examine the solutions presented by the Community to the most urgent problems and then consider the whole problem of equilibrium.

The solutions to the immediate problems
The disposal of existing stocks of skimmed milk powder is certainly very costly, but it involves only a relatively simple choice between a number of possible solutions depending on the market situation.

A short time ago the situation was as follows. The sale of skimmed milk powder at a viable price for use as feed for calves and for pigs and poultry in competition with other protein foodstuffs, meant respectively a loss of approximately 38 and 71 UA per 100 kg, that is 42% and 78% of the intervention price. Exporting it on the world market entailed a loss of 65% UA per 100 kg, or 71% of the intervention price. Sending it to the developing countries as food aid meant a loss of 91 UA per 100 kg, or 100% of the intervention price.

The present reduction in stocks was achieved largely by financing the following measures: incorporation in foodstuffs for pigs and poultry (400,000 tonnes), food aid to developing countries (150,000 tonnes) and exports on the free market (90,000 tonnes). With the help of aids amounting to about 38 UA per 100 kg, 1,200,000 tonnes of powder were incorporated into foodstuffs for calves in 1976.

Moreover, reducing the quantity of skimmed milk powder produced from a given quantity of milk would prevent the continuing accumulation of stocks and is therefore just as urgently necessary as the disposal of existing stocks. This can be done by: (1) increasing the consumption of milk in its natural form, (2) skimming the milk at the farms which then supply cream to the dairies or produce butter themselves, (3) return of the liquid skimmed milk to the farm. Most of these measures are proposed in the action programme for 1977–1980 and a subsidy of about 4 UA per 100 kg of skimmed milk is paid.

Problems of equilibrium
The first point to note is that the target price for milk is between 93% and 96% of the value of its constituent elements—butter and skimmed milk powder—calculated at their intervention price.[4] But the contribution of each of these to the target price for milk has varied. As a result of the periodical surpluses of butter (1968–1970, 1972–1973 and 1976–1977) and the soya crisis (1973), the proportion relating to butter has fallen, from 75% to 54% (the proportion at present), while the proportion relating to skimmed milk increased correspondingly from 25% to 46%.

The intervention price of butter therefore replaces that of skimmed milk powder in achieving a given target price for milk. Since the same quantity of whole milk provides twice as much powder as butter, measured by weight, it is possible for example to obtain the same price for milk by reducing the intervention price for butter by one unit of account per 100 kg on condition that the price for skimmed milk powder is increased by 0.5 UA per 100 kg.[5] An increase in the price of one element for a given target price for milk allows the price of the other to be reduced and stimulates its consumption, while, at the same time, leading to a reduction in consumption of the first element, more particularly when the demand for this product is elastic.

The foregoing observations suggest that it is possible to restore the equilibrium of the market in the constituent elements of milk by adjusting their price, on condition that at least one of them is in short supply.

On the other hand, when over a period of several years both elements are in surplus or even only one of them is—and it is impossible to reduce the surplus without creating surpluses of the other—there can be said to be an imbalance. This has been the situation in recent years, with surpluses of butter and, at present, large surpluses of skimmed milk powder.

This then is the nature of the problem in regard to the equilibrium of the market in milk products—which is in a state of structural surplus. We shall approach it from a comprehensive and long-term angle without referring now to the situation in the beef and veal market. We shall examine in turn the possible measures and the impact they would have either in increasing demand or in reducing supply, while pointing out that this distinction should not be taken to imply that a clear-cut choice must be made between this or that solution: indeed, taken together, the various kinds of measures can either jointly or complementarily help to absorb the surpluses and above all prevent the production of further surpluses at a later stage. Finally, we shall evaluate the measures proposed from the threefold angle of minimizing social costs, distributing the cost among the groups of individuals concerned and tampering as little as possible with the mechanisms of the free market economy.

Measures designed to increase the demand for milk products

This first series of measures implies a given price for milk, accepted by the producers and not affecting the way in which resources are distributed among the various types of production on the farms.

Increasing the price of competitive products

In food for human consumption (margarine)
Taxing the primary commodities used in the manufacture of margarine would, by raising its price, alter the relationship between the price of margarine and butter in such a way as to boost butter consumption.

For the Community's finances this measure has the twofold merit of increasing tax revenue on imported oils while not requiring any contribution for the butter surpluses eliminated thereby. But it places the whole cost of disposing of the surplus butter on the consumer; for this reason, and because of its inflationary implications, it is unacceptable to certain socio-professional groups, and was consequently rejected recently by the Council.

In animal feed
Taxing imported protein foodstuffs (soya) at a rate which would make skimmed milk powder competitive would promote the sale of the latter, particularly in the manufacture of composite feeding stuffs.

34

This measure would have the same advantages for the Community budget as the taxation of the raw materials used in margarine. But it cannot easily be applied. In the first place it would entail repudiating undertakings given by the Community to the soy-exporting countries at the time that common organization of the markets was being established. Quite apart from this difficulty, its effect on costs following its application would pass first from the manufacturers of composite foodstuffs to the farmers, who—temporarily—would suffer a reduction in earnings before transferring the loss in turn to consumers of animal products through increased prices following the necessary adjustments; alternatively there might be a reduction in supply. In short, its inflationary effects and the transfer of the costs involved to the consumers make it hardly acceptable from the social angle.

Expansion of the markets
Expanding the markets entails in the first place a large number of disparate measures to increase the demand for milk products. Most of the following measures are to be found in the action programme for 1977–1980: the exclusive use of milk products in the manufacture of certain foodstuffs, sales promotion and market research, increased consumption of milk in schools, increased consumption of milk on the farms, the introduction of new techniques and new products . . . .

Obviously the research entailed would have to be financed in varying degrees from the EAGGF, as would the measures mentioned above for disposing of surpluses.

Dual price policy
This policy can involve two types of measure:

Fixing prices according to elasticity of demand
The first approach involves allowing a double—or multiple—price for milk according to the purpose for which it is used. This is justifiable insofar as the elasticity of demand for milk varies according to the use made of it (natural milk, butter, cream, cheese . . .). In this case total earnings are maximalized when the quantities sold on the various markets are such that marginal earnings, and not prices, are equal.

The principle is simple. It consists in fixing the price of the milk converted into a product for which the demand is inelastic at a relatively high level: this has the effect of putting up the price of this product without noticeably reducing consumption. By contrast, fixing at a lower level the price of milk converted into a product for which the demand is elastic would noticeably increase consumption of that product.

Working from the demand figures for the various milk products, it is possible to fix the different prices for milk according to the use made of it and to distribute the production of milk among the various uses in such a way as to maximalize the producers' total receipts. The preliminary task of determining the demand curves for milk products in the major consumption areas of the Community is, however, difficult to carry out.

35

Fixing an "in quota" price and an "ex quota" price

A second method would consist in fixing an "in quota" price in relation to the proportion of milk production disposed of on the Community market and an "ex quota" price corresponding to the price at which any surpluses would actually be sold (denaturing, exports, food aid . . .). This system, which places responsibility for surpluses on the milk producers, has the advantages of (1) discouraging production in excess of the requirements of the Community market, (2) reducing the expenditure on price support, and (3) nevertheless guaranteeing a remunerative price for "in quota" quantities.

Measures designed to reduce the supply of milk products

These measures are complementary and not alternative to those just described for increasing the demand for milk products. The difference is that the measures described below are based above all on principles relating to the distribution of resources among the farms.

Lowering the relative price of milk

The farmer allocates the fixed resources at his disposal among the various types of production according to the relationship between the various prices rather than the actual prices. It would of course be politically unacceptable to reduce the absolute price of milk as compared with the price of other products; the answer is to hold the rise in the price of milk to a lower level than the rise in other prices. In accordance with the economic principles of agricultural production this measure would influence the farmers' decisions so that they either allocated fewer factors to milk production and expanded other forms of production correspondingly, or practiced a less intensive form of farming (smaller quantities of concentrated foods for milk cows, less intensive care in the pastures . . .).

This approach, suggested by the economic aspects of the problem, will, we believe, have to be adopted in the long term insofar as the surpluses are of a structural nature or, in other words, if it is found that at existing prices the quantities of milk produced exceed those which the various users have decided to buy at that price, with the result that there is a constant increase in unsold stocks of milk products.

The cost of this measure, borne in full by the milk producers, will be felt more or less keenly, depending on their particular situation and whether it is applied in a discriminatory or non-discriminatory manner.

Non-discriminatory application

The impact of a non-discriminatory method of reducing the relative price of milk will vary according to the type of farm. A number of distinctions may be drawn.

Small producers in an area of grassland with a dairy herd, for whom milk products represent the major part of their gross earnings, will undoubtedly be the most affected by this measure.

The loss to farmers with a dual-purpose breed—that is, producing both milk and meat—would be considerably less, even where bovine products occupy an important place in the farm, and would depend on the variation in the price of beef and veal. It is quite possible that an increase in this price would offset the losses due to the relative reduction in the price of milk, even if the farmer did not change the balance of his production following the modification in the relationship between the different prices. But the commonest reaction following the rise in the relative price of beef and veal will undoubtedly be the adoption of techniques and types of production aimed at producing meat instead of milk.

Finally, on mixed farms, the decrease in the relative price of milk will be felt less insofar as (1) bovine products represent a smaller proportion of the farmer's total earnings, (2) milk production represents a smaller proportion of the earnings from bovine products (there would be no impact at all in the case of nursing cows) and (3) alternative forms of production (cereals, beet crops, . . .) are possible.

In these situations the impact of a decrease in the relative price of milk will vary according to the size of the farm. The smallest farms will suffer the greatest loss, while the larger farms are better able to offset the loss by structural improvements (increased yields, expanding the farm, mechanizing fodder production . . .).

In all these cases complementary measures would have to be taken to lessen the unfavourable impact of the relative reduction in price, e.g., greater use of technical advances (pasture management, foodstuffs, habitat . . .), structural improvements (increasing the average size of the herd . . .). These complementary measures, while ensuring a more efficient use of resources, would have the effect of helping to determine the farms' economic viability by means other than price increases.

Discriminatory method

A discriminatory method of applying a reduction in the relative price of milk according to the size of the farms and the volume of milk produced is justifiable both because of the extremely precarious economic situation of the small farms and because of the fact that the elasticity of the supply of milk varies according to farm size.

On the smallest farms the volume of production is insufficient to ensure a reasonable income level, which makes the farmers' standard of living precarious. Moreover, most of the resources on these farms is allocated to milk production, because it valorizes land, a comparatively rare factor. The result is that the supply of milk is inelastic: the production of milk can hardly be avoided and the volume produced corresponds very little to variations in price.

On larger farms, particularly mixed farms, the supply of milk is much more elastic, i.e., it responds much more to variations in price: milk production is continued, perhaps even intensified, when prices rise, while it is abandoned in favour of alternative products when prices fall. These farms would be less affected by a relative decrease in the price of milk, not only because they are generally in a less precarious situation than the smaller farms but because it is easier for them to transfer the funds previously used in milk production to other forms of production with the result that less milk would be produced.[6] A good many farms have already carried out such an adjustment in their production, mainly in response to social pressures.

A discriminatory reduction in the relative price of milk is therefore justifiable for economic and social reasons. It could be applied in the form of a co-responsibility levy, which would vary according to the size of the surpluses; the proceeds of this levy—fixed at a certain percentage of the price of milk—would be used (as provided in the 1977–1980 action programme) to finance various measures to expand the market, promote sales . . . . But certain types of farm would be exempt from this levy, for instance, small farms and farms situated in less-favoured regions.

The co-responsibility levy, whose amount would be adjustable according to the real or anticipated conditions of the market, would therefore be applied to those farms on which it would have the greatest impact with regard to the supply of milk, but without causing them any serious loss. But it would result in an indirect transfer of revenue from the farms to which it is applied to the small or less-favoured farms to which it is not applied. On no account should it be allowed to interfere with the winding-up of farms which are not viable in the medium-term.

Increase in the price of other products
This measure also alters the relationship of the different prices to the detriment of milk, but in an indirect way by increasing the price of the other products in order to stimulate production and at the same time put a brake on the decrease in milk production.

The repercussions of this measure are easy to assess: by producing a virtually overall increase in agricultural prices it would increase farmers' incomes, but to the detriment of consumers who would have to pay the cost. This fact, combined with the inflationary effects and the risk of surpluses of other products, makes it more difficult to apply this measure.

Freezing technical advances, investment and aids
The research into biological innovations and advances and their development and application (food, genetics, prevention of diseases . . .) are part of a vast apparatus established in the Member States (research, education, popularization . . .), and even if the application of all these activities were to be restricted there would probably be a little reduction in the operating expenditure involved. Such a measure is obviously not feasible. It would reduce supply by keeping costs at a high level and at the cost of deliberately renouncing the benefits to be gained by a more efficient use of resources.

With regard to investments, a distinction has to be made between investment for modernization and investment for expansion. As with the extended use of technical improvements, investment for modernization pure and simple, which has no direct impact on the volume of milk production, should be not only continued but also encouraged and the system of aids for this purpose—national and Community—could be maintained. Only those investments intended for expansion might be blocked, together with the aid allocated for them, although these investments are often at the same time intended for rationalization, the purpose of which is to increase labour efficiency.

To sum up, those aids which have a direct impact on milk production could be suspended while those which promote a more efficient use of resources should be maintained and even encouraged.

Joint equilibria of the market in bovine products

The prospect in the immediate future with regard to the equilibrium of the markets is one of a moderate shortage of beef and veal and a surplus of milk products. In these circumstances it is not appropriate to encourage the slaughter of dairy cows, since this would accentuate the shortage in beef and veal. On the contrary, supposing there is no sign of a disequilibrium in beef and veal in the medium-term, it will be necessary, in order to maintain or accelerate the rate of increase in beef and veal production and the contraction of milk production, to keep the number of cows at the present level, pending the conversion from milk production to beef and veal production. Such a transformation is all the more necessary if surpluses of dairy products are accompanied by a serious lack of demand for beef and veal in relation to production.

The problem, then, is to examine ways by which, for a given number of cows and the same overall volume of resources, it might be possible to reduce the production of milk and increase that of beef and veal. The following measures can serve this purpose.

Action on prices

In recent years there has been a continual modification in the relationship between prices and profits in the case of beef and veal, for which the guide price increased by 75% between 1970/71 and 1976/77, while the target price for milk increased by only 51.4% in the same period. The relationship between the price of beef and veal and that of milk has thus increased from 6.6 in 1970/71 to 7.8 in 1976/77.

As a result of this movement and of some extensification of production, due to the increased size of undertakings and a tighter supply of labour, production of beef and veal and of milk increased in the periods 1970 to 1975 at a rate of 2.5% and 1.7% respectively per year while, with the overall number of milk cows relatively constant there was a changeover from milk cows to nursing cows.

This explains why the changeover from milk production to beef and veal production began and continues—slowly but probably irreversibly—a necessary precondition, in any case, for the establishment of market equilibrium in the long-term.

The technical resources

Of all possible political measures, adequate price-fixing is the most effective means of bringing about this conversion from milk to beef and veal production and furthermore the best way of ensuring an efficient allocation of resources and safeguarding farmers' incomes, at least for those farmers dealing in both types of bovine production. It can be combined with complementary measures to accelerate the change, such as instructions regarding breeding, altering the criteria for selecting animals . . . .

39

There are numerous ways by which this change can be brought about. We may single out the following:

Firstly, the choice of *kinds* of production: the use of breeds suitable for meat production only, changeover—with dual purpose breeds—from milk cows to nursing cows.

Secondly, the choice of production *techniques*: increasing the age at which cattle are slaughtered, reducing the average life of milk breeds, postponing the first calving of young cows to a later age, redirecting national selection policies towards breeds more suited to meat production . . . .

Thirdly, *improving* techniques which have a major impact on meat production: combating sterility and increasing fertility, reducing the mortality rate among calves, increasing the birth rate . . . .

Fourthly, research and development of *new techniques*: ovular transplants, sex induction, induction of twin births . . . .

Equilibrium between bovine production and other types of agricultural production

The most likely assumption in the medium-term is one of a generalized surplus of milk products and of beef and veal. In this event, the number of cows should be reduced: this means reducing the overall volume of resources allocated to bovine production and ensuring that these resources are used more extensively.

Widely varying measures can be combined to achieve this purpose, e.g., (1) a relative reduction in the price of bovine products, achieved either by restraining the rate of increase in these prices as compared with that of other agricultural products, or on the contrary by a sharper increase in the prices of these other products: (2) slaughter premiums for milk cows; (3) grants to encourage farmers to discontinue these forms of production.

CONCLUSIONS

1. The existing surpluses of milk products appear to be the result of radical changes which have characterized recent years. The most significant of these are the improvement in production structures and technical advances made at all levels (farms, dairies, firms producing animal foodstuffs . . .) through considerable investments which produce savings only if the size of the undertakings is increased.

By replacing a large number of walled-off national or regional markets by a single vast open market, the common organization of the markets has led to the production of unusually large surpluses.

Finally, the political decision-making system scarcely favours a Community approach to this problem since the decisions rest with the Council, which consists of national ministers essentially answerable to their respective parliaments.

2. Rationalizing the milk sector and preventing subsequent imbalances will entail costs in both the short- and the medium-term. These can be borne directly either by the farmers, for example through reduced prices, co-responsibility levies . . . , or by the consumers, through increased retail prices.

But they can be borne indirectly by the whole community if they are taken over by the EAGGF. Finally, milk products can be put to new uses without any social cost.

3. Widely varying measures—price adjustments, direct subsidies, customs tariffs, market expansion . . . —can be employed to absorb existing surpluses and prevent new surpluses occurring later. Only those measures which are based on the principles of a free market economy are compatible with the optimum distribution of resources, an increase in the productivity of those resources and finally the achievement of the highest possible standard of living.

Consequently, among the measures which have the effect of modifying economic behaviour, price adjustments are to be preferred to subsidies, since the latter can lead to resources being used for very different types of production from those which ensure the maximum satisfaction for the community at large.

Besides, a given price level, whatever it may be, does not constitute a guarantee of adequate incomes to the small farmers or farmers situated in less-favoured regions, while it may lead to an overall volume of production exceeding demand. This elementary observation underlines the conflict of interest between farmers and the Community at large and, at the same time, the fact that it is impossible for price policy to be an effective instrument both for safeguarding incomes and for maintaining the equilibrium of the market. In other words, an incomes support policy based on prices entails the risk of departing from free market economy principles; it may also result in an inadequate allocation of resources.

This paradox highlights the need for a compromise. It is in the end sounder and undoubtedly less costly to give priority to the equilibrium of the markets and to employ social measures to remedy unpleasant or even painful situations arising from the constant contraction, at least in relative terms, of the milk sector.

4. Is it true to claim that the periodical recurrence of surpluses and the large contributions from the EAGGF for price support purposes indicate that the common agricultural policy in the area of milk products has been a failure? It would be presumptuous to hazard a reply to that question, simply because it is hard to imagine the situation without a common organization of the markets, for example, the difficulties which might have arisen under national policies, the effects of occasional shortages of milk products, or, again, the consequences in other fields without the benefits deriving from inter-regional specialization . . . .

But the examination of present difficulties suggests at least that the policy can be perfected and that any efforts undertaken will tend to lessen its weaknesses.

NOTES

1. Stocks of milk products reached record levels at the end of August 1976 with 1,385,300 tonnes of skimmed milk powder and 423,100 tonnes of butter.
2. This trend has also been observed in most other industrial countries: "In Australia, Canada, New Zealand and the Western European countries, there will

soon no longer be any possibility of increasing milk production because of a decrease in the use of liquid skimmed milk for animal feed", extract from "Skimmed milk powder: situation and outlook", FAO Monthly Bulletin on Agricultural Economics and Statistics, 7/8 July–August 1976, p. 34.

3. About 23 litres of whole milk with 3.7% of fat are required to make one kg of butter; the same quantity produces 22 litres of skimmed milk from which it is possible to obtain 2 kg of powder.

4. The target price is not a guaranteed price. The only prices actually reached are the intervention prices for butter and skimmed milk powder. For other products a similar relationship exists between the target price and the intervention price. Dairies selling their products only at the intervention price are penalized and can pay their farmers only 95% of the target price for milk.

Similarly, the intervention prices for butter and skimmed milk powder take account of the cost of converting the milk into butter and the skimmed milk into powder—these costs being assessed at the same level for all dairies.

The result is that the lower the costs of conversion, for example because of a favourable geographical position, adequate size, efficient organization . . . , the higher the price paid by the dairies to the farmers for the milk.

5. However, strictly speaking this would only be true if all the skimmed milk were converted into powder. In fact skimmed milk is used for other products: lactose, casein . . . .

6. Bublot, G., Villers, A., Crispiels, C., L'Orientation en Condroz de la race bovine de la moyenne et haute Belgique. Les substitutions lait-viande dans l'espèce bovine, Nauwelaerts, Louvain, 1963, p. 186.

III. AGRICULTURAL POLICY COUNTER-REPORT

Milk Policy in the European Community Policy on Surpluses of Powdered Milk

by *Dusan Sidjanski*

I have to thank the members of the Working Party which assembled at Geneva on 17 May 1977 for their contributions which have made it possible to draw up this Report. Those taking part in the meeting of the Working Party were the following: J. G. Becue, ASSILEC; J. L. Chomel, agronomic engineer; R. A. Ketteler, EUCOLAIT; D. Kurrer, AGV-BEUC; E. Libbrecht, Nestlé; F. Muller, Commission of the E.E.C.; A. Rioust de Largentaye, COPA-COGECA; R. Stamenkovic, FAO; Economic Commission for Europe, I. B. Warmenhoven, IMACE-UNILEVER. Mlle. M. Payro has assisted me in assembling the documentation, interviewing representatives of institutions and professional organizations, and preparing preliminary notes for the use of the Working Party. While expressing my thanks to all those who have helped me, I would nevertheless like to emphasize that I accept full responsibility for the conclusions in this survey or any omissions from it.

INTRODUCTION

The purpose of this survey is to depict the main participants and factors influencing decision-making regarding the milk policy of the European Community; with the object of attempting to determine which of these carry the greatest weight as far as the lines on which this policy develops are concerned.

In order to clarify the elements in this policy, we shall begin this survey by referring to some of the historical aspects, together with the scope of the problem and its nature. We shall then attempt to identify the main participants contributing directly or indirectly to decision-making in this field, both at the Community level and as external agents. This will in fact involve evaluating the weight and the attitudes of these participants in relation to certain restrictions, and how the factors relate to decisions taken by the Council of the Community. Finally, we shall try to determine whether an alternative policy is possible; having regard to the pattern of the forces and interests in existence, and likewise the various restricting factors which limit the degree of choice in this sector.

J.-L. Giraudy includes a brief review of how the milk policy has developed in the article devoted to the European surpluses of powdered milk.[1] Until 1972, the six Member States of the Community gave priority to supporting milk indirectly through butter. This support was based on the provisions of the Treaty of Rome regarding agricultural policy; and on the decisions which

Key to main organizations referred to by their French acronyms

Abbreviation	Full French title	Translation
ASSILEC	Association de l'industrie laitière de la CE	Association of the dairy industry of EEC
EUCOLAIT	Union Européene du commerce des produits laitiers	European Union of Traders in dairy products
BEUC	Bureau européen des unions de consommateurs	European Bureau of Consumers Unions
COFACE	Comité des organisations de familles de la CE	Family organizations
CCC	Comité consultatif des consommateurs	Consumer Consultative Committee
CGT CISL	Organisations syndicales	Trade union organizations
CES	Comité économique et social	Economic and social Committee
EUROCOOP	Coopératives de consommation	Consumers cooperatives
COPA	Comité des organisations professionnelles agricoles (de la CE)	Committee of (EEC) professional agricultural organizations
CIAA	Commission des industries agricoles et alimentaires	Commission for agricultural and foodstuffs industries
FNPL	Fédération nationale des producteurs de lait	National Federation of Milk Producers
IMACE	Association des Industries des margariniers des pays de la CE	Association of EEC margarine manufacturing industries
FEFAC	Fédération européene des fabricants d'aliments composés pour animaux	European Federation of manufacturers of composite foodstuffs
FEOGA	Fonds européen d'orientation et de garantie agricole	European Fund for Agricultural Restructure
PE	Parlement européen	European Parliament

have governed the course taken by this policy since 1961, which had been subject to deviations resulting from the pressures exercised by the farmers. In this connection, it is pertinent to recall first of all the milk strike which arose in France on 20 September 1964. This strike was unleashed by the National Federation of Milk Producers (FNPL), who demanded an immediate revalorization of the index price for milk at the production level. This strike is of interest for two reasons. Firstly because its causes are European; and secondly because it provoked expressions of solidarity from milk producers in the countries which are the partners of France. In point of fact, the Dutch, Belgian and German producers refused to deliver milk to France since they were unwilling to act as strike-breakers.[2] This solidarity among the farmers of the six Member States was later to be given forcible expression when they were confronted with the Commission's plans for establishing a medium-term structural balance in the milk market. Subsequently, it was going to make itself felt in relation to the programme which the Commission laid before the Council on 8 March 1968 (the Mansholt Plan). Following this, manifestations were organized by COPA, with the participation of the national federations, on 12 March 1968 and 27 May 1968. According to the observers, the last of these manifestations brought together some five thousand peasants coming from the six Member States—of whom a large proportion were French. During this meeting the Council met the wishes of the peasant organizations on several points, and fixed an intervention price for powdered skimmed milk.

In 1973, the crisis which broke out threw into relief the different elements which influence milk policy within the European Community. The problem of milk surpluses appeared to be directly linked to that of free imports of soya oilcake of United States origin. This freedom of access which had developed since the agricultural policy had been put into effect, has given rise to the creation of an animal-feeding industry (for pigs and poultry) developed on the basis of an external contribution of proteins.[3] Behind this crisis lay a poor soya-bean crop in the United States, and the embargo imposed on exports of the oilcake. At the request of the Western European livestock breeders and the Commission, the United States agreed to resume their deliveries some months later. Faced with the situation of insecure supplies, however, the Nine EEC countries decided to raise the price of powdered milk in order to stimulate production. According to J.-L. Giraudy, "they were then making a fatal mistake in taking no precautions against the possible return of American soya-beans and maize on a massive scale." For the crop sowings were simultaneously going strongly ahead on the other side of the Atlantic.

At the time when "the Nine" were re-expanding their production of powdered milk, soya beans and maize were again reaching the European market on a massive scale and at low prices. Furthermore, the world market for powdered milk was collapsing as a result of over-production in New Zealand and Australia. The economic crisis was reducing the market outlets and the purchases of the developing countries. The situation which has now developed in mid-1976 is thus one which leaves the participants confronting each other without any of them being ready to accept the responsibility for it, or to draw the necessary conclusions.[4]

EEC AND EXTERNAL PARTICIPANTS

Official participants: Institutions and Governments

These official participants can be divided in the first place into those responsible for proposing and taking decisions on behalf of the Community; that is to say, the Council and the Commission. To these two main participants can be added those within the Council who participate directly in the decision-making process by virtue of being representatives of their Member States; that is to say, the ministers and permanent representatives of the Member States. In addition to these official institutions playing an active part, there are also secondary official participants with an advisory role who should be taken into account, i.e., the Economic and Social Committee which ensures that the views of various categories of interests in the European Community are put forward, and the European Parliament which reflects in principle the differing political alignments that exist within the national Parliaments of the Member States. In varying degrees, these official participants forming part of the institutions of the Community make decisions or contribute to these being made.

Semi-official participants:—groups representing Community and national interests

The semi-official participants within the Community consist of the vast network of groups of interests and other associations which act as focal points for the interests existing in the different sectors of the activities of the Community. These participants comprise on the one hand the professional bodies, and the trades union and consumer organizations established at the Community level—amounting to some 350; and on the other, the corresponding national organizations.

Community groups carrying on discussions with the Commission
In its search for sources of support, the Commission has from the outset acted in concert with the professional organizations. Its basic policy in this connection consists of limiting the entitlement to consultation and permanent relations to bodies established at the Community level. This principle came under attack during the last negotiations preceding the enlargement of the European Community, when the Commission in fact held separate consultations with the national federations of the three candidate countries. This practice of direct consultations has resulted in somewhat distorting the process of Community consultations, to the extent that certain national federations belonging to the new members continued at times to make use of this direct channel in parallel with the routing through the Community bodies.

Dominant and important factors in the dairy products sector
An analysis of these factors, and of their potential influence, can be made with the help of an overall picture of the predominant indicators.[5] In this way we can evaluate the importance of the agricultural and dairy products sector in the economy of the European Community. The share of agriculture in the Gross Industrial Product (GIP), at factor costs, represents 5% in 1974, whereas its share in employment is 8.7% for 1975. The number of persons actively engaged in the agricultural sector in 1975 is about 9 million, as compared with a figure of 101 million for the total numbers employed. Thus, 2.9 million are employed in agriculture in Italy, 2.5 million in France, 1.8 million in Germany, and 250,000 in Eire, as compared with 700,000 in the United Kingdom. The highest percentage is recorded for Eire, namely 24.5% of total employment; followed by Italy (15.8%), France (11.6%), and Denmark (9.8%), with this percentage reaching only 2.7% for the United Kingdom. These data provide gross indicators for the importance of the agricultural sector, which in addition represents 7.7% of the value of EEC exports in 1975. At the same time, the European Community continues to be a large importer of agricultural products, which accounted for 20.8% of the total value of imports in 1975.

Milk stands at the substantial level of nearly 19% of the total agricultural production of the European Community. This proportion varies with the different Member States, i.e., 37% for Luxembourg, 28% for Eire, 27% for the Netherlands, 22% for the United Kingdom, 17% for France, and only 10% for Italy. Furthermore, the contribution of the milk sector to the total agricultural production of the Community, in terms of individual products, shows corresponding variation. German milk production accounts for 27% of EEC milk production, and French production for 25%. Germany and France alone produce more than half of EEC milk; followed by the United Kingdom (14%), the Netherlands and Italy (11.1%).[6]

These indicators which can contribute to the structural analysis do not take full account of the actual importance of agriculture and of various products, since they give no consideration to the *rise and fall in the weighting of the sectors*. These sectors of which the food industries are a part are closely linked to the production of milk. It is estimated that the whole range of processing and distributing activities developed in connection with agricultural products accounts for about 20% of the GIP of the Community. It is evident that this interrelation between various sectors constitutes the fundamental objective of the alliances between groups representing them.

Aggregation and representation of interests

This general aggregative and representational function is ensured both at the global level and in the European Community as a whole by central organizations. COPA and COGECA are the spokesmen for the producers and members of cooperatives in various agricultural sectors; the section of COPA which specializes in milk and dairy products comprises the national federations of milk producers and cooperatives. The UNICE Agricultural and Food Industries Commission (CIAA) formed by the central national federations of the industries processing agricultural products, represents the whole of the agricultural foodstuffs industry; independently of the sector sub-divisions which are covered by specialized organizations on a product basis. COCCEE has the function of representing all commerce in the European Community.[7] Because of their general functions, these central organizations cannot devote themselves exclusively to protecting the main activities of the dairy sector of the European Community. There is a degree of convergence, and even an identity of attitudes vis-à-vis the agricultural policy within COPA itself; but such is not the case in industry or commerce, where there is a marked cleavage between products competing with each other.

It is therefore natural that the specific interests of different branches of industry or commerce handling dairy products should be catered for by specialized organizations. The processors on the one hand, and those trading in dairy products on the other, are thus brought together in the Association of the dairy industry of the EEC (ASSILEC) and the European Union of Traders in Dairy Products (EUCOLAIT).[8] Also in existence is a European Federation of manufacturers of composite animal foodstuffs (FEFAC), which represents the bulk of the EEC fodder, and all the manufacturers except the cooperative sector and small manufacturers; and an Association of the industries of margarine manufacturers in the EEC countries (IMACE). These two organizations are directly interested in the problems arising from surpluses of powdered milk and butter.[9]

Alongside these organizations characterized by a high capacity for exerting influence, particularly because of the position they hold in production and distribution activities in the EEC economies, the *consumers* emerge as a group possessing a potential strength that has not been fully utilized. Their principal weakness lies in the lack of definition of the interests of the consumers, the producers or the workers. In these circumstances, the problem is one of the priorities which the person concerned attach to various interests. It nevertheless appears easier to gather together the men on a basis of their incomes rather than their expenditure. The responsibilities of women in this field often make them the dynamic element in this group. The factors of mass consumption and of this group's favourable image where public opinion is concerned mean, however, that it has an enormous potential; as has been demonstrated by the activities of consumers in the United States, Canada and Sweden. For the present, the groups of European consumers lack both an efficient organization and the technical knowledge and resources possessed by the other professional organizations or by large enterprises engaged in production and distribution.

Since their strength varies in the different countries concerned, the consumers are attempting to establish themselves as a third force in relation to their traditional social allies. Their main objective is to obtain consumer goods at low prices, but combined with the highest possible quality. In the European Community, several organizations speak for consumer interests: the European Bureau of Consumer Unions (BEUC), the family organizations (COFACE), the consumption cooperatives (EUROCOOP) and the trades union organizations (CES and CGT CISL).

Following the dissolution of the Committee for contacting the consumers of the EEC, the Commission decided in September 1973 to create a consultative committee of consumers (CCC) which consists of three representatives of BEUC, an equal number of representatives of COFAC and EUROCOOP, six representatives of various trade unions, and ten experts appointed by the Commission; four of the latter being nominated by organizations concerned. The task of the new Committee is put the interests of consumers before the Commission, and to give its views to the Commission on all the problems connected with the formulation and implementation of the policy and activities relating to the protection and information of consumers.

Bearing in mind the still fluid nature and the very variable weight of the national organizations,[10] we can conclude that for the present the likelihood of the consumers playing an important part in the Community's decision-making procedures is still small. But the fact remains that with new bodies representing the public interest (in matters of ecology, health protection and collective assets), we have here a political force that is tending to play a more cardinal part in all the decisions taken at the Community and national levels.

Access to decision-making institutions and centres

The group in the Community possess many ways of access to the Community's institutions, namely: main ways of access to the "active authorities", the Commission and the Council; secondary access channels to the Economic and Social Committee and the European Parliament; indirect access provided

48

through the channel of national governments.[11] In addition to these access channels, the groups can have recourse to a number of methods of exercising indirect influence through public opinion and the political parties.

In order to maintain continuing contact with the interested groups, the Commission has taken special care to develop a vast network of surrounding *consultative committees* in the agricultural field. Half of the places in these committees are allotted to COPA, alongside other groups. Even FEFAC has a seat in the Consultative Committee for dairy products.[12] But whatever the importance of the consultative committees, the most effective influence is exercised directly with the Commission at the time when its proposals are drawn up[13] during the meetings which it convenes, or indeed through semi-official contacts maintained by the groups with the service-staff of the Commission.

There are two channels of access to the Council, i.e.:

1. Groups have the possibility of direct approach to the Chairman of the Council. The Praesidium of COPA, for example, accordingly from time to time communicates directly with the Council, and coordinates the dispatch of messages originating from the member federations.

2. The groups likewise exercise a direct influence on the Governments through the channel of their national federations, when there has been mutual agreement that a situation of converging views and a common approach has been reached. When, on the other hand, there is disagreement between the members or a majority and a minority report, the groups regain their powers of exercising their influence independently and attempt to make the case for their interests with their governments; with the latter frequently defending them before the Council. In practice, however, the less the chances of a national group being defended by its government, the more it will look for support from its colleagues in the sector concerned, and from their organization at the Community level.

As far as secondary channels of access are concerned, COPA for instance coordinates the activities of the agricultural representatives within the economic and social Committee; and likewise interventions with the European Parliament.[14] At present, however, these Community institutions have a consultative function, and only a marginal influence on the process of decision-making at the Community level. Once their views have been formulated, the CES and the PE are seldom associated with the final negotiations which take place within the Council, with the active participation of the Commission.

PROGRAMME OF COMMISSION AND COALITIONS OF INTERESTS

In order to analyse this decision-making process which will lead to the fixing of prices and to some other measures on 26 April 1977, we will examine briefly how this originated; and likewise the positions of the institutions of the Member States and the professional organizations.[15] We will then recapitulate the two phases of the process of negotiation, and the decision to which this protracted bargaining is leading; and finally, the synoptic picture will set out the positions of the principal participants and the measures adopted following the final decision.

Action programme of the Commission[16]

The action programme is the basis for the decision of 26 April 1977. The Commission has perceived that the present situation in 1976–1977 shows a serious lack of balance in the milk sector. In the Community, the milk produced from dairy herds comprising 25,200,000 cows reached some 91.7 million tons in 1975 (91.3 million tons in 1974). In the face of this rising production, the slowly declining human consumption of dairy products was reaching a level equivalent to 85.4 million tons of milk. The deliveries of milk to the dairies amounted to 81.5 million tons, compared with 80.9 million tons in 1974. At the end of the year, stocks of butter were 164,000 tons, and 1.1 million tons for skimmed milk. There will be a tendency for the structural surplus to increase in the future, against the background of rising production faced with static or even slightly declining consumption. The constantly increasing yields, including the permanent effect of a favourable price ratio between milk and soya-beans, the increased ratio of milk deliveries to the dairies, and the end of the current declining phase in the cycle of dairy cows, are all factors which indicate a probable increase in production; and consequently, a surplus in the years to come.[17] This imbalance has direct repercussions on the expenditure of FEOGA (Guarantees Section) on the dairy sector. This expenditure rose from 600 million Units of Account in 1968/69, in the Community of the Six, to 1,521 million in 1973 in the Community of the Nine. The credits scheduled for 1976 amount to about 1.9 million Units of Account. As a result of the various pressure factors, the Commission has tried to develop an overall policy for both the supply and demand applicable to milk products; and likewise for the competitive products. The Commission's programme embodies the following elements:
a. reduction of the dairy herds by introducing throughout the Community a system of premiums for non-delivery of milk and reconversion;
b. suspension of national and Community assistance grants in the dairy sector, for a period of three years;
c. introduction of a co-responsibility levy, including a consultation procedure;
d. expansion of the markets of the Community;
e. measures making it possible to reduce the imbalance referred to in paragraph 4.
In connection with this last point, the Commission proposes to take account of the price trends for imports of vegetable proteins when fixing the co-responsibility levy on milk producers. The Commission considers that the existing imbalance between butyric fats and vegetable fats can be partially remedied by incorporating into the common agricultural policy a tax on vegetable oils and fats (TDC 1507, TDC 1504). This tax should be imposed on both the imported and the domestic product. Its level should correspond to that of the co-responsibility levy on milk.

50

The Commission's action programme has been the subject of comments by the economic and social Committee; which, while not opposing the proposal relating to the suspension of assistance grants, considers that a distinction should be made between grants aimed at creating new herds or new dairy installations, and those taking the form of investment for modernization. The fact is that blocking the modernization and rationalization of the dairies involves the risk of reducing the competitiveness of the existing installations.[18] The CES approve the principle of the co-responsibility tax, but draw the attention of the Commission to the inadvisability of putting this proposal into effect at this time in the regions afflicted by the drought. The CES consider that a distinction must be made between the discussions of the Commission with the representatives of the producers on the amount of the tax paid by the latter, and consultations regarding the formulation and implementation of a policy for milk. The producers should be primarily associated with the first of these aspects. Furthermore, as regards the scope of the consultative committee, the entities economically concerned with the milk sector should be more closely associated with the formulation of the milk policy and the management of the market.[19] In short, the CES take the view that the milk producers could not accept the introduction of a co-responsibility levy unless they were assured that the prices fixed for dairy products would permit a relative expansion of their income. (2.4.4) From the Committee's point of view, co-responsibility is thus linked on the one hand to certain objective factors; and on the other, to the form of consultation and collaboration between the producers and the Commission. Although the CES were initially divided regarding the Commission's proposals for the *fats* sector (2.4.8), they have finally pronounced against this proposal. On the other hand, they record their agreement with the Commission's views as regards seeking and establishing new market outlets for the milk sector. The Commission's action programme has accordingly elicited a number of views and reactions. It has obliged both the institutions and the Member States and groups concerned to define their attitudes towards an overall proposal containing concrete measures.

Supporting coalition

The supporting coalition is composed of the COPA–COGECA complex and ASSILEC, and likewise their associate EUCOLAIT. It includes the Community and national associations of milk producers and processors: COPA and its section of milk producers, the private or cooperative dairies; and likewise the associations of milk-processors (ASSILEC) who fall into line with the position taken by COPA. In point of fact, it is the customary or economic practice for the processors always to purchase all the milk delivered by the producers. Their dependence on each other is such that the processors can only approve any measure that ensures them adequate supplies of milk. The situation of EUCOLAIT is equivocal; while considering that an incomes policy is a necessity and that the surpluses are the result of a misguided marketing policy, it favours free trade just as the commercial world as a whole does so. Despite some divergencies, this complex of associations constitutes a

51

coalition favouring a high price for milk and various support measures guaranteeing a given level of income for the producers and repurchases from the processors.

The incomes policy seems to be made necessary by the existence in the Community of about 1.5 million small operators whose living depends on the price of milk. "Milk is where our pay comes from" is the message proclaimed by the demonstrators in Brussels and Luxembourg, as well as in the national capitals.[20] Despite their limited contributions to the total production of milk in the Community, these small operators introduce a rigid element because of their numbers and the vital importance of selling milk for the incomes of their families. Dispersed and relatively weak, they possess a degree of electoral and political strength. In addition, they are reinforced by an alliance with other producers who have them to thank for a steady source of income. In this way, the converging interests of these different groups lead them to form one vast coalition.

a. *COPA–COGECA*

In their comments on the proposals of the Commission, COPA and COGECA consider that "the persistence of a fundamental imbalance between supply and demand in the milk market is calculated to endanger not only the functioning of the common organization of the markets in the milk sector, and for dairy products, but also the common agricultural policy itself. This is why COPA and COGECA agree with the Commission that it is necessary to mount a very large-scale action programme lasting for several years and embracing a whole series of measures having a bearing both on the supply of, and on the demand for dairy products, with a view to thus restoring a better balance in the Community's milk market."

COPA and COGECA are also strongly critical of the fact that the Commission does not place the emphasis on certain reasons for the present situation, and that it omits any reference to the reasons which derive directly from the policy followed under the procedures of the Community. In this respect, COPA and COGECA have stressed the fact that the present difficult situation in the milk market also results from the absence of a real long-term Community commercial policy and an overall Community policy in the fats and proteins sector; and likewise a Community policy aimed at the exclusive utilization of butyric and nitrogenous fatty substances for the lactic components of dairy products. They emphasize, moreover, the absence of assistance for skimmed milk intended for animal feeding at a level below that corresponding to the cumulative increases in the intervention price for powdered skimmed milk; the non-adjustment of the managerial structure and the errors in market management for the various dairy products, and powdered skimmed milk in particular; the deficiencies in the effectiveness of the policy for assisting foodstuffs, which should meet the requirements of the Third World and should in particular include progressively increasing aid, multi-annual commitments, and stockpiling as a safety measure in order to cope with the demand in periods of shortage, and the effects of imports of dairy products carried out under the terms of Protocol No. 18 of the Treaty of Accession, without regard to the market situation. It is for these reasons that COPA and COGECA reject any responsibility, and especially any financial one, for the running-down of the existing stocks, which should be the responsibility of the public authorities.

For COPA and COGECA, there cannot be any question of accepting the proposals of the Commission regarding the financial co-responsibility of the milk producers, as long as the whole of the conditions and procedures set out in the letter from COPA to Monsieur Lardinois dated 29 June 1976 have not been complied with. Among these conditions, these two organizations mention price guarantees, assumption of the responsibility for the absorption of existing stocks by the public authorities, collaboration with the Commission during the preparation of re-structuring measures; maintenance of a special account which would be controlled jointly by the Commission, the milk producers and the milk-processing sector; continuation of the assistance accorded to dairy operations and milk-processing enterprises. Furthermore, the introduction of a tax on certain fats proposed by the Commission constitutes another essential condition for acceptance of a co-responsibility levy. They also consider that the policy of encouraging investments is indispensable for the rationalization and structural improvement of the milk-processing enterprises.

They deeply regret that the Commission's plans to expand the markets of the Community in the milk sector have not been embodied in proposals for actual regulations. In addition, they call to mind the fact that they have always supported the idea of encouraging the utilization of liquid skimmed milk on the farms and wherever this utilization is technically possible (groups of producers, livestock-raising cooperatives), by measures guaranteeing long-term supplies at a competitive price in relation to proteins providing a substitute for skimmed milk in its entirety. Similar measures for powdered skimmed milk, and likewise measures aimed at encouraging the utilization of powdered skimmed milk in the flour used in bread-making, should also be considered at this time.

Furthermore, COPA and COGECA are of the opinion that the premiums for non-marketing of milk or processing it constitute a very positive factor. They consider, however, that restructuring and reorientation in the direction of beef-rearing cannot be carried out overnight. A substantial injection of funds at the outset is essential. Only the operators with ample finance can consider a reorientation of this type; for the enterprises operating on a modest scale, a reconversion implies reconverting outside the milk sector. The general recession facing the European economy as a whole involves the risk of such a switch being equivalent to creating unemployment. In addition, sales of milk constitute the daily bread of agriculture, and as such fulfil a very definite function. Taken as a whole, however, measure of this type—reconversion premiums—would lead to an extension of the structural policy demanded by all concerned.

b. *ASSILEC*

In general, the processors consider that the distinction between structural and circumstantial surpluses is a difficult one to make; since the incidence of uncontrollable factors has a great influence on production, and since the repercussions of a substantial level of production are intensified where products which can be held in store, such as butter and powdered milk, are concerned.

As far as surpluses are concerned, the processors have attitudes exactly similar to those of the producers, although they consider that it is not for them to make the first moves in this connection. Conscious that there is a real solidarity in being between them and these engaged in the agricultural field, they have attitudes very similar to those of COPA as regards the common agricultural policy, and they support the demands of the latter on the question of prices. As regards the co-responsibility tax, they consider that "there can naturally be no question of the milk processors taking a different view on this point from that of the producers."[21] ASSILEC and its members have associated themselves with the conditions put forward by COPA; but have added further conditions, particularly as regards the methods of ensuring the indicator price for the producers, and the increased importance to be given to exports as one of the means of remedying the existing disequilibrium.[22]

The processors have opted for a tax on imports of proteins, and likewise for a tax on fats which would enable resources to be released—harmonization of the conditions of competition. They consider, however, that these measures have little chance of being adopted; in view of the reservations of certain Member States and the problems that they would give rise to with GATT. In addition, these measures are encountering opposition from the employers, the workers' trades unions and the consumers; all of whom aim at maintaining the low prices in order to avoid resulting pressures on industrial prices.[23] As advocates of encouraging consumption, they take the view that the measures proposed are too restrictive. As regards giving assistance to foodstuffs, while desiring that this be developed, they suggest that the Commission should take steps to avoid disturbing the traditional channels of trade. They also consider that errors of judgment by the Commission (a too limited increase in the export rebate) have damaged the possibilities for disposals on the external market. Moreover, in agreement with EUCOLAIT, they criticize the slowness of the bureaucratic machinery of the Community, and decisions which are at times taken in the face of the trends and results in losses of substantial outlets.

c. *EUCOLAIT*

This association comes into the picture as regards several positions adopted by the producers and processors, while also reflecting the interests and motivations of the large importing and exporting wholesalers.

EUCOLAIT, for example, "cannot fail to note that the basis provided by the Treaty of Rome—that is to say, the guaranteeing of the farmers' incomes —greatly handicaps the prices policy."[24] On this point EUCOLAIT goes no further, while recognizing that the incomes policy is a necessity. In another connection, it considers that the internal trading within the Community has proved to be a much more important development than could have resulted from bi-lateral trading.

As regards the commercial policy, the free-trade principles of EUCOLAIT show divergencies from the views of the industry and the producers; who because of their situation tend to be Protectionist-minded. Nevertheless, they are in agreement in taking note that the entry of the United Kingdom has meant a change in the commercial policy because of the traditional links which that country maintains with New Zealand. As far as the export efforts are concerned, the traders support the processors in their complaints against the slowness and the dissemination of the decisions taken by the Committee of Management as regards export rebates; thereby preventing the products of the Community from competing effectively with New Zealand and Australian products. "Through its cumbrousness, its mechanical nature, and the publicity which takes place in connection with all the implementation decisions (especially the amount of the export rebates), the Community authorities in charge penalize the entire body of European exporters." [25] Together with the producers and the industrialists, the traders regret the absence of a common medium- and long-term commercial policy. On this aspect also, their points of view converge; although the traders lay particular stress on the struggle against the acts of commercial discrimination practised by the United States. While not approving the introduction of the taxes on imports of proteins, EUCOLAIT has protested against the price maintenance for proteins and fats. As traders in dairy products, the members of EUCOLAIT basically constitute a defensive coalition alongside the producers and processors of these products.

Opposing coalition

In opposition to this supporting coalition there are two associations FEFAC, supported by the rearers of calves or pigs and poultry, and IMACE, who have an attitude of self-defence towards certain measures proposed by the Commission.

a. *FEFAC and its allies*
The European Federation of Manufacturers of Composite Foods is opposed to certain measures aimed at reducing soya-bean imports into the European Community. This important Federation, which with the exception of the cooperative sector and the small manufacturers embodies the bulk of the tonnage produced within the Community, has the objective of ensuring cheaper supplies of raw foodstuffs for its members. In these circumstances, we can expect that if milk were to become a competitive product, the members of this Association would not hesitate to make greater used of powdered milk in the manufacture of composite foodstuffs. This incorporation of powdered milk has been practised with the assistance of the Community. At the present time, however, it seems difficult to envisage the possibility of replacing soya-beans with powdered milk. In order to keep soya-bean prices low, the members of this Association are simultaneously fighting any restrictions on imports of soya-beans and all taxes which could be imposed on that product within the Community. With this objective in view, they are finding allies among the poultry, calves and pig breeders, and especially among the large-scale enterprises, which have been established and built up on the basis of cheap foodstuffs. The support of the producers of pigmeat appears to them even more solid against the improbability of pig-breeding being able to absorb higher prices for pig-foods.

In March 1977, FEFAC addressed a letter to the Chairman of the Council of Ministers responsible for agriculture, in which its demands were expressed in these terms:— "We request you to be good enough to promote a freezing of the net price when deciding on an increase in the assistance given to powdered skimmed milk incorporated in milk substitutes, equivalent to the same number of units of account as those applicable to the intervention price for powdered skimmed milk, either at the beginning of the next financial year for milk products, or in September. The Commission is considering laying down new regulations allowing the manufacturers of composite foodstuffs to purchase powdered skimmed milk in bulk on the market, and not from the stocks accumulated under the intervention policy. We request you to delay putting this plan into effect for at least one year, or to transfer the powdered skimmed milk into large capacity sacks at the Commission's expense. We would ask you to be good enough to support the creation of an 'emergency exit' for the manufacturers of milk substitutes, who are already paying three times the price paid by the manufacturers of composite foodstuffs; thereby enabling them to buy powdered skimmed milk at the intervention price at any time, and without paying any supplement. We consider that the introduction of special aid for the pig-breeders amounting to 5.5 Units of Account per 100 kilos of liquid skimmed milk is undesirable when compared with the general aid of 4 Units of Account per 100 kilos for liquid skimmed milk used for feeding livestock."

To the extent that the production of these composite foodstuffs is dependent upon imports of proteins and soya-beans, especially of United States origin, the interests of these associations converge; provided that they become confused with those of other external participants, such as the United States itself and the producers and exporters of American soya-beans and proteins.[26]

There are also other countries exporting agricultural products who find themselves in the same position as the United States, such as Brazil, Argentina, New Zealand and Australia. As long as the governments of these countries act in defence of the interests of their producers and exporters, they try to influence the decisions of the Community in favour of their exports.

The steps they take to bring pressure frequently fall into line with those of the members of FEFAC; their common interest consisting in retaining free access to imports of these basic products in order to obtain them at the lowest possible prices. To their position as semi-official participants, as compared with the institutions and governments of the Community, the governments of these countries also add their abilities to exercise official influence within certain international organizations such as GATT and CNUCED. In particular, by making use of the standards and obligations of GATT they have an opportunity to safeguard the free entry of soya-beans into the Community.[27] According to certain observers, the animal foodstuffs industries have played a part in aggravating the imbalance in the dairy sector; in particular, by putting a brake on exports of powdered milk from the Community during the proteins crisis, and by causing the European producers to lose part of their traditional market in the Third World countries.[28]

Subsequently, the fall in world prices in relation to the Community intervention prices has made it more difficult to dispose of the stocks of powdered milk which are piling up in the Community, and continues to have this effect. This problem of the surpluses thus has not only economic aspects but political ones linked to the weight of the groups of interests and governments and the powers of the Community authorities to make their own decisions; and more generally, to the structure of the political forces.

b. *IMACE*

The European association of margarine manufacturers (IMACE) in its turn opposes any tax on fats, vegetable and marine. On this point, it is interesting to note that the Commission has proposed two alternative solutions, and that in its final decision the Council has decided in favour of measures for disposing of the butter without introducing the tax on fats. It will be remembered that in 1963 the Council of Ministers for agriculture decided to bring in a tax on fats. This decision was approved in principle by all the Member States, but was left in abeyance because of opposition from the Dutch and Belgian governments with which the German government associated itself.

Although its point of view is strongly supported by several governments, IMACE nevertheless sent a letter to the member of the European Parliament at the beginning of 1977, in order to ensure *their support*.

This request is significant for two reasons: firstly, because this is a step which aims at enlarging the basis of support on which IMACE can count, and at consolidating its position; and this public intervention suggests that other preventive measures have been taken to avoid losing the support of certain governments; secondly, because this action is intended to win over to the side of IMACE European Parliamentarians who at present are only rarely the target for the solicitations of such important groups of interests.

c. *Consumers Consultative Committee (CCC)*

For various reasons, the consumers support all the measures aimed at reducing consumer prices. Their interests accordingly coincide at least partially with those of FEFAC and IMACE.

The CCC takes note that there are disequilibriums between structural and social aspects of the common agricultural policy, and likewise basic misconceptions.[29] It considers that the decisions taken, especially on prices, have contributed to preserving the agricultural structure, only 10% of the expenditure having been devoted to the structural policy. This price policy has created unsaleable surpluses, and the cost of these to the Community is increasing year by year; that is to say, 3.7 milliard Units of Account for 1974, 4.5 milliards for 1975, and a probable total of 5.8 milliard Units of Account for 1976. This policy causes disquiet to the Governments, and irritates the third countries, the consumers and the farms themselves, with the exception of a minority of farmers who have the benefit of considerable fixed incomes.

The CCC criticises the practice of uniform production prices for undertakings with high and low productivity. By impeding the selective process in agriculture, this policy has resulted in structural surpluses. "Such overproduction is absurd and accentuates the problems from day to day. Its financing can no longer be guaranteed.

"This drying of milk is an immense waste of money and energy. While creating a new industry, the farmer benefits from only 10% of the milliards

57

spent. The costs alone of the common policy for the milk market will rise further in 1977; reaching a figure of more than 2 milliard Units of Account, or 25% of the budget of the EEC. But thanks to the intervention system and subsidized exports to third countries, agricultural production no longer has any need to be directed only towards the possibilities of disposals in normal conditions, since it has thus found an apparently unlimited artificial outlet."[30]

The CCC is therefore opting for a structural and selective policy which is leading to a blockage, and even to a lowering of prices. "Marginal farming operations which should be maintained for social or regional reasons, or for reasons connected with protection of the environment, should receive direct aid in the matter of incomes."[31]

The consumers consider that a figure of 80% for the level of self-sufficiency is adequate for avoiding both over-production and shortages. The remaining 20% could be supplied by the international market (the United States, New Zealand, Australia and Canada in particular). Furthermore, security of supplies would be ensured by an import and export policy operating through longer-term contracts. This policy should lead to more stable price and supply conditions within the Community and in the world; but without stifling competition to the detriment of the consumer. Finally, the consumers consider that the common agricultural policy has above all been directed towards protecting the interests of the producers, and not towards those of the consumers.

MEMBER STATES AND NEGOTIATIONS ON AGRICULTURE IN THE COUNCIL OF MINISTERS[32]

The member Governments figure as defenders of the interests of the main categories of national activities. The various national groups certainly attempt to influence the positions of their Governments. Nevertheless, the Governments are constrained to arbitrate between the interests of different sectors in order to fix priorities for the negotiations which take place in the Council on the basis of the proposals of the Commission. Certain governments thus give unequivocal support to their milk producers, whereas others adopt a more qualified position, or openly favour the importers; or in the case of the British Government, for instance, even favour the consumers. Against this background, the leverage exerted by agriculture and the milk producers is a prime consideration as regards the Government's choice. Nevertheless, this factor does not make it possible to foresee what the governmental position will be, since this depends on a whole range of multifarious considerations. For example, the fact of having an efficient agricultural sector with a high level of output, and a substantial processing industry, as in the Netherlands, can lead the government in question to opt for a free-trade approach rather than for the protection of the producers. The existence of external participants and international obligations may well influence this choice. The result is that the Government is not simply the natural spokesman for a particular sector, but that its preliminary decision is related to several participating elements and to a global picture. These various governmental points of view formulated unilaterally then find themselves facing a process of dynamic confrontation with those of the other Governments, at the level of the Council. From this moment, the complex negotiating procedure is set in motion on the basis of the formal proposals submitted by the Commission. The last negotiations which led to the decision of 26 April can be divided into two main stages: the negotiations on 15 and 27 March, and the final negotiations on 26 April 1977. These negotiations were also subject to a time-limit imposed by the nature of events, namely the need to fix prices for the 1977/78 agricultural year.

Negotiations of 15 and 25 March 1977[33]

The positions of the member Governments can be summarized as follows: The policy of *France*, the leader of the countries favouring the producers, follows a traditionally logical pattern. The French Government does indeed admit that structural surpluses must be avoided, but considers that within a not distant future the demand for foodstuffs will be such that the prospect of surpluses will give place to shortfalls more difficult to handle than the present surpluses. In the milk sector, price rises are supported and certain adjustments to the common agricultural policy accepted. The French Government favours the granting of direct aid to producers, and opposes its suspension; it accepts the financial co-responsibility of producers on condition that the funds collected are used to improve the situation in the milk market and that the level of co-responsibility is reduced to 1.5% instead of the 2.5% proposed by the Commission. In addition, it insists on the exclusion of the mountain areas.

Holland favours a substantial price increase; it accepts the principle of co-responsibility while considering that a levy rate of 2.5% would result in too small an increase. This involves the danger of different levels of compensation, which would in particular lead the producers to develop their livestock and to increase their output. Holland accepts the ideas of co-responsibility, but rejects the Commission's actual proposal. It also opposes any tax on fats, and supports consumer subsidies.

For *Denmark*, as for Holland, the price policy constitutes the main instrument which can ensure stable markets. The Government favours an increase, has agreed to co-responsibility, and has recorded its opposition to the tax on vegetable fats while suggesting that this be replaced by assistance to consumers. Finally, with a mind to the importance and the high yield of its agriculture, the Danish Government insists on an expansion of the market outlets.

Belgium and *Luxembourg* are in favour of higher prices, but have reservations concerning co-responsibility. They both request that a link be established between this principle and the tax on vegetable fats. This tax should restore the competitive situation between butter and margarine.

Germany declares itself in favour of a slight increase in the price of milk. It gives its agreement to the principle, but not to the level of the co-responsibility levy; which would lead to a lowering of prices in Germany because of the "agro-monetary" situation there. Finally, Germany is opposed to the tax on fats.

59

Eire also favours a price increase; the more so, because dairy products play an important part for the numerous small farmers. As regards co-responsibility, the Eire Government has reservations; it would like to see the exclusions not limited to mountain areas but extended to all areas where conditions are unfavourable.

Italy is categorically opposed to co-responsibility; and likewise to all restrictive measures, in view of its inadequate output of dairy products.

The position of the *United Kingdom* reflects the scepticism which it has shown since the beginning of the negotiations for entry regarding the common agricultural policy. Its attitude expresses its "position as net consumer and importer" which has only retained a marginal agricultural industry. For this reason, and because of the inflation from which the country is suffering, it requests a price-freeze. It wishes prices to be fixed in relation to the income necessary for the efficient and not the marginal producers; and it is firmly opposed, with the support in this respect of large sections of public opinion, to the sale of subsidized surpluses outside the Community. For these various reasons, the British Government—represented, moreover, by its Minister responsible for food supplies who is closer to the consumers than the producers—has declared itself definitely in favour of co-responsibility, and has vigorously opposed any tax on fats or imports.

The truth is that the coalitions of groups and Governments form networks of interests and forces which condition the negotiations. In general, the position of the Governments reflect fairly faithfully the weight and the situation of agriculture and the importance of the agricultural population in the different countries (3 millions in Italy, 2.5 millions in France, almost 2 millions in Germany, 250,000 in Eire and 230,000 in Denmark); and likewise the weight of other interests. It is evident that because of their organizations and the political strength that they represent, together with the scale of the supporting activities involved, the farmers continue to exercise pressure on the political authorities; and that that the latter cannot ignore their legitimate interests and the part that they play in our societies. For this reason, and on account of the common agricultural policy put into effect for years past by the Community of Six, and later with some hesitations by the Community of Nine, the broad lines of a possible compromise have emerged since the beginning of the negotiations. It was accordingly clear that the tax on fats was arousing too much opposition on the part of the United Kingdom, Germany, the Netherlands and Denmark, while international pressures and the interests grouped around FEFAC were making it practically impossible to introduce a tax on imports of proteins.

Despite the disagreement on the method of finance and on butter, a compromise thus appeared possible on the basis of the modified proposal of the Commission, i.e., a moderate price increase, a reduced co-responsibility levy excluding unfavourably placed areas, premiums for non-marketing and encouragements for consumption. This compromise represented some deviations from the policy advocated by COPA; with which even the British farmers—despite their initial reservations—had associated themselves. The actual course of the negotiations, however, has not followed this pattern; the British Government having insisted on blocking the process in opposition to the wish of its *eight* partners to reach a compromise. In point of fact, the marathon of the agricultural discussions from Friday 25 to Tuesday 29 March 1977 resulted, after a final unbroken session of nineteen hours, in the recognition of a deadlock which is attributable to the British refusal pronounced on the instructions of the Prime Minister.[34] This compromise proposed by the Commission envisaged, in addition to an increase of 3% and a co-responsibility rate of 1.5%, adjustments of the "green currencies" and substantial aid for butter consumption in Great Britain.

In these circumstances, the negotiations in the Council at the end of March 1977 were bound to take place in difficult conditions. Britain not having obtained the amount asked for butter consumption subsidies, opposed the whole of the propositions of the Commission and the member countries. In so doing, Britain expressed its dislike for the common agricultural policy and paralyzed the negotiations.

Decision of 26 April 1977

In maintaining its opposition, the British Government has displayed a certain ignorance of the Community system. It has minimized the powers of its eight partners acting in unison, while over-estimating its blocking powers. It is the practice in the Community, even if unanimity is prescribed, to seek a compromise which embodies the points on which the majority of the Member States are agreed. From this point of view, the clear distinction between unanimity and the majority rule tends in practice to become blurred. Nevertheless, as emerges from the instance under examination, the fact of being able to take a majority decision makes it possible to accelerate the process of reaching a decision by pushing the minority State into accepting a compromise more speedily. For their part, the States forming the majority group are seeking a solution which avoids forcing the minority State to accept it despite itself, and later trying to neutralize the implementation of a decision. The upshot is a delicate process of injections and compromises; but one which nevertheless remains within the limits of the obligations imposed by the Treaty of Rome, or created by the common agricultural policy.

Another rule governing these negotiations which is normally observed, has been mishandled by the British Chairman. It is in fact the accepted practice that the Chairman of the Council does not seek to defend his country's point of view, but has a duty to look for a general compromise calculated to render his government's demands more flexible in some respects. The German Minister has expressed his strong regrets that the Chairman in office has not imposed the necessary sacrifices on his delegation, as is the normal practice.[35] On the other hand, the British Chairman has taken the responsibility, after having exerted pressure on other members, of blocking the negotiations. Paradoxically, it is the representative of the country most wedded to traditions whose behaviour has struck a blow at the traditional regulations of the Community. Tradition has died hard. Having postponed for one month the decision on agricultural prices, the British Government has accepted the compromise after a face-saving protestation and a final concession on the amount of the aid for British butter (33 instead of 30 Units of Account per 100 kilos). Having been proposed by the Commission, but limited to the end of 1978 at the request of Germany and France, this aid will have the effect of slightly diminishing the price of butter in the United Kingdom, and of giving satisfaction to British public opinion.[36] It is a gesture with political connotations. In addition, as is normal, the decision of the Council follows the main lines of the initial proposal. In accordance with complex negotiating manoeuvres in the field of prices, the Council is finally doing more, but never less, than what is put forward in the proposals of the Commission.[37] In point of fact, by contriving the concessions, the Council is proceeding with the assistance of the Commission and the special Committee for agriculture to administer allocations of mutual satisfaction in order to obtain a general consensus of agreement.

To sum up, this decision embodies the following points: An increase of 3.5% in common prices expressed as Units of Account. As the vehicle for monetary adjustments, this moderate increase is welcomed by all the members other than the United Kingdom, and particularly by France. It is in fact taking effect in an increase of the order of 6.5% on the 1 May 1977. The amount of the co-responsibility levy is fixed at 1.5% with effect from the 16 September of this year. The premiums for non-marketing and reconversion become the responsibility entirely of FEOGA (60% "Guarantee" and 40% "Orientation"). Additional assistance will be given for liquid skimmed milk used by pig breeders and for powdered skimmed milk used in the manufacture of composite foodstuffs for pigs and poultry, Partial Community financing is planned for the distribution of milk and certain dairy products to certain educational establishments. In addition to the subsidy granted to the United Kingdom, supplementary measures have been taken—as an alternative to the tax on fats—to encourage butter consumption in other EEC countries. The Commission has also authorized subsidized exports of butter to the Eastern-bloc countries, while limiting the quantities to from 10,000 to 15,000 tons per transaction. No action on the proposal to suspend the assistance will be taken for the present. The essential decisions have thus been made, although some items have been left ear-marked for later examination.[38] In spite of the multiplicity of the interests and influences of the Member States and the Community and national organizations, the coherence of the proposal formulated by the Commission has in the main been preserved, with some modifications. In this connection, the experts point out that at times the Ministers of Agriculture introduce certain changes without immediately appreciating the consequences. For example, it seems that the fact of having brought forward the start of the milk season runs counter to the practice of the dairy industry. The producers need increases from the month of September, when production falls.[39] In addition, arbitrations are put through on an emergency basis, favouring certain categories more than others. On re-reading this decision, it appears that the producers and their allies, and likewise the Member States who take their part, are still weighing up the directions in which the decisions will lead. Their influence rests, among other things, on the overriding factor of income, which dominates the preoccupation with surpluses. Nevertheless, this influence is held in check by the opposing coalition, even if some of its members are standing aside from the negotiations. The same is true of the external participants protected by international commitments, and likewise of the group comprised by the margarine industries. Although absent from the scene of the negotiations, these participants remain on the horizon where the decisions are concerned, because of their economic and social strength. It is to some extent a question of an "objective" influence which does not take the form of pressuring activities as long as no threat hangs over the interests which these organizations or States defend; or which shows itself in a preventive light, as in the case of IMACE. This attitude is explained by the fact that the interests of these third countries or of IMACE often have some sponsors among the Member States; there is England, for example, in relation to New Zealand; and likewise several governments which have opposed the tax on fats again put forward by the Commission although the latter, having no illusions, has made provisions for an alternative. Out of this jigsaw puzzle of sector interests and divergent objectives, which covers a whole range of domains and agricultural products, a compromise is emerging. Based on balances between prices, products and various measures of assistance, the compromise takes account of the major priorities of the Member States, and pays regard to the interests of the principal organizations. It inserts itself in its turn into a more global balance within the Community which embraces the main activities of industry, commerce and agriculture. As with other experiments in economic integration, there is a golden rule that guarantees the development of common solidarity: over the medium terms, the costs/profits ratio must be positive for each Member State, and likewise for the Community as a whole.

CONCLUSIONS

In the light of these constraints, is any alternative policy possible? In his report, Monsieur François Muller concedes that the common agricultural policy is the fundamental choice, and erects a coherent network of measures around it. On the other hand, Professor Georges Bublot concludes that it is impossible for "the price policy to be at the same time an effective instrument for supporting incomes and also an effective market stabilizer. In other words, the policy of giving indirect support to incomes through prices risks diverging from the mechanics of the market economy and resulting in an inefficient allocation of resources. This paradox evokes the need for a compromise. It is in the end healthier, and probably less costly, to give the preference to stabilization of the markets, and to remedy constricting situations, or even painful ones, through social allocations, when these finally arise out of the perpetual contraction of the dairy sector, at least in relative terms."[40]

A revision of the common agricultural policy is supported only by the British Government and the consumers. The latter in particular have come out in favour of a selective agricultural industry with low and competitive prices and social subsidies for the small farmers. This policy would have the advantage of eliminating unproductive incomes, together with the butter and powdered milk surpluses. The consumers in fact consider that the rate of self-sufficiency could without danger fall to 80%, for instance; the remaining 20% being more advantageously supplied by the international market. To ensure these external supplies, the consumers propose that the long-term contracts be concluded with the countries of the Third World, which will thereby have a chance to develop their agriculture. In short, they advocate a series of measures and are opposed to any protection, with the object of obtaining the best conditions in the Community markets. They advocate for the Community a healthy and economic food policy which is more in accord with the general interest than an agricultural policy. They are in fact demanding a fundamental revision of the common agricultural policy. But this "European alternative" runs up against a constellation of forces and constraints that we have tried to depict.

The supporters of the prices and incomes policy invoke in their turn the fragility of the estimates for the milk sector, and the difficulty of controlling agricultural production in general. Accepting the limited rate of self-sufficiency would mean accepting the threat of shortages. Who foresaw the 1973 shortage? Furthermore, the transfer of certain activities to outside Europe would only increase its dependence on external sources, without excluding the possible emergence for agricultural products of an organization similar to that created by the oil-producing countries (OPEP). The drama of the energy crisis could thus find a counterpart in the foodstuffs sector. As regards the farmers' incomes, a lowering of which cannot be considered without creating social tensions, the policy of small increases is not practical over a period, while the costs of production and other items are rising. In these conditions, the only choice lies between either higher prices or timely assistance with a Community contribution. In a word, the economic problem is transforming itself into an overall problem; that is to say, a political one.

This analysis of the surpluses certainly confirms the powers of decision possessed by the Commission and the Council; powers which are completed by the Community's financial potentialities in the form of interventions by FEOGA. In this power structure, the national Governments figure as participants in the making of common decisions, and in phases of implementation. Nevertheless, in the face of the pressures exercised by various factors and groups, the Commission and the Council have a tendency to proceed by compromise. The Commission thus seems to base its proposals on an evaluation of the factors, and the combination and shape of the forces, rather than on the conception of a medium- or long-term policy. For its part, the Council negotiates compromises with the help of the Commission; on the basis of the proposal presented by the Commission and the positions of various Member States.

The economic and social Committee emerges as carrying out the functions of an assessor whose frequently over-generalized opinions only rarely lay down precise guidelines. The European Parliament, once its views have been obtained, is no longer drawn into the process of negotiation. Its role could be modified after the European elections. But even on the assumption that these European elections are successful, it does not necessarily follow that this would strengthen the political will and powers of the Council and the Commission. To judge from the experiences of national Parliaments, these are particularly susceptible to the influences of pressure groups; especially where the farmers and various other sectors of public opinion are concerned. The direct elections would nevertheless contribute to giving a legitimate status to the basic source from which the institutions spring; and markedly in the case of the Commission, but without for all that automatically re-inforcing its ability to impose a line of conduct. Similarly, these elections might well give a political dimension and a more open character to the decision-making process.

The example examined shows how difficult it is to carry out a change of policy in order to move from a price policy to a structural policy. From the outset, priority has been given to an incomes policy. Now this incomes policy operating through high prices applied in a linear manner leads to discrimi-nations in favour of the large agricultural enterprises. In these conditions, it may be asked whether a policy of low prices accompanied by subsidies for the small operators and the mountainous and unfavourably situated areas would not constitute a more reasonable solution to the problem of the Community surpluses. Has the Community the capacity to revise its policy despite the rigidities created and the influences of the groups and categories benefiting this policy?

In the agricultural sector, the Community decisions have a direct effect on the persons concerned. This is why the national groups have tried to organize themselves in a way that influences the policy of the Community more effectively. The conflict generated by the problem of the surpluses is giving rise to the formation of two alliances; one between the producers and the processors, supported by the national governments which aim at ensuring the continuation of this price policy; and the other consisting of the governments and groups which seek to exercise a power of veto over any tax on soya-bean imports or on fats. With particular support from the Third Countries, this alliance is becoming a negative restraining factor.

The consumers are still a marginal factor. But they possess considerable potential influence provided that they have the means and the technical knowledge to enable them to carry on discussions with the institutions and the other groups; and on conditions that they are also capable of organizing themselves, and of mobilizing the massive strata of their potential supporters and of the sectors of public opinion which appear to have sensitive reactions to the surpluses and to the subsidized sales of butter to the Soviet Union.

Finally, this survey has made it possible to bring into relief the consultation procedure which has developed in the European Community. In point of fact, the Commission carries on a continuous dialogue with the European groups when preparing its proposals, while the Ministers of Agriculture are in permanent contact with those whom they represent. This process could lead to going beyond mere consultation and reaching, in accordance with the request put forward by COPA regarding co-responsibility, a formula for collaboration or even joint decisions and joint direction of the common responsibilities. But the closer the collaboration with the interested groups, the more necessary it is to assert the *autonomy of the powers of the Community*. It may be asked whether specialization within the Commission, and likewise the fragmentation of the responsibilities of the Council, are in fact contri-buting to this. In contrast to the global approach which characterizes the governmental procedures of the member countries, the Council tends to subdivide itself into specialized Councils. The Ministers of Agriculture, who are more inclined to listen to their connections in this field than to pursue general objectives, thus assume the responsibility for decisions on agricultural questions. It is true that the important decisions are taken with the endorsement of the national governments. But the fact still remains that the various specialized Councils suffer from the disequilibrium resulting from differences between the powers and the actions taken, from one sector to another of the activities of the Community. It is in this sense that the absence of exact spheres of authority and real progress in the field of economic and monetary union holds a threat over the common agricultural policy. There is no doubt that in this case some division of the work within the Council is necessary in order to preserve common policies. Nevertheless, whatever the advantages expected from this specialization, it may be asked whether the moment has not arrived to put an end to the lack of coordination between different specialized Councils, and the fragmentation of authority; by reestablishing, against the background of the elections and European unity, unity of vision and political action within the Community.

NOTES

1. Jean-Louis Giraudy, "The impact of the lobbies"; Review of the Common Market, May 1976, pp. 233–236.
2. J. Meynaud and D. Sidjanski:—"Pressure groups in the European Community"; 1958–1968, 1971, Brussels, published by the Institute of Sociology, pp. 216–219.
3. Giraudy, *op. cit.*, p. 234.
4. *Ibid.*, p. 234.
5. 1. Importance of sector and group in relation to turnover, percentage of workers and sales. 2. Importance and validity of principle or interest defended. 3. Representativeness and number of members, e.g., trade unions, peasants, enterprises. 4. Financial basis. 5. Organization and efficiency: a) numbers of managerial and administrative staff; b) competence of managerial staff; c) their powers and standing. 7. Image and reputation of group. 8. Homogeneity or divergencies. 9. Relations with other groups (coalitions, rivalries). 10. Network of contacts and access to institutions and decision-making centres.
6. This structure is also reflected in the relative distribution of the dairy herds (25,200,000 head) among the member countries.
7. J. Meynaud and D. Sidjanski, *op. cit.*, pp. 41 to 78, 79 to 92, 163 to 234. On the COPA, see William F. Averyt, "Agropolitics in the European Community", New York, Praeger Publishers, 1977, pp. 71–99.
8. ASSILEC includes both the cooperatives and the private industries for all dairy products, amounting to about 20% of the agricultural income. It covers all the member countries, with the exception of Luxembourg and likewise two specialized sections, namely: condensed milk (ASFALEC) and melted cheese (ASSIFONTE). For example, the Nestlé factories in the EEC which process dairy products are members of it. EUCOLAIT represents the large commercial exporting and importing organizations of the EEC member countries; with the exception of the United Kingdom and Eire, where free trade is marginal. In Denmark the trading organization is more flexible, but this in no way prevents 97% of the butter trade from being in the hands of the cooperatives. ASSILEC has three Commissions for specific products: butter, cheese and casein.
9. The members of FEFAC attempt to obtain cheaper foodstuffs, in particular by imports of soya-beans. IMACE, which is affiliated to UNICE, brings together

the national associations specializing in margarine production, including the Dutch one which numbers UNILEVER among its members.

10. For example, BEUC embodies national associations of consumers which range from the relatively powerful organizations in the United Kingdom and the Netherlands to the powerless Italian ones which do not enjoy any governmental support. In addition, there are at least two categories of organizations in existence, namely: the consumer unions centred on the publication of comparative tests (with for instance about 700,000 subscribers in the United Kingdom and 450,000 in the Netherlands), and those coordinating the consumer-policy activities of their various member organizations (such as AGV in Germany, which embodies 36 organizations with a total of 8 million indirect affiliates and with 70% of its budget contributed by the regional and Federal Governments).

11. For the systematic typology of the access channels, see J. Meynaud and D. Sidjanski, *op. cit.*, pp. 467–638.

12. More than one organization criticizes the consultative committees, though they all make efforts to attend these.

13. When price proposals are being worked out, the Commission only consults COPA, and does not approach ASSILEC and EUCOLAIT. During this procedure, the Commissioner responsible receives representatives of COPA, without carrying out this type of exchange of ideas and contact with other Community associations. This gives an indication of the importance that the Commission attaches to the producers represented by COPA where prices are concerned.

14. More recently, BEUC has been particularly active in attempting to coordinate the positions of the members of these interested institutions through the problems of the consumers.

15. For the economic factors and the various restrictions, see the reports of Messrs. Bublot and Muller.

16. "Action Programme", page 14.

17. *Ibid.*, paras. 16 and 19, pp. 9 and 11.

18. *Views* of the economic and social Committee regarding the "Action Programme for 1977–1980 aimed at progressive stabilization of the dairy market"; Brussels, 30 Sept. 1976, paras. 2, 3, 1.

19. *Views* of the Economic and Social Committee, page 7.

20. Giraudy, *op. cit.*, p. 235.

21. ASSILEC, J. G. Becue, Bil 1/10/76 No 368.

22. ASSILEC editorial, Bil No 372.

23. Meeting of 17 May 1977.

24. EUCOLAIT reply to our questionnaire; Brussels, 11 May 1977, p. 2, Q. 2.

25. *Moral Report* presented by Francis Lepatre, the Chairman, to the 1976 annual General Meeting of the National Federation of the Dairy Industry, Paris.

26. In its comments dated 27 January 1977, the Economic and Social Committee says:—"1.3.6. The agricultural policy of the U.S.A. appears increasingly to be directed towards the export of cereals and oil-cake for which there is every likelihood of the external demand remaining at a high level." . . . 1.3.8. The American "agro-alimentary strategy" adopted in recent years has not satisfied everyone even in the United States, as can be seen from certain criticisms regarding the use of "agricultural might" for diplomatic purposes. Any radical change in American commercial policies is scarcely to be expected, since these are supported by the majority of the farmers and by the vast agro-alimentary industrial and commercial complex which accounts for a very substantial proportion of the active population (20% of the total, of which 4% falls under agricultural production as such). This complex indeed has a remarkable hold on the domestic and external markets; in addition, it enjoys the services of the strongest capacity for research and innovation in the world."

27. They also seem to be in a position to put a brake on certain measures taken by the Nine aimed at routing 400,000 tons of powder into animal feeding. See Giraudy, p. 235.

28. Giraudy, *op. cit.*, p. 236.

29. *Draft comments* of the Consumers Consultative Committee on the common agricultural policy; CCC—127/76, Brussels, 7 October 1976, p. 2.

30. *Ibid.*, p. 3.

31. *Ibid.*, p. 5.

32. This chapter is based mainly on data derived from the following sources:— *Agence Europe*, Nos. 2176 and 2205; *Le Monde*, 30.3.77; *Le Journal de Genève*, 30.3.77; *L'Express*, 13.3.77; *Réunion*, 17.5.77; the *Reply* to written question No. 994/76 of Monsieur Martens; *Press communiqué*, Council of the EEC, 25 and 26 April 1977.

33. The Irish, Danish and French producers, for example, are defended in a particularly effective way. This coincidence is paralleled by the place that this social category occupies in these countries. (*Réunion*, 17 May 1977).

34. The article by Lemaitre appearing in *Le Monde* on 30 March 1977.

35. Pierre Collet:—"New agricultural crisis in the Community", *Journal de Genève* of 30 March 1977.

36. In his article entitled "Dear living in Great Britain: EEC named as the scapegoat" (*Journal de Genève* of 31 May 1977), Claude le Saché remarks that "reduced to its most down-to-earth terms—fish, butter, pork—the European Community is getting a bad Press just now in Great Britain ... The re-hashed criticism directed in the most formal terms against an ill-conceived and harmful common agricultural policy, the incessant battles embarked on in Brussels by the Minister John Silkin in order to obtain special dispensations regarding an exclusive fishing zone of 50 miles, the price of butter, subsidies granted to pig breeders, the violent attacks aimed at EEC by individuals and coming both from the Left (Joan Lestor) and the Right (Enoch Powell), all these are signs of a growing dissatisfaction feeding on a basis of rancour and popular mistrust with regard to Europe, that still survives despite a decisive referendum."

37. *Réunion*, on 17 May 1977.

38. For example, the Commission has already drawn up a communication to the Council on 4 May 1977 regarding provisions for powdered milk (150,000 tons of a value of 55.5 million Units of Account) and butteroil (45,000 tons of a value of 47 million Units of Account) under the assistance to foodstuffs programme for 1977. *Informatory memorandum*, Commission, Brussels, May 1977.

39. *Réunion*, on 17 May 1977.

40. G. Bublot, *Report quoted*, conclusions.

ANNEXES

TABLE 1. *Percentage share of agriculture, forestry and fisheries sector in Gross Industrial Product, at cost of factors and percentage of active population employed in this sector.*

Country	% of G.I.P. 1974	% of employment 1975
Germany	3.2	7.3
France (market prices)	5.3	11.3
Italy	9.5	15.8
Netherlands	4.8	6.6
Belgium	3.1	3.6
Luxembourg	3.5	6.0
United Kingdom	2.9	2.7
Eire	16.4[1]	24.5
Denmark	8.9	9.8
EEC of Nine Countries	5.0	8.7

1. 1968 figures.

Source: Eurostat—The situation of agriculture in the Community; 1976 Report, Brussels-Luxembourg; January 1977.

TABLE 2. *Active civil population engaged in "agriculture, forestry and fisheries" sector in relation to total active civil population employed in 1968 and 1975*

Member States	Agricultural employment (000's)[2]		Total employment (000's)[2]		Agricultural employment as % of total employment	
	1968	1975	1968	1975	1968	1975
	2	3	4	5	6	7
Germany	2,523	1,822	25,491	24,828	9.9	7.3
France	3,098	2,452[1]	19,749	21,166[1]	15.7	11.6[1]
Italy	4,173	2,964	18,607	18,818	22.4	15.8
Netherlands	352	299	4,445	4,535	7.9	6.6
Belgium	201	136	3,614	3,744	5.6	3.6
Luxembourg	17	10[1]	139[1]	151[1]	12.2	6.6[1]
Total EEC 6	10,364	7,683[1]	72,045	73,242[1]	14.4	10.5[1]
United Kingdom	763	667	24,903	24,632	3.1	2.7
Eire	310	252	1,055	1,030	29.4	24.5
Denmark	276[3]	228	2,282[3]	2,332	12.1	9.8
Total EEC 9	11,713[3]	8,830[1]	100,285[3]	101,236[1]	11.7	8.7[1]

1. 1974
2. Man-years
3. 1969

Source: Eurostat.

69

TABLE 3. *Share (as %) of products in final agricultural output of the Member States and the Community (provisional figures for 1975)*

Country	Milk	Beef	Wheat
Germany	22.9	18.0	3.8
France	16.9	18.7	7.9
Italy	10.0	10.7	8.9
Netherlands	26.8	13.1	1.1
Belgium	15.6	16.9	2.8
Luxembourg	37.2	28.7	2.1
United Kingdom	22.1	15.2	5.3
Eire	28.0	39.8	1.5
Denmark	25.9	14.9	2.6
EEC of Nine Countries	18.7	16.3	5.8

Source: Eurostat—*The situation of agriculture in the Community* 1976 Report, Brussels–Luxembourg; January 1977.

TABLE 4. *Share of the Member States in final agricultural output of the Community by products (provisional 1975 figures)*

Country	Milk (%)	Beef (%)	Wheat (%)
Germany	26.6	24.1	14.2
France	24.9	31.7	37.5
Italy	11.1	13.7	31.9
Netherlands	11.1	6.3	1.6
Belgium	3.3	4.2	1.9
Luxembourg	0.3	0.2	0.0
United Kingdom	13.7	10.9	10.6
Eire	3.0	4.9	0.5
Denmark	6.0	4.0	1.9
EEC of Nine Countries	100.0	100.0	100.0

Source: Eurostat—*The situation of agriculture in the Community*, 1976 Report, Brussels–Luxembourg, January 1977.

TABLE 5. *Levels of herds of dairy-cows*

Country	1975 (000 head)	1976 (000 head)	Difference (%)
Germany	5,393	5,395	0
France	7,751	7,590	− 2.1
Italy	2,927	2,883	− 1.5
Netherlands	2,251	2,186	− 0.9
Belgium	997	980	− 1.7
Luxembourg	73	70	− 4.1
United Kingdom	3,387	3,249	− 4.1
Eire	1,344	1,300	− 3.3
Denmark	1,130	1,106	− 2.1
EEC of Nine Countries	25,217	24,769	− 1.8

Source: Eurostat—*The situation of agriculture in the Community*. 1976 Report, Brussels–Luxembourg; January 1977.

TABLE 6. *Degree of self-sufficiency in 1974*[1]

Dairy products	G	F	I	NL	UEBL	UK	IRL	DK	EUR 9
Milk	101	101	96	101	100	100	100	101	100
Whole powdered milk	205	167	47	794	261	98	511	3,278	216
Skimmed powdered milk	205	167	2	74	143	143	1,001	206	147
Condensed milk	100	178	86	309	19	98	:	326	:
Cheese	90	115	83	234	44	63	529	285	103
Butter	118	114	61	352	97	14	216	322	97
Vegetable fats and oils	8	29	49	7	1	4	0	0	22

1. Order of countries (left to right) as in Appendix 1 etc.
Source: Eurostat—*The situation of agriculture in the Community*. 1976 Report, Brussels–Luxembourg; January 1977.

TABLE 7. *Price of powdered skimmed milk*

	EEC entry price	World price	EEC price/ world price
Powdered skimmed milk: 1974–75	94.28	67.70	139
Powdered skimmed milk: 1975–76	101.90	38.25	266

Source: Eurostat—*The situation of agriculture in the Community*. 1976 Report, Brussels–Luxembourg; January 1977.

TABLE 8. *Measures and Positions*

Institutions, professional organizations and personalities: measures and positions	1977/80 Action programme:—Proposals and decisions of 26 April 1977				
	Prices	Co-responsibility levy	Premiums for non-marketing and reconversion	Tax on fats	Tax on imports of proteins
1. Commission	Rise of 3%	2.5% in April	Financing:— 40% FEOGA guarantee 40% FEOGA orientation 20% Member States	Introduction of the Tax	
2. Economic and social committee			Agreed	Opposed	
3. COPA/COGECA	Rise of 7%	2.5% Rejected (conditions not met)	Agreed	Agreed	
4. ASSILEC EUCOLAIT	Support for COPA thesis	Reservations on effectiveness as regards surpluses	Qualified agreement	In favour, but tax to be linked to co-responsibility	Need for common policy in fats and proteins sector Need for common policy in fats and proteins sector
5. FEFAC IMACE	No opinion expressed	Slight scepticism (IMACE)	Opposed	Opposed	FEFAC against any reduction of imports; tax opposed
6. Consumers	Blockage, or even reduction	Agreed, higher rate desired		Opposed	
7. Member States	G: slight increase NL: large increase GB: freeze IRL, F, B: increase	G: agreed F: agreed @ 1.5% B, I: opposed LUX: in favor if....... DK, GB: in favour		GB: opposed DK: opposed NL: opposed ....This tax takes place	
8. Council (decisions)	Increase of about 4%	1.5% on 16.9.77	Financing:— 40% FEOGA orientation 60% FEOGA	Laid aside	Laid aside

TABLE 9. *Measures and Positions*

Institutions, professional organizations and personalities:— measures and positions	1977/80 Action programme: Proposals and Decisions of 26 April 1977			
	Foodstuffs aid	Encouragement of consumption	Suspension of aid contributing to increased production	Other measures
1. Commission		Cheap school milk; aid for butter consumption	Suspension of national and community assistance till 31.3.80	Limits for intervention buying of powdered skimmed milk
2. Economic and social committee	Within scope of overall EEC policy		Does not support this proposal	Development of long-term EEC commercial policy
3. COPA/COGECA	Aid to be increased	To be developed (promotion campaigns)	Opposed	External commercial policy; cumbrous bureaucracy; too much publicity
4. ASSILEC EUCOLAIT	To be developed, but under control of commission	Development for all types of milk	Agreement on new, less rigid project. Risk of economic distortions	FEFAC: Increased subsidies for powder incorporated in milk substitutes, to hold stable net price (support price less aid)
5. FEFAC IMACE				
6. Consumers	To be developed, plus agricultural development of 3rd World	General picture:— Reduction in total consumption of fats		Essential developments of social and regional policies
7. Member States		Netherlands:— consumption subsidies	Opposed to suspension of aid	I: Income supplements for weak enterprises; EEC preference B: bold export policy GB: opposed to external sales of surpluses
8. Council (decisions)		Aid for butter consumption; supply of milk at reduced prices	Prohibition of national aid; maintenance of FEOGA aid	Lifting of limits for support purchases; aid for investment necessary for utilization of skimmed milk on the farm

IV. CONCLUSIONS

Beef and Dairy Product Surpluses in the Community

by *John Pinder*

1. Unlike most of the other policies studied by this conference, the agricultural policy has been on a community basis for 8–10 years depending on the sector (though for a shorter time in the cases of Britain, Denmark and Ireland). The alternatives to status quo are therefore either a reform of the present policy or a return to national policies.

2. The arguments against a return to national policies were forcibly presented: the CAP has helped to modernize farms and make processing industries more competitive; it reflects the complementary character of farming in the north, centre and south of the Community and the need for security of supply; it protects the balance of payments of some countries that have difficulty in paying for their oil imports. Above all, the renationalization of agricultural policy would imply the re-emergence of protectionism which could spill over into industrial trade and European integration generally.

3. On the other hand the present agricultural policy cannot be said to be fully communitarian. The mechanism for dealing with fluctuating exchange rates has diluted the concept of a common Community price; and national expenditure on agricultural structures and social aid is still greater than Community expenditure. If Community policy does not overcome some of its deficiencies, a creeping renationalization might undermine the principles of the agricultural common market.

4. In order to remedy defects such as costly surpluses of some products and the excessive variation among farm incomes due to uniformity of agricultural prices in the face of widely differing production costs, some modifications of the common agricultural policy were suggested, including:

a. adjustment of the market organizations so as to avoid structural surpluses and facilitate the marketing of products within and outside the Community;

b. development of the agricultural structures policy, the weakness of which makes it more difficult for the market policy to work properly, which has marked regional effects;

c. income support in some cases, to allow moderation in the increase of producer prices without deprivation for those with the lower farm incomes.

5. Other changes of policy were also suggested, including the extension of Community activity to the distribution networks; the setting of production targets; a more determined export policy; the reduction of the degree of self-sufficiency to, say 80%; and the negotiation of contracts with Third World countries that would enable them to develop their agriculture.

6. The difficulty was brought out of securing reforms in the agricultural policy in view of the weight given to farmers' interests and to certain processing industries in the Community's decision-making. For example the producers' organization and the processors and to some extent the traders in milk products defend the dairy producers price policy, backed by the Commission and most of the Ministers of Agriculture. On the other hand there is opposition to any tax on imports of soya and proteins on the part of the feeding stuffs manufacturers, the margarine producers, the farmers who use cheap feeding-stuffs and the consumers, backed by some Member States and also by the United States and other supplying countries. The effect of these conflicting interests has been to narrow the scope for rational decisions along the lines of paragraph 4 and without unacceptable cost. The development of consultation between the Commission and the European interest groups, and between the Ministries of Agriculture and the national interest groups, has moreover reached the point where it might almost be called joint decision-making and joint management of the shared responsibility; and this may have reduced the autonomy and decision-making capacity of the Community institutions.

7. With the balance of power shifting somewhat in favour of the consumers, a shift towards policies of lower prices combined with more subsidies for small farmers may become possible. But the prospects for changes of policy are also constrained by structural weaknesses in the Community's decision-making process, such as the splitting of the Council into specialized councils (e.g., Ministers of Agriculture) and the degree of specialization within the Commission, as well as the relationship with interest groups mentioned in the preceding paragraph.

8. The need was therefore stressed for the Community to increase its capacity for "globalizing" its decision-taking, that is for facilitating trade-offs of advantages among the different member countries between one policy area and another. The hope was also expressed that the European elections would give the Community the political impulse to reach decisions that were impeded by the resistance of interest groups and governments within the present system, though doubts were also expressed whether the elections might not weaken the authority of the institutions in the agricultural sector. In any case, most members of the group considered the constraints presented by interest groups and national governments' positions to be such that adjustment of the common agricultural policy would be a gradual process rather than a spectacular reform.

ENERGY POLICY

I. Report Robert De Bauw
II. Counter-report Guy De Carmoy
III. Conclusions The Chairman and Rapporteurs

I. ENERGY POLICY REPORT

Oil Policy before the Yom Kippur War

by *Robert De Bauw*

Has energy policy become the Gordian knot of the European endeavour? This is a question one may well ask in view of the number of proposals made on this matter over the past twenty years, the failure in which most of them have ended and the fact that each of these failures has been followed by a resumption of the perennial discussion.

This perseverance is not surprising in view of what is at stake. In 1972, energy investments accounted for 25% of total industrial investments, 6.5% of gross fixed capital formation and 1.5% of the GDP. Energy imports have risen steadily, accounting for 16% of the Community's total imports in 1963, for 20% in 1973, and rocketing to 32.5% in 1974. But the main factor is that a harmonious development of economic and social life is impossible without a regular supply of energy at reasonable prices.

The Community as a whole is fairly poor in energy resources, but the situation varies from country to country. There are likewise differences between the Member States as regards consumption patterns, import flows, the structure of energy-producing undertakings, the extent and the methods of intervention by the authorities, the part played by the multinationals, the taxation situation and the like. In short, the energy policies of the Member States form so intricate a pattern that it is difficult to discern any main elements which are common.

Yet it is necessary to discover and structure those elements, if the goals which the Treaties assigned to the Communities are to be attained. There will be no true freedom of trading as long as energy products do not move freely within the common market. There will be no equality of competition between energy consumers as long as price distortions and tax differences persist. There will be no industrial policy as long as the markets in energy-generating plant remain walled off from one another. There will be no common commercial policy as long as the Member States seek bilateral solutions to their supply problems with non-member states.

The energy policy thus appears at one and the same time to be conditioning a whole series of other policies and to be conditioned by the progress made in other policy areas. Among these, events have shown up the primary role of foreign policy and the still inadequate nature of political cooperation between Member States.

Perhaps it is this dual nature of the problem which explains why all efforts to achieve a common energy policy have been in vain so far and why these efforts must continue.

The first part of this report is a brief summary of events in the energy policy

79

sphere up to 1972 and an account of how things stood in 1973 on the eve of the Yom Kippur War. The main emphasis is on oil, bringing in other energy sources where necessary to give an overall picture.

The second part attempts to evaluate—in the light of later events—the policy proposed by the Commission.

The third part deals with the reception the Commission's proposals received from the European Parliament, the Economic and Social Committee and the ECSC Consultative Committee, and from the industries concerned.

I. HISTORICAL BACKGROUND AND THE STATE OF COMMUNITY ENERGY POLICY IN 1973

The long march towards a common energy policy

There has been talk for close on twenty years of the need for a common energy policy, and yet it seems as difficult and as remote as ever.

And it was nonetheless an energy source—coal, at that time the major source—which was chosen as one of the first two areas for European integration, back in 1950. However, hopes of creating a European energy community on this basis were soon disappointed.

Only a few years after the ECSC was set up, coal found itself faced with increasingly sharp competition from the hydrocarbons (oil and natural gas), which left it with only limited markets. It was this rundown which virtually prevented full implementation of the common market in coal which the ECSC Treaty was meant to create. Furthermore, the EEC Treaty[1] did not provide the machinery which might have solved the new problems presented by the preponderance of imported oil. Lastly, the hopes engendered by the Euratom Treaty[1] concerning the development of nuclear energy were disappointed: the low price of oil prevented this promising source of abundant and reliable energy from becoming competitive, while nationalist attitudes hindered the establishment of effective research mechanisms and a solid industrial base.

The merging of the executive bodies of the three Communities in 1967 engendered new hopes, since the merged institutions (a single Commission and a single Council) were henceforth able to take a comprehensive view of the problems presented by the various energy sources and to arbitrate between them as required.[2] The new Commission presented its ideas on the subject in December 1968 in a communication entitled "First guidelines on a Community energy policy".

Putting the emphasis on the need for the involvement of public authorities in the energy sector, the Commission proposed that the Community should take action at three levels: (a) to work out a framework for joint action (overall and sectoral forecasts and guidelines and emergency measures), (b) to establish a common energy market and (c) to ensure cheap and secure supplies.

In keeping with the first of these three lines of action the Council adopted in December 1968 a Directive on security stocks of oil which had been under discussion for over three years. In 1972 the Commission presented a package of studies and programmes concerned with investigating or determining the future direction of the energy market.

Little progress, was, however, made in the second field despite the efforts made to harmonize energy taxation, pricing systems, concessions to the oil and gas industry, etc.[3] In respect of supplies although the measures proposed by the Commission to provide public authorities and economic operators with more information (primarily to ensure a certain degree of investment coordination[4]) were adopted by the Council, it proved impossible to adopt measures defining supply programmes in keeping with the objectives to be set by the Community.[5] Finally, it should be noted that the Commission is concerned to strengthen the structure of the Community energy industry[6] and to solve the problems of investment financing.

Progress to be made in Community energy policy (October 1972)

The decade 1960–1970 will go down in the economic history of Europe as an era of plentiful and cheap energy. However, various factors gradually appeared which were to impose new constraints on energy policy. These were:

a. the extraordinary growth which took place in world economic activity in 1970 and 1971 which was reflected in a sharp increase in energy demand (particularly for oil) while the traditional flexibility in oil production and transport was unable to operate fully;[7]

b. the more rapid increase in American imports on the world oil market than had been expected;[8]

c. the desire of oil-producing countries to govern the exploitation of their natural resources as far as possible themselves and to control prices;[9]

d. the growing awareness in consumer countries that the public authorities should have a greater responsibility as regards energy supplies and that this was closely bound up with external policy;

e. the public debate about the limits to growth and the depletion of natural resources to which the first report of the Club of Rome in particular gave rise;[10]

f. the new interest in environmental protection.

These facts and the prospects clearly necessitated a searching reappraisal of the energy situation in Europe. This the Commission of the European Communities carried out in 1972 in a series of documents constituting a threefold approach:

Description and analysis

i. Analysis of energy demand between 1970 and 1985: it was predicted that, if economic growth continued at a rate of around 5%, energy demand would double in fifteen years;[11]

ii. Study of the conditions of supply of each of the major energy sources with particular emphasis on the constraints on or dangers to future supplies (both internal and external).[12]

Consolidated analysis of the problem to be resolved[13]

In the Commission's opinion the main problems in the world's energy situation during the period 1975–1985 would primarily involve oil and gas which would be called upon to cover two-thirds of energy requirements.

Although the use of nuclear energy and natural gas could reduce the Community's dependence on imported oil, the latter would remain a key factor in supply. Without minimizing the scale of the problems posed by other energy sources and of the policies which would have to be worked out to solve them (stabilizing coal production and developing nuclear energy) the emphasis should, nevertheless, be placed on the oil policy.

Two different types of uncertainty were pointed out in this connection:
- uncertainties with a long-term effect on the trend in the price of crude oil. Two possibilities were envisaged: that of a stable market and that of a market where prices rose steeply; the latter would have deleterious effects for both the consumer and producer countries;
- uncertainties with a short-term effect on the regularity of supply. Action would have to be taken at two levels to mitigate their effect: improvement of the supply pattern and security measures (storage, production and transport reserves, etc.).

Various means of improving security of long-term supply were mentioned:
- more rational utilization of energy;
- large-scale stockpiling of primary energy, particularly oil;
- diversification of sources with particular emphasis on North Sea oil;
- maintenance of certain outlets for Community coal;
- utilization of greater quantities of imported coal;
- increasing supplies of natural gas from various sources;
- accelerating development of nuclear installations.

Proposed action

In its Communication entitled "Necessary progress in Community energy policy"[14] the Commission outlined the new guidelines which it proposed that the Member States should follow. The first course of action was to find a rapid solution to the environmental problems posed by energy. Secondly, determined efforts should be made to ensure a more rational utilization of energy, even before the effects of any rise in costs was felt. A scientific and technical research policy should be pursued in parallel to improve the conditions of energy production, conversion, transport, storage and utilization and to develop new energies or new uses for traditional energies. Emphasis was also put on questions linked with foreign relations: co-operation between consumer countries (information, joint arrangements for security of supply) and between the Community and energy-exporting countries.

Internally, apart from a number of proposals aimed at preserving the unity of the energy market, emphasis was once again placed on the need for machinery to deal with any oil supply crisis.

The Council considered it difficult to arrive at an agreed position in respect of such a wide range of analyses and of the large number of—more often than not general—measures which had been proposed. The preparatory work did in fact show that the actual scope of most of these measures could generally only be assessed in the light of specific proposals which the Commission might decide to make in the future.[15]

Once again therefore it was a case of the vicious circle which has characterized the common energy policy for so many years—and which it seems is no nearer to being eliminated today. The Member States ask the Commission to propose a cohesive set of measures to form the basis for this policy,[16] but as soon as the Commission complies with this request, the Council finds itself unable to arbitrate successfully between the various interests of the Member States in order to take a decision of principle; and it therefore calls for formal proposals, item by item, on which to reach a decision.

On the other hand, whenever the Commission proposes a concrete measure, its adoption is frequently delayed or obstructed on the pretext that a decision cannot be taken unless the measure is viewed in the context of a set of broader measures.[17]

Guidelines and priority actions under the Community energy policy (April 1973)

In an attempt to overcome the deadlock described in the preceding paragraph, the Commission forwarded to the Council a new communication, the content of which included both guidelines to inspire future activity by the Community institutions and sufficiently detailed principles for specific proposals to be made to the Council without delay.

This communication obviously contained no particularly new proposals but it did concentrate discussion on a number of what were felt to be basic points.[18]

Relations with the energy-importing countries
The Community and the other main energy-importing countries (USA and Japan) should institute mutual cooperation based on the following principles:
– non-discrimination and reciprocity of obligations
– consideration for the particular circumstances of each party and non-interference with specific moves made by individual parties
– respect for the legitimate interests of the energy-exporting countries
– concern for the problems of the developing countries, in particular those which have no energy resources.

Fields for cooperation are listed very openly but with the accent on measures to prevent any oil supply difficulties: stockpiling, apportionment schemes, rationing.

It is suggested that a suitable joint consultation body be set up as a framework for this cooperation, but still taking account however of what is done within the OECD.

Relations with energy-exporting countries
Although it does not go into the content of this cooperation, the Commission does explain that a climate of mutual trust is a guarantee of stability of Community supply.

This cooperation has a firm basis in that there is a matching of interests between the Community and the exporting countries.

Organization of the oil market
In the Commission's view "organizing" the market in petroleum products basically means guaranteeing the existence of a common market in this sector

83

by applying the rules of the Treaty on freedom of movement and competition, and by setting up a framework within which to implement a common supply policy including surveillance of imports, which is justified for security reasons.

This also means that in some cases action should be taken beyond the strict application of the Treaty. For example, it might happen that the *a posteriori* procedures in respect of competition (Article 85 and 86 EEC) are not sufficient to guarantee the requisite market stability. The Commission therefore considers that instruments should be made available which would allow oil mergers to be controlled, information on oil supply costs to be obtained and prices to be harmonized.

Lastly, still in the context of the growing responsibility of the public authorities for supply, it is recommended that a unified system be set up between these authorities and the oil companies to exchange information and policies so as to achieve, by means of flexible procedures, improved cohesion and a more rational use of oil supplies in the short, medium and long term.

Nuclear energy
With its advantages in respect of cost and security of supply, nuclear energy is of vital interest and should be developed more rapidly. Although forecasts for 1985 indicated an installed capacity of 130 GW(e), the Commission plans to fix a more ambitious objective (the 200 GW(e) which was subsequently included in the "New energy policy strategy" in 1974 and aroused much controversy) and proposes the adoption of a plan of action for this purpose.

The main features of this plan of action are the opening of markets, the financing of investment, informing the public (on the need for nuclear energy and its advantages and on safety measures taken) and fuel supply policy.

The Council meeting of 22 May 1973

A detailed discussion at the Council meeting on 22 May 1973 on all the documents outlined above concentrated on an assessment of the situation and the measures proposed.

The Council approved the assessment and emphasized the economic and political importance which energy questions assume for the harmonious development of the Community.

As regards the measures, the Council first reaffirmed the pressing need to draw up a Community energy policy, and then stated that the priority guidelines and actions constituted, in their broad lines, the appropriate basis of discussion for the Community measures intended to ensure security of energy supply.

However, the Council did not specifically agree on any of the proposals put forward and particularly could not agree on the priorities to be selected. One government found itself unable to agree with the proposals on external relations, since the other governments declared that they could not approve the Commission's proposals on the organization of the market in oil products which the former delegation was able to accept in spite of the fact that it felt they were inadequate. The other delegations, on the other hand, felt that emphasis should be placed on problems of relations with other importing and exporting countries, and that the organization of the oil market was comparatively less important. However, one delegation felt that priority in relations with non-Community countries should be given to cooperation with exporting countries.

The communiqué published at the end of the Council meeting[19] could only reflect this basic difference in opinion by postponing the debate until the Commission could put forward formal proposals.

The Council meeting of 22 May did however show a positive approach by approving various specific measures on which it was asked to reach a decision:
- a Regulation on the support of Community projects in the hydrocarbon sector, enabling the Community to grant its support to technical development directly connected with prospecting, producing, storing and transporting hydrocarbons.[20]
- a Directive on measures to mitigate the effects of difficulties in the supply of crude oil[21] whereby Member States had to provide themselves with legal powers and regulations enabling them to make levies on security stocks, to limit the consumption of oil products and to regulate prices.

  The security system introduced in 1968 by the directive requiring Member States to hold oil stocks was thus reinforced—although this was by no means the final step.
- a resolution setting up a Standing Committee on Uranium Enrichment with the basic task of examining the means for promoting the expansion of the Community's industrial capacities and facilitating the coordination of initiatives.[22]

Once again, therefore, the Council could not reach agreement on an overall conception of energy policy. Part decisions showed some progress, but of a limited kind and by no means equal to the magnitude of problems which were becoming increasingly threatening.[23]

The application of the guidelines and priority actions

In July 1973, the Commission presented the Council with a first series of proposals in accordance with the undertakings given:[24]
- measures to supplement Community information on trade in oil products with non-Community countries. These measures were adopted in 1974 and 1975;
- a procedure of consultation between Member States and the Commission within the framework of a Committee on hydrocarbon supplies. This Committee would be able to arrange hearing of the oil companies contributing towards supplies, which would be required to supply information on a number of specific items. No action was taken on this proposal;
- commercial policy measures to enable a check to be kept on hydrocarbon supply whenever necessary. This proposal suffered the same fate as the previous one.

Concurrently, the Commission put forward a number of specific proposals designed to give practical expression to the cooperation between the Community and the energy-importing and -exporting countries. In this context,

85

the Commission stressed the need for a joint approach, the only way to avoid outbidding.

Conclusions (Part I)

Such was the state of the Community energy policy on the eve of the October 1973 crisis. Council experts had just begun to consider the latest Commission proposals but initial discussions revealed major difficulties concerning the proposals for consultations about supply and commercial policy measures for oil.

On 16 October 1973, the producing countries in the Persian Gulf decided to raise the price of crude oil unilaterally and to place a selective embargo on their deliveries. A new page in the history of the oil industry was being turned. From the Community's point of view, this page would no doubt have been written differently if the Commission's long-recommended policy had been applied.

II. ASSESSMENT OF THE PROPOSED POLICY

The discussions on the Community energy policy are frequently marred by ambiguity.

The term "energy policy" sometimes takes on a different meaning depending on the country and period of time involved. For example, some countries stress the need to control external sources of supply while others concentrate on developing internal resources and placing them under the control of the public authorities; for some countries the priority is to fix objectives for the nationalized energy industries, for others it is the role of the multinational concerns, while for others the main consideration is to respect competition and market rules.

Quite clearly it is difficult to even try to merge all these, sometimes contradictory, points of view into a Community policy. The problem is more one of determining the Community's requirements and the measures needed to meet them.

Whereas in 1973 the Community was 61% dependent on imported energy, and whereas oil (59%) and coal (21%) accounted for the bulk of consumption, the situation varied from one Member State to another. Various situations existed (see annexed table):
– two countries, namely Germany and the United Kingdom, are approximately 50% self-sufficient in terms of their consumption;
– four countries (France, Italy, Belgium, Ireland) depend on external supplies for approximately 8/10ths of their consumption. In the case of the first three countries mentioned, it should be remembered that a proportion of their imports come from another Member State, i.e., Dutch natural gas;
– two countries, Luxembourg and Denmark, have no primary energy production;
– the Netherlands are an exception to the extent that the export of natural gas largely offsets their dependence on oil imports, thus making the country apparently self-sufficient.

This alone could justify differences in the approach to an energy policy, particularly if account is taken of the prospects offered by some countries' resources; one only has to compare the case of the United Kingdom, which is staking its future on North Sea oil, with that of the other countries. And then there is the question of how long these resources will last.

Another obstacle to the adoption of a common policy must surely be the differences from one country to another, in the degree of state intervention in the energy sector.

The events of 1973 clearly underlined the links between energy policy and foreign policy. It is understandable, in the case of some Member States, that tactical considerations make "privileged" relations with a non-member country seem more attractive than a European supply policy. Yet the question must be asked whether a joint approach on energy relations with non-member countries would not pay greater dividends in the long run, especially if one looks beyond the energy sector proper and considers an overall strategy. The experience of individual governments in the matter of crude purchasing contracts has been generally disappointing.

Governments and public opinion have too often expected the Commission to put forward global, watertight proposals which could be accepted "en bloc". It is clear, however, that whereas this approach is vital as far as principles are concerned, its application does imply giving up certain short-term interests. Some governments are not prepared to run the risk of agreeing at the outset on the broad lines of the measures, the details of which might not be considered wholly satisfactory at a later date.

The Commission has endeavoured to make a compromise in its approach between principles and pragmatism. Unfortunately, this has too often been confined to a list of proposed measures. Yet each time formal proposals (regulations, directives, decisions) have been put forward, they have given rise to fruitful discussions which have, in many cases, led to the adoption of specific measures.

The assessment of the proposed policy involves the examination of the adequacy not only of measures put forward but also of the Commission's analysis of the energy situation.

This analysis—with the problems it raises[25]—has been borne out by the facts: the Community is, and will for a long time remain, dependent on imported energy, especially oil. Although North Sea oil resources, under British jurisdiction, somewhat offset the degree of this dependence, they do not remove it altogether.

The events at the end of 1973 adequately demonstrated that the Community's energy policy is closely dependent on a world context. Certainly, once could reproach the Commission for not having laid greater stress in its appraisal on the probable sharp rise in oil prices.[26] But it must be remembered, that whereas other agencies considered this possible, no one was able to forecast when or with what force it would occur. Doubtless the cautious attitude by the Commission was designed to avoid "attracting the thunderbolt". Yet this was not enough to prevent it and the lack of effective "lightning conductors" is the result of the failure of the Council to take any decision, since it was unable to give an opinion on the preventive programme which was submitted to it.

So far as the adequacy of the proposals is concerned, since 1973 the Community and the Member States have commenced in the international cooperation on energy proposed in the "Guidelines and priority measures". But they have only done this under pressure of events and under circumstances which have been far less propitious than they would have been if, before the crisis, all the parties concerned had taken the action that was suggested.

On the consumers' side, the International Energy Agency was set up in November 1974 at the initiative of the United States. And yet France does not participate in this organization and the Community as a body is unable to make its voice known. The result is a continuing feeling of malaise among the Nine and diminished effectiveness in an area where, had they taken the initiative, the Community could have played a fuller and more effective role in world energy affairs.

On the producers' side the Community was represented on the Energy Commission of the International Conference on Economic Cooperation, held in Paris since the beginning of 1976, and made a positive contribution. However, this Conference took place under circumstances which were extremely different from those which would have obtained if, from the beginning of 1973 onwards, and "atmosphere of confidence" and "appropriate relations" had been created in line with the Commission's proposals.[27]

Obviously, the political factors which gave rise to the embargo of October 1973 must not be overlooked; there are, however, grounds for thinking that prices would not have been raised so sharply had the machinery existed for producing and consumer countries to consult each other regularly on energy policies. Furthermore, cooperation involving the dovetailing of economies could already have produced positive results.[28]

In fact, the majority of governments has always considered that relations with the producing countries were a purely commercial problem, responsibility for which was left to the oil companies. From 1971 onwards several of these companies had come to think that the public authorities should in future have more say in these relations. Few governments, however, possessed either the willingness or the resources to do so.

The 1973 crisis also showed just how necessary some of the measures put forward by the Commission for organizing the oil market were:
– in the absence of measures designed to ensure free movement even in times of crisis, the Community oil market suffered serious disruption following the selective embargo introduced in October by the producing countries;
– one of the major shortcomings in this respect was the lack of any machinery for ascertaining supply costs[29] and for monitoring supply conditions and structures.

Nevertheless, the lack of any organized consultation with the oil companies led them to use their own initiative in apportioning available supplies. It is unnecessary to repeat the many criticisms from public opinion as to the behaviour of these companies in order to justify the need not only for the public authorities to be better informed of the activities of these companies but also for a tighter control on competition.

The proposals relating to the other energy sectors have retained all their relevance and, whereas some have been followed up since 1973,[30] little progress has been achieved in a number of other fields acknowledged as crucial, such as the policy for developing energy resources offering an alternative to imported oil.[31]

III. IMPACT OF THE PROPOSALS

As mentioned above (particularly, chapter II) although the Council acknowledged the relevance of the analysis carried out by the Commission, it could not agree on an order of priority for the proposals. The other Community institutions, on the other hand, were generally more positive as to what measures should be adopted, although they often expressed a less clear-cut opinion on the analysis. The opinions of the parties concerned (trade organizations and trade unions) usually placed an emphasis on one or other aspects of the opinions of the advisory bodies, and, like the latter, urged that a political decision be taken as soon as possible.

The European Parliament

The European Parliament has always devoted a great deal of time to energy matters; they have been analysed in depth by a specialist committee and discussed at length in plenary session. Parliament has constantly supported the Commission in its efforts to work out and implement a common policy, sometimes going further than the Commission's requests to the Council.

From the resolutions which it adopted in June and December 1973 on the Commission's proposals to the Council one can assess the attitudes of the Parliament:

– Parliament would firstly like to give the Commission all the instruments of an energy policy. It underlines the need for the Communities' powers in respect of research to be strengthened and requests the Council without delay to confer upon the Community the requisite powers. It asks that the Commission be given new powers to carry out the energy policy in accordance with Article 235 of the EEC Treaty so that the Commission can present the requisite proposals for Regulations and Directives without interruption. Finally, Parliament feels that, in this critical period of 1973, the Energy Council should meet every three months.[32]

– Parliament notes the set of proposals presented by the Commission in the Communication entitled "Necessary progress in Community energy policy" but considers that, to be effective, the measures should be put in order of priority with general measures to protect the environment, rational utilization of energy, scientific and technical research and the improvement of relations between importing and producer countries being given top priority.

– Parliament views energy policy as a part of an overall policy and believes that concomitant measures should be taken in the sectors of competition, monetary, external trade, financial and transport policy to ensure the best possible security of supply.

But because of its limited present powers, Parliament has not, however, been able to give an impetus to energy policy.[33]

The Economic and Social Committee

At its plenary sessions on 27 June and 29 November 1973 the Economic and Social Committee had an opportunity to express its views on the two Commission Communications, "Necessary progress in Community energy policy" and "Guidelines and Priority actions under the Community energy policy".

The Committee's opinion on the first Communication was unanimously adopted; this took place in an atmosphere of calm which has not yet been put to the test by the crisis which broke at the end of that year. By this vote, the Committee indicated its approval of the guidelines recommended by the Commission.[34]

The situation was quite different on 29 November, when the Committee was called upon to give its opinion on the "Guidelines and priority actions". A favourable opinion on the Commission Communication was adopted by a nominal vote of 50 to 18 with 5 abstentions.[35] However, the prior rejection (by an extremely small majority of 42 in favour and 50 against with 4 abstentions) of an amendment criticizing the attitude of the oil companies and noting their inability to ensure stable and regular supplies in the future was a precursor to the division which later took place within the Committee between the liberals who favoured a market economy and action by the oil companies, and those who preferred central planning by the public authorities and a stricter control of the activities of the oil companies. This division was subsequently to make it difficult for the Committee to adopt explicit and unequivocal positions on energy questions.

The Committee also stressed the importance for supply policy of relations with the oil-producing countries and the oil companies. The above mentioned amendment went so far as to call for direct negotiations with the producing countries in order to guarantee supplies—in view of the crisis reigning at the time.

The ECSC Consultative Committee

This Committee is made up of representatives of manufacturers, workers and consumers of coal and steel and has, on several occasions, turned its attention to the problems of general energy policy in view of the repercussions which such a policy can have on the coal industry.

With regard to the "Necessary progress", the Committee has been deliberating—and rightly so, as borne out by events five months later—on the reality of the "stable market" hypothesis put forward in the Commission's diagnostic reports. The Committee was also sceptical about the availability of nuclear energy.

As to the guidelines proposed, the Committee regretted that the Commission had not made greater provision for Community coal and underlined the economic security which, in its opinion, this source of energy supplied.

It considered, moreover, that whereas the trend in the price of Community coal can be satisfactorily predicted, it is impossible to forecast the extent to which competitive products would rise in price (especially imported oil and gas), since this depended as much on political as on economic factors.[36] The Committee called upon the Commission to urge governments to take measures chiefly with a view to maintaining substantial energy production in the Community and to make maximum rational use of indigenous resources.

The trade organizations

The European Centre for Public Enterprise (ECPE) has expressed no formal opinion on the proposals put up by the Commission in 1973. In the light of the positions subsequently adopted by this body, it may nevertheless be assumed that, had the Centre reacted at the time, it would have stressed the importance it attached from the domestic point of view to the proposals regarding the maintenance of vigorous competition, and to greater market transparency.

Unlike the ECPE, the Union of Industries of the European Community (UNICE) represents private industry and not public enterprise. And yet, as in the case of the ECPE, the opinions of the UNICE are basically motivated by the fear of restrictions being placed on businesses' freedom of action. This is why, traditionally, the emphasis has been placed on the basic part played by competition, greater involvement of firms in determining energy policy guidelines and on the necessary safeguard of self-financing capacity.

As with the ECPE, the various preoccupations of the affiliated industries make it difficult to obtain a consensus among the producers of energy (especially as they compete with one another) and among the consumer industries for a vigorous policy which would somewhat damage the interests of certain parties. The opinions put forward in May and September 1973 on the "Guidelines and priority actions" reflect this feature.

The trade unions

The European Trades Union Confederation (ETUC) has always supported the Commission's efforts to define and implement an energy policy. It made no formal pronouncement on the proposals of 1972 and 1973 but did make its position clear in the course of several meetings with Commission officials. Official positions were subsequently adopted along the same lines.

In general terms, the Confederation believes that action by the public authorities should be strengthened at the expense of private interests and in particular those of the oil companies and that the Commission's proposals lack vigour in this area.

The ETUC agrees with the broad lines of the Commission's proposals, in particular the development of alternative resources to imported oil i.e., the development of indigenous oil resources, recourse to nuclear energy, re-appraisal of the coal situation, rational utilization of energy sources.

On relations with the producer countries the ETUC recommends balanced

91

cooperation which respects the interests of producers and is generous towards the developing countries.

As far as the industrialized countries are concerned, the ETUC would like a form of cooperation which precluded subservience to the most powerful nations and the creation of a "bloc" against the exporting countries.

On the subject of market organization, the ETUC proposes that the national and Community authorities be given real powers of intervention and price control, especially in the oil sector. It calls for the establishment of a body able to perform these functions, in which the trade union organizations would take part. It considers, moreover, that the basically liberal approach of the policy put forward by the Commission is no longer appropriate to the nature and scale of the problems involved.

General conclusions

It is trite to say that European policies have often depended on the pressure of outside events to give them any forward impetus. As far as energy policy is concerned, the oil crisis of 1973/74 did not have this effect:
– during the last months of 1973 there was no solidarity between the Member States who had been variously affected by the oil embargo, the main reason being foreign policy considerations; since that time only some of the measures have been taken which would, in the event of a new crisis, guarantee such solidarity in the maintenance of market unity;
– whereas the Council has laid down targets for energy consumption and production in 1985, it has taken only a few new measures to encourage the pursuance of these aims.
– the Community has not been able to play the part it should in cooperating with other energy importers.

As against this, it has, since the middle of 1975 and despite the considerable problems, been able to make its voice known in the dialogue with the energy-exporting countries and the developing importing countries.

Can one hope that in the absence of an early agreement on the principles of an internal energy policy the constraints imposed by external relations will gradually break the vicious circle of an energy policy being a "determining and a determined factor" and will enable short-term sectoral rivalries to be put aside for the sake of long-term Community prospects?

NOTES

1. Came into force in 1958.
2. The cooperation between the executive bodies of the ECSC, the EEC and Euratom introduced by the protocol agreement of 7 December 1957 never really got off the ground.
3. Proposal for a Council Directive on the harmonization of the legislation of the Member States concerning the technical security measures in the construction and operation of oil pipelines
OJ No C 123 of 26 November 1968, p. 6.

– Proposal for a Council Directive on the harmonization of the specific consumption taxes of liquid hydrocarbons for use as fuel
OJ No C 14 of 11 February 1971, p. 25.
– Proposal for a Council Regulation concerning cross-frontier oil and gas pipelines
OJ No C 134 of 27 December 1972, p. 22.
4. Council Regulations (EEC) No 1055/72 on notifying the Commission of imports of crude oil and natural gas
OJ No L 120 of 25 May 1972, p. 3.
– Council Regulation (EEC) No 1056/72 on notifying the Commission about investment projects of interest to the Community in the petroleum, gas and electricity sectors
OJ No L 120 of 25 May 1972, p. 7.
– Council Regulation (EEC) No 812/73 of 22 March 1973 delaying application to the United Kingdom of Regulations (EEC) No 1055/72 on notifying the Commission of fuel imports and (EEC) No 1056/72 on notifying the Commission about investment projects of interest to the Community in the petroleum, gas and oil sectors
OJ No L 80 of 28 March 1973, p. 1.
– Commission Regulation (EEC) No 1068/73 of 16 March 1973 applying Council Regulation (EEC) No 1055/72 of 18 May 1972 on notifying the Commission of imports of crude oil and natural gas
OJ No L 113 of 28 April 1973, p. 1/13.
– Commission Regulation (EEC) No 1069/73 of 16 March 1973 applying Council Regulation No 1056/72 of 18 May 1972 on notifying the Commission about investment projects of interest to the Community in the petroleum, natural gas and electricity sectors
OJ No L 113 of 28 April 1973, p. 14/26.
5. Proposal for a Council Regulation establishing a common system for imports of oil and gas from third countries
OJ No C 134 of 27 December 1972, p. 21.
6. Proposal for a Council Regulation concerning the application of joint undertaking status to the activities of the oil and gas industry
OJ No C 106 of 23 October 1971, p. 2/5.
7. For instance, the rapid increase in supplies from North Africa to Europe was not matched by the creation of new transport facilities to meet any accidental shortfall in oil supplies from this area such as that which occurred in 1970.
8. American oil imports (million tonnes):

1965: 127	1971: 201	1973: 316
1970: 176	1972: 242	

9. This gradual control was initially secured through agreements with the oil companies. Teheran and Tripoli (February 1971): revision of pricing system; Geneva (January 1972): increase in prices following the devaluation of the dollar; New York (October 1972): participation of producer countries in concessions; Geneva (June 1973): supplementary agreement. From October 1973 the producer countries fixed their prices unilaterally.
10. Meadows and associates: "The Limits to Growth", Earth Island Ltd, London 1972.
11. Community of Six. See Commission of the European Communities: Prospects of primary energy demand in the Community (1975–1980–1985), Luxembourg (no date), 121 pages.
12. See Commission of the European Communities: Medium-term forecasts and trends for the oil sector in the Community, Luxembourg (no date), 90 pages.

Medium-term forecasts and trends for the gas sector in the Community, Brussels, 1972, 94 pages. Second illustrative nuclear programme for the Community, 1 July 1972 (Doc. EUR 5011), 323 pages.

13. See Commission of the European Communities: The problems, instruments and necessary progress in the Community energy policy for the period 1975–1985, Luxembourg (no date), 59 pages; Part A (problems and instruments).

14. Published in Part B of the document mentioned in footnote 13 and as Supplement 11/72 of the Bulletin of the European Communities.

15. European Communities, Council: Report by the Working Party on Energy to the Permanent Representatives Committee, Doc. R/1182/1/73 of 18 May 1973.

16. Cf. for example,
– the Conference of Heads of State or Government in Paris on 19/21 October 1972: " . . . deem it necessary to invite the Community institutions to formulate as soon as possible an energy policy guaranteeing certain and lasting supplies under satisfactory economic conditions".
– *idem*, Copenhagen, 14/15 December 1973: " . . . agreed on the necessity for the Community of taking immediate and effective action along the following lines".
– *idem*, Paris, 9/10 December 1974: " . . . referring to the Council Resolution of 17 September 1974, have invited the Community institutions to work out and to implement a common energy policy in the shortest possible time".

17. Cf. the recent case of the draft decision on Euratom loans.

18. The items not listed which concern coal, natural gas and environmental conservation do not differ appreciably from what was proposed in the "Necessary progress". The idea of limiting the supply of gas to thermal power stations should be noted however as it subsequently became a Council Directive.

19. Doc. R/1667/72 (ENER 20) Annex 1.

20. Regulation (EEC) No 3056/73 of 9 November 1973, OJ No L 312, p. 1. Thus the Commission proposal on the application of joint undertaking status to the activities of the oil and gas industry, which had already been set out in the "First guidelines" of 1968, was implemented although in a markedly amended form.

21. Directive No 73/328/EEC of 29 July 1973, OJ No L 228, p. 1.

22. At the time, the existence of two rival projects for setting up enrichment plants (Eurodif and Urenco) risked creating excess capacity. Subsequently, market trends and the staggering of investment programmes for each project have improved the chances of the favourable coexistence of both technologies.

23. The Directive 73/238/EEC on measures to mitigate the effects of difficulties in the supply of crude oil specified that Member States should make the necessary provisions by 30 June 1974 at the latest. Some Member States already had the required legal instruments, or some of them at least, in October 1973. The Directive was meant as a guide for *de facto* coordination during the crisis at the end of 1973.

On the other hand the Community did not, in October 1973, have a system for limiting consumption according to common principles and for distributing supplies in time of crisis. The mechanisms of the OECD—an organization to which all Member States belong—would normally have seen to this distribution. As these mechanisms were not implemented, however, the Community oil market was soon in difficulties. The Commission proposed to the Council on several occasions that it take the measures required to re-establish market unity, but this was not done before the end of 1976.

At the end of June 1977, the Council has still not fully made good this lack in the Community system for security of oil supplies. Discussions on a draft decision on reduction of consumption in case of oil supply difficulties are still pending.

24. See OJ No C 92/73.

25. See pp. 81 and 82.

26. See p. 81 and the document referred to in footnote 13.

27. See pp. 82 and 83.

28. Cooperation which is currently developing in many areas, not necessarily concerned with energy: Lomé, Maghreb, Euro-Arab Dialogue.

29. This shortcoming was remedied by Council Regulation No 76/491/EEC, OJ No L 140 of 28 May 1976, p. 4.

30. For example:
- Council Directive of 13 February 1975 (75/404/EEC) on the restriction of the use of natural gas in power stations, OJ No L 178 of 9 July 1975, p. 24.
- Council Directive of 14 April 1975 (75/405/EEC) restricting the use of petroleum products in power stations, OJ No L 178 of 9 July 1975, p. 26.
- Council Directive of 20 May 1975 (75/339/EEC) obliging the Member States to maintain minimum stocks of fossil fuel at thermal power stations, OJ No L 153 of 13 June 1975, p. 35.
- Commission Decision of 25 July 1973 (73/287/ECSC) concerning coal and coke for the iron and steel industry in the Community, OJ No L 259 of 15 September 1973, p. 36.
- Commission Decision No 528/ECSC of 25 February 1976 regarding the Community system of measures taken by the Member States to assist the coal-mining industry, OJ No L 63 of 11 March 1976, p. 1.

These last two Decisions extend and amend the arrangements previously enforced.

31. Cf. p. 94, note 16. See also the conclusions of the European Council meeting in Rome on 1–2 December 1975. Mention should, however, be made of Regulation (EEC) No 3056/73 of the Council of 9 November 1973 on the support of Community projects in the hydrocarbons sector (OJ No L 312 of 13 November 1973, p. 1), under which support was given between 1974 and 1976 to some 50 projects totalling 81 million u.a.

32. In December 1974 the Ministers for Energy decided to meet every two months. In the two years following that date the Council has held only five meetings on energy.

33. As a result of the new budgetary powers conferred on Parliament (as regards own resources), Parliament was able to retain the appropriations entered in the Communities' Budget for 1977 for energy development projects which had been rejected by the Council.

34. Doc. ESC 531/73.

35. Doc. ESC 882/73.

36. Opinion of the Consultative Committee, 156th session, 4 May 1973.

ANNEX
Some Characteristics of Energy Consumption in 1973.

	D	F	I	N	B	L	UK	IR	DK	EEC-6	EEC-9
A. Internal primary energy consumption											
(M tec)	380	256	183	88	66	7	318	11	28	980	1,337
B. Proportion of each primary energy source in consumption (% of A)											
Coal	22.4	15.5	6.0	5.1	25.1	48.7	36.2	7.8	10.9	16.4	20.9
Crude oil	55.0	68.9	74.6	47.7	59.3	32.9	48.6	74.4	89.1	61.7	59.3
Brown coal	8.9	0.5	0.3	—	—	0.4	—	15.3	0.1	3.6	2.8
Natural gas	10.3	7.7	11.3	47.2	16.8	4.4	11.5	—	—	13.5	12.6
Electrical energy (primary)	3.1	7.4	7.6	-0.3	13.5	3.7	2.5	-0.1	4.6	4.3	—
Total	100	100	100	100	100	100	100	100	100	100	100
C. Energy dependence[1]	55	78	83	6[2]	86	100	48	81	100	64	61

1. Net imports excluding bunker oil as % of internal gross primary energy consumption in %.
2. This figure indicates the volume of natural gas exports, which virtually offsets oil imports completely.

Source: EUROSTAT: Energy Statistics, Yearbook 1975.

II. ENERGY POLICY COUNTER-REPORT

Oil Policy before the Yom Kippur War

by *Guy de Carmoy*

M. Robert de Bauw's paper sets forth very clearly the slow progress of the Community towards a common energy policy and contains a careful assessment of the policy proposed by the Commission, from an analytical point of view as well as from that of the adequacy of the proposals. M. de Bauw has provided internal analysis. I propose to treat the subject from a point of view extraneous to the Community, that of the geostrategy of energy.

The energy policy of a country or of a group of countries is simply the optimal use of resources, which are limited although essential to all branches of the economy and to the well-being of the people. The volume of energy consumption at a given time is in direct relation to the degree of industrialization and the increase in the consumption of energy is in direct relation to the increase in overall demand, in other words, of the gross national product.

The first industrial revolution was based upon coal and steel, the second upon oil and the motor-car. While the coal markets in Europe were essentially national, the European oil market was in its essence international because of the distances between the centres of production and those of consumption. This was not the case in the United States which had long been the greatest producer and consumer of crude oil and oil products. It was in the United States that five of the seven great oil companies were created. Quite naturally they swarmed towards the production centres of the Middle East, where two companies, one British and the other Anglo-Dutch, had already started operations, and towards Europe. This movement was accelerated after the Second World War when British influence in the Middle East waned and the Europeans were drawn to the American way of life based on the individual motor car. An unprecedentedly great change in the type of energy used took place in a few years. Domestic coal took second place to imported oil. The increase in the overall consumption of energy became both the cause and the effect of the economic growth of the European countries.

In the oligopolistic market in which the French and Italian national companies had more or less to align themselves with the policy of the great Anglo-American oil companies, the price paid by the industrial consumer or by domestic users was far higher than the development cost of the marginal producer in the Middle East. The difference formed a rent which theoretically could be appropriated by the producing country in the form of a tax upon profits and of royalties, by the consumer country in the form of indirect taxes and by the oil companies in the form of profits. Until 1970, the share of the oil-producing country was far smaller than the two others. Furthermore, the rise in real wages placed the coal industry, with its very high labour intensity,

97

in an unfavourable position compared with the oil industry. Already in 1958 the consumption of coal was diminishing, while the total consumption of energy was growing.

The coal crisis in the European Iron and Steel Community was only a forerunner of the energy crisis which was to strike the European Economic Community. The oil market involved a great number of states and enterprises. The oil-producing countries claimed a growing share in the oil revenue. The process of decolonization was bound to affect the multinational companies, which were themselves a form of colonialism. The strategy of the oil-producing countries, which since 1960 had been grouped in OPEC (Organization of Petroleum Exporting Countries), took its stand upon the Resolution by the General Assembly of the United Nations which was passed in November 1966 by 104 votes to none with 6 abstentions (among which were those of the United States and Britain). This resolution proclaimed "the inalienable rights of countries to exercise their permanent sovereignty over their natural resources in the interests of development". New enterprises queued up to take their share in such an expanding market: the "independent" American companies, not content with the crumbs of the Iranian Consortium, settled in Libya. The European countries, with the exception of Germany, did their best each for their own national oil champion. The Soviet Union exported oil to Europe. The oil market, oligopolistic in the 1950's, became more competitive in the 1960's after the oil-producing countries had asserted their claims, while demand increased constantly in Western Europe, Japan and the United States.

Between 1960 and 1973, the market went through two violently contrasting phases, one of a slow decline, the other of a rapid rise in real prices from 1970, before the Yom Kippur War accelerated this movement. I propose to examine the strategy of the main actors in these two phases.

THE PARTIES INVOLVED AND THE OIL MARKET IN THE 1960'S

The United States

In 1959, President Eisenhower established a quota system for the import of oil. Its aim was to ensure adequate supplies, while protecting the national industry with relative price stability. However, the decline in the reserves of gas and oil resulted in stagnation or a fall in national production while imports continued to increase in absolute value and in percentage of the total consumption of energy, in spite of some adjustments in the rise of domestic prices which took place in 1968 and 1969. President Nixon decided at that date to reconsider the oil policy.

If the rate of self-sufficiency in energy was in decline, the international expansion of the oil industry continued, the American companies controlling half the production of the free world, outside their own territory. The American government was far from averse to such an expansion provided that internally the anti-trust legislation was respected.

98

The major oil companies

The protectionism of the American market benefited the small producers and induced the companies to develop their external markets. Circumstances were favourable in the sense that the volume of crude oil shipped to the industrial countries grew enormously between 1960 and 1970: from 278 mt. to 900 mt. for OECD member countries, from 109 mt. to 406 mt. for the six EEC original member countries.

But the activity of the major oil companies met with some obstacles. The Soviet Union agreed to sales below the prices decided upon by some of the European countries. The large oil companies, however, in February 1959 had operated a reduction in these prices which brought them back to a level below that of the Suez crisis in 1956. In July 1960, the Board of Directors of Exxon decided upon a new reduction in prices. This decision was to mobilize the oil-producing countries. Lastly, the "independent" American companies and some European nationalized companies were disposed to offer slightly more advantageous terms to the oil-producing countries then those of the major companies. Several "independent" companies started to operate, some in the Middle East, others in Libya. In 1967, after the Six Day War, the Arab countries refused to supply Britain, but the major oil companies were able to replace the oil from these countries by Iranian and American oil.

OPEC

The Organization of Petroleum Exporting Countries was created on 14 September 1960 as a reaction to the decision by the major oil companies to lower prices. During the 1960's eight countries joined the five founding countries. The initial aim of OPEC was to maintain the price stability of oil. The long-term goal, still unformulated, was the suppression of concessions by participation in the assets of the companies or by nationalization. The organization's early years were devoted to the study of oil economics and to the training of civil servants and of the executives of the national oil companies created by the producing countries. The strength of the organization stemmed from the fact that its members possessed two-thirds of the world reserves of oil, and ensured half the world production and 85% of world exports. The aim of stabilizing prices was achieved, but circumstances favourable to large-scale action only presented themselves in 1970.

The European countries

Just when their imports of oil were increasing, the European countries found themselves caught between the cartel of the major oil companies, long used to concertation, and that of the producing countries, which was on the way to consolidation.

National oil policies varied from one country to another, according to the degree of dependence on outside sources, the structure of the industry and the traditions of economic policy. Britain and the Netherlands followed a liberal tradition inside their country, welcoming the major companies on an equal

99

footing. Abroad, Shell and BP tended to follow the same line as their American colleagues and this was easier in that the vacuum left in the Middle East by Britain's withdrawal tended to be filled by the United States. Germany had no "national champion" in the oil sector and its market, which in 1970 became the largest in Europe, was also the most widely open to the great multinational groups. France and Italy pursued a policy of dirigisme. The ENI group was the first to obtain crude oil from the Soviet Union and to agree to conditions which were advantageous to the producing countries in the matter of profit sharing. France set up, alongside the *Compagnie Française des Pétroles*, a state group which was intended to be the instrument of several overseas operations, particularly in Algeria. It tightened control over all stages of the activities of the companies, both French and foreign, operating on the national market through the "delegated monopoly" of imports of crude oil and of oil products. These differences in interest and direction are an explanation of the obstacles which the European Communities met with when defining and applying a common energy policy.

The Commission of the EEC

Energy problems were of serious concern to the founders of the European Coal and Steel Community (1952) and Euratom (1957). At the Messina Conference (1955), a discussion took place as to whether the different sectors of energy should be merged in one organization, but this project was dropped. The sectors of oil and natural gas thus came within the competence of the EEC.

A report on the energy situation of the member states, undertaken in 1957 under the direction of Louis Armand, drew attention to the danger for Europe of its excessive dependence on the Middle East.

The merger of the Executives of the three Communities in 1967 gave the impression that a common energy policy could be drawn up. One of the first moves of the new General Directorate of Energy was to prepare a comprehensive, confidential report entitled "Ten years of activity of the oil industry in the Community (1958–1967)" This report described especially the concepts of oil policies in the different member states. It stated that taking into account an average reduction of 15% the oil prices effectively obtaining in 1967 in the Middle East were one quarter lower than those of 1958.

A few months later, in December 1968, the Commission published an important communication entitled "First Guidelines for a common energy policy", containing proposals for a framework of action and for the establishment of the common market. This document recalled that the aims of a common energy policy had been laid down by the Member States in a protocol of agreement of 21 April 1964 which gave priority to a cheap and secure supply. Commenting on these objectives, the report on the "First Guidelines" remarks:

There is no foundation for the assertion that this requirement is a contradiction in terms. It is only true to say that neither security nor a low price can be attained absolutely . . . In the long-term, a rational behaviour consists in fact in including in the determination of the optimum cost the price of a reasonable guarantee against the risk of insecurity.[1]

Here we come to the heart of the problem. It can be asked whether this argument is based on a realistic assessment of the risk deriving from the balance of strength of the parties involved.

In this respect, the Commission's approach was somewhat uncertain. It acknowledged the degree of dependence of the Member States with regard to imports and the insufficient diversification of the sources of supply.[2] It estimated that the consumption of oil within the Community would double in the next ten years.[3] Referring discreetly to events in the Middle East, it observed that there is a complementarity of interest between the importing countries and oil producers.[4] It indicated the methods suitable to measure the risk of a break in supplies and the risk of a rise in price.[5]

These observations, scattered throughout the report in veiled terms, do not make for an analysis of the geopolitical situation such as could be seen in the light of the Israeli–Arab conflict and the pressing claims of the oil-producing countries. But such an analysis would have justified, by an assessment of the risks, a medium-term common energy strategy. The strictly economic attributions of the Commission may explain its reticence on this matter at that time.

The Commission felt on surer ground when it came to the organization of the internal market. The proposals which it drew up in clear terms tended to bring about the free circulation of crude oil and oil products within the Community.

But the obstacles remained formidable. The differences in the basis and the level of indirect taxes from one Member State to another distorted trade conditions within the Community. The gaps in technology were numerous. However, the main obstacle arose out of the French system of "delegated monopoly", which enabled the government to control, as mentioned above, the various activities of the national and foreign companies on the market. The Commission proposed a system not of direct intervention but of supervision, based on information relating to the movement of goods and to investment projects. It could not achieve this because of the French government's refusal to alter its monopoly and the attachment of the Dutch and German governments to the free circulation of goods, the first because of the links of Royal Dutch Shell with the major companies, the second because its politics were based on free enterprise in a market economy.

The Commission stressed in other respects the consequences for the oil market of the Community of the protection of the American market. The companies based in the United States benefited from outlets at remunerative prices and from reduced taxation. Their affiliates in Europe received their crude oil at transfer prices adjusted in such a way that refining and distribution within the Community were not profit making. The Commission thought it desirable for the Community "that a part of its supply should be effected by the Community companies which dispose of oil at cost price or nearly so".[6] It did not think it desirable that the major oil companies alone should supply the Community. To sum up, opposing pressures were brought to bear by the countries with a planned oil economy (France and Italy) supporting their national champions and those with a free economy (the Netherlands and Germany) linked more or less closely to the great Anglo-American groups. These divergences were to persist when the political situation took a new turn due to the reversal of the market trends.

Sent back for scrutiny of the Committee of Permanent Representatives, the "First Guidelines" was only discussed by the Council of Ministers on 13 November 1969. The Council approved the basic principles of the document and invited the Commission to forward it the most urgent proposals. Moreover it authorized the Commission to set up a network of contacts with the high officials of the Member States, the representatives of the oil-producing countries, the representatives of the oil companies, and the United States government.[7]

In May 1972, more than two years after the agreement in principle, the Committee of Permanent Representatives adopted two regulations which required the communication to the Commission of the imports of hydro-carbons and of planned investments in the sectors of oil, natural gas and electricity. Thus, the Commission could be better informed.[8] But it could not draw up a programme of supply which conformed to the set objectives. This should not come as a surprise. In fact, in the course of the session of the Council of 13 November 1969, the Dutch representative declared strongly that any form of intervention must be avoided as far as possible by letting the free play of competition settle the matter.[9] The lack of action of the Council of Ministers was to continue when the reversal of the market trends modified the balance of forces in the international oil game.

THE CRISIS OF 1970–1971 AND ITS AFTER EFFECTS

The real oil crisis, which changed the balance of forces between the oil-producers and the consumers took place in 1970–1971. The events of 1973 were rather a further development.

The change in the international market

The unleashing of the crisis was due to the reduction in supply and the increase in demand. On the supply side, Syria refused in May 1970 to mend the Trans–Arabic Pipeline which carried 25 mt. of crude oil to the Mediterranean. At the same time, Colonel Khadafi, who had overthrown the traditionalist monarchy of Libya, ordered Occidental Petroleum, a newly established and independent company, to reduce its production and to accept an increase in the rates of taxes and the price of crude oil. The major companies consulted the American government in Washington and soon yielded to the Libyan demands, thus depriving Western Europe of 50 mt. of crude oil. At the same time there took place a rise in the rate of freight. The interruption of supplies from Libya and the cutting of the Tapline overtaxed the means of transporting oil from the Persian Gulf, the tankers being forced, since the closure of the Suez Canal, to sail round Africa. In the meantime the demand for oil products was growing rapidly in Europe as well as in the United States. In order to meet it in the medium term, the oil companies planned to bring into production the oil fields of Alaska and the North Sea, regions which were attractive from the point of view of the geographical division of risks, but with high exploitation costs. The international oil market thus passed from the zone of decreasing costs of the 1960's to one of rising costs.[10]

The state of the American market

During the same period the American government became concerned about developments in the domestic market. Faced with the increased demand for oil, the government had to decrease the application of the quota system of production through a reduction of the ratio of reserves to production, and to increase the quota of imports. The dependence on foreign sources grew worse and the United States could no longer supply Europe in a crisis as it had done after the Six Days War in 1967. Faced with the growing deficit in its energy balance, the United States had a choice between two policies, the first to continue to supply itself at the lowest cost with imported oil, as did Europe and Japan, the other to reduce gradually its dependence for energy on foreign sources by encouraging, by higher prices, the development of national sources of energy.

In 1970 President Nixon rejected the suggestions of a Task Force which recommended the first choice. He acted on the advice of the Lincoln Commission which recommended a rise in the price of imported oil in order to stabilize domestic prices at a high level and to encourage investments for the development of national sources of energy.[11] The State Department had criticized the forecasts of the Task Force on the national consumption of energy in 1980 and in 1970 had published its own assessment according to which the price of crude oil in the Persian Gulf, which was then a little below 2 dollars a barrel, would reach 4.50 in 1980.[12] In April 1973 President Nixon launched a message on energy. His aim was to stimulate the oil production in the United States and especially in Alaska by freeing the price of the "new oil". His decision was influenced by developments in the Middle East since 1970.

The Teheran and Tripoli agreements

At the conference of OPEC Ministers in Caracas in December 1970, the Member States, encouraged by Libya's action, recommended the raising of the rate of tax on profits, the general increase of posted prices and the definition of new bases for the calculation of differentials of quality and of location. A resolution was passed that negotiations with the oil companies should start at once. On 11 January 1971, twenty-three companies met in New York and, having been assured that the American anti-trust legislation would not be opposed to them, sent a collective memorandum to OPEC. The Under Secretary of State, John Irwin, was sent to visit the Shah of Iran, the King of Saudi Arabia and the Sheikh of Kuwait. His mission was to assure the moderate states in the Persian Gulf that the agreements on prices would be honoured by the oil companies, provided that the threat to cut deliveries was withdrawn.[13] At the same time, the American government called an extraordinary meeting of OECD in Paris at which the consumer countries made it clear that they were not prepared to resist a rise in prices.[14] They were well aware that were they to refuse, they would be exposed to a break in supplies or the nationalization of the shares of the companies.

The agreements of Teheran of 14 February 1971 on crude oil from the Persian Gulf and of Tripoli on 2 April 1971 on crude oil from the Mediterranean yielded to the claims of the oil-producing countries. The rise in posted prices were respectively 33 and 55 cents per barrel. The share of the oil-producing countries of the Persian Gulf was raised by 33–34 cents per barrel in relation to an initial price in the order of 90 cents,[15] that is to say a rise of about 37%. In the case of Mediterranean oil, the share of the producing countries was slightly higher.

The follow-up of OPEC's action

From this time onwards, events gathered momentum. As far back as February 1971, Algeria had nationalized 51% of the shares of the French groups operating in the country. In December 1971, Libya nationalized 50% of the shares of BP and did the same to the other oil groups in 1972/73 with a rate of 51 to 100%. In January 1972, Syria and Iraq proceeded to an outright nationalization of foreign oil interests. During the same year, Saudi Arabia and the other Gulf states signed in New York an agreement granting them a 25% share in the stock of the concessionary companies. All the OPEC countries obtained from the companies, without any difficulty, in 1972 and 1973, an adjustment in the price of crude oil to the two successive devaluations of the dollar.

At the start of 1973 the oil companies were still discussing with the producing countries, but the latter had achieved their goal. Nationalization or participation enabled them to determine the rhythm of production and to set the price. The concession system was dismantled. The negotiating ability of the companies was reduced and the discussions took a political turn which justified the intervention of the governments. The State Department in the autumn of 1969 had suggested to the Oil Committee of OECD the possibility of a common approach to energy problems. At the ministerial conference of the Council of OECD in May 1970, the Assistant Secretary of State, Philip Tresize, insisted that the energy question should be discussed in a multilateral context. His point of view was supported by only a few countries, Britain and the Netherlands being among them. The United States returned to the charge in the autumn of 1971 and in the spring of 1972 with no greater success.[16]

The commission's position

The Commission was not slow to state the consequences of the 1970–1971 crisis. In a communication to the Council, dated 30 July 1971, it stressed insistently the changes in the nature of the relations between the producing countries, the oil companies and the consumer countries: "Today the producing countries seem to be decided either to fix the level of prices in such a way as to appropriate for themselves the differential rent in relation to the marginal cost, or to take a growing share in the companies which operate on their territory, or to market themselves the crude oil which they produce". The Commission observed that the validity of the statements in the document "First Guidelines" was reinforced by the confrontation with the new situation.[17] On a practical level, it proposed to bring forward the obligatory stockpile of oil products from 60 to 90 days of consumption; it gave notice that it had prepared a system of periodic collection of information on the prices obtaining for the different forms of energy collected from companies cooperating on a voluntary basis; lastly, it proposed to extend to the sphere of hydrocarbons the status of "common enterprise" of the Treaty of Euratom.

At the same time, the Commission prepared a series of documents comprising an analysis of the data on the demand for primary energy in the Community up to 1985, an analysis of the conditions of supply by source of energy for the same period and, lastly, a report of synthesis entitled "The necessary progress of the common energy policy for the period 1975–1985". These documents were available on the eve of the Summit Meeting which was held in Paris from 19 to 21 October 1972. It is doubtful whether the heads of state or of government read them or even had them read. In fact in paragraph 9 of the final Summit communiqué it is stated that these high personalities "estimate that it is necessary to have drawn up by the institutions of the Community as soon as possible an energy policy which would guarantee a sure and lasting supply in economically satisfactory conditions".

The report of synthesis had nevertheless the merit of revealing clearly the geopolitical facts of the energy problem and of recommending a line of conduct. It noted that the Community found itself competing with other purchasers—the United States and Japan—in a sellers' market. "The problems of energy supply" it observed, "are today so linked with a world context that attempts to solve them nationally seem doomed to failure in advance. But the Community decisions themselves, to take into account its own interests, imply a permanent consideration of what is taking place in the Third World". It went on to say that "the essential problem of ensuring the investments in the energy sector cannot be exclusively resolved by the play of market forces". The principle for action which results from this is that the Community should invite the broadest cooperation with all the countries and regions which are interested in it.[18] On the question of the relations between the importing and exporting countries, "the Commission considers that it behoves it to help the progress of the developing countries". It adds: "Europe provides them with the essential outlet for their main production and these supplies are for Europe of primary importance, thus creating a situation of mutual dependence".[19]

These very judicious observations and recommendations of a political nature were followed by sectorial proposals for oil which repeated or amplified the previous proposals relating to common information, to the unity of the market, to the measures to be taken in case of a break in supplies, to investments and financing and to the common import regulations. Lastly, it put forward new proposals of a general nature in regard to the environment and to the rational use of energy.

The weakest part of the report was the analysis of the oil market. The Commission considered that oil would remain in 1985 with 900 mt. of crude oil, representing 65% of the total demand, the main source of the Community's energy supply. It took into consideration several factors of stabilization: oil and natural gas from "safe" areas such as the North Sea and the weight of nuclear energy which should begin to be felt after 1980. Examining two possible trends in the oil market, it seemed to lend some credence to the case of a stable market, according to which "the price of crude oil in 1985 would be along the lines laid down by the Teheran and Tripoli agreements". Against this an appreciable rise in the price of oil is only seen as an academic eventuality in the case of the deliberate restriction of supply or of inadequate investment in oil prospecting. Again, price rises would be restricted by the price of two potential competitors: oil from tar sands and shale and imported steam-coal, both very long-term competitors, it must be stressed.[20]

For the time being, the oil-producing states were firmly decided to exploit to the maximum a sellers' market and the United States came down on the side of high-priced energy. "What obligation has any country to sell its product cheaply when it knows it can obtain a higher price?" wrote an American diplomat, an expert in oil matters, in February 1973. He estimated that "the OPEC governments will probably continue to be able to obtain a very high rise in price".[21] In April 1973, he thought that a price of 7 dollars a barrel in 1980, taking into account the market trend, would seem to be "conservative".[22]

The real ministerial debate on the common energy policy took place during the session of the Council of 22 May 1973. To prepare it, the Commission drew up a working document[23] mentioning the correctives which the enlargement of the Community from six to nine members—effective on 1 January 1973—would bring to the already developed themes and also produced a communication to the Council on the "Guidelines and priority actions for a common energy policy",[24] the aim of which was to concentrate the debate upon a series of fundamental points in the Report of Synthesis of October 1972. This document emphasized the relations to be established between the Community and states, both importers and exporters of oil, and it described the contents and the modalities of the setting up of the common oil market.

The paralysis of the Council of Ministers

On 13 November 1969 the Council debated the 1968 Commission's report "First Guidelines". On 22 May 1973 it met to discuss the Report "Guidelines and priority actions" and the documents prepared for the Summit Conference of 1972. Thus for more than three years—particularly during the 1970-1971 crisis—the Council of Ministers had never discussed in depth the common energy policy.

The debate of May 1973 concentrated on a question of priority. Should or should not the common energy market be set up before developing contacts with the oil importers and the oil exporters? The French delegate thought it premature to negotiate with Third World countries before being assured of the existence of a coherent and firm common position. The other delegations thought it essential to define a common attitude between the three great oil consuming regions—the Community, the United States and Japan—and to bring into focus certain forms of cooperation with the oil-exporting countries, notably in the sphere of development. The view of the Commissioner for Energy was that it would be useless to speak of a common foreign policy if at a given moment no contacts had been made and no talks had been started. The Council was unable to come to an agreement. It merely stated that the Commission's proposals "contained in broad lines the basis for appropriate discussion for the common measures aimed at guaranteeing the security of energy supplies".

The communiqué relating to the debates also stressed "the urgency of drawing up a common energy policy" and noted "with satisfaction" the Commission's intention to present to it before the end of 1973 proposals for putting this policy into practice. According to the German representative, this text was tantamount to the Community's capitulation to the challenge which had been thrown to it. The Council was unable to carry out the mandate entrusted to it by the Summit Conference. How can this deficiency be explained?

The Commission's analysis embraced the fundamental facts of the geo-political problem. The Council was far more fully informed in 1973 than it had been in 1969. The Commission's proposals were coherent. The Community's dependence on suppliers demanded both an internal organization of the market and external negotiations. The motives which had impelled the Community in the 1960's to bring into force a common external tariff and to make contact with its main industrial partners remained valid for the 1970's when it was necessary to guarantee the supply to the Member States of an essential product for all industrial activity.

The Community and the oil-producing countries were in a state of asymmetrical interdependence, in the sense that the goods and services sold in exchange for imported oil were not indispensable to the users and that the Europeans were competing with the Americans and the Japanese in the limited markets of the OPEC countries.

For the partners of France, a concertation between the industrial countries was essential. Its setting was clearly OECD. The preponderance of the United States could be seen in the weeks preceding the Teheran and Tripoli Agreements. The American government had on various occasions since 1969 recommended a multilateral approach to energy problems. France did not want concertation with the United States. One may be surprised that France did not respond to the idea of global negotiations with the oil-producing countries, although her policy since 1967 had been decidedly pro-Arab. Doubtless, her government preferred to have bilateral relations with the Third World. One wonders indeed if the French position at the Council of 22 May was not a prefiguration of the position she was to take in February 1974 at the energy conference convened in Washington, at the invitation of the United States—a conference during which France took a different line from that of her partners in the Community who rallied to the American views.

As for the proposals for controlling the market formulation by the Commission, they were only partly accepted owing to the objections of Great Britain and the Netherlands.

The Council of 22 May 1973 had adopted a regulation on the support of common projects in the sector of hydrocarbons and a directive concerning the measures to lessen the difficulties of hydrocarbon supplies. However the Community did not yet possess a system which enables it to restrain consumption on common bases and to share supplies in a crisis. Two of the Commission's proposals, presented to the Council in July 1973, were not adopted by the Council until December 1973: this was a regulation concerning information on the establishment of energy balances by the Community and a decision to set up an Energy Committee.

Is not the date of the creation of this Committee symbolic?

The attitude of the other institutions of the community

The word institution is taken here in a wide sense. It comprises the European Parliament, the Economic and Social Council, and the trade associations and trade unions which are working at Community level.

The stance taken by these diverse institutions with regard to the Commission's action and the deliberations of the Council are described pertinently by M. de Bauw. I can do no less than refer the reader to his very complete account, mentioning, with him, that the institutions in question, beginning with the European Parliament, have only a consultative role and stressing some points which seem to me to be important. The European Parliament in its resolution of 3 July 1973 regretted that the Council had been unable to draw up guidelines for a common energy policy or to take decisions on commercial policy in the sector of hydrocarbons. It asked for an extension of the powers of the Commission, in conformity with Article 235 of the Treaty of Rome. In the light of the debates of the Council of Ministers, it appeared that such an extension would not be acceptable to most of the Member States.

The Economic and Social Committee in its recommendation of 27 June 1973 also regretted that the Council had given no ruling on the general guidelines presented by the Commission. Although it approved them in broad terms, it declared its conviction that, taking into account the world market trend, the next few years would see a general rise in the cost of energy, especially of natural gas and of oil.

CONCLUSION

Knowing the attitudes and aims of the main actors during the decisive years for OPEC, which preceded the fourfold rise in the price of oil, it is possible, with hindsight, to engage in the exercise of political-science-fiction. This consists in bringing judgement to bear on the Commission's perception of the import of events and on the value of its recommendations, and to assess to what extent these recommendations, had they been followed, would have provided a true European alternative.

The Commission was confronted by a colossal challenge, that of the struggle for the control of raw materials in a politico-economic system directed towards a more and more general and elaborate industrialization. In this struggle, world public opinion, especially in the United Nations

Organization, sided with the developing countries, and Western Europe, poor in fossil energy, was less well placed than the United States. In this struggle, oil had a special place. The economic growth of the industrialized countries was based widely on the exponential growth of consumption of oil products for industrial, transport and domestic use. The motor car had become a way of life, providing transport from the home to the place of work and increasing tremendously the satisfaction of weekend and holiday leisure. The result was that the material progress, the wellbeing of collectivities and the contentment of individuals was based on the uninterrupted supply of ever increasing quantities of cheap oil. The system was fragile. Politicians and consumers lived in a soap bubble, refusing—as they are still doing—to imagine an era in which oil was at first expensive and then perhaps rare, with all its individual consequences.

The Commission was slow to see the extent of the challenge. Having seen it in 1972, it was unable to convince the ministers and to warn public opinion. Some will say that it was not its role to take the place of the governments in denouncing dangers which the latter wanted to ignore or to minimize and that, moreover, it did not have the necessary means to mobilize public opinion.

Be this as it may, the Commission carefully stressed the relation between the internal organization of the common energy market and the ability of the Community to negotiate with the suppliers of OPEC and with the United States, leader of the industrial countries and guarantor of the truce in the Middle East. Organized internally, the EEC would have been able to play on the external plane its role as the largest consumer. Equally, it could have asserted the solidarity between its members in the case in which some of them were discriminated against by the oil-producing countries. To be sure, the organization of the market, as it was proposed in 1972, would not have been entirely set up in 1973 but it would have shown to the oil-exporting countries and to the United States a common will which was utterly lacking.

The rules governing the debates of the Council of Ministers and in particular the rule of unanimity do not permit that body to arbitrate between the positions taken by the Member States. On the energy question, as in many other areas, the Council looked for the lowest common denominator. It found this in quasi-inaction. It did not debate the energy policy between November 1969 and May 1973. At that moment it divided between two trends and came to no decision. Its failure is that of all the governments of the Community Member States. This continues in 1977.

The Chronology of the oil crisis 1960–1973 is summed up in the following table.

NOTES

1. "First Guidelines for a common energy policy", p. 11.
2. *Ibid.*, Appendix.
3. *Ibid.*, Appendix 1, p. 95.
4. *Ibid.*, p. 100.
5. *Ibid.*, Appendix 2, p. 164.
6. *Ibid.*, Appendix 2 as above pp. 175, 176.

7. Note of the General Secretariat of the Commission, 31 October 1972.

8. The information was, however, far from complete in the fields of imports of oil products, of distribution and of marketing.

9. General Secretariat SEC (69) 4019 Report on the 88th session of the Council, devoted to energy problems.

10. Jean-Marie Chevalier, *Le Nouvel Enjeu Pétrolier*, Calmann Levy, Paris, 1973, p. 77.

11. Nicolas Sarkis, *Le Pétrole à l'heure arabe*, Stock, 1975, p. 60.

12. James E. Akins, "The Oil Crisis: This time the wolf is here", *Foreign Affairs*, April 1973, p. 464.

13. James A. Akins, *op. cit.*, p. 473.

14. Anthony Sampson, *Les Sept Soeurs*, Alain Moreau, 1976, p. 342.

15. Michel Grenon, *Le Nouveau Pétrole*, Hachette, Paris, 1975, p. 239.

16. James E. Akins, *op. cit.*, p. 486.

17. Communication from the Commission to the Council on the opening of the "First Guidelines for a common energy policy", COM (71) 810 final, pp. 2, 3.

18. "The necessary progress of the common energy policy for the period 1975–1985", pp. 35, 36.

19. *Ibid.*, pp. 44, 45.

20. *Ibid.*, pp. 44, 45.

21. James E. Akins, "New Directions in Foreign Policy", *Financial Analysis Journal*, Jan–Feb. 1973, pp. 61, 62.

22. James E. Akins, "The Oil Crisis", *Foreign Affairs*, April 1973, p. 487.

23. ESC (73) 128, "The main characteristics of the supply of primary energy in the enlarged Community", 8 Feb. 1973.

24. ESC (73). 1481 final, 19 April 1973.

ANNEX
Chronology of the oil crisis 1960–1973

	OPEC—Middle East	United States—Oil Companies	Commission, Council of EEC
Aug. 1960		Reduction of official oil prices	
Sept. 1960	Creation of OPEC		
April 1964			Protocol of agreements on energy problems
Nov. 1966	Resolution ONU on natural resources		
June 1967	Six days war		
1967			Merger of executives
Dec. 1968			Report "First Guideline" directive on security stockpiling
Jan. 1969	Revolution in Libya		
Nov. 1969	Resolution OPEC Caracas		Council of energy ministers
Jan. 1970			
Jan. 1971	Teheran agreement Nationalization in Algeria		
Feb. 1971		Irwin mission	
April 1971	Tripoli agreement		
Dec. 1971	Nationalization of BP in Libya		
1971		Report Lincoln commission	

(continued)

ANNEX (cont.)

	OPEC—Middle East	United States—Oil Companies	Commission, Council of EEC
Jan. 1972	Nationalization in Syria and Iraq Geneva agreement after first devaluation of the dollar		
May 1972			Regulation on imports of hydro-carbons
Oct. 1972	New York agreements on participation		Regulation on investment projects Report "Necessary Progress." Paris summit
April 1973		Nixon message on energy Article Akins, *Foreign Affairs*	
May 1973			Report "Guidelines and Priority Actions," Council of energy ministers Directive on supplies of hydro-carbons
June 1973	Geneva agreement after second devaluation of dollar		Regulation on community projects
Oct. 1973	Yom Kippur War Unilateral rise of official oil prices		
Nov. 1973		Nixon "Project independence"	
Dec. 1973	Second unilateral rise of official oil prices		Regulation on energy balance-sheets Creation of an energy committee

III. CONCLUSIONS

Energy Policy of the European Community

by the Chairman and Rapporteurs

Group IV, Energy Policy, under the chairmanship of Mr. John Pinder, agreed with the parallel conclusions of the reports of Mr. de Bauw and Professor Guy de Carmoy on the causes and developments which led to the oil-crisis of 1973. The discussion concentrated therefore on the general, past and present, problems faced by a European Energy Policy.

The problems are on two levels:

a. on the level of national politics where it is impossible to cope with all aspects of the situation as we have known it since 1973 (in fact since 1970/71);
b. on the level of public opinion which does not realize the need to change its consumption pattern (energy saving, motor car);

- The economic growth of the industrial countries was conditioned by the proportional growth of the consumption of oil products. The public at large does not seem to realise how important it is to reduce the consumption of imported energy and, most specially, to limit the use of motor cars.
- Public opinion is afraid of the development of nuclear energy. Yet the increase of consumption of nuclear energy combined with energy saving and, to a certain extent, the use of coal, provides the only possible practical solution to the energy crisis;
- Finally, public opinion is unaware of the economic and political implications of the rise in prices of energy .(There are three types of countries in the Community: those Northern European countries which are well supplied with hydrocarbons; the countries whose high level of exports of manufactured goods compensates for their possible lack of energy resources (e.g. Germany and certain neighbouring countries); and finally, the countries of the Mediterranean, which are basically lacking in primary energy resources. The growing balance of payment deficits of the countries in the third category can have serious social consequences.)

What can the community (and especially the commission) do to solve this problem?

a. The Commission must inform the public clearly and objectively (even if this does not always please the national governments). In this context, a "shock technique" consisting of announcing a drastic change in living standards and conditions was considered by most of the group to be neither advisable nor compatible with European traditions.

b. The Commission must take a long-term view and show that, by the end of the century, when presumably even the North Sea oil reserves will be exhausted, all Member States will find themselves in a grave situation of economic dependence. This requires the organization of a basic economic solidarity.

c. The need for the European Parliament to inform the public was stressed, as was the Parliament's role as a sounding board for the Commission's message.

Several approaches could contribute considerably to the progress in the community's energy policy:

a. more information should be made available to the public at large, which clearly shows the relations between energy policy and other policies, such as the consequences of certain choices (e.g. oil, nuclear, coal);

b. increased efforts should be made towards adopting a common foreign policy for the Community's relations both with oil-exporting countries and with other major consumer countries,

    i. in the case of the former, attention was drawn to the asymmetric interdependence between the Community and those Third World countries which provide it with oil, which is essential to the functioning of the Western economies;

    ii. in the case of the latter, it was stressed that the European Community depends on the USA for its military security and for assuring its source of oil supply. It ought to be able openly to discuss this problem which the Member States cannot solve separately. The fact that the Community has joined the International Energy Agency shows the Member States' common interests in this respect.

Institutional and political aspects:

a. The weakness of the governments of the member states may explain their inability "to pass the message to the public" but hardly justifies it;

b. It also explains the Council's inability to take decisions;

c. Experience suggests that it will be difficult to make rapid and real progress in energy policy, unless the Commission makes increasing use of those courses of action which are open to it in the context of the Treaties, and unless the Council starts to take more decisions by majority vote.

The progress which could be made in these two areas depends on an evolution of the way in which these institutions function, which might be facilitated by direct elections to the European Parliament.

COAL POLICY

I. COAL POLICY REPORT

Coal Policy of the European Coal and Steel Community

by *Karlheinz Reichert*

The special features of the ECSC Treaty

This report on the coal policy of the European Coal and Steel Community (ECSC) was drawn up as a case study at the request of the Research Committee on European Unification of the International Science Association as part of a research project entitled "The European Alternatives". The organizers classed coal policy among "policies being implemented by the Commission". The author would like to begin by stating that he regards this classification as somewhat euphemistic. It would be possible to reverse the argument and prove that coal policy is among those economic policies which have in the course of time largely been re-nationalized, although it has always been an area of lively activity on the part of the High Authority and the Commission. The reader is invited to decide for himself.

To understand this opening statement, it is necessary to take a look at the special position of the ECSC Treaty and review the evolution of the ECSC, for vital political decisions about coal date back ten years or more. Although the Commission did, in fact, try to reorient coal policy after the oil crisis, that policy is not yet fully implemented.

The ECSC Treaty came into being in 1950/51, when hard coal accounted for 70% of the energy consumed in the six-nation Community and the world economic situation was dominated by the Korean War. It differs from the later EEC Treaty in that it confers direct responsibility for coal, iron and steel undertakings upon the executive (formerly the High Authority, now the Commission), in particular by means of Articles 51, 54, 55, 56, 60, 61, 64, 65 and 66. In the fields covered by these regulations the Member States have retained little, or no, responsibility. In other areas (Articles 53(b), 58 and 59) the Commission requires prior Council approval for its decisions. Only if the powers of the Commission are inadequate, can—and must—the Governments of the Member States take a hand, e.g., in the field of trade policy.

The ECSC Treaty is a "traité de règles", i.e., the treaty text actually contains the major regulations, so that the institutions have little scope to create new regulations. Since the Treaty is restricted to two basic industries, the Commission cannot evolve an economic policy of its own, nor indeed can it even influence that of the Member States, whose Governments remain autonomous in the fields of currency, taxation, wages, social security, transport and last but not least, trade policy (Articles 71–75). The link between the

117

overall economic policies of the Governments and the Commission's coal (and steel) policy is—leaving aside cases of serious market disturbances—to be found in the provision for constant exchange of information or formal consultation in the Council (Article 26). As regards the evolution of an industrial policy of its own, the Commission is limited to the mechanisms provided by the Treaty, such as intervening in respect of prices and restrictive practices, setting up general targets, granting loans and providing research grants.

The EEC Treaty, on the other hand, is a "traité cadre", which contains few directly-applicable regulations, apart from a number of programmatic phrases in Article 3. Substantially, it contains organizational provisions related to trade within the Community, but not procedural dispositions like the ECSC Treaty. It apportions responsibility and offers a broad framework for action, thus providing an opportunity to create new substantive law to fill out this general framework, law which establishes a basis for implementing the wide-ranging goals of the EEC Treaty. As a result, it is possible to go beyond the areas, such as agriculture, transport, turnover tax and freedom of movement of production factors, which are mentioned in the Treaty. For this reason a joint energy policy can be developed within the terms of the EEC Treaty.

From the founding of the common coal market to the oil crisis

In the first years of its existence, the High Authority of the ECSC concentrated on setting up and extending the common market for coal, as from 10 February 1953. Its efforts were concerned with removing quantity restrictions (there were no coal duties), eliminating obvious discrimination in the transport tariff field, setting up a Community price control for coal (publishing price lists and sales conditions) with the aim of unimpeded access to coal (non-discrimination), enforcing the ban on restrictive practices set out in Article 65 and applying Article 66 in the field of mergers, introducing direct international railway tariffs, introducing an obligation to report investments, working out quarterly forecasts and medium-term overall goals for production and sales, drawing up a Council protocol on means of implementing a coordinated energy policy, etc.

From 1958 onwards, the High Authority's efforts concentrated on dealing with the coal crisis. However, the Governments of the Member States rejected commercial policy measures as a limitation of their sovereignty. Only Belgium and the Federal Republic of Germany imposed a limitation by quota on their coal imports. In addition a number of other—mostly *ad hoc* but nevertheless important—measures were taken.

In May 1959, the Council rejected the comprehensive crisis plan worked out by the High Authority on the basis of Article 58 of the ECSC Treaty on the grounds that there was no "manifest crisis" on the common coal market. This negative decision was justified in the sense that the reasons for the crisis were structural and not cyclical, so that—literally—Article 58 was not applicable. However, with this decision the Council nipped in the bud all attempts at concerted action to deal with crises. For the High Authority had no other really effective means of intervention at its disposal.

At this point, however, mention must be made of the minor revision of the ECSC Treaty done jointly under the third and fourth paragraphs of its Article 95 by all four Community organs, which extended the provisions of Article 56 on the adaptation of labour to cover all cases involving basic changes in the sales conditions for coal and steel. Before that, sales difficulties arising from the setting up of the common market could only be recognized as a reason for granting adaptation allowances from the ECSC budget during the so-called transitional period, i.e., from 1952 to 1958.

The previously-mentioned measures taken under Article 58 would have permitted action only in the coal sector, although a problem affecting the whole energy market was involved. However, a design for a joint energy policy did not exist at that time. The result was that the coal-producing countries began taking measures of their own to master the coal crisis, measures which were neither uniform in character nor coordinated in application; moreover, they certainly did not stay limited to the coal sector. It was impossible to coordinate these measures, because the Treaties did not provide for such a thing and because other Member States openly opposed any attempt at coordination.

The High Authority took all the measures it could take within the bounds of the ECSC Treaty, i.e., measures limited to the coal sector. The decisions it made between 1958 and 1964 were mainly intended to keep within tolerable limits the effects of the crisis on the common market, on employers and employed. In this it was successful.

A degree of clarification was not achieved until 1964 in the discussion on energy policy, after the High Authority had had extensive consultations with the EEC and Euratom Commissions and the three executive bodies had repeatedly had conclusive discussions with the Special Council of Ministers of the ECSC. All involved agreed that the time would come when imported forms of energy would considerably increase their competitive pressure on domestic hard coal and capture an increasing share of the Community's energy requirement. They therefore demanded that adequate protection be provided for Community coal, as this still represented the largest domestic source of energy, provided employment for hundreds of thousands of workers and was the basis for industrial development in large areas of the Community.

On the other hand, it was important to ensure that the Community—as the world's second largest trading bloc—was able to cover its energy requirements at prices allowing it to compete with the other industrial powers. One school of thought held that priority should be given to assuring energy supplies, while an opposing school of thought contended that more importance should be attached to obtaining those supplies at the lowest prices.

The inter-executive working group, composed of members of the High Authority and the two Brussels Commissions, attempted to reconcile the widely divergent points of view by opposing exaggerated protection at the frontier, urging harmonization of the competition rules applying to the individual energy sources and advocating support for the Community's own sources of energy. The idea was that this new system should take shape by 1970 and be the prelude to a common commercial policy in respect of energy.

However, when the Governments of the Member States were faced with these aims in the Council, they were reluctant to commit themselves. To impel them to make the requisite amendments to the Treaties, strong political pressure would have been needed, and such pressure was not there in 1962.

On 21 April 1964, the Community Member States finally agreed on a "protocol of an agreement concerning energy questions".[1] In this they agreed first of all on a number of energy goals, such as, for example, cheap supplies, security of supply, progressive substitution, free choice by the consumers, competition between energy sources, undertook to coordinate their measures in the interests of the Community and recognized the necessity of state aid for coal mining.

The protocol was a political admission of an economic fact, the fact that coal had declined in importance and, since 1962, had been accounting for less than 50% of energy consumption. De facto, the agreement laid down that hard-coal mining should shrink to a level where it could compete with heavy fuel oil and imported coal. The official version was more cautious:

"As far as coal is concerned, the Governments are considering the necessity of providing state support through appropriate legal channels for measures by the hard-coal mining industry aimed at adapting to prevailing market conditions, particularly rationalization measures, and to supplement this by generally degressive protective and support measures intended to assist the mining industry . . ."

The protocol also stressed the problem of the long-term provision of the Community with coking coal, because it was generally felt that supplying the steel industry with coking coal was less an energy problem than a raw material problem and because even then the supply situation on the world market was not seen in very optimistic terms.

These decisions ended years of political discussion on whether and how the strict ban on subsidies contained in the basic articles of the ECSC Treaty could be lifted. The High Authority was instructed to draw up proposals for a Community system of state aids.

In 1965, after invoking the first paragraph of Article 95 of the ECSC Treaty, the so-called loophole clause, and after consulting the Consultative Committee, the Council unanimously adopted Decision No 3/65,[2] which—in bold outline —contained the following provisions:
- aid may be granted only after prior approval by the High Authority;
- aid may be granted by the High Authority only if this does not affect the proper functioning of the common market;
- in principle, aid may only be used for rationalization so that undertakings may more easily reduce their costs;
- aid may also be granted so that pits may be closed at a suitable rate, taking into account economic and social factors.

When the Decision expired at the end of 1967, the economic situation of the hard-coal mining industry showed no substantial improvement. The system was therefore extended to the end of 1970.[3] But even then hopes that production could be limited to the economically-sound—i.e., fully competitive pits and the payment of subsidies terminated, remained unfulfilled. The aid system was supplemented in a number of points and extended to the end of 1975.[4] The basic idea that aid should serve only to alleviate temporary difficulties was retained.

The coking coal aid system introduced in 1967 was basically different in conception.[5] It was based on the idea of maintaining temporarily the capacity for producing the coking coal needed to supply the steel industry so that the steel industry would make a decision about its own provisionment, either paying cost-covering prices for Community coal or turning to other sources on the world market. Decision No 1/67, also adopted on the basis of the first paragraph of Article 95 of the ECSC Treaty, was valid for two years, was extended until the end of 1969 and then replaced by Decision No 70/1/ECSC, which ran until the end of 1972.[6] After protracted negotiations, a new Decision, No 73/287, went into force covering the 1973–1978 period.[7]

The coking coal Decision makes it possible to close the gap between production costs in the Community and the lower world market prices (for long-term supply contracts) by means of national subsidies. A further subsidy, limited to specific sums, is jointly financed by a levy on the steel industry and by contributions from national budgets and the ECSC budget. This subsidy is intended to facilitate deliveries from Community mines to customers in areas at some distance from the coalfields or in trade inside the Community.

The objectives aimed at with the decisions on subsidies and coking coal were in the main achieved. However, the expenditure had to be increased considerably in the course of time; it was only 0.57 UA per ton in 1965 but had risen to 6.06 UA per ton in 1974, for the original six-member Community only. Including the British mining industry, the average expenditure for the Community was 3.85 UA per ton in 1974 and 2.51 UA in 1975.

The Commission's new energy strategy

The conditions under which the Community obtained its supplies of energy were so profoundly changed by the oil crisis at the end of 1973 that they necessitated a modification of the aims of Community energy policy.

The Commission reacted to the situation in mid-1974 by presenting the Council with a comprehensive communication entitled "Towards a New Strategy for an Energy Policy for the Community".[8] Along with it went proposals for two Directives on reducing natural gas consumption and limiting the use of petroleum products in power stations.

The "new strategy" evolved by the Commission was based on the reflection that past crises and what was likely to happen in the future, should cause the Community to reduce as far as possible its dependence on the rest of the world in the energy sector. In fact the Commission had pointed to the risks involved in dependence on imports long before the 1973 crisis. But now it called for the following objectives to be set for 1985:
a. In the demand sector: by means of more rational utilization a reduction of 10% in the energy demand originally expected in 1985; an increase in electricity

consumption by intensified development of nuclear energy to give it a share of 35%, instead of 25%, of total energy consumption;

b. in the supply sector: provision of 50% of the electricity requirement from nuclear sources and creation of a nuclear energy capacity of 200 GWe; maintenance of the present production of solid fuels (coal, brown coal, peat) and increase in imports; a reorientation of demand on the part of thermal power stations, having them use coal as often as possible and always when nuclear energy was not available; a greater use of natural gas, doubling domestic production and having greater recourse to imports; a reduction in the share of oil in energy supplies by concentrating its consumption on specific markets (fuels and raw materials) and promotion of domestic production (North Sea).

In all, the Commission's plan was that these measures would reduce the Community's dependence on imports in the energy sector from 63% in 1973 to 40% in 1985.

After intensive discussions, the Council, in several consecutive Decisions,[9] came down heavily in favour of the objectives set by the Commission, although it made a number of amendments or at least changes of emphasis. In the solid fuel sector the Community set itself the following objectives:

1. Maintenance of coal production in the Community at its present level (180 mtce in 1985) *under satisfactory economic conditions,*
2. an increase in coal imports from non-Community countries (40 mtce in 1985),
3. an increase in the production of brown coal and peat to 30 mtce.

A subsequent Council resolution on measures for achieving these objectives stated that "reliable energy sources should be developed as soon as possible under satisfactory economic conditions, which means:

– applying Community support measures in certain cases,
– facilitating access to financing for the necessary investments in certain cases,
– making it possible for prices to cover, gradually and to the fullest extent feasible, the costs of making energy available and the amortization of the necessary investments".

The Council approved the following guidelines for the policy to be implemented at both national and Community level in the solid fuels sector:

"The maintenance of coal production at its current level and the development of brown coal and peat production, as mentioned in paragraph 5(2) (A) of the Council resolution on Community energy policy objectives, require the definition and implementation of a solid fuels policy which takes into account the principles set out in paragraph 1 B above, particularly in respect of carrying out the necessary financial investments and having available a suitable labour force.

The commitment of such investments and the recruitment of the requisite labour force presuppose a stable and regular outlet for Community solid fuels under satisfactory economic conditions which take account of consumer interests. Consequently, it might be necessary to take measures to ensure their rational use in satisfactory economic conditions which take account of consumer interests in the principal sectors of consumption, namely the iron and steel industry and thermal power stations, and to build up stocks to offset the effects of fluctuations in demand and to avoid the interruption of supplies.

"Free access to the world market should, in a manner consistent with the attainment of Community production targets and in satisfactory economic conditions, be progressively extended to all Community coal consumers who do not at present have free access."

The proposals specifically related to coal were discussed in detail in the "Medium-term Guidelines for Coal 1975–1985", which were sent to the Council in November 1974.[10] In this document the Commission defined the role of hard coal in the Community's energy supply and set out the main lines of a coal policy. It estimated the size of the market in 1985 at some 300 mtce, of which 149 would be used in thermal power stations, 115 in coking plants and 40 in the domestic/sundry industries sector. Two hundred and fifty mtce of the demand would be covered by Community production, the rest by imports from non-Community countries.

The "Medium-term Guidelines" may be summarized under the following ten headings:

Demand:
1. Fullest possible utilization of existing coal- or lignite-fired power stations and the conversion to coal of dual-fired power stations in so far as this is technically and economically possible. In so far as nuclear energy is ruled out, investment to be directed into the construction and modernization of solid-fuel-fired power stations, with long-term stabilization of sales of Community coal to power stations through the creation of an appropriate system of support.
2. Maintenance of a system of aids for Community coking coal used by the Community's steel industry.
3. Assistance from public funds towards coal stockpiling to even out cyclical fluctuations in demand. Compulsory security stocks to be drawn on in the event of interruptions in the flow of energy supplies.

Supplies:
4. Maintenance of Community hard coal production at about 250 mtce with due regard to geological, technical and economic conditions in the different coalfields. Continuous efforts by the coal industry to maintain or regain competitiveness with competing sources of energy through increased productivity, rationalization and reduced costs.
5. Pursuit of an active manpower policy to maintain a stable, young and productive labour force through the creation of attractive working conditions at all levels. Re-establishment of confidence in the long-term security of coal mining as a career.
6. Immediate increase in current investment to balance depreciation and maintain productive capacity and assets. Additional investment in coalfields suitable for the development of existing and the sinking of new pits.
7. Strengthening of the financial position of the coal industry through a pricing policy which enables undertakings progressively to cover amortization as well as costs of production. Provision of capital under Article 54 of the ECSC Treaty and investment assistance by the respective Governments.
8. Increased technical research in coal mining, coal preparation and upgrading, and conversion of coal into hydrocarbons. Provision of additional

research funds for this purpose from the general budget of the Community and closer cooperation between the research institutes involved.
9. Gradual development of a Community import policy designed to give all consumers access to the world market and to secure mutually satisfactory commercial relations with the exporting countries, and connected therewith, monitoring of imports at Community level. Participation in joint ventures in the coal industries of non-member countries by Community firms and industries (including the coal industry).

General:
10. Efforts to re-establish a climate of confidence and genuine cooperation between all parties concerned (producers, employees, consumers, authorities), to enable the coal industry to fulfil its tasks as the presently most important indigenous source of energy.

Communications and proposals on a Community coal policy

The conformity with the Council Decisions and its own "Medium-term Guidelines", the Commission published, at the beginning of 1975, a communication to the coal undertakings in the ECSC,[11] in which it urged them to pursue a pricing policy "which enables undertakings progressively to cover amortization as well as costs of production". The purpose of this was to limit subsidies "to those which are strictly necessary and do not involve indirect aid to industrial consumers" (Decision No 3/71). In fact, the spasmodic rise in prices on the energy market made it possible to improve revenues and thus to reduce subsidies.

To increase technical research in the coal sector, the Commission decided to increase financial support from the ECSC budget (Article 55 of the ECSC Treaty) in the 1975 and 1976 budget years. Because these decisions are made shortly before the beginning of a budget year, no data can at present be given for subsequent years. Since the expansion of the Community, funds made available for coal research from the ECSC budget have been as follows:

1973	6.0 million UA
1974	7.1 million UA
1975	18.0 million UA
1976	17.0 million UA

In their applications for financial support from the Commission, applicants such as institutes, universities, industrial firms, etc. are guided by the "Medium-term Research Aid Programme 1975–1980".[12] Some two-thirds of these research funds are allocated to the further development of mining technology, while the remainder goes mainly to coking technology.

The Commission's efforts to arouse the Council's interest in Community support for research on converting coal into hydrocarbons have so far failed, because there is no hope of getting the necessary funds from the Community's general budget. Financing with funds from the limited ECSC budget is out of the question because of the expense involved.

Since the general aid Decision No 3/71 (see point 9 above) expired at the end of 1975, the Commission sent a new Decision to the Council in September of that year. In this Decision it made some basic changes in the approach hitherto applied, which could be summed up as adaptation of the hard-coal mining industry to the conditions on the energy market. Mindful of the conviction expressed in the "New Strategy" and "Medium-term Guidelines for Coal" that it would be wise to assure a fixed contribution of indigenous coal to the Community's energy supply and, for this reason, to stabilize coal output at the 1973 level, the Commission modified the trend of the preceding aid decisions. With this objective in mind it suggested going beyond the aids provided by the old Decision by

- permitting aids for rationalization measures which would increase the output from economically sound coalfields to compensate for output declines in areas yielding a low return;
- permitting investment aids to create new output capacity in the economically healthy coalfields;
- permitting reimbursement of stockpiling costs, including depreciation, for at least 1/24th of annual output;
- permitting aids for the accumulation and maintenance of security stocks of coal and coke;
- permitting aids for the recruiting and training of staff;
- setting the period of validity of the aid system at ten years (up to 1985).

The European Council (meeting of heads of state and government) of 1–2 December 1975 in Rome agreed on a number of energy policy principles, including measures to protect and promote the development of the Community's energy sources. Subsequently, the Commission sent to the Council a communication entitled "Implementation of the Energy Policy Guidelines drawn up by the European Council at its Meeting in Rome on 1 and 2 December 1975".[13] In this communication, the Commission asked the Council to give its opinion on various systems for protecting and promoting energy sources, including coal. The communication did not contain finished proposals or draft decisions, but was intended, rather, to clarify by means of discussion in the Council what practical approaches could be made with any prospect of success.

As far as hard coal was concerned, the idea was to reduce the financial burden on the mining industry represented by the growing stocks of coal, a purpose for which a maximum of 50 m.UA would be made available from Community funds.

Secondly, the Commission suggested that Decision No 73/287/ECSC (see point 10 above) be extended until 1985 to cover the whole period affected by the Council Decisions on energy policy objectives made in 1974 and 1975.

Thirdly, the Commission urged the Council to conduct a policy debate on increasing the use of coal in thermal power stations and to take appropriate Community measures, e.g., to grant investment aids for the building of coal-fired power stations or subsidies to ensure that coal could compete with fuel oil.

All three suggestions were explained in greater detail in working papers drawn up by the appropriate departments for the benefit of the Council's

Energy Committee or its Energy Working Party. At the time of completion of this report,[14] formal Commission proposals were not yet available.

Reasons for Commission proposals

The new Decision 528/76/ECSC on a Community system for measures by Member States on behalf of the coal mining industry (see point 16 above) amended and expanded the subsidy rules which have existed in the ECSC since 1965 in one decisive point, for it enjoins the Commission to examine the financial measures taken by the Member States from the point of view of whether they help to achieve the objective of stabilizing the Community's overall output under satisfactory economic conditions. This means that a new "philosophy" has been postulated, one which no longer pursues the aim of adapting output to the conditions of the energy market ("shrinking to an economic level").

In addition, the Decision was set to run for ten years to ensure the Community's energy supplies and enable the coal mining industry to take the appropriate measures. Previous Decisions had been valid for only three to five years.

With this basic orientation towards a longer time-scale and in its individual provisions, Decision No 528/76/ECSC performs the functions of a safety net, created as a precaution and ready for use when this seems economically necessary and sensible from the energy policy point of view. At the same time, it provides the means of avoiding serious economic or social upsets when mines are shut.

Of course, Decision No 528/76 provides a Community system only in the sense that the criteria for national aids are the same for all, and that the Commission has to monitor and approve them, to ensure that state measures do not go beyond what is strictly necessary and deviate from the normal rules of the ECSC Treaty any more than is unavoidable to achieve solutions to the problems. Furthermore, indirect aids to industrial consumers of coal have to be avoided.

On the other hand, participation by all Member States or the Community budget in finding the necessary funds (1.36 thousand m.UA in 1973) could not be envisaged. What was needed, in the first place, was to set up in good time a new system of coal aids. Community financing would have taken much longer to prepare, quite apart from the fact that, in view of the utter lack of unanimity on the part of the Member States in matters of energy policy, a Community contribution to subsidizing the coal mining industry is a utopian idea.

Nevertheless the Commission attempted to bring the Governments of the Member States closer to an attitude of solidarity. However, the figure of up to 50 m.UA per year to finance coal stockpiling mentioned under point 17 had not progressed beyond an initial discussion in the Energy Committee by mid-1976 and had not yet been embodied in an official Commission proposal to the Council.

This measure aims above all at easing the financial position of coal mining undertakings in periods of declining sales, thus enabling them to maintain production. Taking a Community average, it costs some seven UA annually to stockpile a ton of coal. With 50 m.UA in Community funds—a relatively modest sum compared with other Community financial transactions—it would be possible to cover a subsidy of, for example, 2.5 UA per ton and thus make possible a coal stockpile of 20 million tons.

Two forms of stockpiling would be possible: either strategic stocking, i.e, the stockpiled coal or coke would be made available only in a previously-defined emergency, or the stocks would fluctuate cyclically, allowing the mining industry to adapt to changes in the sales situation. Costs exceeding the sum of 2.5 UA per ton would have to be financed either by the undertakings themselves or from national aids.

The Commission hopes for an understanding attitude on the part of the Member States towards its proposal that Decision No 73/287/ECSC on coking coal and coke for the steel industry be extended until 1985—the current system expires at the end of 1978. The system described under Point 10 has twice already proved its usefulness in times of shortage. Although it may be assumed that the Community's coking coal requirement—estimated at between 104 and 111 million tons in 1985—can be covered without major difficulties, the prerequisite for this is that consumers undertake long-term purchasing commitments for as large a portion of the output as possible and thus make possible the investments needed to maintain capacity.

The overall volume of the Community's supplies of coking coal and coke and the supplies from the various sources are unlikely to change substantially between now and 1985. The increased demand caused by the rise in the production of crude iron will be balanced by a decline in the specific coke consumption. The world market for the classical type of coking coal will continue to be of importance, but will remain limited as regards volume and elasticity. Community output will continue to be able to cover most of the demand under conditions which must be considered as eminently satisfactory from the point of view of reliability, regularity and quality. In addition, there are available stockpiling facilities which—as experience showed in 1974 and 1975—provide an effective cushion in the event of cyclical deviations, whether upward or downward. The boom year 1974 showed up the dangers inherent in excessive dependence of Community demand on the world coking coal market.

Events which have come about since the promulgation of this Decision (1973)—the accession of new Member States, new energy policy guidelines, the general objectives set by the Commission for the steel industry and the general trend of the world energy market—justify its extension. As early as 1972 the Commission had demanded a ten-year period of validity when the coking coal Decision was renewed, but was unable to get this accepted by the Council. The Commission's reasons remain unchanged:
– the wish to place the investment and promotion programmes for the coal mining industry on a solid and lasting basis,
– to maintain the common market for coal, which has shrunk considerably in other market sectors, the prerequisite for this being that all market partici-pants be placed on the same footing,

– to implement measures which enable the steel industry to bear the full costs of obtaining supplies of coke after this subsidy Decision has expired.

Under the present system based on Decision 73/287, Community aid amounts to some 33 m.UA. (In addition, a national production subsidy may be paid, where necessary, if production costs are above the long-term world market price.) This Community aid is financed mainly out of contributions from the steel industry—on the basis of the actual coke consumption of blast furnaces—and by the budgets of the Member States involved and the ECSC budget.

In the case at issue it may be said that a relatively major effect can be achieved with relatively little financial aid. Consumers do in fact cover roughly three-quarters of their requirement within the Community, i.e., from reliable supply sources of excellent quality. More than one-quarter of the demand is satisfied by intra-Community trade. During the 1973/74 steel boom, Community consumers were able to rely on stable delivery conditions as regards both quantity and price.

Although the supply situation on the world market in coking coal is not regarded as a cause for concern, it is not regarded as simple either. The supply cannot be expanded indefinitely, since the number of suitable deposits is limited. The tendency of consumers in Europe and the rest of the world to enter into long-term contracts or acquire their own sources of supply is obvious. The result is that the price of long-term contract coking coal free in Europe tripled between 1970 and 1975 and did not decline even during the exceptional recession on the steel market.

The Commission's second proposal of January 1976 is concerned with a Community contribution to the expense of maintaining stocks of coal and coke. Since economic development and energy consumption go hand in hand, there are cyclical consumption fluctuations in the coal sector, which are accentuated even more by the traditional attitudes of consumers in times of crisis or boom.

Every mining undertaking in the world is faced with natural, technical and economic facts which oblige it to seek the most nearly continuous working method possible, particularly for its underground operations. When sales are down, output is stockpiled. If these stockpiles threaten to exceed a certain size, the mining undertakings attempt to limit the growth by instituting short-time working, but social reasons and reasons of staff policy set severe limits on such measures. If sales difficulties persist, the undertakings have no choice but to reduce capacity (shutdown).

Since the common market for coal was set up, there have been four cycles of cyclical fluctuation, each of which lasted between six and seven years. The stocks accumulated during the periods of downward trend were in every case cleared in the subsequent upswing. This cushioning effect proved useful not only for the producers and for the continuity of production, but also for the consumers, as it made up for the industry's inability to increase output.

The Commission's ideas in connection with Community aid for coal stockpiling start from the fact that the Community energy policy gives clear priority to security of supplies (Council Resolution of 17 December 1974) and aims at ensuring and developing alternative energy sources. Stabilizing the production would be the most important measure in this connection, since only a productive pit can contribute to security of supply. Another step is the creation of a cushion between production and sales in the form of stocks. In addition, such stocks provide additional security if supplies should be interrupted.

Sizeable stockpiles, at the very least those which exceed half a month's output, are an extraordinarily heavy burden on the firms. However, only a financially sound mining industry can, in the long run, perform the task allotted to it by the Community.

Stocks of some 50 million tons (mid-1976) and average annual costs of seven UA per ton mean an annual financial burden of 350 m.UA on the mining companies. The Commission's proposal that 50 m.UA annually of this burden be borne out of Community funds cannot therefore be regarded as excessively generous, but could be regarded as a genuine expression of solidarity if it were provided.

In 1975 the Community took measures affecting the use of primary energy in power stations and aiming at a limitation of the use of natural gas and petroleum products. However, there should be no illusions about the limited effect of these measures. The two Directives[15] adopted by the Council in February and April 1975 cannot undo all the investment in oil-fired and natural gas-fired power stations, which were begun in the years before the oil crisis and which are now gradually becoming operational. It will be some years before any effect is felt at all from the slowdown in the rise of electricity consumption and the advance of nuclear energy. Furthermore, the Directive on the limitation of the use of petroleum products in power stations was, at the insistence of some Member States, so phrased that exceptions, i.e., a deviation from the objectives, can be conceded with relative ease.

Under these circumstances and in view of the fact that the market for power-station coal is the only sector, apart from the steel industry, where coal can still play a part from the energy economy point of view and can be used sensibly in the energy policy sense, the Commission thought it all the more urgent to point out to the Member States in its communication to the Council on the "Implementation of Energy Policy Guidelines"[16] the necessity for promoting the use of coal in power stations. And this despite the fact that in some Member States measures have already been taken to promote such use of coal in power stations.

It has become impossible to predict the electricity industry's situation in the medium-term view, in the energy pattern. For the first time in 30 years the recession has interrupted the steady increase in electricity consumption; uncertainty prevails regarding the future growth of consumption, for while higher electricity prices and the resulting efforts to use electricity more rationally have a retarding effect, efforts are also under way to promote nuclear energy and achieve a "penetration of electricity". The growth rate for electricity generation depends on the rate of general economic growth, a subject on which expert opinions differ greatly. There is likewise uncertainty— for a whole series of reasons—about the actual development in the capacity of power stations, whether they are nuclear, coal-fired or dependent on some other fuel. Another factor is the obscurity of the primary energy market in the medium and long term as regards prices and quantities; the glut of energy prevailing in 1976 does not exactly make it easy for entrepreneurs to obtain a clear picture.

Even though the forecasts lead us to expect a rising demand for coal in the electricity sector, the experience of the past few years shows that, without increased energy policy safeguards, periods of declining demand for coal may well occur. This is particularly true of cases where Community coal is unable to compete with heavy fuel oil or natural gas, and with coal imported from non-Community countries.

However, as long as coal is regarded only as a cushion and is used as a stopgap to cover the demand which still exists after full utilization of other power stations, the security of this market is inadequate for the coal mining industry; this is why coal cannot perform the function of security base for electricity supplies which has been allotted to it. It is less the relation between nuclear energy and coal which is decisive here than the positions accorded to coal and the hydrocarbons.

There is reason to fear that, if no coal-fired power stations are built, more than half of the current coal-fired capacity will be shut down in 15 years time. This is why the Commission is thinking along the lines of ensuring an appropriate and up-to-date electricity generating capacity in the eighties on the basis of coal and of framing the necessary promotion measures in such a way that existing supply levels are maintained and, if possible, expanded. In other words, investment inducements would be linked to long-term purchasing commitments. In so far as an offset is needed for the higher costs of coal in comparison with cheaper fuels, solutions must continue to be sought at the national level because of the financial and administrative problems involved.

Opinions of the European Parliament

The European Parliament and, more particularly, its Committee on Energy have always devoted considerable attention to coal policy. The Committee on Energy prevailed on the Commission to have the Parliament consulted on all questions related to coal policy, particularly Commission proposals and decisions, although—unlike the EEC Treaty—the ECSC Treaty does not prescribe such ad hoc consultation. On the whole, it may be said that the Parliament emphatically supports the Commission's ideas on coal policy and has sometimes advocated even more far-reaching protective and support measures for Community coal.

Since the 1973/74 energy crisis the following reports dealing, though not exclusively, with coal questions have been discussed by the Parliament:

1. Report on the Commission's communication and proposals to the Council on a new energy policy strategy for the Community (rapporteur: Mr. Jean-François Pintat) of 10 July 1974 (Doc. 184/74)

2. Report on the need for and the feasibility of a Community policy to promote the production of coal gas (rapporteur: Mr. Friedrich Burgbacher) of 11 November 1974 (Doc. COM 325/74)

3. Report on the potential and limits of a Community policy on promoting the liquefaction of coals for the manufacture of synthetic fuels (rapporteur: Mr. Friedrich Burgbacher) of 12 December 1972 (Doc. 407/75)

4. Report on the Commission proposal on the "Medium-term Guidelines for Coal 1975–1985" (rapporteur: Mr. Friedrich Burgbacher) of 27 June 1975 (Doc. 147/75)

5. Report on the future planning of Community coal policy within an overall energy policy (rapporteur: Mr. Gerd Springorum) of 10 June 1976 (Doc. 133/76).

The Pintat report (Doc. 184/74) gave a large measure of approval to the new strategy for an energy policy for the Community proposed by the Commission and noted that its major points coincided with opinions previously expressed by the European Parliament; it went on to state that there should be as much encouragement as possible for Community energy sources.

Regarding supplies of hard coal, the report expressed fears that substantial imports of coal from non-Community countries could not be expected and that Community output would therefore have to be boosted beyond the point which the Commission considered possible. In the plenary session debate on the report, Parliament acknowledged that the Commission's ideas on the coal sector were clear and realistic.

Mr. Burgbacher's two reports on the gasification and liquefaction of coal (Doc. 325/74 and 407/75) were highly technical in nature, although they did not neglect the economic and political aspects of these matters. Neither report was drawn up in reaction to Commission communications but on the initiative of the Parliament's Committee on Energy. Both reports were based mainly on conditions in the Federal Republic of Germany.

Mr. Burgbacher expressed the opinion that the demand for upgraded energy was increasing and the use of coal and lignite by the application of new technologies, was acquiring increasing importance, that the Community's dependence on imported energy could be reduced through increased use of indigenous energy, particularly coal, through improved exploitation of imported raw energy-carriers and through energy conservation, and that for these reasons research efforts in these fields should be intensified, should be coordinated by the Commission and that the necessary funds should be made available by the Community to finance research and experimental plant. In addition, the Council should generously apply Article 235 of the EEC Treaty, the so-called "loophole clause", in those areas where the Community appeared to have no jurisdiction.

In the debate on the coal gasification report, members of Parliament again pointed out the need to develop alternative sources of energy in view of the Community's dependence on energy imports and to avoid thinking that the energy crisis had been overcome once and for all.

The debate on the liquefaction of coal report did not take place until April 1976, when there were references to the rather scientific nature of the report and cautious wording of its title. All speakers regarded the report as a warning to all involved to take a more long-term view of the problems of the various energy-carriers.

The Burgbacher report on the "Medium-term Guidelines for Coal 1975–1985" (Doc. 147/75) once again put into words the doubts felt about the energy supply structure at which the Commission and Council are aiming, above all about the proposed scale of the nuclear energy industry and/or natural gas imports, and complains that the absolute share of oil in Community energy supplies will not decline, but remain constant, and perhaps even increase. For this reason, the report said, coal should make a greater contribution than what it termed the "modest minimum target" set by the Council and Commission, though this would require long-term preparation. Coal policy would have to look beyond 1985 to develop the necessary potential (investments, application of new technologies) needed to reactivate the mining industry. For these reasons the Commission should see to it that a controlled ratio between Community and imported coal was established, the successful aid systems expanded to become instruments of a Community energy policy, and all appropriate measures taken to stabilize the sales of a substantially increased output of hard coal.

In the debate in plenary session there was wide support for the rapporteur's argument, which broadly followed the coal policy guidelines of the Commission, particularly the proposal to go beyond the stabilization of output envisaged by the Commission and expand production. The long-term safeguarding of sales, particularly in view of employment problems, was described as urgent. Other topics discussed were research, the protection of Community coal against imported coal at times when the market was weak, a policy of stockpiling financed by the Community, employment policy, safety measures in mines and ways of boosting productivity in the coal mining industry.

In mid-1976, the Chairman of the Committee on Energy and Research, Gerd Springorum, submitted a report on the future planning of Community coal policy within an overall energy policy. The starting point for this report was Decision No 528/76 on the Community system of measures by the Member States on behalf of the coal mining industry (see point 16 above). The basic attitude of the report as regards energy and coal policy was in line with previous statements by Parliament. However, this report has a different emphasis in that it demanded that the general Community aid system, which subjects national subsidies to prior Commission approval, should be made obligatory and the subsidies themselves made uniform to avoid distortions of competition. In addition, it called on the Commission to introduce specific aids for training personnel and to build up a coal reserve using Community funds. It urged that proposals be made to encourage the hydrogenation of heavy fuel oil, thus producing lighter derivatives and safeguarding the sale of power-station coal.

In the plenary session debate on this report, concern was expressed that, if the demand for energy rose again, coal would be neglected and used as a cushion to offset the effects of the market cycle—something which the aid system was meant to prevent. Referring to the long-term importance of coal in supplying the Community, a number of speakers demanded that attention be paid to the value of coal as a raw material for the chemical industry or for conversion into gaseous or liquid fuels. Others referred to the important role of the miners' unions and the price-boosting effect of the exigencies of environmental protection. Once again those responsible were accused of negligence and the Council was reproached for its failure to take decisions; all were following the principle of "passé le péril, adieu le saint".

The attitude of the ECSC Consultative Committee

The Consultative Committee of the ECSC has also taken up the topic of energy policy, particularly the contribution of coal to energy supplies, on every possible occasion. It has presented the following resolutions and opinions in the most recent past:

1. Resolution on coal policy in the Community (6 November 1973)[17]
2. Opinion on the new strategy for an energy policy for the Community (3/4 October 1974)[18]
3. Opinion on the medium-term guidelines for coal 1975–1985 (6 December 1974)[19]
4. Report by Mr. Reintges on implementation of the "Medium-term Guidelines for Coal 1975–1985", which were drawn up at the end of 1974 (10 June 1976).[20]

In its resolution on coal policy in the Community, the Consultative Committee—after considering a number of energy policy factors—"urged that the energy supplies of the European Community be assured:
– by intensifying prospecting for hydrocarbons in the territory of the Community,
– by speeding-up the development of nuclear energy,
– by fully maintaining its own productive capacity, in particular in the coal industry, which can in fact contribute substantially to security of supplies, especially to the iron and steel industry and for the production of electrical energy, in as far as this does not compromise the consumer industries' competitiveness vis-à-vis others on the world market".

In its opinion on the new strategy for an energy policy for the Community, the Consultative Committee was unusually terse, endorsing the long-term objectives for the coal industry set by the Commission (see point 12 above), though at the same time describing them as minimum requirements.

In its opinion on the medium-term guidelines for coal, the Consultative Committee repeated its view that the output target of 253 mtce was a realistic one, though it must be regarded as a minimum. As regards output and related problems, it fully endorsed the Commission's view. It stressed the importance of stable and regulated sales outlets for the Community's coal industry under conditions which covered costs even when the market was slack. Additional sales-stabilizing factors were the financial aid systems, particularly for supporting sales to the steel industry and the electricity works, stockpiling and ensuring imports. However, these would have to be as simple and as flexible as possible. With regard to the structural differences between power stations in the Community, the administration of financial aids for this consumer sector should be left to the individual Member States under Commission supervision.

With regard to imports from non-Community countries, the Consultative Committee said that "it will admittedly be necessary for consumers to enter into commitments abroad to make up their coal requirements". On the other hand, the supplanting of Community coal would have to be avoided so that the output target could be reached.

Finally, the Committee expressed the opinion that 40 m.UA was the minimum amount required for research.

The Reintges report is unusual in that it was not requested by the Commission. The Consultative Committee based its discussion on Commission document COM(76) 9 of 16 January 1976 entitled "Report on the Implementation of the objectives of the Energy Policy for the Community 1985".

The Reintges report on implementation of the Community's coal policy brought out very clearly the disappointment of the economic circles involved over the fact that domestic energy production would be lower in 1985 than the minimum target set up 18 months ago by the Commission and the Council and that net imports would be higher in 1985 than they should be in the light of the "50% dependence" figure which had been set. If there were higher growth rates for the demand for energy, the volume of imported oil and the Community's dependence might be considerably higher.

The Reintges report also expressed doubts as to whether the Community could achieve a nuclear energy capacity of 150–160 GW in 1985 and noted that indigenous oil and natural gas production would also be considerably less than the figures aimed at.

This provided an occasion to stress once again the importance of the indigenous coal mining industry in filling future energy needs. Unlike the other energy carriers, the report said, Community coal was even now capable of meeting the output target for 1985. However, the prerequisite for this was that energy policy measures by the Community and the Member States provided the necessary basis for appropriate investment, labour force and production planning on the part of the mining undertakings. In this context the report referred to the Decision of 6 December 1974 and stressed that the mining companies were not demanding a sales guarantee for every ton they mined.

Representatives of labour and management in the coal industry were in favour of a Community policy on imported coal, so that there should be no threat to the stabilization of domestic output as regards price and quantity.

Finally, the report, which was essentially a summary of an extensive discussion in the Consultative Committee's "General Objectives" sub-committee, discussed the proposals made by the Commission in its communication to the Council on 16 January 1976 regarding coal (see point 17 above), proposals which were—in general—welcomed, though their reception in consumer circles was more varied.

Conclusions

To sum up, it must be said that the Community still does not have a Community coal policy worthy of the name. Only in the coking coal sector has it been possible to achieve a modest degree of solidarity, mainly due to the interest of the steel industry in *all* Member States in a regular supply of this raw material, which is in short supply all over the world and for which no substitute has been found.

134

The function of coal as an energy-carrier in the Community has been recognized only on paper, i.e., in the Council's guidelines for energy policy of 17 December 1974. Support measures exist only at the national level; the only thing the Community has done is to place national aids under Commission supervision. The obligation to supply consumers on a non-discriminatory basis which the ECSC Treaty imposes upon the hard coal mining industry has not so far induced consumers to respond in kind with an assurance of purchase.

NOTES

1. OJ No 69, 30 April 1964.
2. OJ No 31 of 25 February 1965.
3. OJ No 261 of 28 October 1967.
4. OJ No L 3 of 5 January 1971.
5. OJ No 36 of 28 February 1967.
6. OJ No L 2 of 6 January 1970.
7. OJ No L 259 of 15 September 1973.
8. Bulletin of the European Communities, 4/74.
9. OJ No C 153 of 9 July 1975.
10. OJ No C 22 of 30 January 1975.
11. OJ No C 15 of 22 January 1975.
12. OJ No C 60 of 25 May 1974.
13. Document COM(76) 20 of 16 January 1976.
14. 30 June 1976.
15. OJ No L 178 of 9 July 1975.
16. Doc. COM(76) 20 of 16 January 1976.
17. OJ No C 103 of 27 November 1973.
18. OJ No C 133 of 29 October 1974.
19. OJ No C 10 of 15 January 1975.
20. Doc. No. A/2005/1/76.

II. COAL POLICY COUNTER-REPORT

Coal Policy of the Federal Republic of Germany

by *R. Hrbek*

The task facing the authors of the following study[1] was to assess European Community policy in a specific sector (coal), as outlined in the report by a Commission expert[2] and, in particular, to contrast it with national model solutions. In the short space of time available they have had to confine themselves to an account of coal policy in the Federal Republic of Germany, and even this would not have been possible without the assistance of third parties.[3]

It becomes apparent relatively quickly that one of the premises of the draft research project "The European Alternatives" (i.e., that coal was a policy area implemented by the Community) is not tenable. Possibly this premise was valid in the case of the ECSC Treaty, which treated coal as a Community matter. The EEC Treaty provides for no corresponding Community competence in the field of energy policy. For many years coal policy has had to be looked at, analysed and assessed in the overall energy policy context. Consequently, the coal policy exists only as an element in the framework of the energy policy. Since to date there is no European Community energy policy, it is possible to speak of a common coal policy in the EC only in a very limited sense. In other words, there is no Community approach to a solution of the problem which can be compared with the national approach, i.e., where coal is understood and treated as an element of the energy policy.

Nevertheless, an analysis of the coal policy of the Federal Republic of Germany—presented below—can perform an important function in the context of the research project "The European Alternatives", i.e., it may help towards an understanding of the difficulties of successfully pursuing the integration process in the framework of the EC. Treating coal policy—i.e., a sectoral policy—as being in the tangible decision-making process an element in a wider area—namely energy policy as a whole—which must be analysed by us accordingly, makes the demands which such an extension of Community competence and activities would make on those involved quite clear and comprehensible. The difficulties of extending the functional scope of the EC—in the Lindberg/Scheingold sense, an aspect of the integration process—become even clearer if we also bear in mind the foreign policy and security implications of energy policy—not to mention the economic significance of this policy area, which we propose to examine briefly below.

For the purposes of this survey, references to coal and coal policy are restricted to hard coal. Lignite is not dealt with since, being mined in completely different conditions from those which apply to hard coal as well as having a constant production capacity, it presents no problems.

Since the following account concentrates on coal policy over the last 10 years, it may be useful to include in the introduction just a brief outline of developments since the end of the war.

In the early post-war years coal was almost the only source of energy which came under "central administration", as it were. Despite the considerable ravages of war, coal production—backed up also by "special bonuses" (food allowances) for miners—increased once more. As the almost exclusive source of energy available, coal was the subject of excessive demand on an enormous scale. The occupying powers and—insofar as they were already empowered, to take decisions—the German authorities distributed the output in quotas, largely on the basis of planned economy principles of demand. Prices exercised virtually no influence whatsoever. Coal deliveries to victorious European powers had the character of reparations.

In the years that followed coal as energy-carrier took on the role of a vehicle of integration. The transition (marked by the currency reform) to a market economy system, which gave wider scope in the coal sector, too, for prices to exercise a steering function, was accompanied by a noticeable rise in productivity. Earlier movements towards establishing overriding safe-guards against the seizure of coal as an energy and raw materials source (Ruhr Statute) gave way to a proposal by the French, who had a vital interest in Ruhr coal, for the setting-up of a European Coal and Steel Community. In this way controls (rules) for these sectors, which also provided for direct action, were "superimposed" on basic principles of free enterprise. Political insight into the impracticability of French claims, in particular, in the Ruhr and Saar produced, by intelligent control of economic interests, and impetus for integration which was further sustained by a widespread acceptance of the notion of European unity. Obviously a further crucial factor in France's renunciation of an alternative model for safeguarding coal supplies was the negative outcome of the occupation of the Ruhr in the 1920's. As a source of energy coal still stood in the forefront, until around 1958 a new situation developed.

Lastly, it will help the understanding of the following account of coal policy in the Federal Republic of Germany and the conclusions to be drawn therefrom to give a rough outline of coal policy in an international and overall economic framework.

The fact that hegemonic factors figured originally in the period immediately preceding European economic integration and to a much greater degree in the "revolt of the oil states" (subsequently merges in OPEC) against the industrial nations is attributable, first and foremost, to the following fundamental reasons.

1. The historical and economic development of the principal industrial nations is closely bound up with the availability of energy and changes in sources of energy.[4] The (phenomenal) economic expansion of the industrial nations was from the start characterized to a decisive degree by the increase in energy supply and by the replacement of one source of energy by another.[5] As long as coal was the main source of energy, the chance of achieving economic growth (a vital interest for France) continued to depend on the possibility of procuring this source of energy. The economically-acceptable uses (reasonably priced and capable of being financed from foreign exchange)

of substitute sources of energy reduced dependence on coal, so much so that for a time there was even a risk that coal might be relegated to a position of relative unimportance among the potential sources of energy. ("Imported" growth of the industrial countries on account of the flexible supply of efficient and cheap sources of energy,[6] i.e., petroleum and natural gas.) Coal is still suffering essentially from its disadvantages in the "substitute-competition" situation, in that it is a relatively expensive source of energy, a fact attributable to comparatively unfavourable geological mining conditions in the Federal Republic of Germany with its high labour intensiveness and high wages—even despite considerable progress in mechanization.

2. The, as it were, "classic" connection between political power and energy availability can be seen in the exemplary economic expansion which had brought the industrial states not only prosperity and internal stability but also economic superiority and political hegemony vis-à-vis the rest of the world;[7] the amalgamation of the oil-exporting countries to form a powerful supplier group—OPEC—is a further example. As in the days when capitalism was at its height, availability of the dominant sources of energy seems today, too, to be a decisive factor in the distribution of economic and political power.[8] At the same time, however, coal has lost its dominating position and dependence on oil as a source of energy exposes Western industrial nations to possible pressures which can be countered only with difficulty through "self-sufficiency" in coal or nuclear energy (as well as energy saving).

Apart from this "power-policy" aspect, a number of other predominantly economic effects of the overall world economic situation may be mentioned.

The increased cost of imported energy has repercussions on price levels and price structures in the purchasing countries and hence on their economic growth, their employment situation (unemployment) and on their current-account balances (terms of trade). In view of the fact that, given the gradual fall-off in national product annual growth rates, there is also an increasing long-term tendency for the growth cycles of the Western industrial nations to move towards concurrence (synchronism), the danger arises that economic recessions may occur simultaneously and become additive as a result ("world-wide economic crises"). The favourable overlapping (particularly for the Federal Republic of Germany with its very high proportion of exports) of non-synchronized fluctuations in the trade cycle in the potential importing countries vis-à-vis the trade cycle in Germany itself (export-led boom stimuli cushioned the downward tendencies in the economic situation at home) may give way to a mutual reinforcement of amplitudes in both directions (boom and slump). The accompanying recessions—overlaid, moreover, by structural changes—assume considerable proportions, a fact which is clearly demonstrated by the example of the fall-off in demand and the world market price slump in the steel industry—where hard-coal coke increasingly has much more the character of a raw material.

The following survey on coal policy is divided into three sections. The first section will be devoted to the identification and explanation of various essential aspects considered by the parties concerned in the course of their coal-policy deliberations and decisions. In this way we attempt to clarify the multiplicity of coal policy interests and objectives. The second section sets out the position of the major protagonists in the coal policy arena, in order to highlight the decision-making machinery in all its complexity. The third section explains the tangible measures in the context of the national coal policy, which is an element of the national energy policy. Lastly, an attempt will be made, on the basis of the survey findings, to present a number of conclusions and the prospects for the integration process.

THE COAL POLICY IN ITS VARIOUS ASPECTS

Coal as an energy-carrier

We shall begin with a percentage breakdown of the individual sources of primary energy in the gross consumption pattern of the Federal Republic of Germany, in order to give a clear picture of the position of hard coal as an energy-carrier.

TABLE 1

Hard coal	Lignite	Oil	Natural gas	Primary electricity	Other	
19.7	10.1	51.2	14.4	4.3	0.3%	1975
20.0	9.3	52.4	14.3	3.7	0.3%	1976

Source: Commission publication.

On the one hand, this table indicates the heavy predominance of oil as a source of energy and, on the other, shows that hard-coal accounts for about one-fifth of the total.

Fig. 1 traces the development of the individual sources of energy from 1957 to 1976. Particularly striking is the sharp oil increase which, after 1964, led not only to a decline in the share of hard coal in the overall energy consumption but also to a reduction in the absolute output of hard coal. The oil crisis at the end of 1973 represented a turning-point, inasmuch as greater importance was again attached to the security of supplies. This is reflected in the table by a slight decline in the position of oil and by a steadying in the position of hard coal.

Having established the share of hard coal in the overall energy consumption, we may now refer to Fig. 2 for a breakdown of the major German hard-coal consumer groups.

This figure shows a growing concentration of sales of hard coal on the steel industry and electricity supply services. Whereas in 1960 the steel industry and electricity supply services accounted for 47% of the total sales of hard coal, in 1975 the figure had risen to 76.5%.[9]

In view of the dominant market position occupied by these two consumer groups, we propose from now on to confine our analysis of coal as an energy-carrier to these two groups.

140

FIGURE 1. *Primary Energy Consumption in the Fed. Republic*

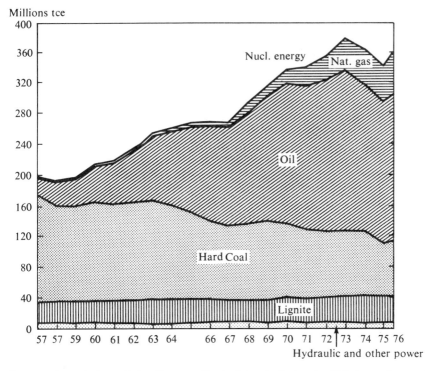

Source: Association of the German Coalmining industry (publ.) Annual report for 1975/76, p. 33.

Coal in power stations
In order to be able to assess the position of hard coal in the electricity supply industry, we must consider the part it plays in meeting the requirements of the thermal power stations.

In 1976 the thermal power stations accounted for 88.3% of the net generation of current.

TABLE 2. *Percentage of Total Energy Production per Fuel*

	1975 %	1976[10] %	1977[11] %
Hard coal	30.0	33.6	32.8
Lignite	33.1	31.8	31.2
Petroleum products	10.7	11.0	11.8
Natural gas	20.6	18.2	18.5
Others	5.6	5.4	5.7

Source: Commission publication.

FIGURE 2. *German Hard-Coal Sales Broken Down by Consumer Groups*

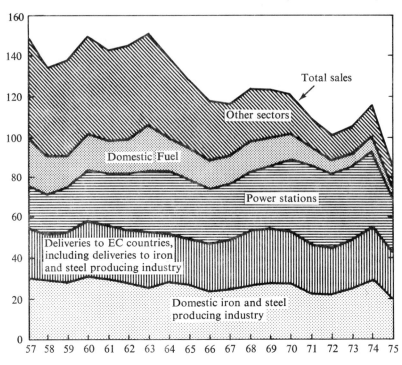

Source: *Ibid*, p. 46.

Since, in addition to hard coal, more and more nuclear energy is being used in power stations, it is proposed to take a brief look at the various problems involved (see also pages 162–166).

After the oil crisis of 1973, and in addition to a stabilization of hard-coal output, particular hopes had been pinned on nuclear energy. The main arguments in favour of nuclear energy at the time were environmental acceptability, security of supply and substantially more attractive prices.

Recently, however, these arguments seem to be increasingly questionable. Among the reasons for this are the growing resistance of those opposed to nuclear power stations, who cast doubts on the environmental acceptability and safety of such stations. In addition, the embargo on uranium deliveries by the United States and Canada has raised doubts about security of supplies. Nor can we any longer take for granted substantially more attractive pricing arrangements for nuclear energy, since the forecasts in this sector differ very widely. Thus it has been established, for example, that hard coal is cheaper than nuclear energy for medium- and peak-load operation. However, nuclear current is cheaper for base-load operation.

In view of these developments it was necessary to rethink energy policy, in the sense of reassessing the role of hard coal, with special reference to the power station sector (see page 165ff).

Coal as a raw material in the production of steel
Only coking coal is required for the production of steel. The German hard-coal mining industry supplies 54% of the European Community steel industry's coking coal requirements, 64% of the requirements of the old Community of Six and almost 100% of the German steel industry's requirements.

It will be clear from the foregoing that, as far as coking coal is concerned, the German hard-coal industry is heavily dependent on economic cycles in the steel industry. This problem has been accentuated following attempts by the steel industry, wherever possible, to keep its own coking plants (metallurgical coking plants) operational and restrict outside supplies in the event of production cutbacks. As a result, there has been a disproportionately heavy increase in pithead stocks at the colliery coke ovens.

The steel industry continued to step up production at its metallurgical coking plants. In 1975, production stood at 8.9 million tonnes and by 1976 the figure had gone up to 9.6 million tonnes.[12] Furthermore, the steel industry's dependence on coking coal was diminishing in view of constant reductions in the specific amount of coke used in the blast furnaces as a result of technical progress. This can be seen from the following synoptic table:

TABLE 3. *Average specific consumption of coke per tonne in the EEC Member States*

	Community of Six	*Community of Nine*
1960	883 kg	
1965	703 kg	
1970	582 kg	
1971	554 kg	
1972	526 kg	
1973	526 kg	534 kg
1974	528 kg	536 kg
1975	508 kg	522 kg

Source: Commission publication.

The following factors are also important in connection with the use of coking coal in the steel industry:
– High-grade coking coal, as supplied by the German hard-coal industry, will continue to be scarce worldwide.
– There is a tendency for prices to rise (despite the fall-off in sales resulting from the economic recession in the steel industry since 1975).

In view of rising prices, the blast furnaces in the Federal Republic of Germany have been eager for quite some time to meet part of their needs from imported coal. On this point they were accommodated by the Federal Government to the extent that the latter made provision in its projected energy programme for a special tariff quota of 3,000,000 tonnes a year for metallurgical coke.

Safeguarding jobs and regional structural policy in the coal sector

This is an aspect to which special importance must be attached, in view of the fact that hard-coal mining in the Federal Republic of Germany is concentrated in two narrowly-defined geographical areas.

Problems arose in these areas with the start of the coal crisis in 1957 and the resulting process of contraction in the numbers employed.

TABLE 4. *Trends in employment levels in the hard-coal industry*

1957: 607,300 employed (including 12,100 foreigners)
1975: 202,300 employed (including 29,400 foreigners)

Source: Annual report for 1975/76, p. 75.

However, in what was in varying degrees a rather favourable overall economic climate, the Federal Government and the Land Governments succeeded in largely overcoming these problems by taking the appropriate structural measures.

The situation today calls for a different assessment, in view of the following two factors:

– On the one hand, because of the current labour market position, as a result of which steps have had to be taken to stabilize the numbers employed in the mining industry. Thus a DIW report published on 1 December 1976 established that electricity-from-coal production involving 2,000,000 tonnes of coal a year would safeguard 11,000 jobs, of which only 4,000 were in the mining sector. Forecasts such as these were bound to attract the attention of the politicians responsible in the Ruhr and the Saar. The North Rhine/Westphalia Minister for Economic Affairs, Herr Riemer, defined his Government's attitude as follows: nuclear power stations for Bavaria and Schleswig-Holstein, but coal for North Rhine/Westphalia.

– On the other hand, taking into account the uncertainties of future energy consumption, coupled with doubts about whether these needs can be covered by the individual sources of energy, it would be unwise to run down the number of men employed still further, as this could jeopardize supplies in the event of an increase in energy consumption. If we are to be in a position to fulfil these future technical requirements, the personnel structure in the German hard-coal industry must be changed.

In this connection, special mention should be made of the problem of the rise in the proportion of older workers making up the labour force. The following table may serve to illustrate this.

144

TABLE 5. *Age pyramid in the German hard-coal mining industry (1975)*

Age group	Percentage of labour force
15–19	8.7%
20–24	5.4%
25–29	8.3%
30–34	9.5%
35–39	13.1%
40–44	15.9%
45–49	21.0%
50–54	13.9%
55–59	3.7%
60 and over	0.5%

Source: Annual report for 1975/76, p. 83.

As a consequence of the rise in the proportion of older workers in the mining industry, the 1980's will witness a sharp increase in the number of retirements. However, the need to create a more attractive job image in the mining industry had arisen not only against the background of an ageing labour force but also as a result of the present shortage of apprenticeships. The Federal Ministry of Economic Affairs has made its own contribution by enacting on 30 June 1976 a regulation on vocational training for miners, i.e., modernization of the existing job description for the miners.

Coal and the drive for independence and security of supply in the energy sector

As mentioned earlier, the oil crisis was the signal for a reorientation of energy policy. The time had come to lay new foundations which would bring the rundown of the coal-mining industry to an end. The uncertainties of the energy market—with oil being used as a political weapon—underlined the need to stockpile larger quantities of coal and coke as a safety reserve than before the crisis. This raised the question of who was to pay the bill for storage.

In this situation the Federal Government expressed willingness to finance a national coal reserve of 10 million tonnes in association with the Länder North Rhine/Westphalia and Saarland. These stocks were to serve not merely as a safety reserve, but to absorb any production surpluses that might occur from time to time, and thus help to safeguard employment in the mines. Proposals for the financing of coal stocks by the Community as a means of relieving the financial burden of storing coal in times of recession have recently been put forward by the Commission.

Figure 3 illustrates the rise and fall of stockholdings in the German hard-coal industry. Among the reasons for these ups and downs were alternative energy sources (oil), economic cycle fluctuations and the oil crisis.

FIGURE 3.   *Coal and Coke Stocks in the German Hard-Coal Industry*

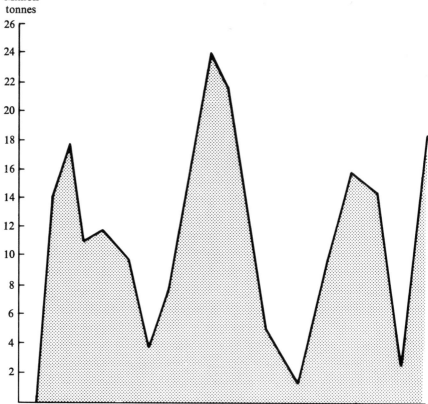

Source: Annual report for 1975/76, p. 35.

Equality of competition in the community coal sector

In this context we shall confine our remarks to measures taken by the Governments of the Community countries which might affect the balance of competition. Such measures take the form of subsidies, and in the paragraphs that follow a distinction will be made between subsidies that are not related to current production and subsidies for current production.

The legal basis for these subsidies is provided by Decision 528/76 of the Commission of the European Communities regarding the Community system of measures taken by the Member States to assist the coal mining industry.

Subsidies not related to current production
These related to social security benefits and the payment of inherited liabilities resulting from the closure of pits in earlier years.

146

In the case of social security benefits, the measures taken are considered compatible with the common market "provided that, for undertakings in the hard-coal industry, they bring the ratio between the burden per miner in employment and the benefits per person in receipt of benefit into line with the corresponding ratio in other sectors."[13]

Figures prepared by the Commission in 1976 show that the Federal Republic of Germany, Belgium and France have kept within the limits laid down in this Article, whereas in the United Kingdom those limits have been exceeded.

In the case of inherited liabilities, measures are compatible with the common market provided that they do not exceed the amount of such liabilities (Decision 528/76, Article 5). Aids that fall within this category are the following: pit closure premiums, "burden-equalizing" aids in respect of water handling charges, aids to the financing of the rundown measures for the industry, aids to cover inherited liabilities and aids in respect of pit closure depreciation (affecting only the RAG).

The Commission found that the measures taken in the countries concerned were in accordance with the provisions of Decision 528/76.

Aids to current production
Here a distinction is made between direct and indirect aids to the undertakings.
a. Direct aids
Direct aids have to be reported to the Commission and are approved in accordance with the provisions of the ECSC Treaty. In the Federal Republic the first electricity-from-coal law comes under this heading; the Commission found that this law did not involve any contravention of the ban on subsidies imposed under Articles 4 of the ECSC Treaty.
b. Indirect aids
In the Federal Republic of Germany the following aids come within this category:

TABLE 6

Measure	Total aid	Aid per tonne of production
Investment aid	DM 273.0 million	DM 2.90
Backing for first-time innovations	32.8	0.35
Mine-workers' premiums	115.0	1.22
Aid in respect of safety stocks	80.0	0.85
Assumption of RAG amortization instalments	67.2	0.71
TOTAL	DM 568.0 million	DM 6.03 = 2.08 EUA

Source: Commission publication.

The table below shows how the subsidies granted for current production (per tonne) in the Federal Republic compare with the subsidies granted in the other Community countries:

TABLE 7

Country	Aid per tonne of production in EUA
FR Germany	2.08
Belgium	12.12
France	13.88
United Kingdom	0.26[14]

Source: Commission publication.

Organization of coal-mining undertakings in the Federal Republic of Germany

Since the merger of 24 Ruhr mining companies in 1969 to form the Ruhrkohle AG, the German hard-coal industry has consisted of six undertakings. Four of them operate as private companies, namely the Gewerkschaft Auguste Victoria, the Eschweiler Bergwerksverein, Preussag AG Kohle and the Gewerkschaft Sophia Jacoba.

The Ruhrkohle AG holds a special position.[15] Its sixteen shareholders are companies which have put their mining assets into the holding company in accordance with the "Grundvertrag zur Neuordnung des Ruhrbergbaus" (Outline Agreement on the Reorganization of the Ruhr mining industry) of 18 July 1969. Most of the shareholders are linked with Ruhrkohle AG by long-term agreements on the supply of coke and power station coal.

The management of the coal mines, coke works and subsidiary operations is in the hands of six regionally-organized management companies.

Steag AG, of which shares Ruhrkohle AG holds more than 66%, looks after that company's electricity generating interests.

The Saarbergwerke AG is under public ownership, the share capital being held by the Federal Government and the Saarland with 74% and 26% respectively.

Table 8 gives the breakdown of overall production between the various undertakings.

Research and technology in the coal sector

Bearing in mind that world supplies of natural oil and gas will be used up within a few decades, and that substantial price increases will be resultant, research and development in the coal sector takes on special importance, the more so in view of the ample supplies available at home and the steady improvement in relative costs.

TABLE 8. *Hard-coal mines. List of mining enterprises*

Undertaking	Place	(1,000 tonnes)					
		1969	1970	1971	1972	1973	1974
FR Germany	Total	117,035	116,970	117,143	108,690	103,654	101,484
Lower Saxony							
Preussag		2,780	2,917	2,918	2,695	2,486	2,200
North Rhine-Westphalia		103,029	103,327	103,289	95,330	91,731	89,999
Ruhr		96,027	96,204	96,424	88,866	85,487	83,838
Ruhrkohle AG	Essen		89,374	89,904	82,659	79,399	77,786
Gewerkschaft Auguste Victoria	Marl	2,924	3,189	2,987	2,942	2,819	2,772
Eschweiler Bergwerks-Verein (Ruhr)	Kohlscheid		3,641	3,534	3,266	3,269	3,280
Gewerkschaft Alte Haase		54	—	—			
Aachen		7,002	7,123	6,865	6,464	6,244	6,161
Eschweiler Bergwerks-Verein	Kohlscheid	5,123	5,268	5,114	4,968	4,606	4,487
Sophia-Jacoba Gewerkschaft	Huckelhoven	1,878	1,855	1,751	1,496	1,638	1,674
Saarland							
Saarbergwerke	Saarbrücken	11,075	10,554	10,677	10,429	9,175	8,930
Small pits		150	172	258	237	260	355

Source: Energy Statistics Yearbook for 1970–1974, Verlag Bundesanzeiger (1975).

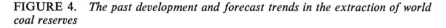

FIGURE 4. *The past development and forecast trends in the extraction of world coal reserves*

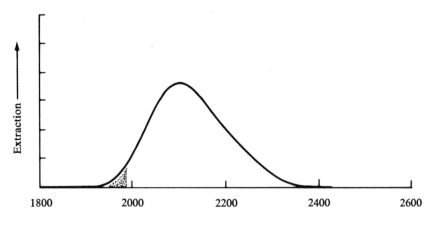

FIGURE 5. *The past development and forecast trends in the extraction of world petroleum reserves*

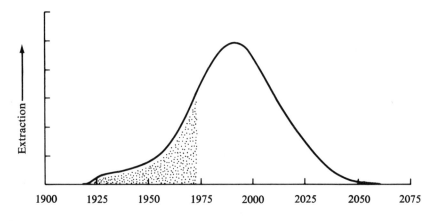

Source: Fig. 4, 5: Outline programme of energy research 1974–77, p. 20

Comparison with Fig. 4 shows that a relatively large proportion of the petroleum reserves has already been used up: the downward trend in production begins much earlier than for coal.

150

FIGURE 6.   *Development of the production per working point, the output per man and shift underground, the overall production and the number of producing pits in the coal industry of the Federal Republic of Germany (1957 = 100)*

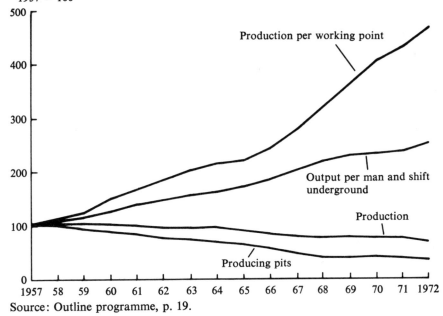

Source: Outline programme, p. 19.

The rationalization achieved by progressive mechanization of the industry is clearly apparent.

The efforts being directed to the refinement of coal are aimed at presenting the product in as economic and environmentally innocuous a form as possible. Considered in relation to lower investment costs, greater efficiency and increased profitability, there are two processes in particular that hold out good medium-term prospects. These are pressure gasification and fluidized-bed combustion, both in combination with a gas-steam turbine process. Taking a long-range view, new technologies are being developed for the production of both gas and oil from coal; these could well be the answer to the vagaries of the oil supply situation and above all offer an alternative to the increased use of natural gas which will otherwise be necessary in the 1990's.

The intensive research and development activity in mining engineering is aimed at improving on the rationalization already achieved. Thanks to these efforts, the German coal industry is holding its position as the most efficient in the European Community.

The Federal Government's "outline programme for energy research 1974–77", together with the energy technology programme of the Land North Rhine/Westphalia, similar action in the Saarland and increased research grants from the European Community, has given a powerful boost to research in the fields of coal gasification and liquefaction as well as to mining technology.

The Government's "energy research and energy technologies programme 1977–80", which was adopted at the end of April, is intended to give a special fillip to research projects that tend to improve the techniques of coal production and the clean generation of electricity from coal. In the allocation of funds, this programme reveals a marked change of emphasis in favour of the development of non-nuclear forms of energy.

MAKERS OF COAL POLICY

Having outlined the main aspects of coal policy in the first section, we will now go on to consider the protagonists in its formation and their basic viewpoints. Our purpose in so doing is to give a better understanding of the measures adopted by the Federal and Land Governments (discussed under Government Measures) by pointing out the interests and requirements of the parties concerned that go into the making of coal policy. These have to be taken into account by the politicians in reaching their decisions.

In this connection, the Federal Government—and up to a point the Land Governments as well—have a special role to play. Apart from the very specific requirements of the parties involved, there are more general internal and external factors which must be considered (e.g., environmental problems, security of supplies and the question of growth).

Needless to say, the positions of the various parties have undergone some modification over the years (see Government Measures), and in the remarks that follow only the present situation will be examined.

The Federal Government

In general terms, what the Federal Government seeks to do is to ensure the utilization of German coal for the benefit of the economy as a whole and the energy economy in particular.

In the Government's view, specific objectives (e.g., for sale to the electricity generating industry) should be set only for a medium-term period, say five years. Among the reasons given are the uncertainties in the energy market—lately the difficulties encountered in expanding nuclear energy—which make the security of supplies a crucial factor in energy policy.

The production of electricity from coal is regarded as a sector which gives a vital place to the German coal industry in energy policy. With the third electricity-from-coal law, an attempt was made to ensure an adequate share of coal for this sector. Since the law was unable to ensure the required level of sales, the Federal Government pressed for an agreement between the electricity producers and the coal industry on long-term supply agreements. After long and difficult negotiations, this agreement came into being at the end of April 1977.

The Federal Government take the view that, to meet the expected rise in electricity consumption, a combination of nuclear and coal-fuelled power stations will be required; the Government is therefore continuing to support a balanced expansion of nuclear power stations.

152

In the steel industry, support is given to the use of Community coke under the system of EEC aid, and the Government does not see how any further intervention is possible. Nevertheless, the expensive home-produced coking coal is protected against low priced imports from non-Community countries by national action under the Kohlezollkontingentgesetz[16] (Law on customs quotas for coal).

In the course of the adaptations of the German coal industry in the sixties, the Federal Government evolved a comprehensive social "safety-net" (e.g., an overall social security scheme, tideover allowance arrangements, compensatory payments by the miners' provident fund). Even today, this is still regarded as an essential component of coal policy. Problems of regional structure were handled by measures designed to promote industry and create new jobs (e.g., by the grant of investment premiums). One important consideration underlying these measures is that the Ruhr carries considerable weight at election time.

In view of the vital importance of a secure, uninterrupted supply of energy, the Federal Government is conscious of a special responsibility in this sector and feels that more active intervention by the State is called for. This places the energy policy in a rather special position in the overall organizational policy.

In view of the importance of energy policy and the worldwide nature of the problem, the Federal Government regards international cooperation as essential. Whereas it views the possibilities within the Community with some scepticism, it is more optimistic in its approach to the International Energy Agency (IEA). It feels that the cooperation within that organization to date has yielded satisfactory results, and points in particular to the adoption of an allocation system for oil in the event of a crisis.

Land Governments

In contrast to other countries, the federal structure of West Germany is such that the Land Governments, too, have a share in the making of coal policy decisions. The Länder in question are North Rhine/Westphalia and the Saarland—the latter being a very small land which depends heavily on mining.

Despite the different party-political make-up of the Governments in these two Länder, both of them take a firm stand for the stabilization, if not expansion, of coal production. This attitude is dictated by reasons of social policy and regional economy. On this matter of principle, the Governments are backed up by the opposition, who tend to favour even stronger action in support of mining. Underlying this political harmony is the fact that, in these Länder, mining and the associated industries hold decisive vote-winning potential.

Both Länder are going all out in the effort to develop new technologies, both in collaboration with the Federal Government[17] and on their own account. North Rhine/Westphalia alone is to support research and development in the coal sector with DM 120 million in 1977.

A point of interest in this connection is that there are considerable differences between the Federal Government and the Länder in the matter of assessing energy policy requirements.

Discord prevails in particular over the future contribution of nuclear energy and coal to electricity supplies. Whereas the Federal Government, in its document "Grundlinien und Eckwerte für die Fortschreibung des Energie-programms" of 23 March 1977, maintains that 30,000 MW of nuclear power in 1985 is absolutely essential, the Minister for Economic Affairs of North Rhine/Westphalia, Herr Riemer (FDP), contends that 10,000 MW would be more realistic. However, his fellow party-member, Friderichs, (Federal Minister for Economic Affairs) believes that with such a low proportion of nuclear energy in 1985 rationing would be unavoidable, as the other energy sources would be unable to fill the gap. To which Riemer retorts in an interview with the "Spiegel" of 2 May 1977:

"The lights won't be going out anywhere. In fact the prospects are quite different. They look more like this: We are promoting the construction of power stations, but we shall have a job to sell the power they produce. Nobody wants it. And we are capable of generating still more power. To my mind, as long as this situation lasts, the theory of the energy gap is just a theory and no more."

The political parties

In the party-political debate in the Federal Republic of Germany, coal is not one of the points at issue, one of the reasons being that differences of organizational policy have no bearing on it. Government intervention is not merely approved but demanded by all political factions.

The overall energy policy on the other hand is a bone of contention, with discussion concentrating on the following questions:
– How much extra energy will be needed?
– What should be the role of nuclear energy?
– How much can be achieved by energy savings?

It is obvious, of course, that the position of coal will be affected by the answers that are given to these questions. If, for instance, we start from the assumption of an increased energy requirement, but wish to keep the proportion of nuclear energy as low as possible, the conclusion is virtually inevitable that the production capacity of the mines should be stepped up. In answering these question, there is no clear line-up of the parties. What is agreed, however, is that any further rundown of coal would be irresponsible, and cannot be contemplated.

The undertakings of the German coal industry

To illustrate what the German coal industry expects from the Federal Government's coal policy, we shall consider the demands made by the mining undertakings with respect to the continuation of the 1977 energy programme. The central points are as follows:
– In regard to output, a further stabilization of the production capacity is called for (currently at least 94 million tce);

- In the electricity-from-coal sector, the demands of the mining undertakings with respect to long-term supply contracts and a target quantity of 33 million tonnes/year have been largely met by an agreement concluded at the end of April by the electricity producers;
- In order to achieve better and longer-term planning between coal and steel producers, the mining undertakings wish the European Commission to extend the Regulation on the coking coal subsidy up to 1985;
- The restrictive coal imports regulation of the Federal Government is in line with the wishes of the mining industry; the volume of imports permitted is considered acceptable;
- Government aid to research and development in the coal sector is thought by the mining industry to be in line with the vital future needs of our national and energy economy, and all the more necessary in order to catch up after the long years of preoccupation with other energy sources (nuclear energy).

The attitude of the undertakings to the European Community and the International Energy Agency is marked by scepticism:

"If, in the vitally important sector of energy supplies, neither the European Community nor the association of Western industrial nations in the International Energy Agency have sufficient power of integration to introduce a scheme that could serve the common interest, Community policy in this, as in other areas, can only be regarded with scepticism".[18]

Hence the Federal Government is still looked upon as the proper authority to whom to address their demands.

The electricity industry

In this connection, one can first state quite broadly that the relationship of the electricity industry either to the Federal Government or the mining industry is not free of problems. In both cases, this arises from the fact that the electricity industry—an unreserved advocate of nuclear energy—seems to regard other energy sources only as stopgaps. On account of the overall economic aspects involved (security of supply, job security, etc.), the Federal Government cannot comply with such one-sided demands from the electricity industry. Instead, through a series of legal measures (third electricity-from-coal law), it has had to try to ensure that coal receives an adequate share in the production of electricity.

This led to opposition in the electricity industry, which refused to accept such "dirigistic measures". When the target quantities under the third electricity-from-coal law were not reached and the Federal Government threatened, as a result, to take new measures, the electricity industry declared itself willing to negotiate with the mining undertakings on long-term supply contracts. Dr. W. Tegethoff, the Executive Secretary of the Vereinigung deutscher Elektrizitätswerke (association of German electricity producers) made the following statement on 5 October 1976 in an interview on the German radio station, Deutschland-funk:

"We hope that it will be possible, in accordance with free-market principles, to solve these questions which are extremely difficult ones both for the coal industry and for us, and that we can avoid dirigistic interference on the part of the State, as happened last year."

A particular bone of contention during the negotiations between the coal and electricity industries was the amount of coal to be supplied. The electricity industry continually stressed that German hard coal, as the most expensive energy source available in the Federal Republic of Germany—even when the special coal subsidies were taken into account—could only be used in electricity generation to cover medium- and peak-load demands. Since, however, the anticipated increase in demand would occur almost exclusively in base-load operations, where nuclear power has the undoubted advantage of lower cost, the electricity industry did not believe that the consumption of 33 million tonnes of hard coal, as required by the mining industry, could be achieved.

As a result, mainly of the pressure exerted by the Federal Government, the electricity industry gave in to the demands of the mining concerns.[19]

In contrast to the mining industry, and also to statements made by Herr Riemer, the Minister for Economic Affairs of the Land of North Rhine/Westphalia (see page 154), the electricity industry believes that any shortfalls in nuclear power production—such as those currently appearing on the horizon—could not be offset by coal or any other primary energy source.

The steel industry

The main demand of the steel industry, which has continually been made for years, is for the gradual removal of the tariff quotas.

When Ruhrkohle AG was founded, the iron and steel works were guaranteed cost equalization for 20 years in respect of the disadvantages incurred by purchasing the more expensive domestic coal. In fulfilling this guarantee, the Federal Government pays the difference between the cost-covering list price of Ruhrkohle AG and a so-called "Competitive" price.[20]

The steel industry is now of the opinion, however, that this price is higher than that which must be paid by its Italian, French, Belgian and Netherlands competitors for coking coal from third countries and that they thus suffer from a disadvantage in competition.

Two aspects that have already been mentioned in Part One should also be brought up once again in this connection:

Firstly, the success of the steel industry in its efforts to lower specific coke consumption[21] in blast furnaces and, secondly, the increasing capacity of the steelworks' own coke ovens.

Both of these points indicate the importance of coking coal as a cost factor and the efforts being made here to lower costs.

156

Indubitably, the strongest and most influential pressure group in the coal sector in the Federal Republic is IG Bergbau und Energie (IGBE). Because of the regulations governing co-determination in the mining industry, this body is represented in the management of the undertakings and participates in fixing the prices. With a union membership rate of 86.7% (on 31 December 1975), and of 91.8% in the coal-mining sector, the IGBE possesses strong backing and excellent means of action. It is represented in parliament by its chairman Adolf Schmidt.

The IGBE regards coal as an element in the overall context of power supply and the energy policy. To achieve its most urgent aim—long-term job security—the IGBE is pressing for coal to be allotted a specific part in the energy concept of the Federal Republic. To this end, it is supporting the intention, under the programme of the Federal Government, of maintaining an annual output of about 95 million tonnes. Specifically, the IGBE is adopting the following standpoint:[22]

- In the field of electricity generation, the IGBE complains that, from 1974 to 1975, the consumption of hard coal suffered a disproportionate decrease (of 26% with a decrease in overall electricity generation of only 3.8%), while the consumption of nuclear energy and natural gas, by comparison, increased disproportionately (by 73% and 9.3%, respectively). The third electricity-from-coal law, which lays down that a specific amount of hard coal must be used, is continuously supported. The IGBE is also pressing for rapid continuation of the construction programme.
- With an eye on the efforts being made to increase the use of nuclear energy, the trade union is demanding that the position of coal in the league table also be safeguarded in the long term. This is to be promoted and/or achieved by the development and application of new technologies enabling coal to be put to more modern and better uses and by appropriate investments in the opening-up of new deposits.
- Where coking coal is concerned, the interest of the trade union lies in stabilizing sales. Accordingly, the IGBE rejects any opening of the market and any change in the import arrangements; it does not see any reason even to discuss the removal of the tariff quotas laid down by the Federal Government.
- In the eyes of the IGBE, the existence of a national hard-coal reserve (of about 10 million tonnes) is a further element in its concept of maintaining a permanent place for coal in the energy supply policy.
- The IGBE misses no opportunity to stress one employment-policy aspect of the coal policy for which it is jointly responsible: with an overall increase in the unemployment rate, in 1974 and 1975 Ruhrkohle AG managed to create 9,000 new jobs annually; in addition, about 6,000 apprentices were accepted each year.

The IGBE sees the main reason that the energy market continues overall to function properly in the Federal Republic despite the energy crisis and recession—and in its view this means precisely the maintenance of the "league table" position of coal—in the readiness of all the participants to cooperation. It has in mind here only the protagonists in a national context, and is clearly placing its trust in national decisions and measures; on no occasion has it ever demanded that the coal policy should become a Community matter. The IGBE obviously does not believe that the Community can offer a better basis for solving the problem; in addition, it occupies a very strong position in the national decision-making system. Since the IGBE ascribes the quality and the success of the coal policy in the Federal Republic in large measure to the type of company constitution characterized by the pattern of co-determination in the mining industry, a further obstacle in the way of Community solutions becomes evident: differences in company constitutions and in the concept of trade union strategy and policy.

GOVERNMENT MEASURES

Starting with the coal crisis, the measures taken by the governments in the Federal Republic of Germany can be divided into four phases.

The period from 1958 to 1973 is characterized by the appearance of alternative energy-carriers, particularly oil, which, on the one hand, were cheaper and, on the other, it was presumed, were available in sufficient quantities.

Attempts were made in the period 1958–1968 to resolve the resulting coal crisis by protecting German hard coal against cheaper imported coal and ensuring a market for the hard coal in the important area of electricity production; rationalization measures were also taken. When all this failed to cope with the structural crisis, the decision was made in the period from 1968 to 1973 to turn to more trenchant measures. It was clear that considerable cutbacks were necessary to adapt coal production to the market situation; to achieve these cutbacks in a controlled—and socially and structurally acceptable—manner, far-reaching State intervention was necessary.

Under the shock of the oil crisis, those responsible for the energy policy began a fundamental rethinking of the problem. It became clear that oil, as an energy-carrier—which accounted for 55.4% of the primary energy supply in the Federal Republic of Germany in 1972—was exposed to considerable risks where its availability was concerned. In addition, the enormous increases in the price of oil, and the further rises which could, at the time not be estimated, led to new assessments of the competitiveness of the other energy-carriers.

For hard coal this called for measures intended to lead to stabilization. Further, research funds were made available, particularly for research into coal gasification and hydrogenization.

Although, after the oil crisis, in addition to stabilizing the use of hard coal to reduce dependence, a considerable increase in the role of nuclear energy in particular was planned, a new development, has recently occurred.

Further expansion in the field of nuclear energy seems doubtful for two reasons:
– the increasing activity of the citizens' action group opposed to nuclear power plants, together with relevant court decisions, gives reason to doubt the political feasibility of expanding the nuclear power plant programme;
– the difficulties encountered in obtaining uranium supplies, particularly

158

from Canada and the USA, show that even nuclear energy is dependent to a large extent on foreign trade.

This had to lead to a return to the secure domestic energy sources, which, for example, was evidenced by the provision of new research funds for coal technologies and is reflected, in particular, in the key figures for carrying forward the energy programme of 23 March 1977.

First phase (1958–1968): Ensuring sales and rationalization

The measures taken in this phase, which represent an initial attempt to cope with the coal crisis, have three aspects:

a.   Foreign trade aspect

In 1959, the import of hard coal from third countries was subjected to licencing and, in addition, a coal tariff of DM 20/tonne was introduced, with an exception covering a duty-free quota of 5 million tonnes per year. It is significant in this connection that this was a measure taken independently by the Federal Government on a national basis.[23] In our opinion, this step marked the beginning of a development towards re-nationalization in the coal policy.

b.   Ensuring sales within the country

To ensure sales of hard coal in the field of electricity production, electricity-from-coal laws were passed in 1965 and 1966.

Under the "first electricity-from-coal law", tax relief was accorded to firms which could prove that, over a specific period, they had utilized exclusively hard or bituminous coal produced within the ECSC.

More trenchant measures were laid down in the "second electricity-from-coal law". On the one hand, certain eligible firms were granted a contribution towards the cost of the Community coal and, on the other, under specific conditions, the utilization of fuel oil in power plants required a license.

c.   Rationalization

To increase the competitiveness of hard-coal mining, to improve the production facilities and processes and to adapt the coal mining industry to the marketing realities, the "Rationalisierungsverband des Steinkohlebergbaus" (Association for the Rationalization of Coal Mining) was founded in 1963.

From 1963 to 1965, this public-law entity granted loans and guarantees, and closure premiums of DM 25/tonne net production, half of which was borne by the Federal Government.

For closures and for adaptation of production to marketing realities, the "Aktionsgemeinschaft deutsche Steinkohlenreviere GmbH" (German Coalfields Association), founded by German industry in November 1966, paid further closure premiums. In addition, tax advantages were granted for this purpose.

Second phase (1968–1973): Outbacks

After the measures described above had proved inadequate to cope with the coal crisis, the Government increased its efforts in 1968. The aim here was to achieve adaptation to the market by consolidating individual measures in the coal mining industry.

Increased supervision on the part of the State (Kohlebeauftragter: Commissioner for coal), was intended to ensure that the undertakings geared their production capacity to the given market realities and that they concentrated their production on the most rationally operating and highest yielding pits.

A further important step was the creation of a new type of undertaking—the Ruhrkohle AG. This was a merger of most of the pits operating in the Ruhr region, in which the State (Federal Government and Land) undertook the guarantees for the responsibilities of Ruhrkohle AG towards the previously-existing firms.

These deep-going measures were aimed, in particular, at achieving:

– Rationalization through pit closures and increase in productivity;
– A reduction in the number of undertakings:
– Greater powers of intervention for both the Federal and Land Governments.

Where foreign trade was concerned, these measures were supported by prolonging the quota system for imported coal.

The coal adaptation law

This law, the most comprehensive yet in respect to coal policy, was particularly intended to ensure that the mining undertakings adopted uniform practices in the field of sales promotion, of investments and of employment policy. The Commissioner for coal played a central role. He was responsible for the following tasks:

– establishing sales estimates;
– registering information from the mining undertakings in respect of production capacity, number of employees, pithead stocks and other important factors;
– receiving reports on anticipated recruitment, dismissals and reallocation of employees.

On the basis of this information, the Commissioner for coal is empowered to make recommendations to the mining undertakings. If these recommendations are not followed, he can then, to some extent as a sanction, withdraw subsidies (e.g., closure premiums, etc.).

A further important element of the coal adaptation law is the overall social plan, which provides for uniform social measures in the hard-coal, pitch-coal and lignite sectors.

A further measure accompanying the adaptation process is designed to improve the economic structure of the areas affected by pit closures (assistance in the creation and expansion of industrial plants and in the acquisition of land for industry).

In parallel with the reorganization of the Ruhr mining industry, the Saar mining industry also received Federal assistance. In this case the following measures were taken:

– guarantees for the Saarbergwerke AG for restructuring investments;
– interest subsidies for these guaranteed loans;
– subsidies for inherited charges.

About six months after publication of the coal adaptation law, a "Verordnung über die Masstäbe für die Ermittlung der optimalen Betriebsgrössen im Steinkohlenbergbau—Order Concerning Criteria for Determining the Optimum Size of Undertakings in the Coal Industry" was issued; in the formulation of this regulation, the information acquired by the Commissioner for coal had played a substantial role.

This way, the Commissioner for coal was provided with criteria for determining the optimum size of undertakings. Undertakings that did not fulfill these prerequisites could have the subsidies withdrawn from them.

The Ruhrkohle AG

Like the coal adaptation law, the foundation of Ruhrkohle AG was a fundamental and extremely important step, which was aimed at achieving the requisite adaptation of hard-coal production to the market by concentrating on the collieries with the highest economic yield potential.

The mining assets, together with the debts with which they were saddled, were to be transferred to the overall company, and certain investments in affiliates that served the mining industry were brought in. The previously-existing companies received a total compensation of DM 2 100 million, two-thirds of which was guaranteed by the Federal Government while the Land Government of North Rhine/Westphalia guaranteed one-third; the same system held in respect of the DM 1 200 million of the transferred outside liabilities. This sum was to be repaid in 20 annual instalments and interests of 6% paid.

The codetermination policy of the mining industry was to apply to the overall company.

Pithead power stations, which provide a substantial proportion of the power supply for the mining industry, and several of the power stations associated with the mining industry in the Kraft-Wärme-Verbund (power-heat association) (900 MW), were also taken over by the joint company.

For the other major power stations there was concluded a 20-year contract which bound the previously-existing companies to give adequate regard to the overall company in the allocation of new power station projects.

In addition, a blast furnace was to be concluded (also for a 20-year period) governing the coal and coke purchasing obligations incumbent on the previously-existing companies for their iron and steel works and the corresponding supply obligations on the part of the overall company.

All the real estate necessary to the industry were transferred to the overall company at book value. Similarly, the overall company was also to obtain right of occupancy for an unlimited period in respect of the miners' living accommodation.

Two years after the foundation of Ruhrkohle AG, the supervisory board adopted an overall adaptation plan to contribute to the recovery of the German coal industry; the most important points of this plan were:
– concentration of production on particularly high-yield mines, with the concomitant closure of certain pits;
– transfer of production from lower-yield pits to better pits;
– formulation of social plans as supporting measures.

To enable the overall adaptation plan of Ruhrkohle AG to be implemented together with a series of other measures, the government of the Land of North Rhine/Westphalia had increased its guarantees in the 1972 budget by a further DM 1 000 million in view of the worsening sales situation in the Ruhr coal mining industry. Furthermore, additional assistance to the Ruhr coal industry was decided on by the Federal Government at the end of 1972.

161

Despite this wide range of measures, real adaptation to the market situation could not be achieved, and Ruhrkohle AG still had to receive subsidies.

Coal tariff rules
The retention of the existing coal tariff arrangement should also be seen against this background (see page 159). Because of the competitive conditions, it is necessary to protect the German mining industry for a further period against imports from third countries.

Third phase (1973–1976): Stabilization

How unprepared the Federal Republic was when the oil crisis struck is shown by the most important points of the overall energy policy programme formulated by the Federal Government; this was published two weeks before the oil crisis began on 3 October 1973. Although certain risks in the field of energy supply—particularly those due to the high degree of dependence on petroleum imports—had actually been identified, very few practical conclusions were drawn. (See Table 9.)
   The following measures were thought necessary in respect of the coal industry and were based on the overall estimate of the situation in respect of the energy policy (before the oil crisis):
– further adaptation of production in relation to the achievable sales (further pit closures);
– support of the concomitant supporting measures in the socio-political field;
– stabilization of the amounts supplied to the most important sales sectors (iron and steel industry and electricity industry).

Repercussions of the oil crisis: re-assessment of the 1974 energy programme
   In order to identify the decisive repercussions resulting from the oil crisis, a comparison must be made of the forecasts set out in the following tables of the proportions of various energy-carriers in the overall primary energy consumption; Table 9 was published in the 1973 Energy Programme, Table 10 in the first extension (1974).

TABLE 9. *Forecast of Proportions of Energy-carriers in Overall Energy Consumption*

	1972		1975		1980		1985	
	Million t.c.e.	%	Million t.c.e.	%	Million t.c.e.	%	Million t.c.e.	%
Crude oil	196.4	55.4	230	57	275	54	330	54
Hard coal	83.7	23.6	72	18	58	11	50	8
Natural gas	30.6	8.6	48	12	82	16	92	15
Lignite	31.0	8.7	35	8	39	8	38	6
Nuclear energy	3.1	0.9	12	3	45	9	90	15
Other	9.5	2.8	9	2	11	2	10	2
Total primary energy consumption	354.4	100	406	100	510	100	610	100

Source: Overall energy policy programme of the Federal Government, 1973, p. 4.

TABLE 10. *Forecast of Proportions of Energy-carriers in Overall Energy Consumption*

	1973		1980		1985	
	Million t.c.e.	*%*	*Million t.c.e.*	*%*	*Million t.c.e.*	*%*
Crude oil	209	55	221	47	245	44
Hard coal	84.2	22	82	17	79	14
Natural gas	38.6	10	87	18	101	18
Lignite	33.1	9	35	7	38	7
Nuclear energy	4	1	40	9	81	15
Other	9.7	3	10	2	11	2
Primary energy consumption	378.6	100	475	100	555	100

Source: First extension of the 1974 energy programme of the Federal Government p. 6.

Table 10 clearly shows that natural gas and nuclear energy have high growth rates, and also that the contribution of hard deep-mined coal to the overall energy supply should remain fixed within the existing order of magnitude up to 1980.

This new forecast should be regarded as a repercussion of the changes brought about by the oil crisis. The competitiveness of oil versus the other energy-carriers has thus become highly distorted as a result of the considerable price increases made by the OPEC countries; the relative price positions of other forms of energy have improved. New technologies for the generation of energy and ways and means for the efficient use and the recovery of energy have become more prominent.

The inferences in respect of energy policy were:
– The share of crude oil in the energy supply pattern will be forced down;
– Speed-up of the use of nuclear energy, natural gas and lignite;
– New "league table" position for hard coal;
– Intensification of energy saving;
– Higher priority for energy research;
– Intensification of crisis—precaution measures.

These new circumstances have brought a whole series of consequences for hard coal:
a.   Coal stocks
Coal stocks from domestic production, amounting to about 10 million tonnes, were deemed essential. In view of the resultant burden on the mining companies, the Federal Government was prepared to shoulder the costs of establishing such stocks of hard coal; the basis taken was that the mining Länder would bear one-third of these costs.
b.   Stabilization of sales to the electricity industry
An average power station consumption of hard coal of 33 million tonnes a year was planned up to 1980. Refer to page 164/65 as regards the legal provisions in this connection.

c. Stabilization of sales to the iron and steel industry

The average consumption of coking coal over the period up to 1980 was expected to be about 25 million tonnes a year. This should be almost completely covered by German coking coal. In order to compensate for the disadvantageous competitive position of German hard coal, selling aid for coking coal was granted if the free market price on the international coal market fell below the break-even price for the German coal.

d. Investment aids and social measures

The target outputs assumed that the necessary labour would be available and that the requisite capital investments would be committed by the undertakings. The Federal Government was therefore prepared to raise its investment aids from DM 160 million to DM 210 million. In addition, the ceiling for Rationalization Cooperation Association was raised and the existing social aids continued. Here again also the mining Länder were to bear one-third of the costs.

e. Energy research

Hard coal was also assigned greater prominence in the 1974 "Energy research outline programme". Encouragement was given primarily in the following areas:

– Conversion of coal into products of high economic value (hydrogenation and gasification);
– Mining techniques and coal preparation, especially work on the development of fully mechanized and automated system that open up, win and prepare the coal.

The special position of the Ruhrkohle AG company

The special position of Ruhrkohle AG is attributable to a whole set of factors, namely:

Participation of the Government in the responsibility for, on the one hand, the joint initiation of the founding of the overall company and, on the other hand, the underwriting of guarantees. Owing to the fact that the undertaking is concentrated in a small geographical area, special significance is attached with regard to job security and regional structural policy.

Against this background it is understandable that, with a continuously worsening sales situation, the governments—and indeed already before the oil crisis broke—were constantly constrained to intervene to stabilize the situation. The most significant measures adopted in this connection were:

– stabilization programme in 1972 with the entering of a debt register claim of DM 1 000 million;
– Underwriting of additional guarantees;
– The parent companies and the Rationalization Cooperation Association waived their rights to the payment of interest on the sums due to them.

Securing of sales to the electricity industry

A number of legal measures have been adopted to ensure that the target quantity of 33 million tonnes prescribed in the first re-assessment of the 1974 Energy Programme is consumed annually in the electricity industry.

Mention should first of all be made here of the third electricity-from-coal law of 13 December 1974. Under this there was set up an "equalization fund

164

to ensure that deep-mined hard coal is used" from which the following measures were financed:
- Compensation to meet the additional costs incurred in using coal of Community origin in the production of electricity as against using heavy fuel oil;
- Grants towards investment costs;
- Grants towards electricity transport costs.

The money for this equalization fund were mainly raised by the electricity supply undertakings which then, however, pass on the additional costs to the consumer ("Kohlepfennig" levy).

In addition, the building of power stations designed to operate on heavy fuel oil or natural gas were subject to a licensing procedure.

Moreover, on 10 December 1975 the Federal German Cabinet adopted more incentives to increase the use of hard coal in the electricity industry, which was to receive a bonus of DM 213 million in the form of a bigger "Kohlepfennig" levy.

Regulation of customs tariffs for coal

Owing to the foreseeably weak demand for German hard coal and the aim of stabilizing the domestic output, the tariff quota for coal, which was originally only to have applied up to 1976, was extended on 2 April 1976 up to the end of 1980. The quota adopted for solid fuels was 5.5 million tonnes a year and, in addition, a special quota was approved of 3 million tonnes of hard coke a year for the iron and steel industry.

Stage Four: latest thinking on the "league table" position of hard coal

Recently, the politicians responsible have been increasingly obliged to take account of the difficulties encountered in expanding nuclear power stations. Pointers in that direction can be discerned in the "Guidelines and angles of approach for the extension of the energy programme" of 23 March 1977.

TABLE 11. *Forecasts of the proportions of various energy-carriers in the overall consumption of primary energy*

	1975 (actual)		1980		1985	
	Million t.c.e. (%)					
Crude oil	181	(52.1)	216	(50)	226	(45)
Hard coal	66.5	(19.1)	72	(17)	73	(15)
Lignite	34.4	(9.9)	35	(8)	35	(7)
Natural gas	48.7	(14.0)	73	(17)	87	(18)
Nuclear energy	7.1	(2.0)	28	(6)	62	(13)
Other	10	(2.9)	11	(2)	13	(2)
Total	347.7		435		496	

Source: "Guidelines and key figures for the extension of the energy programme 1977" in Bulletin der Bundesregierung (Federal Government Bulletin) No. 30, p. 268.

Comparison with Table 10 shows that, whereas the expected growth rates for nuclear energy are no longer very high in the case of hard coal an increase in output is forecast. In addition, a preliminary forecast was made of a 10% lower overall consumption of primary energy by comparison with the first extension of the 1974 Energy Programme.

Against this background German hard coal will in future be assigned a supply-securing function; the present output of about 94 million tonnes should therefore be henceforth maintained.

In view of the cost disadvantages resulting from the geological conditions and in consideration of the appreciable capital investments which will continue to be required to maintain its output capacity, the German coal mining industry will still be granted government financial support in the future.

The sales of German hard coal are becoming more and more concentrated into two markets, namely, the iron and steel industry and the electricity industry.

a. Electricity industry

As regards the contribution made by hard coal to the generation of electricity, the Federal Government makes at the following forecast:

	1975	1980	1985	1990
Hard coal	24.4	30	32	40 (million tce)[24]

This forecast is based on the demands to meet a total installed capacity of about 115,000 MW(e) in 1985. In the opinion of the Federal Government, this can only be done by a combination of the increased (!) use of hard coal and the moderate, steady expansion of nuclear energy.

Since the consumption of hard coal (33 million tonnes a year) provided for in the third electricity-from-coal law has not been achieved, in the opinion of the Federal Government—especially in the light of the new situation prevailing in the nuclear power station field—it would be necessary to ensure this condition by means of a long-term supply agreement between the coal industry and the electricity industry. This the partners agreed at the end of April.

The agreement reached moreover means that the 6,000 MW(e) programme for new coal-fired power stations will be increased accordingly.

b. Iron and steel industry

It is in this sector that the Federal Government is striving to bring about a prolongation of the EC coke subsidy scheme in line with the interests of the German coal industry.

The coal policy measures seen from the point of view of organization policy

To conclude an attempt will here be made to relate to the above-mentioned stages, the change in economic policy concepts which has decisively affected the economic area in the Federal Republic of Germany to the above-mentioned stages.

In its early stage (1949 till about 1958) German coal policy was strongly orientated towards an economic policy of the social market economy marked by neo-liberal ideas. The coal policy did indeed operate within the framework laid down by the ECSC, which achieved a definite influence on German coal policy.

During the economic policy era of overall control (Stages One and Two), the structural aids (intended not just to be adapted but also to maintain the potential of coal) increased in importance. This seems to have been due more to the "need of the hour" and the pressure exerted by the powerful coalition of the representatives of the mining industry and the mineworkers, rather than to a renunciation of market economy ideas to that extent; one can speak rather of a change of style in the economic policy approach. In EC circles the German side emphasized its voluntary dedication to a free market economy; the German coal market did not initiate in the light of its conception of its own position any measures which went beyond the Commission's proposals in a direction out of line with the market.

The economic policy landscape of Stages Three and Four might well throw up a unique polarization of areas of policy: The strong profession of free market economic principles and the orientation of the general economic policy (strongly influenced by neo-liberal ideas) along these lines would then —in the fields of energy and raw materials—find its counterpart in a situation where greater weight would be given to the principles of central "steering" (even reaching as far as direction of investments such as has already been in part achieved in private industry).

The advocates of the directed achievements of objectives should nevertheless not necessarily be labelled with a particular ideology: much rather do decision-governing factors of a pragmatic kind and belonging to an interest group have an effect in the direction. It would therefore be wrong to assume that the Federal Government would deviate in other areas from its free market economy stance.

The change of style described above is reflected more and more clearly in the economic policy proposals being submitted to the national and EC authorities that decide economic policy. How far these proposals will be met (in the structural and competition policy) remains to be seen.

SUMMARY AND CONCLUSIONS

Just as Reichert did, we also come to the conclusion that no common coal policy exists among the Nine. The structural crisis in the coal mining industry that set in with the beginning of the 1958 coal crisis and the resultant run-downs resulted in the measures required in the field of coal policy being restored to the national level. The reason was mainly that the varying interests of the individual EC Member States ruled out any Community settlement of the crisis; this aspect will be touched upon again later.

Having outlined in our remarks the interests in Germany in respect of coal, we showed our attempt to pinpoint the reasons for the lack of a Community coal policy.

Finally, an effort will be made to draw general conclusions as regards the process of integration.

The first and most important reason for the lack of a common coal policy can be said to be differences in the basic organization policy tenets of the Member States of the European Community. Full statement would seem at first not very discerning since Germany, like other States too, was and is prepared to apply sectoral controls in this field; basically, despite all arguments, Germany is attached to the principles of free market economics. It is therefore—in the case of the Federal Government's coal policy decisions—not a question of a change in the basic ideas on organization but a pragmatic reaction to the difficulties of the coal mining industry described above. The application of similar rulings in other fields is therefore not a current problem for the Federal Government.

An essentially different attitude can be seen in other EC Member States, especially the "Coal States" (Britain, France and Belgium).

A further aspect is the varying pattern of interests in the separate States, which is determined by their specific situations any given time.

There, in the case of Germany, special mention should be made of the difficult conditions of coal mining which result in high costs. Attempts have been made to overcome the resultant competitivity problems with a whole series of measures (import quotas, guaranteeing sales in important fields, financing of stockpiles, etc.).

In this connection it is interesting to note that there is considerable harmony between the Commission's proposals and the measures adopted in Germany.

The outside is faced with the question as to whether a common coal policy —against the background of a completely changed energy policy—would be possible at all, since coal policy should always be viewed in the overall context of energy policy.

The considerable structural differences between the coal States is not the least important factor to be mentioned. Germany is characterized by its federated structure and, e.g., in contrast to Britain and France, the private enterprise organization of the undertakings. The result is that there are more protagonists on the coal scene (e.g., the Federal Länder and the coal mining undertakings).

It can therefore be concluded that considerable limitations affective against a common policy exist in respect of coal.

We shall now try to arrive at certain more general conclusions regarding the process of integration. Owing to the worldwide complex of energy policy problems, the first question to be asked is whether or not the decision-making framework of the European Community is sufficient for the purpose of reaching adequate solutions. There are, after all, international organizations equally concerned with energy questions; for example, NATO, the OECD Energy Committee and especially the International Energy Agency (IEA).[25]

The attraction of the IEA, is due among other things, to the fact that it seems more appropriate as a framework for solving problems. This is nevertheless only one aspect; much more important—as regards the European Community—is that the eight Member States, excluding France, represented in the IEA obviously prefer the form that intergovernmental collaboration takes in the IEA. The proof of this is, for example, that discussions on the

Commission's proposal for a set of rules to meet the crisis, put forward immediately after the oil crisis, have not yet been concluded.

In the IEA, however, a similar proposal was approved in short order.

The fact that forms of intergovernmental collaboration have been recently preferred more and more to the EC decision-making process is also manifest in other fields such as European Political Cooperation (EPC) as well as the rising importance of the European Council.

As we see it, there are two essential reasons for this, namely, the greater flexibility of this kind of collaboration and the possibility inherent in this procedure of greater consideration being given to the attitudes adopted by the separate Member States.

Since it is obvious that each Member State of the European Community attaches great importance to energy policy, the question arises why this field is not a suitable one for initiating and promoting the process of integration as was the ECSC at the beginning of the 1950's.

We believe answering this question throws up ideas which in quite general terms help to explain the stagnation at present affecting the process of integration.

Considerable changes in the internal and external fields of force: Whereas coal was the clearly dominant energy-carrier at the beginning of the 1950's, therefore and that consequently, it was a vital interest of all six ECSC countries to pool—and thus to control this sector by means of a Community —the energy policy landscape, and hence also the pattern of interests of the separate countries, have fundamentally changed. Coal is now one of several energy-carriers which has a very varying share in the primary energy consumption of the EC Member States; these states are consequently dependent to different degrees on imports (e.g., as is the case with petroleum). Another problematic factor here is Britain's new role as an oil producer.

Doubts on the flexibility of the Community system: Thus there is hesitation to relinquish authority to the Community in the field of energy policy since it is believed that reaction to unforeseen developments can be quicker under a national administration.

General reservation over closed markets: Mainly because the CAP is regarded as a "deterring example"; the great structural differences in the case of coal would complicate a similar organization of the market still more.

Great reluctance to relinquish authority in view of the development of the decision-making process in the EC ("package deal"): The fact that today many Community decisions come about through the "package deal" process deters Member States from bringing other fields under the Community system. They fear an "overloading" of the decision-making process which would even more heretofore hinder arriving at realistic decisions.

Great reluctance to take further steps towards integration in view of the expected accession of new members: Since additional difficulties, especially in the decision-making process, are expected from the accession of new Member

States to the Community, nobody is currently prepared to introduce initiatives for Community solutions in such a complex field as that of energy policy.

The reasons demonstrate that coal policy as an item by itself is not suitable for promoting integration. Nevertheless it also remains true that each Member State of the European Community assigns paramount importance to energy policy. For the advancement of the development of the Community within the framework of the EC, our deciding factor will consequently be whether there is success in deriving from this interest some new motivation potential and new impulses for the continuance of integration.

THE MOST IMPORTANT MEASURES AFFECTING THE COAL MINING INDUSTRY, IN CHRONOLOGICAL ORDER

1959   Law on the tariff quota for solid fuels
1963   Law on the furtherance of rationalization in the coal mining industry
1965   Law on increasing the consumption of hard coal in power stations (first electricity-from-coal law)
1966   Law safeguarding the use of hard coal in the electricity industry (second electricity-from-coal law)
1968   Law on the adaptation and streamlining of the German coal mining industry and German coal mining areas
1969   Regulation on the criteria to be adopted for determining the optimum sizes of production units in the coal mining industry
      Signature of the agreement to set up the Ruhrkohle AG
1970   Amendment to the petroleum taxation law
1971   Complete plan published for the adaptation of Ruhrkohle AG
      More funds made available for Ruhrkohle AG by the Government of Land North Rhine/Westphalia
1972   Coal produced in the Ruhr subsidized by the Federal Government and the Government of Land North Rhine/Westphalia
1973   Federal Government's overall energy policy programme
1974   Technology programme published by the Government of Land North Rhine/Westphalia
      First extension of the Federal Government energy programme
      Law further ensuring that coal produced within the Community is consumed by the electricity industry (third electricity-from-coal law)
1975   Additional incentives for consuming hard coal in the electricity industry
1976   National reserve stock of coal set at 10 million tonnes
1977   Key figures for extending the energy programme;
      1977–1980 programme of energy research and energy technologies.

NOTES

1. The Working Party consisted of: Prof. Dr. Rudolf Hrbek, Bärbel Burkhardt and Wolfgang Schumann of the Institute of Political Science, University of Tübingen, and also Dr. Lothar Rall of the Institute for Applied Economic Research.

2. Dr. Karlheinz Reichert, ECSC Coal Policy, Brussels, 1976.

3. Our thanks go to Dr. Joachim Grawe, Head of Section in the Baden-Württemberg Ministry of Economic Affairs and to Dr. Karlheinz Reichert, Director responsible for coal in the Directorate-General for Energy of the Commission of the European Communities for a wealth of useful advice. We are also indebted to Prof. Dr. Fritz Burgbacher, Director Gerd Springorum and the German National Coal Mining Association (Gesamtverband des deutschen Steinkohlenbergbaus) for supplying material.

4. Wolfgang J. Mückl, Die Auswirkungen der Energieverteuerung auf die Wirtschaft der Bundesrepublik, in: Der Bürger im Staat, 1976, Vol. 1, p. 3 et seq.

5. Wolfgang J. Mückl, *loc. cit.*, p. 3.

6. Cf. Wolfgang Mückl, *loc. cit.*, p. 4.

7. Wolfgang J. Mückl, *loc. cit.*, p. 4.

8. Wolfgang J. Mückl, *loc. cit.*, p. 4.

9. Of this the electricity supply services accounted for 16.6% in 1960 and 31.7% in 1975, thus almost doubling their share.

10. Estimates.

11. Forward estimates.

12. The colliery coke ovens produced 26.9 million tonnes in 1975 and 1976, while the independent coke ovens produced 35.8 million tonnes in 1975 and 36.5 million tonnes in 1976.

13. Commission Decision 528/76 ECSC, Article 4 (1).

14. This very low figure reflects the different social security system in the United Kingdom, and to that extent is not a reliable yardstick.

15. One reason being that the Federal Land Governments undertook substantial guarantees when it was founded.

16. See also on page 159.

17. The coal Länder cover one-third of all the Federal Government's measures in the coal sector.

18. Gesamtverband des deutschen Steinkohlebergbaus (publisher), Annual Report 1975/76, page 72.

19. See, in this connection, section 3.4.

20. This price was calculated by a Court of Arbitration and is adjusted in accordance with the fluctuations in the price for American coking coal.

21. See table 3.

22. For comparison, see Industriegewerkschaft Bergbau und Energie: Jahrbuch 1974/75, Bochum 1976.

23. Only Belgium temporarily took similar measures.

24. "Guidelines and key figures for the extension of the energy programme 1977" in Bulletin der Bundesregierung (Federal Government Bulletin) No. 30, p. 269.

25. The IEA, without France, was set up in 1974 with the aims of uniting consuming countries, normalizing relationships with OPEC and adopting rules to meet the crisis.

III. CONCLUSIONS

Findings of the Group on Coal Policy

by *Jean Rey*

1. The group, under the chairmanship of Mr. Jean Rey, concluded that a fully implemented coal policy of the Community does not exist. In comparison to the early years of the ECSC when the energy source coal was the vehicle of the integration, coal policy is renationalized. There are two main reasons for that:
- coal policy today is part of the energy policy which again does not exist as a Community policy,
- coal policy in the national framework is, due to the structural change of the energy market (substitution of coal by oil), a policy aiming to maintain indigenous coal production or to direct its run down. Contributions from the treasuries are necessary. The one making the necessary funds available dictates what is to be done.

2. The non-existence of a common energy policy figuring on the Council's agenda since 1957 has many reasons (see also the discussion in the group "Energy policy"):
- links with foreign, defence, research, economic growth and employment policies. In these fields the interests and attitudes of the Member States are not parallel. There is no sufficient scope for a consensus necessary for the self-advised rule of unanimity
- the basic economic philosophies of the Member States (free market economy/dirigism) differ widely. This is reflected in the organization of the national energy markets (role of competition, monitoring via prices, governmental interference in the undertakings' policies, etc . . .)
- the enlargement of the Community—the first and the coming—furthers the diversity of interests thus diminishing the scope for consensus
- the uncertainty about the long-term development of the economy and the role of energy therein is growing. It is believed that unforeseen problems can be tackled more flexibly and efficiently within the national framework and much less on Community level. One can tend to close the eyes before the fact that a Community energy policy would aim to avoid negative surprise
- the weak majorities carrying present Governments lead to an incapacity to act or a lack of readiness for sacrifice (= ability to compromise) on Community level.
This enumeration is not exhaustive.

3. Since the shrinkage of the Community coal mining industry until the 1973 energy crisis hard coal holds a share of only 20% in the primary energy consumption—in some countries more, in others much less. Although

Community coal together with on-shore hydrocarbons represents on the supply side the most secure energy source, its importance apparently is not very appreciated because of this (still shrinking) share.

4. Only four out of nine Member States are coal producers. In Europe coal policy always carries components of employment and welfare policy. Since there does not yet exist a Community employment policy (EMU) some Member States tend to look at the coal problem in the other coal producing countries as a problem of national responsibility rather than a question of common energy policy.

5. The question is justified if the existence of direct and far reaching powers (in former days one was allowed to speak about supranational powers) of the executive within the framework of the ECSC Treaty does not enable the Commission to design a dynamic coal policy which might lead via a spill-over-effect to a progress in Community energy policy. But this possibility is not real because the supranational powers of the executive prevail in those sectors where they cannot influence the present situation and role of Community coal (non-discriminatory access of consumers to coal, provisions for cartels and mergers, etc . . .) or these powers alone do not suffice to realize the objectives (investment loans, grants for technical research, grants for redundant miners, etc . . .).

Measures considered necessary today to develop a common coal policy can be based only on Art. 95 of the ECSC Treaty (an Article for cases not foreseen within the Treaty) which supposed the unanimous assent of the Council before the Commission's decisions. It is obvious that this is not the way and means by which to realize a dynamic Community coal policy—with or without a spill over.

COMMODITIES POLICY

I. Report   S. Bertoletti
II. Counter-report   Geoffrey Goodwin and James Mayall
III. Conclusions   David Marquand

I. COMMODITIES POLICY[1] REPORT

Commodities in the Developing and Industrialized Countries

by *S. Bertoletti*

This report deals with commodities, i.e., those products which go through the minimum of transformation required to qualify them as merchandise (e.g., cereals, bulk minerals) and playing a specific part in world economy, particularly in world trade. But those commodities which are mainly used for the production of energy (coal, oil, etc.) will not be dealt with here.

Commodities are at the basis of the very sharp contrast between industrialized and developing countries. But one should not assume that the specific role of commodities is due to the fact that developing countries are the exclusive or principal suppliers of the industrialized countries: with the exception of tropical products, such an assumption is false. The role of commodities is to be found in the very nature of underdevelopment. Underdevelopment deprives developing countries of the *possibility* of transforming the commodities they produce. The result is that commodities provide the most part, and in some cases almost the totality, of the export revenues of those countries.

This situation is often aggravated by the dominant position held by a single commodity in the exports of one or another of these countries. This is illustrated in Table 1 based on the list (picked as a sample) of the developing countries taking part in the CIEC.

In the case of the industrialized countries, outside dependence for the supply of commodities varies according to the country and commodity concerned. This is illustrated by Table 2 covering the EEC, USA and Japan which lists—again as an example—the commodities selected by the Fourth UNCTAD Conference held in Nairobi in May 1976. One notes above all the particularly fortunate position of the USA with regard to oil seeds, cotton, phosphates, iron ore, copper and to a lesser extent tin. It should be added that certain figures for import dependence for the USA are misleading in that only small quantities of the products in question are imported as they can be replaced without difficulty by local products (e.g., jute, hard fibres and tropical wood). EEC and Japanese import dependence is fairly comparable except for tea, sugar, meat and bauxite, and on the whole much higher than that of the USA. However, in the case of the EEC, compared to the USA, meat and sugar figure as exceptions.

It would also, of course, be wrong to oversimplify matters by assuming from the outset that the problem of commodities arises only with regard to the relations between industrialized countries and the developing countries which supply them.

For this purpose, the sample of commodities shown in Table 2 is not quite representative, either for the EEC (see e.g., the commercial problems raised by the common agricultural policy) or for the developing countries (see e.g., the marked dependence of the latter on industrialized countries for food products from temperate climates).

However, it can be assumed that in the relations between the industrialized countries themselves or in their role as suppliers of the developing countries, commodities form only one category of merchandise among others, and the problems they involve are usually not the most overwhelming.

In the light of the present international situation, this report purposes mainly to deal with the question of commodities in relations of the EEC and other industrialized market economy countries with developing countries. For this reason we shall base the discussion on the list of commodities selected by the UNCTAD—Nairobi.

HISTORICAL BACKGROUND

Introduced at the end of the 18th century, industrialization very rapidly put Western Europe in a position of growing dependence on many commodities, such as cotton. In spite of technological break-throughs (e.g., the development of the sugar beet industry in France during the First Empire), the dependence of Western Europe increased steadily up to the present day because of the limitations of the temperate climate and of its moderate mineral resources. This was one of the reasons for the great colonial enterprises of the 19th century.

In the period between the two wars, the instability of the raw materials market, which was caused particularly by the economic crises of the thirties, had already shown that remedial action was called for in this field; however, the enduring colonial order maintained those powers most directly concerned in the illusion that the problem could be dealt with in the context of their empires.

Immediately after the Second World War, the supply of commodities still remained an acute problem; with the recent shortages still in mind, this question was the subject, along with that of liberalizing international trade, of the UN Conference on trade and employment held in Havana in 1948.

Looking back on it now, it can be said that those responsible for drafting the charter project (named the Havana Charter) proved to be remarkably far-sighted, as at the time the very concept of "developing countries" had not emerged. Still even less had emerged the collective expression and "class" solidarity in international organizations like the UNO of countries now described as developing countries.

The emancipation of the colonies and, more recently, their determined refusal of economic subordination—which in many cases could have replaced colonization, as it had long done in the cases of ancient empires dismantled in the 19th century—progressively transformed the question of commodities into one of the major international problems.

The non-ratification of the Havana Charter actually counts amongst the events with the most serious repercussions in the field of international relations and especially of the relations between developing and industrialized countries in particular.

Indeed, the merits of free enterprise and free trade provided excellent arguments against proposals frequently put forward to mitigate the defects of the raw materials market, proposals which met and still meet with objections of principle on the part of the most influential market economy countries. It is true that, at worst, the commodities market presented limited drawbacks for industrialized countries, taking into account the persistent development and economic prosperity achieved during the greater part of the period up to 1974. Yet, existing product agreements are often the purpose of consultation and mutual information only.

On the other hand, over the past 10 years or so, the developing countries, and especially those most recently decolonized, have frequently tried to join forces in order to secure an improvement of the terms of trade. There are slightly more organizations of developing countries alone, than organizations grouping both developing and developed countries together (see Table 3). It is even more remarkable that the most active amongst them, like CIPEC or the association of natural rubber producing countries (counting in, of course, also OPEC and OAPEC) are organizations of developing producing countries. A certain propensity toward confrontation was naturally felt in such international organizations.

With the Middle East crisis in 1973, the oil embargo, the price of crude oil unilaterally fixed at 4 times its previous value, and finally with the world economic crisis starting in 1974, commodity markets first experienced a general but short-lived increase in demand and prices, which then dropped again and durably stayed at very low levels. The effects of the crisis, especially on commodity prices, have demonstrated the strength of the oil producers and have only slightly eroded their initial advantage, although in the meantime an International Energy Agency (IEA) has been set up, according to American wishes, within the OECD, whose aim is to examine ways of protecting the interests of developed energy consuming countries. But, in reality, the circumstances are now different from what they were before 1974.

The Fourth UNCTAD Conference was held in Nairobi in May 1976, where the developed countries were faced with a successful coalition led by the developing countries of the "77" Group who called for a "new world economic order" with the support of the socialist countries. The developed countries had to agree to their demand to set up an Integrated Programme applicable to the 18 commodities of most interest to them.

Simultaneously the Conference for International Economic Cooperation (CIEC) was in progress between the 8 principal developed countries and the 19 developing commodity (including oil) producing and/or consuming countries. This conference came to a close on 2 June 1977, with a partial success; the developed countries actually confirmed their undertaking to implement the Integrated Programme without being given assurances as to oil supplies, but also without making concessions on the problems of indebtedness of developing countries.

THE PHILOSOPHY OF THE COMMISSION

The Commission's philosophy as to commodities is still in formation and cannot be defined. But it must be seen in relationship to the EEC treaty. As such, and in consideration of the above, particular reference should be made to: paragraphs d, g, and k of Article 3, part 1: Principles Articles 113 and 116, chapter 3: Commercial Policy, heading II, part 3; and part 4: Association of Overseas Countries and Territories.

The Commission is therefore responsible for paying particularly close attention to the problem of commodities in the light of world affairs and also its particular relationship with the African, Caribbean and Pacific countries (ACP) and submitting relevant proposals to the Council.

Generally speaking, the Commission's attitude to commodities was first illustrated in the following documents: "The supply of raw materials to the Community" (Bulletin of the European Communities, Supplement 1/75) and "Development and raw materials-current problems" (Bulletin of the European Communities, Supplement 6/75).[2]

Certain general principles emerge therefrom, for instance:
1. The search for balanced counterparts (stabilization of revenues and prices, access to markets and supplies, industrial cooperation and investment regimes, etc . . .) with reference to the demands of the developing countries.
2. The comprehensive approach, i.e., taking into account the specific characteristics of commodities and of producing countries.
3. The need to give due regard to past experience, including the merits of the existing set-up.

Following the agreements of Yaounde and Arusha, the Lomé Convention, concluded between the EEC and the ACP and effective as of February 1975 for a period of 5 years, is, in fact, an important experiment in organizing the relations between the EEC and the developing countries, especially as far as commodities (Title II of the Convention) and industrial cooperation (Title III) are concerned.

In terms of commodities, the essential instrument lies in a system of compensation (STABEX system), product by product, for the eventual decrease in export earnings of the ACP countries. To qualify for compensation, these decreases must
1. Apply to products shown on a list of 12 commodities or groups of commodities.
2. Exceed a certain minimum percentage (variable according to the ACP country concerned) in relationship to the average value of export revenues exceeding a certain minimum (variable according to the ACP country in question).
3. Apply to products which, during the year previous to the year of application, represented a percentage of total export revenues exceeding a certain minimum (variable according to the ACP country in question).

Taking these two threshold-minima into account, compensation is awarded by means of payments, the total amount of which cannot go beyond, for any beneficiary under the Convention, and over a period of 5 years, the sum of 375 million units of account received from the European Development Fund. The beneficiaries should theoretically reimburse these compensatory payments out of future revenues when these have reached an appropriate level. It should be added that, as sugar does not belong to the STABEX commodities, the EEC has, in the terms of the Lomé Convention, given certain ACP countries purchase guarantees of a fixed level and at the price guaranteed within the EEC.

Industrial cooperation is based on the context of commercial cooperation (Title I, especially: Unilateral Customs Franchise) and financial and technical cooperation (Title IV, especially: Project or Programme; Financing by the FED) established by the Lomé Convention, and provides for the setting up of an Industrial Cooperation Committee and an Industrial development Centre.

Whatever lessons can be learned from the results of the Lomé Convention and from the STABEX system in particular, the doctrine of the Commission cannot, of course, be a mere generalization of the practices which they introduced. In fact, the new doctrine of the Commission, which is gradually taking shape, is more influenced by the atmosphere of international discussions and negotiations which have been intensified since 1973.

COMMODITIES IN THE INTERNATIONAL FRAMEWORK AND THE REPRESENTATION OF THE COMMUNITY

Among the organizations dealing with commodities, particular mention must be made of:
- the OECD. This group of developed, market-economy countries pre-existed the Community, and fulfills, in fact, the part of a coordination forum. These countries constituting the "Western Side" are thus in a position to assess the extent to which concerted action is compatible with their particular interest and still compatible with the principle of loyal competition, which is part of their common doctrine. In the framework of OECD a specialized group is responsible for coordination as to commodities.
- the trade rounds of the GATT ("Multilateral Trade Negotiations", MTN). In the current round of the MTN, entitled "The Tokyo Round", the Commodity exporters have obtained an agreement that the general problem of access to the market will be examined for products requiring initial transformation and in exchange, the Community has requested that access to supplies be guaranteed.
- then, there are the UNO and the UNCTAD, where the most important of the developing countries and now most numerous have, since 1964, made themselves heard more and more forcefully in debates on commodities, until May 1976 when the Fourth Conference held in Nairobi was mainly devoted to this question. Parallel with UNCTAD one must mention another UNO organization, FAO, where commodities are examined especially from the point of view of adequate production levels and food security.
- finally, mention must be made of the North-South dialogue (Conference for International Economic Cooperation, CIEC) whose specialized commissions have held frequent sessions since February 1976, particularly the commission dealing with commodities. The CIEC represents a parallel

181

attempt to try to handle objectively the problems arising between developed and developing countries by limiting the number of participants to the most representative amongst them. The following split in 8 industrialized nations and 19 developing countries:

Industrialized countries	Developing countries	
EEC	Iran	Brazil
USA	Saudi Arabia	Mexico
Japan	Iraq	Argentina
Australia	Algeria	Venezuela
Canada	Nigeria	Peru
Spain	Egypt	Jamaica
Switzerland	Zaire	India
Sweden	Cameroon	Indonesia
	Zambia	Pakistan
		Yugoslavia

In the UNCTAD and CIEC there is the same sort of coordination as in the OECD between industrialized market-economy countries belonging to "Group B" of the UNCTAD and "the 8" of CIEC.

On the other hand, representation of the 9 Member States of the Community is different than that of UNCTAD and the CIEC.

At the CIEC, the community is represented by a single but two-headed delegation, the Commission/Council.

At the UNCTAD, although the Member States have their own delegations, the Community, which already for some time has had the status of observer in the UNO fora, is equally represented on its own. This representation is ensured both by the Council and by the Commission. In this hybrid scheme, the roles of the EEC Member States and of their two-headed organization (Commission/Council) are not perfectly defined.

In practice, however, in UNCTAD as in the CIEC, the position of the Community is elaborated through coordination in the groups of the Council on draft proposals generally prepared by the Commission.

THE UNCTAD RESOLUTION 93 (IV) AND ITS FOLLOW-UP

As a result of the Fourth Conference of the UNCTAD (Nairobi, May 1976) with regard to commodities, the main legal basis is now Resolution 93 (IV) of that conference. The adoption of this resolution has started off a process of preparatory work involving at least the following 18 commodities:

bananas	manganese
bauxite	meat
cocoa	phosphates
coffee	rubber
copper	tea
cotton and cotton yarns	tropical timber
hard fibres and products	tin
iron ore	vegetable oils including
jute and products	olive oils and oil seeds

This preparatory work is in theory aimed at the conclusion of a set of individual product agreements for all or part of the above-mentioned commodities as well as the creation of a common fund before the end of 1978, thus forming the "Integrated Programme".

Resolution 93 (IV) (document TD/RES/93 (IV)) should be situated—especially with regard to the subject we are dealing with here—in the background of the set of resolutions adopted at Nairobi, and most specially, Resolutions 94 (IV), and 87–88–89 (IV) (TD/RES/94 (IV) and TD/RES/87–88–89 (IV)), which deals respectively with the problems of indebtedness of the developing countries (the CIEC was implicitly put in charge of finding a compromise regarding this question) and the problems of transfer of technology.

The Community and the "Group B" countries (developed) approached the Nairobi Conference in a rather disorganized way. Even the coordination between Member States was never really effective during the course of this conference.

Indeed, the Community found itself committed because some of its Member States, together with the "Group B" countries, which were the least in favour of the Integrated Programme idea accepted at the last moment, "for the sake of peace", the solution which permitted the adoption of Resolution 93 (IV). In these circumstances, the adoption of Resolution 93 (IV) provoked interpretative declarations from several countries, and especially from the Federal Republic of Germany and from the USA, which define very precisely the bearing of their commitment. In this connection it must also be noted that the USA remained attached in principle to their proposal of an "International Resources Bank" which they had hoped to carry as a complement, if not an alternative, to the Integrated Programme.

It is therefore during the consultations and negotiations initiated by Resolution 93 (IV) and even more so in CIEC that it became and still will be necessary to iron out substantial residual differences, in particular between Member States, with regard to the bearing of commitments deriving from Resolution 93 (IV). At this stage we must therefore regard the report of the CIEC with its annexes (ref. document nr. 16) as complementary to the Nairobi resolutions already mentioned and as constituting bases for the question of commodities.

ACTION TO BE CONSIDERED

It would no doubt be helpful to review the measures which may be contemplated for international action and to outline their possible role in the present circumstances.

Financial co-operation

Financing of Action (Common Fund: Section III Para. 1 and Section IV Para. 1–3, Resolution 95 (IV))

The application of any intergovernmental measure implies appropriate financing. The very concept of an Integrated Programme is based on the idea that all commodities present similar problems. This could justify the setting up of a specific organ for the purpose of financing the measures to be decided upon. An alternative would have been to resort to the benefit of financially autonomous commodity agreements or arrangements and, in case of necessity, to the services of existing financial organizations, such as IMF, IBRD, private banks etc., and to drop the idea of setting up a new fund specifically for the financing of commodity action; there is no doubt that this alternative, although obviously ruled out by Resolution 93 (IV), would have been the preference of several Member States of the Community as well as the USA and Japan. No doubt, in spite of results achieved at the CIEC, their preferences will still bear on the work in progress to implement the Integrated Programme.

Compensatory Financing (Table 6, col. A; Section III. Para. 2–f, Resolution 93 (IV))

Where the producer-exporter countries of a particular commodity play a significant part in international trading, compensatory financing granted to these developing countries and ensuring the stabilization of the export revenues of this commodity could bring a solution to the drawbacks of the market. In favour of compensatory financing it could also be said that it could, in addition, aim at introducing some degree of compensation between producing countries with more or less favourable conditions as to production costs, and easy conveyance means for the product.

The idea of a generalized STABEX, though on the list of measures envisaged by Resolution 93 (IV), was the object of no serious proposal or study by the secretariat of UNCTAD. It did not get through at the CIEC either, in spite of a proposal by Sweden and the support of some Community countries for whom such a solution could theoretically represent an alternative or a complement to the Integrated Programme. One might therefore ask oneself if the STABEX idea to be applied either to all the commodities of the Integrated Programme and to all developing countries, or only to certain of these commodities and/or countries, should continue to be considered. It seems, unlikely, at the time of writing, that the Common Fund will be responsible for its financing.

Guarantees of investments and access to the capital market

The US proposal to create a specialized financial organ, called the International Resources Bank, was made without sufficient warning at the start of the Nairobi Conference. While the Integrated Programme is orientated towards measures acting on supply and demand, the IRB would bear on investments: apparently, it would provide financial motivation (participation in the financing of mining investments in particular) to harmonize investments (which is also, in a sense, part of industrial co-operation). It would also provide cover for "non-commercial risks" for the benefit of the investors and facilitate access to the private capital market.

184

As the USA continued to show a certain scepticism towards the very concept of the Integrated Programme, their proposal was regarded as a counter-initiative and was not adopted. The USA, however, fought back and put the matter before the CIEC, claiming that their proposal intended to fill a gap in the Integrated Programme (see ref. document: Interpretative declaration by the US delegation on Resolution 93 (IV)).

Looking now at the substance of the idea of guarantee of investments it is likely that the non-commercial risks involved in these investments, because of the changing circumstances in the host countries may, in some cases, have a dissuasive effect on the investors; similarly, it would perhaps be helpful to give technical assistance to the investors of the developing countries in turning to foreign capital markets and mobilizing their own domestic savings.

However, there is no apparent reason why the action called for by such problems should be limited to commodities. In the event, it is unlikely at this stage that the Community will give firm support to the USA's proposal of an IRB, partly, and in particular, for reasons of timing. It seems indeed difficult, in view of current circumstances, to establish a balance between advantages for the developing countries (who are only too prone to see themselves as targets of neo-colonialist design) and advantages for the industrialized countries. The CIEC did not reach a favourable conclusion on any one of the points covered by the US proposal, anyhow.

Technical and economical co-operation

Agreed, Guaranteed Outlets (Table 6, col. B, 1, Section III Para. 2–d, Resolution 93 (IV))

According to the terms of Resolution 93 (IV), only a complementary role would be attributed to measures of this kind which are merely referred to as "multilateral purchase and supply commitments". It is, in fact, hardly conceivable that this particular type of intergovernmental measure could be generally adopted among market-economy countries to remedy the drawbacks of the commodity markets. This very fact should, on the contrary, make one think of the stabilizing effect that both long-term "capitalist" and/or contractual ties and regular trade connections have on commodity trade flows. The cases of bauxite and iron ore illustrate this point, as does that of copper, in the case of the relationship existing, for instance, between the Canadian and US industries or that of Japan's copper supply policy.

It is perfectly conceivable that intergovernmental commodity measures aiming at putting a premium on the most stable and organized forms of commercial relations, that is, relations governed by commercial law, would be likely to bring about a generalization of practices which would contribute directly to the stabilization of export incomes and indirectly to that of the actual price level, without affecting the functioning of the terminal commodity markets. In this matter, views were not hopelessly divergent at the CIEC, nor especially contrary to the principles of free trade and free enterprise.

The European Community might be well advised to take initiatives at the right moment in order to fill one of the gaps in Resolution 93 (IV) and in the UNCTAD doctrine.

Production and Export Limitations (Table 6, col. C; Section III Para. 2–d, Resolution 93 (IV))

The laws guaranteeing free enterprise and competition in industrialized market countries are normally opposed to enforced or combined limitations to production. But exceptions to this principle are frequent—the sugar policy of the Community for example. In general, however, control of world supply by this method can hardly be envisaged. As the protectionist policy of slowing down or even restricting imports clashes with the principle of free trade, the industrialized countries and especially the Community, when confronted with structural surpluses will tend to be in favour of export controls; except, of course, if they export on a large scale themselves, which again, for instance, explains the Community's position in negotiating its participation in the sugar agreement.

Stabilization Stocking (Table 6, col. D; Section III Para. 2–a,b,c, Resolution 93 (IV))

Stabilization (buffer) stocking or combined stocking policies are in keeping with the principles of market economy, the most orthodox instruments. Accordingly, these kinds of measures, apparently also in response to a natural propensity, especially in UNCTAD, were chosen to form the foundation of the Integrated Programme. This is all the more remarkable in that such forms of action become less attractive when one considers that
1. Many commodities are not suited to any form of stocking.
2. Stocks are, by definition, unproductive (even if a profit is shown on paper, this profit represents a "painless" disguise for contributions made by purchasers and suppliers).
3. Stocking does not offer a direct solution to structural imbalances between supply and demand. In particular, the action of defending a "remunerative" price floor for long periods of excess production capacity is a difficult exercise.
   Moreover, setting up a buffer stock also implies choosing the price range which will have to be maintained. There is no doubt that periodic renegotiation of this price range, depending on world inflation, relationships between supply and demand, fluctuations in exchange rates, production costs etc., would always be both tricky and uncertain, it being well established that an inadequate price range would soon make the scheme ineffective because it would either run out of stocks or funds. In any case, the extent to which the CIEC fell short of bringing together the views of opposite parties on price stabilization can be judged by comparing the following alternative formulations:

"That all commodity agreements within the framework of the UNCTAD Integrated Programme or arrangements outside of it should include price or price ranges which should be periodically reviewed and automatically revised. Such revisions should take into account, *inter alia*, the movements in the prices of manufactured goods and services imported by developing countries from developed countries, prices of imported inputs, exchange rate changes and imported inflation from developed countries".

– proposed by the 19 developing countries

"That price stabilization around the long-term market trend could be sought in the context of individual commodity agreements where the producers and consumers concur that such agreements are appropriate and desirable. In this regard, the participants agree that where commodity agreements have pricing provisions these provisions could be periodically reviewed and appropriately revised taking into account, *inter alia*, levels of production and consumption, exchange rates, world stocks, and production costs including movements in the price of imported manufactured inputs".

– proposed by the 8 developed countries

In spite of the probable drawbacks and especially the ones mentioned above, one cannot *a priori* claim that buffer stocks or combined stocking policies could not work for certain commodities and under certain conditions. One can, therefore, say that the Community's attitude towards these measures will remain cautious and vary according to the commodity involved. Also, perhaps, the usefulness of stocks conceived as a relay or fly-wheel, specifically for long-term contractual purchase and supply commitments, should be examined. A more precisely limited range of application is implicit in such an idea and if it could be established that this advantage is real in terms of necessary financial means, this idea could also be considered as one of the measures to be applied under the "agreed or guaranteed outlets" mentioned above.

Concertation (Table 6, col. E; Section III Para. 2–e, Resolution 93 (IV))

No one apparently doubts the utility of continued contacts between the countries in a given commodity in order to discuss the current situation and prospects in the light of the latest facts, to compare points of view and to eventually arrive at a consensus on one or another line of action.

It seems taken for granted that such contacts or consultations, described here as "concertation", should, in order to be really effective, take place between producers and consumers and exclude as much as possible "political" distinctions such as developing-developed countries, market-economy countries and state-trading countries, and so on.

It must be noted, however, that in many cases, a country is concerned both as a producer and as a consumer and as exporter and importer of a given commodity. As for the modern capitalist industries themselves, organized as they are beyond geographical frontiers and sometimes on the basis of vertical integration, these can hardly be classified as producers or consumers only.

In any case, concertation on a given commodity cannot take place without an appropriate institutional set-up; once this is done the set-up will tend to become organized on a permanent basis, as is apparent in Table 3.

The Tables also show that no producer-consumer consultative body exists for most of the mineral commodities in the Integrated Programme or, indeed, for tropical wood. This could lead one to say that among the measures envisaged in the Integrated Programme, the organization of concertation on a commodity by commodity basis is of a very special nature as the purpose of such concertation is to achieve operational results, even if only with a limited scope each time.

In these circumstances, if the organization of such concertation precedes the conclusion of an agreement, it may tend to become a substitute for it, thus eschewing more binding or longer-term commitments which would justify an agreement. On the other hand, if and when concertation were envisaged in the framework of an agreement, this would mean that most commodity agreements would also, *ipso facto*, serve to organize the mechanisms of concertation on the commodity concerned. Thus, it is hardly surprising that whenever the industrialized countries, and especially the EEC, insisted on the necessity of organizing the concertation as soon as possible (e.g., in the case of copper, from the very beginning of the preparatory work under the Integrated Programme) even on a provisional basis, they failed, and the other side demanded that an agreement be first concluded. In the present conditions it seems probable therefore that concertation will mostly be a by-product of the preliminary work under the Integrated Programme.

What is perhaps even more important to stress is the fact that the option concertation v. commodity agreement could not be solved easily because it involves in reality a choice between two philosophies of action. We should therefore ask ourselves if we would be well advised to try and overcome it. From this point of view, it is relevant to observe that an important drawback —the worst perhaps—of permanently binding measures established under an international agreement for a (by necessity) relatively long period is due to the scarce reliability of economic forecasts. The experience of existing commodity agreements invariably shows that at some moment or other, and since their very entry into force, the measures provided for are found grossly ineffective or perhaps inapplicable under the prevailing circumstances.

It could thus be asked whether it would not be wiser to come out in favour of evolutive or, indeed, "à la carte" commodity agreements. Parties to the agreement would then essentially be committed to participate in the appositely established fora, and deliberate there on the measures most suitable for each period and for the particular case of each party, and also on the sharing of the corresponding burden.

With such a conception, it would probably be necessary to include in the agreement an exhaustive catalogue of the measures to which it would be permissible to resort, and for which the parties should waive the right to refuse to discuss or at least to take into account.

The agreement should provide for setting up monitoring and surveying means so as to provide the necessary information for the debates and also lay down the principle that the parties would be left, to the largest possible extent, with the responsibility to implement on an autonomous basis the agreed measures. This should result in limiting, to the largest extent possible, the needs for international financing.

Industrial Co-operation—Access to the Market (Table 6, col. F; Section III Para. 2–g,h,i,j, Resolution 93 (IV))

Industrial co-operation covers a group of actions which should result in enabling the exporting developing countries to increase the value of their commodity-based exports. This amounts to exporting processed commodities by installing the required transformation industries. This implies co-operation in technology transfer, concertation on the creation of new capacities which might involve the necessity for reconversion operations elsewhere, etc. In particular, it implies the principle that the raising, lowering or elimination of tariff and non-tariff obstacles to imports of the relevant processed products should also be subject to concertation. However, as Resolution 93 (IV) explicitly states, GATT is competent for these particular matters.

The place of industrial co-operation in commodity agreements or arrangements might, of course, vary considerably according to the commodity involved and it is difficult to give any indication at this stage except point out that the EEC countries could only agree to facilitate the transfer of activities if smooth transitions were assured. It should also be borne in mind that access to resources should be guaranteed to the developed countries as a counterpart for the concessions which the latter may be called upon to make in implementing the Integrated Programme; and this principle should therefore be emphasized whenever the occasion is appropriate. As a matter of fact, however, the 8 developed countries did not succeed in having this principle acknowledged at the CIEC even when they largely acknowledged the demands of the 19 developing countries on the points we are examining here. The problem of access to resources is of the highest importance for the Community, because of its dependence on imports. But because it goes beyond the domain of the study it cannot be done justice here.

The common fund—the cost of the Integrated Programme

If the conclusion of commodity agreements raises many problems, the nature and the role of a "common fund", leaving aside the principle of its being set up, is even more controversial.

As previously stated, Resolution 93 (IV) attributes a special role to this fund: that of financial pivot of the Integrated Programme. Actually, this fund is conceived as being called to finance all the measures taken under the commodity agreements resulting from the implementation of the Integrated Programme; as such, its intervention in the management of agreements and on the commodity markets would be paramount and would give its administrators such a considerable power, that some commodity producing countries themselves might well be reluctant to back the ideas.

On the other hand, one might ask whether the creation of a new source of finance specifically devoted to commodities is justified when there are already numerous international finance institutions, especially the IBRD and the IMF. Many of the industrialized countries, including members of the EEC, would have preferred this approach. Apart from these two extreme positions, one can at least see the merit of studying the possibility of a financial department bound by strict working rules which could, as a limited and subordinate

189

instrument, serve the purpose of a relay or link in the financing at market conditions of commodity agreements or perhaps only of certain kinds of measures taken under the commodity agreements.

Roughly speaking, this formed the initial position of the Community at the start of the negotiating conference opened in March 1977.

A reconciliation between the extreme points of view on a mutually acceptable definition of the Fund cannot be hoped for very soon, particularly because of the impossibility of making even an approximate estimate of the number or of the scope of the agreements or arrangements which will actually result from implementing the Integrated Programme. Accordingly, the conference must be suspended for the preliminary work to be resumed and more progress achieved.

On the part of both the Community and the USA, the positions gradually became more favourable (or less hostile) to the Common Fund (cf. European Council of 25-3-77), which, as already mentioned, enabled the CIEC to confirm the undertaking of setting up a common fund.

The EEC, in particular, is now engaging in the exercise of evaluating a Common Fund project covering stocks and eventually other measures. The possibility, which was once considered, that the Fund should include financing has been abandoned for the time being.

As for the UNCTAD secretariat, the last studies have been issued under references (TD/B/IPC/CF/L2,L3,L4). The UNCTAD evaluations are obviously quite inadequate to determine the means required for the whole of the Integrated Programme. Purely for information's sake it may be mentioned that, according to the following evaluations:

1. Financing the setting up of buffer stocks for 10 commodities, cocoa, coffee, tea, sugar, cotton, jute, sisal, rubber, copper and tin, would require globally an investment of $5 billion in the case of common financing (about $7 billion in the case of separate financing of 10 corresponding commodity agreements) at 1976 conditions. But if the number of products were reduced, the financial covering would also be reduced according to the economic weight and to the fluctuations of the respective commodities.
2. As a purely illustrative and arbitrary hypothesis, programmes for jute, hard fibres, tea, bananas and rubber, should make available financial aid on the order of $200 million a year to the producer countries.
3. Compensatory financing was not examined.

Obviously, other relevant studies, more often than not on specific topics or for specific purposes, may have been published and/or circulated in various places and capacities but generally committing only their authors. The estimates made out in such studies are neither comparable nor entirely in agreement. For some time already this subject was also the object of much reflection in the services of the EEC Commission where the current thinking is that:
1. It is arbitrary to put into account the financing for commodities covered by existing agreements.
2. The forecasting of the commodities which may qualify for future commodity agreements entailing measures and involving multilateral financing is still too doubtful—with the exception perhaps of forecasting their number

190

which could not amount to more than a few units, especially if one thinks in terms of buffer stocking.

3. It is impossible to forecast with reasonable accuracy (even being optimistic about it) the date of entry into force of possible new commodity agreements. This makes it impossible to project cost estimates for the measures which would eventually have to be implemented, in view of world inflation and especially in view of the evolution of the prices of the commodities concerned.

Thus, by mentioning here the estimates made by the UNCTAD secretariat, it is not intended to accept them as likely, and even less as accurate, but at most to indicate the orders of magnitude which have to be borne in mind when discussing the overall financing of the Integrated Programme. Indeed, the sheer bulk of this financing shows the extent to which the preparation of relevant decisions is still inadequate.

COMMODITY REVIEW

At this point it is necessary to characterize, even summarily, the commodities we are concerned with. This characterization includes two main features: the intrinsic properties of the commodity and their trade peculiarities, not forgetting the inconveniences involved in such trade. On the basis of a precise characterization, it will then be possible to discern by what means and with what practical applicability an international policy of commodities could be based. The method is not very original but, apart from the cases where measures are more or less obviously inapplicable, it can provide sufficient elements for political choice.

In so far as it would take too long to examine in detail the characteristics of the commodities and the possible means of action, we have summarized diagrammatically our findings in Tables 4 and 5.

First of all, one must stress that such terms as "agreement", "arrangement" or "measures" have no exact definition. All one can say is that "agreement" refers to an arrangement involving relatively far-reaching contractual commitments and subject therefore to ratification in the signatory countries. In any event, it is clear that the objective of an "agreement", or arrangement, is the establishment of certain measures which will be applied in given circumstances, but this in no way presupposes the nature of the measures involved.

Therefore, for example, to accept the principle of negotiating a commodity agreement in no way implies the *a priori* acceptance of setting up a buffer stock.

Similarly, we must emphasize that in the general schematic examination made here, in envisaging certain measures, we are ignoring the vast range of methods which could be adopted in the application of such measures.

These comments apply to this document as a whole, but it is particularly important to mention them before making any comments on individual commodities.

With this in mind, Table 6 aims at showing broadly the Community position at the present time in relation to the measures envisaged in Resolution

93 (V) of Nairobi, with the exception of the Common Fund. The table also shows that even at the UNCTAD, attention has up to now been almost exclusively limited to intervention on prices by means of buffer stocks, possibly completed by appropriate restrictive supply appointment measures, in spite of the fact that stocking is practically possible only for certain commodities. But, on the contrary, compensatory financing and outlet guarantees have been, in general, practically ignored although they are more broadly applicable.

In view of the wide range of measures envisaged in Resolution 93 (IV), this fact means, without doubt, that a useful discussion on operational details is still a long way off.

In fact, commodity agreements already exist for the following four commodities: tin, coffee, sugar and cocoa.

As for sugar, partial or bilateral agreements/arrangements existed already for a long time. These include, for instance, the Commonwealth Sugar Agreement, the USA preferential agreement, and the USSR-Cuba agreement. The "International Sugar Organization" (consultative with the EEC as an observer) and a multilateral sugar agreement have also existed since 1968, although the EEC rejected the export quotas in effect between 1969 and 1974. As the Commonwealth Sugar Agreement and the Community's own arrangements have been consolidated in the CAP and the Lomé Convention since the 1973 accession, the EEC is now prepared in theory to participate in the international sugar agreements, the negotiation for the renewal of which (at present temporarily discontinued) started in UNCTAD, 8 April 1976. The previous participants still stick to the idea of export quotas being the essential instrument of the agreement, but nonetheless strongly disagree between themselves. The EEC, on the contrary, proposes stocking measures as its principal tool; if quotas were to prevail, the EEC might propose an argument using the precedent of the special circumstances invoked in the special case made for the participation of the USSR that, in the terms of the agreement, the EEC should not be committed to comply with a quota but to bear the responsibility of an appropriate stocking policy.

It also must be pointed out that the EEC took the initiative to propose negotiating a framework agreement on meat, cereals and dairy products within the Multilateral Trade Negotiation of GATT.

As for the other commodities in the Integrated Programme, it is far more difficult to assess the Community position.

The advantages to the Community of well-balanced and efficient commodity agreements can be measured by taking into account:
1. The highly negative balance of foreign trade showing in the balance of payments for specific commodities of the Community.
2. The "sensitivity" of the markets of specific commodities.
3. The "vulnerability" of supplies (which is high if the producers are few, especially if most of them are at the same time developing countries).
4. How susceptible a given product is to be dealt with by regulations.

These criteria point particularly to copper, manganese, phosphates and rubber.

Actually, a rubber agreement can optimistically be envisaged in view of the limited number of producers of natural rubber and the proportion of the market that they are able to maintain because of its very specific properties compared to synthetic rubber.

Phosphates and, even more so, manganese are irreplaceable and "vulnerable". The Community would be wise to avoid finding itself confronted with a coalition of producer countries.

Finally, copper involves the most important interests and therefore also presents the biggest problems. On the Community's side, the need to establish the concertation is strongly felt. Being ready to envisage a formal agreement is perhaps a precondition to set up the framework of such concertation. The difficulty resides in the choice of the nature and the initial contents of such an agreement which would render it acceptable to all interested parties.

Schematically, the following comments can be made on the other commodities:

Iron ore and bauxite. Although the EEC negative trade balance is high as far as these commodities are concerned, especially iron ore, they are plentiful and accessible in many countries. Actually, the market of these commodities is fairly stable and, even if they are not completely subject to vertical integration, their market is in fact dependent on the evolution of the production of the corresponding metals.

Cotton, vegetable fats. The EEC negative trade balance is high for these commodities but they are very heterogeneous and there are numerous substitution products. The production of cotton fibre and cotton oil extracted from seeds are linked together just as the production of most vegetable fats also takes place in connection with the production of proteins. The principal world exporter of all these commodities is the USA.

Tropical timber. Although again the EEC negative trade balance is high, this is a very heterogeneous commodity which generally competes with wood produced in countries with temperate climates. Almost all paper pulp is also produced starting from the latter which is therefore at a greater economic advantage.

Jute, hard fibres. These commodities present moderate negative trade balance for the Community; as they are easily substituted, they are on the decline or at least stagnant.

Bananas, tea. These again present moderate negative trade balances and although they cannot be substituted, they are not indispensable. The possibility of a developing production means that, in many countries, the supply of these commodities cannot be considered as vulnerable.

For these commodities, the above comments do not, of course imply that the EEC would refuse to do anything. In certain cases it would seem to be reasonable to envisage *ad hoc* action to the advantage of the producers directly concerned: for example, jute and tea. In other cases, the Community could be satisfied with an agreement between producers, e.g., bananas. All in all, in most cases modest arrangements could be sought.

To conclude, it should be stressed that, speaking very generally, looking for overall solutions, however useful this is, will not exclude looking for partial solutions to be agreed upon by the important trade partners of the Community.

POSSIBLE DEVELOPMENT OF A EUROPEAN POLICY ON COMMODITIES

Should each Member State define its orientations and take part in multilateral negotiations by itself, or should all nine of them act jointly as a Community?

We have already shown that, mostly for historical reasons, the Member States have adopted divergent policies at the Nairobi Conference, as well as the difficulties which resulted from this. Although there would be little point in analysing here individually the national orientations and the ensuing disadvantages, it is fair to say that while the problem of supply in commodities is posed in very similar terms for all Member States, some of them are more inclined to envisage introducing international monitoring or international administrative control over the commodity market and would even be prepared to set up institutional operators, while others are only concerned with limiting to a minimum any interference with market forces. Others are mostly interested in preserving the advantage of their position as hosts to trade places of international importance for the price formation of given commodities, or in protecting the position of their own industry in the processing or the first manufacturing of given commodities.

These attitudes, all of which are quite legitimate, can no longer ignore demands with regard to commodities from outside Western Europe.

For the EEC, before the 1973 oil embargo, the negative balance in commodity trading was compensated for by the equally important and negative balance in oil product trading (in 1973, $14,9 million or so for the 18 commodities of Nairobi and $16,100 million for oil).

The abrupt increase of the oil balance to three or four times its value ($43,500 million in 1974, $50,000 million estimated for 1976) somewhat overshadowed the commodities where, on the contrary, prices generally slumped during the crisis years.

If growth was to become again a feature of the economic situation, the commodities balance could again become a serious handicap and even really harmful if the prices of some important commodities were to soar as the oil products did in 1973. The problem of commodities would be brought then before public opinion, the most concerned section of which is, of course, made up of the professional, commercial or industrial milieux.

These circles, because they instinctively mistrust any decision which might upset the practices they are accustomed to, are up to now very hostile to the notion of the Integrated Programme and to the stabilization of export revenues (compensatory financing) which, in their view, would bring about surpluses.

Their main concern, however, is supply security. Consequently, if the latter should be threatened by disorders affecting the commodity markets, they might accept living with multilateral measures as a lesser evil as long as these were applied empirically on a case by case basis and even industrial co-operation, including (admittedly, to a safely controlled extent) access to the market, but accompanied by serious guarantees concerning investments abroad.

As for public opinion in general, apart from the obvious manifestations of discontent and demands on the part of the "third world"—in the name of "a new world economic order"—it is probably not clearly aware of the changes which have occurred in the relations of force. In the new situation the potential solutions to many world problems, especially that of commodities, will also have to be thought out anew.

For a European country, the chances of success of defensive tactics lie obviously in the intrinsic merits of proposals or counter-proposals made, but perhaps to a larger extent still, in their convergence with those of neighbouring countries, acting in a spirit of solidarity.

The necessity to elaborate on these bases of Community attitude as to commodities results just as much, if not more, from the general necessity for solidarity (on which the Treaty is based) than from the obligations actually laid down in the Treaty. In fact, third countries often seem to expect solidarity to manifest itself in all fields as a natural, inevitable consequence of the existence of the Community.

Although the background of the problem of commodities is largely the same for all the Member States, there exist very distinct national attitudes, due to historical circumstances. These differences make the formulation of a Community policy much more difficult. As in many other cases, it is the practical necessity for each Member State not to remain isolated in international discussions or negotiations, which progressively might lead to a common Community position.

Since the Community has the natural function of ensuring this convergence in view of conducting a Community action (or at least, common actions, in the sense of Article 116 of the Treaty), there is no doubt that it guarantees the best possible chances of success. Were this its only merit, the CIEC would have been permitted to establish this principle, the validity of which applies unquestionably to the negotiations on commodities at large.

Although the elements available at present still present many gaps, we can realistically assume that by going from harmonizing national positions to progressively defining piecemeal Community positions, the pieces of the jigsaw puzzle can be sorted out to form a coherent European policy on commodities.

At the present stage we can, of course, only try and guess what direction this will take and even then, only very generally.

The general guidelines might be the following:

1. Make a general rule of the participation of the Community, *qua* Community, in the negotiation and application of all multilateral measures (or agreements) relative to commodities, independently of the continuation of other eventually more stringent commitments undertaken by the Community within a policy of association with certain countries (ACP countries and global Mediterranean policy for instance).

2. As a general rule, aim at satisfying the demands of balance and continuity, by means of permanent structures of concertation on each individual product involving both producers and consumers. These structures themselves may differ according to the cases at hand, varying from simple study groups to commodity agreement management councils.

3. Applying the principle of Community participation in taking over the burden deriving from the implementation of arrangements or agreements

(along with other consuming/importing countries and the producing/exporting countries).

4. Introduce corrective measures to the freedom of the market with caution and resorting, as much as possible, to self-discipline and co-operation between the economic operators involved.

5. Make it a general rule, in the examination of problems and solutions, to give due importance to the developmental aspect and to the necessarily progressive transformation of industrial and commercial structures of all the countries concerned.

6. By preference to the application of a pre-established uniform scheme, seek out individual commodity-by-commodity-solutions to be adjusted, if necessary, according to the parties and the periods concerned and making any changes from the present situation as smooth as possible.

NOTE

1. This report was originally prepared during the first half of 1977. Even in its present slightly revised form it could not be expected to perfectly reflect later developments. Also it should be regarded as presenting the author's personal views, expressed in a purely personal capacity.

2. This document consists of 4 surveys concerning international development strategy for the second decade of the United Nations, the problems of raw materials and the relationship with the developing countries, product agreements, and international action for stabilizing import revenues.

TABLE 1. *Part of exports (in value) of the developing members of CIEC, by principal commodities (average 1970–1972)*

Developing countries	Total Exports in value (10^3 $)	By commodities %
Iran	3,275.0	Oil 77.2, Cotton 2.1: Total 79.3
Saudi Arabia	3,120.0	Oil 94: Total 94
Iraq	1,335.0	Oil 94: Total 94
Algeria	1,022.7	Oil 76.1, Iron 1.2: Total 77.3
Nigeria	1,743.7	Oil 73.4, Cocoa 10.4, Arachide 3.8, Rubber 1: Total 88.6
Egypt	792.0	Cotton 46.9, Rice 7.8: Total 54.7
Zaire	699.7	Copper 64.2, Coffee 6.8, Palm oil 3.4, Zinc 3.6, Tin 2.8, Rubber 1.7: Total 82.5
Zambia	812.7	Copper 94.1, Zinc 1.6: Total 95.7
Cameroon	218.7	Coffee, 26.5, Cocoa 22.8, Wood 9.1, Cotton 5.1: Total 63.5
Brazil	3,211.0	Coffee 28, Sugar 7.1, Iron 7, Cotton 5, Meat 3.5, Wood 2.7, Cocoa 2.1: Total 55.4
Mexico	1,566.0	Cotton 8.3, Sugar 7, Coffee 5.7, Meat 3, Silver 1.9, Oil 1.7: Total 26.6
Argentina	1,818.0	Meat 17.4, Corn 14.5, Wheat 5.2, Leather 5.1, Wool 3.8: Total 46
Venezuela	3,169.7	Oil 86.8, Iron 4.5: Total 91.3
Peru	952.3	Fish 28.1, Copper 21.7, Sugar 7.4, Silver 6, Iron 6.7, Tin 5.7, Cotton 5: Total 80.6
Jamaica	351.3	Bauxite 25.5, Sugar 11, Bananas 4.1, Oil 2.6: Total 43.2
India	2,154.7	Iron 7.1, Tobacco 2.7, Coffee 1.8, Cotton 1.2: Total 12.8
Indonesia	1,255.7	Oil 43.4, Rubber 17.5, Wood 12.7, Coffee 5.4, Tin 5, Tea 2.1: Total 86.1
Pakistan	680.3	Cotton 15.2, Rice 7.2, Tobacco 3.1: Total 25.5
Yugoslavia[1]	2,852.6	Meat 5.6, Wood 5.5, Copper 3.1, Corn 1.4, Zinc 0.9: Total 16.5

1. 1973

TABLE 2. *Dependence of the EEC, USA and Japan on external sources of supply for commodities of the UNCTAD Integrated Programs for Commodities (net imports as % of consumption)*

Commodities	EEC	USA	Japan
Coffee	100	100	100
Cocoa	100	100	100
Tea	100	100	~18
Sugar	<0	45.6	70.6
Bananas	100	100	100
Oleaginous	78	<0	95
Meat	2	1.9	23
Cotton	100	<0	100
Jute and products	100	100	100
Rubber	100	100	100
Tropical wood	100	100	100
Phosphates	100	<0	100
Bauxite (Primary Aluminium)	36 (65)	100 (100)	100 (100)
Iron ores	63	35	90
Manganese	~100	~100	~100
Copper	99	8.1	92.7
Tin	~94	~83	~92
Hard fibres and products	100	100	100

N.B. <0 applies to exporting countries.

TABLE 3. *Intergovernmental organizations of producers or of producers and consumers of commodities* (*Organizations of research, of consultation or of management of agreements*)

| Commodities | Organizations of producers | | Producers and consumers organizations |
	Developing only	Developing and developed countries	
A. *Metals*			
Tin	International Tin Research Council[1]	—	International Tin Council (agreement body)
Lead/Zinc	—	—	Lead and zinc International Study group
Copper	CIPEC	—	—
Tungsten	—	primary Tungsten Assoc.	Tungsten committee UNCTAD
Mercury	—	International Mercury producers Assoc.	—
Silver	Assoc. of exporting countries silver[2]	—	—
B. *Minerals*			
Iron	—	Assoc. of Iron ore exporting countries	—
Bauxite	—	International Bauxite Assoc.	
Phosphates	—	World Phosphates Institute	—

1. An organization both intergovernmental and private.
2. Only Peru and Mexico.

TABLE 3. (Continued)

Commodities	Developing only	Developing and developed countries	Producers and consumers organizations
		Organizations of producers	
C. *Refreshing produces, spices*			
Coffee	Several regional organizations[1]	. . . . . .	International Coffee Council (agreement body)
Cocoa	Cocoa producers Alliance	. . .	International Cocoa Council (agreement body)
Tea	—	. . .	FAO[3] Intergovernmental group
Tobacco	—	—	FAO Ad hoc meetings
Pepper	Asian Pepper Community	. . .	FAO Ad hoc meetings
D. *Natural Fibres*			
Wool	—	Intern. Wool Secretariat[2]	International group study wool
Cotton	—	International Cotton Institute[3]	International Cotton consultative committee
Jute	—	—	FAO[3] Intergovernmental group
Hard Fibres	—	—	FAO[3] Intergovernmental group
E. *Basic Vegetable food products*			
Cereals	—	—	FAO Intergovernmental group
Wheat	—	—	International Wheat Council (agreement body)
Rice	—	—	FAO Intergovernmental group
Sugar	—	—	International Sugar Council (agreement body)
Oleaginous & fat matters of vegetable origin	—	—	FAO Intergovernmental group

1. African, Central-American, Latin-American.
2. Intergovernmental organizations financed by voluntary contributions, private or public, also by consumers.
3. Informal group to prepare measures eventually to be taken.

TABLE 3. (Continued)

| Commodities | Organizations of producers | | Producers and consumers organizations |
	Developing only	Developing and developed countries	
Arachides	African Arachide Council	—	—
Coconuts	Asian coconuts Community	. . .	—
Olive Oil	—	—	International Olive Oil Council
Wine	—	—	FAO Intergovern-mental group
F. Raw materials of biological origin			
Rubber	Association of Natural Rubber producing (Asian) countries	. . .	International Rubber Study group
Leather	—	—	FAO and UNCTAD Ad hoc meeting
G. Perishable foodstuffs			
Meat	—	—	FAO Intergovern-mental group
Milk products	—	—	OECD Consultations
Bananas	Union of Bananas exporting countries	. . .	FAO Intergovern-mental group
Citrus fruit	—	—	FAO Intergovern-mental group

Sources: Documentation of the Commission of the European Community.

TABLE 4.   *Characteristics of commodities. Properties and 1973 Production. . .:*
characteristic meaningless or value existent; –: not assessed or useless

Properties	Congestion[1]	Danger of degradation	Homogeneity	Stocking possibilities	Renewable, affected by weather conditions	Possibility of recuperation/substitution	Vertical ties from natural sources up to commercial form	World Produc Quantity (thousands of t)	Average yearly growth
Metals									
copper	0.15	weak	high	easy	no	high	modest	7,509	
tin	0.18	weak	high	easy	no	weak	weak	219.8	
Ores									
iron	0.33	...	modest	possible	no	...	notice-able	326,100	
manganese	0.32	...	modest	possible	no	...	weak	22,287	
bauxite	0.64	...	modest	prohibi-tive	no	...	notice-able	72,750	
phosphates	0.5	...	modest	prohibi-tive	no	...	modest	25,161	
Refreshing beverages									
coffee	1.5	modest	notice-able	easy	yes	...	...	4,193	
cocoa	1.5	modest	notice-able	easy	yes	...	...	1,355	
tea	2.5	impor-tant	modest	possible	yes	...	...	1,535	
Natural Vegetables Fibres									
cotton	1.7	weak	notice-able	possible	yes	modest	weak	13,080	
jute	1.7	weak	notice-able	possible	yes	modest	weak	3,961	
hard fibres	1.7	weak	notice-able	possible	yes	modest	weak	905	
Basic vegetable foodstuffs									
sugar	1	weak	high	easy	yes	...	weak	78,917	
oleaginous	1.1	modest	modest	possible	yes	...	weak	135,022	
Vegetable raw materials									
tropical wood	1.5	modest	weak	possible	no	...	weak	999,213	
rubber	1.2	impor-tant	modest	possible	yes	weak	weak	3,453	
Perishable foodstuffs									
bananas	3	high	modest	prohibi-tive	yes	...	notice-able	34,978	
meat	2	high	modest	prohibi-tive	yes	...	notice-able	109,751	

1. Apparent specific volume for transport (and stocking) m³/t.
2. Of quantity index base 73.

OECD %	GINI Index 1963–1975%	EEC Production			US Production			Production of Japan		
		Quantity	Yearly average growth 1963–1975	GINI Index 1963–1975	Quantity	Yearly average growth 1963–1975	GINI Index 1963–1975	Quantity	Yearly average growth 1963–1975	GINI Index 1963–1975
40.9	3.6	1,515	...	...	1,558	2.6	10.5	91	—1.7	5.5
8.2	3.1	4.1	—	—	...	...	...	0.8	...	...
40.5	—	72,900	—	—	88,600	—	—	1,000	...	...
26.6	—	25.6	—	—	—	—	—	189	—	—
30.9	6.1	3,022	1.3	6.6	1,909	2.3	6.7	...	...	...
64.7	4.8	4,891	3.7	4.5	6,232	5.3	5.4	736	0.6	5.5
/0	16.3	...	...	...	0.9	...	...	...	...	...
)/0	10.1	...	...	...	...	...	...	...	...	...
6.2	4.4	...	...	...	...	...	...	95	2.1	—
24.0	4.2	...	...	...	2,821	1.7	—	...	...	...
—	8.5	...	...	...	...	...	...	...	...	...
.2	5.5	...	...	...	...	...	...	...	...	...
28.7	3.5	9,940	1.9	—	5,397	1.5	—	630	2.2	—
44.9	3.3	3,881	3.6	—	48,830	4.7	—	217	0.0	—
)/0	2.7	...	...	...	...	...	...	...	...	...
)/0	3.9	...	...	...	...	...	...	...	...	...
.2	3.9	...	...	...	...	...	...	...	...	...
48	—	17,361	3.3	—	22,259	2.1	—	1,856	11.9	—

TABLE 5. *Characteristics of commodities: 1973 trade*
(...: meaningless)

	Prices		World Exports					EEC Balance		USA Balance		Balance of Japan	
	Formation	Level 1973	Quantity (millions of t)	Value (millions of $)	Average yearly growth 1963–1975	GINI Index 1963–1975[1]	Concentration of exports[2]	Quantity	Value	Quantity	Value	Quantity	Value
Metals													
copper	Supply and demand	1,82[3]	4.6	6,000	—	14.6	6	−1	−2,000	−0.14	−250	−0.9	−1,200
tin	Supply and demand	4,834	0.2	950	—	—	3	−0.1	−500	−0.05	−200	−0.04	−160
Ores													
iron	Producers	25	337.3	3,411	—	—	6	−120	−1,600	−40	−500	−135	−1,700
Minerals													
manganese	Producers	36	13.0	560	—	—	3	−3.5	−104	−0.7	−35	−3.4	−92
bauxite	Producers	8[4]	28.1	230	—	—	5	−4.5	−77	−13	−158	−5.5	−63
phosphates	Producers	...	55.5	600	—	—	4	−16.6	−310.8	+13.3	+171.0	−3.2	−74.5
Refreshing beverages													
coffee	Supply and demand	1,160	3.7	4,223.0	6.5	8.4	13	−1.2	−1,497.0	−1.4	−1,567.8	−0.1	−119.7
cocoa	Supply and demand	1,060	1.1	942.1	13.0	17.1	5	−0.5	−453.2	−0.3	−277.2	−0.05	−66.9
tea	Supply and demand	900	0.7	668.4	2.0	4.7	7	−0.2	−200.6	−0.08	−68.3	−0.02	−32.6

Natural Vegetables Fibres											
cotton Substitution	1,590	4.7	4,095.9	8.2	7.3	10	−1.4	−1,178.2	+0.9	+948.2	−0.9	−770.2
jute Substitution	340	1.0	222.1	4.1	10.7	2	−0.3	−700.9	—	—	−0.07	−26.0
hard fibres Substitution	410	0.5	156.3	10.9	22.0	4	−0.3	−107.0	NA	−12.4	−0.06	−21.8
Basic vegetable foodstuff											
sugar Supply and demand	200	18.2	3,373.7	25.1	16.4	8	−0.7	−15.2	−4.8	−927.8	−2.3	−422.4
oleaginous Supply and demand	...	19.4	4,551.4	16.0	9.2	21	−10.0	−3,175.2	+14.6	+2,666.4	−5.0	−1,137.9
Vegetable raw materials											
tropical wood Supply and demand	...	50.6 (miom 3)	1,895.2	18.0[5]	7.2[5]	4	−8.3	−1,205.3	NA	−105.2	−25.8	−1,581.3
rubber Substitution	680	3.4	1,910.1	8.5	10.8	3	−0.8	−443.4	−0.6	−334.5	−0.4	−202.7
Perishable foodstuff											
bananas Supply and demand	140	6.9	649.4	4.6	4.8	10	−2.1	−419.3	−2.0	−197.6	−0.8	−122.5
meat Supply and demand	1,900	4.3	5,610.1	13.0	6.9	14	−0.4	−1,797.3	−0.4	1,226.9	−0.4	−819.4

1. % export value index basis 73.   2. Number of countries providing 75% of world exports.   3. U.S. Price: 1,320.
4. In 1977, purchases U.S. (Jamaica) and Japan (Surinam) on basis of 20 $/t.   5. Interval 1963/1974.

Sources: Trade Yearbook FAO (1974); Trade and Price Trends 76 (BIRD)EC/166/76; Int. Tin Council—Tin Prices 1956-1973; Statistics UN. 1974 Yearbook; Statistics OECD—Series C 1973. Unctad papers on Iron ore, Manganese and Phosphate.

TABLE 6. *The diagram endeavours to schematically provide a general view of the directions which developing (mainly) producers and the EEC seem to be willing to take in the application of the UNCTAD Integrated Programme—as well as indications on the content of agreement on already existing agreements*

How to read the table:

Blank case: matter settled in existing agreement;

? : matter open, no clear positions;

Grey case: impossible

each cell shows:

developing producers orientation / existing agreement / EEC orientation

agreement in existence: Tin

agreement probable in near future: Rubber

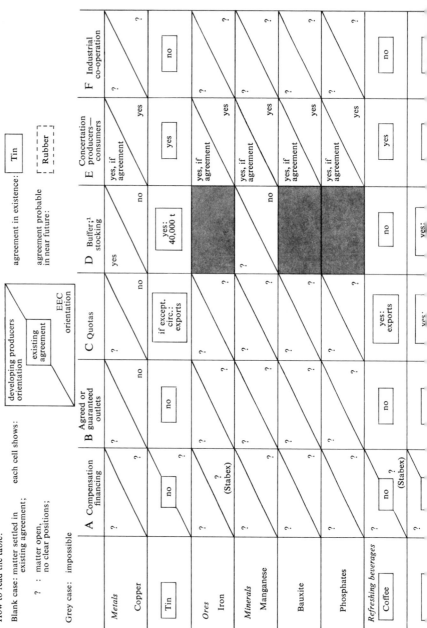

	A Compensation financing	B Agreed or guaranteed outlets	C Quotas	D Buffer;[1] stocking	E Concertation producers—consumers	F Industrial co-operation
Metals						
Copper	? / ?	? / ?	? / ?	yes / no	yes, if agreement / yes	? / ?
Tin	no	no	if except. circ.: exports	yes: 40,000 t	yes	no
Ores						
Iron	? (Stabex) / ?	? / ?	? / ?	*(grey case)* / ?	yes, if agreement / yes	? / ?
Minerals						
Manganese	? / ?	? / ?	? / ?	? / no	yes, if agreement / yes	? / ?
Bauxite	? / ?	? / ?	? / ?	*(grey case)*	yes, if agreement / yes	? / ?
Phosphates	? / ?	? / ?	? / ?	*(grey case)*	yes, if agreement / yes	? / ?
Refreshing beverages						
Coffee	no / ? (Stabex)	no	yes: exports	no	yes	no

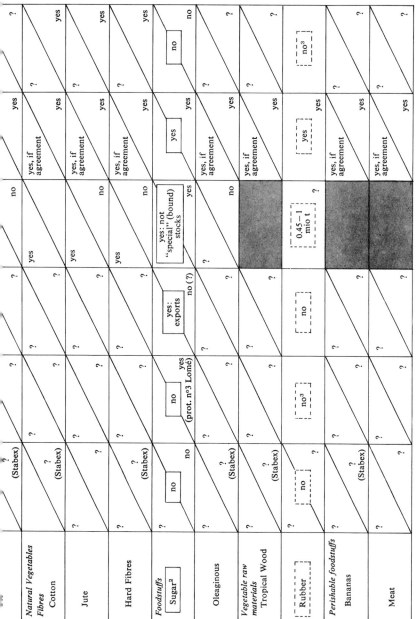

1. In some studies by the UNCTAD secretariat concerning the implementation of the IPC the following buffer stock sizes were used, in mio t: Copper: 1; Tin: 0.037; Coffee: 0.7; Cocoa: 0.5; Tea: 0.1; Cotton: 0.5; Jute: 0.4; Hard fibres: 0.1; Sugar: 4.3; Rubber: 0.6.
2. In the case of sugar the EEC does not participate but might join if more favourable, CAP compatible, conditions were offered.
3. U.S. are strongly against but insist for a B.s. of 1 mio t.
4. Vertical ties presently existing between producing and consuming industries are equivalent to agreed-guaranteed outlets.

II. COMMODITIES POLICY COUNTER-REPORT

EEC Policies and Options

by *Geoffrey L. Goodwin* and *James B. Mayall*

The emphasis of this paper is on the political economy of international commodity problems and on the political context within which EEC commodity policy is being shaped. This is not to discount the often crucial importance of purely economic and technical considerations. But the Commission Dossier Commodités (DG1–UCPEE of April 1977) necessarily, and rightly, focuses on these. By highlighting the political dimensions this paper will, it is hoped, usefully complement the Commission paper.

BACKGROUND

At the outset it is as well to recall that much of the international debate on commodity problems over the last 50 years has been dominated either by the pleas of those countries that considered they were denied an "equitable" share of the world's resources or by security considerations, including the security of supplies. The first to plead for an "equitable" share immediately after World War I, were Italy and France who pressed for the "international distribution of food stuffs and raw materials." The plea was rejected and in the League of Nations discussion concentrated on "equal access." In the 1920's this was not, in practice, a serious problem. Most of the colonial powers in whose dependent territories key materials were located practised "open door" policies, and the barriers to commodity trade though sometimes inconvenient were rarely insurmountable, while being for the most part non-discriminatory they only infrequently provoked serious political friction. Moreover, in the 1920's the main problem was one of surpluses which was generally met by producers' schemes to control output and keep prices up.

The picture changed dramatically in the 1930's with the economic depression and the challenge from the "revisionist" powers (Germany, Italy and Japan) which faced by the unwillingness of producers to accept payment in their currencies and by a battery of discriminatory tariffs and exchange controls found it increasingly difficult to gain access to the raw materials needed for their rearmament programmes. Nazi Germany's concept of "Versorgungs-raum" (of "tied sources of supply") or the Japanese vision of a "Co-prosperity Sphere" were in part reactions to this situation. Meanwhile, the initial inclination in, for instance, Britain to accept some measure of "economic appeasement" was gradually stifled both by the realization that what was sought by the revisionist powers was "war materials rather than raw materials" and by the demands of its own "economic rearmament" programmes.

209

In the 1930's security considerations, therefore, tended to overshadow "welfare" schemes designed to relieve the acute distress caused to producers by the sharp decline in the level of economic activity in the industrial world and by the volatility of world commodity prices. The history of the producer agreements intended to alleviate this distress is sobering. The relative success of the International Tin Agreement of 1931 was consequent upon special circumstances, particularly the existence of an independent buffer stock and the willingness of producers to police production controls; but agreements on, for instance, rubber, wheat and coffee were beset by difficulties over membership (including in most instances the absence of consumer interests) and the appropriate level of production quotas. In any event they were unable to withstand the onslaught of the depression, the retreat to economic nationalism, and the readiness of many members to put short-term domestic considerations before long-term international commitments.

World War II called into being the Combined Raw Materials Board which cut its teeth on the acute problems of raw material scarcity created by the sudden Japanese conquests. Its allocation system was essentially Anglo-American even though its membership was opened up as victory came in sight. The point to stress here is that it was the shared war aims and the meshing together of the two countries' war efforts which were the guarantee of the CRMB's success. In the immediate post war period of acute shortages such bodies as the International Emergency Food Council went some way to negotiating "fair shares" of essential supplies, as did the International Materials Conference during the Korean War, which secured some measure of agreement on "fair shares" for all at a time when United States stockpiling and Western rearmament programmes threatened further to inflate prices by competitive bidding for scarce supplies. Even so, the importance of United States stockpiling programmes in setting the general level of world prices for a wide range of primary commodity prices was underlined, while the search for synthetic or domestic substitutes was notably accelerated by the increased prices of natural products. Moreover, the relative success of the IMC stood out in sharp contrast to the early demise of Boyd Orr's proposals for a World Food Board (1946) and those in 1949 for an International Commodity Clearing House intended to forestall the accumulation of commodity surpluses in hard-currency countries in face of need in soft-currency countries. In neither case were the main prospective donors, and especially the USA, acutely aware of Congressional hostility, prepared to place the large funds needed to finance such schemes in the hands of an international agency over whose operations and price policies they might have little direct control.

This brief sketch of the highlights of the interwar period and of war-time experience is emphatically not intended to suggest any close parallels with the contemporary scene, except in so far as it draws attention to the importance of the political dimension of international commodity control. Thus national "security" policies and alliance needs were usually decisive in shaping broad governmental strategies, while those called upon to bear the main financial burden for any international commodity management scheme were often inhibited from doing so by domestic pressures as well as by doubts about the use to which funds might be put. In this period also it became clear how much individual commodity needs might differ, and how fragile even such agreements as were reached often proved: any sudden shift in political and economic circumstances, for instance, a sharp rise in commodity prices, was generally accepted by producing countries as an invitation to ignore their long-term commitments. In the current debate, the political context has, of course, changed, but the relevance of these political considerations has not.

COMMODITIES IN NORTH/SOUTH RELATIONS

From the end of the 1950's, and particularly from the first UNCTAD in 1964, much of the debate between the industrial and developing countries has not only reflected the coming to independence of many formerly dependent commodity producers but it has also concerned two arguably related questions in international commodity trade. The first is a widely acknowledged price volatility in many commodity markets. In an age when the belief in planning is widespread, the uncertainty about receipts is said to represent a permanent threat to the economies of many developing countries whose economies depend on the production of a few (often one) commodity. The second is the alleged, and much more controversial, long run tendency of the terms of trade to move against primary producers. But while most of the underlying arguments have been a feature of North/South relations for several decades, it is only since 1973, and notably since the success of OPEC in raising oil prices and the simultaneous boom in commodity prices generally, that the major industrial states have been persuaded that they must at least be prepared to consider changes in international policies for commodities other than oil.

A NEW POLITICAL CONTEXT

Put bluntly, the success of OPEC scared the industrial West; it also convinced the Group of 77 that they possessed new potentialities for political leverage. There were now two possibilities which could threaten the future economic security of the industrial countries—the producers of other commodities might attempt to follow the OPEC example, or the oil producers might provide an effective lead to the Group of 77 by linking concessions on oil to a Western commitment to a New International Economic Order.

This briefly is the essential background to the current debate about a new international regime for commodity trade. It is important to recognize at the start that what has changed is not so much the problem as the political context in which decisions must be taken or avoided: for not only have most studies of the problem since 1973 confirmed that oil is a special case and that the industrial world is unlikely to be held to ransom by new producer cartels, but there is little evidence that the governments of most of the industrial countries have *either* altered their traditional policies on commodity trade *or* have accepted the "terms of trade" argument which was set out as long ago as 1964 by Dr. Raoul Prebisch in his report to the first UNCTAD and which is still current amongst many of the Group of 77 even though it is not official UNCTAD policy. It is true that in some instances there is a willingness on political grounds to reconsider existing positions; but it is too early to say whether this is mainly a matter of presentation.

The demand for a New International Economic Order, in which the UNCTAD Integrated Commodity Programme and Common Fund proposal form the centre piece, was advanced in the immediate aftermath of the oil crisis; so too were the various responses of the industrial countries. Now more than three years later it remains uncertain whether there is sufficient common ground between the major industrial powers and the LDC's, or just as important between the industrial countries themselves, to introduce substantive rather than cosmetic changes in the management of international commodity trade. Admittedly the EEC Heads of State have now committed themselves to support a Common Fund, but it is clear that there is no general acceptance of the Group of 77's scheme and the opposition to it was such as to suggest that the final outcome of the negotiations is unlikely to be far reaching. Certainly, our own discussions with those involved have served to underline the problems involved in any major innovation in the commodity field, and the practical difficulties in reconciling different national policies, rather than the possibilities for making "progress" along lines which seem not merely economically desirable but also politically feasible.

Apart from the technical problems associated with the negotiation and operation of ICA's (International Commodity Agreements) there are two political problems which stand in the way of a coherent response by the industrial countries to the demands of the developing countries. The first arises, oil notwithstanding, from an asymmetry in bargaining power, which is accentuated by a somewhat different kind of reliance on economic and statistical argument by the two sides. The second is the more parochial, but just as intractible, problem of aligning policy within the EEC (as indeed within the industrialized world generally), where the members have different historical attitudes and alignments, and where consequently it is more than usually difficult to arrive at agreement on the nature of the problem or the extent of the threat to European interests. Moreover, the problem of alignment is compounded by the fact that many industrialized countries are themselves major commodity producers.

POLITICAL PRESSURE AND TECHNICAL ARGUMENT IN THE NORTH/SOUTH DIALOGUE

LDC's strategy

Consider first the position of the LDC's. The leitmotiv of all their efforts since 1964 has been "solidarity". The fact that the Group of 77 is still known by its original name, despite a current membership of well over 100 states, is more than a light-hearted joke; it also reflects a collective awareness of the importance of fixing, institutionalizing and providing an historical identity to this solidarity. In this context, the Group of 77's preoccupation with the integrated approach to commodities and with the Common Fund in particular is not merely a slogan but the logical outcome of an internal negotiating procedure which puts a premium on the *aggregation* of LDC interests, and a deliberate emphasis on their common predicament within the international economy. Thus their case is built up by statistics of the kind which establish that more than 60% of LDC earnings are derived from commodities, that only 27 developing countries do not depend for more than 50% of their export earnings on commodity receipts and which purport to show a positive correlation between poverty and dependence on commodity trade. Such statistical portraits have a double purpose: they justify the LDC alliance to itself and, in the absence of a compelling sanction, they establish an interpretation of reality which the industrial countries must at least answer.

It may be questioned, of course, how deep the solidarity of the 77 goes. Certainly there are quite deep divisions within the group. In the UN Law of the Sea Conference, for example, there was no concealing the conflict of interest between the geographically disadvantaged and the coastal states, the latter going so far as to denounce the "unholy alliance" between the developing and developed landlocked states, (*Ocean Development*, 1976, p. 189). Similarly, in the negotiations over the Common Fund there is a conflict between the African group, which is generally in favour of an institution with substantial resources of its own and powers of direct intervention in the market, and the Latin American and some Asian countries which favour a more modest fund operating through and in support of individual commodity agreements. There is an obvious temptation for the industrialized countries to play upon these differences. But there are also dangers in doing so; for whatever the conflicts of interest and perception amongst the 77—and there is no doubt that they exist—in the last analysis they have never been prepared openly to breach their common front, to abandon their collective demand for structural reform.

How, then, does the integrated commodity programme fit into the Group of 77's overall strategy? According to Gamani Corea, the Secretary General of UNCTAD, its purpose is twofold: to improve the terms of trade of developing countries (considered as a whole) and to encourage orderly growth in world commodity markets in the interests of both producers and consumers. Only the second of these objectives has much support amongst industrial countries, most of which are prepared to consider commodity agreements where such a mutual interest has been shown to exist and on a "commodity by commodity" basis. From the LDC point of view, however, this approach has already been tried and has already failed. Nor, from their point of view, is the Western insistence on separating action to stabilize markets from action to improve LDC terms of trade persuasive; on the contrary they argue that given existing factor proportions it will be extremely difficult for developing countries to diversify out of primary production—the course of action which is almost universally advised. In any case the foreign exchange cost of diversification programmes requires a steady and remunerative, not a declining, return from traditional exports.

It is therefore because they believe that corrective action must come from within the commodity sector itself that the UNCTAD secretariat has devised and continues to insist on the integrated approach. At the same time while the argument is often highly technical—on the terms of trade for example much depends on the starting and cut off dates chosen for statistical analysis —in a fundamental sense it is also about the idea of an international political community, in which the "poor" as well as the "rich" have rights, including in particular the right to share in policy decisions about the management of the international economy. For the 77 the test is whether the industrial world is prepared to abandon thinking about developing problems mainly in terms of charity, in order "to help the developing countries get out of the poverty trap with dignity". This conviction that the dignity of the Third World is at stake was clearly behind Corea's veiled threat in his report to the UN General Assembly. "If the current negotiations fail, the developing countries may well question the validity of the concept (of consumer-producer cooperation) as a means for regulating and strengthening the markets for their commodity exports". Whether this was an empty threat remains to be seen. By the time of the Nairobi UNCTAD, however, it was clear that the LDCs had chosen their ground and that their attachment to the principle of an integrated commodity programme was not merely, or even perhaps primarily, a question of empirical analysis. (Indeed, it could not be since such an approach being untried there was no data about how it might work; only interminable projections and hypotheses). It is an attachment which directly reflects their resentment of their long-standing position as "suitors" in a world economic system hitherto run mainly by the rich industrialized countries; UNCTAD itself is a symbol of dissatisfaction not only with GATT but with a Bretton Woods system in the shaping of which they have had little voice.

INDUSTRIALIZED COUNTRIES: ANALYSIS AND COMMITMENT

For obvious (and perhaps unavoidable) reasons the industrial countries have difficulty in coming to terms with the fact that LDC governments employ the apparatus of rational policy debate for symbolic as well as analytic purposes. Admittedly, in other contexts, they often do this themselves but the problem for the industrial West is that it is being asked, on the basis of these arguments, to introduce what could be costly and often unpalatable changes in the existing arrangements for international trade. But, it is easy to see how, from an LDC viewpoint, the British position may seem particularly disingenuous. The British can no doubt argue that because of their long experience of commodity trade, they can speak with authority on the sheer technical difficulties of any grand design for commodity trade as a whole. At the same time for historical reasons (during the imperial period they were often producers as well as consumers, e.g., in the case of tin) the British, unlike, for example the West Germans, have never been opposed to commodity agreements in principle. As a result in the recent CIEC and UNCTAD negotiations British officials have emphasized that despite their reservations they have a relatively open mind about the principle of a Common Fund while simultaneously working to maintain the dialogue by stressing the need for detailed and specific analyses of the UNCTAD proposals. The hope is that detailed analysis will close the communication gap between rich and poor countries. But no analysis can transcend the premises on which it is based, which is why the LDCs want a prior commitment to the Fund. Whatever the outcome of the detailed studies they want a direct management role in a new commodity regime which will have resources of its own and a capacity to intervene directly in commodity markets.

This objective may seem far fetched but it is not altogether without precedent. Practical agreements need not necessarily wait upon an analytical consensus. Although much of the evidence suggests that tin, like oil, is a special case, once the ITA had been established, it was able to function even though the French frequently advanced different analyses of the Tin Market and therefore advocated different policies from the other consumers. In the present case the primarily political nature of the initial decision has possibly now been recognized (at the meeting of the European Council at the end of March 1977), but it remains true that once this decision was taken the only feasible way of making progress on the detailed questions of function, finance and management is through negotiations on the separate issues involved. This is both because the issues, while linked, *are* separate, and because any detailed negotiations requires a manageable agenda. In other words, while the LDC achievement in forcing a change in the political context has been accomplished through aggregating LDC problems, perceptions and interests, if there is to be any substantive change in existing arrangements, it must involve a process of disaggregation between countries, commodities and instruments of management and control.

THE PROBLEM OF FORMULATING AN EEC POLICY

If the problem for the LDCs is how to consolidate their gains in detailed negotiation, for the EEC it is just the opposite: how to give effect to the compromise commitment to the Common Fund at the March 1977 summit without surrendering the principle of "damage limitation" to the separate national interest of the Member States, which in recent negotiations has sometimes seemed to be the only common strand uniting their efforts. It will clearly be an uphill task.

The case for developing a coherent Community position rests on four arguments. First, like Japan but unlike the United States, the EEC Member States are highly dependent on imports of raw materials. And in the case of some of the most important of these, e.g., minerals where imports already account for 75% of consumption, there is likely to be an increasing degree of dependence in the future. Admittedly, only 50% of EEC imports come from LDCs but this is still a significant figure and it is an obvious EEC interest to maintain security of supplies. This indeed might reasonably be regarded as the essence of damage limitation. Second, since there is already a Common Commercial Policy, it would seem logical, irrespective of external pressure, to assert a common Community position on trade in primary products. Third, although this is also a complicating factor, the Community already has a compensatory finance policy directly related to primary commodity exports in the shape of the STABEX scheme and sugar agreements negotiated within the context of the Lomé Convention. Fourth, there is a somewhat incoherent but widely felt need both to insure against the possible political risks involved in alienating much of Third World opinion (a point to which politicians are usually more sensitive than officials) and to consolidate the political identity of the Community, particularly in its external relations. But while each of these arguments is reasonably persuasive in theory there are formidable practical obstacles in translating them into an overall Community position. Not the least is the fact that on matters of doctrine, some Community members feel closer to the stance of industrialized countries outside the Community than to that of their fellow members within the Community, (e.g., West Germany with the U.S.A. and Japan, the Netherlands with the Scandinavians).

DEPENDENCE AND DOCTRINE

Since there is a tendency amongst the industrialized countries as a whole to counter the generalist LDC approach by insisting on the detailed analysis of specific issues, it is perhaps not altogether surprising that Member States have not been overly impressed by the more pessimistic projections of Europe's growing dependence on Third World sources of supply. The long run supply position still causes some anxiety, but once the political threat of OPEC type pressure had receded a more comforting thought has tended to reassert itself in Western policy debate; so long as the demand for Third World commodities persists in the West, the mechanism of the market place will ensure that they are sold there. Where else, after all?

This is an area in which policy debate is still heavily coloured by national interests and traditions rather than by European supranationalism. The reasons for this are not merely to be found in the residue of imperial trading systems and habits, important as these are, but also in the position adopted by the leading European states on the most fundamental issue of economic ideology, i.e. the debate between those who favour an international system derived from classical laissez faire principles, and modified as little as possible, and those who favour the principles of *dirigisme* either across the board or on a sectoral basis. LDC spokesmen point out with some justice, that all industrial countries have intervened in domestic markets by establishing farm support policies to prevent the impoverishment of domestic agriculture; and they argue by analogy that similar statistics should now lead to a similar response on the international level. But it was, of course, not the statistics which established the case for agricultural protection, but the political pressure which farmers (and not an heterogeneous collection of primary producers either) were able to bring to bear on their governments. It may be anomalous but it is also largely true that since 1945 Western governments have become increasingly involved in the management of the domestic economy, while attempting to uphold an international commercial system based on non-interventionist, neo-classical principles. The tension between these two objectives lies behind many of the crises of the contemporary Western international economy, but to the extent that the commitment in principle to an open, liberal economic system remains part of the general political philosophy of several governments, it is obviously difficult to generate wide support for the proposition that economic security requires a switch to the *dirigiste* principles favoured by the Group of 77.

RAW MATERIAL POLICY AND THE CCP

The argument that the CCP should be extended to cover raw materials is vulnerable on two counts. First, the creation of international machinery to manage international commodity trade calls for a far more positive alignment of Member States policies in favour of intervention than was the case with the commercial policy itself. The creation of the Common External Tariff was provided for in the Treaty, and the evolution of the Community's negotiating position in the Kennedy Round and Tokyo GATT negotiations concerned the degree of liberalization that the EEC was prepared to concede to reach agreement with the United States and Japan. Even then, where there was no question of changing the ground rules of the liberal market economy, it was difficult to reach agreement, and consensus has always had to be built at the pace of the most reluctant member. If that principle is applied to the Commodity problem it is difficult to forecast significant movement. But the argument is vulnerable also on the grounds that the UNCTAD proposals deliberately link commercial with development policy, which for historical, technical and institutional reasons most EEC Member States have always insisted on keeping separate.

Of the three leading EEC powers the British position is roughly midway between the French government's public enthusiasm for *dirigisme* and West Germany's strict adherence to laissez-faire. However, it is perhaps worth noting that while French governments have traditionally favoured "the management of markets" in their public utterances about commodity trade and have been less concerned than some EEC members to draw the distinction between commercial arrangements and development aid, they have also been the principal advocates within the Community not only of a continuing dialogue with the developing countries but also of protecting the special interests of those developing countries with which France (and now the EEC) has historical and institutional ties. But while there is no doubt a bias against universalism in French thinking on North/South relations, the interventionist tradition in French foreign economic policy may give the executive a relatively free hand from domestic political pressure and opinion in this area also. It may be significant, for example, that it is the French proposal of a Common Fund organized as a holding bank for buffer stock surpluses which at the time of writing seemed to offer a possible basis for an intraEuropean compromise although it was already doubtful whether it would satisfy the LDCs.

Although it is also true of Britain that commodity policy has generally been left to the professionals, the emphasis is different. From 1945 the principles of British foreign policy—that is support for a liberal economic order subject to the constraints imposed by a long succession of balance of payments crises—have been endorsed by both major parties. Admittedly there have been periodic attacks on this policy by those who advocate more direct control by the state of Britain's involvement in the international economy (most recently by the Cambridge group of economists), but so far at least these attacks have always been fended off. Moreover, policy towards the developing countries has not featured prominently in this debate and is consequently fairly secure from serious political challenge.

One reason for the security of the official view from outside pressure is probably that a high degree of consensus exists—at least so far as the commodity problem is concerned—between those in charge of formulating the policy and what may reasonably be called the main-stream position within the British economics profession. If anything, official opinion, which is characterized by a "willingness to negotiate on a case by case basis" on any commodity where consumer/producer cooperation appears possible, is more flexible than the views of many leading economists who remain hostile to commodity agreements in principle. There are, of course, influential dissidents. Lord Kaldor, for example, speaking in his personal capacity in his 1976 presidential address to the Royal Economic Society (*Economic Journal*, December 1976), argued the case for commodity buffer stocks as the most promising line of action for introducing greater international growth and economic stability which would be to the benefit of both producers and industrial countries. It is, however, common ground among professional economists that it is undesirable in principle, because inefficient, to use commodity agreements as a vehicle for *transferring* resources from rich to poor. The official argument here tends to be slightly different, namely that aid should follow a political decision and not be concealed in an automatic mechanism for fixing commodity prices. In recent years British aid has been aimed deliberately at the least developed developing countries, whereas aid channeled through ICAs might be arbitrarily directed at producers at the expense of other states in greater need.

While the British proposed, first at the Kingston *Commonwealth Congress, 1975* and then at the Nairobi UNCTAD, both "to establish improved schemes for the stabilization of export earnings" and to give new impetus to the conclusion of ICAs to stabilize commodity prices (particularly for those products of most interest to the LDCs), they continue to have serious reservations about the role of the Common Fund proposed by the Group of 77—hence the insistence on specific analyses referred to earlier. They have for example made it clear that any financial contribution to a Fund would almost certainly be at the cost of other regular programmes of assistance to the LDCs. British spokesmen have conceded for some time that some Common Fund is likely to be introduced, because of the political pressures surrounding the issue, but since they also insist that price indexation is neither feasible nor desirable, that ICAs are not suitable mechanisms for resource transfer and that the pattern of international trade is not likely to be substantially changed in any case, it is far from clear what role they do envisage for a future organization.

Within the EEC the West German attitude on Commodity policy has been the most restrictive, and until the last minute at the March 1977 summit, towards the Common Fund as proposed by the Group of 77, the most hostile. "The basic attitude of the West German government to raw material policy is that it is the concern of private enterprise." Moreover West German opposition to government intervention in commodity markets is more deeply engrained in West German experience and public philosophy than is the case with other EEC Member States. Originally, free enterprise was part of the political consensus in Germany, which reflected resistance to any creed that smacked of the kind of central planning pursued either under Nazism or in the GDR. Consequently the steady encroachment of the German State into economic management has increasingly become one of the most sensitive issues in German politics. In general, despite West Germany's heavy depen-dence on imports (she mines only 12% of her domestic consumption of iron ore, 12% of lead and 35% of zinc) raw material procurement was not tradition-ally regarded as a serious problem. In this, as in other areas, West German policy was confidently based on the Pax Americana, support for which was reflected at all levels of Federal policy-making. This assumption is clearly less tenable now than in the past, particularly at a time when a new US admini-stration has hinted at a more positive response to LDC demands. The trouble is that for West Germany this shift in the American perspective has come at the wrong time: there is already mounting discontent about the growth of the public sector and strong political resistance to increased government expendi-ture; indeed in 1974 it was made a public condition of West German raw materials policy that it should not cost any money.

The opposition to allowing aid considerations to change the conditions of trade is also even stronger in Germany than in Britain, and with the exception of the Development Ministry (whose views are apparently not taken very seriously in German policy-making) the political and official élites regard the commodity problem as almost wholly a welfare issue, and the UNCTAD integrated approach as merely an inefficient way of transferring resources to the poorest countries. These views and the policy based on them have been repeatedly and vigorously argued in public. The present danger, therefore, seems to be that if West German public policy changes (and there are indica-tions that it has already begun to do so as a result of the EEC compromise on a Common Fund) the domestic credibility of the government and the stability of the FDP/SDP coalition might suffer. Once again these are hardly circumstances favourable for stitching together any very innovative or far-reaching EEC policy.

THE EEC'S EXISTING POLICY

An important reason for holding that the EEC should, on its own account, develop a coherent raw materials policy is that it has in existence a policy already, albeit limited by both product and geographical coverage. Under the Lomé Convention the EEC is now operating the STABEX scheme, which provides for automatic transfers to Lomé signatories whenever their earnings in the EEC market from a particular commodity fall below the reference price. From the point of view of the economic philosophy of most Member States compensatory financing has certain advantages as a general approach in that it does not operate in the market, interventions taking place after transactions and thus having no influence on market prices. It was a pre-ference for this kind of measure to stabilize LDC export earnings over more direct market intervention which led the British to suggest some extension of the principle in their Kingston initiative and which lies behind West German support for a compensatory financing scheme distinct from both STABEX and the IMF facility, and which would be confined to the commodity component of the export earnings of the LDCs.

Apart from its implications for future policy, the establishment of STABEX (and the same point can be made of the Lomé Sugar Protocol which was negotiated simultaneously) provides a further disquieting insight into the process of EEC decision making. This is simply that policy on issues such as these is most easily formulated under a compulsion *internal* to the EEC than in response to external pressures. The coincidence in time of British accession and the expiration of the second Yaoundé Agreement meant that the Community had to make some provision for the Commonwealth states which would otherwise lose preferential access to the British market, and that they also had to put forward some proposals which would both meet the criticisms of existing Associates of the previous agreement and stem their fears that they might suffer from association with stronger Commonwealth African states. Similarly, as a further consequence of enlargement, a solution had to be found—although it is true it has not proved an altogether satisfactory one— to the problem of Commonwealth sugar. Not only is the present—in mid-recession—a difficult time to generate enthusiasm for policy innovations when the external sanctions are so unclear, but in the North/South dialogue none of these inner compulsions are at work. In the spring of 1976 a Commission report showed an examination of 22 commodities in which 20 different solutions had been proposed. There has apparently been only a limited convergence between national viewpoints since then.

RISK AND OPPORTUNITY: POLITICAL CALCULATION IN EEC POLICY

The final reason for maintaining that the Community should develop a common, and defensible, position on raw materials concerns its political identity, and hence credibility, in the wider international environment. It may be that had North/South relations (including the handling of commodity problems) been left to officials there would have been even less "progress", or at least development, than has in fact occurred. But European politicians have sometimes been more sensitive than their advisers to the need to maintain the dialogue for its own sake irrespective of the force or weakness of particular technical arguments. This is an area in which inevitably the evidence is more than usually insubstantial; nevertheless it is possible to identify, if only tentatively, positive and negative incentives which are likely to influence the political leaders of the Nine (and have no doubt already done so) in favour both of concerting their policies and reaching some accommodation with the LDCs.

On the positive side of the argument it is only necessary to make two points. The first is that politicians naturally, and quite reasonably, prefer to be associated with successful negotiations than with failure. This is perhaps particularly the case in the present context, partly for historical reasons and partly because of the general feeling of unease felt by the stronger side in an unequal contest. It is one thing to stand up to the Russians, or the Americans, or even to each other; quite another to appear unyielding in the face of Third World demands, especially when other industrial countries may be adopting a more accommodating position, and perhaps picking up influence in the Third World in doing so. The second point is that for some admittedly fairly fortuitous reasons the Community has already adopted a reasonably coherent and positive approach in relation to the ACP countries, and it is obviously politically attractive to consolidate this position in the wider North/ South dialogue. Moreover, as in the negotiation of the Lomé Convention, part of the attraction lies in the opportunity offered the EEC for strengthening its own institutions and capacity for action—for example, perhaps by asserting a Community role in any future Common Fund. (See below, p. 228.)

But there is also a strong negative argument for political accommodation with the Third World, namely a perceived need to hedge against political uncertainty by avoiding so far as possible political conflict with primary producers. This argument persists despite the widespread acceptance, referred to earlier, of the technical case against any general emulation of OPEC by other commodity producers. It may be that the changed political context to which we have also referred may seem somewhat illusory to those actually involved in the negotiation of trade and development issues which have after all been on the international agenda for two decades or more. But what is clear is that the Bretton Woods/GATT framework of the Western international economy has been severely if not irretrievably weakened over the past five or six years, and that no similarly coherent set of principles has been advanced in its place. In the meantime, if it is accepted—and it generally is—that in any future international economic system it will be important for the industrial West to retain access to Third World markets and sources of supply, it follows that European states will wish to avoid wherever possible alienating the LDCs and may even in special circumstances wish to develop special relations with some of them.

The dialogue, and Western concessions to keep it in being, can thus be seen as a kind of holding operation, in place of a universal system which no longer operates (if it ever did) and to protect by political means Western economic interests against the day when a new political and economic dispensation may seem feasible. Hence the insistence on keeping the show going, even when some of what is proposed is regarded by certain European governments as bad economics or technically unsound. It was, after all, a French initiative, with which the others subsequently concurred, that led to the setting up of the CIEC with its deliberate bridging of the energy and wider development issues. Moreover, among many West European social democrats there is a strongly held, if unproven, assumption that Third World economic development is likely to contribute to future international, as well as national, political and economic stability. In the case of CIEC this kind of argument, has led to the offer of $1,000m in aid to the LDCs. It can be argued that the same kind of broad political considerations should (and indeed probably will) govern the EEC approach to the UNCTAD negotiations.

POLICY OPTIONS

The circumstances in which negotiations for some kind of Common Fund are opening can hardly be described as propitious. Yet evidently there have been shifts in political attitudes as indicated by the EEC compromise commitment to a Common Fund. Whatever else, this presumably registers that some change, however minimal, to existing arrangements must be introduced in the foreseeable future, and it is, in fact, claimed that it reflects a willingness to consider the "real needs" of LDCs in the broader context of North/South relationships. In particular, what appears to have been agreed is to study the possibilities of a Fund in terms of three "windows" (partly with a view to estimating the costs of each): (i) the financing of stockpiles for appropriate commodities; (ii) equivalent measures for commodities not appropriate to buffer stock management, e.g., presumably production controls, research into alternative uses, investment incentives, diversification, etc; (iii) residual problems. Since it is inevitable that progress in each of these areas will be slow, partly because the information on which to base policy decisions is incomplete, and partly because of the low level of intellectual and political commitment to the integrated approach as such in the industrial countries, it may be worth while examining some of the policy options open to the Community and the areas which merit further exploration. The discussion in this section is mainly by way of a commentary on section 4 of the Commission Dossier Commodités (DG1-UCPEE of April 1977).

The first point to make is that commodity issues command a lower priority amongst the economic preoccupations of most Community members than, for example, the problems of unemployment, inflation, monetary control, the external balance, the immediacy and urgency of which are only too evident and which provide a yardstick against which any commodity proposal will be measured. Particular commodity policies will consequently be tested against and subordinated to the dictates of these other preoccupations. Whatever their potential long-term merit, commodity policies that threaten to aggravate these other more immediate preoccupations, e.g., those that by raising the short-term prices of commodity imports threaten to bring a deterioration in the current terms of trade and accentuate inflationary pressures, or by according readier access for processed foods threaten to disrupt domestic industries and fuel unemployment, will receive short shrift. The long-term need for international commodity arrangements which can secure prices equitable alike to consumers and producers, may be accepted, in principle, but particular arrangements which run the risk of delaying the recovery of the industrialized world from the present recession will have little chance of acceptance, not only on economic grounds but because the political health of the Western democracies is significantly dependent on their ability to overcome their present economic ills and this is inevitably seen as a higher priority than cultivating better North/South relations.

Nevertheless, although as the Commission rightly recognizes, most Community members would prefer to build on existing measures of support offered by such institutions as the IMF, IBRD and private commercial arrangements, there is general recognition not only that these need to be strengthened and perhaps supplemented, but that the demand of the "77", for a greater say in the general oversight and management of the North/South economic relations cannot be gainsaid. On the exact modalities for achieving this end, however, there is no consensus. One of the difficulties is a genuine doubt about the ability of the integrated programme to achieve its declared objectives. It can plausibly be argued, for example that to implement the main elements of the UNCTAD integrated programme and, in particular, the kind of Common Fund envisaged by the "77", would be a disservice to the LDCs; for it might cause a diversion of resources from more worthwhile measures and might, by falling far short in its operations of the initial hopes placed in it, lead to a measure of disillusion within the developing world which would merely accentuate present resentments. This cannot be proved in advance, of course, but the precedent of the protracted negotiations on the GSP scheme, now widely regarded as of only marginal relevance to LDC needs, suggests that it cannot be easily dismissed.

For the EEC there is also the further danger of exacerbating precisely those tensions which they wish to avoid in the present failure to reach a clear and unequivocal position on the issue of *additionality*. Although it no longer represents the formal position of the Group of 77, several industrial states are convinced that for many of the "77"—and for the African group in particular —the main attraction of the Common Fund is as a source of *additional* aid. So far this question, while present in the minds of the delegates, has not been confronted at all in the negotiations. For their part, of course, what EEC governments resist is any demand that they should increase the burden on their own taxpayers. Yet, since the EEC is now committed to a Fund, it is obviously important that a Community position be hammered out soon (i.e., does the Common Fund concept as a political option imply additionality, and if so how much is the Community prepared to concede?) if a major misunderstanding is to be avoided. At the very least, assuming as seems likely, that the clearing house proposal is unlikely to provide the basis of a compromise with the "77" (as distinct from among the Nine themselves—see p. 221 above) there will be a need to examine alternative proposals which might have a better chance of satisfying the "77" while avoiding the political and intellectual quagmire represented by the entire debate over additionality.

COMPENSATORY FINANCING

In addition to the possibility of extension and strengthening much of the existing IMF compensatory financing scheme the possibilities of an extended STABEX scheme has attracted some attention. Two possibilities have been suggested: the first is to extend country coverage, i.e., (a) to include all developing countries but with different intervention thresholds which would automatically exclude some countries; or (b) to limit the benefits of the scheme to, say, those countries with a per capita GNP of $200–$300. This has financial attractions, but several countries in this group have no significant primary commodity exports; consequently an extended STABEX of this kind would not help them. The second possibility would be to extend the product coverage to all commodity earnings, i.e., including mineral products. But iron ore is the only mineral presently covered by STABEX and that is primarily a result of political pressure.

In short, the STABEX scheme was primarily designed as an instrument for offsetting losses in marketing non-mineral raw materials; extending the list of commodities and countries would be likely to increase the level of conflict amongst producers, could displease the Lomé signatories, and might endanger the flexibility of the scheme by introducing new and complex management problems. It is true that drawings under the STABEX scheme are in theory recoverable and that strictly speaking it cannot be criticized as a "hole in the ground", one of the hard-line objections to the 77's Common Fund proposal. But the fact that STABEX is financed out of the EEC's development budget nevertheless may now confirm some Community members—who are already opposed to additional aid—in the view that the UNCTAD proposals will consist of an even larger tax on their aid resources rather than a commercial arrangement to stabilize markets in the interests of both consumers and producers. Attention has in fact shifted to the third alternative of creating a separate compensatory financing scheme directed to commodity exports of LDCs (see p. 220 above), which also has the attraction of providing a means of wooing support away from the more ambitious versions of the Common Fund current amongst the 77. A scheme of this kind would almost certainly offer the most attractive negotiating position for the Nine.

INVESTMENT GUARANTEES

The "International Resources Bank" proposed by the USA was designed not only to provide greater security of supplies but also to facilitate a variety of modes of association between private corporations and developing countries, which would facilitate the transfer of technological and managerial know-how as well as of capital resources. Otherwise it was feared that higher prices could lead to developed countries expanding their own production of a range of commodities—or of synthetic and other substitutes—whilst output in the developing countries stagnated. It has also been argued that the lower price levels experienced in the most recent past could lead to shortages since they might bring an insufficient return to finance new developments in LDCs or the replacement of exhausted capacity. The presentation of the American proposals may have been inept and not designed to allay suspicions of neo-colonialism, but the proposals were directed to a real anxiety about the long-run supply of several commodities; they deserve not to be ignored.

The fourteen European mining companies submission to the European Commission in 1976 focused more directly on the question of guarantees against the political risks involved in many "host" countries. The need to secure adequate long-run raw material supplies for Europe was recognized, but the political risks and uncertainties in many "host" developing countries were such, it was alleged, as to encourage a tendency to shun Third World countries and to concentrate on "safe" areas (e.g., the USA, Brazil, Canada and Australia). This posed, it was claimed, a possible conflict between "the desire for a geographical diversity of mineral supplies for security reasons, and the equally strong preference for secure investments . . ." (*The Times*, 21.3.77). The possibility of providing some guarantee system on a European, as well as a World Bank, level merits further exploration. Attention might be drawn, in parenthesis, to the state support given in West Germany for exploration by German firms. Exploration for minerals has been made part of the German technical assistance programme to developing countries. The co-ownership of mining and refining ventures has also been favourably viewed and these have somewhat lessened West Germany's previous dependence upon the international mining companies. Moreover, the reliance on bilateral treaties with "host" countries of German mining investments has worked quite well as "nationalizations" have not seriously hit German companies.

AGREED OR GUARANTEED OUTLETS

Bulk purchasing agreements are not the exclusive prerogative of the socialist countries and Keynes was at one time a powerful advocate of their merits. In many commodities it is already an error to think of a free market situation. While market prices have some, though not a widely known, bearing on commodity trade in general, and on government policies in particular, the actual amounts traded are in many cases merely residual. In sugar, wool, wheat, copper and iron ore, to mention only a range of commodities, bulk purchase agreements have been, or were for a time, the norm. Sir Ronald Prain also points out that "A high proportion of the copper trade between the producers in the six major exporting countries and their consumers is arranged under direct contract" covering such matters as prices, delivery dates and embracing the bulk of supplies ("Copper, the Anatomy of an Industry", p. 74). He also records that Japan has eschewed "mining enterprises of their own in foreign lands, and concentrated on offering long-term purchasing contracts, thereby providing security for the miners to raise development capital elsewhere (*ibid.* p. 75). In some minerals (bauxite, aluminium, iron ore, and, up to 1965, copper), moreover, the situation of oligopolistic competition with a high degree of vertical integration (as, *mutatis mutandis*, in the oil industry) goes some way to ensuring secure outlets and it may be suspected that the international companies concerned (as with the oil "majors") are at least as sensitive to the "host" countries' interests as they are to those of the consumer. Given the importance of the operations of international companies to the development and the external trade of developing countries this whole area, as well as the relationship between commercial and intergovernmental arrangements, merits further exploration. In the process it may be found that the producer countries' bogy of neo-colonialist exploitation by international corporations is misplaced and that it is consumer interests which tend to be downgraded.

EXPORT AND PRODUCTION QUOTAS

The size of buffer stocks, and the financial resources they would need to make them viable, is directly affected by the kind of provision, if any, that is made for production and export constraints where surplus situations threaten. Without some such provision the buffer stock size might become quite unmanageable. Some would argue that quota arrangements are only too likely to be the subject of unilateral action by producers which pay insufficient heed to the interests of consumers; others—and not only in developing countries—argue that unilateral action by producer cartels, designed to increase their bargaining power and to raise prices, coupled possibly with export taxes and/or increased royalties, are a surer way of securing more equitable treatment for producers, and interfere less with the workings of the market. This is not to generalize the OPEC model, but it is to accept that in a market system of collective bargaining gross inequalities of bargaining strength may provoke political animosities and that such devices may do something to mitigate present asymmetries.

STOCKPILING

Concertation

The Commission paper sets out the problem very clearly and comment is deferred to the section on the Common Fund and concluding section.

MARKET ACCESS

One of the most vexed questions is that of market access not only for semi-manufacturers and textiles but also for processed goods. Although recently further liberalized, the GSP still tends to favour imports from the more advanced developing countries and even the STABEX scheme is, for the most part, limited to first stage processed products. Producing countries' acquisition of the "knowhow" for manufactures and for more sophisticated forms of processing is of little avail if, as the Commission paper recognizes, the products themselves are subject to crippling fiscal or customs dues. This is a matter to which the Community should give its attention. A first step would be for the Nine to examine more seriously the scope for compensatory action through the Regional Development Fund and the Social Fund to guard against the possible disruptive effects of readier access accorded to imports from developing countries. At present the Community's GSP scheme operates on a quota basis. Since most LDCs sell up to the quota anyway, it is their ability to sell beyond this point that is likely to determine investment decisions. What is needed on the EEC side, therefore, is less preoccupation with protectionist safeguards and more with compensatory action to facilitate necessary domestic adjustments. Some of the bitterness at present felt by several developing countries might then be assuaged. Yet this is not a new concept and it must be admitted that it would require a particularly close and sympathetic relationship between policy areas and instruments within the Community which would go well beyond the Community's present approach to commodity problems. Since most Community members have scarcely come to grips with these possibilities at the national level, any co-ordinated Community policy along these lines is particularly difficult to envisage in the near future.

COMMODITY MARKETS

One facet of commodity questions which has been little explored is the possible impact that UNCTAD'S integrated Commodity Programme might have on commercial commodity Markets. This is of particular concern to Britain for it has been calculated that total "invisible" earnings from trade in three groups of commodities (foods, fibres and other industrial materials, including copper, lead, silver, tin and zinc) amounted to something like £200–£250 million for 1975/76. The news that the International Lead and Zinc Study Group has moved to London from New York has also renewed interest in proposals to establish a World Commodity Centre in London. The relation between commercial markets and current intergovernmental discussions merits closer attention for this and other reasons. For instance, whether they have a stabilizing or destabilizing influence on commodity prices is uncertain and when assessing the size of international stocks it is as well to remember that commodity speculators (e.g., the copper stocks held by speculators on the LME) may command stocks of anything up to three months. Or there may be stockpiling by private firms of 2–4 months supply with or without government encouragement. Mandatory stockpiling can, of course, add to industrial costs and may be resisted for that reason. But this is not true of the mandatory reporting of stocks, a possibility which might be considered as a necessary basis for better informed governmental policies. It would then be possible, for example, to consider the effect of commercial stockpiling on the desirable size of intergovernmental buffer stocks. Some buffer stock schemes, might, for instance, merely switch inventory from the market place to an internationally-managed organization and the cost from private to governmental funds.

The existence already of national stocks in most of the developed countries has also led to the proposal for a scheme of national buffer stocks within an international structure. National buffer stock managers would execute policy, but the policies, in which they would have a direct voice, would be formulated internationally between both consumers and producers. Such a scheme would be effectively run by the developed countries; it would afford greater security of supplies; and it could ensure that these were less exposed to speculative attack. The developed countries would have to bear the main financial burden, but they would have more direct control. The developing countries would be relieved of financial contributions, but they would have a direct voice in the concertation of national policies. The merits of the scheme for the industrialized countries are evident; but the details might prove difficult to agree. In particular, it might prove difficult to sell a scheme to developing countries in which they would quite clearly be the subordinate partners. The exact form of producer-consumer cooperation is thus the first and most critical question which would need to be explored both within the EEC and in discussion with the LDCs.

THE COMMON FUND

To the Group of 77 the Common Fund is symbolic of the kind of restructuring of the international economy they seek. They are not primarily concerned with the specific issues of what kind of activities should be conducted under its aegis or what particular management regime might be appropriate. Whatever their internal divisions, collectively they insist that the Common Fund should be the central source of funds for international commodity agreements and buffer stocks and many would extend its competence to cover such measures as research and development, diversification aid, and commercial aid generally. They see it as having its own source of funds and as playing an active role in promoting, guiding and assisting new international commodity agreements. Some, particularly the African states, also see it not merely as a means of stabilizing prices in line with a long-term equilibrium between supply and demand but as a means of transferring *additional* resources from the developed to the developing countries (see p. 223 above), although this no longer is the official position of the Group of 77.

It would seem (July 1977) that there are signs of an emerging consensus on six points:
  i. that the CF should operate through individual ICAs;
 ii. that it should respect the autonomy of the ICAs;
iii. that the CF should be financially viable and that government commitments should not be open-ended;
 iv. that individual ICAs should be involved in the CF decision-making process;
  v. that management of the CF should be based upon producer-consumer cooperation;
 vi. that agreement is necessary on the modalities for borrowing against stocks.

These points of consensus still leave any number of issues open. Amongst most of Group B (i.e. industrialized countries) there is a strong suspicion that the UNCTAD proposals seriously underestimate the size of buffer stocks required, for instance, for tin and copper, and therefore the level of finance required for the CF (see below). They do not accept the premise that price movements over a range of commodities would diverge sufficiently to ensure substantial savings in total costs; nor is there any reason to suppose that the "swings and roundabouts" would necessarily balance each other out. Moreover, they would hope to devise a management system within which the balance of control might differ according to the particular kind of responsibilities being exercised.

The whole issue of the "management" of the Common Fund has, in fact, been hardly touched upon, e.g., whether it should operate solely through individual ICAs, or have the power itself to buy and sell, as the African states argue. If the latter, who would authorize the operations? Is the Common Fund to operate on the principle of parity as the "77" insist or on some form of weighted voting as in the IBRD? According to what scale would governmental contributions, if any, be elicited (if contributions to the Fund were based on the import figures of the commodities involved, several Community members might believe that they would be paying more than their fair share)? And the question may have to be faced of whether any separate Community contribution is to be envisaged, or whether Community involvement would be restricted to administrative coordination and "clearing house" functions. The desirability of a collective Community response to this as to other measures is a function of the broader need for the Community to develop a collective identity in its external relations. Nevertheless, the Group B countries and the "77", despite these uncertainties and the very considerable gulf that still separates them, do appear to be edging towards agreement on some kind of Common Fund (see the March 1977 Communiqué of the European Council). The fact is that easy as it is for economic analysts to identify the weaknesses in the whole concept of a Common Fund, this is now a major political issue of North/South relations and it is increasingly seen by Community members in that light. To be sure, it is possible to conceive of a Common Fund that might help to ensure greater stability of commodity prices, give greater assurance of long-term supplies of non-substitutable commodities, and by underpinning the economies of the poorly endowed producing countries, contribute to the health of the world economy generally. But devoutly though such a consummation may be desired, it is unlikely to be achieved. It is in practise easier to discern the economic risks and possible costs than to be altogether clear about the political costs of a breakdown in the negotiations. Nevertheless, the assumption seemingly now shared, though in very different degrees, by all of the Nine is that the economic risks can be reduced to the point where they are unlikely to outweigh the political desirability of bridging present North/South differences and achieving a more satisfactory long-term relationship.

On the individual commodity arrangements there is little to add to the Commission paper. On *tin* it is claimed that the buffer stock envisaged in the 5th International Tin Agreement is far too small and that to be effective in keeping prices within an agreed range it needs to be at least 2–3 times as large; alternatively it needs to be backed by a battery of production and/or export controls which could negate the main purposes of the agreement. Here, of course, the role of the US GSA is crucial. If any tin buffer stock were to be financed through a Common Fund the present agreement might have to be drastically modified and it is difficult to envisage producers agreeing to contribute to a fund over which they might have little control. If the Common Fund were to raise money by other than direct contributions this difficulty would be less acute.

On *copper* there is a considerable gulf between developing and developed countries. The former seek a fully fledged copper agreement within the UNCTAD structure, the latter prefer what would mainly be a study group outside UNCTAD which could study the problem in detail but which would not commit them at this stage to any firm proposals for action. They also claim that the buffer stock suggested by UNCTAD of 5–800,000 tons is far too small; the size required for an optimal price stabilization role has, in fact, been estimated at $1-1\frac{1}{2}$ million tons, a stock that would rapidly exhaust the $5–6 billion proposed to finance the Common Fund. A smaller stock would require greater reliance on supply restrictions to which both producers and consumers appear opposed.

On *sugar* some surprise has been expressed that the Community appears to favour a version of the international coordination of nationally held stocks, an arrangement based on the guaranteed intervention system operated within the Community under the Common Agricultural Policy, whereas the developing country sugar cane producers seek a pact similar to the 1968 ISA export quotas divided amongst producers and related to three wide price bands, the "general principle being that quotas would be increased whenever prices moved higher and cut where there was a need to withhold supplies and bolster the market".

To some observers the Community buffer stock system would be geared to creating unnecessary surpluses (as the CAP itself has only too often done) and would be of little benefit to sugar cane producers. The explanation appears to be that the Community, i.e., France and Belgium, is likely to have sizeable exportable surplus (if imports from the Lomé ACP countries are taken into account) and that it is opposed to any scheme which might restrict sales to third countries. The EEC was not a member of the 1968 pact and, given probable USA support for a quota system, its adherence to any new pact is not crucial.

On *cocoa* and *coffee* agreements are, of course, already in force. On *tea* the main problem appears to be the differences between the producers themselves, particularly the traditional Asian and the rapidly growing East African producers. On *jute* the danger is that if prices are substantially raised, the greater part of the market is likely to be lost to substitute products. On *rubber* two proposals have been under discussion: one has been tabled by the UNCTAD Secretariat, but it has received scant attention and discussion has concentrated on the proposals of the newly-formed association of national rubber producing countries. These do not appear to be greatly interested in the Common Fund, unless by sheltering under it any stockpile could be increased from the 100,000 tons at present contemplated (which is recognized to be far too small and is to be financed by four producing countries) to something of the order of 3–400,000 tons. But the main stress of Association members is on increased productivity and supply rationalization and here the second "window" finance of a Common Fund could prove attractive.

One aspect of International Commodity discussions has focused on the needs of the least developed countries; particularly with regard to tea, jute, rubber, hard fibres and copra, which in the view of the UK and others should be given priority. Some stocking arrangements might be appropriate for jute to even out and ensure supplies and the World Bank's tentative proposals to improve productivity in jute, sisal and tea are thought deserving of Community support.

CONCLUSION

In conclusion, it must be admitted that it is not easy to discern anything more than the bare outline of an emerging consensus within the Community on the issues discussed, while the gulf between developed and developing countries remains intimidating. Nor do the internal decision-making processes of the Community offer much confidence that an overall policy based upon agreed economic objectives can be worked out within a reasonable span of time. It is not only that there are differences both among and within member governments, but these are reflected in differences within the Community itself, between, for instance, DG I and DG VIII. Moreover, the Community's existing commitments (especially those associated with the Lomé Convention and the Mediterranean agreements) will inevitably impinge on the course of the commodity negotiations. Nevertheless, these continued differences of approach, conflicts of interest, and disagreements of both principle and detail are to be expected. Their existence should not conceal the growing awareness within the Community and its members that if the North/South "dialogue" at times tries the patience of its participants it is at least to be preferred to the acrimony and bitterness which unmitigated "confrontation" would engender.

Dr. Owen aptly put a too neglected dimension of the issues when, speaking as President of the Council of Ministers to the European Parliament, he recognized that "an international economy in which one third of the world population has an annual per capita income of less than $100 and in which the gap between the poorest and richest nations is growing is morally unacceptable, demeans human dignity and is a force for unpredictable tensions, economic and political, worldwide. Stability in Europe cannot be isolated from world stability. It says a lot for the Community that it has always recognized that fact." (*The Times*, 21 April 1977).

III. CONCLUSIONS

Findings of Group III on Commodities Policy

by *David Marquand*

Group III's afternoon discussion on commodity policy was marked by fewer disagreements than its morning discussion on aerospace policy, but was perhaps more aggressive. This, it should be stressed, did not arise from any lack of lucidity on the part of the participants. On the contrary, it was precisely the clarity with which the experts present described the complexities of the problem that made the non-experts—and particularly the Chairman, as the most obvious of the non-experts—realize just how intractable the issues are and how difficult it is to make progress.

The group readily reached agreement on three points. The first was that commodities differ so sharply from each other that it is hopelessly unrealistic to try to treat them all in the same way. To do so, in the graphic phrase of one participant, would be rather like treating elephants in the same way that one treats mice. The second point of ready agreement was that the attitudes, ideologies and interests of the Member States of the Community also differ strongly from each other, and often extends beyond the Community's boundaries. To some extent, we were told, the three differences are philosophical—some countries having a dirigiste philosophy and others a laisser faire one. Behind these philosophical differences, however, lay genuine differences of interest: the leading exponent of the laisser faire philosophy believes in laisser faire because she has done well in the market; the leading exponent of dirigisme, on the other hand, has benefited from a dirigiste approach. All this, it was agreed, made it extremely difficult to adopt a composite Community policy.

On the other hand, the group also agreed that in spite of all these difficulties, a European alternative was necessary. It was pointed out that all Member States are importers, and that this furnishes the foundation for a common policy. More important, the Community has certain assets, which no Member State possesses in isolation. As one participant put it, Europe is affluent enough to be able to afford an external policy, heterogeneous enough to understand the heterogeneity of the exporting countries, and has suffered enough to recognize the need for generosity. At a more mundane level, important economies of scale would result from the adoption of a common policy—purely economic economies of scale which resulted from the existence of the Common Market, and political economies of scale resulting from the fact that if nine countries pull together they will get further than if they pull separately. Finally, the very divergences in national experience and tradition were, in a sense, complementary.

Though it agreed that this provided the basis for a European alternative, however, the group found it less easy to agree on the nature of that alternative. It was agreed that there was a strong case for establishing the machinery by which the commercial interests concerned in commodities could be brought into close and continuous consultation with Governments —the point having been made that in the absence of such machinery, the commercial interests often ignore agreements reached by Governments. On the more fundamental question of whether or not the Community's policy is now following the right lines, however, it seemed to the Chairman that the Group was divided. One view, developed with great force and lucidity by one of the Commission representatives, was that, *de facto*, a common Community policy was beginning to emerge; that its premises and philosophy could not be publicly spelt out since that would merely wake philosophical dogs which would be better left sleeping; that in any case, the problems were too complex for global generalizations to be made. In spite of these inhibitions, the really remarkable thing about the recent past was the progress which had been made, and that the fact that the Community had, after all, had a common position in the North/South conference was a pivotal point. The other view was that, on the contrary, the Community had nothing that could properly be called a policy: that its actions were simply *ad hoc* responses to events: and that the Commission's duty was to draw up a coherent policy for the Community and campaign publicly for its adoption. That difference of opinion apart, the group ended its labours with the sense that, although the tunnel ahead was very long, light is visible at the end of it.

FOOD AID POLICY

I. Report   Klaus von Helldorf
II. Counter-report   Hélène Delorme
III. Conclusions   John Taylor and G. K. Roberts

I. FOOD AID POLICY REPORT

Food Aid from the European Community

by *Klaus von Helldorf*, with *Ch. Bossard, P. Hoguet* and *A. Szarf*

In response to an invitation from the Council (of 16 July 1974) to give its thoughts on Community cooperation with the Third World in the coming years, the Commission transmitted to the Council (on 5 November 1974) a "Fresco of Community action tomorrow".[1] The document's main idea may be summarized in the formula, which has since become the "leitmotif" of all the Commissions' proposals:

"To each according to his *needs*, by bringing *all our means* to bear".

Food aid has become one of these means—and certainly not the least important.

Rapid progress . . . towards a coherent policy yet to be declared

The only area in which the Community has made appreciable progress in recent years is that of relations with third countries, and above all with the Third World. Food aid provides a striking example of this progress, but also of the limitations of its real scope.

The aid, initiated in 1968, without any specific warrant from the Treaty, only nine years later has come to represent over 75% of the total value of supplies from the Nine to the developing countries.

What is more, though instigated mainly as a result of growing agricultural surpluses, this aid is now no longer merely a morally expedient method of disposing of excess stocks.

It is also a sign of considerable progress that food aid today is recognized to be an important instrument of overall development policy, commitments under which ought to be integrated with the agricultural policy and also with a common commercial policy.

Nevertheless, internal conflicts of the interests and hence the approaches, of the Member States persist, despite the generally favourable attitude of the Council towards various proposals transmitted to it by the Commission on this subject since 1974.

Fundamental differences have more frequently been concealed than genuinely resolved by the compromises that have been achieved.

There is no prospect of agreement on two essential matters: the size and the continuity of the aid to countries with serious food shortages to which the Community would be prepared to commit itself. This is why, in fact, on 22

March 1977 the Commission chose to withdraw its latest proposal on the subject (triennial programme), rather than pursue a deadlocked debate.

The refusal to commit itself in the medium term makes it impossible for the Community to correlate its aid effort with a trade policy of agricultural surplus disposal such as is practised successfully by the United States. Yet regular contracts for supplies at competitive prices, in addition to food aid, would be in the interest both of the developing countries, with their large food requirements, and of Europe, in its search for new markets for its agricultural surpluses (notably milk).

However, certain principles are already being applied in drawing up Community aid programmes without their having been unanimously adopted by the nine ministers: they include the principle of concentrating aid on the poorest countries (per capita GNP less than $300) and a definition of the needs to be met.

Thus, while the Community's food aid activities in practice conform more closely to the guiding principles laid down by the Commission than the opinions expressed by the nine governments in the Council, the divergences nevertheless give rise to one of the most serious shortcomings of Community food aid: the fact that Commission staff are so tied up with internal administrative tasks resulting from the complexity of the procedures followed that supplies often arrive at their destinations too late and their utilization is controlled inadequately, or not at all.

One of several means

Before proceeding to analyse the development of food aid, it would be useful to indicate briefly its place among other instruments of Community development policy.

The chief of these instruments for the EEC is constituted by the trade arrangements granted to the developing countries for their exports to Community markets. Since the introduction of the Common External Tariff, 18 months in advance of the deadline laid down in the Treaty (1 July 1968), the Community has had sole responsibility for external trade (Article 113 of the Treaty) and hence also for the application of the *"Generalized System of Preferences"* to the developing countries.

This is far from being the case in the area of *financial cooperation*. Despite considerable progress made since 1975, it is still the Member States who control the bulk of public resources allocated for development under their national policies.

In 1975 net transfers from the Nine to the developing countries (including food aid) totalled US $6,000 million,[2] broken down as follows (in million $):

TABLE 1

national actions:	4,300	=	71%
multilateral actions:	1,700	=	29%
including EEC	670	=	12%
others (UN, etc.)	1,030	=	17%

238

The value of food aid in that year was about $330 million, or 5.5% of the total, but represented nearly 50% of Community financial aid.

These comparisons will show:

– that an extremely small proportion of the resources available has so far been devoted to the implementation of the Community's development policy, although, admittedly, it will tend to increase in coming years as the provisions of the Lomé Convention and of the financial protocols to the cooperation agreements concluded with eight Mediterranean countries come into effect;

– that food aid is of negligible importance (5.5%) in the overall aid effort of the Nine, but of first-order significance for the Community (approximately 50%).

I. EEC FOOD AID FROM ITS INCEPTION TO THE 1973 CRISIS

Initiated to meet commitments entered into under GATT in July 1967, the European food aid policy developed until 1973 along essentially pragmatic lines. This is reflected both in the provisions governing its implementation and in the annual programmes of supply of the products concerned.

The origins of food aid in the form of cereals: International Convention on Food Aid

One of the items of the overall agreement which emerged from the trade negotiations of the 1964–1967 Kennedy Round, was an arrangement on cereals, which was to contribute to the stabilization of the world market in grains. The international grains arrangement consisted of two separate legal instruments, the Wheat Convention and the Food Aid Convention, preceded by a common preamble. The Food Aid Convention, which came into force on 1 July 1968 for an initial three-year period (1968/69, 1969/70, 1970/71), laid down the minimum quantities of *cereals* which each contracting party undertook to supply under the Convention to developing countries as a gift, for sale on favourable terms, or as a contribution in kind calculated in accordance with a predetermined convention rate). The EEC's contribution was fixed at 1,035,000 tonnes, or 23% of the total amount, as against 42% to be contributed by the United States. The Food Aid Convention was renewed for another three years in 1971, then for another one-year (1974/75) and a further two-year (1975/76 and 1977/78) period.

Implementation of the European food aid policy

The legal background to the implementation of the commitments entered into under GATT was rather complex.

(a) *Aid in cereals is not determined solely by the community*

By an internal decision it was agreed that the Food Aid Convention would be implemented partly by Community measures and partly by national measures, for which the Member States would have sole responsibility. The latter's share has steadily diminished, falling from 70.9% in 1968/69 to 60% in 1972/73 and only 44% in 1967/77. The tonnage supplied under national actions is shared out among the Member States according to a "cereals key" which was empirically fixed in 1968 and has since varied each year.

(b) *Food aid should combine humanitarian objectives and the fight against hunger with the economic objectives of expanding local agricultural production* This dual aim can be seen in the three forms of food aid provided by the EEC:
– the first is humanitarian: emergency aid supplied in the form of free gifts;
– the second has nutritional objectives and takes the form of free distributions to particular population groups;
– the third, over and above its humanitarian aspect, has economic objectives: it is the "normal" aid in the form of supplies to be sold on the beneficiary countries' domestic markets for the dual purpose of:
> saving foreign currencies, which can thus be used for development purposes (aid to the balance of payments),
> the building up of a counterpart fund to be used for the implementation of development projects, particularly in agriculture.

(c) *The cost of national actions is partly covered from the EEC's annual budget (through refunds)*[3]

The evolution of food aid in the form of cereals

(a) *The first Convention (1968–1971)*
The total EEC commitment for the three years (1968/69, 1969/70, 1970/71) *of the first Convention* amounted to 1,035,000 tonnes. The part provided under national measures was fixed by Council decision at 70.9% for 1968/69 and subsequently reduced to 65.9% (1970/71). In the initial stages the implementation of these commitments was marked by a certain amount of pragmatism due to the lack of criteria for the allocation of the quantities agreed and lack of coordination between Community and national measures.

In this period the contribution of international bodies was relatively small (6.3% of the total in 1969/70). There were striking divergences in the geographical distribution of counties benefiting under national and under Community actions: in 1968/69, 61.8% of Community aid went to the Far East as against 42.4% of the total under national actions, 20.6% of which were concentrated on the Middle East (16.6% in Egypt alone), for which no Community aid was granted. It should be noted that the bulk of Community aid (95.6% in 1968/69) was drawn from the stocks of intervention bodies and that approximately 90% of aid commitments were delivered by the end of September.

In the face of this empirical approach the Commission was moved to emphasize the *need for a more coherent approach* in its food aid programme for 1970/71. Further reasons were the rapid rise in the number of requests received by the Commission (19 applications involving a total of 2,650,000 tonnes, in addition to the 85,000 tonnes for previously agreed emergency measures) and the fact that the aid granted was found to interfere with trade patterns.

The 1969 compromise adopted by the Council stipulating that Community actions arise from a convergence of the intentions of the Member States meant that coordination could apply only to joint actions. National measures would be the exclusive responsibility of the States, which were to keep each other informed. In order to remedy the situation the Commission proposed a single programme, drawn up without regard to the division between Community and national actions, which would be coherent as regards:
– both the applicants for food aid, in order to ensure that overall EEC actions corresponded to the applicants' real needs: the applicants' import requirements would have to be examined also in the light of the volume of trade it was necessary to maintain;
– *and* as regards the total volume of requests, so as to coordinate the needs identified with the amount of aid available, bearing in mind the beneficiaries' ability to pay and their relations with the Member States.

Only then would the amounts assigned to each country be divided between Community and national actions.

Under this arrangement applications for food aid were assessed according to four criteria:
a. required imports of wheat and wheat flour
b. food aid received from non-EEC countries
c. official gold and foreign currency reserves
d. the effect on trade patterns of food aid granted previously

The criteria proposed by the Commission did not receive the approval of the Council, which made significant alterations in the apportionment proposed under the programme.

There was some delay in the implementation of the measures for that financial year: by November 1971 only one half of Community aid had been delivered. The implications for the effectiveness of the aid granted have ever since been a matter of growing concern for the Commission.

(b) *Provisions of the second convention (1971–1974)—Enlargement of the EEC*
When the Convention was renewed for a further three-year period in 1971, the EEC commitment remained unchanged. It was the enlargement of the Community which resulted in an increase in the total contribution, which rose to 1,287,000 tonnes from the 1973/74 tranche onwards, with an intermediate figure of 1,161,000 tonnes in 1972/73 consequent on the "coming into effect" of this increase on 1 January 1973. The accession of the United Kingdom—a grain-importing country with a declared preference for aid in the form of finance and with historic links to the countries of the Far East—was to introduce new elements into Council discussions on the problem of food aid.

During this period the Community's share of the aid rose gradually from 40% to 45% (in 1973/74) and the Commission's global approach crystallized, especially as regards the scrutiny of aid applications received by the EEC.

The four criteria listed above remained essentially unchanged.

It was during this period that trends, subsequently to be firmly established, in the apportionment of the total aid granted—among geographical regions, between direct and indirect aids, and between Community and national actions—began to emerge.

Both the portion assigned to international bodies (23.4% of Community actions in 1971/72 and 15% of total aid in 1973/74) and the relative share of the WEP in this increased during this time.

The EEC was receiving a growing number of requests, especially for emergency aid, which it was able to satisfy only partially.

TABLE 2

	1972/73 Programme	1973/74 Programme
Normal aid measures	206,000 t (44.4%)	400,000 t (69%)
Emergency aid measures	258,400 t (55.6%)	180,000 t (31%)
Total Community action commitment	464,400 t	580,000 t

The Community emergency actions in 1973 concerned principally Bangladesh (175,000 tonnes), the Sahel and Ethiopia (117,955 tonnes) and Pakistan (20,000 tonnes); in 1974; the Sahel (together with Ethiopia, the Gambia and Somalia) (147,000 tonnes), and India (30,000 tonnes).

It should also be noted that the value of the total volume of food aid increased (29.4 million UA in 1971/72 to 110.2 million UA in 1973/74). Two factors account for this:

1. In view of the extent of the Sahel disaster, the principle that the Community covers transport and distribution costs for emergency aids was extended to exceptional costs, for which a commitment of 46.6 million UA was made.

2. Prices rose in parallel with the growing volume of aid supplied. This point brings out the specific nature of EEC food aid, which, unlike that provided by the United States, is not reduced when world prices rise appreciably.

Evolution of food aid in dairy products—Origins

On 21 and 22 April 1969, the Council decided to include dairy products in a Community food aid programme. The primary and avowed reason for this was the financial burden of maintaining stocks of these products in the Community (350,000 tonnes of skimmed milk powder and 300,000 tonnes of butter on 31 December 1969) and the problems involved in maintaining the butter at the minimum quality standards required for the industrial utilization of butter fat. Given that, in the existing market situation, these stocks could not be disposed of in the normal way and that the revenue which the Community could derive from their sale was roughly equal to the cost of additional storage, it was considered that the best solution was to supply these products to certain developing countries, as the cheapest way for the Community of diversifying its food aid. Requests for aid in the form of dairy products had, in any case, been received by the Community from the developing countries and from international bodies.

242

This form of food aid, which was supplied for the first time in 1970, independently of any international commitment and as stocks became available on the Community market, initially lacked the continuity and regularity characterizing food aid in cereals. It has, however, subsequently become more regular as the Commission's policy has achieved firmer shape.

The expenditure on this form of food aid was borne by the EAGGF under the heading of intervention provided for by the common organization of the market. Only in 1974 did the Council adopt a proposal from the Commission for the harmonization of the system of aid financing, whereby, for all agricultural products supplied as food aid, expenditure exceeding the difference between internal EEC prices and world prices was to be covered from the food aid title of the budget.

In implementation of the Council's decisions, the Commission, depending on the level of stocks, instructs one of the intervention bodies to supply the products from stocks and to organize invitations to tender for the processing (necessary for the conservation of the product) of butter into butter oil and for its transportation.

While aid in dairy products was an independent EEC initiative and was a Community action from its inception, there were not well-tried channels for its distribution, such as already existed for cereals. Aid in dairy products was therefore subject to certain delays.

Criteria for granting aid in dairy products
In drawing up its proposals the Commission has taken the following three factors into consideration:
1. Applications received by the Community. These have been rapidly growing in number and reached 30 for milk powder and 24 for butter oil in 1974.
2. The Community market situation (output, public and private intervention stocks, internal consumption, export opportunities), which is carefully examined to see how much of the product can be given in aid. This is why Community dairy products aid appears in the initial stage to be a direct function of the internal market situation.
3. The developing countries' requirements, which are assessed in the light of criteria, varied during the period under consideration.

Unlike aid in cereals, that in the form of dairy products was initially supplied primarily through *international bodies*: not only the WFP (which received 95% of all dairy product aid in 1970 and 57% in 1972), but also the International Red Cross Committee, UNRWA and UNICEF. From the beginning of 1973 the Community decided to apportion a greater share to direct aid (55% in 1974).

Food aid in other products

By Council decision of 19 December 1972, *sugar* was included in Community aid under an UNRWA triennial programme (approximately 6,000 tonnes).

There was also an isolated Community contribution of 500 tonnes of *egg products* to the WFP in 1973.

II. TOWARDS A DEFINITION AND RATIONALIZATION OF THE COMMISSION'S POLICY

The seriousness of the food crisis in many Third World countries and the 1973 crisis on world commodity markets called for action by the industrialized world. This began with the World Food Conference in November 1974, at which the United States asked its partners to increase their food aid effort.

In the absence of a clear common policy, and with the Member States' individual policies insufficiently convergent, the Europe of the Nine was ill-prepared to meet this challenge. The Commission's proposal[4] of March 1974 for a Community food aid policy was a first step towards this end; it was followed, at the Council's request, by a comprehensive study on development aid[5] in November of the same year.

Discussion of these two documents have still not, however, resulted in the adoption of a definite policy by the Council. Nevertheless, since 1974 all the food aid programmes proposed by the Commission have followed the main lines of these two basic documents. Since the Council usually adopts the programmes without major change, it can be said that these guidelines are being applied in practice, though they continue to be debated in principle.

Requirements set out in the memorandum

The food crisis which broke out with two great famines in 1972/73 and was to intensify as a result of the fall in world grain output and the energy crisis, seriously weakened the position of many developing countries, especially the poorest. As a succession of years of bad weather reduced their own agricultural output, they found it increasingly hard to satisfy their growing food requirements on the world market (where the prices of wheat and rice tripled from 1972 to 1974) and were hampered in their efforts to increase agricultural production by increased costs of imported inputs, mainly fertilizers and energy. In addition, widespread inflation, monetary upheavals and an often alarming population growth created an ever-present danger that output would not keep pace with demand. In this situation, the Commission considered that Europe had to face responsibilities in several areas.

As regards the developing countries. There were responsibilities above all towards the poorest, the MSA countries,[6] who found themselves simply shut out of world markets by prices sharply rising at the very time when the aid granted to them was shrinking.

The first task, then, was to divert aid to these countries from those who were raw materials producers.

As regards the industrialized countries. The developed countries' economies can, for their part, benefit from this situation since, on the one hand, increased revenues from higher raw materials prices will create considerable demand in the recipient countries and, on the other, appropriate aid transfers may be transformed into capital and consumer goods for the MSA countries.[7]

In overall economic terms, the Community, being highly dependent for its raw materials on external sources, must contribute to the stabilization of the

244

international market while ensuring that its own producers, faced with stiff competition, retained adequate outlets for their goods.

The Community does not have unlimited aid resources to achieve all these objectives; it must therefore adopt a selective approach in its policies and objectives.

The policy proposed by the commission

If the Community is to achieve its objectives with respect to the developing countries, three features are essential to its food aid policy:

a. *Continuity of supplies*, rationally planned on the basis of a *three year indicative programme*, which would provide the recipient countries and organizations with useful indications for the planning of their own policies. These quantitative targets should be integrated in the agricultural policy and in the stockholding policy required to ensure such continuity.

b. *Diversified product range*. The Commission would like to see the present product range, considered as corresponding to the developing countries' needs and the EEC's capabilities, extended to include products such as processed cereals, egg powder, etc., to be used in emergency actions and thus not subject to forward planning.

c. *Increased size of the commitment*, which, in the final account, is the only means of ensuring that the Community's food aid policy achieves the desired impact and influence, especially in relation to the programmes implemented by other donor countries.

TABLE 3. *Indicative programme proposed for the period 1974/75 to 1976/77 (tonnes)*

Product	Annual commitment bracket (in tonnes)	Firm commitments for 1973/74 (in tonnes)
Cereals	1,700,000 to 2,500,000 (including 700,000 in national actions)	1,287,000 (including 707,000 in national actions)
Skimmed milk powder	80,000 to 120,000	55,000
Butter oil	45,000 to 65,000	45,000
Sugar	10,000 to 40,000	6,094
Other[8] products	— —	—

Aid administration

No genuine Community policy can, however, be effected unless two closely linked conditions can be realized:

a. The principle of *progressive communitarization of cereals aid* should be adopted. Only in this way can aid administration be improved through faster decision-making, closer coordination with the commercial and agricultural policies, more effective control of the aids' destination and impact, and the use of counterpart funds.[9]

b. If food aid is to be effective, the relevant *procedures* must be *efficient.*
Experience shows that procedures must be made more flexible and the
Council's administrative involvement (at present extending to the smallest
details in consequence of point (a) above) reduced. The Commission has
proposed, therefore, that in future the *Council* should decide on the indicative
programmes, the annual programmes and the apportionment of aid among
the recipients, and on the basic conditions of the granting of aid and that it
would then *delegate* (pursuant to Article 155 of the EEC Treaty) to the
Commission, assisted by a management committee, the *power to commit the
Community vis-à-vis beneficiary countries and organizations.*

In emergency situations the Commission wishes to have the authority to
decide on the first, limited, amounts of aid to be despatched during the early
days following a disaster.

Forms of aid

The principles governing the utilization of food aid in the beneficiary
countries are those which have emerged pragmatically, but there have been
so far no safeguards to ensure that they are applied. *Counterpart funds* in
local currencies arising from open market sales of aid products should be
placed in a special account and used for projects or programmes chosen by
the developing countries and approved by the EEC, before the delivery of the
products, in the light of certain criteria, particularly their contribution to
increased agricultural output. Primarily with the aim of simplifying administrative procedures, the beneficiary countries are left considerable freedom in
the management of these funds and flexibility in their utilization. Countries
short of development credits are recommended to use them in development
projects, while more advanced countries are encouraged to adopt the programme approach.

Direct aid should be an essential instrument of action by the Community,
which has an identity of its own to establish on external markets, particularly
as food aid is virtually the only method of cooperation available to it with
regard to non-associated countries. *Multilateral aid* nevertheless should
remain substantial and even be increased, especially through the WFP. The
different approaches[10] of the EEC and the WFP to food aid result in differences
in the geographical distribution of aid provided by them: in 1972/73 50% of
all EEC aid, but only 14% of the total WFP commitment, was directed to the
least developed countries (as defined by the UN). These actions being to that
extent complementary, it would be in the interests of the developing countries
if cooperation on them could be increased and improved.

The divergences existing *within the Council* will be reflected in the difficulties
encountered in the implementation of the policy proposed by the Commission.

III.

From 1974/75 to the 1977/79 three-year programme: difficulties in the
implementation of the Commission's policy.

246

AID IN CEREALS

Results achieved

Requests for food aid to the Community are constantly growing:[11] in 1974/75 the applicant countries' total requirement was 25 million tonnes and the requests totalled over 2.4 million tonnes.

Breakdown by countries. Consistently with its analysis of the crisis and the principles of its policy the Commission has been *concentrating aid on the MSA countries:* 81% of direct aid proposed under the 1974/75 programme (as against 72% previously) and 82% subsequently reduced to 80%, for 1976/77. The composition of this group of countries, however, has varied from year to year, reflecting the flexibility considered by the Commission to be essential to the Community's food aid policy.[12]

– Thus, in 1975/76 the share of the Far East countries was over 55% of the total (with increased aid for India, 175,000 tonnes and Pakistan, 35,000 tonnes), while there was an improvement in conditions in the Sahel countries. The remainder of the aid went to the poorest countries of Africa (not only Ethiopia but also Somalia, Sudan and Tanzania) and Latin America (Haiti and Honduras);

– There was a change in the food situation before the 1976/77 programme: hence aid to the Sahel countries[13] and India gave way to a special effort in favour of the Middle East and East Africa.

Criteria for granting aid. Applications for aid were systematically *analysed* throughout the period in the light of three criteria for *normal actions*:

– the existence of a *food shortage*, a necessary but not sufficient condition for the granting of aid. Import requirements which could not be covered by commercial purchases were determined. A closer analysis of the needs was performed where free gifts were envisaged.

– *an annual per capita income of less than $300.* If the other two conditions were fulfilled, a certain amount of flexibility was admitted, of which Peru, Syria and Honduras were able to take advantage.

– the existence of a *balance of payments deficit*—a criterion which made allowance for the consequences of the food and energy crises.

Emergency aid, of which the sole aim is to feed certain population groups, and not to make good persistent shortages, was granted according to the one criterion of whether there was a danger of famine.

In consequence of the application of strict criteria, some countries, although experiencing serious food shortages, became ineligible for Community aid. This applied in 1974/75 to Tunisia, Lebanon, Indonesia, Syria and Malta:[14] the first three of these did not find it necessary to re-apply in the following year.

Forms of aid

Community actions have played a growing role in the implementation of the Food Aid Convention which was extended each time for one year (1974/75, 1975/76 and then 1976/77, following the Council's decision of 1 June 1976), providing for a total commitment of 1,287,000 tonnes. However, the share

247

of *aid in cereals* in total Community aid fell from 49% in 1974 to 46.7% and then to 40% in 1976 under the combined effect of a relative fall in world grain prices and the increasing amount of aid in the form of daily produce.

It would seem, moreover, that the share of aid in cereals for specifically humanitarian purposes has not increased at the rate envisaged in certain recommendations addressed to the Commission.[15] Each programme, nevertheless, provides for a sizeable priority reserve for *emergency actions* (130,900 tonnes for 1976/77, of which 20,900 tonnes was allocated to WFP, Red Cross and UNICEF emergency actions), thus contributing to the achievement of the objectives of world food security[16] laid down by the 7th Extraordinary Session of the United Nations General Assembly.

The share of *indirect aids* in the Community total rose from 13.2% in 1974/75 to 16.7% in 1976/77, mainly as a result of an increase in the amounts allocated to the WFP (55,000 tonnes under the last programme).[17] This was the logical consequence of discovering that the WFP project approach was complementary to Community actions and that the WFP had significantly reapportioned its aids in favour of the poorest countries. To facilitate the WFP's task the Council agreed to a procedural modification: it would confine itself to laying down the regional distribution[18] of aid granted through WFP; decisions on apportionment among individual countries would be only indicative and could be altered by the Commission (only the inclusion of new beneficiary countries being referred to the Council). The possibility of joint WFP-EEC projects was mentioned but has not materialized.

Difficulties in implementation

Two major difficulties, attributable to the Member States, and vigorously stressed in all the Commission's programmes, reduce the efficiency of its actions.

Deadlines for decisions on Community programmes are not observed and so result in delays in implementation. The fact that some Member States were not able to finalize their plans for national actions in good time has made it impossible to test in the course of the last three programmes the consistency of Community actions with national ones and has led to irretrievable delays in the administration of the aid. Thus the 1975/76 programme, which was forwarded to the Council in November 1975, was agreed upon only five months later.[19]

The resources allocated for the food-aid programme by the Council's budgetary decisions have been inadequate to meet the needs of the developing countries or satisfy the guidelines laid down by the World Food Conference. For each programme, the Commission, with Parliament's support, has asked the Council to revise upwards its budgetary decisions: the amount of Community aid should never have been less than 1 million tonnes, whereas in fact it was only 643,500 tonnes in 1974/75, raised subsequently to 708,000 tonnes and 720,500 tonnes under the 1976/77 programme.

248

Aid in dairy produce

This follows the main lines of the cereals programme, particularly as regards
the need to bring forward deadlines for which the Council has been asked.
Unquestionably, aid in dairy produce has become more stabilized: it amounted
to 45,000 tonnes of butter oil and 45,000 tonnes of skimmed milk powder
under the last three programmes. Following repeated requests from the
Commission, an additional 95,000 tonnes of skimmed milk was granted by
the Council in 1976.[20]

The 1975 and 1976 programmes (first milk powder tranche)
a.   *Geographical distribution.* The concentration of aid on the MSA countries
continued: they received 86% in 1975 and 81% (first tranche) of the milk and
73% in 1976 of the butter oil.
b.   *Second tranche of the 1976 skimmed milk powder programme.* At its
meeting of 2 and 3 March 1976 the Council agreed to the Commission's
request and increased the maximum quantity of powdered milk for the 1976
programme to 200,000 tonnes (of which 50,000 tonnes will be financed in
1977).
   In view of the size of the programme the Commission felt bound to draw
attention (notably in Parliament) to the risks associated with the consumption
of skimmed milk powder (lack of vitamin A) and its improper use (inadequate
nutritional mix, discouragement of breast-feeding). Beginning with the
current programme[21] it is proposed to supply enriched milk and, if the risks
prove genuine, recipients can be asked to ensure proper use of the product.
   Aid in the form of other products was confined to sugar supplied to
UNRWA (6,100 tonnes in 1975 and 6,094 tonnes in 1976). On 22 September
1975 the Commission was instructed by the Council to negotiate the renewal
of the triennial Convention concluded with that organization.

The 1977/79 indicative three-year programme

No action was taken on the proposal made in the memorandum for forward
planning for the period 1974/75 to 1976/77 until 9 June 1976, when the
Council adopted the principle of medium-term planning. This entails two
sensitive questions: increasing the size of the overall commitment and
increasing the volume of Community actions in cereals. On these, the
Commission, despite support from Parliament and some Member States, has
not yet been able to obtain the Council's agreement.
   In view of the lack of enthusiasm on the part of certain Member States,
especially for increasing the overall commitment (FRG), the Commission
withdrew the proposal at the meeting of the Council of Development Ministers
on 22 March 1977. Unless the Council changes its attitude, therefore, the
Commission will continue to submit annual programmes.

Aid in cereals
The Community has been frequently criticized in international fora for not
having responded to the World Food Conferences' appeal: it was to have

increased the amount of aid in 1977 (the minimum of 1,650,000 tonnes proposed in the indicative programme should have been adopted). The Commission has proposed as a possible solution that the increase should take place outside the Convention, and solely within the ambit of Community actions, national actions remaining unchanged at the 1976 level.

Aid in skimmed milk powder
The Commission emphasizes that this form of aid is not purely charitable in nature; it has been more than "creating its own demand" and has produced a spin-off by stimulating investment in the dairy industry and infrastructures.

Aid in butter oil
The proposals were drawn up on the basis of conservative estimates of the consumption capacity of the developing countries and of the European industries' capacity to transform butter into butter oil.

It should be noted that the European Parliament approved the proposed three-year programme, while warning that it must not be allowed to encourage the production of even greater surpluses in the Community. In the light of the experience of some countries which have traditionally been suppliers of food aid, Parliament sees the programme as a stimulant to Member States' exports of agricultural produce and possibly also of other products (such as equipment for dairy establishments). It considered, on the other hand, the proposed quantities of dairy produce to be too low compared with the volume of requests received and of the surplus stocks existing in the Community (150,000 to 175,000 tonnes of milk, 45,000 to 65,000 tonnes of butter oil).

The 1976/77 programme

The three-year programme having been withdrawn in view of the impossibility of obtaining the Council's agreement to an increase in the volume and the duration of the proposed commitments, the 1977 programme now stands as follows:

By Council's decision of 8 February 1977, 1,287,000 tonnes (720,500 tonnes under Community actions and 566,500 tonnes under national actions) will be delivered to 42 recipient countries and 6 international organizations (WFP, ICRC, UNICEF, UNRWA, the Catholic Relief Service and the League of Red Cross Societies).

On 4 May 1977 the Commission adopted for submission to the Council, aid programmes involving 150,000 tonnes of milk and 45,000 tonnes of butter oil.

CONCLUSION
AN UNAPPROVED POLICY THAT IS LARGELY APPLIED
IN FACT

As regards increased regularity in tonnage supplied, diversified range of products, ability to meet emergency situations, concentration of aid on the countries most affected by the crisis, the EEC's food aid policy has been a success. But, nearly three years after the memorandum, the same obstacles still impede the policy it proposed. Debated among Member States on the significance to be attached to the decision [22] of 9 June 1976 adopting medium-term pluri-annual planning—whether it should be regarded as planning for increased aid or for its qualitative improvement—show that the Community's food aid policy remains a policy of compromise among diverging opinions. In the sense in which it is understood by the Commission, a genuine food aid policy cannot be said to exist. Nevertheless, despite the obstacles to its adoption, the annual programmes which have been adopted since 1974 are clearly marked by a consistent respect of the principles laid down in the memorandum. The Council debates could thus be regarded as merely academic, were it not for the fact that they serve to cloak the participants' preoccupation, all too familiar in relation to other sectors, with protecting strictly national interests, whatever the cost.

National policies still to be reconciled

It will be seen from a comparison of the 1968 and 1969 figures in the table below that before acceding to the Convention, none of the Nine pursued a food aid policy of any importance,[23] whether because they themselves were net food importers (United Kingdom, Italy) because they were not convinced of the principle and effectiveness of this type of aid (Netherlands, United Kingdom) or because they accorded it a low priority (notably France).

Thus. paradoxically, it is within the framework of EEC membership that the national policies have developed, reinforcing in the process both their consonant and their discordant features.

Differences between national policies are illustrated by several indices.

The volume of aid supplied

TABLE 4. *Volume of food aid and cumulative totals (net contributions in $million)*

Country	1968	1969	1970	1971	1972	1973	1974	1975	Total 1969/75
Germany	3.2	25.7	33.5	49.9	44.5	91.9	144.4	131.4	525.5
France	1.0	21.2	26.3	34.0	32.5	66.0	105.2	83.7	368.9
Italy	0.5	23.7	29.6	31.1	20.4	29.6	47.6	45.1	227.1
Netherlands	0.1	13.8	17.1	15.7	20.3	33.0	47.8	44.5	192.2
United Kingdom	1.9	17.4	16.0	17.3	2.7	14.3	49.2	60.0	177.2
Belgium	0.2	3.8	4.7	7.5	11.1	16.0	36.4	28.7	108.2
Denmark	2.5	9.4	6.7	7.3	8.0	13.9	20.9	20.0	86.2

Source: OECD 1968–1973, Food aid, 1974
 1974–1975, Statistical annex 1976

– The cumulative totals show the leading part played by Germany and France in the period under consideration;
– Variations in individual annual contributions follow the general trend, but differ from country to country;
– The following table shows in greater detail the relative importance attached by each country to food aid.

TABLE 5.

Food aid as percentage of:	D	F	I	NL	UK	B	DK
development aid from public sources (1972–1973 average)	6.9	3.5	17.7	8.4	1.4	6.3	9.6
food exports (1972)	2.4	0.7	1.2	0.5	0.2	0.7	0.5

Source: OECD, Food aid, 1974

For the United Kingdom, and to a lesser extent for France and Belgium, food aid is a relatively insignificant method of providing development aid.

It takes a more important share in the development aid effort of Italy, Denmark and the Netherlands, but only for Germany does it amount to more than 2% of food exports.

These differences of practice are translated into differences of attitude in debates within the EEC, in which Member States prepared to increase the volume of food aid (Belgium, Ireland, the Netherlands and United Kingdom) confront those who have reservations (France—which makes an increase conditional on the conclusion of commodity agreements under GATT, and Denmark) and those which oppose it (Italy—determinedly, essentially for budgetary reasons, and Germany—indirectly, in proposing that in the three-year programme's upper, instead of lower, limits should be set on the volume of aid).[24]

Again, some delegations (United Kingdom) agree to an increase in aid in cereals, but want that in milk powder to be maintained at the 1975 level (55,000 tonnes). The question of the diversification of the product range, particularly by the inclusion of processed products, is also in dispute, some States pressing for disposal of the products in processed form, others expecting the developing countries' processing industries to provide the necessary demand.[25]

This persistent conflict of national views is all the more surprising in that the sector involved is a relatively marginal one, and the differences are largely theoretical, since in Community practice they are ironed out. They have the unfortunate consequence of preventing food aid from playing its full part as an important instrument of the Community's development policy as well as of its commercial policy.

As regards the form of food aid
There are two opposing schools of thought, championing, respectively, the principles of:
– *aid in kind*. The objectives of mainly wheat-producing countries with, principally, France and, until 1973, Germany, but subsequently to a lesser

252

extent, in the leading roles, differ from those of the group in which other productive sectors, especially dairy farming (the Netherlands and Denmark) predominate.

– *financial aid.* This is favoured by countries which are net food importers. In the Community, this approach is ardently sponsored by the United Kingdom, which, having no surpluses to dispose of, put forward in its memorandum of 18 October 1976[26] proposals for making food aid an instrument of development aid for agricultural production in the developing countries. Italy especially, and also Ireland demand that the Member States should be free to fulfil their commitments under the Convention by contributions in kind.[27] These debates in the Community led to the sort of compromise that is habitually reached when differences remain but a common declaration must be made, on this occasion, in the course of the North/South Dialogue (September 1976), to be subsequently endorsed by the Development Ministers (March 1977): they were in principle in favour of the purchase of developing countries' products (triangular transaction), but only "in appropriate cases" (non-availability in the EEC), and only in very limited quantities.

The distribution of food aid

Each State has its own "clientele" to which it is anxious to provide aid, bilaterally, but also through multilateral efforts to which it contributes, especially those of the EEC.

– *The geographical distribution*[28] of the aid depends on the donor country's relations with particular developing countries and on the role it assigns to food aid.

Thus, until 1971 France regarded food aid as a means of diversifying the geographical distribution of its trade outlets and Tunisia, Egypt, Indonesia, Pakistan, Bangladesh and Sri Lanka were the principal beneficiaries. Only later was a special effort to aid African countries made.[29]

Germany concentrated its bilateral aid in 1973 on Bangladesh (52%), Indonesia (18%), Sri Lanka, Egypt, Chile, the countries of the Sahel and Ethiopia (30%).

Between 1969 and 1971 nearly 80% of Italian bilateral aid was directed to African countries, with 36% going to Egypt. Belgium sends the bulk of its aid to Zaire, Rwanda and Burundi and to countries with which it has signed cooperation agreements.

The United Kingdom directs what little bilateral food aid it grants to countries with which it had special relationships: India, Sri Lanka, Pakistan, Indonesia and Mauritius.

In the Council's *ad hoc* Working Party on Food Aid discussion on this distribution turns particularly on the selection criteria for the granting of applications: the British delegation considers that per capita income should be the sole determining criterion, thus enabling the aid to be concentrated on the MSA countries (primarily in Asia), while France insists on greater flexibility and complete freedom of decision for the Council.

The above table brings out the Netherlands' and Denmark's clear preference for multilateral[30] aid, provided mainly through the intermediary of the WFP.

TABLE 6. *Relative shares of bilateral and multilateral aid*
Breakdown of net food aid contributions, averages for 1972–1973

	Total bilateral aid in '000$	Total multilateral aid (including the EEC) in '000$	Aid supplied through the WFP as % of total multilateral aid
Germany	26,100	42,100	25.4
France	17,900	31,500	0.3
Italy		25,000	4.0
Netherlands	5,500	22,600	43.4
United Kingdom	500	8,000	21.3
Belgium	7,700	8,800	3.4
Denmark	1,300	9,700	90.7

Source: OECD, Food aid, 1974.

The geographical distribution of WFP aid is another factor determining the preferences of the donor countries. The World Programme's bias towards the countries of the Far and the Middle East, some of them with relatively high per capita incomes, is favoured by the United Kingdom and Germany. On the other hand, France, anxious to keep control of its aid to countries with which it has special links, shuns the WFP, though declaring that it would be prepared to reconsider its attitude if the Programme did the same for the geographical distribution of its aid.

Unwieldy administration procedures

These antagonisms both account for, and make use of, the many stages of Community procedural machinery. In the absence of a delegation of executive power to the Commission under a clearly defined policy, the decision-making process is cumbersome and complex. It entails long delays and the elaborate compromises which make it possible to achieve the unanimity that is always required in the Council. Two principal stages can be distinguished in the process of drawing up a food aid programme.

The formulation of a programme
Since the Member States still cling to their share of national actions in cereals aid, the Council has been laying down in the first instance, for each year of operation of the Convention, the ratio of the volume of Community to national actions.

It then approves an annual implementation schedule on the basis of programmes proposed by the Commission for each product (cereals, milk, butter oil). These programmes specify the amount granted to each country or intermediary organization, the method of distribution (gift or sale), and the financial arrangements (whether fob, cif, or delivered to place of destination).

The average time lag between the examination of an application received by the Commission and the Council's decision is 6 to 8 months, and another 6 to 7 months elapse before the goods are actually on their way to the country of destination.

a. *For normal actions*: under the "simplified procedure" adopted by the Council on 14 April 1975 the Commission (instead of the Council) is authorized to negotiate delivery agreements with the beneficiary countries, keeping the Member States, however, permanently informed.

b. *For emergency actions*: by the decision of July 1975 the Commission is authorized to allocate directly certain quantities of products to countries stricken by *sudden and unforeseeable natural disasters*, with the provisos, however, of:

– prior consultation of the Member States, who have two days to present their comments;

– ceilings on the overall amount and on individual products which are fixed at: 5,000 tonnes for cereals, 500 tonnes for skimmed milk powder, 500 tonnes for butter oil—the total of emergency aid mobilized in a year by this method not to exceed 5% of the volume of the programme agreed by the Council;

– submission by the Commission to the Council of proposals for decision under the usual procedure whenever the necessary supplies are not available from existing reserves or if additional quantities have to be released.

By the decision of 22 March 1977 (S/534/77) this procedure was extended for a trial period to emergency actions following *disasters other than natural disasters* (for instance, military operations)!

In these circumstances is it any wonder that, once again, at the Council's meeting of 22 March 1977 "note was taken of the difficulties of staff availability facing the relevant Commission department in view of the size of the task entrusted to it?"

NOTES

1. Bulletin of the European Communities, Supplement 8/74.

2. It is interesting to observe that this is nearly 50% more than the contribution of the United States ($4,300 million).

3. See Regulations (EEC) 2052/69 of 17.10.1969 and 1073/72 of 3.8.1972.

4. Food crisis and the Community's responsibilities towards developing countries. Memorandum on food aid policy of the European Economic Community. Communication from the Commission to the Council, 6 March 1974 (COM(74) 300 final).

5. "Development aid. Fresco of Community action tomorrow." Communication of the Commission transmitted to the Council on 5 November 1974, Bulletin of the European Communities, Supplement 8/74.

6. "Most seriously affected".

7. Consequently special attention should be given to aid for the agricultural sector, whose share was no more than 9% for the DAC Member States and under the EDF rose from 16% (first EDF) to 37% (3rd EDF).

8. 20 to 30 million UA would be earmarked for the purchase of these other products.

9. The control function will be the responsibility of EDF delegates and, in non-associated countries, of *ad hoc* missions and will be exercised on the basis of information provided by the embassies of Member States; an expansion of the administrative infrastructure would thus not be necessary.

10. Aid granted under WFP projects is largely governed by the beneficiary country's ability to satisfy the project requirements, and so tends to be directed towards countries already possessing fairly advanced infrastructures.

11. In contrast to requests for national actions, which some Member States are not receiving at all.

12. 1976/77 programme.

13. With the exception of Senegal, for which a 20,000 tonne reserve remained available from the previous programme.

14. The Commission has declared them eligible for aid from other sources (national actions, WFP).

15. In the 1974/75 programme the share of normal actions (including those with nutritional objectives) was over 80% of the total.

16. The donor countries were to provide a total of 500,000 tonnes for the emergency actions reserve.

17. The relative share of aid going to the WFP is, however, greater in national actions.

18. From 1975/76 onwards allocations for emergency action reserves were made within the WFP allocation; if the Commission so decides they may be added to the regional totals.

19. Similarly, the 1976/77 cereals programme proposed in October 1976 was not adopted by the Council until 8 February 1977.

20. 150,000 tonnes have been proposed (4 May 1977) for 1977.

21. Especially for allocations to UNICEF and the WFP.

22. Forced by the need to present a declaration at the World Food Council and the subsequent negotiations in the Development Committee of the CIEC (North-South Conference).

23. The 1972 and 1973 United Kingdom contributions were made outside the Convention.

24. Attitudes on the communitarization of aid are reproduced in another form in discussions on the volume of aid: here, there are reservations on the part of Germany and France, the latter seeking, in addition, to remain free to direct its aid to a geographical area which does not coincide with that covered by EEC aid.

25. The compromise reached by the Council at the end of February 1977 is characteristic of this type of balanced agreement with which such conflicts conclude: the Council agreed to increase the share of processed products, but only to a limited extent, on condition that this was what the beneficiaries wanted and that this measure would not prevent the growth of industries in the developing countries.

26. New strategy for Community food aid to developing countries.

27. In accordance with a Council decision of 30 April 1974, which has never been implemented.

28. Source: OED, Food aid, 1974.

29. Countries outside the franc area received 82% of French food aid in 1969, 70% in 1971, and 37% in 1973.

30. Denmark has consequently opposed the principle of food aid products being sold on the recipient country's domestic market.

II. FOOD AID POLICY COUNTER-REPORT

European Community Food Aid Policy

by *Hélène Delorme*, with *J. P. Chabert* and *J. Egg*

The concept of food aid on which this study is based is that it is a specific but not autonomous sector in the system of economic and political relations of which it forms a part.

Hence, taking food aid as a form of export of agricultural products through a specific market regulated mainly by the states concerned, we shall attempt to identify the relationship between this market and the "normal" commercial markets, which in theory are competitive but in practice are governed by the combined or conflicting action of the states (or groups of states) and a limited number of multinational and national undertakings (private and cooperative).

This concept, which is similar to the one adopted by the main organizers of food aid—the United States[1] and the international organizations[2]—is based on a theoretical pattern of relations between the various operational sectors which takes the following form:

Food aid must first of all increase agricultural exports, since by changing habits of consumption in the recipient country it helps to create a commercial demand. In addition to (or as a consequence of) this commercial objective, food aid also has an economic purpose. The change in consumption patterns encourages the recipient country to reorganize its agricultural structure to bring it into line with that of the donor country. This creates a demand for the industrial goods needed for agriculture, which in turn extends the markets open to the industries of the donor countries.

It is only in recent years that the EEC has had any experience in this field. The Community's food aid policy became operative in 1968, when the agreements concluded under GATT in July 1967 entered into force. The regulations governing this policy are of a fairly flexible nature:

– The volume of aid depends essentially on the economic and political situation in the EEC.[3] The only firm commitments are those that the EEC entered into in 1967 when it signed the International Grains Arrangement of which the Food Aid Convention is a part.[4] It should be also noted that since 1974 the validity of these commitments has been merely temporary, since the negotiations on the renewal of the International Grains Arrangement are still in progress. The Community has no legal obligations as regards the other products exported as food aid (chiefly skimmed milk powder and butter oil and more rarely, and in smaller quantities, eggs and sugar).

– The form of food aid also depends on any agreements that may be reached by the ministers concerned. They are allowed full discretion in deciding on the list of products, the amount of each product to be supplied as aid and the amount of financial aid; the amount of aid to be distributed directly by the EEC or the Member States and the multilateral aid to be distributed through the international organizations; the proportion which is to be donated (in the form of emergency or nutritional aid) and the proportion to be accounted for by sales in local currencies, together with the establishment of counterpart funds.

– The arrangements for the distribution and administration of the aid are determined on an equally pragmatic basis. Although, in March 1977, the Council adopted the criteria for the selection countries proposed by the Commission in 1974, these do not apply to national aid which accounts for a proportion also fluctuating of aid in the form of cereals.[5] Furthermore, there are no rules governing the use by the developing countries of products imported as food aid, or the use of counterpart funds in local currency.

This report is divided into two parts.

Its primary aim is to provide a summary of Community measures since 1968. What is the relationship between exports of agricultural products as food aid and "normal" commercial exports of agricultural products on the one hand, and the industrial products used for agricultural production on the other? Having established this, it should be possible to determine whether or not the EEC's food aid policy is an integral part of a commercial policy designed to promote the external expansion of the European Community, both in the agricultural and in other sectors, by encouraging the development of agriculture in the recipient countries on the pattern of European agriculture.

On the basis of this assessment an outline can then be given of the discussions that have been in progress since 1974, chiefly within the Community's select committees. The same criteria will be used in evaluating the points of view expressed by the politicians, as with the summary of Community action: we shall give a description of the projects involved, indicating whether or not they establish any links between the commercial, economic and political objectives to be achieved by food aid.

In the light of these factors we shall conclude by offering a few observations on the ways in which the EEC's policy differs from the policies of the Member States and its partners and the expediency of the various possibilities available in the field of European politics.

FOOD AID AND COMMERCIAL AGRICULTURAL EXPORTS

Since 1968 there has been a diversification of the products exported by the EEC as food aid (see Table 1). Since 1970, dairy products (skimmed milk powder and butter oil) have been exported in addition to cereals; sugar and eggs have also been exported, but less frequently and since the United Kingdom joined the EEC there have been regular cash payments.

The bulk of the aid is made up of two groups of products:
– first, cereals, mainly wheat and wheat flour,[6] which constituted 54% of the food aid for the period in question;

258

TABLE 1. *Food aid provided by the EEC, France and the United States, 1969–1975 (in millions of dollars and as a percentage)*

1969–75	Cereals	%	Other products Total	%	Dairy products[1] %	Cash payments %	Total	%
EEC[2]	450.76	53.9	377.51	45.1	367.80 44.0	7.06 0.8	835.33	100
France[3]	411.40	82	88.0	18	— —	— —	449.40	100
USA[4]	4008.10	60	2639.3	40	— —	— —	6647.4	100

1. Powdered milk and butter oil.
2. In the case of cereals, the figures related only to Community aid and not to national aid—Source: EEC Memorandum to the DAC–OECD.
3. For cereals, payments per marketing year (1 July to 30 June) for Community and national aid; the 1969–1970 marketing year is incorporated in the 1969 figures. Source: ONIC. The value is calculated on the basis of the value per tonne of Community aid. For other products: proportion of Community aid financed by France (22.9%), per calendar year—Source: EEC Memorandum to DAC–OECD.
4. For the USA: 1968–1973, per tax year, 1968—1 July 1967 to 30 June 1968:

   Source = Almeida et al. *op. cit.*

– second, dairy products, constituting 44% of Community food aid between 1971 and 1975.

French and American policies are also geared primarily to cereals, including wheat and wheat flour. Table 1 shows that cereals made up 83% of the aid provided by France during the same period. Between 1955 and 1973 cereals accounted for 61.4% of the aid provided by the United States.[7]

In view of the predominance of these products in the EEC's food aid, the analysis concentrates on wheat and wheat flour and dairy products.

Wheat and wheat flour

EEC. Table 2 provides data on exports of wheat and wheat flour by the EEC as food aid between 1969 and 1975 (national and Community aid) in thousands of tonnes (value of grain) and as a percentage of total exports (commercial exports + food aid) of the same products to the same countries.

A comparative analysis of the fluctuations in food aid exports and total exports (whose frequency is attributable to the instability of world markets) shows that there is only a tenuous link between these two types of export.

a. In the areas with which the EEC has a special relationship, either because they comprise countries on the periphery of Europe with which the Community is associated (e.g., Turkey) or has plans for association (e.g., Portugal) or because the countries concerned are one with which the EEC Member States have maintained trade relations established under an earlier colonial system (the Maghreb, the Middle East, Africa), food aid is not effective in preventing a certain erosion of the commercial advantages already obtained. This erosion, which is more marked in some cases than others, takes a different form in each group of countries.

TABLE 2. EEC: Wheat and wheat flour—Food aid exports—Payments in thousands of tonnes (grain value) and as a percentage of total exports of the same products to the same countries

Country or group of countries	1969 1000 t	%	1970 1000 t	%	1971 1000 t	%	1972 1000 t	%	1973 1000 t	%	1974 1000 t	%	1975 1000 t	%	1969-75 1000 t	%
Europe	104.2	44	161.8	71	38.9	55	0	57	10	10	7	2	11.52	8	333.4	27
Maghreb	87.9	41	119.1	92	56.0	88	147.0	nd	111.0	25	104.0	18	27.5	10	652.6	19
Tunisia	78.5	64	114.0	100	46.0	88	104.0	nd	55.0	53	39.0	93	27.5	39	464.0	78
Africa	49.5	10	80.8	12	28.8	5	40.5	7	118.8	17	152.0	28	138.5	24	609.0	14
Sahel	20.4	9	34.6	13	7.5	5	18.0	11	82.3	33	75.0	39	38.2	22	276.0	19
Middle East	160.7	10	260.0	15	251.0	22	132.1	9	163.0	9	176.5	9	159.2	8	1302.5	11
Egypt	127.0	9	172.0	12	185.0	23	93.1	9	132.0	9	100.0	6	123.2	7	932.3	10
Far East	323.9	63	287.8	61	163.3	51	294.1	62	399.7	58	443.5	70	657.2	28	2569.7	46
Bangladesh	0	0	0	0	0	0	*	0	240.5	95	207.5	94	286.8	67	734.8	81
Indonesia	90.0	nd	102.0	nd	58.0	nd	92.4	nd	58.1	77	102.0	nd	17.5	48	520.0	nd
Pakistan	87.9	nd	137.0	94	83.0	nd	145.5	83	46.2	70	48.0	nd	58.3	17	605.9	68
India	115.0	nd	0	0	0	0	0	0	0	0	30.0	nd	237.5	19	382.5	28
Latin America	0	0	20.0	nd	0	0	1.5	26	46.9	nd	33.5	82	14.0	68	115.9	87
International Organizations	145.6		43.7		72.3		169.2		87.0		154.2		189.0		861.0	
TOTAL	871.8	28	973.2	30	610.4	27	784.4	30	936.5	25	1070.7	25	1196.9	17	6544.1	25

* aid included with aid to Pakistan
nd = percentages over 100%

Sources: EEC: Statements of food aid (broken down by calendar year)
OECD. International trade figures.

- In Europe, the reduction in food aid in 1972 was more substantial but was accompanied by a reduction in exports, notably those to Turkey and Portugal.
- In Africa, food aid has increased more rapidly since 1973 (aid to the Sahel countries suffering from drought) than exports, which are still at more or less the same level as in 1969[8].
- In the Middle East, food aid exports have since 1972 stabilized at more or less the same level as in 1969, while total exports are once again showing an upward trend.
- The decline—in relative and absolute terms—in aid to the Maghreb reflects the trend away from trade with Tunisia, the main recipient country, towards trade with Algeria and Morocco, whose purchases have been increasing since 1973.

b. In the areas with which the EEC does little or no trade in the agricultural sector (the Far East and Latin America), total exports are closely linked with food aid. There is ample evidence of this in both the Far East and Latin America; exports to these countries are connected exclusively with food aid projects; when such aid is reduced or terminated, total exports show a corresponding decline.

France. The tenuous connection between commercial exports and food aid exports is not peculiar to Community policy; the same applies as in the case of French food aid policy.

Table 3 shows the amount in tonnes of wheat and wheat flour exported by France as food aid since 1968 (Community and national aid) and as a percentage of total exports (commercial and food aid exports) of the same products to the same countries.

Dairy products

EEC. Table 4 shows the exports of dairy products and eggs by the EEC under the heading of food aid in millions of dollars and as a percentage of total exports (commercial and food aid) of the same products to the same countries.

Although the relationship between the two kinds of export is of a quite specific character, Table 4 shows a similar result to that obtained in the case of wheat and wheat flour.

a. In the case of the areas with which the EEC has maintained trade relations over a number of years, two main trends are to be observed:

- *With the Maghreb and the Middle East* the EEC is consolidating its trade relations. The situation is most encouraging in the case of the Maghreb, where food aid is on the decline in absolute and relative terms, while total exports are increasing, notably exports to Algeria, the main recipient of aid. The same trend has been observed in the case of Egypt.

It is true that in the latter case the proportion of exports accounted for by aid represents a high percentage of total exports. In the other Middle East countries, food aid is increasing slightly in absolute terms, but not as fast as total exports, which are increasing more rapidly and at a comparatively regular pace.

261

TABLE 3. *France: Wheat and wheat flour—Food aid exports—Payments in thousands of tonnes (grain values) and as a percentage of total exports of the same products to the same countries*

Country or group of countries	1968-69 1000 t	%	1969-70 1000 t	%	1970-71 1000 t	%	1971-72 1000 t	%	1972-73 1000 t	%	1973-74 1000 t	%	1974-75 1000 t	%	1975-76 1000 t	%	1968-76 1000 t	%
Europe	0	0	0	0	0	0	3.2	23	1.8	50	2.5	2	7.0	2	5.0	5	19.5	2
Maghreb	30.0	11	64.7	63	46.3	89	13.7	99	37.5	19	112.5	38	17.5	2	20.0	2	342.2	11
Tunisia	30.0	50	64.7	63	46.3	100	3.6	100	37.5	80	62.5	84	17.5	25	20.0	13	282.1	50
Africa	0	0	25.5	6	24.8	6	17.2	4	37.5	8	80.7	21	66.3	16	55.0	13	307.2	8
Sahel	0	0	19.8	8	19.0	11	8.0	5	26.5	14	53.0	31	37.5	24	25.5	16	189.4	13
Middle East	72.0	7	73.1	10	225.1	47	26.1	7	90.0	8	92.0	8	54.5	4	28.0	3	660.8	8
Egypt	72.0	7	73.1	11	225.1	50	18.5	6	90.0	8	51.0	5	54.5	4	28.0	3	612.2	9
Far East	14.9	9	62.1	38	82.3	76	54.3	34	64.6	54	154.0	39	422.0	34	92.0	8	946.4	27
Bangladesh	0	0	0	0	0	0	0	0	15.0	34	55.0	nd	225.0	55	12.5	13	307.5	53
Indonesia	0	0	47.1	100	22.5	nd	21.3	nd	15.0	84	39.0	100	11.0	70	10.0	31	165.9	89
Pakistan	0	0	15.0	nd	44.8	nd	15.0	100	10.0	100	35.0	nd	10.0	13	10.0	12	139.8	55
India	0	0	0	0	0	0	0	0	0	0	0	0	163.0	34	30.0	6	193.0	16
Latin America	0	0	0	0	0	0	0	0	0	0	26.5	98	5.0	84	1.5	100	33.0	50
International Organizations	0		12.9		15.2		3.9		3.0		3.0		20.3		75.4		133.9	
TOTAL	116.9	5	238.4	16	393.9	36	118.4	12	234.4	12	471.2	19	592.6	13	276.9	8	2443.3	14

Source: ONIC
nd: percentages over 100%

TABLE 4.   *EEC: Food aid in the form of dairy products (skimmed milk powder, butter oil and eggs). Payments in millions of $ and as a percentage of total exports (food aid and commercial exports)*

	1971 Mill. $	%	1972 Mill. $	%	1973 Mill. $	%	1974 Mill. $	%	1975 Mill. $	%
Europe	5.7	51	4.6	36	1.2	8	1.17	6	1.05	9
Turkey	5.2	74	4.2	76	1.1	23	—	0	0.12	6
Maghreb	4.28	7	6.34	11	2.15	3	2.49	2	0.32	0.3
Algeria	3.88	11.5	6.33	15	2.12	4	2.49	3	—	0
Africa	6.94	10	7.91	10	13.76	13	27.76	18	23.03	12
Sahel	1.13	11	0.49	38	10.99	53	26.42	67	13.89	32
Middle East	10.36	25	14.53	33	15.17	16	9.05	9	12.77	11
Egypt	5.76	nd	8.77	57	8.16	40	2.77	38	4.45	21.5
Far East	13.46	30	24.43	59	17.25	21	42.44	32	47.49	46
Bangladesh	—	—	—	—	6.62	63	13.58	nd	11.54	50
Indonesia	0.13	3	1.56	26	0.44	6	0.43	4	0.77	11
Pakistan	1.64	48	2.59	50	2.55	22	4.69	25	13.97	nd
India	10.81	76	19.69	51	5.88	36	22.35	51	17.31	65
Latin America	7.87	15	15.11	28	4.41	5	4.91	4	7.03	17
TOTAL	48.61		72.92		53.94		87.82		91.68	

Source: Commission, Report on food aid 1971, 1972. 1973. Memorandum to DAC–OECD for 1974 and 1975 (the conversion rates are those used by the OECD) OECD—International trade figures.
nd: percentages exceeding 100% and therefore not calculated.

– Food aid to *countries on the periphery of Europe* is on the decline, but this is affecting exports, which are showing a corresponding decline.
– Total exports to *Africa* are increasing, but at the same rate as food aid, so that the ratio of food aid to total exports remains constant.
   Food aid to the Sahel countries, which have received the major share of aid to the African countries since 1973, is increasing more rapidly than total exports.
b. Food aid has had no effect on the situation in areas with which the EEC has only limited trade relations:
– In the *Far East*, the proportion of total exports accounted for by aid is increasing rapidly.
– In *Latin America*, although food aid exports account for a lower percentage of total exports than in the Far East, the two are closely related, and any reduction in food aid exports results in a corresponding decline in total exports.
   France. The figures currently available relate to exports under the heading of food aid in the form of skimmed milk powder for 1975 (see Table 5). They do not reflect any particular trend but they do indicate a relationship (or rather the lack of relationship) similar to that observed in the case of the EEC.
   a. The ratio of food aid to total exports is lowest in the case of the Maghreb (the main external market) and the Middle East. In the case of Africa, (the second most important external market), aid accounts for a considerably higher proportion of total exports, particularly aid to the Sahel countries.

TABLE 5. *France: Dairy products (skimmed milk powder) Food aid exports and total exports (milk and cream)—In thousands of tonnes and as a percentage*

	1975		
	Food aid 1,000 t. 1	*Total exports* 1,000 t. 2	% $3 = 1/2 \times 100$
Europe	0.55	1.35	40.5
Maghreb	0.10	52.22	1.0
Africa	7.25	21.75	33.3
Sahel	5.22	8.49	61.4
Other countries	2.04	13.25	15.3
Middle East	0.06	8.98	7.0
Far East	5.89	7.55	77.9
Bangladesh	2.0	2.0	100.0
India	2.5	3.51	71.4
Pakistan	1.39	1.39	100
Latin America	0.80	2.41	33.1

Source: OECD—International Trade Figures. Interlait

b. In the case of the Far East, aid often accounts for 100% of total exports (as with Bangladesh and Pakistan), while in the case of Latin America it represents one third of the total.

FOOD AID AND DEVELOPMENT COOPERATION

Although statistics on this point vary, "normal" food aid projects, i.e., goods sold to a recipient country to establish a counterpart fund in local currency, account for an increasing proportion of the EEC's food aid. According to the von Helldorf report, "normal" aid has increased from 56% of the aid in the form of cereals in 1969 to 80% in 1974 (excluding national aid); in the case of dairy products the same trend has emerged since 1974, although it is more marked in the case of butter oil than in the case of powdered milk.[9]

A similar situation is to be observed in American food aid policy, but the circumstances are slightly different: it is not so much that the aid sold to the recipient countries is increasing in proportion to the aid donated as that dollar sales are increasing in proportion to sales in the non-convertible currencies which are abolished in 1971.[10]

But for the EEC the increase in the volume of counterpart funds does not signify a qualitative improvement. In fact, in the absence of adequate supervision and consultation structures the EEC cannot coordinate the use of counterpart funds with its development cooperation policy.

Inadequacy of supervision and consultation structures

It is generally acknowledged by the Community authorities that the administration of the counterpart funds is unsatisfactory.

At present supervision and consultation structures are inadequate, if not totally lacking. The EEC does not have a specific administrative structure like the American Development Agency (US AID) which, in close collaboration with the governments of the countries concerned, administers the distribution of food aid and the use of the related counterpart funds through a network of offices covering all the recipient countries (over 100). In the case of the ACP countries (the countries of Africa, the Caribbean and the Pacific), the EEC can use the services of the Commission representatives responsible for the administration of the European Development Fund.[11] In other countries there are no permanent supervisory bodies.

The Commission sometimes sends officials to these countries on missions; in the case of aid provided in conjunction with the WFP, it relies on the latter organization to exercise control; cooperation with the external economic departments of the Member States is rare.

It should be noted that in France the administration of the counterpart funds relating to food aid is equally fragmented. Three departments are responsible: the Ministry of Finance (Treasury Department) for countries that have financial protocols with France (Tunisia and Egypt), the Ministry of Cooperation for Africa, and the Foreign Affairs Ministry for other areas, in particular the Far East and Latin America. Only in exceptional cases does coordination between these three departments go beyond the allocation of the budgetary appropriations set aside for food aid.

At Community level too, control of counterpart funds is limited: ". . . the Community does not in fact supervise the implementation of projects. It merely satisfies itself that counterpart funds are in fact used on the projects to which they are allotted".[12] Virtually none of the EEC's food aid agreements are coordinated with the development project or projects on which they are theoretically based.

Uncertainty of effects

At present there is no complete list of projects financed from the counterpart funds relating to the food aid provided by the EEC.[13]

Since we have no information as to the breakdown of investment between recipients and donor countries and between the various sectors, we shall confine ourselves to an overall assessment of the relationship between the EEC's development cooperation and food aid policies.

To determine whether or not the latter has brought the food production/consumption structure in the recipient countries into line with the pattern in the EEC and the industrialized countries with market economies, and hence created markets for the industrial products manufactured in the EEC, we have compared the exports of fertilizers and agricultural equipment[14] to these countries with exports of the same products to the developing countries as a whole.

This is a general comparison, but also partial in the sense that it is confined to four countries: Egypt, Tunisia, Pakistan and India. These four countries, two of which are among the MSA,[15] have received the bulk of the EEC's food aid since 1969. On the other hand their resources, particularly manpower, offer the best scope for the development of a commercial demand.

Table 6 reveals a similarity between the trend in the EEC and the trend in France and at the same time indicates that the economic effects of food aid are still uncertain.

It shows first of all that exports of the products in question to these four countries are increasing more rapidly than exports to the developing countries as a whole: the proportion of exports to all developing countries accounted for by these four countries rose from 2.9% in 1969 to 17% in 1974 in the case of the EEC, and from 2% in 1969 to 31% in 1974 in the case of France.

However, Table 6 also demonstrates the irregularity of the results obtained in each of the countries in question, and hence the uncertainty of the economic effects of food aid. In fact, exports from the EEC and France to Egypt and India are increasing steadily, but exports to Pakistan are more or less

TABLE 6. *Exports of Fertilizers, Agricultural Machinery and Equipment by the EEC, France and the USA to Egypt, India, Pakistan and Tunisia 1969 to 1974. In M.$ and as a percentage of exports of the same products to the developing countries as a whole.*

	Egypt		Tunisia		Pakistan		India		Total Developing Countries
	M.$	%	M.$	%	M.$	%	M.$	%	M.$
a. EEC									
1969	0,059	0	1,589	0.6	6,021	2.3	0,195	0	252,500
1970	5,662	1.9	3,513	1.2	3,562	1.2	9,893	3.4	286,690
1971	4,034	1.7	4,652	2.0	1,290	0.5	7,845	3.4	229,041
1972	11,778	4.1	7,345	2.5	2,991	1.0	11,907	4.2	283,401
1973	18,401	3.0	14,385	2.3	17,479	2.8	41,539	6.8	606,603
1974	94,237	6.9	18,543	1.3	29,376	2.1	91,190	6.7	1351,714
TOTAL	134,171	4.4	50,027	1.6	60,719	2.0	162,569	5.4	3009,949
b. France									
1969	0,006	0	0,707	1.9	0,031	0.1	0,012	0	37,874
1970	3,553	6.0	1,631	2.8	0,050	0.1	0,848	1.4	59,166
1971	0,114	0.3	2,310	6.3	0,093	0.3	0,984	2.7	36,735
1972	2,782	7.0	4,516	11.3	0,258	0.6	0,580	1.5	39,840
1973	3,45	6.0	6,411	11.1	0,058	0.1	1,536	2.6	57,979
1974	17,364	10.7	6,768	4.2	2,997	1.8	23,243	14.3	162,408
TOTAL	27,269	6.9	22,343	5.7	3,487	0.9	27,203	6.9	394,002
c. USA									
1969	0,235	0.1	0,761	0.3	7,875	3.0	4,517	1.7	265,056
1970	0,014	0	0,394	0.1	22,134	5.4	18,312	4.5	407,078
1971	0,050	0	0,363	0.1	0,384	0.1	27,755	8.0	347,446
1972	0,717	0.1	1,071	0.2	17,568	3.6	28,804	5.8	492,682
1973	0,764	0.1	0,714	0.1	26,821	4.4	31,477	5.2	608,161
1974	0,554	0	1,354	0.1	12,974	1.1	69,630	6.1	1144,291
TOTAL	2,334	0	4,657	0.1	87,756	2.7	180,495	5.5	3264,714

Source: OECD: International Trade Figures

constant and in 1973 exports to Tunisia showed a relative decline, these trends having in all cases a more marked effect on exports from France than on exports from the EEC.

CONCLUSION

The above assessment shows that the EEC's food aid policy is still not an integral part of commercial agricultural policy and development cooperation policy.

Its autonomy in relation to commercial agricultural policy is particularly noticeable. Although in the case of dairy products there is a certain relationship between food aid exports and commercial exports (to the Middle East and Maghreb countries), in the case of wheat and wheat flour, which with other cereals are the main agricultural products that the EEC exports to third countries, there is generally no connection between the two kinds of exports: food aid exports are no help in preventing the erosion and stagnation of total sales. The relationship between food aid policy and development cooperation policy is also irregular and random. This does not apply specifically to Community policy as compared with the policies of the Member States, or at least France, which is used here as an example. In fact there is just as little connection (and sometimes less) between French food aid policy and agricultural export and development cooperation policies. In France, too, food aid is closely and strictly related to political factors. It is used as a short-term means of maintaining or reorganizing the pattern of external relations inherited from an earlier period, and is adapted when necessary to bring it into line with agreements reached with the other Member States whose policies appear to be based on the same principles.

European food aid policies differ from American policy in that they are of marginal character. Since 1945 American policy has been part of an economic and commercial strategy,[16] which has achieved satisfactory results in many areas, including Japan, Brazil and Spain, and more recently Morocco and Tunisia.[17] Because of its scale and its original administrative structure,[18] American food aid is not simply a diplomatic instrument; it is an integral part of agricultural and economic policy, both internal and external.

DISCUSSION WITHIN THE EEC INSTITUTIONS

It is only recently that food aid policy has become a subject of discussion within the EEC. The Community institutions began to review the policy and its reform in 1974 in conjunction with the preparatory work for the World Food Conference. Discussion is still at an embryonic stage and continues to be conducted within a restricted framework even though there are now signs that the issues are beginning to be taken up by a wider circle of interested parties.[19] The Council of Ministers' *ad hoc* Working Party on Food Aid[20] continues to be the main forum for the consideration of measures adopted or envisaged. The work undertaken by this body will therefore constitute our main source of documentation. Where further clarification is needed, however, we shall turn to the studies carried out by other bodies.

267

The question that arises is whether food aid is destined to remain a minor and ancillary area of Community policy or whether it can be developed as a major and separate policy in its own right, capable of integrating its various objectives in a consistent and clear-cut way into European policy as a whole.

There are three different approaches to this question. Firstly, there are those who believe that economic objectives should be given priority over commercial objectives in the EEC's food aid policy. Then there are those who maintain that food aid policy should be integrated within an agricultural commercial policy. In the third camp are those who would like to see the creation of a policy managed independently of economic or commercial considerations. Each of these theories will now be considered in turn.

FOOD AID AS A TEMPORARY INSTRUMENT OF DEVELOPMENT COOPERATION

The first approach has proven to be the most popular as it ties in with the guidelines adopted by the UK, Netherlands and German governments, which, although admittedly different in detail, are generally convergent.[21]

Food aid in response to crisis situations

All three governments begin with a criticism of the food aid policy applied in the EEC since 1968. This is implicit in the Dutch memorandum and couched in general terms in the German text, but is explicitly expressed in the UK memorandum, which claims that:

"it is clearly necessary to change the *basis* of the EEC's food aid policy so that it is no longer simply a means of orchestrating the disposal of the Community's food surpluses, but becomes an instrument of development aid."[22]

Bearing in mind that the worsening of the world agricultural crisis is making this form of aid even more essential, the UK, German and Netherlands memos do not suggest that it should be abandoned, but rather that it should be rationalized through integration into the development cooperation policy, which they see as being a more appropriate framework than the agricultural policy which hitherto has served as its legal basis.[23] The Deutch Mémo is entirely dedicated to measures of emergency and humanitarian aid. This priority given to emergency actions, which are seen as "a vital area for the development process", emphasizes the possible link between catastrophies and the take off of a modernization process. Catastrophies, by shaking the social, economic and political fabric, may determine strategic moments during which both the necessity of aid and its chances of success are increased: in a way disorganization open the door to restructuration.[24]

Differences as regards implementing procedures

Although they share the same views on food aid, the UK, Netherlands and German governments differ over the implementing procedures. In this respect, four issues will be examined, the first two bearing on the commercial and economic aspects of food aid, the second two relating to its political aspects.

a. *Volume of aid and multi-annual programming.* The positions adopted by the three governments show that, while priority is given to economic objectives, this neither precludes an increase in the amount of food aid granted, nor does it mean that the amount is fixed. Even though the UK has displayed more readiness than Germany[25] in the European negotiations to accept an increase in the amounts exported as food aid (particularly in the case of cereals), both countries nevertheless wish to reserve the right to change the amounts exported and are reluctant to commit themselves for more than one year at a time.

b. *Development of the agricultural production of the developing countries.* The three governments take a somewhat different stance on the importance to be attached to counterpart fund loans as compared with gifts, as also on the form in which the loans should be made (in kind or cash payments allowing of "triangular operations"). However, such differences must not be allowed to obscure the really essential point, which is that all three governments consider it necessary for the granting of food aid to be closely linked to development schemes (individual projects or overall programmes) drawn up in collaboration with the recipient countries to foster agricultural production.

Despite the general nature of the documents under consideration, it may be said that the preference given to the policy of promoting agricultural production in the developing countries reveals, or confirms, that in the three countries concerned agricultural processing is more important than agricultural production: processing would be boosted by the prospect of markets being expanded by the increase in solvent demand this policy may trigger off in the developing countries; agricultural production, on the other hand, is seen in the light of competitive pressure from the assisted countries.

c. *Improved management in the present political situation.* As regards the questions which come under the general heading "management procedures" and which relate to the power of decision, the three memoranda lay great stress above all on the need for stronger coordination between the national policies themselves and between them and Community policy, so as to avoid "an undesirable accumulation of aid"[26] and to ensure a more rational use of the counterpart funds. The Netherlands and German governments urge that the "cooperation with the non-governmental institutions",[27] which they cultivate extensively in their countries, should be encouraged since their "knowledge of local habits and customs is a valuable asset[28] for the distribution and management of food aid.

However, none of these governments wishes to see a radical change in the existing balance of power between the Council and the Commission. The Netherlands memorandum is the only one to propose that the Commission should be made the "centre of coordination" for emergency aid as a whole. The UK and German texts continue to advocate inter-governmental procedures. Thus, while the UK memo considers it useful to increase the Commission's staff, it entrusts the task of coordination to the Council's *ad hoc* Working Party on Food Aid. Lastly, and most importantly, the three texts all favour retaining the existing duality between areas "reserved" for individual decisions of the Member States and areas amenable to collective decisions.

d. *Globalism or Regionalism?* On this aspect of food aid policy, which is of fundamental importance inasmuch as it affects all the facets of the external relations of the Member States, and is one of the conditions for increasing the effectiveness of Community action, the UK and Netherlands governments part company with Bonn, adopting a "globalist" approach and linking their policies to those of the UN and the WFP (in the belief that the international organization is better equipped), to the various programmes for displaced persons and to the work of the CAL (Committee for food aid policies and programmes). A further reason for this globalist approach is, as mentioned by the UK memo (point 18), the international character of the food crisis.

EEC FOOD AID: A POLICY WHICH SHOULD FORM PART OF AN AGRICULTURAL COMMERCIAL POLICY

The idea of food aid as a temporary and partial remedy to be used only in crisis situations to point the way to a country's recovery and future development is opposed by those who would like to see food aid policy developed as a significant and permanent element of an agricultural commercial policy. The analyses carried out in France in the reports of the VIIth Plan and, more recently, by the Economic and Social Council form the basis of this second, alternative, approach.

Food aid as a permanent element of an agricultural export policy

The report drawn up by the Committee on Agriculture and Food under the VIIth Plan, which lays down the economic policy guidelines for the period 1975–1980, merely draws attention to the need to define a Community agricultural trade policy as well as the need for "better integration of food aid into trade policy while respecting its own specific objectives".[29] The arguments set out in the report submitted by Mr Bienaymé on behalf of the Economic and Social Council on 26 January 1977[30] are more elaborate. It criticizes the EEC's food aid policy for being merely a series of "operations whose purpose is to dispose freely or cheaply of unsaleable surpluses",[31] and rejects it as being "expensive" for the donors and "inadequate" to the needs of the recipients.

While, like the UK memo, the Economic and Social Council's report is critical of the link established by the EEC between food aid and agricultural surpluses, it stresses, in common with the Commission (see below), the damage caused by the irregularities to which this link gives rise. In contrast to the position adopted by the UK Government, the Economic and Social Council takes the view that food aid must first form part of an agricultural export policy before it can become an instrument of a development cooperation policy. This viewpoint is in line with the three principles on the basis of which the Economic Council proposes that the CAP should be reformed:
1. Europe must assert its presence on the international cereal markets.

2. It must negotiate with the Mediterranean countries the bases of a concerted adjustment of "sensitive" products.
3. The philosophy behind, and the organization of, European food aid must be revised.[32]

The main inference here is that food aid cannot be restricted to a set of *ad hoc* "humanitarian" projects.

"All too often humanitarian aid masks the deficiencies of a system of international trade, the human objectives of which are frequently neglected. The humanitarian objectives of granting aid too often serve as a pretext for arousing the sympathies of a largely disinterested public and for launching spectacular, but short-lived, projects".[33]

Implementing procedures

The priority accorded to the commercial rather than the economic objective is reflected in the procedures for implementing the food aid policy proposed by the Economic Council.

a. *Volume and programming of aid.* The Economic Council would seem to attach more importance to programming food aid exports than to increasing their volume.[34] It points out that programming enables first the commercial effectiveness and then the economic effectiveness of food aid to be assessed by identifying the conditions under which it might be progressively distributed:

a. through the gradual emergence of an additional solvent demand on the part of the third countries, and

b. through an upturn in per capita food production in these countries.

The first stage of this procedure gives an indication of the size of the foreign markets accessible to the European farmer, and the second an indication of the external market capacity for the industrial goods and services provided by the European countries.[35]

The Economic Council points out that the programming of food aid must make provision for a strengthening of the supply lines and provide in particular for "an active storage policy in Europe and in the countries of destination".[36]

Like the UK memo, the Economic Council's report maintains that cereals, and most importantly French wheat, should constitute the main foodstuffs for exportation in the form of food aid. It justifies this argument by reference to the central role played by these products in the food production/consumption pattern of the industrialized countries. Thus:

"There can be no question that the developing countries must obtain sufficiency in food supplies by achieving real autonomy as soon as possible. However, these considerations in no way detract from the importance of the contributions which the advanced agricultural countries (the United States, France, Canada, Argentina Australia), which provide 80% of cereals and wheat exports, can make in cereals and food products. Moreover, cereals represent the main source of human food as they provide the raw materials for other processed products (stock-farming, raising of poultry), when not used directly as foodstuffs. Finally, cereal production is an essential factor for large industrial units. There can be no doubt that at the present time cereals provide the best means of remedying the world food shortages".[37]

271

b. *The economic objectives of food aid.* It is evident from the foregoing quotations that the Economic Council is conscious of the part played by food aid as an instrument of development in the developing countries. They also show, however, that this role is subordinate to the commercial objective. The report says very little in fact about the methods of using the counterpart funds, the existence of which is not even mentioned. It merely points to the advantages of promoting the development of the agricultural products processing industries in the developing countries and stresses the potential value of establishing technical cooperation founded on the direct participation of the "European smallholder" on the grounds that the latter

"possesses a valuable fund of unique experience which the specialized engineers and technicians often fail to put over: a lifelong attachment to the land, practical knowledge of farming and an accumulated fund of professional experience".[38]

The fact that little attention is paid to the agricultural development techniques to be propagated in the developing countries seems to us to be proof of an internal balance in the French farming structure in which the interests of the producers prevail over those of the related sectors. The food aid policy proposed by the Economic and Social Council is directed first and foremost towards affirming France's role as a supplier of the major primary agricultural products of the temperate zones (cereals and animal products). The need for a "concerted" adaptation of production in the Mediterranean area is, however, also recognized.[39]

c. *Food aid management and partners.* The approach of the Economic Council's report to management problems is similar to that of the UK and German texts, the view being that the diversity of the present aid distribution channels, e.g., FAO, the EEC and "the bilateral channels" should be retained.

As for the question of the partners for European food aid, the Economic Council's report differs from the VIIth Plan, which adopted an all-embracing strategy,[40] and opts for the order of priority chosen by the German Government:

"External aid must do more to promote the regular development of the food standards of the developing countries, especially those with which (the Europe of the Nine) maintains special relations of the kind that the Lomé agreements have recently consolidated".[41]

EEC FOOD AID: A POLICY WHICH SHOULD SUBORDINATE COMMERCIAL AND ECONOMIC OBJECTIVES TO HUMANITARIAN OBJECTIVES

Shortly after the October 1973 war, when the world economic and political crisis was at its peak, the Commission turned its attention to defining an EEC strategy adequate to meet the new economic situation.[42] Since the food crisis posed the most urgent problems, the Commission first concentrated on devising appropriate machinery for their solution. The Memorandum of

March 1974[43] proposes a policy which, unlike the two previous approaches, avoids weighing the advantages of the commercial against the economic objectives, subordinating both to humanitarian objectives.

The objectives of EEC food aid: to meet the requirements of the developing countries

The Memorandum of March 1974 also criticizes the existing link between food aid projects and surpluses (at least for products other than cereals), not because this link reveals the lack of an EEC commercial or development policy, but because it conflicts with what should be the primary objective of these projects, which is to meet the food requirements of the developing countries.

The arguments used to justify this order of priority are not altogether convincing. Is the priority given to the requirements of the developing countries a means of dissociating food aid from the agricultural commercial policy and of tying it to the development cooperation policy?

The policy procedures proposed

Adopting a somewhat non-committal approach, the Commission avoids ruling out any of the possible objectives of food aid, even while giving priority to the humanitarian objective. Nevertheless, the policy procedures proposed seem inadequate to the execution of the project as a whole.

a. *Volume and programming of the aid.* The Memorandum of March 1974 proposes a massive supply programme. Believing that the "food shortage has gone beyond the warning point",[44] the Commission recommends expanding, regularizing and diversifying supplies of food aid.

b. *The development of the partner countries.* However, the supply programme is not accompanied by an equally well planned development cooperation programme. The Commission merely proposes that the EEC should use the existing machinery, but avoids making a specific choice which would denote a clear conception of the type of development which food aid must aim at promoting. The Memorandum maintains that most of the aid must continue to be granted as direct aid, especially as:

"The Community is not a simple intergovernmental institution. In the eyes of the world, it has an identity and a personality of its own".[45]

Indirect aid granted under the auspices of the international organizations, must, however, also be increased.

c. *A management procedure which calls for political reinforcement in Europe.* The Memorandum stresses the need for a significant improvement in food aid management. In order to meet the requirements of the developing countries, decisions must be taken more rapidly so that emergencies can be dealt with under the best possible conditions. They must also be better coordinated with the commercial and agricultural policies, so as to contribute more effectively to development.[46] The two changes which the Memorandum deems "essential"[47] would alter the decision-making structure in the EEC.

The first of these changes aims at restricting the Member States' margin of autonomy in relation to the EEC by reducing (at least partly, if not completely, for an initial period) the proportion of national projects. The second change is designed to "re-allocate . . . responsibilities . . . between the Council and the Commission"[48] by entrusting to the latter the management of the food aid policy.

The management of the expanded supply programme proposed by the Commission presupposes that direct relations will have to be established with, and a choice made between, the various categories of private agents (undertakings, cooperatives, farmers' unions, charitable institutions, etc.) interested in its implementation. However, the Commission does not specify its intentions on this point in its Memorandum of March 1974. The "Fresco" refers to the "driving forces behind public opinion", which suggests that the Commission has only a vague notion of the various agents with which it intends to work, since it defines them only in terms of their functions: "members of parliament, manufacturers, businessmen and trade unionists".[49]

d. *The partner countries.* Here, the Commission believes it should maintain its customary practice (see point 45 of the Memorandum) and to conclude food aid agreements only with the poorest of the developing countries.

CONCLUSION

The specific character of the European food aid policies

The foregoing assessment of the European food aid policies shows that their specific character lies in the fact that they are not linked to the commercial and economic objectives which are likely to be attributed to this form of public aid. From the commercial point of view, the difference is even more striking in the case of cereals than in the case of milk products, exports of which occasionally reflect general trends in food aid projects. From the economic point of view, too, the same phenomenon may be observed, since sales of industrial products necessary for agriculture to recipient countries tend to increase in some cases, but to diminish or remain unchanged in others.

Both the analysis of the alternative projects proposed by this report and the description of the decision-making process in the von Helldorff report suggest that we should look for the reason for the discrepancies between food aid policy and commercial and development policy in the pluralistic system of the EEC.

Pluralism is first of all reflected in the theories propounded in regard to the policies to be followed: these divide into three broad and usually conflicting alternatives, which never cover exactly the same group of projects.

Pluralism is also evident in the relationship between the implementers of Community policy. Decisions can only be taken unanimously, which means finding compromises acceptable to all the interested political participants and precludes any arrangement whereby one alternative is able to override the others. Furthermore, the division of responsibilities is such as to leave each

Member State an area of policy over which it has ultimate discretion. Two of the three schemes considered adhere to this decision-making procedure. The third, that of the Commission, endeavours to replace it by a less pluralistic decision-making procedure, advocating some narrowing of the sphere in which the Member States exercise ultimate authority and an increase in the decision-taking power of the Commission.[50]

Applicability of the alternatives proposed

However, which of the three alternatives discussed in the ruling bodies of the EEC would be the most favourable to a significant development of European policy? This brings us back to the question of the internal consistency of the three schemes or, in other words, their degree of applicability.

The first two alternatives considered set against each other the commercial and economic objectives of food aid. The first, which has the strongest support, conceives of food aid as a temporary instrument of development cooperation policy, to be used in the event of some social or natural "catastrophe" and as a means of expediting a process of economic modernization capable of expanding the external markets open to European industry. The second alternative, which has so far only been propounded in France, aims at integrating food aid into a commercial policy, the objective of which is the expansion and regularization of the external markets of European agriculture.

Our view is that both these schemes lack consistency in economic terms. Because they assume the requirements of the commercial agricultural policy to be incompatible with those of the development cooperation policy, they conceive of agricultural expansion in Europe as a process independent of, if not contrary to, the agricultural expansion of its underdeveloped partners. However, developments since 1945 have shown that the two processes are linked and complement each other. The emergence of surpluses in the industrial countries has resulted in an expansion of their agricultural exports, particularly in the form of food aid. These exports, by altering consumer habits in the developing countries, have also encouraged the establishment in these countries of modern agricultural sectors organized along the lines of those of the industrial countries. This process of modernization, based on the techniques introduced by the agricultural processing industries of the industrial countries, has contributed to the expansion of the markets for their products.

It is perhaps because it recognizes that exports depend on expansion and vice-versa, that the Commission has proposed another criterion for rationalizing the EEC's food aid policy. The way in which it justifies the priority given to humanitarian objectives over commercial, economical, political ones suggests in any event this interpretation of its approach. The Commission often emphasizes the political, commercial and economic interest of a policy which aims primarily at the satisfaction of the food requirements of the Third World. While the idea as a whole is an attractive one, if only because of the generous spirit which informs it, the methods suggested by the Commission for its implementation nevertheless do not carry conviction. Although its proposal contains a programme for expanding, regularizing and diversifying supplies, the Commission does not specify the links that have to be

275

forged with the agricultural commercial policy to enable food aid operations to help towards the expansion of "normal" agricultural exports, nor those which have to be established with the development cooperation policy to enable food policy to promote an increase in exports of industrial products. The Commission evidently believes that a food aid programme geared to the requirements of the developing countries will automatically correspond to the commercial and economic interests of the EEC. However, the ideas put forward by the Member States after the publication of the March 1974 Memorandum demonstrate that this theory of an automatic dovetailing of the humanitarian, commercial, economic and political objectives of food aid is not accepted and indeed is thought to be either too optimistic or too simplistic.

This report has been prepared by a study group working at the Centre d'études et de recherches internationales Fondation nationale des sciences politiques in 1977.
    The members of the group were:
    Mme Françoise Rastoin
        Fonds d'organisation et de régularisation marchés agricoles—FORMA
    M. Rohrbacher
        Office national interprofessionnel des céréales—(ONIC)
    M. Jean-Paul Chabert
        Institut national de recherche agronomique—(INRA)
    Mme Hélène Delorme
        Centre d'études et de recherches internationales—(CERI)
    M. Johny Egg
        Research associate CERI
    Were also consulted for special problems:
    M. Sylvio Almeida (Research-associate INRA)
    M. Marcel Marloie (INRA)
    M. Jean-Pierre Lafaurie, Director, Caisse nationale de Crédit agricole.
    Mrs. Delorme and Mssrs. Chabert and Egg, the editors of the report, are responsible for any mistakes or omissions in the report.

NOTES

1. On American policy, see Almeida, S., Chabert, J. P., von der Weid, J. M., *Les Exportations des Etats-Unis au titre de l'aide alimentaire*, Paris, INRA, 1975, p. 219.
2. In particular the UN, which administers the World Food Programme (WFP) and under whose auspices the World Food Conference was held in November 1974.
3. The agreement reached in the Council in June 1976 on the principle of multi-annual planning of food aid exports has not yet been put into effect.
4. See "International Grains Arrangement 1967 and Rules of Procedure (Wheat Trade Convention)", International Wheat Council, London, p. 63.
5. See minutes of the Council meeting of 22 March 1977—Council, S/534/77 (ALIM 21).

6. As an indication, in 1975 wheat and wheat flour accounted for 68% of aid in the form of cereals. It should be noted also that the figures in Table 1 do not reveal the true proportion represented by cereals, since they do not take account of national aid in the form of cereals.

7. The tables drawn up by Almeida *et al.*, *op. cit.*, show that between 1955 and 1973 dairy products accounted for 7.9% of the United States' total food aid (Tables I and IV, pp. 59 and 73).

8. This applies particularly to the Sahel countries, which accounted for a higher proportion of total aid than is indicated in our tables since the substantial aid to these countries in the form of sorghum is not taken into consideration.

9. On the variations in the rate for "normal" powdered milk exports, see the von Helldorf report, art. cit., p. 24.

10. The proportion of aid sold between 1955 and 1973 represented 71% of total food aid. See Almeida, *et al.*, *op. cit.*, p. 3.

11. The counterpart funds for food aid often provide additional finance for EDF projects in these countries.

12. Answer to Written Question No. 828/75, OJ No C 139, 21 June 1976.

13. The answer to Written Question No. 353/76 gives some information on the development projects financed in 1975. See OJ No C 269, 15 November 1976.

14. This corresponds to sections CTCI 56 and CTCI 712 of the OECD's International trade figures.

15. M.S.A.: most seriously affected countries, of whom India and Pakistan.

16. The diplomatic and military objectives of America's food aid policy are mentioned here simply as a reminder, since these are not considerations which enter into the EEC's policy.

17. See the classification of recipient countries drawn up by Almeida, S., Chabert, J. P., von der Weid, J. M., *op. cit.*, pp. 23–26.

18. The appropriations relating to PL 480 are fixed for four-year periods, at the same time as the domestic agricultural prices; they are adjusted each year to keep pace with the economic situation.

19. The spread of interest in food aid policy has been particularly marked in France: see the report of the Economic Council quoted below. There have also been developments in the EEC: see the views of the Committee of Professional Agricultural Organizations in the EEC, published in the 9 June 1977 (French) edition of *Agra-Europe*.

20. The task of the *ad hoc* Working Party on Food Aid is to carry out preparatory work under the direction of the Permanent Representatives Committee and with the assistance of the Commission, for the meetings of the EEC Council of Ministers.

21. See the UK delegation's memorandum concerning a new Community food aid strategy vis-à-vis the developing countries, dated 18 October 1976. The Netherlands paper relates to the EEC's emergency aid and humanitarian aid programme and was submitted on 4 November 1976. The German government's position is analysed in four documents: (1) The Second Federal German Government report on cooperation policy; (2) Annex C to the latter report comprising the "25 principles regarding political cooperation with the developing countries adopted by the Council of Ministers at its extraordinary meeting of 9 June 1975"; (3) Annex D to the same report entitled "Revised approach of the Federal Republic of Germany towards development cooperation policy" 1975 revised version: *A Development Cooperation Policy*. Federal Ministry for Cooperation-Information Service—Bonn, Nov. 1975; (4) Memorandum by the Federal German Government advocating an action programme aimed at further integrating Community development cooperation policies, 3 March 76.

22. "New strategy . . .", point 2.

23. Food aid is not specifically covered by the Treaty and is implemented on the basis of Articles 39 and 43, which govern agricultural policy.

24. Deutch Mémo.

25. See report by Klaus von Helldorf, art. cit., pp. 30–32.

26. Memorandum by the Federal German government advocating an action programme aimed at further integrating Community development cooperation policies, doc. cit., p. 5.

27. The German Government refers to the workers' unions, the cooperatives, the womens' organizations, the youth and student associations, the employer's associations and the churches—see "Revised approach . . ." art. cit., point 92. The Netherlands Government mentions international organizations such as the International Red Cross.

28. Netherlands memorandum, point 6.

29. Report by the Committee on Agriculture and Food (VIIth Plan), Paris, "La Documentation Francaise", 1976, p. 31.

30. *The prospects for world food supplies and the European agricultural policy*— Opinion on the report by Mr Alain Bienaymé adopted by the Economic and Social Council at its meeting of 26 January 1977.

31. *Id.*, chapter 3, section 3.

32. *Id.*, chapter 3, introduction.

33. *Id.* chapter 3, section 3, paragraph 2.

34. This order of priority reflects the position of the French negotiators in Brussels, who refuse to commit themselves on the volume and the programming of food aid on the grounds that it is one of the instruments by means of which the world agreements currently being negotiated will have to stabilize the agricultural products markets.

35. *Id.*, chapter 3, Section 3, para. 2.

36. *Id.*, chapter 3, section 3, para. 3 and 4.

37. *Id.*, opinion, p. 5.

38. *Id.*, chapter 3, section 2, para. 6.

39. See report by Mr. Bienaymé, chapter 3, section 2.

40. The report of the Committee on Agriculture and Food proposes that measures should be taken to "adjust to the different geographical zones concerned and to their individual requirements", *op. cit.*, p. 31.

41. Report by the Economic Council, *op. cit.*, general conclusion.

42. *Development Aid. Fresco of Community action tomorrow.* EEC Commission, 5 November 1974.

43. *Food Crisis and the Community's responsibilities towards Developing Countries. Memorandum on Food Aid Policy of the European Economic Community. Commission, 6 March 1974.*

44. Development aid . . . , *op. cit.*, p. 11.

45. Memorandum, point 41.

46. This requirement is discussed in point 20 of the paper on "The Food Crisis and the Community's responsibilities", which prefaces the Memorandum.

47. Memorandum, point 49.

48. *Id.*, point 49.

49. *Development aid, op. cit.*, p. 9.

50. It should be pointed out here that while the Commission, like the Council, endeavours to establish a unanimous consensus, it resorts more often than the Council to majority voting.

III. CONCLUSIONS*

The Policy of Food Aid

by *John Taylor* and *G. K. Roberts*

1. The meeting was agreed that the exercise of policy analysis and criticism that had been undertaken was valuable.

2. It was clear that food aid policy was particularly appropriate for discussion in a Conference on Commodity policy-making, touching as it did directly on general issues of world peace, of the development of Third World countries, and of foreign trade. However, the speakers emphasized that trade encouragement, if it occurred, was a "spin-off" from food aid policy, not a criterion or major purpose of such a policy.

3. After lengthy discussion, the consensus opinion was that the food aid policy of the Community was a specific, multinational policy, even if it was parallel to, and not unaffected by, national food aid policies. The Commission applied three criteria to the determination of which countries should be recipients of Community food aid:
- the need of the country for such aid,
- its level of per capita income,
- its balance of payments situation,
and the policy of the Commission was based solely on these criteria. The opinion of the authors of the University report was that other criteria, such as trade benefits and agricultural stabilization, could not be separated from Community policy-making on this matter.

4. Concerning the question of the feasibility of the Community policy, there was no doubt about the practicality of the existing food aid policy. There were divergences of view concerning the question of how useful this form of policy was, and it was suggested that a case could be made for concentrating aid more on technical assistance or other forms of aid. However, in times of crisis (such as a sudden food shortage) food aid was of great significance.

5. There were problems of monitoring the efficacy of food aid, including the difficulties of deciding upon appropriate indicators and of obtaining data.

6. It was agreed that the current state of food aid policy could be considerably improved, in particular, with regard to the following points:
a. a substantial increase in the volume of aid, especially in cereals;
b. the adoption of pluri-annual planning of food aid policy;
c. an increase in the degree of communitarization (rather than national action) of cereals food aid;

* The conclusions were completed and presented by Dr. G. K. Roberts.

d. an increase of staff in the Commission division responsible for the policy of food aid;

e. simplification of the procedures of Community decision-making for this policy sector.

Given such improvements, it would be easier to attain the objective of aiding the development and the viability of recipient countries. More attention could also be given to data acquisition, to monitoring of the effects of policy, and to consideration of the cross-impacts of food aid policy with other areas of Community responsibilities.

AIR INDUSTRY POLICY REPORT

I. AIR INDUSTRY POLICY REPORT

Political Choice in the Aerospace Sector

by *Richard Nobbs*

ORGANIZATION OF AND LEGAL BASIS FOR THE COMMISSION'S ACTIVITIES IN THE AEROSPACE SECTOR

Questions relating to aerospace manufacturing are covered within the Services of the Commission by Directorate General III (Internal Market and Industrial Affairs). Military affairs are in principle not part of the Commission's terms of reference. But since 70% of the aerospace manufacturing industry's turnover is military, the Commission believes that some linking of civil and military decision-making is necessary and inevitable.

A working group of the Council of Ministers was set up to report on this matter, although the Council confined themselves to considering that aspect of the Commission's proposals relating to a common civil aircraft manufacturing programme. On 14 March 1977 the report of the Working group led to a Council Declaration on the desirability of common activities and consultation in civil aircraft matters.

Apart from aerospace manufacturing, airlines and air transport aspects are covered by Directorate General VII (Transport). Space activities as such are covered by the European Space Agency and the Commission maintains a peripheral role in this field. Military affairs are a matter of national policies and involve NATO, Eurogroup and other organizations.

Scope of the commission under the treaty

It is necessary to refer to the Treaty to understand why the Commission makes certain proposals and not others, and what are the margins of the competence of the Commission. It may be thought for example that the Commission would be closely involved in the Concorde programme. In fact the Concorde programme is a bi-lateral one between Britain and France who have not required action on the project from the Community, dealing with it purely from two national viewpoints. The Commission can only work in areas referred to it in the common interest of the Community, where there is firm legal basis in the various Treaties, or where the Commission is given latitude under the Treaty which it believes are in the Community's interest and are not already covered.

It is worth noting, therefore, that not only does the Treaty setting up the EEC make no reference to aerospace, it makes no specific reference to industrial matters at all, merely confining itself to calling for fewer barriers to trade.

Although the Treaty calls for a Transport Policy (Articles 74–84), saying that this may be interpreted to include air transport by unanimous agreement it does not call for an Industrial Policy. The situation of Air Transport has been clarified lately by the European Court of Justice Ruling 67/74, which found that air transport matters were within the competence of general rules of the EEC Treaty and the Commission has in fact made proposals in this respect (Draft Decision 3 October 1975).

With respect to industrial policy, various summit meetings have called for concerted action in key industrial sectors. These sectors have been primarily those undergoing crises, which are strategically important, and in which the States have a major participation notably aerospace, nuclear power production, steel, conventional energy, shipbuilding, telecommunications and data-processing.

Apart from this direct declaration of interest the Treaty itself calls for harmonization of State Aids to industry, and concertation on commercial policy, including export credits. Both these issues affect the industry.

THE WORK OF THE COMMISSION 1967–1976

As seen, the Member States have declared a direct interest in aerospace. At the same time the nature and industrial difficulties of the industry have prompted the Commission to make various proposals.

In 1967, the Commission asked several international consultants to prepare a comprehensive study of the state of the industry in the EEC (then the Six) in comparison with that of the USA and the UK. The first major document by the Commission on aerospace matters was a Communication from the Commission to the Council dated 19 August 1972. It analysed the employment and work situation, the barriers to closer collaboration and the measures necessary to promote growth. Although the Council was supposed to debate and act on the draft legal implementing texts, the Communication was forwarded neither to the European Parliament nor to the Economic and Social Committee and no decisions were reached by the Council until March 1975 so that the Commission was unable to take further action until that date. However, on 4 March 1975 the Council passed a Resolution calling for "concerted action and consultation" amongst the Member States on matters of aeronautical policy. This Resolution *called upon the Commission to submit a further report by 1 October 1975* "on the conditions in the industry and the measures necessary for its development".

The latter Report was entitled "Action Programme for the European Aeronautical Industry". It was a fairly comprehensive set of proposals for a common civil aircraft programme, and called for urgent decisions to be taken by the Community in view of the difficult situation faced by the industry. The Programme was forwarded to the European Parliament and the ESC who received it with generally favourable opinions. Progress in the Council, however, was slow, and no proper discussion took place until 12 March 1976 in COREPER, at which time it was agreed to form a working group within the Council of senior national government officials whose role was to report on the market prospects for civil aircraft and in relation the possibilities for a joint programme.

The detailed proposals of 1972 and 1975 are described in the following sections.

DESCRIPTION OF THE COMMISSION'S PROPOSALS OF 19 JULY 1972 AND 1 OCTOBER 1975

The Communication from the Commission to the Council on "a policy for the promotion of industry and technology in the aeronautical sector" dated 19 July 1972 was still concerned with the industry of "the Six", although the UK's aerospace statistics were included where appropriate. The document took the form of: a review of the EEC industry; a discussion of the reasons for its weak position in the civil market plus recommendations for improving its performance; five "implementing texts" which embodied the recommendations mentioned above; and a statistical annex to provide backing for the arguments in the previous parts.

The very weak position of EEC manufacturers in 1970 in the world civil market (3.8%) and in the European market (15%) was attributed to:

a. the competitive edge given to US manufacturers by having a large, dynamic home market (50% of the world market).

b. A fragmented home market, where the users—airlines and governments—made their policies on an individual basis rather than a Community basis.

c. a fragmented industrial effort—i.e., too many, frequently competitive projects launched by governments, and duplicated Research and Development.

d. the economies of scale achieved by US companies with their large turnover.

e. the financial strength of the large US companies.

f. dynamic support from the US authorities and EXIM bank in particular in helping with export marketing.

g. the devaluing of the dollar in relation to European currencies added to un-harmonized commercial efforts by European, credit—assurance, agencies.

h. difficulties involved in cross-border collaboration.

To improve this situation long-term objectives were laid down which were defined as being the need to agree on a co-ordinated air transport policy and to encourage trans-national mergers of manufacturers into bigger and stronger industrial groups.

More immediately the Council was called on to consider and take action on:

a. agreement on a small number of civil aircraft programmes to form the basis of a common programme.

b. a better and more co-ordinated approach to financing of civil international programmes, both at the Research and Development and the marketing phases.

c. joint work on Certification, Standards and advanced Research.

Four implementing texts were submitted to the Council which, if adopted would have required Member States to consult each other and to co-ordinate their efforts in making aeronautical policy; to co-ordinate financial aid both for Research and Development and for marketing; to harmonize export credit insurance, exchange guarantees and guarantees against inflation during manufacture; and finally they would have required the Commission to attempt to have the 5% tariff on imports of aircraft into the USA removed by the US authorities.

THE COMMISSION'S PROPOSALS OF 1 OCTOBER 1975

After two and a half years of discussion of the Commission's previous proposals, the Council finally passed a resolution on 4 March 1975 agreeing to "co-ordinate their civil aeronautical policies", and calling for yet another Commission report by 1st October of that year which should examine "the operating conditions obtaining in the Community aircraft construction industry and on the measures necessary for its development". The resulting document was duly forwarded on 1 October. It took the form of a brief introduction and conclusions; five annexes dealing with particular aspects of the industry; a draft decision for the Council on civil aircraft; and a draft Resolution for the Member States on military aircraft.

The introduction to the document summarized the reasons for the industry's weakness and laid them mostly at the door of the individual governments viz:
– Resources spread over too many programmes,
– No co-ordinated marketing strategy
– Inadequate marketing support for existing projects
– No co-ordination of decision-making.

It then called for a co-ordinated air-transport policy and collaboration on military procurement as long-term objectives. As short-term objectives it called for agreement at a Community level on a civil aircraft programme, including agreement on the development of a range of aircraft; finance through the Community; and joint work on certification, standards, environmental pollution and basic research.

Most important it called the attention of Member States to the fact that a situation had arisen in the aircraft market where there appeared to be a powerful opportunity open to EEC manufacturers if they collaborated together, rather than competed against each other as in the past.

The five annexes examined in some detail the situation in the manufacturing industry in the EEC. Despite the air-transport market suffering a declining growth rate since 1970 (which had hit the industry in both the USA and the EEC); and the fact that during the period 1970–1974 all the EEC's new projects had reached the marketing stage; nevertheless *no progress had been achieved since 1972 in either co-ordination of decision-making or of marketing existing projects.*

Even though virtually all projects involved international co-operation, on the major projects (the A300 airbus and the MRCA) the Member States were not collaborating but rather competing with each other.

The annexes went on to examine the future market and reached two conclusions:
a. that the USA's home market would become a declining percentage of the world market with the consequent opening up of opportunities for the EEC.
b. That the major markets for the period 1975–1990 required aircraft which the EEC industry was well placed to supply.

286

The Commission therefore proposed the establishment of a joint civil transport programme based on existing aircraft or derivatives of existing aircraft aimed at supplying the main requirements which had been identified i.e., aircraft of 100 seats, 150 seats, 200 seats (approx.). It offered as a suggestion that the above programme could be filled by:

a. the F28 with refanned Spey engines,

b. a derivative of either the BAC 1-11, HS Trident or Dassault Mercure,

c. the A300 B10,

and called for urgent discussions on this subject at a Community level. At the same time it suggested that financing should also be on a Community basis.

For the medium term it proposed that agreement should be reached on objectives related to structures, employment and levels of productivity and that there should be a Community programme for basic research and development.

A draft Decision was submitted in respect of the adoption of a common programme, common financing, common Research and Development, harmonized financial support and harmonized laws, tariffs, regulations, standards, etc. It called for the disappearance within 5 years of national aids to the industry in favour of Community agreed aid.

In the field of air-transport it stated the objectives to be firstly, the creation of a European airspace managed on a Community basis with the aim of Rationalizing Route structures and services and secondly, negotiations of traffic rights with non-Member States to be done on a Community basis.

A draft Resolution called for the creation of a European Military Aircraft Procurement Agency to co-ordinate weapons procurement and to deal with the USA with a view to achieving reciprocity in arms purchase.

OPINIONS OF THE EUROPEAN PARLIAMENT AND THE ECONOMIC AND SOCIAL COMMITTEE ON THE PROPOSALS

Three committees of the European Parliament prepared opinions on the Commission's proposals: the Political Affairs Committee; the Committee on Regional Policy and Transport; and the Committee on Budget. These three opinions were transmitted to the Economic and Monetary Affairs Committee who prepared the final opinion.

Political Affairs: this opinion considered the strategic implication of a common aircraft policy. It concluded that it was vital to co-ordinate civil and military technology, and welcomed the Commission proposals although calling for closer collaboration with NATO and other military aircraft planning groups, plus a formal cooperative structure with the USA.

Regional Policy and Transport: this opinion reviewed the failure of Member States to achieve a common air transport policy, and welcomed the Commission's proposals although calling for greater emphasis on the need for a rationalized air transport system. It accepted, however, that without the basic political will in the Member States to have a common equipment manufacturing programme, there was little point in the Commission making detailed proposals for air transport rationalization.

Budget: this opinion felt that the proposals needed exhaustive study by the Council, so that the full details of the various proposals could be examined. Without these details it was not possible to formulate opinions on budgetary estimates or mechanisms for financial management of a common programme.

The final opinion was therefore a positive support for the Commission activities and was adopted after debate by the Parliament.

Prior to the opinion of the Parliament the Economic and Social Committee produced an opinion which was favourable to the Commission's proposals, but suggested that the objectives should be approached in two stages.

The first stage should take into consideration the political difficulties involved in creating an EEC "market". It required that the Commission study in greater depth all aspects of a common civil aircraft programme including effects on employment, market prospects, etc. and get this accepted by Member States. Parallel with this, concrete Community action could be taken on aligning sales finance practices, common technical and airworthiness standards, and on setting up a common basic research programme.

The second stage should be mainly a function of the speed with which the EEC moved or otherwise to Economic and Monetary Union. The management and financing of a Common Programme should be a function of the will of Member States to organize things on a Community basis rather than on a national basis but the Commission should nevertheless make clearer its proposals on how centralization of policy making and management might be achieved.

EVALUATION OF THE FEASIBILITY OF THE PROPOSALS AND THEIR ALTERNATIVES

The Commission's 1975 proposals were based on the following premises:
1. The civil aircraft manufacturing industry in the EEC has been in steady decline.
2. Future market projections indicated that opportunities existed for non-US manufactured products in the growing market of the Third World.
3. Industry in the EEC has a base of technology and projects suited to the large markets of the next decade.
4. The industry has had long experience of collaboration, particularly within Europe.
5. Industry and unions showed support for efforts towards greater European collaboration.
6. Strategically the Community risked an enormous balance of payments deficit and the *possibility* of complete dependence on a single US manufacturer if its own industry gave up civil aircraft manufacture.
7. The Member States were heavily involved in providing state aids to their aerospace industries.

Based on these premises the Commission pointed out that there was general world agreement on markets for:
- a 100 seat aircraft
- a 150 seat aircraft
- a 220 seat aircraft

288

The only differences of opinion were on the precise aircraft configuration and the timing of the market forecasts. Moreover, it was generally felt that economy demanded that new projects should be derivative versions of existing aircraft. The EEC industry had existing aircraft which could well form the basis for derivatives to fill the above market slots. (The F28, the Mercure, the BAC 1-11, the HS Trident, the A300 Airbus).

Encouraged by the work of the major EEC airlines in trying to define common requirements and by the work of the main European manufacturers in "the Group of 7" in trying to define a common set of proposals to fill these requirements, the Commission proposed that the Council should agree on the need for a common programme and negotiations should take place on the projects themselves, the breakdown of work and the effect on employment. It was assumed to be a logical step forward to propose that if the Member States could agree on the need for a common programme, the latter should be financed centrally in whole or in part out of the Community budget. This would actually make the financing easier for the Member States since from 1978 the Community budget would be financed from its own funds ("*fonds propres*") and the Community budget is currently heavily out of balance due to the large percentage devoted to agriculture. The level of financing needed was assumed to be roughly equivalent to the total of 1973/74 national aids.

It was further assumed that a central programme would rationally require central management. The intention, however, was not to create a large technical organization, such as the European Space Agency, but to use the existing skills and personnel of the Member States governments who would form project-based teams, and who would deal contractually with a permanent industrial structure, on the lines of an expanded Airbus Industrie. Some form of permanent industrial structure was thought to be necessary to provide continuity in the market for customer airlines, an advantage possessed by Boeing and Douglas which could not be attained by continually changing industrial consortia.

In the much longer term the Commission proposed an EEC Military Procurement agency and a common air transport policy, but more closely related to the Common Aircraft Programme were proposals for aligning sales financing, basic research programmes, work on airworthiness and standards.

Reception of the commission's proposals

Although the proposals reflected fairly accurately the wishes and requirements of industry, the Commission's proposals for centralization of decision-making and financing at a Community level were not well received. The main objections might be summarized as follows:
1. Collaboration by the EEC Member States would exclude collaboration with the USA and would bar Europeans from access to USA technology.
2. The proposals would lead to "committee aeroplanes", whereas it is industry who should decide which aeroplanes to build.
3. It is not desirable to create another "faceless bureaucracy", which, in order to run something as big as a common Civil Aircraft Programme, would

need to have thousands of employees, and would be outside the direct control of Member States.

4. Centralized financing would mean that decision-making would be situated outside the control of Member States and such problems as sustaining employment or using state aid to the industry as an instrument of industrial or regional policy would no longer be possible.

5. The Commission should confine itself to central technical areas, such as the alignment of export credit and insurance matters, or agreement on a common certificate of airworthiness, and not make proposals on important issues.

6. If the Community were to build commonly agreed aircraft, the Member States airlines will be "forced" to buy European and lose their commercial independence.

7. The major part of the industry's turnover being military, the Member States could not surrender their authority over their defence interests and therefore could not delegate authority over the civil part.

Whereas the Commission found widespread support, the above objections are a synthesis of some of the opinions encountered within industrial, political and official circles, in the process of consultation it engaged in after publication of the proposals. It was hoped that discussion in the Council would air these points, and enable the Commission to put up counter arguments.

Since the alternatives to the Commission proposals largely revolved around the above points it is proposed to discuss them in some detail.

USA Technology. The Commission favours collaboration with the USA. However, it feels that Member States would serve their interests better by dealing on a united basis, with a common policy, rather than on several bi-lateral bases. The Commission feels that bi-lateral collaboration between say France/USA, Britain/USA would: result in splitting the EEC domestic air transport market; weaken European technology because the USA does not believe in technology transfer, and might become even more reluctant in this area should Europe perhaps in the future become more socialist; lead for this reason to EEC firms increasingly becoming subcontractors to USA industry; mean that EEC unions would have even less say in major decisions effecting employment; not necessarily guarantee access to the American market.

On the other hand for technical reasons collaboration with the USA is vital, inevitable and exists to a considerable extent already, for example, in aero-engines (SNECMA/GE, Rolls-Royce/Pratt and Whitney).

The main point is that US industry also needs to collaborate with Europe, and Europe should seize this opportunity to establish a firm negotiating base to avoid the situations listed above and to ensure, for the consumers in the EEC, that airlines are not soon faced with a situation where there is no choice of aircraft manufacturer—just one or two large US monopolistic suppliers.

"Committee aeroplanes". This is a specious but often made implication that the Commission's proposals would lead to bureaucratic decisions. In fact although aircraft projects arise from years of market study and technological solutions and although these will always be the prime function of industry,

it is a fact that all large civil projects are now collaborative and mainly government financed. Collaborative efforts have already begun (The Group of 7, the quadripartite talks between France, UK, Germany, Holland) and the Commission's proposals would alter nothing of these contacts, but in fact should improve the decision-making process by providing a forum where decisions would become part of a continuous process rather than being made on an *ad hoc* uncommitted basis, with a strong background of mutual suspicion.

Centralized bureaucracy. The Commission has studied the workings of the Netherlands Institute for Aeronautical Research, which runs a large, profitable aircraft and space programme with 20/30 employees.

The Commission feels that far from creating a new bureaucracy, the existing skills and competences of officials in Member States could be welded together in some semi-permanent governmental organization not centralized anywhere, with a small central bureau modelled on that of the Netherlands to administer the work. Financing could be done by existing institutions such as the European Investment Bank or the Commission itself, always under the control of the Council and of the European Parliament through the Budget procedure.

In fact for all collaborative projects (MRCA, Jaguar, Transall, Airbus, Concorde, etc.) there exists groupings of officials. Since the Commission feels that one of the main needs of the European industry is to have a permanent industrial marketing and product support organization (on expanded Airbus Industrie lines) it believes that its proposals could in fact rationalize the present system and make it less haphazard.

Lastly, it is worth pointing out that the principle of a centralized organization has already been accepted by Member States for the European Space Agency, and that the Commission is not at present proposing the same thing for the aeronautical sector.

Centralized financing. If Member States agree on a common programme it is logical that they should seek to have the financing of this programme centralized and make use of the already voted "fonds propres". It is also logical that they should try to phase out national aid which might otherwise lead to interests conflicting with the Common Programme. If they have problems of a social or regional fund nature the Community has its own mechanisms already in use for assisting with these; no new institutions need to be set up.

On the other hand, if there are worries that project expenditure and control would be weaker if done on a Community basis, the Commission would point out that these situations are satisfactorily handled by Member States for current collaboration projects, and under the structure envisaged, the same personnel would be involved, all under the control of the Member States themselves through the Council.

Export credits, C. of A., etc. As explained earlier in this paper the Member States themselves called for proposals of a basic kind situation. Previous to the "Action Programme" in 1975 the Commission had already made proposals about export credits but the Council has found itself unable to act and these proposals have never been withdrawn. Ideally, however, any work done at a Community level should be geared to long-term aims. Basic research for example should be geared to the precise needs of a Common Programme. As a result therefore the Commission has called for a *prior decision on projects before making more detailed proposals.*

On the question of export credits the Commission feels that the EEC exporters should be in the same competitive position as US exporters with Eximbank, and has made proposals that the Eximbank's role should be played by a European Export Bank. For financing within the Community it is hoped the European Investment Bank may play a greater role. On the other hand there is little value in making such proposals if European industry has no products to finance.

Commercial freedom of airlines and industry. Airlines already have limited commercial freedom, because there are a limited and decreasing number of manufacturers and aircraft. The worst situation the airlines could be in is at the mercy of a single monopolistic US manufacturer. It is in their interest therefore that they work towards maintaining a situation of competition. What has been proposed is that they would work closer with industry and amongst themselves in defining specifications (as happens in the USA). Clearly, if European airlines define a specification and European industry builds it, the airlines would be expected to buy, all things being equal. European aircraft are technically equal to US aircraft and if the manufacturers failings lie in product support, the remedy is in the hands of the airlines to specify what they require, and the manufacturers to produce it.

Whilst not therefore proposing to shackle European airlines to a "buy European" requirement, the Commission feels that the long-term interests of the airlines themselves is in supporting a strong European industry. Furthermore cooperation between airlines should lead to rationalization of air transport policy, greatly benefiting the European consumer.

Military. Member States already take military decisions in a plethora of international organizational structures, so there would be no loss of sovereignty. On the other hand a strong civil programme has benefits industrially— spreading the overheads, retaining costly scientists, technologists and engineers, improvement of manufacturing processes and productivity.

Since Member States will wisely continue to maintain a military capability, it would seem sensible not to throw away their civil capability and thus make military technology more expensive just at a time when there is high inflation and defence budgets are shrinking.

SUMMARY OF THE ATTITUDE OF THE MEMBER STATES

From contacts made at various levels in the Member States, one can draw the following impression of the attitude of the Member States in matters of air policy. Eire, Luxembourg and Denmark have no large aerospace interests, although the latter have an electronics and equipment industry and have been involved in subcontract work, for example on the recently purchased American military F16. One might summarize their position as being favourable in principle to the proposals of the Commission provided the solutions proposed are rational and in the interests of the Community as a whole.

France has a major industry. Projects such as the Airbus—which is being assembled in France—the Mercure, which although not commercially successful is one of the few new airframes developed since 1967, and the CF6 and CFM56 engines—developed with General Electric in the USA—are key elements in all project negotiations. These projects are central to the various discussions currently taking place.

Faced, however, with a serious employment problem in its factories caused by the general recession in airline purchases, the French became visibly impatient with European efforts to agree on projects, for example in the "Group of 7". Furthermore they had a situation of industrial rivalry between Aérospatiale (a nationalized company and, officially the vehicle for all civil aircraft development) and Dassaulit, (a private company and with an interest in pushing its own civil project—the Mercure).

This situation let to contacts being made with US industry and links being formed between Dassault/Douglas and Aérospatiale/Boeing to study various aeroplanes. It was announced in early 1976 by the French Administration that a review of the studies would be made in June 1976, and a decision taken by the President as to which course to follow. Although in isolation either of the two collaborations seemed attractive, the internal contradictions were such as to make a decision more difficult than at first appearance. For example, the two collaborations were mutually exclusive; choosing the Dassault/Douglas Mercure would mean not being able to concentrate on the Airbus; choosing the Boeing collaboration would mean problems with European Airbus partners. In any case the state of the market did not allow sufficient confidence to be placed in freezing a design. The result of the announced French deadline however was to spur activity by all countries and to create a situation where, because everyone was involved in bi-lateral contacts, it was not possible to raise the Commission's proposals within the Council until 12 May 1976.

The UK was occupied up to April 1977 with nationalization procedures and, with the French, on getting Concorde into the USA. Its main European energies are spent on military projects and it has no governmental stake in the Airbus. On the contrary, the UK had competed with France both through the RB211 engine on the Tristar and the MRCA. UK industry and the unions, on the other hand have supported the idea of increased European collaboration. The position of the authorities appears to be roughly in favour of more European collaboration, notably through the airbus programme, without necessarily accepting a long-term need for action at a Community level.

Germany has recently reviewed its aerospace policies through the Grunner Report. Its conclusions were that it should continue with its present collaborative European policies, notably in the Airbus, the MRCA, and the FVW-Fokker 614. Recently, too, Lufthansa has come out in favour of the Airbus B10 project which is the cornerstone of the Commission's proposals. As might be expected the Germans are not, in principle, in favour of centralization of project finance and administration in the framework of a common programme. However, the Commission feels confident that once it is given the opportunity of showing that its proposals are based on providing a practical solution to problems which must arise if the Community adopts a common programme, and which are based on a successful working model as in Holland, and which keeps financial control in the hands of the Member States, then the Germans will be in favour of a fully Europeanized Programme. For them the disadvantages of following a policy of bilateral arrangements (even if these are European ones) are that, whereas they may have some bargaining power on the A300 project they have little elsewhere, and this could mean that the UK might take unilateral decisions to launch for example the HS146, or an M45-engined version of the HS748, both of which projects would hurt their interests in the VFW-Fokker F28, VFW 614.

The Dutch have consistently followed a policy of European collaboration. They have interests in all the major European projects. Whilst initially not impressed by the centralized aspects of the Commission's proposals, because they believed that it was proposed to take all decision-making out of the hands of the Member States and rest it in a large Commission bureaucracy, it is felt they will strongly support any practical proposals for management of a common programme, particularly when such proposals are based on the Dutch system itself.

Italian industry has strong links with US industry, notably in the collaboration with Boeing on the 7X7 project. They also have interests in several European collaborative ventures, notably the MRCA, and this together with the fact that Boeing have appeared to postpone the 7X7, together with the recent Lockheed affair, has made them more receptive to a European joint programme, particularly should it include helicopters.

Finally, the Belgians have supported strongly the basic idea of greater European collaboration.

SUMMARY OF THE ALTERNATIVE POLICIES OPEN TO THE COMMUNITY AND THE LONG-TERM FUTURE FOR THE INDUSTRY

This section is divided into a consideration of the two main questions: With whom to collaborate? How to organize such collaboration?

With whom to collaborate?

As can be seen from the previous sections the aerospace industry has been characterized over the past fifteen years by increasing collaboration. European industry now has various alternatives:
- to collaborate on a European level to a greater extent,
- to collaborate with the USA to a greater extent,
- to extend collaboration increasingly to third parties such as Canada, Japan, Sweden, Spain, the developing countries.
- to continue on an *ad hoc* basis with a mixture of all these.

294

Apart from the above choices there is a *parallel* one which has been growing in importance for a decade, which is: should *European* collaborative arrangements continue to be *ad hoc*, relying on bilateral or multilateral project arrangements, such as for example with the A300, Concorde, Jaguar, MRCA, and so on, or should there be some more formal, concerted, long-term basis? The latter principle is one which has been accepted by Europeans in other spheres, such as for example Euratom and the European Space Agency.

The Commission's analysis of the recent history of Community aerospace industry (Annex 1 of "Action Programme for the European Aeronautical Sector") is that, apart from the collapse of the market, the decline of the industry has been due to an over-fragmented effort by Member States. Although there has been much collaboration it has frequently been self-competitive. For example Europe has launched 10 jet transport civil programmes compared to the 9 of the USA, and has had an average production run of 86 compared with 461 for the Americans (figs. to 31 December 1974).

In 1976, however, the technological gap between the USA and the Europeans has narrowed. With the decline of the space and military effort in the USA fewer launch bases are provided for civil programmes, whereas European technology has been advanced in civil technology by expenditure on Concorde, VFW 614, Airbus and Mercure. In a submission by Boeing to the US Senate in January 1976, Boeing declared that it was now necessary for US companies to seek access to European markets and European government-funded technology for new programmes.

Now the main attraction of collaboration with the USA for Europe lies in the access to markets, since the USA represents half of the world civil air-transport market itself and the USA manufacturers dominate the market as a whole. There is a natural desire in some Member States to achieve long production runs and strengthen their industry by bi-lateral collaboration with the USA. But resistance to European products by American airlines is still very strong, quite apart from the existence of tariff and other barriers, which together with higher levels of inflation and lower levels of productivity in Europe, make trans-Atlantic collaboration, at an industrial level, difficult. This is less true of the aero-engine side which is now moving toward two large groupings for civil engines, namely GE/SNECMA and P&W/Rolls-Royce.[71]

The other attraction is that of building up one's own industry with American help. Collaboration in the long term should however be on the basis of equality, and there is an obvious disparity in the relative size of US and European manufacturers. The Americans do not willingly give up project leadership nor do they willingly exchange technological know-how on an equal basis, and this has been not infrequently stated by Boeing themselves. Unless long-term agreements are balanced, the European partner of such a deal must inevitably become more and more in substance a subcontractor.

On the other hand, EEC manufacturers have a long history of collaboration. The industry and the unions both recognize the need to retain some measure of control over decision-making, and that immediate efforts to strengthen cooperation should be at the European level. The technology exists, the market opportunities exist, the industrial framework exists. Provided that a long-term plan can be worked out, and an industrial and administrative framework created, European industry could then be sufficiently strong to negotiate with the USA on an equal footing, or, if necessary, bring in partners such as Canada or Japan.

The answer then to the three or four alternatives outlined above is that the Community should create a European aeronautical policy first, from which point of strength the EEC could negotiate with the USA or third parties as conditions warranted.

How to organize community collaboration?

If the policy proposed by the Commission is adopted, various alternative methods of organizing collaboration suggest themselves.

- For the major aeronautical countries to negotiate themselves, bringing in other Member States as expedient,
- For major aeronautical decisions to be taken at Council level, but the existing industrial and governmental procedures and machinery to be used,
- For some form of central co-ordinating agency to be created exterior to the Community,
- For the latter to be created within the Community.

The advantage of the first option is that it allows continuing freedom of choice for the partners to continue their partnership or go separate ways on succeeding projects. The disadvantage of such a method is that it implies continued fragmentation of effort notably in the area of Research and Development and marketing. One of the main advantages which Boeing and Douglas retain is the fact of continuity in the eyes of the market. Selling an aeroplane is one thing, but keeping it in the air is another, and for the latter any airline depends on a complicated relationship between people and organizations. Airbus Industrie has been slowly building up this required network, which already exists for BAC, HSA and Fokker. In the long term, it would be infinitely desirable to see some kind of stable and continuous grouping of these resources, rather than have them re-created for each new project; but pooling of these facilities would only be possible, and desirable, if work was continuous and successor aeroplanes to the original projects could be counted upon. This, however, requires political continuity and for this one must look at the other two options.

The introduction of a Common Civil Aircraft Programme within the Community framework should have the advantage of widening the industrial, political, and financial framework in which decisions on aerospace would be taken. One would be likely to get, for example, support for a continuous European point of view from the smaller countries. One could also begin to develop a coherent relationship with other major sectors influencing the manufacturing industry, such as air-transport. On the other hand one would again be dependent on an *ad hoc managing* organization totally dependent on shifting political requirements in the participating countries.

Furthermore airline clients are equally anxious to have a known identity to deal with when negotiating things like guarantees, and permanent governmental organization at the European level is necessary to provide this.

For this reason the Commission feels that a realistic initial solution could be to create a small central administrative unit whose job would be to coordinate the Common Civil Programme. However the Commission feels that the main problem is to obtain agreement on the nature of the programme and organizational questions will follow naturally from the technical nature of the programme. Nevertheless management of the programme on a day-to-day basis *could* be done by an industrial organization (built up perhaps from the existing Airbus Industrie) dealing with inter-governmental project teams who themselves would be of a semi-permanent nature and would be comprised of existing governmental experts in the Member States. Interface with the Commission and the Council of Ministers could be by means of the small central unit mentioned above.

For, and let this be stated as a general conclusion, the great advantage of a Community approach would be to give coherence and stability to an industry which is largely international in character and needs twenty-year timescales in its decision-making process. Allied to this would be a coherent approach to related areas such as Research and Development, air-transport, and military aspects. This is the sole aim of the Commission's proposals and it is the belief of the Commission that this approach is vital for the maintenance of Europe's capabilities in one of the commanding-height technologies.

II. AIR INDUSTRY POLICY COUNTER-REPORT

Air Industry Policy in the European Community

by *Martin Edmonds* and *Roger Williams*, with *M. Dillon* and *K. Hayward*

The European Commission has responsibility to investigate and propose remedies when Community performance lags Community potential. There can, therefore, be no denying its right to become involved in European aerospace questions. Unless more positive measures are adopted, the probability of further deterioration in this sector creates a sense of urgency; and the various summit pronouncements conveniently provide a specific legitimacy. With only cursory analysis, it is apparent that the "Action Programme" of 1975 when compared with the "Communication" of 1972 reflects significantly increased sensitivity on the part of the Commission to the harsh, and often contradictory, realities of the current situation. What remains at issue is whether the Commission is still too exhortatory and idealistic, or whether it does indeed now display "The rugged brow of careful policy".

This is what we have to examine here. We are not required to consider how the aerospace sector compares with other industries in terms of its contemporary appropriateness for a Community initiative. That is a separate matter, and indeed an even more fundamental one. We probably should remark here, however, that the Commission's proposals in respect of aerospace unfortunately cannot draw strength from the one advanced technology sector in which a formal European approach was initially attempted, nuclear energy. In that case the civil-military division and hardened national positions have for twenty years proved particularly insuperable obstacles. There is thus no reserve of demonstrated success on which the Commission can capitalize in addressing another advanced technology industry. But by the same token, the European collaborative process has historically been most harmonious and most successful when political and industrial pressures have been least.

THE PREMISSES OF THE COMMISSION'S PROPOSALS

It is basic to the Commission's proposals that the aerospace industry can make a major contribution to the European Community. An alternative view has been voiced—that the Community would be better without high technology industries, or perhaps even all industries, which seemed to call for indefinite state, and eventually Community, assistance. We are certainly not unaware of the damaging distortions which public subsidies can encourage, and we also recognize that Europe need not always slavishly follow the American and Soviet examples in its technological and industrial policies. Despite this, neglect of an aerospace capability where it already exists would

299

seem ill-advised and short-sighted. The employment aspects alone should give pause in current circumstances; but if further justification is wanted, then balance of payments and military considerations, and technological spin-off possibilities provide them.

Beyond all these essentially pragmatic considerations we feel there is an even more critical concern: what kind of society does future Europe want to offer its citizens? One of spreading prosperity undoubtedly, but also surely one of technological challenge, because science and technology effectively controlled, have clearly shown their ability to contribute to the adventure as well as the utility of human experience. It is our conviction that aerospace is an exceptionally visible and demanding form of advanced technology. The people it attracts are the very ones Europe cannot afford to lose.

Two other of the Commission's premises are that the European industry has the capability and the opportunity to excel, and that more is required to realize its existing potential than a straightforward intensification of existing co-operation. Taking aerospace within Europe as a whole, we are confident that the capability is there. We can also see that there is urgency if that capability is to be maintained without its becoming a growing burden for each of the separate Community members, without their having increasingly accepted collaboration with the United States on American terms, or without a retreat to narrow national specialization by product or component. It is not so easy to be sure about the opportunities. It is readily apparent that European aerospace not only starts from a weaker, because fragmented, position than does the American, but is also disadvantaged by having no captive domestic market.

We acknowledge that market opportunities cannot be considered in isolation, but are vitally dependent upon the organizations, products and deals available to exploit them and, especially in the case of aerospace, also on political leverage. It is bound, in present circumstances, to be something of an act of faith to postulate that the demand would be there if the supply were right, but it must be admitted that if there is no European supply, then European and Rest-of-the-World demand will in practice be met by American products designed initially to meet American needs.

Does it follow though that there must be a qualitative change in existing bi- and multi-lateral co-operation? It is highly probable that such a change, if it could be engineered, would greatly enhance the overall prospects of European aerospace; but we identify below some of the taxing realities which confront it, and would not want to limit ourselves to the view that there were no worthwhile alternatives.

ASSESSMENT OF THE COMMISSION'S ANALYSIS

The Commission's analyses of the circumstances of European aerospace in 1972 and 1975 are, on the evidence we have been able to collect, sound. There is naturally room for argument about the relative importance of the problems identified by the Commission, and in some respects we might wish to go further. Thus the financial strength of even the largest US companies can be overestimated, and dollar devaluation probably belonged in a different category from the other factors itemized in 1972. We would certainly also agree that there have been too many and frequently competitive projects, but would add that some of these projects have been the wrong ones—wrong both in themselves and in their impact on alternatives. Unlike the Commission we feel there is little risk of European dependence upon a single US manufacturer; the US airlines, military and government have, in general, too immediate an interest to allow such an eventuality.

The Commission's analysis underlines the unsatisfactory circumstances facing European aerospace very effectively. There is, nonetheless, an appearance that linguistic inconsistency has been used to avoid some tough realities. In the first place, there is no such entity at the present time as a European aerospace industry, except conceptually. Any analysis has, therefore, to be concerned with national aerospace industries. Whilst the Commission's strategy is essentially teleological, in that it sets the goal of European aerospace as the paramount objective and relates all strategies and proposals to that, the approach of the national aerospace industries is basically ontological. These industries accept the reality of their position, at least as they perceive it at any given time, and correspondingly try to optimize their decisions over both the short and longer terms. The shortening of the "Action Programme" lay in the representation that its strategic proposals were realistic steps towards the attainment of a specified goal when they were in fact, and were seen to be, hypothetical possibilities distanced from the realities with which the aerospace industries within Europe were and are faced.

For any progress towards the creation of a European aerospace industry, however it may ultimately be defined in terms of size, structure, expertise, and scope, a clear appreciation must be gained first of the current realities of the aerospace industries of Europe, and second of how these are perceived by those most likely to be affected by change and who are expected to decide upon and implement that change. Our focus of attention here is on the British aerospace industry, though our research to date suggests that in general terms the realities perceived by members of the British aerospace industry have their parallels on the continent. The differences are more of degree than kind.

It is an old adage that what one sees depends largely upon where one stands. Thus, British aerospace manufacturers recognize both a British and a European context. It is important therefore to examine in some detail not simply the situation facing a "European aerospace industry", but the structure and salient characteristics of the separate national aerospace industries. It is upon the latter that perception of the former should largely depend.

How do the British aerospace manufacturers see their industry relative to those of their continental counterparts? Bearing in mind that there has been collaboration between most aerospace companies within Europe over the past fifteen or so years, the basis for comparison and judgement is, *ceteris paribus*, well founded. Whilst according full and proper recognition to the advanced technical skills and notable managerial achievements of their continental colleagues, there remains some general feeling within the British aerospace industry that, rocketry apart, Britain is the only country in Europe with an indigenous, balanced, across-the-board capability in facilities, skill and size, to undertake simultaneous major civil and military aircraft programmes.

301

Those who think thus argue that, in particular, within Europe only Britain has, independent of the United States, state-of-the-art technology in aerospace propulsion. They regard Britain as also having some useful leads in many equipment, avionics, and airframe production fields. These views are not universally shared within Britain, and they are certainly questioned abroad. Two general conclusions may be drawn: firstly, within any strategy intended to lead towards European aerospace, due recognition needs to be given to the dominant position of Britain, as perceived by some, and especially politicians, both in the politically sensitive context of size and employment, and in the psychologically sensitive one of national prestige and capability; and, secondly, if the strategy of creating a European industry is to make real progress, and be internationally credible, it must in the final analysis be recognized that it can be built only out of the technical strengths of the extant industries located predominantly, though not exclusively, in Britain, France, and Germany.

DIVERSIFICATION AND ORIENTATION

It is misleading, or at least premature, to talk of a "European aerospace industry". It is also rather imprecise to suggest that there is a British, or any other aerospace industry, as such and in isolation. There are many companies within the United Kingdom engaged in producing components for aerospace products and they have varying degrees of diversification and aerospace orientation. There is a small number of companies involved in airframe manufacture and assembly and only one producing engines. It is thus preferable and more accurate to talk of the aerospace sector of British industry. The critically important point here is that national aerospace policy and strategic plans for "Europeanization" impact differently on different fields within the aerospace sector, and appreciation of what that impact means for the commercial, employment, and technological futures of each sphere of activity and each company varies significantly.

In the interests of simplicity, the British aerospace sector can be conveniently divided between the airframe, aero-engine, avionics and equipment spheres of activity. Each sphere has different employment levels, capital requirements, elasticities of demand, options for diversification, competitive positions, structural complexity, production lead times, and so on, leaving quite aside the wider political connotations of its activities. Upon all these collaborative European strategies will necessarily impact. As a broad generalization, the attractiveness of collaboration is proportional to the degree of aerospace-orientation of the company plus a combination of total product launch costs and length of lead time. The airframe and aero-engine elements of the aerospace sector tend therefore to be more receptive to collaborative proposals. Yet even here there are noticeable differences, the most significant of which is the felt imperative for the aero-engine industry to secure a world-wide civil and military market. If the latter means collaboration whether within Europe or with the United States, then these options would be treated on their commercial merits. Expressed another way, the opportunity costs of collaboration with European partners are greater for the manufacturers of avionics and equipment than they are for those of engine and airframe production and assembly. Until essentially commercial incentives can be provided to lower these opportunity costs, some divergence of attitude and policy towards collaboration will persist within the British aerospace sector as a whole.

From a purely structural standpoint, several other factors also influence the outlook of those who must take decisions for the future. Space permits only brief mention of them here. Of particular significance, and especially because it differentiates aerospace within Europe from that of the United States, there is the division between publicly and privately owned companies. The full implications of the publicly owned British Aerospace cannot yet be ascertained, though the experiences of Rolls Royce (1971) and, indeed, of Aérospatiale, could be expected to serve as a guide. It is still not really sufficient to imply, as did the Commission in its 1972 proposals, that the industry can be directed towards Europe because of the monopsonist position of the Government, public ownership and the dependency of the aerospace sector, whether private or public, on public financial support. A case could conversely be made that public ownership constitutes a greater constraint on collaborative proposals since it adds an overtly political dimension to the mainly commercial preoccupations of private industry. With public ownership, the Government and the relevant Departments become accountable to the public, unlike a Board of Directors, which is answerable principally to shareholders. Public interest in the performance of the aerospace sector is considerably more comprehensive in its concerns than the basically commercial preoccupations of shareholders. In the British case, the size of British Aerospace might even constrain flexibility, and the assumption that wider control means a broader range of feasible programme options is, at the least, debatable.

The British Government's position that each aerospace programme will be considered on its own commercial merits, whether in conjunction with a European partner or not, could be held to give inadequate weight to other, largely political, considerations. The relevance of these other considerations, for example prestige and independence, must be seen alongside figures of employment in each of the spheres of activity of which the British aerospace sector is comprised, and in the light of demographic and regional economic circumstances.

MILITARY AND CIVIL CONTRACTS

A further structural distinction of importance is the division within British Aerospace between military and civil contracts. Approximately sixty per cent of British Aerospace turnover per annum is military. Without this steady source of work it is well understood that aerospace as a whole throughout Britain would be in serious difficulties. The real significance of the division as far as the Commission's proposals for Europe are concerned is less clear. On the one hand, the military dimension is outside the Commissions' brief; but if the objective is the creation of a rationalized European aerospace industry, then a current 60% military turnover cannot be ignored. On the other hand

303

it can be argued that the inter-operability of military and civil aerospace products and technological spin-off from the one to the other are so limited that effectively it is not of fundamental importance that the one is excluded from the Commission's remit. Furthermore, the military dimension is the focus of attention elsewhere. The real situation, we believe, lies somewhere between the two propositions: technological transfer from military to civil aerospace is not as great as is commonly assumed, but collaboration in military programmes helps reduce unit costs for participating nations, and has distinct military advantages, which have been recognized by the Independent European Programme Group (IEPG) and the Western European Union.

The significance of the civil-military division varies both between companies and between aerospace spheres. With the establishment of British Aerospace this significance will diminish as the opportunity to transfer skilled employees from one project to another will increase. This has long been so in the case of engines. For the avionics and equipment spheres the significance will remain higher, partly because ownership has remained in private hands and partly because of their degree of product specialization. For them, perhaps, it is more important that overall schemes for European collaboration include the military side, primarily to ensure that military programmes continue to provide a basic stimulus and cash flow for further product developments.

In many respects, the military side of European aerospace has moved further in the direction of collaboration than has the civil. Although there have been notable exceptions, in particular the Dassault range of Mirage fighters, the Nimrod maritime reconnaissance aircraft and AWACS variant, and the new British Aerospace (Hawker Siddeley) Hawk, most indigenous aerospace systems in operation with European and NATO forces have been developed and produced on a collaborative basis. From this experience, a number of important lessons have been learned, the principal among which is that, at the technical level, collaboration works well; assumed barriers such as language and work methods have proved no incumbrance. Other insights which have emerged are that with organizations such as PANAVIA, Europe has at least the blue-print for the effective management of future collaborative programmes, and that perhaps because of its unique position Europe has already in Rolls-Royce, particularly on the military side, virtually a "European" company. At present, the British Government supports the principle of continued collaboration on European military programmes. The eventual form these might assume will still nevertheless be conditional on the responses of the other members of the Community, especially France, on the progress of the IEPG towards agreeing common specifications, and on United States defence and strategic policy.

Whilst we recognize the principle of national sovereignty in defence and security matters, the choice of the F16 by the Netherlands and Belgium must be seen as detrimental to the longer-term goal of European aerospace, even if it was thought at the time by these nations to have been in their best security interests. Yet it must at the same time be recognized that neither Belgium nor the Netherlands has any obligation to "buy European" merely to help the development of what would, anyway, be a European industry based largely upon only three of the Community partners. It follows that if the commercial, technological and financial trade-offs and benefits offered by the Americans were calculated by these nations to be greater by buying the F16 than by participating in a European programme or buying European, then their decision cannot be considered as other than correct.

THE EXPERIENCE OF COLLABORATION

One of the most effective opinion-forming influences on collaboration is the experience of collaboration itself. British experience has been mixed, having varied between one sphere and another of the aerospace sector. Generally speaking, future aerospace collaboration at the technical level is thought to give little cause for concern; the same cannot be said for the political level where the experience in monitoring and controlling escalating costs has been far from reassuring. No hard evidence can be brought to bear in support or refutation of the effect of collaborative experience on government leaders and officials. This can only be left as an open ended question. There is, however, evidence that some British equipment and avionics manufacturers feel that collaboration with counterparts on the continent is all too often costly, inefficient and generally detrimental to the competitiveness of the final product. The sentiment behind this sort of assessment stems above all from the effect of collaborative arrangements on past European civil and military programmes, which have emphasized a British aero-engine and/or airframe contribution.

On the credit side, enough has been learned about aerospace collaboration within Europe for the parties concerned to recognize fully that while design leadership is important, it is not overwhelmingly so. They have also come to accept that it is imperative, given the nature of the international competition which this industry faces, that all involved—individuals, companies and governments—should give close attention to the proposals and abilities of all others so that the technically best solutions and a politically lasting consensus can be found. This is the price of credibility.

When examining the possible strategies which might further the objective of extending collaboration within Europe, a paramount factor must be the provision of finance for aerospace production, development and research. The aerospace sector of British industry, no matter which sphere is under scrutiny, is highly skilled and labour intensive. Aerospace products are technically advanced, complex and expensive. They involve long lead times, a high degree of technical and financial risk, and face relatively elastic markets in which there are strong, generally American, competitors. The problems facing companies in the aerospace field necessitate strict management and financial control if there is to be any profit margin at all. The requirement to keep the different stages of design, development and production in aerospace manufacture balanced where the workloads of employees are concerned, is a major task. It calls for, among other things, a regular flow of military and civil contracts, adequate capital reserves and relatively easy access to credit facilities. But the sunk costs in most aerospace programmes and the time taken before a positive cash flow is generated on a project together make it very difficult to raise the necessary credit, and in time of inflation especially, extremely expensive. As a consequence, the aerospace sector has looked to the British Government for assistance at both ends of the process—the market and development and production finance. The absence of any overall Government strategy for the sector has meant that its financial problems have been exacerbated. Some respite has been found in recent years in overseas military markets. For collaboration to lead to the establishment of a European aerospace industry and for it to have real attraction to those immediately involved, the financial aspects of aerospace would have to be looked at in much greater detail than has yet been done.

THE MARKET OR THE INDUSTRY?

The "Action Programme" recognized that the market, rather than the industry, was a more expedient place from which to begin. Here again, the realities, and industrial perceptions of them, differ from the suggestions and observations of the Commission. The market for military aircraft has been referred to above, though it is not inaccurate to add that it continues to be more fragmented within Europe than it need be, acknowledging that military traditions place national security interests first. It remains the civil market which is critical for European aerospace; yet this also is so complex and fragmented that the Commission's proposals of 1975 appear too general.

Before considering the market for civil aircraft, the highly sensitive nature of the air transport industry must first be understood. It is a service industry with high costs, notably in labour, and is especially vulnerable to inflation, fluctuations in the economy, and other cost increases over which it has little control including fuel, ground handling charges and interest rates. It is also regulated; the free operation of market forces in determining air fares, air routes, etc., is therefore largely prevented. Finally, it is an industry with a highly seasonal demand, with peaks and troughs of profit and loss. Over the past ten years it has, as a result, had to be particularly careful in its choice of equipment. Upon future choices depend not only each airline's competitiveness but also the fine line between profit and a potentially substantial loss. There is considerably more to the selection of a civil airliner than merely defining the number of passengers and range. No airline is going to commit itself to high capital costs on equipment merely to support the principle of European aerospace.

Only with this background can the harsh realities of the civil aerospace market within Europe be grasped. It is no coincidence that 80% of the aircraft in the current inventory of the European airlines were manufactured in the United States. The unit cost of American airliners is less, the line of credit for purchase is more favourable, the operating and service support costs are lower, and the American manufacturers have demonstrated over time that they are sensitive to the support requirements of the European airlines. Those civil aircraft which have been built by Britain have been sold mainly to British Airways and its predecessors, in more than one case to their specifications, and export markets for these aircraft have been difficult to find. For this reason, no British civil airliner project, with the possible exception of the Viscount, has made a significant profit.

THE PROBLEMS FACING THE AIR-INDUSTRY IN EUROPE

The problem facing Britain and the rest of the Community is the need to agree on a market and on an initial minimum order, before beginning to talk about the structure of collaboration. If this proves to be impossible, the only alternative, if public money is not to continue to be lost on civil aerospace programmes, is separately or jointly to seek participation in United States civil airliner programmes, with the limited objective of participating with American manufacturers in the lucrative United States' domestic market. For the aero-engine and airframe companies this option can be as attractive a prospect commercially as a purely European project to meet, essentially European demand. Negotiations with US companies can be a bruising experience and it is obviously desirable to proceed from a clear basic position. The argument that such negotiations would produce better results if conducted on a European basis is persuasive, but the reservation must be entered that to obtain a clear basic position would first require intra-European agreement both as between national interests and as between subsector and company interests.

The consequence for future European aerospace, however, of any collaboration with United States' corporations are imponderable, though it seems clear that an eventual outcome could be to extend United States' dominance over Western civil aerospace.

How realistic is it to consider that a European civil aircraft market can be established? A number of factors suggest that it would not be easy. First, the upper end of the market—long range high capacity aircraft—is precluded for the European manufacturers because total orders barely give sufficient opportunity for any manufacturer to break even. Among the remaining markets, all things being equal, current requirements are for replacements of 200–220 seat medium haul, 140–180 short/medium haul, and 100–130 seat short haul first generation jet aircraft currently in service. Current analyses of these markets suggest that at the bottom end total projected sales are limited but within the remaining two a realistic European market has been projected. What then stands in the way of the European manufacturers' meeting this demand?

The American grip on the European market has already been alluded to, as has the critical nature of airline choices. One of the main barriers against "buying European" is the lack of financial incentive for the European airlines. Except for those European states with a stake in the programme by way of employment, technological investment and regional economic advantages, the remaining European national airlines, many of which are not within the Community anyway, have little to gain. With long standing prejudice against imported aerospace equipment and a tariff barrier to emphasize the fact, the American airlines are unlikely to buy European save in exceptional circumstances. One such exceptional circumstance could be highly favourable credit facilities, though the tendency for United States' airlines to lease aircraft from (generally conservative) American financial institutions, and the track record of at least British export credit policy make this extremely unlikely. Without access to wider markets, at any rate larger than an initial European launch figure could guarantee, unit costs are likely to be uncompetitive compared with those of United States' manufacturers, despite significant differences in labour costs. This is when the market in the world outside Europe and the United States becomes extremely important.

The realities of the European civil aerospace market are such that whilst they make collaboration imperative, they also make it unattractive. There continues to be residual user resistance to collaborative projects. Assurances that liability for damages can be determined without difficulty have not entirely mitigated this attitude. If Europe is going to collaborate on a civil programme, and if Britain is going to be part of that programme, a *sine qua non* would have to be agreement between Lufthansa, British Airways, and Air France on specification and initial launch numbers. It would then be a further matter of hope or persuasion that the ATLAS and KSSU groups would alter their procurement policies to fall in line.

Failing any such agreement the alternatives are either transatlantic collaboration on an inter-state basis, or a go-it-alone assault on the specialist, feeder-liner and executive/light aircraft markets which do not involve high capital risk, or some combination of these. The initiative has to lie with Governments and airlines in the first instance to determine whether the market properly exists.

THE WAY FORWARD

The way forward for European aerospace can be seen to include a number of policy elements. First, or perhaps first and second, would be the definition of common requirements (civil and military) and steps to secure adherence to these definitions, including means of preventing competitive duplication. These moves could be paralleled by others designed to ensure that manufacturing arrangements were on an appropriate footing; or alternatively these arrangements could be left to the individual initiative of the aerospace companies. Next, the financial dimension (launch aid, credit guarantees, etc.) might be put on a firm basis and any uncertainties regarding legal liabilities be ironed out. Long-term provisions for an efficient marketing, support and service infrastructure would then fall naturally to be considered. Taken as a whole such a package could establish both coherence and confidence. Alternatively, there are policy options involving, for instance, development of particular competences, concentrations on specialist or restricted markets, and collaboration with whichever partners, and for whatever projects, circumstances dictated. These two groups of options—and they are not put forward as exhausting the possibilities—may not necessarily be mutually exclusive; but neither do they look comfortably compatible.

There is a continuing role for the Commission in monitoring the emerging problems, and evolving opportunities of the European aerospace industries. This role can usefully be combined with another—the stimulating, catalysing and servicing of initiatives, whether governmental, industrial or commercial. These are jobs worth doing and ones which the Commission, more than any other single agency, is able to perform. They are not, however, terribly glamorous jobs. They call for sensitivity, thoroughness, patience and flair; they do not amount to a central function, though by no means are they entirely peripheral. Properly carried out, they would allow the Commission gradually to become the repository of valuable information and a source of practical wisdom. To expect or require the Commission to do more is to pitch ambition further ahead of achievement than is prudent—or perhaps helpful. To be taken seriously in matters of high politics—and that is exactly what aerospace necessarily is—requires the possession of at least one of three resources: influence, finance or expertise.

The Commission has begun to develop expertise, expects shortly to have some limited research funds, but otherwise carries as yet no significant independent clout. Experience of research co-operation naturally cannot by itself be expected to generate momentum for more thoroughgoing co-operation, but it should certainly help towards this end, as well as being eminently desirable in itself as a means of spreading unavoidable costs and strengthening the European research capability.

These are substantive considerations which are bound to limit the Commission when (if) it comes to the provision of any institutional framework for European aerospace. The Community's non-military orientation is, as we have implied, another such consideration. Finally, a latent suspicion of the Commission's motives, in this as in other cases, hardly helps.

To recapitulate, the survival and health of the European aerospace sector is unequivocally important when judged against any one of several criteria, and the time available is far from unlimited if the best policies for its future are to be found and adopted. From the European supranational perspective a convincing case can be made, and arguably has been made by the Commission, for those policies to be ones of far-reaching industrial integration. Difficulties arise only when one transforms co-ordinates to the various European capitals. There, "European" solutions must compete with a mix of national ones, some involving balanced calculations, others only seductive expediency. In short, all industrial, commercial, and even technical, problems have it within them to become political. Furthermore, for the immediate future nationally-oriented policies, with a certain amount of *ad hoc* European or American co-operation, cannot really be dismissed as totally non-viable. It has then to be faced that the extrapolation of past practice is the easy option; full-blown European co-operation is significantly more demanding politically.

What hope there is of breaking through this impasse depends upon operating simultaneously at the political and the commercial levels and, we think, operating in detail even more perhaps than in general. It follows from what we have said that we are not optimistic that the best solutions from the European point of view will be applied: some of those implemented may not even be the best available from the national point of view. But at least it cannot be said that the Commission has not tried.

NOTE

1. The background work for this study would not have been possible without the aid of a grant from the Council of the Society of British Aerospace Companies to whom the group would express their gratitude.

The group was helped by a panel of consultants: Norman Boorer, British Aircraft Corporation, Weybridge; Derek Brown, Hawker Siddeley Aviation, Hatfield; John Franklin, Department of Industry; Christopher Harlow (Management Consultant); Eddie Kemp, Hawker Siddeley Aviation and Richard Nobbs, he European Commission.

In the course of its research, representatives of the following organizations and nstitutions generously gave up valuable time for formal and informal discussion: Aérospatiale (SNIAS) (Paris); Aerospatiale (SNIAS) (Toulouse); Airbus ndustrie (Blagnac); British Aircraft Corporation (Weybridge); British Airways; Boeing Aircraft Company; Confederation of Shipbuilding and Engineering Unions (CSEU); Dassault-Breguet Aviation (Blagnac); Dassault-Breguet Aviation (Vaucresson); Department of Industry; Dowty Rotol Ltd., (Gloucester); Hawker Siddeley Aviation Ltd., (Brough); Hawker Siddeley Aviation Ltd. Hatfield); Interavia (London); Marconi-Elliot Avionic Systems Ltd. (Rochester); McConnell-Douglas Corporation; Ministry of Defence, Procurement Executive; Office of the Secretaire d'Etat, Ministry of Transportation (Paris); National Westminster Bank Ltd. (London); Rolls-Royce Ltd. (Derby); Smiths Industries, Aviation Ltd. (Cheltenham); Society of British Aerospace Companies; University of Southampton, Department of Aeronautics and Astronautics, Department of Electronics, Department of Politics.

A particular debt of gratitude is owed to Professor Lucien Mandeville of the Centre d'Etudes et de Recherches sur L'Armée of the Université des Sciences Sociale de Toulouse for facilitating arrangements on the group's behalf in France.

Despite the wealth of expert advice and assistance the group has received, all views expressed within this paper are the responsibility of the authors alone.

III. CONCLUSIONS

Aerospace and the European Community

by *David Marquand*

The discussion on the aerospace industry began with brief statements by the rapporteur and counter-rapporteur, designed to identify the main points of agreement and disagreement, and to isolate the political issues and choices about which the voters of Europe will have to make up their minds when the campaign for a directly-elected Parliament begins. At first, there seemed to be a fairly sharp difference of emphasis between the Commission experts and the academics, particularly over the extent to which the British aerospace industry could be said to have a dominant position in the European industry as a whole. The Commission experts pointed out that the extent to which the British industry could be said to have a dominant position depended on the criteria used, and argued that in some areas the French were more dominant than the British. To this, the academics replied that the British alone had a balanced capability, and that, in any case, the British thought they were dominant and that British policy could not be understood or influenced unless that psychological factor was taken into account.

Despite these initial differences, however, a consensus gradually began to emerge along the following lines. First, it was agreed that it is essential to retain a strong European aerospace industry and that policy should be framed to achieve this overriding objective. The only realistic alternative was seen to be total dependence on the United States, and this would lead to a situation in which the Americans could shut down the European aerospace industry whenever it suited them. This was unacceptable, both on social grounds, because of the fierce hire-and-fire policies of the American industry, and in view of the balance-of-payments implications for the long term.

Secondly, it was agreed that the Community and/or the Member States concerned must have a coherent strategy—that it is not enough to respond *ad hoc* to the needs of the moment, as has been done up to now. The group then identified three strategies between which the European electorate would have to choose: first, complete national self-sufficiency, with no international collaboration at all; secondly, a combination of national self-sufficiency and collaboration with the Americans, each Nation-State having separate agreements with the Americans; and thirdly, a European strategy. Option No. 1 was ruled out as not feasible. Option No. 2 was ruled out on the grounds that it had been tried and failed: the British, French, Germans and Italians had all had bloody noses when they tried to collaborate separately with the Americans. Thus, only a European strategy was left.

On the question of what the European strategy should actually be, there was a sharp difference of opinion between one member, who argued strongly

311

in favour of a tariff on American imports, and the rest of the group, who argued that, to be effective, a tariff would have to be enormous, that it would run diametrically counter to the Community's overall trade policy, that it would have damaging political repercussions and that the objectives it was supposed to achieve could be attained more successfully in other ways. On the other hand, there was general—though not universal—agreement that other methods of encouraging the industry would have to be used, and that the central objective of a strong European industry could not be achieved by relying wholly on free competition. In this connection, great stress was laid on the fact that the Americans protect their aerospace industry in a whole variety of ways; and it was agreed that the Community should push hard for a revision of the "Buy America" policy in the military field. At the same time, however, it was recognized that in some quarters there was strong and vocal, if minority, opposition to any suggestion that public funds should be used to encourage the aerospace industry, and that this opposition was a political factor of great importance, particularly in the United Kingdom.

Finally, the group discussed the role of the Commission in all this. It was unanimously agreed that it had a crucial role to play as a mediator, as a guardian of the Community interest and as a provider of impartial and expert advice. It was also agreed that it would have to do a great deal of behind-the-scenes persuasion if a European strategy was to become a reality. On the question whether behind-the-scenes persuasion should be complemented by public propaganda on stage, and whether public propaganda might make behind-the-scenes persuasion less effective, the group seemed, at least to the Chairman, to be somewhat ambivalent. The Chairman's efforts to get the group to give him a clear-cut answer to this question having failed, the discussion was adjourned, on a note of surprisingly optimistic consensus.

TEXTILE POLICY

I. TEXTILE POLICY REPORT

Textile Policy in the European Community

by *C. Friz* and *J. Scheele*

The textile industry, despite its reputation as an old-fashioned industry remains extremely important in terms of the national economies of the Member States of the Community. It will suffice here to point out that the textile and clothing sectors together account for 8% of net output and 11% of industrial employment. Employment of women is extremely high at 50% in textiles and over 80% in clothing, and the industry is concentrated in a limited number of regions where it may account for as much as 80% of industrial employment.

Since the mid-1960's the EEC industry has laid off an average of 40,000 workers per year (2.4% of the total work force). This is due partly to an effort by the industry to modernize itself, improve its productivity and hence its competitiveness with imports from low-wage countries, and in part to a distinct decline reflecting a loss of its markets to the growing industries of the developing world. The effects of this decline in employment have been particularly severe in the regions where the industry is most heavily concentrated (N.E. England, Roubaix-Tourcoing).

The phenomenon of the growth of the industry in the developing countries has shown an accelerating tendency in recent years. It reflects the relatively low barriers to entry into this primary industry which can initially substitute for imports from the developed countries and subsequently permit the development of significant exports. It has now reached the stage where certain of the developing countries in S.E. Asia have textile industries which are more modern and more efficient than any in the developed world, with wage costs well below half of those in Europe and the USA. Clearly this type of competition seriously threatens the Community's industry.

The importance of the textile industry has been clearly demonstrated at national level by the actions of the governments of the Member States. Clearly it would be undesirable for the development of a Common Market that such actions continue in an uncoordinated manner without any policy framework at Community level.

THE COMMISSION COMMUNICATION

Background

On 21 July 1971, the Commission laid down the orientations of a Community textile policy in a Communication on a Sectoral Policy for the Textile

Industry (Annex I), the so-called "Spinelli Memorandum". The document was transmitted for information to the other institutions of the Community and also to the social partners of the industry, with whom discussions were subsequently held on the basis of the Memorandum.

The history of the Memorandum goes back to 1966 when COMITEXTIL (Coordination Committee of the EEC Textile Industries) presented the Commission with a note describing the problems of the sector and suggesting that a trade policy which protected the industry against *abnormal* competition from imports was a precondition for the harmonious development of the industry.

Following the reception of this note the Commission held numerous consultations with the social partners both on a bilateral and on a tripartite basis. The Commission's services had produced a number of monographs on various branches of the industry but it was decided in 1968 to commission a study of the perspectives of the textile industry to 1975—the De Bandt Report.[1] This was followed in 1970 by a similar study of the clothing industry —the Capelin Report.[2] Although these reports differed in their conclusions on the advisability of a wider opening of the Community markets to imports, both noted the necessity of major restructuring in the sector. It was also clear that trade liberalization would inevitably lead to a further decline in employment in the sector.

On the basis of these reports and further consultations with the social partners, the Commission formulated the Spinelli Memorandum. It should be noted that the Memorandum was presented to the Council of Ministers not for approval but merely for information. This was a deliberate action on the part of the Commission to avoid, as has happened with a similar policy document for another sector, the rejection by the Council of the document as a whole and hence of the individual actions proposed. This pragmatic approach has permitted the Commission to introduce proposals within the framework of the Memorandum which have then been approved by the Council.

Content

After an assessment of the textile/clothing industry and of its prospects in the medium term, the Memorandum acknowledges the need for increased competitiveness in the industry which must be obtained by:
– technical and technological progress and its exploitation;
– restructuration by concentration, conversion and scrapping.

It is the role of the public powers to create an environment which will encourage the industry to take the necessary restructuring initiatives without causing serious social difficulties. In the field of general Community policy, the textile industry would benefit, like other sectors by the progressive creation of a true Common market at Community level. Specific policy in the textile sector should, on the trade side, reconcile a progressive opening of the Community's markets with the sector's need to adapt progressively. On the internal side, measures should be adopted which would tend to accelerate restructuring while limiting the social and regional difficulties which would arise.

316

In more detail, on the commercial policy side, the Community policy of a progressive opening of markets, particularly to developing countries, was confirmed. However, this policy would be limited by the following considerations:
- the volume of GSP quotas would rise by a maximum of 5% per annum;
- the liberalization of import quotas would take account of the attitude of other trading partners, and should in any case move progressively downstream from yarns to cloth before affecting made-up goods;
- the establishment within the GATT framework of an international code of fair conduct for textile trade would be vital, failing which unilateral restrictive action might become necessary.

Internally, Community action should aid in all possible ways research and the utilization of technological progress. In particular Community financing was envisaged for a common research programme to be proposed by the industry. The Commission also foresaw the creation, with Community sponsorship, of a Cyclical Observation Centre (COC) at Community level, to establish the short- and medium-term economic forecasts necessary in view of the cyclical nature of the textile sector.

The Memorandum also established broad guidelines for the assessment of state aid to the industry and its compatibility with the Treaty of Rome. Three types of aid were distinguished:
- aid to collective actions, aimed at developing research or improving short-term economic forecasts;
- aid in restructuring (elimination of over-capacity, concentration, conversion outside the sector);
- aid with capital expenditure (modernization, conversion within the sector).

In general it was felt that the third type of aid would need to meet stricter criteria of non-increase of capacity, acute social problems, and the need to examine the situation of the branch at Community level.

Finally, the Memorandum emphasized the need for the application of the European Social Fund to the industry, in line with certain criteria which should also apply to the other Community financial instruments (Regional Fund, European Investment Bank).

Reactions

Since the Memorandum was not submitted for opinion to the other Community institutions, no official reactions were forthcoming and they can best be judged by the success or failure of the individual proposals. However, an informal consultation of governmental textile experts revealed general support for the outlines of the Commission's policy.

From the social partners, the reception was mixed; from the unions' side there was complete opposition. They felt that the objective of the document was to give the Commission and the Community an alibi for the adoption of an open trade policy by proposing various measures, in particular the application of the Social Fund, which would in no way solve the problems caused by the opening of markets. They felt that there was no assurance from the Community regarding a long-term future for the industry inside the EEC.

The industry as a whole was never able to comment formally because of the widely differing views which were expressed, including some of the same fears as the trades unions. There was, however, a very positive welcome to the proposals for joint scientific research and for the ideas which were to lead to the Multi-Fibre Arrangement. The proposal for the Cyclical Observation Centre was criticized for its concentration on short-term phenomena to the exclusion of medium- and long-term prospects. Doubts were also expressed regarding the efficiency of such a centre which would be under governmental rather than industrial control. Finally, there was concern about the Community's thinking on state aids since it was feared that the lack of transparency in many national aid measures would make impossible the application of the aid guidelines.

THE SITUATION OF THE INDUSTRY SINCE 1971

In examining the development of the Community's textile policy since 1971, with particular regard to the implementation of the various aspects of the Spinelli Memorandum, a very important factor is the evolution of the economic situation of the industry during that period.

Briefly, there have been two phases, one of expansion until early 1974 followed by the most serious recession since the Second World War. In mid-1976 a sustained recovery seems to be established although output levels are still well below available capacity.

The recession has meant that many of the long-term measures taken by the Community to promote an ordered restructuring of the industry have been overshadowed by the severe short-term decline in employment. Similarly, on the commercial side, the cut-back in demand on a worldwide scale has resulted in severely increased competition from low-priced imports which have exacerbated the recession within the Community, and created problems in the administration of a commercial policy in the long term.

DEVELOPMENT OF THE COMMUNITY'S COMMERCIAL POLICY

The most significant event in the field of commercial policy has been the signature in December 1973 of the Arrangement regarding International Trade in Textiles (the GATT Multifibre Arrangement). While intended to promote the liberalization of international trade in textiles, the Arrangement provides for limits to this movement where disruption or the threat of disruption due to imports exists on the markets of importing countries. These limits go beyond the normal rules of the GATT.

The conclusion of this Arrangement, to which all the major textile trading countries, both importers and exporters, are signatories, was envisaged in the Memorandum when it referred to the establishment of a GATT code of conduct for textile trade. While fulfilling this role it has also had a major effect on all other aspects of commercial policy.

It commits the Community internationally to the principle of a wider opening of our markets to imports, especially from developing countries, a principle which has been further underlined by the conclusion of the Lomé agreement (and of the agreements with the Mediterranean countries). However, since the Agreement permits under its Articles 3 and 4 bilaterally agreed import quotas where market disruption or the threat of market disruption exists, it has resulted in the establishment or re-establishment of quotas on a wide range of products imported from specific sources. The objective expressed in the Memorandum of the progressive elimination of quantitative restrictions is thus far from being realized and in some cases there has been a retrograde step, as with Brazil, where imports of cotton yarns, already liberalized by the Community, are subject to quota.

The Community is not alone, however, in modifying its objectives of liberalization as a result of the Arrangement, and the bilateral agreements concluded by the Commission are only restrictive of certain specified products where those concluded by, for instance, the USA are very much more global in application, covering almost the entire range of textile products. It should also be remembered that the Arrangement prescribes an annual growth rate in textile imports of 6% even where these imports are subject to quantitative restrictions. Thus, while it has been possible to agree a reduced growth rate for specific products where severe market disruption exists, this has had to be compensated by concessions in the growth rate for other products.

A very significant feature of the Community's policy in connection with the bilateral restrictions has been the idea, proposed by the Commission's services, of "burden-sharing". At present the greater part of imports from South East Asia are taken by Germany and the UK, with France and Italy taking a share well below that which their economic importance would suggest. It was agreed by the Member States that the increase in imports should be taken mainly by those best able to absorb it rather than by those already heavily supplied by imports, with the ultimate objective of arriving at a distribution of imports to Member States in line with their economic importance.

The Community's application of the Arrangement has been subject to a good deal of criticism both inside and outside the EC. Within the EC, the industry has become increasingly critical on the grounds that the agreements concluded have been too liberal and too late. Outside the EC the criticism has been that agreements are too restrictive and too late. This criticism has been a result of the serious textile recession which began almost as soon as the Arrangement was concluded and it seems likely that an Arrangement concluded at the end of 1974 would have been more restrictive with a lower average growth rate for imports.

It is certain that the Community, by comparison with other trading partners, has been very slow to conclude bilateral agreements. The first negotiations only began in December 1974, eight months after ratification of the Arrangement, the first bilateral agreement (with India) was only concluded in May 1975 and, in mid-1976, twelve agreements have been concluded, with three more still under negotiation. The validity of these agreements can only run to the end of 1977. Our negotiating partners have taken advantage of this slowness to increase their exports to the Community and ensure a high

319

reference level in the establishment of quotas, which must be based on imports in the most recent 12-month period.

The major blame for this delay must be laid at the door of the Member States who, because of conflicting attitudes to trade liberalization, significantly retarded the establishment of the Commission's negotiating mandate. Only the rapidly developing recession caused some realization of the urgency of measures. The Commission did not, however, give a sufficiently strong lead in this matter and omitted to undertake the statistical preparation of negotiations at an early enough stage, thus slowing down the progress of the negotiations. Finally, the Community was faced by blatant bad faith in the case of some negotiating partners—one agreement in particular came ten months after the opening of negotiations, which took place in five rounds and were only completed under the Community's threat of unilateral urgent safeguard measures on a wide range of products.

This delay, in the climate of 1974/75, meant that the quotas are much higher than was envisaged when the Arrangement was signed in December 1973. This has led the industry to re-examine their attitude to the renewal of the Arrangement when it expires at the end of 1977. The perspectives for this renewal will be examined later.

In the context of commercial policy, mention must also be made of the work towards a harmonized policy vis-à-vis the State-trading countries. In the textile field this work is complicated by the fact that some of these countries (Romania, Poland, Hungary) are also signatories to the Multi-Fibre Arrangement. Work is still under way on a Community negotiating position, but it is clear that this must take account of our obligations under the Arrangement.

To conclude the examination of commercial policy, the GSP scheme has essentially remained unaltered, with annual growth in textile imports under this scheme restricted still to 5%, as proposed in the Memorandum. Some difficulties have been experienced due to the dominance of some developing countries in the textile field and the mechanisms have been modified to allow a fairer distribution of the benefits of the scheme. Finally, in the Commission's proposal for the 1977 scheme, Hong Kong becomes for the first time eligible for preferences on all textile products, following continued pressure from both the UK and Hong Kong.

DEVELOPMENT OF POLICIES TO AID RESTRUCTURING

Research

Following the publication of the Memorandum consultations were held between the Commission's services and COMITEXTIL regarding a possible common textile research programme. These culminated in the submission by COMITEXTIL on 12 June 1972 of a programme containing three projects, for partial Community financing.

After some modifications to the programme, in particular the changing of one of the projects, the Commission approved on 17 September 1974 a proposal for a Council decision setting up a common textile research programme. Following favourable opinions from the CREST (30 October 1974), the Economic and Social Committee (28 November 1974) and the Parliament (8 January 1975), the Council approved the Decision on 14 April 1975.

The three projects in the programme cover the following fields:
- heat treatment of chemical fibres;
- treatment of textiles in organic solvent media;
- fireproofing of textile fibres by radiation-grafting.

The research work, to be co-ordinated by COMITEXTIL, will be carried out in nine different textile-research institutes throughout the Community. Work commenced in 1976 and will last three years. The Community is contributing one-third of the programme's costs up to a maximum of 250,000 units of account.

It is hoped that, as well as providing direct benefit from the research programme, the scheme will also act as a catalyst to promote further co-operative research and to increase the level of co-operation generally within the European industry. A particularly important aspect of the programme is that it is of a global nature and should yield results which will be valuable to all branches of the industry and to all sizes of firm, particularly small and medium-sized ones.

Cyclical Observation Centre

The Memorandum proposed the creation of a Community-level Cyclical Observation Centre to produce short- and medium-term economic forecasts. This would be particularly important for small and medium-sized firms who were unable to afford the necessary expenditure individually and where the necessary restructuring would be inhibited without this knowledge.

The Commission accordingly commissioned in 1972 the Centre for Economic and Management Research at Lille to carry out a study on this proposal and covering the following areas:
- analysis of the root causes of the cyclical fluctuations in the textile sector;
- determination of the information which should be collected and published to supplement short-term forecasts;
- inventory of statistical information available;
- proposals for the work and organization of a Cyclical Observation Centre.

The report, which strongly supported the creation of such a Centre, was received by the Commission in June 1973. Consultations were held shortly afterwards with representatives of the Member States' governments. The scheme was strongly supported by the smaller states but the outright opposition of one major member of the Community meant that the project would stand little chance of success. The idea has lain dormant since then with the exception of moves by the Statistical Office of the EC to give priority to the textile and clothing sectors in harmonizing production statistics. Although this harmonization is making slow progress, it is an essential part of the development of a common industrial policy. At national level, in France, Germany, the UK and Italy some initiatives have been taken in this field. It is possible that these may lead to some form of co-ordination at Community level to achieve the objectives of the Centre as originally laid down.

Financial aids to the textile industry

At the same time as the Memorandum, the Commission also published some Community guidelines in the field of aids to the textile industry. These gave a more detailed interpretation of the orientations contained in the Memorandum which was intended to aid both the governments of Member States in the formulation of textile aid policy and the Commission's services in their examination of proposed national aid schemes. This was particularly important in view of the growing tendency towards the use of aid for restructuring in this sector and the risk that this constituted for competition within the EC.

Since then the Commission has undertaken an examination of all existing textile industry aid measures at national level, both producing an inventory of these measures and obtaining a statistical picture of their importance for the different industries. At the same time all new proposals for national aid have been examined before their introduction. The examination of existing measures was completed in 1973 for the Six and during 1974 for the new Member States. With one important exception, this examination has not revealed the need for any major modifications to national measures either existing or proposed, although some modifications of detail and accent have been made.

Only in the case of the Italian law No. 1101 has the Commission needed to take serious action. This case predates the Spinelli Memorandum since the Italian government communicated the proposed law to the Commission on 24 April 1969 although the Commission's reaction was entirely in line with the principles laid down in the Spinelli Memorandum. The measure was intended to promote the restructuring, reorganization and conversion of the Italian textile industry and gave significant fiscal and credit advantages to textile firms and others taking advantage of the scheme, particularly those in the so-called "textile regions" of Italy.

On 27 May 1970, the Commission issued a preliminary decision ordering the Italian government to remove from the proposed law the 10-year direct tax exemption on income from investments approved in the framework of the law and made in textile zones. In addition the Commission requested a modification of the criteria for application of aid to ensure an appreciation of the production capacity situation, not simply, as proposed, on a national basis but at Community level.

The law was subsequently passed with these modifications on 1 December 1971. However, during its passage through the Italian Parliament, a clause was added which gave a three-year partial reduction of the social charges payable by textile and clothing firms. In its Decision of 25 July 1973 the Commission ordered the Italian government to withdraw this measure, and this Decision was confirmed, following an appeal by the Italian government, by the Court of Justice on 2 July 1974. Following this, the Italian government withdrew the measure and the Commission finally approved the law, as modified, on 7 March 1975.

Aid from community financial instruments

The Memorandum concluded that important problems would arise regarding the conversion of labour both within the textile sector and towards other sectors, due to the regional and social repercussions of restructuring combined with the rise in productivity. It regarded the application of the European Social Fund to these problems as crucial.

In this connection the Commission had carried out in 1971 a study of the likely evolution of the industry in areas where the textile industry predominates,[3] together with the structure of these regions. This report was followed up in 1973 by reports on two particularly critically-placed areas—Prato in Italy and the Roubaix-Tourcoing complex in France. In addition the original study was completed for the new Member States.

The information obtained from these studies has been utilized in the application of the Council's decision of 19 December 1972 opening up the possibilities of Article 4 of the European Social Fund Regulation to the textile sector—"social problems resulting directly from the creation of the common market". This Decision, which also followed directly from the Spinelli Memorandum, has so far made available finance for training textile workers for new more secure jobs either within the textile sector or outside. The validity of this Decision expired at the end of 1975 but was renewed by the Council for a further period of eighteen months and its field of application extended to the clothing sector.

In examining projects for aid from the Social Fund as well as from other Community investments (Regional Development Fund, European Investment Bank), the Commission's services have tried to ensure that this aid is only given to projects which provide stable future employment and which will not tend to affect unduly employment prospects in other firms within the EC, whether as a result of long-term overcapacity problems or a declining market.

Clearly such analysis is not easy but it will become even more important as Community financial interventions increase, and the Commission's services are at present preparing a detailed examination of some fifty sub-branches of the textile/clothing sector with the objective of a definition of the suitability of each sub-branch for aid. It must be remembered that such an analysis of the industrial aspects of a project is accompanied by a similar assessment of the social and regional aspects and that these latter aspects may sometimes be sufficiently positive to outweigh the negative industrial aspects—this political judgement is made by the Commission itself.

Finally, it is worth noting the doubts which have been expressed by both sides of industry, particularly the union side, regarding the opening of the Social Fund to the textile sector. They fear that the fund constitutes an alibi for the Community, authorizing it to follow a policy of unconditional opening up of the market without any real alternative choice being possible since the limited sums of money allocated in the budget would preclude an active employment policy.

SPECIFIC PROBLEMS

Man-made fibres

The man-made fibre sector is a relatively new industry and grew at a very high rate from a consumption within the EEC in 1950 of 9,000 tons to a level of over 2 million in 1973. Synthetic fibres account now for over 50% of all fibre consumption in Europe, and constitute a significant positive factor in the Community balance of payments.

Until 1970, growth was sufficiently rapid to avoid the creation of surplus capacity but a flattening out of demand growth allied to the large number of investment decisions taken in the favourable years of 1968 and 1969 led to serious overcapacity problems. These are complicated by the increasing size of economic production units, which has resulted in a "step" growth in capacity. The Commission was made aware of this situation following the announcement in April 1972 by the Dutch AKZO group of a rationalization plan in its synthetic fibre plants threatening some 6,000 jobs throughout the Community. Following two debates in the Parliament during the second half of 1972, and a request from the Dutch government for Community action in this field, the Commission's services prepared a working document which after consultations with the social partners and the governments was modified to constitute, in May 1973, a basis for action. The document proposed that the Commission should obtain fibre demand forecasts in the short and medium term and that it receive notifications from the producers, on a voluntary basis, of investment plans. On the basis of an analysis of these two parameters the Commission would discuss with the interested parties any modifications to investment plans which might prove necessary.

This idea was broadly approved by both sides of industry and by the member governments, although slight reserves were expressed by one Member State. On the basis of this approval the Commission's services prepared in September 1973 a draft Commission Recommendation to synthetic fibre producers on the declaration of investments. However the reserves expressed by one Member State had by this time become outright opposition due to fears that this action could create a *de facto* cartel in this sector.

This total opposition rendered the chances of success of the scheme so small that it was temporarily abandoned despite strong pressure both from the Dutch government and from both sides of industry.

This pressure was redoubled when, during the recent recession capacity utilization in the industry fell to around 50%. While it seems unlikely that the proposed Community measures would have made much difference in this particular crisis, it is probable that they would prove valuable in the future. The Commission's services are at present re-examining with the social partners the possibilities of Community action in this field.

The tights industry

In April 1974, the Commission was informed, via a Parliamentary question and a letter from the Belgian industry, of the serious situation of the tights industry following sales of tights produced in other Member States at very low prices. The situation was confirmed by the Dutch government's intervention in August 1974 to rationalize its industry by merging the two largest companies following the near bankruptcy of the largest.

In view of this situation, the Commission had carried out by consultants a study of the industry which was completed in July 1975.[4] Consultations with the social partners took place in September 1975 and with the member governments, beginning in December 1975. A Commission Recommendation in this sector should as a result appear very shortly.

The report showed up a situation of severe overcapacity (some 30–40%) in a branch which had undergone very rapid growth and technological progress during the short period of its existence. The situation was exacerbated by the development in Castelgoffredo (Italy) of a totally new major centre of production entirely devoted to this industry. The industry here is to a large extent composed of small family units with minimal overheads. Furthermore, because of their small size, the producers are subject to very strong pressures by the wholesalers, with the result that prices are forced down to an unrealistically low level. Another factor in reducing prices to uneconomic levels has been the practice of outward processing in State-trading countries, particularly by the German industry.

The general recovery of the textile industry has not aided the problems of this sector in the slightest and, even in Italy, one of the largest firms has recently gone bankrupt as a result of the competition from Castelgoffredo.

Faced with these circumstances, the Commission's possibilities for action are limited by its powers. The proposed Recommendation, which has formed the subject of consultation with the Member States, suggests the following actions:
– non-encouragement of new investments in this sub-sector;
– the creation of suitable means for a rapid surveillance of intra-Community trade in tights (prices and quantities);
– non-encouragement of outward processing in low-wage cost third countries.

It is recognized that this recommendation will only have an effect in the medium term and there is very strong pressure from the German and French industries, in particular, to take national measures to restrict imports from Italy.

However, the Italian government is supporting efforts by the industry in Castelgoffredo to rationalize its structure and its pricing policies to raise the general price level and also to constitute a form of buffer stock to prevent price levels deteriorating too sharply during the slack summer months. It is hoped that these measures will have a positive short term on the EC market, and hence prevent any recourse to national measures contrary to the objectives of the common market.

The textile labelling directive

One other Community measure, conceived in the framework of the harmonization of national laws, has also had an effect on the industry. This is the Council Directive of 26 July 1971 on textile labelling. While imposing obligations on the industry to label goods far more accurately as regards fibre content, it also permits the sale of products in the entire Community under the same conditions.

The provisions of the Directive are extremely complex and include definition of fibres; subsidiary directives regarding analytical methods have also been promulgated. The entire legislation was elaborated in very close consultation

325

with the industry's experts, but despite this a number of modifications to the original Directive have been necessary. The implementation of the Directive occurred on 1 January 1975.

THE FUTURE

The most important factor affecting the Community's textile policy in the near future is the termination of the Multifibre Arrangement at the end of 1977. It seems clear that the arrangement must be renewed in some form, but there is strong pressure from several quarters for modifications. In particular, parts of the European industry would prefer some form of "globalization" of import quotas to limit the market share of imports from all sources to a given level as well as a form of "recession clause" which would restrict the growth rate of imports (at present 6%) in times of recession, so that damage to the European industry is reduced in this situation.

The European trades unions have suggested that the opening of the Community's markets should be restricted to those countries which apply the various ILO agreed provisions regarding safety at work, social security, etc. They feel that the profits to be made by a developing country's exports should go to improve the worker's conditions as well as to the entrepreneur.

Finally, the developing countries are likely to request a number of modifications all tending to ensure more unrestrained access to the markets of the developed world. The USA, on the other hand, has already announced that it would like to renew the Arrangement unchanged.

In the face of these conflicting interests, there is a risk that any attempt to make significant changes to the provisions of the Multifibre Arrangement will run into severe difficulties and may even threaten its renewal altogether. In particular the idea of globalization of import quotas raises problems since it implies the establishment of import quotas administered by the import country. This is contrary firstly to the principles of the MFA, in that the quotas are not based on the existence or risk of market disruption, and secondly to the principle of bilateral negotiation based on export self-restraint agreements. In addition, the principle of globalization is contrary to the objective of progressive trade liberalization and the underlying precepts of GATT. Finally, it seems very unlikely to receive international acceptance because of the inherent inequalities resulting from the imposition of a static overall limit on a dynamically changing picture.

In the long term, it seems likely that the growth of the textile industry in the developing countries will continue, although perhaps in other geographical zones than those where it has so far been concentrated. In this connection, the textile industry has tended to become less attractive for developing countries in recent years as a result of the continuing overcapacity on a worldwide scale and the changing comparative advantages resulting from the higher levels of technology in use. However, the ease of entry into the textile industry combined with the availability of raw materials in developing countries means that the sector still exerts an attraction as a first step in industrialization in those countries where the sector is not yet well-established.

326

In these circumstances, it seems highly likely that, whatever the results of the renegotiation of the Multifibre Arrangement, the European industry will continue to change, showing a quantitative decline, albeit at a less rapid rate than in the recent past, but a qualitative improvement towards an industry which is viable in the long term. Almost certainly the industry will be forced to rely even more on its major assets of design and marketing know-how together with the development of advanced technology.

CONCLUSIONS

The case-study confirms the disparity between the Community's and the Commission's strength in the area of commercial policy, and its relative weakness in that of industrial policy, as a result of the lack of provision for a common industrial policy in the Treaty of Rome. However, it was in the light of these limitations that the Spinelli Memorandum was formulated and, with the exception of the Cyclical Observation Centre, the Commission has had a good deal of success in implementing the policies proposed in the Memorandum.

The question remains as to the relevance of the Community's actions to the problems of the textile sector. On the commercial policy side, there seems little doubt that the policies carried out have had a very significant effect on the attitude and development of the industry. Equally, the delay in negotiating bilateral restraint agreements under the Multifibre Arrangement contributed to the difficulties experienced by the industry during the recent recession. The experience gained in these negotiations will no doubt reduce the delay in a future series.

In the field of industrial policy proper, the recent problems in the man-made fibres and tights sectors have demonstrated the difficulties of Community action, particularly in the short term. Similarly, the proposals in the Spinelli Memorandum were of an indirect type and are very much long-term measures. In particular the significance of Community financial instruments is, by comparison with national means, very limited, particularly given the restrictions placed on the Commission's freedom of action in this field.

However, in the field of orienting national policies towards a common set of principles, the Community has had some success. The guidelines on aid have been rigorously applied, and informal discussions are at present in progress, which are designed to develop common guidelines for general industrial policy measures, with particular reference to the clothing sector. This initiative by the Commission, together with the realities of a common commercial policy, will, it is hoped, lead to a further rapprochement of national policies so that in the future one will genuinely be able to talk of a common industrial policy. The question of its institutionalization and formalization then becomes secondary.

The need for a common textile policy has become clearer in recent years as the worldwide evolution of the textile industry and trade has rendered policies at a national level irrelevant. It seems certain that any policy can only be effective if it is applied at Community level, in a world context.

The main requirement of the European industry is to be able to plan for the future in the knowledge of a stable environment; a Community policy can only provide the environment for progressive change, and not attempt to dictate actions by private firms. It is in this framework that the Community's textile policy over the next decade must be developed.

ANNEX I

The Textile Industry of tomorrow

Trends for a textile policy according to the EEC commission's report

The EEC Commission examined thoroughly the EEC textile industry's situation and the economic policy which it is intending to develop in the future in this field.

The conclusions will be found in the following document, which has been transmitted to the Member States as well as to the employers and workers.

TEXTILE SECTOR POLICY

In 1969 the textile and clothing industries represented, in terms of value added, 9% of the production of the whole of industry (13.4 thousand million dollars); they employed 11.8% of the manpower (3,160,000 persons). In 1969 textile and clothing imports represented 7% of Community imports (2,748 million dollars) and exports 7.5% (2,947 million dollars). In the last three years the textile-clothing trade has shown a credit balance of around 300 million dollars, as against a deficit of some 200 million ten years ago. This reversal of the tendency is explained by the substitution of man-made fibres for imported natural fibres.

For some years the textile industry has been laying off, on an average, 40,000 persons a year, mainly in the wool and cotton branches. The reason for this lies in the restructuration effort made to improve productivity, in view of the increased pressure of competition within and outside the Community. That effort is expressed by the laying-off of manpower mentioned above and by a moderate increase in production.

The textile industry currently plays an important part in the Community economy, particularly in the regions where it is concentrated. Some 70–80% of this industry lies in a limited number of regions, where it employs up to 30% of the active population. They are often mono-industry regions where, taking into account the laying-off of labour in the primary sector, the economic and social function of the textile industry will remain essential to economic balance as long as the structures of those regions have not evolved.

Although the consumption of textile fibres (wool, cotton, man-made fibres) will, in the next few years, progress at a rhythm slightly less than that of the individual income, it is to be expected that this consumption which, in 1969, was around 13.6 kg/inhabitant in the Community, will very likely reach 18–19 kg/inhabitant in 1980 (it was already 21.9 kg/inhabitant in the USA in 1969).

Taking population increase into account, a very substantial margin of increase may reasonably be reckoned on in the course of the next ten years. At world level, also, a big development in consumption is to be envisaged, especially in the less developed countries where at present the consumption per inhabitant figures remain relatively low (2.7 kg/inhabitant in 1969).

329

It is to be expected, however, that the laying-off of labour will continue in the textile sector in the forthcoming years at a rhythm comparable to that which characterized recent years, since the need for increased competitiveness will be expressed by the necessity of pursuing, and even accelerating, the restructuring movement that is already well under way.

Technologically, a tendency has been noticed for some years now to replace natural fibres by Community-produced man-made fibres, the latter coming from the expanding chemical industry. Their rhythm of progression depends however, largely on the future development of the textile and clothing industries. At present, man-made fibres represent 50% of the consumption of the three principal textile fibres processed in the EEC (cotton, wool, man-made fibres); according to some estimates, this percentage should reach 75% by 1980. This tendency improves the competitive position of Community textile industries vis-à-vis less industrialized countries.

It is to be expected that, in the years to come, one of the conditions of maintaining or improving the competitive position of Commodity industries is technical progress and technology, as well as the exploitation of that progress.

Technological progress in the Community may enable it to some extent to maintain its competitive position vis-à-vis industrialized countries rapidly evolving in the same field. It may also enable it, under normal conditions of competition and in numerous sectors, to make up for the divergence currently existing in labour costs, in relation to some less developed countries.

Bearing in mind the preceding considerations, the evolution of the textile sector towards increased and adequate competitiveness requires, at company level, the continuation, and even the acceleration, of the restructuration movement already begun. This restructuration will proceed by concentration, conversion and absolescence and will prove all the more necessary in that the application of new technologies (in the field of fibres, processing materials, products, and management), the utilization of which is indispensable, will require structural adaptation.

The public powers can accompany this restructuration by economic policy measures and appropriate specific measures.

In effect, whilst initiatives regarding restructuration must remain a matter for those who undertake them, it is for the public powers, both national and Community, to create adequate conditions in order to encourage the necessary evolution. It is also necessary to avoid structural adaptations causing serious social difficulties, especially in regions where the textile and clothing industries are more particularly concentrated.

The objects set out above can be pursued at Community level by the following actions.

Like the other sectors of economic activity, the textile industry will benefit, in its adaptation effort, by all the measures of a general nature aimed at ensuring for the Community market characteristics that are equivalent to those of a national market. It is a matter of continuing fiscal alignment and the elimination of obstacles to the free circulation of products, of improving the capital and security market, of ensuring adequate financing sources for industries, and of pursuing the actions of a general nature set out in the Memorandum of Industrial Policy.

Specific textile sector actions can be grouped as follows:

a. the implementation of a trade policy able to conciliate the progressive opening of the Community market with the adaptation requirements peculiar to the textile sector:

b. The adoption of measures likely to accelerate restructuration and, whilst directing the latter towards increased productivity, to palliate social and regional difficulties that may arise.

Generally speaking, the Community's trade policy will continue to be characterized in the future by progressive opening of the market to imports from outside countries and in particular the developing countries.

This choice follows, above all, from the constantly affirmed wish of the Community to participate in the development of the emergent countries. Economically speaking, it is also justified by the fact that the development of commercial traffic, within the framework of the principle of international work distribution, conditions for the Community the very continuance of its growth.

As regards textile and clothing articles, this choice of general policy was confirmed when the Community included textiles in the generalized preference offers made to the developing countries. However, the very fact that most of the other industrialized countries excluded textiles from their preferences shows the difficulties that this sector experiences in adapting itself quickly and easily to the competitive conditions ruling on the world textile market.

The smooth orderly structural adaptation of the textile industry to the conditions of an open market policy pre-supposes several conditions and, in particular, sufficient indications to social partners as regards the envisaged trade policy calendar.

a. As regards generalized preferences, the Community's decisions are expressed by specially fixed terms of application for textiles and clothing, and comprise the establishment of quotas and buffers for sensitive products and a special surveillance system for semi-sensitive products. For a period of five years, any subsequent tariff concession should, in general, come within the framework of this system. When the present offer is completed for the beneficiary countries in the sense of the Council decision of 30 March, (i.e., for countries belonging to the 77 group and not having signed the A.L.T.), the volume of the Community offer should not be subject to a progression exceeding 5% per annum of the total offer,[5] whether because of the extension of the regime to other countries or because of a ceiling rise.

b. As regards quantitative restrictions, subsisting limitations will be progressively eliminated taking into account the attitude of the other trading partners. The liberation calendar, spun goods being largely freed already, should affect cloths before touching more elaborate articles. Such concept is coherent with the process of the progressive industrialization of the developing countries.

c. The establishment of worldwide fair competition in terms of rules to be defined within the scope of GATT, capable of avoiding the permanent threats weighing on world textile commercial currents and of progressively achieving the conditions of an orderly worldwide division of work.

Should it prove impossible to define a code of good conduct with the principal partners, it is to be feared that, on both sides, one would be faced with the necessity, either successively or concomitantly, of falling back on restrictive policies.

In the course of the forthcoming years the Community will be characterized by a gradual opening to imports and more especially those from the developing countries. The strengthening of healthy competition, both inside and outside of the Community, will constitute the principal incentive to restructuration.

Faced with the necessity of progressively improving firms' competitiveness, capital expenditure should primarily aim at increasing productivity and to adapting supply qualitatively to consumers' requirements.

a. Research and the utilization of technological progress will be two essential factors in achieving objectives.

Both as regards the production of man-made fibres and their processing and finishing, research plays an essential part in reducing cost prices and in the qualitative adaptation of supply to the foreseeable evolution of demand.

Man-made fibre producers generally proceed independently with research in order to discover new fibres.

Research conditioning technical progress in textile machinery, closely linked with the productivity of the processing industry, is efficiently carried out within the more general framework of the mechanical engineering industry, frequently in liaison with the utilizers.

Textile research proper is situated at the stage of fibre treatment, processing and finishing. Some firms or groups of firms carry out independently the research in which they are more specially interested. However, the low profitability of most firms does not generally allow them to free the financial means indispensable for continued research. At inter-professional level, co-ordinated research has been begun for all the branches grouped within Comitextil, but this action is far from having satisfactorily solved the problems in question.

In some Member States, research institutes are partly financed by the public powers.

The Commission will be interested to learn of any programme the textile industries may envisage. It will then be able to judge whether, within the scope of general advanced technology policy, any particular backing by the Community should be envisaged and proposed to the Council.

The Commission could also act in the coordination of individual and collective research.

Community research begun in 1964 within the framework of activities promoted by the Eurisotop Bureau for the application of nuclear techniques in the textile industry should be continued.

b. The important fluctuations of market conditions which take place periodically in the textile industry constitute a serious handicap to indispensable restructuration and modernization operations. They also seriously affect firms' finances. The extent of these movements results from the difficulties, in this sector, of making very short-term forecasts. It is important to set up, at Community level, a Cyclical Observation Centre with adequate means for getting together all the data necessary for the establishment of such forecasts and palliating such difficulties. The financial intervention of the Community to encourage this action should be envisaged. The Commission undertakes, by coordinating and centralizing such initiatives, to back any professional initiative taken to this end.[6]

c. The Commission considers that national aid should contribute more especially to speeding up restructuration and directing it towards the Community objects already stated.

In the appraisal of national aid under Articles 92 to 94 of the EEC Treaty, the Commission will take into account the acute social problems that may accompany possible contractions of sector activities and cause serious deterioration of regional situations.

It considers, however, that these problems cannot be finally solved without the combined action of the Community regional and social policy instruments.

Setting up this Community policy would have the effect, *inter alia*, of reducing the need for recourse to interventions in the form of national aid and thereby of attenuating the negative effects of such interventions.

The Commission distinguishes between three types of government intervention:

i. aid to collective textile actions aimed at developing research or improving the short-term economic prospects;

ii. aid in arranging textile structures (elimination of over-capacities, conversion out of the sector, concentration of businesses);

iii. aid with textile capital expenditure (modernization, conversion within the sector).

Whilst fully reserving its power of appraisal, the Commission considers that, subject to various terms and conditions, and in particular not impairing competition more than is indispensable, interventions i. and ii. above would benefit by a presumption in their favour whereas those under iii. would have to meet much stricter exigencies, e.g., be justified by acute social problems, not lead to increased capacity, and take into account the situation of the branch concerned at Community level.

Taking into account, on the one hand, regional and social repercussions of restructuration and, on the other hand, a productivity increase exceeding the foreseeable development rate of Community production, it may be concluded that important problems will arise as regards labour conversion, not only within the textile sector but also towards other sectors of activity.

The Commission is aware of these problems and considers the textile sector as one of the most sensitive industrial sectors as regards the social aspects.

The "Fonds Social Européen Renové" could play a determinant part in facilitating the indispensable manpower conversions both within the sector and outside of it, provided that its action is founded on very strictly selected criteria, and that it is given the financial means adequate for the accomplishment of this task and the other functions entrusted to it. In order to evaluate the means that could prove necessary, a survey is being made to appraise the probable evolution of the various sectors of the textile industry, their personnel and their regional context. The "Fonds Social" could give priority to actions complying with the following criteria:

1. Conversion within the textile industry will enable the development of textile branches in which—in an open market—Community production can

more easily meet outside competition by reason of its specialization and competitiveness.

Definition of activities liable to present these characteristics is under consideration and the results will be submitted for appraisal by the profession, with full hearing on both sides.

2. The operation of laying-off manpower in the textile industry is coordinated within the scope of an action carried out jointly with textile firms destined to lose their personnel and firms belonging to other sectors that could absorb this manpower provided it is first given appropriate training.

3. Restructuration operations within the textile sector. In these operations the training of the labour force would be accompanied by an equipment and technology conversion programme such as to ensure the optimum utilization of this retrained manpower.

Among actions complying with one of the three criteria mentioned above, priority would be given to those which, in addition, meet the exigencies of regional policy. Within the scope of regional policy measures proposed by the Commission to the Council on October 17, 1969, it would be expedient to ensure conditions favourable to the locating of industries other than the textile industry in regions where this need is felt, in particular because of a one-industry situation, by thus rendering easier the carrying out of operations complying with the criteria set out under 2.

These criteria will be communicated to the European Investments Bank to guide those of its interventions which may be complementary to the actions of the "Fonds Social Européen Renové".

In view of the heavy concentration of the textile industry in certain regions, the Commission considers that all industrial restructuration and manpower conversion actions, if they are to be developed without causing serious social problems, necessitate the Community being provided at the earliest possible date with an appropriate range of instruments and financial means of regional policy.

NOTES

1. III/69/5885-F "L'industrie Textile de la CEE—Analyse et Perspectives (1975)".

2. III/70/12734-F "Les industries de la Confection dans la CEE—Analyse et Perspectives 1975".

3. III/471/72-F "Etude préparatoire à des actions visant à faciliter l'adaptation et le progrés dans l'industrie textile européenne".

4. III/75/750-F "L'industrie des bas et collants dans la CEE".

5. The terms of application of the generalized preferences regime will have to be adapted before their application to the expanded Community, particularly as regards sensitive products, so as not to prejudice the advantages or limits of the decisions put into application w.e.f. July 1, 1971.

6. The Commission can make any arrangements with a view to adapting the OSCE programme so that information can be collected and handled for utilization by the Centre.

II. TEXTILE POLICY COUNTER-REPORT

EEC Industrial Policy and the Textile Industry[1]

by *D. C. Hague, T. A. J. Cockerill* and *G. K. Roberts*

The output of the textile and clothing industries[2] of the European Community has fallen sharply in the period since 1973, reflecting the onset of the recession in the wake of the energy crisis and the rising penetration of imports. In order to safeguard the long-term survival of the industry, there are pressures for modernization and rationalization, for greater co-ordination between the industries of the Member States, and for some protection against imports. At the same time, the trend decline in job opportunities in the industry, and the difficulty of offering alternative employment, are providing social difficulties in each nation, and these are particularly severe in certain regions.

In Section II of this paper, the initial report on the EEC textile industry is summarized. Sections III and IV are a case-study of the industry in the UK, and an appraisal of government policy. In Section V, an evaluation is given of Community policy towards textiles.

THE TEXTILE INDUSTRY IN THE EUROPEAN COMMUNITY

We have reviewed with interest the initial paper and subsequent notes submitted by the textile division of the Directorate-General for industry of the Commission. In our view, the salient points can be summarized as follows:
- Despite the recent recession, the textile and clothing industries remain an important segment of the Community's economy, accounting for 8% of net manufacturing output and 11% of employment.[3] Table 1 shows that in terms of net output, the industries are largest in West Germany and France. Employment is highest in West Germany, but the next largest nation in employment terms is Italy.[4]
- In the Community as a whole, the textile and clothing sector experienced growth of output until 1973, after which the effects of the recession were felt, with output levels in 1975 below those of 1970.[5]
- Imports, especially from South-East Asia, have risen sharply in recent years, and in some sectors of the markets of Member Nations account for 50% of supplies. With the exception of textile products (SITC 65), the balance of the Community's external trade has worsened over the period 1970 to 1975, and in 1975 there were deficits in the raw materials and clothing sectors, whose combined effects were not offset by the surplus for textile products.[6]
- The starting point of the Community's commercial and industrial policy towards the textile and clothing industries in recent years has been the Spinelli Memorandum of 1971. This recognized (a) the need for increasing

335

TABLE 1. *Key Indicators of the EEC Textile and Clothing Industries 1972–1975*

Country	Net Output 1972 (*million units of account*)	Employment 1975 (*in thousands*)	
		Textiles	Clothing
West Germany	6,417	357	292
Belgium–			
Luxembourg	1,132	84	59
Netherlands	719	49	25
France	5,484	337	206
Italy	4,735	354	215
Denmark	276	16	14
Eire	158	20	14
UK	4,130	460	310
EEC "9"	23,051	1,677	1,135

Source: *The Textile Industry*, Annex 1.

the efficiency of the industries through restructuring and the encouragement of technical progress; (b) the need for progression towards an integrated Common Market within the Community for textile products; (c) accompanying this, the opening of the Community's markets to outside imports, together with an effective policy for containing the disruptive short-run effects of imports; (d) the need for improved short- and medium-term forecasting to assist the industry to deal better with cyclical market movements; (e) the harmonization of aid to the textile industries by the Governments of the Member States for the purposes of improved forecasting and research, industrial restructuring and capital investments. A principal concern in the case of the latter would be to ensure that there was no net increase in capacity in the medium term.

– The memorandum met opposition mainly from the labour unions (who were concerned about the impact on employment within the Community of the liberalization of the market to outside supplies) but also from the industrialists who were concerned about government influence on forecasting and also the difficulty of applying harmonization guidelines to ensure the transparency of State financial aids to the industry.

– Some parts of the commercial objectives of the Memorandum were achieved when the Member States became signatories to the GATT Multi-Fibre Arrangement (MFA) in 1973. While the long-term objective of this is to encourage the progressive liberalization of markets in textile products, under Articles 3 and 4, it also allows for quantitative limits on imports to be agreed bilaterally when there is disruption, or the threat of disruption in the markets of the importing nations. At the same time, however, the MFA allows for imports to increase at an annual rate of 6% even in cases where restrictions apply.

– Recognizing that import penetration is more severe in some Member States (especially the Federal Republic of Germany, and the UK), than in others, the Council of the European Communities has instituted a system of burden sharing, the long-term objectives of which are to seek to equalize the impact of imports on the markets of the individual Member States.[7]

- It was noted that, as a result of delays in negotiating the Community's position in regard to the MFA, import quota levels are probably higher than they would have been had agreement been reached earlier.[8]
- In regard to policies for industrial restructuring, it was observed that a start had been made on a coordinated programme of technical research, on reviewing the transparency of the various aid schemes available for the industry from the governments of the Member States (to guard against hidden subsidies) and on examining the possibility of Community aid to the industry to assist with the relocation, retraining and re-employment of labour displaced by restructuring.[9] It is also noted that severe difficulties have been encountered in the development of Community-wide forecasting for the textile industry.
- Two of the three case-studies presented (on man-made fibres and the tights industry) emphasize the difficulty for the Commission in establishing a coordinated and effective industrial policy in circumstances of excess capacity and aggressive marketing from a Member State. It is too soon to judge the impact of the textile labelling directive.

THE TEXTILE INDUSTRY IN THE UNITED KINGDOM

Since 1966 the demand for textile goods (including clothing) in Britain has increased very slowly. Sales of textile end-products in 1973 (a year of relatively high demand) were 36% above their 1966 level, and over the same period, output of textile yarns was up by only 7%.[10] Consumers' expenditure on textile end-products, in real terms, has similarly shown slow growth over the period, and expressed as a proportion of total consumers' expenditure, has remained more or less static at around 9%.[11]

As a whole, the UK textile and clothing industries in 1974 accounted for 7.8% of the net output of all manufacturing industry, 12% of employment and 8.5% of capital expenditure.[12] In the period since 1963, the trend has been for the two industries' share in total manufacturing output to fall, and for the numbers employed also to reduce: in 1963 the industries employed 1,143 thousand people, or 14.3% of the total in manufacturing industry, but by 1974 the number had fallen to 923 thousand. Capital expenditure has been more stable in relation to total investment in the manufacturing sector as a whole, at between 8 and 9%.[13]

This relative decline, however, disguises some significant changes within the textile sector as a whole. Table 2 gives comparative details of output, employment and capital expenditure for each sector of the textile industry in 1974. The predominant sectors in order of their net output, are hosiery and knitwear, man-made fibres, woollen and worsteds, and cotton and allied textiles, each of which have net outputs of around £300 million or between 16 and 17% of the industry's total output. The cotton, woollen, and hosiery and knitwear sectors tend to be relatively labour intensive, accounting in each case for between 18 to 22% of industry employment, and this contrasts sharply with the man-made fibres sector, which to a large degree is a chemical process operation, accounting for less than eight per cent of total employment.

TABLE 2. *Output, Employment and Capital Expenditure in the UK Textile and Clothing Industries, 1974*

	Net Output		Employment		Capital Expenditure	
	£m	% of all Textiles	thousands	% of all Textiles	£m	% of all Textiles
Man-made fibres (MLH 411)[1]	308.4	16.8	45.4	7.9	40.0	16.9
Cotton and allied textiles (MLH 412/13)	298.0	16.2	110.2	19.1	56.5	23.9
Woollen and Worsted (MLH 414)	302.4	16.6	104.7	18.2	33.8	14.3
Hosiery and Knitwear (MLH 417)	311.0	16.9	127.6	22.2	35.1	14.8
Carpets (MLH 419)	177.5	9.7	45.9	8.0	19.4	8.2
Household Textiles (MLH 422.1)	68.6	3.7	22.6	3.9	9.6	4.1
Textile Finishing (MLH 423)	121.4	6.6	44.6	7.7	20.2	8.5
Other Textiles (MLH 415/16/18/21/22.2/29)	250.5	13.6	75.1	13.0	22.1	9.3
All textiles (except clothing)	1837.8	100.0	576.1	100.0	236.7	100.0
Clothing	684.6	n.a.	347.0	n.a.	35.7	n.a.

1. Minimum List Headings (MH) refer to the basic industrial categories of the UK Standard Industrial Classification.

Source: Joint Textile Committee, *Textile Trends 1966–75*, (London: National Economic Development Office) 1976, Tables 1.5 and 1.7.

In 1974, capital expenditure was particularly large in the cotton and allied textiles sector (24% of the industry total).

The most striking developments within the industry since 1963 have been the growth of the man-made fibres and carpets sectors. Between 1963 and 1974, man-made fibres increased their share of total textile net output from 13.8% to 16.8%, and in 1971, accounted for over sixty per cent of the fibre consumption of textile mills in the UK. The growth of these fibres can be attributed to two principal factors. One is the sharp fall in the relative price of man-made fibres, especially the non-cellulosics. Appendix A (Figure AI and Table A1) indicates UK prices of wool, cotton and rayon and Japanese f.o.b. export prices for non-cellulosic fibres (nylon, polyester and acrylics) expressed in UK New Pence.[14] The price of nylon fell by 41.3% between 1962 and 1971, and the reductions for the other non-cellulosic fibres were even more pronounced. The second factor has been improvements in the characteristics of man-made fibres, as a result of which they have been blended with other natural and artificial fibres and applied to an increasingly broad range of end-uses, particularly industrial ones.

The expansion of the carpets sector, the sales value of which rose by 48% at constant prices between 1966 and 1974[15] is attributable in part to a general increase in living standards, and in part to the steady growth of sales of tufted carpets, which improved both in quality and in the range of designs available. Hosiery and knitting enjoyed persistent expansion during the 1960s, but have suffered a considerable set-back in the 1970s. Market share had fallen by a full two percentage points in 1974 as compared with the 18.8% of 1968. Hosiery manufacture has encountered very strong competition from imports, especially of tights from Italy and South-East Asia. The growth of knitted garments, including men's suits, has also been considerably reduced in recent years. Household textiles have exhibited strong growth, but this has been from a small initial base, and the sector accounted for less than 4% of total industry output in 1974. Elsewhere, and especially in the woollen and worsted and cotton and allied textiles sectors, the story has been one of continuing relative decline.

In spite of its modest growth, the textile industry as a whole succeeded in achieving a higher rate of growth of productivity as measured by the value of net output per head, than manufacturing industry as a whole in the period 1963 to 1973. However, in 1974, output and productivity fell back sharply with the onset of the recession. The rise in the industry's productivity can be attributed to three main factors: (a) the relatively faster growth of the high productivity sectors of man-made fibres and carpets; (b) increases in capital expenditure per head and reductions in manning levels as new equipment was brought into operation, and (c) trading-up into higher added-value product areas.

There has been a substantial reduction in employment in the industry. In 1963 the textile industry (excluding clothing) had 749,300 employees, but by 1974 this had fallen to 576,100, a reduction of 23.1%. The sharpest decline was in the cotton and allied textiles sector (down from 193,400 in 1963 to 110,200 in 1974) but, against the general trend, employment increased in the man-made fibres and carpets sectors. At the same time, the composition of the labour force has altered. Traditionally an employer of female labour, by

339

TABLE 3. *UK trade balance in textiles and clothing 1966 and 1975. £ million*

	1966			1975		
	Imports	Exports	Trade balance	Imports	Exports	Trade balance
Textile (SITC 65)						
EEC	61	69	+8	296	233	−63
EFTA	15	33	+18	145	133	−12
Other W European countries	3	14	+11	14	18	+4
Comecon	4	3	−1	13	36	+23
Other developed countries	19	86	+67	90	136	+46
Developing countries	53	47	−6	125	142	+17
Total: the World	159	261	+102	683	698	+15
Clothing (SITC 84)						
EEC	21	16	−5	123	110	−13
EFTA	5	8	+3	77	64	−13
Other W European countries	—	2	+2	15	5	−10
Comecon	1	1	—	17	4	−13
Other developed countries	5	15	+10	18	43	+25
Developing countries	32	6	−26	255	39	−216
Total: the World	69	53	−16	505	265	−240

− less than £2m

Source: *Textile Trends 1966–75.*

June 1974, women formed 45.6% of the total workforce in textiles.[16] This reflects the increased capital intensity of the industry and the need to work shifts. Earnings within the industry have increased at a slightly slower rate than for manufacturing industry as a whole. The differential between male and female earnings, as elsewhere in the economy, has narrowed rapidly in recent years.

The trade balance for textiles and clothing worsened considerably between 1966 and 1975. Table 3 shows that the UK achieved a positive balance on trade in textiles in 1975 although this was much reduced as compared with 1966. But this was quite inadequate to match the large and increasing deficit on clothing. The principal sources of imports of textile goods are the other countries of the EEC, but the bulk of clothing imports (32.7% in 1975) come from Hong Kong. Figure 1 shows import penetration for the principal items of production of the UK textile and clothing industries in 1975 and 1976. In 1976, imports took over 50% of the domestic market for cotton and polyester/cotton cloth, and for certain categories of clothing, particularly shirts.

The major problems which have faced the textile industry since the 1950's have been:

i. Chronic over-capacity in many sectors. As demand has fallen, production has become concentrated on the more efficient manufacturers, and redundant capacity has remained in the industry;

ii. The high average age of much equipment in the industry and the need to replace it with modern machinery incorporating technical developments;

iii. Low profitability which has reduced the availability of funds for capital investments;

iv. The rising penetration of imports in many sectors, especially imports received free of duty from the Commonwealth and those coming from within the EEC.

FIGURE 1

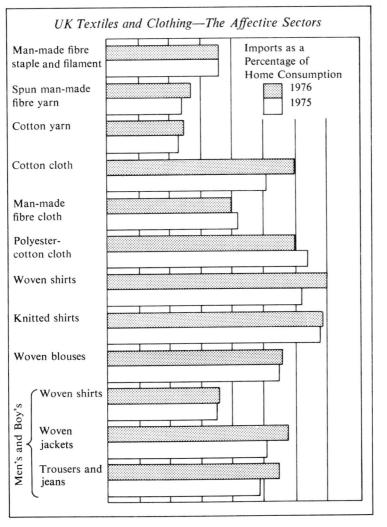

Source: *Financial Times*, 23 March 1977

These two classes of problem—structural and trade—are inter-related. Strong competitive pressure from overseas weakens the domestic industry, lowers its production in relation to its capacity, reduces its profitability and in turn makes more difficult the problem of reorganization. As a consequence, much of the pressure for Government assistance has come initially from the textile industry itself. To tackle the structural question, the Cotton Industry Act 1959 was designed to speed the rate at which redundant capacity was eliminated by providing financial encouragements to firms to leave the industry, rather than wait until they went bankrupt. The Textile Council, in its report of 1968[17] found that in both the cotton and the woollen sectors of the industry, machine utilization rates could be increased through longer running, allowing a reduction in the number of machines, and a corresponding reduction in the labour force. Between 1966 and 1970 the Industrial Reorganization Corporation took an interest in the industry, looking for ways in which the industry might be restructured through mergers, but little was achieved. To lead this, it was hoped to involve companies other than the existing major textile producers, but while, in most cases, the latter had sufficient funds, other companies did not. Moreover, with the cotton and man-made fibres sector already strongly concentrated on Courtaulds, Carrington Viyella, Tootal and Coats Patons, the government feared that any further rationalization would reduce competition too far and the industry feared triggering action under the competition legislation. The woollen and worsted sector of the industry undertook a number of vertical mergers, covering a wide range of activities, but their operations remain essentially fragmented and horizontally managed.

The rising tide of imports has led to the inevitable pressures for protection, which have been largely achieved through bi-lateral agreements. Restrictions still continue on imports of certain cotton goods from Eastern Europe, Japan and other Asian countries, and more recently controls have been imposed on goods from other countries including Taiwan, Spain, Portugal, South Korea, Thailand and Colombia.[18] Since 1973, the UK has been a signatory to the GATT Multi-Fibre Arrangement, and is currently participating in its renegotiation.

PUBLIC POLICY AND THE UK TEXTILE INDUSTRY

We have considered the problems of the UK textile industry and the contribution of public policy towards their solution. Our conclusions are as follows:

1. The efficiency of the industry has been raised during the last fifteen years, in spite of the severe contraction of demand in some sectors. This improvement has been aided both by Government legislation and by the rationalization activities of firms within the industry, particularly the larger ones. However, there is still room for further improvements, and these are vitally necessary if the continued loss of home markets to imports is to be stemmed.

2. Very little of the restructuring which has taken place has been the result of direct intervention in the industry by Government. Indeed, as noted above, the majority has been initiated by the leading companies through

342

mergers or licensing arrangements (for example the "Crimplene Club" of eight throwsters licensed to process textured filament yarn produced by ICI). While there may be dangers to the level of effective competition in the market through such arrangements, we feel that, overall, the effects of these developments have been beneficial. In any case, the pressure of imports is more than sufficient as a check on the undue exercise of market power.

3. It was our general opinion that there is a need to protect the domestic textile industry against imports. The price advantage of imports comes from three principal sources. One is the lower input costs which some countries (especially those in Asia and in certain parts of the Commonwealth) enjoy. In several cases, this advantage vis-à-vis the UK is being steadily eroded as wages rise. Another source is the ability which some nations have to discriminate in their prices between their home markets—which offer secure and growing demand and which are often effectively protected from imports—and the world market. A final source is the policies of many centrally-planned economies, whose prices are partly set with a view to earning hard currencies, rather than to demand conditions in world markets.

4. Imports entering developed economies under these conditions can have a very destabilizing effect on their domestic industries and, our view is, can destroy them unless protective action is taken. There is clearly a case for tariffs or quotas to counter short-term inflows of imports at times of low demand, but, in view of the majority of the Study Group, there is also a longer-term justification.

5. One aspect of long-term policy is that adequate supplies of textile goods may not be available, in times of high world demand, to a developed nation which has chosen to rely predominantly on imports. A second, but equally important, consideration is that the free play of international market forces, reflecting comparative advantage between nations, seems no longer able to provide an effective distribution of the textile and clothing industries within the developed world, and between it and the less developed countries (LDC's).

In this respect, the position of the textile industry is complicated by the high degree of vertical integration which characterizes it. There may be a *prime facie* case for permitting substantial sections of the labour-intensive sectors of the textile industry—for example cotton spinning, fabric production and the manufacture of textile end-goods, especially clothing—to migrate to the LDC's in which labour costs are lower. But this process will separate them from the capital-intensive upstream operations of basic chemical production and the manufacture of man-made fibres. The expanding textile industries of the developing nations are likely to change considerably the pattern of demand for fibres supplied by the developed nations, and this could damage seriously the chemicals and fibres industries of some, if not most, of the developed nations. In the view of several members of the group, and especially those concerned with the maintenance of production and employment in the British textile industry, it is not feasible under present-day circumstances, to separate the many highly-integrated processes, and to leave a commercially viable core of fibre production.[19] The fear has also been expressed that, in countries such as the UK where mobility of factors of production is slow and difficult, the effects of a declining industry cannot easily be offset by expansion elsewhere in the manufacturing sector. This is one cause of the process of "de-industrialization" and on which some observers have commented.[20]

6. This view is qualified to some degree by those members of the group who referred to the interests of the final consumers of textile goods. It was pointed out that, all else equal, low-priced goods—whether coming from domestic or foreign sources—increased the real income of consumers. At the same time, however, the difficulty of the correct balance between short-term benefits from lower prices and longer-term gains from security of supply and more stable prices was recognized.

7. It was also pointed out that protection against imports and assistance to domestic industries by the developed nations have impacts on the LDC's, and that one dimension of an optimal policy must take into account the interests of the Third World. It is important to ensure that the protection of EEC markets does not nullify aid given by the Community to the LDC's. The opportunity exists for the Community to differentiate in its tariff and quota policies between nations, and use of these powers could be considered as a means of safeguarding the interests of the LDC's.

CONCLUSIONS—THE EFFECTIVENESS OF COMMUNITY POLICY

The textile group was able to reach substantial agreement on the analysis contained in the study group's report. The principal conclusions are as follows:

1. Effective application of policy has occurred mainly in the field of international trade. This has been particularly the case so far as the UK is concerned, on which the analysis is primarily based. However, significant contributions have also been made by the Commission in other areas, in particular the provision of funds to aid industrial restructuring and to promote research. In other areas, such as research coordination and harmonization of descriptions, the initiatives of the Commission are at a very early stage, and appraisal is impossible.

2. As to the problem of trade policy, the majority of the group recognizes the need for some restrictions in imports from outside the Community, at least in the short term, for the reasons summarized in Section IV of the contra-report.

3. Nevertheless, there is concern about the means by which the Community's policy has evolved. It was noted that the MFA was a GATT initiative, the impetus for which came from all major industrialized nations and not just those of the Community. While the MFA clearly meets some of the objectives of the Spinelli Memorandum, the Group question whether a more positive and individual initiative on the problem of imports could not have come from the Commission.

4. The Group note with concern the delays which have occurred—and which are readily admitted by the Commission—in the negotiation of the original MFA, due largely to the problem of achieving common agreement between the various Member States, and the suspicion that in some cases, the

hesitation of Member States was designed to improve their own individual situations under the arrangements. The delays encountered are in sharp contrast to the fast and efficient way in which the United States establishes its position, and there is little doubt that the collective interests of the Community have suffered as a result.

5. Indeed, some consideration was given to the question of whether the overall outcome of the original MFA, from the point of view of the Community, was better than would have occurred with uncoordinated bilateral negotiations by the individual Member States, but it was not possible to reach a definite conclusion. On the one hand, there is great potential for effective negotiation in the size of the Community. But on the other hand, the difficulties of developing a co-ordinated approach are profound.

6. In the light of this, there are considerable doubts about the effectiveness with which the renegotiation of the MFA, in 1977, will be carried out. It was noted that the United States wishes the MFA to continue unmodified, but the general feeling was that some increase in protection for the markets of the Community is essential, and it is hoped that in view of the effective protection which the US market has enjoyed in recent years, some accommodation of the Community's interests will be possible.

7. The reasonableness of the Council's initiative on import burden-sharing was also questioned, especially in the context of the UK. It was noted that the problem of clothing imports from Hong Kong is essentially the result of commercial policy in the period before accession to the EEC and in the view of some of the Group, should be dealt with unilaterally by the UK.

8. The fears of exclusion from the extensive markets of the major industrialized nations on the part of the LDC's is fully recognized, but at the same time the maintenance of an efficient and commercially viable textile industry within the Community is clearly a principal priority, for reasons both of security and of employment. Protection against short-term disruption is therefore legitimate and essential. Indeed, it was argued by some of our members that the maintenance of a sound industrial structure in the developed nations in itself guarantees continuing access to a profitable market by the LDC's. However, while the need for some short-term protection against imports is necessary, it is also important to ensure that consumers have considerable freedom of choice in making their purchases and to recognize that low-cost imports initially raise living standards by increasing purchasing power. At the same time, little attention has been paid to the net increases in welfare of different groups of the population brought about by a policy of aiding consumers with lower prices and against a policy of employment protection. Some research in this area is urgently needed.

9. Further enlargement of the Community to include low-cost producing nations (for example Portugal and Greece) will have profound implications for policy towards the textile industry and the Group was pleased to note that the Commission is aware of this. It was agreed that a coordinated and consistent policy towards the accession of other textile producing nations was vital.

10. Bearing in mind the need for some protection together with ensuring sufficient international mobility of productive factors to increase overall living standards, it was considered that the Commission should give serious attention to the evolution of an integrated trade and industrial policy.

11. The Group was also concerned about the apparent lack of progress towards a common Community industrial policy on textiles and by the evident reluctance of some Member States to participate constructively in the evolution of such a policy.

12. At the same time, it would not be appropriate to encourage an undue amount of *dirigisme* on the part of the Commission in regard to the textile industry. The founding philosophy of the Community is based upon the operation of free-market competition; but this cannot be expected to operate (if at all) until the entire Community is fully integrated. Until that time, some interventions on the part of national or Community authorities will be necessary.

13. The Group was disturbed to note, therefore, the absence of *de jure* powers in the Treaty of Rome for the formulation and application of Community-wide industrial policies. If it is possible to rectify this situation by obtaining a mandate from the Council, this should be done forthwith. It may be essential to persuade Member States progressively to accept the jurisdiction of a central authority over industrial matters before an effective policy can be framed. In the Group's view, this is currently a major obstacle in the way of the progressive development of a community-wide industrial policy, which is regarded as an essential step.

14. At the same time, the Group would like to know more about the philosophy and the effectiveness of the Community's regional and social policies as applied to textiles. These are clearly potential instruments for restructuring and modernizing the industry.

15. The Group is also concerned to observe the extent to which the Commission's activities in recent years have been dominated by questions of import protection and industrial restructuring, important as these are. In its view, the Commission should take a broader view to encompass the interests of consumers and, to a greater extent than is presently achieved, also of the labour unions.

16. It is of the greatest importance that the various policies proposed by the Commission, and which impact upon the textile industry, should be developed in a consistent and co-ordinated manner, and it is to be hoped that the close co-operation which exists between the various departments of the Commission will continue to be fostered.

17. The question was also considered of whether there were actual potential sources of conflict between Community policy and the policies of the Member States. To date, for the UK, the Group were unable to identify any serious areas of difficulty, but this may be in large part due to the short time that Britain has been a member of the Community. For the future, it seems likely that difficulties for the UK may be caused by any pressure on the part of the Community for a more liberal attitude towards imports from outside, and by movements towards the harmonization and increased transparency of Member States' aid to industry.

18. The work of the Commission in regard to the textile industry is currently hampered by a lack of adequate data. It is to be hoped that this will receive urgent attention.

TABLE A1. *Japanese Unit Export f.o.b. Values for non-cellulosic fibres; UK domestic prices for rayon, cotton and wool, 1960–1971*

Year	Cotton[1] with devaluation effect	Cotton[1] without devaluation effect[4]	Wool[2]	Nylon[3]	Acrylic[3]	new pence/kg Polyester[3]	new pence/kg Rayon[3]
1960	22.14		85.00				15.70
1961	22.73		87.00				15.73
1962	21.96		89.00	62.08	62.80	87.77	16.49
1963	21.15		101.00	59.35	68.64	80.44	16.41
1964	21.44		109.00	56.27	59.49	78.49	15.05
1965	20.56		96.00	52.09	49.60	54.23	16.62
1966	19.84		97.00	45.16	44.08	49.82	18.87
1967	25.18	(21.72)	91.00	45.29	46.12	52.35	21.25
1968	24.61	(21.03)	101.00	43.20	41.52	46.97	19.64
1969	24.18	(20.08)	94.00	41.24	39.16	45.00	19.98
1970	27.40	(28.51)	82.00	40.94	39.27	40.53	
1971	31.07	(28.52)	73.00	36.44	36.05	30.17	

Notes and Sources:
1. Orleans/Memphis M1 at Liverpool; Bureau of Agricultural Economics, *The Fibre Review 1971/72*, (Canberra) October 1972.
2. 64's Merinos, UK, Commonwealth Secretariat, *Industrial Fibres*, (London), 1973.
3. *The Fibre Review.*
4. at 1966 mid-point exchange rate of £1 = £2.7902.

347

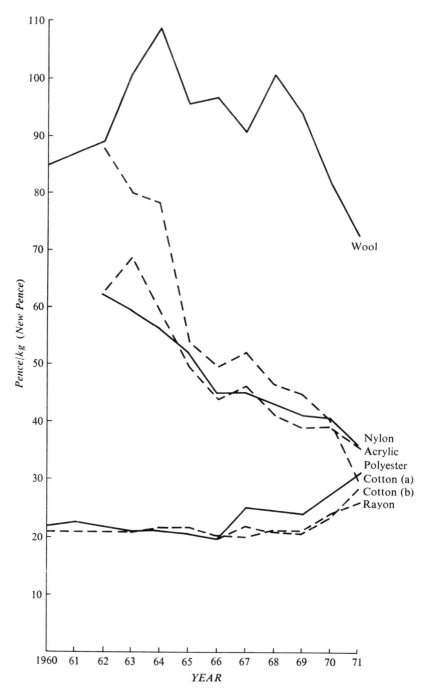

FIGURE 2. *Japanese unit export f.o.b. values for non-cellulosic fibres. UK domestic prices for rayon, cotton and wool, 1960–1971*

MEMBERSHIP OF THE STUDY GROUP

Mrs. C. Brierley, National Economic Development Office
Mrs. L. Briscoe, Department of Economics, University of Manchester
Mr. T. A. J. Cockerill, Department of Economics and Geography, University of Salford
Mr. J. Evans, Courtaulds Limited
Mr. A. J. Godden, ICI Fibres Limited
Professor D. C. Hague, Manchester Business School
Professor G. Ionescu, Department of Government, University of Manchester
Dr. D. Jacques, Courtaulds Limited
Mr. J. Knapp,* Department of Economics, University of Manchester
Miss L. L. Lowne, Department of Industry
Dr. K. Norris, Department of Textile Technology, University of Manchester Institute of Science & Technology
Mr. C. M. Purvis, British Textile Confederation
Dr. G. K. Roberts, Department of European Studies and Modern Languages, University of Manchester Institute of Science & Technology
Professor J. Taylor, Department of Government, University of Manchester
Mr. P. G. Walker, Amalgamated Textile Workers Union

The starting point of the group's work was the report on the textile industry prepared by the European Commission. In addition the Group was fortunate to receive valuable contributions from Mr. Jonathan Scheele of the European Commission, Mr. Alan Godden, Chief Economist of ICI (Fibres) Ltd., Miss L. L. Lowne, of the UK Department of Industry, and Mrs. Caroline Brierley of the National Economic Development Office.

    * Deceased.

ANNEX I

Statistical information on the textile and clothing sector

1. *Employment (1,000's)*

EEC (9)	Textile Industry	Clothing Industry	Total
1965	2,242		
1970	2,117	1,308	3,425
1971	2,019	1,313	3,332
1972	1,929	1,281	3,210
1973	1,878	1,260	3,138
1974	1,806	1,186	2,992
1975	1,677	1,135	2,812

Textile Employment

Year	D	B/L	N	F	I	DK	IRL	GB
1965	547	123	86	395	393	22	21	655
1970	500	109	68	359	415	21	26	619
1972	457	105	65	360	375	22	23	522
1974	394	93	55	355	370	16	21	502
1975	357	84	49	337	354	16	20	460

Clothing Employment

Year	D	B/L	N	F	I	DK	IRL	GB
1965								
1970	381	65	49	204	200	14	18	377
1972	374	68	41	219	204	17	17	341
1974	312	64	33	206	220	16	16	319
1975	292	59	25	206	215	(14)	14	310

Sources: COMITEXTIL, AEIH, OECD

2. *Net Output (million UA)*
(Gross value added at market prices (current) for NACE Branch 42)

Year	D	B/L	N	F	I	DK*	IRL*	GB	EEC
1970	5,637	911	612	4,265	3,888	244	146	3,792	19,495
1972	6,417	1,132	719	5,484	4,735	276	158	4,130	23,051

* Gross value added at factor cost

Source: SOEC, National Accounts

350

3. Production Index (1970 = 100)

Year	Textile Industry	Clothing Industry	Manufacturing Industry
1969	101		
1970	100	100	
1971	103	103	
1972	109	106	
1973	112	107	
1974	107	103	
1975	97	97	

Sources: OECD, SOEC

4. External Trade

Year	Raw Materials (SITC 26)	Text. Products (SITC 65)	Clothing (SITC 84)	Total (SITC 26 + 65 + 84)	Fin. Products (SITC 65 + 84)
1970	−1,208.5	+1,444.6	+141.2	+377.3	+1,585.8
1971*	−1,078.7	+1,559.8	−115.5	+405.6	+1,484.3
1972	−1,429.5	+1,444.5	−399.3	−384.3	+1,045.2
1973	−2,022.4	+1,893.8	−937.5	−1,066.1	+956.3
1974	−1,990.0	+2,197.6	−1,500.5	−1,293.9	+697.5
1975 (est.)	−1,213.0	+1,235.0	−1,578.0	−1,551.0	−338.0

* Excluding Ireland.

Sources: OECD and National Statistics

5. Fibre Consumption

Year	Mill Consumption	Final Consumption
1969	3,510	3,497
1970	3,460	3,469
1971	3,499	3,521
1972	3,585	3,784
1973	3,789	4,058

Sources: CIRFS

ANNEX II

Arrangement regarding international trade in textiles

Preamble

Recognizing the great importance of production and trade in textile products of wool, man-made fibres and cotton for the economies of many countries, and their particular importance for the economic and social development of developing countries and for the expansion and diversification of their export earnings, and conscious also of the special importance of trade in textile products of cotton for many developing countries;

Recognizing further the tendency for an unsatisfactory situation to exist in world trade in textile products and that this situation, if not satisfactorily dealt with, could work to the detriment of countries participating in trade in textile products, whether as importers or exporters, or both, adversely affect prospects for international cooperation in the trade field, and have unfortunate repercussions on trade relations generally;

Noting that this unsatisfactory situation is characterized by the proliferation of restrictive measures, including discriminatory measures, that are inconsistent with the principles of the General Agreement on Tariffs and Trade and also that, in some importing countries, situations have arisen which, in the view of these countries, cause or threaten to cause disruption of their domestic markets;

Desiring to take cooperative and constructive action, within a multilateral framework, so as to deal with the situation in such a way as to promote on a sound basis the development of production and expansion of trade in textile products and progressively to achieve the reduction of trade barriers and the liberalization of world trade in these products;

Recognizing that, in pursuit of such action, the volatile and continually evolving nature of production and trade in textile products should be constantly borne in mind and the fullest account taken of such serious economic and social problems as exist in this field in both importing and exporting countries, and particularly in the developing countries;

Recognizing further that such action should be designed to facilitate economic expansion and to promote the development of developing countries possessing the necessary resources, such as materials and technical skills, by providing larger opportunities for such countries, including countries that are, or that may shortly become, new entrants in the field of textile exports to increase their exchange earnings from the sale in world markets of products which they can efficiently produce;

Recognizing that future harmonious development of trade in textiles particularly having regard to the needs of developing countries, also depends importantly upon matters outside the scope of this Arrangement, and that such factors in this respect include progress leading both to the reduction of tariffs and to the maintenance and improvement of schemes of generalized preferences, in accordance with the Tokyo Declaration;

Determined to have full regard to the principles and objectives of the General

Agreement on Tariffs and Trade (hereinafter referred to as the GATT) and, in carrying out the aims of this Arrangement, effectively to implement the principles and objectives agreed upon in the Tokyo Declaration of Ministers dated 14 September 1973 concerning the Multilateral Trade Negotiations;

THE PARTIES TO THIS ARRANGEMENT have agreed as follows:

Article 1

1. It may be desirable during the next few years for special practical measures of international cooperation to be applied by the participating countries[21] in the field of textiles with the aim of eliminating the difficulties that exist in this field.
2. The basic objectives shall be to achieve the expansion of trade, the reduction of barriers to such trade and the progressive liberalization of world trade in textile products, while at the same time ensuring the orderly and equitable development of this trade and avoidance of disruptive effects in individual markets and on individual lines of production in both importing and exporting countries. In the case of those countries having small markets, an exceptionally high level of imports and a correspondingly low level of domestic production, account should be taken of the avoidance of damage to those countries' minimum viable production of textiles.
3. A principal aim in the implementation of this Arrangement shall be to further the economic and social development of developing countries and secure a substantial increase in their export earnings from textile products and to provide scope for a greater share for them in world trade in these products.
4. Actions taken under this Arrangement shall not interrupt or discourage the autonomous industrial adjustment process of participating countries. Furthermore, actions taken under this Arrangement should be accompanied by the pursuit of appropriate economic and social policies, in a manner consistent with national laws and systems, required by changes in the pattern of trade in textiles and in the comparative advantage of participating countries, which policies would encourage businesses which are less competitive internationally to move progressively into more viable lines of production or into other sectors of the economy and provide increased access to their markets for textile products from developing countries.
5. The application of safeguard measures under this Arrangement, subject to recognized conditions and criteria and under the surveillance of an international body set up for that purpose, and in conformity with the principles and objectives of this Arrangement, may in exceptional circumstances become necessary in the field of trade in textile products, and should assist any process of adjustment which would be required by the changes in the pattern of world trade in textile products. The parties to this Arrangement undertake not to apply such measures except in accordance with the provisions of this Arrangement with full regard to the impact of such measures on other parties.

6. The provisions of this Arrangement shall not affect the rights and obligations of the participating countries under the GATT.

7. The participating countries recognize that, since measures taken under this Arrangement are intended to deal with the special problems of textile products, such measures should be considered as exceptional, and not lending themselves to application in other fields.

Article 2

1. All existing unilateral quantitative restrictions, bilateral agreements and any other quantitative measures in force which have a restrictive effect shall be notified in detail by the restraining participating country, upon acceptance of or accession to this Arrangement, to the Textiles Surveillance Body, which shall circulate the notifications to the other participating countries for their information. Measures or agreements which are not notified by a participating country within 60 days of its acceptance of, or accession to, this Arrangement shall be considered to be contrary to this Arrangement and shall be terminated forthwith.

2. Unless they are justified under the provisions of the GATT (including its Annexes and Protocols), all unilateral quantitative restrictions and any other quantitative measures which have a restrictive effect and which are notified in accordance with paragraph 1 above shall be terminated within one year of the entry into force of this Arrangement, unless they are the subject of one of the following procedures to bring them into conformity with the provisions of this Arrangement:
   i. inclusion in a programme, which should be adopted and notified to the Textiles Surveillance Body within one year from the date of coming into force of this Arrangement, designed to eliminate existing restrictions in stages within a maximum period of three years from the entry into force of this Arrangement and taking account of any bilateral agreement either concluded or in course of being negotiated as provided for in (ii) below; it being understood that a major effort will be made in the first year, covering both a substantial elimination of restrictions and a substantial increase in the remaining quotas;
   ii. inclusion, within a period of one year from the entry into force of this Arrangement, in bilateral agreements negotiated, or in course of negotiation, pursuant to the provisions of Article 4; if, for exceptional reasons, any such bilateral agreement is not concluded within the period of one year; this period, following consultations by the participating countries concerned and with the concurrence of the Textiles Surveillance Body, may be extended by not more than one year;
   iii. inclusion in agreements negotiated or measures adopted pursuant to the provisions of Article 3.

3. Unless justified under the provisions of the GATT (including its Annexes and Protocols), all existing bilateral agreements notified in accordance with paragraph 1 of this Article shall, within one year of the entry into force of this Arrangement, either be terminated or justified under the provisions of this Arrangement or modified to conform therewith.

4. For the purposes of paragraphs 2 and 3 above the participating countries shall afford full opportunity for bilateral consultation and negotiation aimed

at arriving at mutually acceptable solutions in accordance with Articles 3 and 4 of this Arrangement and permitting from the first year of the acceptance of this Arrangement the elimination as complete as possible of the existing restrictions. They shall report specifically to the Textiles Surveillance Body within one year of the entry into force of the Arrangement on the status of any such actions taken or negotiations undertaken pursuant to this Article.

5.   The Textiles Surveillance Body shall complete its review of such reports within 90 days of their receipt. In its review it shall consider whether all the actions taken are in conformity with this Arrangement. It may make appropriate recommendations to the participating countries directly concerned so as to facilitate the implementation of this Article.

Article 3

1.   Unless they are justified under the provisions of the GATT (including its Annexes and Protocols) no new restrictions on trade in textile products shall be introduced by participating countries nor shall existing restrictions be intensified unless such action is justified under the provisions of this Article.

2.   The participating countries agree that this Article should only be resorted to sparingly and its application shall be limited to the precise products and to countries whose exports of such products are causing market disruption as defined in Annex A taking full account of the agreed principles and objectives set out in this Arrangement and having full regard to the interests of both importing and exporting countries. Participating countries shall take into account imports from all countries and shall seek to preserve a proper measure of equity. They shall endeavour to avoid discriminatory measures where market disruption is caused by imports from more than one participating country and when resort to the application of this Article is unavoidable, bearing in mind the provisions of Article 6.

3.   If, in the opinion of any participating importing country, its market in terms of the definition of market disruption in Annex A is being disrupted by imports of a certain textile product not already subject to restraint, it shall seek consultations with the participating exporting country or countries concerned with a view to removing such disruption. In its request the importing country may indicate the specific level at which it considers that exports of such products should be restrained, a level which shall not be lower than the general level indicated in Annex B. The exporting country or countries concerned shall respond promptly to such request for consultations. The importing country's request for consultations shall be accomplished by a detailed factual statement of the reasons and justification for the request, including the latest data concerning elements of market disruption, this information being communicated at the same time by the requesting country to the Chairman of the Textiles Surveillance Body.

4.   If, in the consultation, there is mutual understanding that the situation calls for restrictions on trade in the textile product concerned, the level of restriction shall be fixed at a level not lower than the level indicated in Annex B. Details of the agreement reached shall be communicated to the Textiles Surveillance Body which shall determine whether the agreement is justified in accordance with the provisions of this Arrangement.

5. i. If, however, after a period of 60 days from the date on which the request has been received by the participating exporting country or countries, there has been no agreement either on the request for export restraint or on any alternative solution, the requesting participating country may decline to accept imports for retention from the participating country or countries referred to in paragraph 3 above of the textiles and textile products causing market disruption (as defined in Annex A) at a level for the 12-month period beginning on the day when the request was received by the participating exporting country or countries not less than the level provided for in Annex B. Such level may be adjusted upwards to avoid undue hardship to the commercial participants in the trade involved to the extent possible consistent with the purposes of this Article. At the same time the matter shall be brought for immediate attention to the Textiles Surveillance Body.
    ii. However, it shall be open for either party to refer the matter to the Textiles Surveillance Body before the expiry of the period of 60 days.
    iii. In either case the Textiles Surveillance Body shall promptly conduct the examination of the matter and make appropriate recommendations to the parties directly concerned within 30 days from the date on which the matter is referred to it. Such recommendations shall also be forwarded to the Textiles Committee and to the GATT Council for their information. Upon receipt of such recommendations the participating countries concerned should review the measures taken or contemplated with regard to their institution, continuation, modification or discontinuation.
6. In highly unusual and critical circumstances, where imports of a textile product or products during the period of 60 days referred to in paragraph 5 above would cause serious market disruption giving rise to damage difficult to repair, the importing country shall request the exporting country concerned to cooperate immediately on a bilateral emergency basis to avoid such damage, and shall, at the same time, immediately communicate to the Textiles Surveillance Body the full details of the situation. The countries concerned may make any mutually acceptable interim arrangement they deem necessary to deal with the situation without prejudice to consultations regarding the matter under paragraph 3 of this Article. In the event that such interim arrangement is not reached, temporary restraint measures may be applied at a level higher than that indicated in Annex B with a view, in particular, to avoiding undue hardship to the commercial participants in the trade involved. The importing country shall give, except where possibility exists of quick delivery which would undermine the purpose of such measure, at least one week's prior notification of such action to the participating exporting country or countries and enter into, or continue, consultations under paragraph 3 of this Article. When a measure is taken under this paragraph either party may refer the matter to the Textiles Surveillance Body. The Textiles Surveillance Body shall conduct its work in the manner provided for in paragraph 5 above. Upon receipt of recommendations from the Textiles Surveillance Body the participating importing country shall review the measures taken, and report thereon to the Textiles Surveillance Body.
7. If recourse is had to measures under this Article, participating countries

shall, in introducing such measures, seek to avoid damage to the production and marketing of the exporting countries, and particularly of the developing countries, and shall avoid any such measures taking a form that could result in the establishment of additional non-tariff barriers to trade in textile products. They shall, through prompt consultations, provide for suitable procedures, particularly as regards goods which have been, or which are about to be, shipped. In the absence of agreement, the matter may be referred to the Textiles Surveillance Body, which shall make the appropriate recommendations.

8. Measures taken under this Article may be introduced for limited periods not exceeding one year, subject to renewal or extension for additional periods of one year, provided that agreement is reached between the participating countries directly concerned on such renewal or extension. In such cases the provisions of Annex B shall apply. Proposals for renewal or extension, or modification or elimination or any disagreement thereon shall be submitted to the Textiles Surveillance Body, which shall make the appropriate recommendations. However, bilateral restraint agreements under this Article may be concluded for periods in excess of one year in accordance with the provisions of Annex B.

9. Participating countries shall keep under review any measures they have taken under this Article and shall afford any participating country or countries affected by such measures adequate opportunity for consultation with a view to the elimination of the measures as soon as possible. They shall report from time to time, and in any cases once a year, to the Textiles Surveillance Body on the progress made in the elimination of such measures.

Article 4

1. The participating countries shall fully bear in mind, in the conduct of their trade policies in the field of textiles, that they are, through the acceptance of, or accession to, this Arrangement, committed to a multilateral approach in the search for solutions to the difficulties that arise in this field.

2. However, participating countries may, consistently with the basic objectives and principles of this Arrangement, conclude bilateral agreements on mutually acceptable terms in order, on the one hand, to eliminate real risks of market disruption (as defined in Annex A) in importing countries and disruption to the textile trade of exporting countries, and on the other hand to ensure the expansion and orderly development of trade in textiles and the equitable treatment of participating countries.

3. Bilateral agreements maintained under this Article shall, on overall terms, including base levels and growth rates, be more liberal than measures provided for in Article 3 of this Arrangement. Such bilateral agreements shall be designed and administered to facilitate the export in full of the levels provided for under such agreements and shall include provisions assuring substantial flexibility for the conduct of trade thereunder, consistent with the need for orderly expansion of such trade and conditions in the domestic market of the importing country concerned. Such provisions should encompass areas of base levels, growth, recognition of the increasing interchangeability of natural, artificial and synthetic fibres, carryforward, carryover, transfers from one

product grouping to another and such other arrangements as may be mutually satisfactory to the parties of such bilateral agreements.

4. The participating countries shall communicate to the Textiles Surveillance Body full details of agreements entered into in terms of this Article within 30 days of their effective date. The Textiles Surveillance Body shall be informed promptly when any such agreements are modified or discontinued. The Textiles Surveillance Body may make such recommendations as it deems appropriate to the parties concerned.

Article 5

Restrictions on imports of textile products under the provisions of Articles 3 and 4 shall be administered in a flexible and equitable manner and over-categorization shall be avoided. Participating countries shall, in consultation, provide for arrangements for the administration of the quotas and restraint levels, including the proper arrangement for allocation of quotas among the exporters, in such a way as to facilitate full utilization of such quotas. The participating importing country should take full account of such factors as established tariff classification and quantitative units based on normal commercial practices in export and import transactions, both as regards fibre composition and in terms of competing for the same segment of its domestic market.

Article 6

1. Recognizing the obligations of the participating countries to pay special attention to the needs of the developing countries, it shall be considered appropriate and consistent with equity obligations for those importing countries which apply restrictions under this Arrangement affecting the trade of developing countries to provide more favourable terms with regard to such restrictions, including elements such as base level and growth rates, than for other countries. In the case of developing countries whose exports are already subject to restrictions and if the restrictions are maintained under this Arrangement, provisions should be made for higher quotas and liberal growth rates. It shall, however, be borne in mind that there should be no undue prejudice to the interests of established suppliers or serious distortion in existing patterns of trade.

2. In recognition of the need for special treatment for exports of textile products from developing countries, the criterion of past performance shall not be applied in the establishment of quotas for their exports of products from those textile sectors in respect of which they are new entrants in the markets concerned and a higher growth rate shall be accorded to such exports, having in mind that this special treatment should not cause undue prejudice to the interests of established suppliers or create serious distortions in existing patterns of trade.

3. Restraints on exports from participating countries whose total volume of textile exports is small in comparison with the total volume of exports of other countries should normally be avoided if the exports from such countries represent a small percentage of the total imports of textiles covered by this Arrangement of the importing country concerned.

358

4. Where restrictions are applied to trade in cotton textiles in terms of this Arrangement, special consideration will be given to the importance of this trade to the developing countries concerned in determining the size of quotas and the growth element.

5. Participating countries shall not, as far as possible, maintain restraints on trade in textile products originating in other participating countries which are imported under a system of temporary importation for re-export after processing, subject to a satisfactory system of control and certification.

6. Consideration shall be given to special and differential treatment to re-imports into a participating country of textile products which that country has exported to another participating country for processing and subsequent re-importation, in the light of the special nature of such trade without prejudice to the provisions of Article 3.

Article 7

The participating countries shall take steps to ensure, by the exchange of information, including statistics on imports and exports when requested, and by other practical means, the effective operation of this Arrangement.

Article 8

1. The participating countries agree to avoid circumvention of this Arrangement by trans-shipment, re-routing, or action by non-participants. In particular they agree on the measures provided for in this Article.

2. The participating countries agree to collaborate with a view to taking appropriate administrative action to avoid such circumvention. Should any participating country believe that the Arrangement is being circumvented and that no appropriate administrative measures are being applied to avoid such circumvention, that country should consult with the exporting country of origin and with other countries involved in the circumvention with a view to seeking promptly a mutually satisfactory solution. If such a solution is not reached the matter shall be referred to the Textiles Surveillance Body.

3. The participating countries agree that if resort is had to the measures envisaged in Articles 3 and 4, the participating importing country or countries concerned shall take steps to ensure that the participating country's exports against which such measures are taken shall not be restrained more severely than the exports of similar goods of any country not party to this Arrangement which are causing, or actually threatening, market disruption. The participating importing country or countries concerned will give sympathetic consideration to any representations from participating exporting countries to the effect that this principle is not being adhered to or that the operation of this Arrangement is frustrated by trade with countries not party to this Arrangement. If such trade is frustrating the operation of this Arrangement, the participating countries shall consider taking such actions as may be consistent with their law to prevent such frustration.

4. The participating countries concerned shall communicate to the Textiles Surveillance Body full details of any measures or arrangements taken under

this Article or any disagreement and, when so requested, the Textiles Surveillance Body shall make reports or recommendations as appropriate.

Article 9

1. In view of the safeguards provided for in this Arrangement the participating countries shall, as far as possible, refrain from taking additional trade measures which may have the effect of nullifying the objectives of this Arrangement.

2. If a participating country finds that its interests are being seriously affected by any such measure taken by another participating country, that country may request the country applying such measure to consult with a view to remedying the situation.

3. If the consultation fails to achieve a mutually satisfactory solution within a period of 60 days the requesting participating country may refer the matter to the Textiles Surveillance Body which shall promptly discuss such matter, the participating country concerned being free to refer the matter to that body before the expiry of the period of 60 days if it considers that there are justifiable grounds for so doing. The Textiles Surveillance Body shall make such recommendations to the participating countries as it considers appropriate.

Article 10

1. There is established within the framework of the GATT a Textiles Committee consisting of representatives of the parties to this Arrangement. The Committee shall carry out the responsibilities ascribed to it under this Arrangement.

2. The Committee shall meet from time to time, and at least once a year, to discharge its functions and to deal with those matters specifically referred to it by the Textiles Surveillance Body. It shall prepare such studies as the participating countries may decide. It shall undertake an analysis of the current state of world production and trade in textile products, including any measures to facilitate adjustment and it shall present its views regarding means of furthering the expansion and liberalization of trade in textile products. It will collect that statistical and other information necessary for the discharge of its functions and will be empowered to request the participating countries to furnish such information.

3. Any case of divergence of view between the participating countries as to the interpretation or application of this Arrangement may be referred to the Committee for its opinion.

4. The Committee shall, once a year, review the operation of this Arrangement and report thereon to the GATT Council. To assist in this review, the Committee shall have before it a report from the Textiles Surveillance Body, a copy of which will also be transmitted to the Council. The review during the third year shall be a major review of this Arrangement in the light of its operation in the preceding years.

5. The Committee shall meet not later than one year before the expiry of this Arrangement in order to consider whether the Arrangement should be extended, modified or discontinued.

Article 11

1.   The Textiles Committee shall establish a Textiles Surveillance Body to supervise the implementation of this Arrangement. It shall consist of a chairman and eight members to be appointed by the parties to this Arrangement on a basis to be determined by the Textiles Committee so as to ensure its efficient operation. In order to keep its membership balanced and broadly representative of the parties to the Arrangement provision shall be made for rotation of the members as appropriate.

2.   The Textiles Surveillance Body shall be considered as a standing body and shall meet as necessary to carry out the functions required of it under this Arrangement. It shall rely on information to be supplied by the participating countries, supplemented by any necessary details and clarification it may decide to seek from them or from other sources. Further, it may rely for technical assistance on the services of the GATT secretariat and may also hear technical experts proposed by one or more of its members.

3.   The Textiles Surveillance Body shall take the action specifically required of it in articles of this Arrangement.

4.   In the absence of any mutually agreed solution in bilateral negotiations or consultations between participating countries provided for in this Arrangement, the Textiles Surveillance Body at the request of either party, and following a thorough and prompt consideration of the matter, shall make recommendations to the parties concerned.

5.   The Textiles Surveillance Body shall, at the request of any participating country, review promptly any particular measures or arrangements which that country considers to be detrimental to its interests where consultations between it and the participating countries directly concerned have failed to produce a satisfactory solution. It shall make recommendations as appropriate to the participating country or countries concerned.

6.   Before formulating its recommendations on any particular matter referred to it, the Textiles Surveillance Body shall invite participation of such participating countries as may be directly affected by the matter in question.

7.   When the Textiles Surveillance Body is called upon to make recommendations or findings it shall do so, except when otherwise provided in this Arrangement, within a period of 30 days whenever practicable. All such recommendations or findings shall be communicated to the Textiles Committee for the information of its members.

8.   Participating countries shall endeavour to accept in full the recommendations of the Textiles Surveillance Body. Whenever they consider themselves unable to follow any such recommendations, they shall forthwith inform the Textiles Surveillance Body of the reasons therefor and of the extent, if any, to which they are able to follow the recommendations.

9.   If, following recommendations by the Textiles Surveillance Body, problems continue to exist between the parties, these may be brought before the Textiles Committee or before the GATT Council through the normal GATT procedures.

10.   Any recommendations and observations of the Textiles Surveillance Body would be taken into account should the matters related to such recommendations and observations subsequently be brought before the contracting

parties to the GATT, particularly under the procedures of Article XXIII of the GATT.

11. The Textiles Surveillance Body shall, within 15 months of the coming into force of this Arrangement, and at least annually thereafter, review all restrictions on textile products maintained by participating countries at the commencement of this Arrangement and submit its findings to the Textiles Committee.

12. The Textiles Surveillance Body shall annually review all restrictions introduced or bilateral agreements entered into by participating countries concerning trade in textile products since the coming into force of this Arrangement, and required to be reported to it under the provisions of this Arrangement, and report annually its findings to the Textiles Committee.

Article 12

1. For the purposes of this Arrangement, the expression "textiles" is limited to tops, yarns, piece-goods, made-up articles, garments and other textile manufactured products (being products which derive their chief characteristics from their textile components) of cotton, wool, man-made fibres, or blends thereof, in which any or all of those fibres in combination represent either the chief value of the fibres or 50% or more by weight (or 17% or more by weight of wool) of the product.

2. Artificial and synthetic staple fibre, tow, waste, simple mono- and multi-filaments are not covered by paragraph 1 above. However, should conditions of market disruption (as defined in Annex A) be found to exist for such products, the provisions of Article 3 of this Arrangement (and other provisions of this Arrangement directly relevant thereto) and paragraph 1 of Article 2 shall apply.

3. This Arrangement shall not apply to developing country exports of handloom fabrics of the cottage industry, or hand-made cottage-industry products made of such handloom fabrics, or to traditional folklore handicraft textiles products, provided that such products are properly certified under arrangements established between the importing and exporting participating countries concerned.

4. Problems of interpretation of the provisions of this Article should be resolved by bilateral consultation between the parties concerned and any difficulties may be referred to the Textiles Surveillance Body.

Article 13

1. This Arrangement shall be deposited with the Director-General to the contracting parties to the GATT. It shall be open for acceptance, by signature or otherwise, by governments contracting parties to the GATT or having provisionally acceded to the GATT and by the European Economic Community.

2. Any government which is not a contracting party to the GATT, or has not acceded provisionally to the GATT, may accede to this Arrangement on terms to be agreed between that government and the participating countries. These terms would include a provision that any government which is not a

contracting party to the GATT must undertake, on acceding to this Arrangement, not to introduce new import restrictions or intensify existing import restrictions, on textile products, in so far as such action would, if that government had been a contracting party to the GATT, be inconsistent with its obligations thereunder.

Article 14

1. This Arrangement shall enter into force on 1 January 1974.
2. Notwithstanding the provisions of paragraph 1 of this Article, for the application of the provisions of Article 2 (2) (3) and (4) the date of entry into force shall be 1 April 1974.
3. Upon request of one or more parties which have accepted or acceded to this Arrangement a meeting shall be held within one week prior to 1 April 1974. Parties which at the time of the meeting have accepted or acceded to the Arrangement may agree on any modification of the date envisaged in paragraph 2 of this Article which may appear necessary and is consistent with the provisions of Article 16.

Article 15

Any participating country may withdraw from this Arrangement upon the expiration of 60 days from the day on which written notice of such withdrawal is received by the Director-General to the contracting parties to the GATT.

Article 16

This Arrangement shall remain in force for four years.

Article 17

The Annexes to this Arrangement constitute an integral part of this Arrangement.

Done at Geneva this twentieth day of December one thousand nine hundred and seventy-three in a single copy in the English, French and Spanish languages, each text being authentic.

ANNEX A

I. The determination of a situation of "market disruption", as referred to in this Arrangement, shall be based on the existence of serious damage to domestic producers or actual threat thereof. Such damage must demonstrably be caused by the factors set out in paragraph II below and not by factors such as technological changes or changes in consumer preference which are instrumental in switches to like and/or directly competitive products made by the same industry, or similar factors. The existence of damage shall be determined on the basis of an examination of the appropriate factors having a bearing on the evolution of the state of the industry in question such as: turnover, market share, profits, export performance, employment, volume of disruptive and other imports, production, utilization of capacity, productivity and investments. No one or several of these factors can necessarily give decisive guidance.

II.   The factors causing market disruption referred to in paragraph I above and which generally appear in combination are as follows:

i. a sharp and substantial increase or imminent increase in imports of particular products from particular sources. Such an imminent increase shall be a measurable one and shall not be determined to exist on the basis of allegation, conjecture or mere possibility arising, for example, from the existence of production capacity in the exporting countries;

ii. those products are offered at prices which are substantially below those prevailing for similar goods of comparable quality in the market of the importing country. Such prices shall be compared both with the price for the domestic product at comparable stage of commercial transaction, and with the prices which normally prevail for such products sold in the ordinary course of trade and under open market conditions by other exporting countries in the importing country.

III.   In considering questions of "market disruption" account shall be taken of the interests of the exporting country, especially in regard to its stage of development, the importance of the textile sector to the economy, the employment situation, overall balance of trade in textiles, trade balance with the importing country concerned and overall balance of payments.

ANNEX B

1.   a. The level below which imports or exports of textile products may not be restrained under the provisions of Article 3 shall be the level of actual imports or exports of such products during the 12-month period terminating two months or, where data are not available, three months preceding the month in which the request for consultation is made, or, where applicable, the data of institution of such domestic procedure relating to market disruption in textiles as may be required by national legislation, or two months or, where data are not available, three months prior to the month in which the request for consultation is made as a result of such domestic procedure, whichever period is the later.

b. Where a restraint on the yearly level of exports or imports exists between participating countries concerned, whether provided for under Article 2, 3 or 4, covering the 12-month period referred to in paragraph (a), the level below which imports of textile products causing market disruption may not be restrained under the provisions of Article 3 shall be the level provided for in the restraint in lieu of the level of actual imports or exports during the 12-month period referred to in paragraph (a).

Where the 12-month period referred to in paragraph (a) overlaps in part with the period covered by the restraint, the level shall be:

i. the level provided for in the restraint, or the level of actual imports or exports, whichever is higher, except in case of overshipment, for the months where the period covered by the restraint and the 12-month period referred to in paragraph (a) overlap; and

    ii. the level of actual imports or exports for the months where no overlap occurs.

c. If the period referred to in paragraph (a) is specially adverse for a particular exporting country due to abnormal circumstances, the past performance of imports from that country over a period of years should be taken into account.

d. Where imports or exports of textile products subject to restraint were nil or negligible during the 12-month period referred to in paragraph (a), a resonable import level to take account of future possibilities of the exporting country shall be established through consultation between the participating countries concerned.

2. Should the restraint measures remain in force for another 12-month period, the level for that period shall not be lower than the level specified for the preceding 12-month period, increased by not less than six per cent for products under restraint. In exceptional cases where there are clear grounds for holding that the situation of market disruption will recur if the growth rate is implemented, a lower positive growth rate may be decided upon after consultation with the exporting country or countries concerned. In exceptional cases where participating importing countries have small markets, an exceptionally high level of imports and a correspondingly low level of domestic production and, where the implementation of the above growth rate would cause damage to those countries' minimum viable production, a lower positive growth rate may be decided upon after consultation with the exporting country or countries concerned.

3. Should the restraint measures remain in force for further periods, the level for each subsequent period shall not be lower than the level specified for the preceding 12-month period, increased by six per cent, unless there is further new evidence which demonstrates, in accordance with Annex A, that implementation of the above growth rate would exacerbate the situation of market disruption. In these circumstances, after consultation with the exporting country concerned, and reference to the Textiles Surveillance Body in accordance with the procedures of Article 3, a lower positive growth rate may be applied.

4. In the event any restriction or limitation is established under Article 3 or 4 on a production or products as to which a restriction or limitation had been suppressed in accordance with the provisions of Article 2, such subsequent restriction or limitation shall not be re-established without full consideration of the limits of trade provided for under such suppressed restriction or limitation.

5. Where restraint is exercised for more than one product the participating countries agree that, provided that the total exports subject to restraint do not exceed the aggregate level for all products so restrained (on the basis of a common unit to be determined by the participating countries concerned), the agreed level for any one product may be exceeded by seven per cent save in exceptionally and sparingly used circumstances where a lower percentage may be justified, in which case that lower percentage shall be not less than five per cent. Where restraints are established for more years than one, the extent to which the total of the restraint level for one product or product

group may, after consultation between the parties concerned, be exceeded in either year of any two subsequent years by carryforward and/or carryover is 10% of which carryforward shall not represent more than five per cent.

6.   In the application of the restraint levels and growth rates specified in paragraphs 1 to 3 above, full account shall be taken of the provisions of Article 6.

ANNEX III

Burden-sharing

There are wide discrepancies in imports from specific countries by different Member States, by comparison with the importance of their textile industry, and therefore of their ability to bear the burden of import growth. For instance, for many products, UK and Germany import some 60–70% of the Community total from Hong Kong and Korea.

As a result, it was agreed by the Council that the distribution of Community quotas among Member States should be done in such a way as to equalize in the long term the load borne by the different Member States. Thus where imports into a Member State from a particular source were very high, the rate of growth would be very low, compensated by a very much higher growth rate for those Member States who were not bearing their share of the import burden. At the limit, the lowest rate of growth is 0.5% and the highest rate 50%, and over a period, this should ensure the gradual convergence of actual quotas with the levels of imports which a country can theoretically bear.

A worked example below shows, for three countries, the effects of this system over a four-year period starting from a base in 1975.

		1975 Base	*1976*	*1977*	*1978*	*1979*
TOTAL	Quota	1,000	1,060	1,124	1,191	1,262
	Growth Rate (%)		6.0	6.0	6.0	6.0
A	Quota if 6% growth	350	371	393	417	442
	Theoretical Quota	450	477	506	536	568
	Actual Quota	(350)	384	417	452	489
	Actual Growth		9.7	8.6	8.4	8.2
B	Quota if 6% Growth	300	318	337	357	379
	Theoretical Quota	350	371	393	417	442
	Actual Quota	(300)	322	347	373	400
	Actual Growth Rate (%)		7.3	7.8	7.5	7.2
C	Quota if 6% Growth	350	371	393	417	442
	Theoretical Quota	200	212	225	238	252
	Actual Quota	(350)	354	360	366	373
	Actual Growth Rate (%)		1.1	1.7	1.7	1.9

ANNEX IV

II
(*Acts whose publication is not obligatory*)
COUNCIL

COUNCIL DECISION
of 14 April 1975
establishing a programme of technological research in the textile sector
(75/266/EEC)

THE COUNCIL OF THE EUROPEAN COMMUNITIES,

Having regard to the Treaty establishing the European Economic Community, in particular Article 235 thereof;

Having regard to the proposal from the Commission;

Having regard to the Opinion of the European Parliament;[22]

Having regard to the Opinion of the Economic and Social Committee,[23]

Considering the Council resolution of 14 January 1974[24] on the co-ordination of national policies and the definition of projects of interest to the Community in the field of science and technology;

Whereas the final communiqué of the conference of Heads of State or of Government meeting in Paris on 19 and 20 October 1972 envisages the joint implementation of projects of interest to the Community in the context of the development of a common policy in the field of science and technology;

Whereas, pursuant to Article 2 of the Treaty, the Community shall have as its task *inter alia* to promote throughout the Community a harmonious development of economic activities and a continuous and balanced expansion;

Whereas the research to which this Decision relates aims at a variety of objectives, such as the reduction of manufacturing costs, the testing of new fibres, the solution of certain environmental problems, as well as consumer safety and protection, and represents a fundamental step in the development of the textile industry which is an important economic sector of the Community;

Whereas preliminary research carried out by the textile industry has demonstrated the value of a programme of technological research and whereas, therefore, the textile industry intends to join in the programme with a financial contribution twice that of the Community;

Whereas, therefore, this programme appears necessary in order to achieve the above-mentioned Community objectives in the framework of the common market;

Whereas the Treaty does not provide all the powers necessary to achieve these objectives,

HAS DECIDED AS FOLLOWS:

Article 1

A research programme for the European Economic Community in the textile sector as set out in the Annex hereto is hereby established for a period of three years commencing on 1 December 1974.

Article 2

An amount of 250,000 units of account shall be allocated for the realization of this programme, the unit of account being as defined in the Financial Regulation on the establishment and implementation of the budget of the European Communities and on the responsibility of authorizing officers and accounting officers.

Article 3

The Commission shall implement the programme by means of contracts.

Article 4

Inventions, whether patentable or not, and know-how resulting from the implementation of the programme shall be subject to Council Regulation (EEC) No. 2380/74[25] of 17 September 1974 establishing the conditions of use of know-how applicable to research programmes undertaken for the European Economic Community.

Done at Luxembourg, 14 April 1975.

For the Council
The President
G. FITGERALD

ANNEX

Programme of technical research in the textile sector

A maximum of 250,000 units shall be provided for implementing the programme which is concerned with the three following themes:

1. Thermal treatment of chemical fibres

   Main objectives:

   Optimization of production methods to improve the yield and the quality of products, especially in small- and medium-sized textile undertakings, which generally lack the required research facilities.

   Programme:

   Structural modification of chemical fibres, e.g. polyamides, polyester, acrylic and modacrylic, olefin, di- and tri-acetate, under different conditions of thermal treatment (under tension or not, under tension with twist).

   Changes, as a result of thermal treatment, in dyeing, mechanical, physical and shape properties.

2. Textile processing in organic solvents

   Main objectives:

   Reduction of water pollution and energy consumption. Use of organic solvents instead of water in production methods.

   Programme:

   Fibre/solvent interaction:

   types of fibre: polyester, polyamide, wool;

types of solvents: perchlorethylene, dichloromethan, hydrocarbon fraction, isopropyl alcohol.

Interactions: solubility of fibre in the solvent;

solubility of solvent in the fibre;

variation in fibre structure.

Rheology in the solvent medium: two-phase effects (fibre/solvent), three-phase (fibre/solvent/water—fibre/solvent/dyestuff), four-phase (fibre/solvent/water/dyestuff).

Mechanical, physical, shape and surface properties.

3. Fireproofing of textile fibres by radiation grafting

Main objectives:

Consumer protection by reducing flammability in clothing and household textiles.

Programme:

Types of fibre: cellulosic, wool, polyamide, polyacrylic.

Type of flame retardant: various monomers of vinyl, or acrylic groups, epoxides and others, halogenated, phosphorized or nitrogen-containing compounds.

Irradiation carried out on a pilot scale by electron accelerators.

Physico-chemical control of fire-retardant textiles, and tests of flammability and combustibility in accordance with methods and standards laid down by Member States and certain third countries.

ANNEX V

ENCADREMENT, SUR LE PLAN COMMUNAUTAIRE, DES AIDES A L'INDUSTRIE TEXTILE

NÉCESSITÉ ET PORTÉE DE LA PRÉSENTE INITIATIVE

1. La Commission constate que la situation et les perspectives de l'industrie textile préoccupent de plus en plus les Etats membres, La tendance se manifeste d'accorder à cette industrie une place particulière dans la politique industrielle, notamment sur le plan des aides.

Les aides textiles, inconnues il y a encore quelques années, se sont multipliées depuis lors. D'importants programmes d'aides sont actuellement envisagés dans certains Etats membres. Un renforcement de cette tend n'est pas à exclure dans les prochaines années.

Faute de coordination, les initiatives adoptées en ordre dispersé dans la Communauté sont de nature à réduire l'efficacité des aides tout en étant susceptibles d'affecter les échanges et la concurrence dans une mesure contraire à l'intérêt commun. La Commission souhaite, par ailleurs, prévenir entemps utile toute escalade en matière d'aides textiles.

2. La Commission estime dès lors nécessaire de préciser un certain nombre de conditions que les aides textiles doivent respecter. L'établissement de ce conditions n'a aucunement pour objet d'inviter les Etats membres à intervenir en faveur de l'industrie textile de leur pays, mais doit simplement, pour le cas où les Etats membres tiennent l'octroi d'une aide pour indispensable:

a. orienter les Etats membres dans la conception de pareilles mesures,

b. donner à la Commission des indications pour son appréciation de semblables projets d'aides. La communication de ces critères ne porte évidemment pas préjudice aux dispositions du Traité CEE, notamment à celles de l'article 93 § 3. Elle ne substitue en aucun cas aux prises de position que la Commission est amenée à prendre à l'égard des aides en vertu des pouvoirs qui lui sont dévolus par le Traité CEE.

Les critères dont il s'agit ont été élaborés par la Commission qui en por la seule responsabilité; ils ont néanmoins été établis avec le concours experts nationaux.

3. La Commission a décidé de recourir à une telle communication en fonction caractéristiques particulières de l'industrie textile, d'où le caractère "ad hoc" de la solution retenue qui ne préjuge en rien l'attitude de la Commission à l'égard des aides à d'autres secteurs. Ces caractéristiques particulières sont:

a. secteur en difficulté d'adaptation:
   les difficultés structurelles qui se posent à cette industrie ont une double origine; le développement de certaines productions dans des pays en voie de développement, lié à la tendance fondamentale à l'ouverture progressive des marchés textiles sur le plan mondial; les évolutions technologiques qui pourraient transformer dans l'avenir, les conditions de production et de commercialisation de l'industrie textile;

b. en faveur duquel il y a une tendance dans la Communauté à intervenir par voie d'aides:

la place occupée par l'industrie textile, notamment sur le plan de l'emploi et des exportations est considérée comme importante par la plupart des Etats membres; les aides existantes ou projetées ont pour objet de faciliter l'adaptation de cette industrie aux nouvelles exigences du marché et de la technique.

Cette tendance pourrait encore se renforcer à la suite des répercussions que la politique commerciale de la Communauté pourrait avoir sur les textiles;

c. et dans lequel les aides ont une répercussion parfois extrêmement sensible sur la concurrence et les échanges dans la Communauté:

la concurrence intracommunautaire pour les produits textiles est très vive; les échanges dans la Communauté y sont élevés et en constante progression; quoique les problèmes d'adaptation soient largement communs dans la Communauté, la situation peut être sensiblement différente d'un pays à l'autre selon le degré d'adaptation déja atteint dans chacun d'eux; malgré l'étroite interdépendance des différentes branches textiles, les problèmes d'adaptation ne se manifestent pas partout avec la même acuité.

4. Il paraît à la Commission hautement souhaitable, lorsqu' un Etat membre estime devoir aider le textile de façon plus ou moins particulière, qu'il le fasse par un régime spécifique à ce secteur.

Si toutefois, il estime également nécessaire, pour la détermination de l'aide, de prendre en considération des problèmes extra-sectoriels, notamment régionaux, les conditions d'attribution qu'il fixe doivent permettre, d'une part, d'orienter chaque décision d'aide à l'industrie textile, ou à une de ces entreprises (motivation sectorielle et extra-sectorielle) et, d'autre part, permettre l'appréciation communautaire de chacune de ces aides.

Les orientations dégagées dans cette communication visent uniquement l'aspect sectoriel des aides citées dans l'alinéa précédent, mais il est clair que dans la mesure ou celles-ci répondent aussi à des motivations extra-sectorielles, notamment régionales, elles appellent une appréciation du point de vue régional. L'aspect régional doit être conçu et apprécié à la fois en fonction des problèmes de développement régional et en fonction de leurs effets sur le secteur du point de vue de la concurrence et des échanges intra-communautaires.

CONDITIONS D'ORDRE SECTORIEL RELATIVES AUX AIDES TEXTILES

Dans sa note concernant la "Politique sectorelle pour le textile", qui est transmise en même temps que la présente communication, la Commission admet que, dans certains cas, des interventions des Etats membres sous forme d'aides peuvent se justifier, en particulier pour résoudre des problèmes sociaux aigus. Elle rappelle cependant que des aides dans ce secteur, qui est caractérisé par une concurrence très vive sur le plan communautaire, risquent de conduire à des distorsions de concurrence intolérables pour les concurrents non bénéficiaires de ces mesures. Ceci est valable notamment pour les aides à la modernisation et la rationalisation. Ces aides ne peuvent donc pas être admises sauf si elles remplissent certaines conditions, et notamment:

– ne conduisent pas à des augmentations de capacité,
– tiennent compte non seulement de la situation nationale de cette industrie, mais également de celle de la Communauté. De l'avis de la Commission, des aides textiles éventuelles devraient être
conçues et appliquées dans le respect des catégories et des conditions suivantes. Elles seront, de toute façon, appréciées le moment venu par la Commission en fonction ce celles-ci.

1. Aides à des actions collectives textiles

Cette première catégorie regroupe les aides en faveur d'actions collectives assurées par des organisations publiques, scientifiques ou professionnelles et qui visent soit:
– à développer la recherche, tant fondamentale qu'appliquée, consacrée aux fibres nouvelles, à l'amélioration due traitement des fibres existantes et aux procédés de transformation;
– à améliorer les prévisions à court terme destinées à pallier les fluctuations cycliques d'activité particulièrement prononcée sur le marché textile.
L'octroi de ces aides devrait être lié à une participation importante du secteur industriel bénéficiaire aux frais des opérations aidées. Elles ne peuvent affecter la concurrence et les échanges plus qu'il n'est indispensable de la faire.
La Commission souligne tout l'intérêt d'une coopération, sur le plan communautaire, des actions collectives dont il s'agit.

2. Aides à l'aménagement des structures textiles

Par aides à l'aménagement des structures, ont entend les aides à des entreprises textiles qui ont pour but soit:
– de faciliter l'élimination des surcapacités dans les branches ou sous-branches où elles se manifestent;
– de favoriser la conversion des activités marginales vers d'autres activités que celle du textile;
– d'améliorer la structure industrielle et commerciale du secteur textile dans le sens de la concentration horizontale ou de l'intégration verticale pour autant que de telles aides ne conduisent pas à des accroissements de capacités de production.
Les modalités de ces aides devraient satisfaire aux conditions suivantes:
– ne courir qu'une courte période d'application;
– impliquer une participation importante des bénéficiaires aux frais et risques des opérations aidées;
– présenter une liaison directe entre l'octroi de l'aide et les opérations aidées;
– permettre une appréciation aisée de leur impact sur les opérations aidées une comparaison de celui-ci sur le plan communautaire;
– et, de toute façons, ne pas affecter la concurrence et les échanges plus qu'il n'est indispensable de le faire.

3. Aides aux investissements textiles

Cette catégorie comprend les aides à la modernisation du secteur textile ainsi qu'à la reconversion à l'intérieur du secteur.

Ces aides ayant des répercussions particulièrement sensibles sur la position concurrentielle, leur octroi doit être conçu de façon très restrictive.

Outre les conditions énoncées dans le premier alinéa du chapitre II (à savoir la non-extension des capacités de production et la prise en considération de la situation communautaire de la branche bénéficiaire), elles devraient être motivées par des problèmes sociaux particulièrement aigus.

Elles devraient en outre satisfaire aux conditions générales déjà exposées pour les aides à l'aménagement des structures textiles (II, 2), ainsi qu'aux exigences suivantes:

– avoir un champ d'application strictement limité aux seules activités textiles affectées à la fois par des problèmes sociaux particulièrement aigus et par de graves problèmes d'adaptation;

– avoir pour objectif de donner à bref délai aux bénéficiaires un niveau de compétitivité suffisant pour affronter avec succès le marché international des textiles, compte tenu de la tendance fondamentale à l'ouverture progressive des marchés sur le plan mondial;

– dépasser les seuls critères d'appréciation sectorielle par la prise en considération également des exigences d'un développement dynamique des structures dans la Communauté.

Les conditions précitées seront précisées, le moment venu et en fonction des besoins, avec le concours d'experts gouvernementaux dans le domaine de la politique économique générale et du textile. Elles pourront, le cas échéant, faire l'objet de communications complémentaires.

NOTES

1. The Study Group met under the chairmanship of Professor D. C. Hague of the Manchester Business School, and drew its members from representatives of the textile industry, management and trade unions as well as from the Universities. The membership of the group is set out in Appendix B.

2. Because of its importance as an outlet for textile fibres, whether processed within the Community or outside, we include the clothing industry in our analysis.

3. *The Textile Policy*, Mimeo, 1976, p. 1.

4. *Ibid.*, Annexe 1.

5. *Ibid.*

6. *Ibid.*

7. *Ibid.*, Annex IV.

8. *Ibid.*, p. 10.

9. *Ibid.*, pp. 11–16.

10. Joint Textile Committee, *Textile Trends 1966–75*, (London: National Economic Development Office) 1976, Table 4.1.

11. *Ibid.*, Table 1.2.

12. *Ibid.*, Table 1.5. The ratios for all shares of the textile industry alone are net output 5.7%, employment 7.5% and capital expenditure 7.4%.

13. *Ibid.*, The fall in employment has been most marked in the textile sector, where numbers declined from 749,300 in 1963 to 576,100 in 1974, a fall of 173,200 or 23%.

14. Japanese f.o.b. export prices are selected as giving a more accurate indication of prevailing prices for non-cellulosic fibres than manufacturers' list prices (see Australian Bureau of Agricultural Economics, *The Fibre Review, 1971–72*). Cotton prices at Liverpool are quoted in US$; column 2 shows the corresponding prices in UK New Pence, converted at the appropriate mid-point exchange rate for each year. Column 3 indicates prices from 1967 onwards assuming the exchange rate to have remained constant from 1967: when compared with the previous column, it thus gives a rough impression of the effect of the November 1967 sterling devaluation on cotton imports.

15. *Textile Trends, op. cit.*, Table 4.5, p. 29.

16. *Textile Trends, op. cit.*, Table 7.4.

17. Textile Council, *Cotton and Allied Textiles*, (Manchester) 1969 (2 volumes).

18. *Textile Trends, op. cit.*, p. 59.

19. It was also noted that technical developments may soon allow small-scale production of man-made fibres, which could be located close to indigenous supplies of feedstock in developing countries.

20. For example, R. W. Bacon & W. Eltis, *Britain's Economic Problem: Too Few Producers*, (London: Macmillan) 1976.

21. The expressions "participating country", "participating exporting country" and "participating importing country", wherever they appear in this Arrangement, shall be deemed to include the European Economic Community.

22. OJ No. C 32, 11. 2. 1975, p. 8.

23. OJ No. C 16, 23. 1. 1975, p. 10.

24. OJ No. C 7, 29. 1. 1974, p. 2.

25. OJ No. L 255, 20. 9. 1974, p. 1.

III. CONCLUSIONS

The Textile Industry and EEC Industrial Policy

by *Jean Rey*

The meeting, under the chairmanship of Monsieur Jean Rey, approved the conclusions of the report of the Study Group (pp. 20–24) with the following amendments:

a. Section 1: it is recognized that the conclusions of the Study Group are based mainly upon the experience of the UK industry. Community policy has operated mainly in the context of international trade, but significant contributions have also been made in other areas, in particular the provision of funds for restructuring and the promotion of research.

b. Section 8: While the need for some short-term protection against imports is necessary, it is also important to ensure that consumers have considerable freedom of choice in making their purchases and to recognize that low-cost imports initially raise living standards by increasing purchasing power. At the same time, little attention has been paid to the net increases in welfare of different groups of the population as a result of a policy of aiding consumers with lower prices, backed up by a policy of employment protection. Some research in this area is urgently needed.

c. Section 9: It is recognized that the Commission is aware of the implications for the textile industry of an enlargement of the Community. A coordinated and consistent policy towards the accession of other textile-producing nations is vital.

d. Section 12: The underlying philosophy of the Community is better expressed as one of "free market *competition*".

e. Section 13: The progressive development of a Community-wide industrial policy is a major requirement.

f. Section 16: This section to be recast as follows: "it is of the greatest importance that the various policies proposed by the Commission which impinge upon the textile industry should be developed in a consistent and coordinated manner, and it is to be hoped that the close cooperation which exists between the various divisions of the Commission will continue to be fostered".

g. Section 17—Additional: The work of the Commission in regard to the textile industry is currently hampered by a lack of adequate data. It is to be hoped that this will receive urgent attention.

ENVIRONMENT POLICY

I. ENVIRONMENT POLICY REPORT

European Policy of Protection of Rivers and Water against Pollution

by *C. Pleinevaux*

PROPOSALS AND COMMUNICATION OF THE COMMISSION

Since the Commission first took up the protection of the environment, it has always been concerned with the problem of water pollution.

As long ago as July 1971, in its first communication on the environmental policy of the Community, the Commission indicated that "problems such as the pollution, purification and management of water and rivers like the Rhine and its tributaries which flow through several Member States or problem of the fight against the pollution of seas, such as the Mediterranean or the North Sea, which are a common asset of the Member States as a whole, need immediate and urgent attention. Such an undertaking can only be validly carried out by drawing up and putting into operation joint decisions on the objectives to be aimed for, the solutions to be found and the means to be used".[1]

In March 1972, after consulting political, economic and social circles, the Commission specified its intentions in a second communication to the Council on an environmental programme for the European Community.[2]

The Commission's proposals, as this communication pointed out, were designed "to create a common framework of assessments, actions and, if need be, of regulations to which the Community, the Member States and the local group could refer when making their decisions".[3]

This was in particular concerned with:
- creating an objective basis for the evaluation of the risks caused by pollution to human health and to the environment;
- setting common health standards and defining the common environmental quality objectives;
- drawing the inferences from the application of these standards and objectives to the sources of pollution (products and economic activities) and taking special measures in certain areas of common interest and with regard to certain pollutants;
- defining in common the principles, methods and ways of evaluation and attribution of costs of the fight against pollution;
- ensuring that the regulations and limits set were effectively applied and respected.

These objectives were taken up and more clearly defined during further debate of the Council, which led to the formulation of an action programme for the European Community on the environment which was adopted by the Council on 22 November 1973 within the framework of a "declaration by the

Council of the European Community and the representatives of the Governments of the Member States meeting in the Council on the programme of action for the European Community on the environment". The protection and improvement of fresh and salt water figured in this programme as one of the priorities. The Community's action was to take three forms:

The first was to set scientific criteria, that is to try to express a relation between the concentration of a pollutant in a specific milieu and the effect of this concentration on a particular target (man, fauna, flora, etc.).

The second was to define the *objectives of quality*, that is the whole range of conditions which should be met at a given time by a milieu or by a part of a milieu. In the present case, namely that of water, the objectives of quality will define the quality of water according as to how it is used, this quality being one which the public authorities will try to attain at a given moment. Such objectives will be concerned with, for instance, fresh water intended for the abstraction of drinking water, water for irrigation, for industrial activities, for fish raising, for sea-bathing or for shellfish raising, etc.

These Community quality objectives which become emmission norms or norms of quality as soon as they are made legally binding by the competent public authorities (national or regional), constitute the terms of reference drawn up by common agreement, which the national or regional authorities must use when they decide to attain a certain quality in the water of a river or of a reach of river, for instance. The implementation of the quality objectives will in turn bring about the application of economic and legal means in order to limit the discharge of pollutants: i.e., establishing emission norms, collection of charges and the drawing up of plans for the siting of industry, etc.

The third will consist of establishing the norms and regulations in those cases where general protection of the environment seems necessary and feasible via this method, and also when the correct functioning of the Common Market requires it. Thus, the specifications for the composition or use of certain polluting products will be approximated with a double purpose in mind: the protection of the environment and the removal of the technical barriers to trade. Thus, norms for fixed installations, also called "production process norms", will be set up in certain industrial sectors for some particularly dangerous pollutants.

These actions will be carried on and completed by the Community and the Member States within the framework of international organizations, conferences and Conventions.

Definition of criteria

The objective assessment of the risk to human health and to the environment caused by some pollutants is a long-term task which presents many difficulties. Among them is the absence of or scarcity of scientific information and of sufficient trustworthy statistics, the use of different and often non-comparable measurements, the divergent views of experts and the complexity of the research to be carried out.

The Commission has undertaken research on a series of water pollutants, among them lead, organo-compounds and organo-phosphorous compounds, hydrocarbons, inorganic micro-pollutants and phenols. While criteria are being prepared for the organo-phosphorous compounds, mercury and cadium, it seems impossible to establish criteria for the other pollutants referred to at the moment.

While fully appreciating the benefit of setting up at Community level criteria which are as strict and complete as possible, it must be said that such an undertaking will take time. For this reason the Commission has decided not to wait until such criteria have been set before proposing measures to prevent pollution which can later be revised in the light of improved scientific knowledge.

The objectives of quality

The approach by quality objectives was conceived in the 1973 programme as a flexible instrument to be used in the struggle against water pollution in the Community. It aims at limiting the presence of pollutants in the water while leaving to the Member States a wide choice as to how to apply these objectives and as to the legal and administrative methods by which the objectives could be reached.

Quality objectives have already been established at Community level for surface water intended for the abstraction of drinking water, and for bathing water. Work is in progress on the quality of drinking water, water for aquatic life, for fish raising, for shellfish raising and for agricultural use.

One of the first directives adopted within the Action Programme on the Environment concerns the quality of surface water intended for the abstraction of drinking water in the Member States. According to the terms of this directive, the Member States are to fix the requirements which surface waters used or intended to be used for the abstraction of drinking water must satisfy. These requirements are defined in the directive. They differ according to the three categories of surface water which are themselves determined by three large purification categories. As soon as a Member State has decided to use the water of a river or of a reach of a river for the abstraction of drinking water, it must, according to the purifying process used, fulfil the quality requirements set out in the directive.

Moreover, for the category of water fulfilling the least severe requirements (category A3), the Member States must lay down plans of action at the national level and substantial improvements must be made during the next ten years. The Commission will then examine these plans in depth and will in general follow closely the way the Member States put into practice the different provisions in the directive. Surface water which has characteristics which are inferior to those in category A3 cannot generally be used for the production of drinking water, except under exceptional circumstances, which must be correctly notified to the Commission.

Exceptions are provided for in the case of floods or natural disasters or for certain parameters involving stagnant waters or when the water is naturally enriched by certain substances.

The directive contains some characteristic features. For each category of water, it defines parameters classified in two columns, I and G. The values indicated in column I constitute a limit of concentration of pollutants which the Member States are obliged to observe, and they may not fix values which are less strict. When the values of the parameters appear in column G they should be taken as non-obligatory guidelines. However, if a Member State decides to include these parameters in its legislation, it must be in accordance with the G values of the Community. It is laid down that the list of parameters and their numerical values shall be reviewed or completed in the light of technical developments and scientific knowledge.

The provision allowing the Member States to set stricter values than those indicated in the directive enables the Member States to take into account regional differences (differences of an economic, social and geographical kind).

Another interesting characteristic is the "standstill clause" which expressly lays down that the implementation of the directive should not lead to a deterioration in the present quality of surface water. This means that less strict requirements cannot be applied to water which at present reaches a higher standard. For example, a river with category A1 water will remain in this category and cannot later be downgraded.

Another article contains a provision according to which the Member States will apply the directive without discrimination to national water and to water flowing across frontiers. This provision concerns transfrontier pollution. It reflects the concern of some Member States which lie downstream on an international river and thus could find that they were unable to respect the provisions of the directive because of the poor quality of the surface water originating in another Member State situated up river. In practice, this means that a Member State cannot apply to international waters less strict requirements than those which it imposes for its national waters.

In order to harmonize the results of the tests and the measures which the competent authorities of the Member States must carry out in order to control the quality of the surface water intended for the abstraction of drinking water, the Commission is preparing a directive on the frequency of sampling and measurement methods. This complementary directive will specify the measurement methods to which the Member States can refer in order to express the numerical values of the parameters of surface water. The Member States will not be obliged to adopt exclusively the methods proposed in this directive; however, if other methods are used a calibration must be effected vis-à-vis the methods stipulated in the directive, in order to ensure that the results obtained will enable the control of the application of the values set up by the first directive to be carried out.[4]

Another quality objective directive adopted by the Council concerned the quality of bathing water. Adopted by the Council on 8 December 1975, this directive follows the same scheme as the directive on the quality of surface water intended for the abstraction of drinking water. It establishes a set of parameters and of numerical values which corresponded to the minimal quality required for bathing water. It must be noted that bathing in the sea and in fresh water present similarities because both involve direct human contact with the water in an area in which bathing takes place.

The main differences between the two directives is the importance given to the local examination of conditions and to regular sampling of the quality of the water.

As regards the examination of local conditions, its object is to determine the geographical and topographical factors, the volume and nature of all the pollutants and effluents discharged upstream, as well as their effects, depending on the distance in relation to the bathing area.

Several other directives concerning the quality of the water are in an advanced state of preparation. One of them deals with the required quality of fresh water suitable for fish life and another with the quality of salt water needed for shellfish raising. Both were forwarded to the Council by the Commission in the autumn of 1976.[5]

These two proposed directives ran up against a certain number of difficulties. While it is relatively easy to establish the relationship between the concentration of a substance and its effect upon a fish or a mollusc, it is more difficult to establish such a relationship when several substances are involved (which is normally the case in water) and which interact either by neutralizing each other or, on the contrary, by increasing their specific effects. Very special care is therefore necessary in such cases to establish quality objectives i.e., norms which take into account as far as possible effects which are still little or poorly understood.

Other quality objectives will be prepared for water for agricultural use, for industrial use and for the protection of aquatic life in general.

The implementation of these directives on water quality will require a supervisory network for the control of pollution of fresh and sea water. This network already exists in most of the Member States. It may be foreseen that in the course of the years to come these networks will be extended and will form an important element in the development of a strategy for water management and in the evaluation of the results obtained by the implementation of the anti-pollution measures taken at Community or national level.

For this to happen, however, the national networks must supply information comparable to that of other networks which exist in the Community and the value of the information collected must not be limited to local or regional areas. It is therefore necessary to set up and develop technical exchanges between such networks and to adopt the appropriate measures to improve the efficiency, the precision and the reliability of the information collected. It is with this aim that the Commission sent to the Council a draft decision setting up a common procedure for the exchange of information gathered by the supervisory networks controlling the pollution of water in the Member States. The Council approved this decision, during its meeting, on 12 Dec. 1977.

The setting up at Community level of such information exchange will make it possible to determine the levels of pollution in rivers, to know the evolution in time and space of these levels as well as to assess the results of the regulations against water pollution undertaken at national or Community level. In a first phase, the exchange will be concerned with the values measured for 18 parameters. Other parameters will be taken into consideration later in the light of experience.

Lastly, another directive intended to protect fresh water is being discussed in the Council; it concerns the quality of drinking water and it is designed to protect public health. Clearly, there is a close relationship between the objectives for drinking water and those for surface water intended for the abstraction of drinking water.

Action to control pollutants at source

The protection of the environment against pollution entails actions which cannot be restricted to the control of the quality of the environment, but must in some cases concern the sources of the pollutants themselves. In this point, the programme of action on the environment stipulates that the Commission must study the pollution caused by the main industrial polluting sectors and send the results of this research to the Council, accompanied if need be by specific proposals. The aim of this research is to evaluate:
– the exact nature of the pollution;
– the technology to be employed, developed or still being studied;
– the measures already taken by the Member States or envisaged by them.

This research must equally reveal the additional measures to be taken by Member States in order to reduce the pollution caused by the industry under consideration, taking into account the situation of the said industry, the cost of these measures, as well as the economic, financial, commercial and social consequences.

The first studies dealt with the paper-pulp and the titanium dioxide industries. Using the results of this research, the Commission forwarded to the Council at the beginning of 1975 a technical report and a draft directive restricting the discharge of pollutants into water by the paper-pulp industry.

According to the terms of this proposal, the pollution caused by the existing factories should be reduced to the levels indicated in the proposed directive over a period of ten years. These levels are established taking into account the manufacturing process used and the size of the enterprise, and are expressed in quantities of effluent by ton of pulp produced. This pollution load can be converted into concentration of pollutants by volume of water, care being taken to consider only the water employed in the manufacturing process, excluding all other water which could be used to dilute the effluents.

New factories should observe these levels within one year after their establishment. Exceptions are allowed for discharge into sea water, provided that the quality of this water is not appreciably reduced. Such exceptions can only be granted for a period of five years.

It should be noted that the proposal sets up emission norms rather than environmental quality objectives. Such an approach, aimed at reducing pollution, at the place of discharge, is more effective in combating industrial pollution where large quantities of water are used and contaminated.

The Council of Ministers has twice examined this proposal, but has not managed to reach any agreement.

Another of the Commission's proposals concerns titanium dioxide. Most industries manufacturing titanium dioxide discharge their wastes into the sea or into estuaries. They rely on the sea's ability to neutralize the acid parts of the waste and to convert the iron sulphates. Three aspects of this directive merit consideration. All discharges are subject to an authorization which takes account of the type of waste and the area in which the discharge is made. Discharge into the sea can only be carried out in certain circumstances and waste can only be deposited on land if specific conditions are respected. During the period in which discharge into the sea is allowed, an ecological control of the environment must be undertaken. The directive envisages four phases covering a period of ten years to allow industry to adapt itself to the standards. During the first phase old and new plants can discharge their waste into the sea provided they receive permission to do so. During the second phase, the existing plants must be equipped in such a way that their pollution be reduced by 30%. The third phase envisages a reduction of 70% in pollution for old plants and of 30% for new ones. Finally, the last phase should lead to a reduction of 95% of pollution. This proposal has also been intensively discussed by two meetings of the Council of Ministers. A possible basis for further discussion might be as follows:

In the case of *existing plants*, Member States would undertake to draw up, within one year, programmes for progressive reduction of the pollution of the environment caused by titanium dioxide industries. These programmes would set general reduction targets to be achieved within ten years and appropriate intermediate objectives, and would cover both liquid and solid waste; undertakings would be free to employ the most suitable methods (use of new processes, enriched ores, re-utilization techniques, etc.). The programmes would be sent to the Commission, which, within one year of their being notified of it, would propose an alignment of the various programmes including measures intended to improve the environment and conditions of competition in this industrial sector.

In the case of *new plants* (or extensions to old ones involving an additional 10% or more of the original capacity), their construction and operation would be subject to prior authorization by the relevant authorities of the Member States. These authorizations could be granted only to firms willing to undertake to use the materials and techniques available which were the least harmful for the environment.[6]

As well as the decisions taken and the work at Community level which have just been described, the Council in May 1976 adopted a directive of great political importance concerning the reduction of the pollution caused by certain dangerous substances discharged into the aquatic environment. This directive has a twofold aim: to harmonize the application within the Community of certain international conventions concerning water pollution which are either in force or under negotiation and to complete the action programme in relation to the reduction of water pollution caused by the discharge of certain toxic or dangerous substances.

This directive applies to inland surface water, to territorial waters, to international coastal waters, and ground water. All discharges into these waters which may contain the substances set out in list I of the directive, which have been chosen by reason of their toxicity, their persistence and their bio-accumulation, are subject to an administrative authorization which sets emission limits. These emission norms must not exceed the limit values set by the Council, on the Commission proposal taking into account the best technical means available. If such means cannot be found, then it is forbidden to make any such discharge.

For the same dangerous substances, the Council will set quality objectives which are differentiated depending on whether they refer to salt or fresh water.

The limits will have to be applied in all the Member States with the exception of cases in which a Member State can prove to the Commission that the quality objectives have been reached and permanently maintained by the action undertaken by the Member States in the area affected by the discharge, in accordance with a control procedure adopted by the Council upon the Commission's proposal. The Commission will report to the Council the cases in which it has accepted the implementation of the method of quality objectives.

On the basis of the Commission's proposals, the Council will re-examine every five years the exceptions which have been approved by the Commission. The discharge of less dangerous substances appearing in list II (substances with a damaging effect on the aquatic environment, although their impact is restricted to a certain zone and which depend on the characteristics of the water concerned) will also be subject to prior authorization.

For this category of substances the Member States will draw up programmes to reduce discharges. These programmes will set out the quality objectives to be achieved and the time limit set for them. The Commission will regularly organize comparisons of these programmes in order to ensure sufficient co-ordination in their implementation and will present, if need be, proposals to ensure better co-ordination.

While awaiting the adoption by the Council of a directive on ground water which has already been prepared by the Commission, the Member States apply the rule of zero discharge to ground water of the substances listed in list I, as well as the arrangements laid down for the substances in list II.

International action

The Member States and the Community itself are very active on the international level, in relation both to fresh water and sea water.

In the case of fresh water, in 1975, the Council stated that it was in principle in favour of the Conclusion of the Convention (known as the Convention of Strasbourg) for the protection of international waterways against pollution, which has been drawn up within the Council of Europe for several years. On 8 December 1975, the Council, on the Commission's draft, adopted a decision concerning the Community's participation in the negotiations to conclude a convention for the protection of the Rhine against chemical pollution. These negotiations which dragged on for several years without any tangible success have recently borne fruit. The Commission's action and the compromise reached by the Council on the directive of 4 May 1976 described above have certainly played a decisive part. On 20 September 1976 the Council was informed by the Commission of a draft decision by which the Community signed this convention as well as an additional agreement to the Berne Agreement ensuring the Community's participation in the work of the International Commission on the Rhine. The signature of these texts took place on 3 December 1976.

In relation to marine pollution, the programme of action takes account of four main sources of pollution: the discharge of effluents from land (land-based pollution), the exploitation of marine and sea-bed resources, the deliberate dumping of waste into the sea, and lastly transport and shipping.

In the case of land-based pollution, the Commission took an active part, together with the Member States concerned, in the negotiations for the Paris Convention for the prevention of marine pollution from land-based sources in the North-East Atlantic. On 3 March 1975, on a proposal of the Commission, the Council authorized the Community to sign this convention, which provides for the partial or total elimination of a certain number of pollutants classified according to their toxicity persistence or bio-accumulation. The signature and conclusion of this convention by the Community took place on 23 June 1975.

In the case of marine pollution caused by the exploration and exploitation of the sea bed, the Community is taking part in the work of a special study group, created within the framework of the Paris Convention, which is drawing up the measures to be taken as regards the pollution caused from drilling platforms. The Community also participates as an observer in the work of the London Conference of 1973–1975 on the problems of security and of protection against pollution during research and production operations on the marine mineral resources of North-West Europe. One of the working groups involved is dealing with the problems of civil liability for this type of pollution. Finally, the Commission is following attentively the work on marine pollution undertaken within the framework of the 3rd Conference on the Law of the Sea.

After the accident which occurred in the North Sea on the "Bravo" platform, the Commission forwarded to the Council on 9 June 1977 a draft Resolution on measures to prevent, monitor, and reduce pollution caused by accidental discharges of hydrocarbons into the sea.

In the field of the pollution of the seas caused by the deliberate dumping of waste, the Commission participates as observer in the work of the Commission whose task it is to put into practice the Oslo Convention concerning the dumping of toxic waste in the North-East Atlantic. Furthermore, on 8 December 1975, the Council adopted a decision on the Community's participation in the negotiations of the inter-governmental meeting in Barcelona in order to enable the Community to conclude a framework Convention with its protocols for the prevention of marine pollution in the Mediterranean. Once these negotiations had been successful, the Council on the Commission's proposal adopted on 25 July 1977 a decision by which the Community concluded the Convention for the protection of the Mediterranean Sea against pollution and a Protocol on the prevention of pollution of the Mediterranean sea by dumping from ships and aircraft. This Convention and Protocol were signed on 13 September 1976.

The Commission also sent to the Council on 20 December 1975 a draft directive concerning the dumping of waste at sea. This draft directive corresponds to the desire expressed by the Council to approximate insofar as is necessary for the smooth functioning of the Common Market and for the carrying out of the action programme, the application of the provisions of international conventions by trying to establish a sole certification procedure. The directive differentiates between three categories of waste. Firstly, it establishes the categories of particularly dangerous substances, whose dumping is to be forbidden. It then lays down the categories of waste and material which can only be discharged under specific authorization given by the competent authorities. Lastly, it establishes the principle according to which the discharge into the sea of all other waste should be subject to the grant of a general permit by the competent authorities. The criteria to be taken into consideration for the granting of specific and general permits are proposed in the draft directive as well as a common model of the form for the request for permits. Nevertheless, in order to allow some flexibility in the implementation of the directive, the Member States are able to allow exceptions from these rules in grave circumstances.

Concerning marine pollution caused by the transport of polluting substances and by shipping, the Commission participates as an observer in work in this field undertaken by the Intergovernmental Maritime Consultative Organization (IMCO). It attaches importance to harmonization in this field to ensure that the international conventions concluded in this field will be fully implemented.[7]

Finally, the Commission forwarded to the Council on 14 March 1977, a recommendation for a Council Decision authorizing the Commission to open negotiations with the non-Member States bordering the Baltic Sea with a view to the accession of the European Economic Community to the Helsinki Convention of 22 March 1974 on the protection of the marine environment of the Baltic Sea area.

These then are the direct actions which the Commission has undertaken for the protection of fresh and sea water in the Community.

In order to be complete, one must also mention other actions which have an indirect influence on the battle against water pollution.

On a proposal by the Commission, the Council adopted on 16 June 1975 a directive on the disposal of waste oils which banned amongst other things the discharge of used oil into internal surface water, ground water, coastal waters and drainage systems.

In the economic field, the Council adopted on 3 March 1975 a recommendation to the Member States regarding cost allocation and action by the public authorities on environmental matters. This recommendation was the first step towards a uniform application of the polluter-pays principle throughout the Community. On 7 November 1974 the Commission had informed the governments of the Member States of the conditions under which it could consider State Aids for the environment as compatible with the Common Market. Such grants—provided that they are limited, for a given period of time and decreasing, can facilitate the adaptation of the existing enterprises to the new obligations imposed upon them by the Community or national environment policies.

The Community is also presently preparing a draft directive designed to harmonize the legislation of the Member States applying a system of charges for water pollution. The Council has also asked the Commission to draw up a report on the possibility of harmonizing national legislation on civil liability. The Commission has also agreed to submit to the Council all necessary proposals for the implementation of the polluter-pays principle, notably concerning the harmonization of the methods of carrying out the principle and for its application to the problems of transfrontier pollution.

The work undertaken in the framework of the research programme of the Community is being actively pursued in the CCR establishment in Ispra and via contracts. It deals in particular with the epidemiological research into the effects of water pollution, the ecological effects of water pollutants, and the analysis of the systems applied to the eutrophization of lakes.

In its resolution of 3 March 1975, the Council invited the Commission to present proposals concerning the policies to be followed by the Community and the Member States, concerning thermal discharges. As follow-up to this resolution, the Commission has undertaken research into the effects of thermal discharges, the recycling of heat lost as well as the environmental problems presented by the cooling towers of the electric power stations. The Commission has also proposed creating for the Council the exchange of information on the siting of power stations, taking into account the risks of pollution.

Lastly, the Commission has undertaken a series of studies on the water pollution from various industrial sectors, and on the availability in the medium and long term of water resources, taking into account increased consumption and its utilization.

For the opinions of and debates in the European Parliament see the essay *Environment Policy* by Mr. B. Kuster.

ASSESSMENT OF THE FEASIBILITY OF THE PROPOSALS

Two methods can be used to reduce water pollution: that of quality objectives and that of emission norms. Both have advantages and disadvantages. They can also be applied in a complementary way.

The first method consists in creating a common basis for the evaluation of the facts as well as a common frame of reference and methods. What has to be done first is to establish scientific criteria of harmfulness for the main water pollutants and the methods of sampling, of measuring and of analysing these pollutants must be regulated or harmonized. Subsequently quality objectives can be established, fixing the different requirements which the water must satisfy, taking into account the use to which it is put, and technical exchanges of information between the regional or national networks of supervision and of control of water pollution can be set up.

This first way seems logical and would undoubtedly be the best if there already existed objective scientific information which would assure a full assessment of the short- and long-term effects of pollution upon man and the environment.

The method of emission norms is more arbitrary, more centralized, but given the lacunae in scientific knowledge is far more effective and rapidly set up.

It can, however, lead to some difficulties of an institutional kind, when the responsibility for the water protection is not on the national level, but is decentralized on the level of federal states or of states with regional autonomy. Also, it does not take into account the possible ability of the natural element to purify itself and so could in theory indirectly penalize the States in which this self-purification could take place. About this possibility very little is known, and in any case it is only a relative possibility in the case of substances, which are toxic, non-biodegradable and persistent.

Several arguments are in favour of the signature of the international conventions on water protection by the Community.

These arguments are both political and economic. The Council has on several occasions stressed the importance of the environment policy in the Community, underlining the exceptional importance of the aquatic environment. The Community as a whole is therefore anxious to contribute to the success of the various Conventions by taking part from the beginning in the negotiations, all the more so since the tasks undertaken within the framework of the Conventions are in many respects the same as those entrusted to the Community by the action programme. The Community must thus assume its own responsibilities in this field in order to ensure the necessary coherence between its own work and that of the international conventions and thus avoid distortions of competition and investment.

As has already been mentioned above, it is precisely in the action programme that it is stated that the application of the international conventions "will necessitate the implementation within the Community of legislative rules which will have to be harmonized so as to avoid the creation of distortions in trade and the distribution of investments"; it is added that "such harmonization would be facilitated by the Commission's participation in the work of the Commissions set by these agreements with a view to ensuring their implementation". In fact, it is probable that some measures of an economic nature will be adopted in the framework of these conventions. The presence of the Community amongst the contracting parties to these conventions will ensure that these economic measures will be directly adopted and will thus avoid the inevitable difficulties of an *a posteriori* harmonization. Such difficulties are of course aggravated when all the Member States do not take part in the international conventions.

Finally, a last and by no means negligible argument for the environment policy, the presence of the Community alongside the Member States enables it to propose, to have adopted and to put into force the provisions of the international Convention far more rapidly than if the Member States alone were the contracting parties. To sum up, in the regulatory field as well as in the international one, the Community's action concerning the environment reinforces the coherence of the Community as well as the solidarity of the Member States.

It is by no means easy to proceed to an economic evaluation of the Commission's proposals or of the measures taken by the Council, especially when it is a matter of decisions in the international field or of directives on the quality objectives.

The same cannot be said of the proposals concerning the emission norms. In this respect, the Commission has carefully studied the economic consequences that these proposals for norms could entail in the industrial sectors concerned. The reports which the Commission has forwarded to the Council on the paper-pulp industry and on the titanium dioxide manufacturing industries contain in this respect precise economic evaluations.

What undertakings have been made by the institutions and the publicity given to their action in the field of environment?

Apart from the political commitment, the results of which have been fully described above, it would perhaps be helpful to mention that the Council, the European Parliament and the Economic and Social Committee have created special structures which have been given the task of dealing with environmental problems. Meetings are arranged twice to four times a month by the Council, once a month by the Parliament and the Economic and Social Committee. The Commission's proposals are fully debated and important contributions to the framing of Community measures are made.

However, the actions of the institutions are little known to the public. None of the institutions fully inform the European public, which remains unaware of the reasons why the protection of the environment is also a European concern and do not know the progress which has been made in implementing this policy. And yet the European citizen places the protection of the environment and the improvement of the quality of life among its most important concerns, as is shown by the results of the Eurobarometer of December 1975.

It cannot be denied that a great effort should be made in future, especially by the Commission, so that the European citizen should no longer be under the impression that the building of Europe is merely the business of bureaucrats who are isolated from public opinion.

TIME SCHEDULE

The time which elapsed between the conception of the action programme by the Commission, and the decisions upon the first implementing measures taken by the Council can be said to be short when compared with the other actions undertaken at Community level.

The first reflections of the services of the Commission on an environmental policy took place in February 1971. The first communication of the Commission was issued in July 1971. It was followed by consultations with political, economic and social groups which led the Commission to present a draft programme in March 1972, which was modified in April 1973. It was this draft which the Council approved on 19 July 1973 and adopted definitively on 22 November of that year. The first measures taken in relation to water under this programme were adopted:
– 3 March 1975 for the decision by which the Community concluded the Convention for the prevention of marine pollution from land-based sources;
– 16 June 1975 for the directive concerning the quality required of surface water intended for the abstraction of drinking water;
– 8 December 1975 for the directive concerning the quality of bathing water;
– 4 May 1976 for the directive relating to the reduction of pollution caused by certain dangerous substances discharged into the aquatic environment;
– 25 July 1977 a decision on the conclusion of a Convention on the protection of the Mediterranean Sea against pollution and a protocol on the prevention of pollution of the Mediterranean Sea by dumping from ships and aircraft;
– 25 July 1977 a decision on the conclusion for the protection of the Rhine against chemical pollution;

- 12 Dec. 1977 a decision establishing a common procedure for the exchange of information on the quality of surface fresh water in the Community.
  The Commission has also forwarded to the Council on;
- 20 January 1975 a draft directive on the reduction of water pollution caused by the paper-pulp industry;
- 18 July 1975 a draft proposal on the waste from the titanium dioxide industry;
- 31 July 1975 a draft directive on the quality of water for human consumption;
- 12 January 1976 a draft directive concerning the dumping of wastes at sea;

The time schedule for implementing these actions varies from one to another. The decision of 3 March 1975 took effect immediately. However, in the three directives adopted by the Council, provision is made for a delay of two years for the Member States to adapt their legislation so that it shall conform to the Community directives. It is therefore only in June 1977 that the first national legislation applying a Community directive will be applied.

It must also be recalled that some of the directives have provisions for a time-table which is spread out over several years.

ASSESSMENT OF THE REACTIONS OF THE MEMBER STATES AND OF NATIONAL SOCIO-ECONOMIC GROUPS

It is impossible to examine in detail the many reactions which were observed among the Member States as regards the Commission's proposals in the environmental field. We shall restrict ourselves to assessing the reaction of four Member States which are of special interest for different reasons. These are the French reactions, which at first were fairly negative, the German, which were interesting from an institutional angle, the Dutch, who have always been very interested in a common water policy, and the British who were opposed to the establishment at Community level of emission norms.

France

The first reactions of the Member States to the Commission's proposals came from France in January 1972 in a first memorandum which stated that European co-operation in the field of environmental protection was a necessity. This co-operation, however, had, in the view of the French government to be restricted to a few judiciously chosen actions in accordance with the following criteria of efficiency:
- concern for maintaining the European economic area and, consequently, vigilance in relation to the smooth running of the Common Market;
- the need to combine financial resources and scientific knowledge in an area in which co-ordination of the national efforts would seem most likely to be fruitful.

394

These efficiency criteria led the French government to propose to its partners:
- the setting up of an information procedure concerning draft legislation in the field of the environment which could influence the working of the Common Market;[8]
- if in fact the smooth working was in danger, the adoption *using resolutions*, of common objectives for environmental protection.

In relation to water, the French government deemed it desirable to invite its partners in the Community, together with the Commission, to collate their experience and to compare the economic effects of their action in the fight against water pollution.

The first objective of this concertation which necessitated the adoption of a common terminology was to bring about a gradual co-ordination of methods; in particular to sort out the common principles for the attribution of the financial costs incurred by the fight against water pollution.

The Member States were also to compare the ways of drawing up the quality objectives which they assigned to the different sections of their hydrographic network.

It is clear that the results of this work should be particularly useful as a guide for the activity of each of the Member States in the different specially set up international organizations, within which the States concerned could pool their efforts to combat pollution of water in some of the great international rivers and adjoining seas. These bodies, which are the framework within which the solidarity and efficiency deriving from the common efforts could be most naturally exercised, would gain clear advantages from this work.

The French government also proposed to its partners that they first should start by *reflecting* on the economic and technical limits inherent to some industrial branches which are particularly polluting and to include the protection of the environment among the themes which lend themselves to concerted European action (comparison of plans, scientific programmes and budgets, in order to choose the research actions which would be harmonized at the European level but financed by national budgets).

Lastly, in order to work for the development of European co-operation on environmental questions the French government proposed that the Ministers involved should meet regularly in the Council in order to organize the method of collaboration between the Council and the Commission to define the guidelines for the work and to make sure that it was properly carried out. To this effect, the French government proposed the creation of a Committee of High Level Officials, subordinate to the Council, from which it would derive its attributions and its mandates, which would be given the task of organizing the co-operation and preparing the concertation between the Member States.

These first reactions, which would have restricted the field of action and involved little from the political point of view, were perceptibly modified in November 1972, shortly after the meeting of the Heads of State and government held in Paris in October 1972 and the inter-governmental meeting of the Ministers of the Environment held in Bonn in October 1972.

In its observations on the proposed action programme of the Community on the environment, the French government widened somewhat the field of European co-operation.

Thus, it proposed to harmonize at Community level the methodology (that is to say, the principles and methods) enabling the quality objectives for waters to be set, and the methodology for fixing the individual emission norms to be set for each source of pollution so that these quality objectives could be observed. However, the quality objectives themselves and the norms which result from them, must be able to differ from region to region according to their ecological economic and social characteristics.

The French government admitted that in the case of health norms, which result from an objective evaluation of the effects of pollution on human beings, have no reason to vary between the Member States and should therefore be uniform for drinking water, water for bathing, fish raising and shellfish raising.

Exchanges of technical information between the supervisory networks for water pollution concerning anti-pollution techniques were also to be carried out but it was indicated that it would be easier to conduct such exchanges on a bilateral level.

Action affecting existing industrial establishments in some branches with a high degree of pollution, should be proposed on two levels:
– a harmonization of policies with regard to paper-pulp, food-starch, wool-combing, washing and carding industries;
– an exchange of technical, legislative, economic and financial information on a series of less polluting industries.

In relation to problems concerned with maritime pollution and the management of water quality in the frontiers areas, the French government indicated that only methodological problems should be examined at Community level, and that practical methods for solving such problems should instead be examined within the geographical framework concerned.

After the programme of action was adopted in 1973, France obtained from her partners that the legal instrument appertaining to the programme itself should include a declaration by the Member States and the Council stating that some of the actions envisaged in the programme would have to be put into operation by the Member States. The other Member States and the Commission were opposed to this point of view without success, arguing that the existence of actions within the competence of the Member States did not prevent the adoption of a legal instrument by the Council, since the latter is always able to act, in respect of such actions as a co-ordinator, as is laid down by the Treaty. It was clear at this time that the actions in question were those to be undertaken within the framework of the international conventions. Four years after this stand, it can be seen in the light of the results which have been obtained that the French position has been perceptibly modified. The support given by France for the directive of 4 May 1976, and to the participation of the Community in the Convention of Paris and the Convention on the chemical pollution of the Rhine bear witness to this change of attitude.

It is well-known that in Germany, responsibility for the management of water is in the hands of the Länder.

This special institutional situation has led the Federal German Republic to adopt a reserved attitude towards some of the Commission's proposals.

In 1973, the FGR thought that there would be no special problem concerning the main questions involved in the fight against water pollution, notably the problems which arise out of the definition of quality objectives and the fixing of limit values for the discharge of effluent in frontier areas.

In so far as some special problems could arise, it was recommended that they should be resolved within the framework of multilateral commissions (Rhine, Constance, Moselle, Sarre). The Federal German Republic recommended however that there should be some collaboration between the Commission and the International Commission for the Rhine.

The FGR also indicated that as far as it was concerned, it was necessary to protect ground water as well as surface water, since both categories have to satisfy the requirements for drinking water supply and for industrial water and, consequently, being obliged to achieve the conditions of high quality. It was therefore not surprising to find the Federal German Republic was opposed to any drawing up of quality objectives in the form of a classification of surface water according to its different usage.

As for the supervisory and control networks, Germany considered that exchange of information between the various supervisory networks was already provided for in the Strasbourg Convention in which the creation of commissions for frontier waters and for international waters was envisaged, and that in consequence the exchange of information between the various national control networks would represent one of the tasks which must be taken over by these commissions.

All these attitudes were motivated by the special responsibilities of the Länder in relation to water protection. The Länder feared that via the Community legislation the Federal Government would arrogate to itself new powers in the field of water management.

This situation led to an interesting legal peculiarity. At the request of the German government, the first directive adopted by the Council concerning water, that of 16 June 1975, was based jointly on Articles 100 and 235 of the EEC Treaty.

Legally, one can contest the reference to both these articles, since the first provides for the harmonization of legislation in order to avoid serious distortions in the functioning of the Common Market, and the second serves as the legal basis for actions which are concerned with the attainment of the objectives of the Treaty.

The German government considered, in fact, that the implementation of the directive, which might necessitate very large investments in purifying and treatment stations, could distort the conditions of competition within the Community and, consequently directly affect the functioning of the Common Market.

The other Member States considered, on the contrary, that this directive was intended solely as an action to improve the environment and thus should be exclusively based upon Article 235 of the Treaty.

It must also be said that most of the criticisms of Community environmental action came from the German Länder which consider—contrary to what had been politically agreed upon at the Paris Summit in October 1972—that article 235 was not a sufficient legal basis for action at Community level, and that a revision of the Treaty must be undertaken in order to include a special chapter devoted to this policy.

One wonders what would be the fate reserved for such a revision of the Treaty at a time when, unfortunately the centrifugal tensions often lead the Member States to adopt individualistic attitudes towards problems treated at Community level.

On the other hand, in the industrial field, the Federal German Republic proposed that the Commission should study the methods to achieve the harmonization of the existing national provisions, basing its position upon the most strict national legislation. To this end the Commission was requested to proceed with its activities with a view to establishing the foundations of a long-term environment policy.

This German firmness in favour of emission norms was demonstrated in the Council of October 1975 in the course of the debate on the draft directive concerning the pollution of water by dangerous substances. On that occasion, the Federal German Republic indicated its preference for emission norms as an instrument which can easily be put into operation and which leads to a perceptible improvement of the environment and enables distortions of competition to be avoided.

The Netherlands

The Netherlands were from the outset the most fervent supporters of a Community environment policy, in particular in relation to water. It was they who made their partners accept the need for research and the determination in common of the minimal quality requirements which would be satisfactory in the long term, for all the different milieus which constitute the Community environment.

It was also the Netherlands who were the most demanding concerning the numerical values of the parameters which define the quality of surface water.

In relation to Community action for the improvement of the quality of waters of the Rhine, the sentiment of the Netherlands was for a long time divided between the wish not to hinder the progress of the work carried out within the framework of the International Commission of the Rhine, and the wish to develop the Community's action on the environment. The Netherlands also always expressed the fear that the Community action would lead to the establishment of minimal norms which would not be adequate to improve the quality of the waters of the Rhine. The adoption by the Community of the directive of 4 May 1976, the drawing-up of the Convention relating to the chemical pollution of the Rhine, which had been facilitated by the Directive, and the determined attitude of the Commission in relation to the environment seem to have somewhat reassured the Dutch authorities, who nevertheless remain vigilant in this matter.

From the end of 1971, the United Kingdom had been associated with negotiations to establish a programme of action on the environment. In 1972 the United Kingdom agreed to draw up at Community level quality objectives for water, taking account of the different uses to which it was to be put.

The United Kingdom also approved the development of exchanges of technical information between monitoring and control networks, provided that the exchange concerned uniform data.

In relation to emission norms, the United Kingdom is convinced of their practical value provided that they are applied to individual sources of pollution in their local environment and take account of the totality of the characteristics of that environment, including the particular economic factors of that environment (best practical means). These local norms should be established in such a way that they can be modified to take account of the advances of scientific and technical knowledge without the necessity of having recourse to a procedure of legislative amendments.

In the debate upon the directive of 4 May 1976, in which it was opposed to its partners, the United Kingdom stressed the advantages presented by the quality objectives as compared with the common emission norms by pointing out that the establishment of quality objectives leaves the Member States free to decide upon the means by which they can be attained and to take into account the utilization of the milieu, and that this system allows a better utilization of resources "given the pollution-absorbing capacity of the waters". (This latter argument was contested by the other Member States, especially so far as dangerous, toxic bio-accumulative and non-biodegradable substances are concerned.)

The United Kingdom also did not share the point of view expressed by the other Member States according to which a system of uniform norms is necessary to avoid the distortions of competition which would result from differences between the emission norms.

According to the United Kingdom, it is in fact unacceptable for the continental industries, which in its eyes already enjoy a privileged position as to access to supply and to the market, should oblige industries in a less favourable location to support burdensome investments, which are not strictly necessary, taking into account the "self-purifying capacity of water" in order to ensure the protection of the environment. This last argument was not accepted by the other Member States when dealing with toxic or dangerous substances which present a grave danger to human health. Moreover these same Member States argued that it was for the Member States to give proof of their solidarity since the dangerous substances, for example in the Channel or the North Sea, come from industries situated in the Member States bordering the sea.

The directive of 4 May 1976 is at present the most acceptable compromise to all the Member States, taking into account the differences of opinion which have been mentioned above.

399

PRESENT SITUATION AND ASSESSMENT OF THE LONG-TERM EFFECTS OF THE DEVELOPMENT OF THE POLICY UNDER CONSIDERATION

After four years of implementation of the programme of action of the Community on the environment, it can be said that some successes have been achieved in the field of protecting water against pollution. But these successes are still to be consolidated. In this field, the differences in intensity of political concern, the diversity of national approaches to the resolution of these complex problems, the differences concerning the assessment of priorities, the disparity between administrative structures and the different nature of the legislation in the Member States make it difficult to undertake a common policy. The decision-making procedure at Community level tends to be slow because of this. The present economic situation and the rarefaction of natural resources, in particular of resources of good quality water, should nevertheless incite the Member States in the future to pursue an environmental policy which is both determined and well-considered.

Very often, however, short-term political considerations prevail over the long-term advantages which could be gained by measures designed to improve the environment. This phenomenon can clearly be explained by the fact that the direct and immediate costs can be more clearly perceived by the economy than the advantages which could be gained in the future.

It must be emphasized that a precise evaluation of the costs to be borne by all the sectors of the economy arising from measures taken to protect and improve the environment are sometimes difficult to quantify, because of the scarcity of reliable data, the subjective nature of some pollution damage, and from the fact that such an assessment must take into account the long-term effects.

Besides, one should not try to conceal the fact that the common programme still has lacunae and that its implementation runs up against many difficulties. In the first place, as we have seen, the rule-making function which differentiates the Community from conventional international organizations is not accepted without some difficulty.

In the second place, it is not enough to enact rules, they must be effectively applied and their application must be made via controls and sanctions. In this field, the Community has as yet only reduced powers. It is in fact the Member States that have the task of supervising the correct implementation of Community directives and of putting into operation, according to their own systems, the measures of control and supervision and, if need be, the sanctions. These systems vary from country to country and are not even always comparable amongst themselves. A far more determined effort to harmonize them will be necessary and this will doubtless be facilitated by the setting up of exchanges of information between the centres supervising and controlling pollution.

Lastly, it must be recognized that the environment policy and water protection is an integral part of a more general set of policies undertaken at Community level and that its success is closely linked with that of the Community itself. The economic and political union, a common attitude of the Community and of its Member States to many international problems must be achieved as soon as possible in order to make this Community stronger and more coherent than it is at present. International and Community problems must be approached with the aim of achieving reciprocal objectives and the common solidarity of the Member States.

The environment policy and, in particular, the action to protect and improve water must bring its contribution to the construction of a Community, which has a common feeling not only for its economic objectives, but also for social ones. In order to achieve such a Community, public opinion must take part. In this respect it is regrettable that the institutions of the Community have been so parsimonious in their efforts and with their enthusiasm, in the task of arousing public opinion and making it understand the results achieved, and the efforts still to be undertaken at Community level, in order to improve the aquatic milieu in the Community. It is to be hoped that on the occasion of the coming election to the European Parliament by universal suffrage, the European parliamentary candidates will make their personal contribution to the arousing of public opinion by showing how a better quality of life cannot be dissociated from the building of an integrated Europe.

NOTES

1. Doc. SEC (71) 2616.
2. Doc. SEC (72) 666.
3. *Ibid.*, p. 14.
4. This proposal has been sent to the Council in August 1978.
5. The first one has been adopted by the Council on 18 July 1978.
6. This directive which has been adopted by the Council on 25 February 1978 differs notably from the original proposal. For further details see OJ No. L 54 of 25.2.78.
7. Following the AMOCO-CADIZ disaster, the Council adopted on 26 June 1978 a resolution concerning an action programme on the control and the reduction of the pollution due to accidental discharges of hydrocarbons into the sea.
8. Such a procedure was set up by the Member States in 1973. As well as the reciprocal information provided for in the French proposal, the Information Agreement of 5 March 1973 enabled the Commission, in certain conditions to require the Member States to postpone the adoption of the measures which were envisaged whilst awaiting the adoption at Community level of corresponding measures.

II. ENVIRONMENT POLICY REPORT

European Policy of Protection of Rivers and Water against Pollution

by *B. Küster*

THE RECOMMENDATIONS OF THE EUROPEAN PARLIAMENT

The European Parliament had put forward proposals in the field of environmental policy even before implementation began of the Community policy in this sector, adopted at the Paris Summit Conference of 19/20 October 1972 by Heads of State or Government. The report of 11 November 1970 drawn up by Mr. Boersma on behalf of the then Committee on Social Affairs and Health Protection, on the purification of inland waters with particular reference to the pollutions of the Rhine[1] is especially relevant here. The subsequent resolution of 19 November 1970[2] began with the point that the increasing pollution of the Rhine was posing a serious threat to the population of the Rhine basin and was, moreover, causing large-scale economic damage. Its final paragraph stated that the riparian states must undertake a *collective* battle against the pollution of the Rhine to ensure real success. With this in mind the Commission was called upon to take a number of measures, which may be summarized as follows:

- the submission of appropriate harmonization proposals relating to the purification of the Rhine;
- the negotiation of agreements with Switzerland and Austria with a view to securing from these riparian states an undertaking that they would comply with regulations which are binding in the Community;
- a ban on the discharge of waste salts into the Rhine;
- the drawing up of mandatory quality standards for water;
- the supervision of compliance with the harmonization provisions for the purification of waters;
- the regular publication of data on the pollution of inland watercourses in the Community;
- the realization of a Community regulation on the transport and unloading of dangerous substances (such as highly poisonous chemicals) in the field of goods transport by inland waterway;
- rational coordination between the Member States when planning sites for their nuclear power stations in order to avoid the danger of excessive thermal pollution of rivers through the discharge of cooling water.

These proposals made by the European Parliament were even at that time based on the European Treaties, in particular on Articles 92, 100, 101, 117, and 235 of the EEC Treaty and Articles 35–38 of the EAEC Treaty.

The European Parliament considered the Rhine as a test case for joint action in the European context. Commissioner Spinelli said in the debate of

19 November 1970 that the Commission was well aware of the decisive importance of these problems for the future of the European nations, and that it would accept responsibility for them.

However, since no practical proposals were submitted by the Commission, in December 1971 an oral question was put to the Commission by Mr. Oele, on behalf of the Socialist Group, on the fight against the pollution of the Rhine.[3] The Commission was asked if it did not feel that more energetic measures were essential to protect the Rhine against pollution, and what action it intended taking in this matter. The Commission was also asked what means it intended using with a view to full-scale action in this field in co-operation with the riparian states and the appropriate international organizations. In its reply to Parliament of 16 December 1971, the Commission, while recognizing the need for Community measures, drew attention to some political difficulties which could only be overcome "once the Community has decided on the new powers which the Community in general and its institutions in particular must be given in order to fulfil the new tasks facing us today".[4]

After the debate a resolution was adopted[5] which contained a call to the Commission to do everything in its power to encourage and coordinate the riparian states' programmes for the protection of the Rhine. The Commission was also requested to work out ways of cooperating more actively in the work of the International Commission for the Protection of the Rhine against Pollution, whose powers would need to be extended.

On the basis of the instructions given by the Paris Summit Conference, the Commission submitted in 1972 and 1973 communications and proposals for a Community action programme on the environment. The European Parliament then delivered a detailed opinion on these proposals. Independently of this, Mr. Armengaud, on behalf of the Committee on Legal Affairs, drew up an own-initiative report on the possibilities for taking measures against environmental pollution under the Community Treaties and on the modifications which might have to be proposed to those Treaties in this connection.[6] On the basis of this report, the European Parliament adopted a resolution[7] on 18 April 1972, which not only set out the legal possibilities but also put forward the basic premise "that a really efficient Community environmental policy depends primarily on the *political will* of Member States first to apply existing laws and regulations strictly, and to tackle the problems involved in the fight against pollution and the protection of the environment jointly".

The three reports which Mr. Jahn submitted, on behalf of the Committee on the Environment, Public Health and Consumer Protection, on the Commission's proposal for a European Communities' programme for protecting the environment,[8] refer once again to the existing *legal principles*. In the corresponding resolutions of the European Parliament of 18 April 1972,[9] 6 July 1972,[10] and 3 July 1973:[11]
- the Commission and Council were urged to base Community legal acts in the environmental protection sector predominantly on Articles 100 and 235 of the EEC Treaty, which, in the majority of cases, provided a suitable basis;
- the fact was deplored that in its communication of 22 March 1972[12] the Commission took no account of these two important Treaty Articles as a legal basis;
- the basic premise was stated, in agreement with the Commission, that the

Council's optional consultation of the European Parliament about the action programme was in fact obligatory since this programme was based on Article 235 of the EEC Treaty, according to the instructions given by the Paris Summit Conference of October 1972.

As regards the fight against the pollution of rivers and watercourses, the demands contained in the above three resolutions of the European Parliament may be summarized as follows:

– immediate implementation of measures at Community level against the dangerous increase in the pollution of the Rhine;
– involvement of the Community in the proposed Convention of the North-East Atlantic States on the purification of the North Sea and the Atlantic coast;
– agreement in principle with the proposal for a Council recommendation to those Member States which are signatories to the Berne Convention on the International Commission for the Protection of the Rhine against Pollution; at the same time it was pointed out that if the recommendation were implemented, no improvement in the quality of the water in the Rhine could be expected for at least three to five years;
– a request to the Commission to include setting up a European agency for the Rhine, which it anticipated doing at a later date, in its draft recommendation and to give this agency a flexible legal form, so that it could adopt the status of a joint undertaking at a later date;
– the immediate commencement of preparatory work to set up a method for establishing quality objectives including those for ground waters and lakes.

Apart from these specific demands, the European Parliament had a number of *general requests* which refer to both water pollution and the general policy on the environment:

– the encouragement of greater public awareness of the environment through a comprehensive and resolute information programme drawn up by the Commission (such as by the publication of an easily understandable summary of their communications on the environment);
– the need for Members of the European Parliament to assist in the break-through of the concept of a Community environmental policy by taking appropriate steps in their national Parliaments and by approaches to their governments;
– the early development of contacts and continual cooperation with the competent institutions and organizations in third countries in respect of all environmental problems that extend beyond the Community's boundaries;
– the need to adopt general regulations (framework laws) at Community level and to transfer their implementation to national and local authorities, taking account of the climatic and demographic variations and the differing stages of industrial development in individual areas;
– the need for Community and national bodies to bear in mind environmental aspects when taking decisions and measures in all areas of social and economic policy;
– the consideration of the aspects of environmental policy and environmental improvement when granting financial assistance from Community funds;
– the allocation by the Council of adequate funds for the Community's environmental policy;

– support for the "polluter pays" principle, with the proviso that in certain cases a different form of cost allocation was inevitable and that public funds must be used for solving special problems;
– the wider application of the "polluter pays" principle so that the polluter not only pays for, but must make good the damage he has caused and that he removes the cause of the pollution;
– approximation and *tightening up* of regulations on the environment as well as sanctions against any infringements;
– the development of pioneering and progressive environmental measures in individual Member States and the extension of these innovations to the Community as a whole.

THE PROPOSALS OF THE COMMISSION AND THE OPINIONS OF THE PARLIAMENT

In implementing the programme of action of the European Communities on the environment,[13] adopted by the Council on 22 November 1973, the Commission submitted a series of proposals including some concerning the fight against the pollution of rivers and inland waterways. The European Parliament's opinions on these proposals will be summarized below.

On 12 November 1973[14] the Commission proposed that it should be authorized to participate jointly with the Member States concerned in the negotiations for the conclusion of a Convention in Paris for the prevention of sea pollution from land-based sources.

The aim of the negotiations was that the Commission should sign the Convention enabling the Community to become a member without accession being conditional on the unanimous approval of the contracting parties. In its resolution of 9 January 1974,[15] based on the Martens report,[16] the European Parliament gave full support to the Commission's proposal and called on the Council to give the negotiating mandate to the Commission without delay. It also insisted that the Commission should sign the Paris Convention on behalf of the Community so as to avoid any political difficulties which might arise from the Community's later accession.

In similar vein, by its resolution of 14 March 1975,[17] adopted on the basis of a report by Mr. Della Briotta,[18] the European Parliament approved the Commission's proposal,[19] submitted to the Council in January 1975, for a decision concluding the European Convention for the protection of international watercourses against pollution.

On 21 January 1974 the Commission submitted a proposal for a directive concerning the quality required of surface water intended in the Member States for the abstraction of drinking water.[20] Given the increasing demand for potable water, this aimed in particular at preventing the pollution of watercourses and at purifying polluted water, as well as protecting public health by monitoring surface water intended for the abstraction of drinking water and its purification treatment. On the basis of a report by Mr. Premoli,[21] the European Parliament adopted a resolution on 13 May 1974[22] approving this proposal, subject to the following reservations:

- that the directive should be supplemented as soon as possible by a regulation on the waters of hydrographic basins providing for an interdisciplinary approach to all the related problems;
- that nuclear power-station wastes must be discharged at a safe distance from the points of abstraction of water intended for drinking;
- that the level of radioactivity of such water should be limited by laying down Community standards;
- that water not possessing the minimum characteristics defined in the proposal for a directive should not be used at all for drinking purposes;
- that the frequency of sampling must be stipulated and should be carried out at least every six months, since the characteristics of surface water may be altered by natural phenomena;
- that closer surveillance was needed of the level of contamination of water to be rendered potable, of the possibilities of reclamation and of possible financing at Community level.

It was further suggested in the debate that European water authorities should be created to deal with the abstraction and purification of water in the catchment basin of a river, irrespective of national boundaries, and with waste waters which empty into it.

In October 1974 the Commission submitted a proposal for a Council decision on the reduction of pollution caused by certain dangerous substances discharged into the aquatic environment of the Community.[23] This proposal aimed at standardizing the provisions contained in the international Conventions (Paris, Strasbourg and the Convention for the protection of the Rhine against chemical pollution) and coordinating them with the Community's programme of action on the environment. The European Parliament welcomed this proposal on the basis of Mr. Premoli's report[24] in its resolution of 13 December 1974.[25]

In this resolution it:
- approved the time limits laid down for the application of the various limiting values and the use of the qualified majority in Council deliberations on this subject;
- called on the Member States to forward to the Commission the inventory of proposed discharges into the aquatic environment of the Community not later than 31 December 1975;
- hoped that Member States would extend their global approach to all other aquatic problems.

In February 1975 the Commission submitted a proposal for a directive relating to pollution of sea water and fresh water for bathing (quality objectives).[26] It started from the premise that it was essential for the protection of the environment and public health to protect water from pollution and to clean up polluted bathing water. To do so, Member States were obliged to lay down limit values corresponding to certain parameters for water including bathing water, so that bathing waters would conform to the quality criteria within eight years after the entry into force of this directive. On the basis of a report by Mr. Premoli,[27] the European Parliament, in its resolution of 13 May 1975,[28] approved the proposal for a directive as a whole, considering it as a useful instrument for the realization of the European Community's quality goals in the field of improvement in the conditions of life and the harmonious development of economic activities. But it also:

– regretted that the omission concerning bathing in swimming pools had not been rectified, given the serious danger of the transmission of infectious diseases;
– proposed that bathing be strictly forbidden in water with a higher level of pollution than that stipulated in the directive;
– felt that the provisions concerning the quality criteria of water intended for bathing should be extended by Community measures to improve quality and by Community financing for the purchase by local communities of diffusers and purifiers;
– proposed that in view of the correlation between sea pollution and tourism the Community should align itself with international organizations with a view to introducing on a general basis the protective measures laid down in this directive.

On the basis of a motion for a resolution tabled by Mr. W. Müller on behalf of the Committee on Public Health and the Environment,[29] the European Parliament adopted on 20 June 1975 an important resolution on the acute danger of further pollution of the Rhine.[30] In the motion it regretted that despite the constantly increasing pollution of the Rhine, which, with the rising temperature of the summer, could lead to the breakdown of the ecological balance in some parts of the Rhine in 1975, the previous negotiations between the Member States had produced no effective results. It therefore called on the Commission to offer to act as intermediary between the three riparian states of the Rhine, France, Germany and the Netherlands, all members of the Community, with a view to achieving agreement on immediate, practical and coordinated measures to avert the impending disaster. It further urged the Parliament of these three Member States to give their full support to the Commission in its role as intermediary so that the necessary measures could be brought into effect as soon as possible. It further proposed that the possibility should be investigated of providing Community financial support for specific projects to assist the construction of purification plant and other suitable equipment at the most seriously threatened points of the Rhine.

Finally, it requested the Commission to intensify its participation in the work of the International Commission on the Protection of the Rhine against Pollution.

In the debate it was pointed out that the relevant bodies could learn valuable lessons from the United Kingdom's experiences in cleaning up the Thames 10–15 years ago. It was also regretted that the problem which has existed for some years now of the discharge into the Rhine of waste salts resulting from the exploitation of the Alsace potash mines had still not been solved. The construction of an underground disposal pit was recommended so that the salt could be put back into mine shafts. The Commission pointed out in the debate that there was no reason for them to intensify their activities, since these were continuing.

A further step taken by the European Parliament, not least with the aim of purifying rivers, was the resolution of 13 January 1976 on the conditions for a Community policy on the siting of nuclear power stations taking account of their acceptability for the population.[31] In this resolution, based on a wide-ranging report by Mrs. Walz,[32] attention was once again drawn to the danger of the thermal pollution of rivers by the discharge from nuclear power stations. Here the view was taken that the problems connected with the use of cooling towers (dry and wet processes) needed thorough examination.

In July 1975 the Commission submitted a proposal for a directive on waste from the titanium dioxide industry.[33] This should contribute substantially to the reduction of the pollution of watercourses, lakes and the sea caused by waste substances from the titanium dioxide industry. On the basis of a report by Mr. Premoli,[34] the European Parliament adopted a resolution[35] on 13 January 1976 in which the proposal for a directive was welcomed as a further step forward in the fight against environmental pollution by certain sectors of industry. Parliament regretted, however, that in its proposal the Commission had not taken account of the request expressed earlier by the European Parliament for detailed quality objectives for the environment to be laid down on a regional basis. It also asked the Commission to investigate the possibility of reducing the transitional period from ten to eight years, since the overall level of marine pollution called for speedy action by the Member States. Finally, it urged the Commission to reformulate the authorization procedure so that it took the final decision itself on the coordination and supervision of the discharge of waste and ensured that the characteristics of the various watercourses, lakes and seas into which waste was discharged were homogeneous in all the Member States.

In July 1975 the Commission also submitted a proposal for a directive relating to the quality of water for human consumption.[36] It aimed at setting standards for the quality of water intended for human consumption in order to ensure greater and more effective protection of public health. In its resolution of 15 January 1976[37] based on a report by Lord Bethell,[38] the European Parliament approved the proposal for a directive but urged the Commission to ensure that analyses of the water, particularly microbiological analyses, should be carried out frequently enough to provide sufficient protection for the health of the population and that a continuous check on the presence of bacteria and certain dangerous substances should be carried out. Furthermore, the hope was expressed that the fixing of Exceptional Maximum Admissible Concentrations should be subject to overall limits and bear relation to the particular conditions of the locality. Finally, the Commission was requested to complete as soon as possible its study of analytical methods for a number of parameters and to notify Member States of the results at the same time as they were notified of this directive.

In the debate it was requested that the limitation of certain elements should be extended to mineral waters. Their composition should in any case be stated on the bottle.

The question of the addition of fluoride compounds to drinking water to combat tooth decay was also raised. The Commission had, however, taken no official position on this matter.

Finally, it should be noted that the European Parliament had not only delivered an opinion on the Commission's proposals but also on the petition submitted by individuals pursuant to Rule 48 of the Rules of Procedure.

This was the case with Petition No. 3/74 of May 1974 which Mr. Virgile

Barel tabled on the protection of the Mediterranean.[39] In the petition, the lack of social conscience of the directors of the Montedison Company was particularly criticized; they were poisoning the north-western part of the Mediterranean by the discharge of harmful substances, in particular by the "red mud" effluent from the production of titanium dioxide in the Scarlino factories. It was therefore proposed to urge the states bordering on the Mediterranean and industrial undertakings to put an end to the imminent pollution of the environment, of which, in the last analysis, they themselves would be the victims, alongside effective supplementary measures which, however, could not be implemented at a moment's notice.

On the basis of a report by Mr. Premoli[40] on behalf of the Committee on Public Health and the Environment, the European Parliament in its resolution of 10 March 1975[41] drew the attention of the Community institutions to the danger which the high level of pollutions in the Mediterranean represented to the flora and fauna as well as to the peoples living along its shores. The hope was also expressed that the Council would shortly approve the proposal for a directive on the limitation of discharges into the sea of titanium dioxide waste and of all other similarly polluting substances.

In the explanatory statement it was furthermore pointed out that in view of the increasing pollution of beaches, as evidenced by serious infections to which children in particular are subject, greater attention should be paid to cleaning up the beaches and to setting up sanitary installations.

Finally on 24 March 1976 the Commission submitted a draft resolution and a report on the continuation and implementation of a European Community policy and action programme on the environment.[42] This comprehensive document is at present being considered by the Committee on the Environment, Public Health and Consumer Protection as the committee responsible. There also exists a draft report[43] which Mr. Jahn drew up on behalf of this committee. In it the following position was taken on the Commission's programme relating to the protection of rivers and watercourses.

It was noted with satisfaction that the Community's work in the field of the prevention and reduction of the pollution of fresh and sea water concentrated on the following topics:
– the setting up of quality objectives for water;
– joint research to establish minimum quality requirements which would be satisfactory in the long term;
– the exchange of information between the surveillance and monitoring networks dealing with water pollution in the Community;
– the prevention and reduction of marine pollution from land-based sources;
– the application of international conventions on fresh water which the Community had signed or was to sign;
– steps to ensure the collaboration in programming the construction of water treatment plants and pollution monitoring and control stations.

In the motion for a resolution the committee stated that it:
– considered that the action so far taken by the Commission to prevent pollution of the Rhine was inadequate and reiterated its request for the Community to act on its own and adopt immediate concrete measures;
– considered it desirable for the Commission to concentrate its efforts aimed at solving the problems of water distribution and purity primarily on

concrete proposals for the transfrontier areas where there was an urgent need for the rational coordination of measures.

The Commission was also called upon to give priority to measures for limiting the absorption of nutrients by ground and surface water and to submit appropriate proposals by 1977 at the latest, since their implementation was urgently necessary for the protection of public health. The committee also stressed that the preliminary studies, investigations and research at present being carried out or planned must lead rapidly to concrete proposals for directives, in particular on the prevention of overheating caused by thermal discharge from power stations and the subsequent eutrophication of the Community's rivers. The Council was finally requested to adopt as soon as possible the proposal for a directive on waste materials resulting from the production of titanium dioxide, taking account of the demands made by the European Parliament, so that the proposed measures could be put into effect at an early date.

The final paragraph of the motion for a resolution made the concrete request that the Commission submit a suitably amended and completed proposal for the Second Environment Protection Programme, taking into account the comments contained in the report.

The written questions submitted by individual Members of Parliament, especially those by members of the Committee on the Environment, Public Health and Consumer Protection, pursuant to Rule 45 of the Rules of Procedure, also belong with the European Parliament's opinions. A comparatively large proportion of these questions has been devoted to problems of environmental protection in general and the protection of water resources in particular. They clearly demonstrate the wide public interest in these problems.

Finally, it should be noted that the Commission is, in general, receptive to the requests made by the European Parliament and complies with them to a large extent. The difficulties arise, however, in keeping to deadlines, since the Commission has at its disposal neither sufficient staff nor adequate financial resources to carry out the numerous tasks imposed on it concerning the protection of water resources.

On the other hand it must be deplored that the Council, which has the key role as the decision-making institution of the European Communities, only relatively rarely takes account of the requests made by the European Parliament.

NOTES

1. Doc. 161/70.
2. OJ No. C 143, 3.12.1970, p. 30.
3. No. 14/71.
4. Official Journal of the European Communities, Annex, No. 144, p. 48.
5. Doc. 223/71, OJ No. C 2, 11.1.1972, p. 22.
6. Doc. 15/72.
7. OJ No. C 46, 9.5.1972, p. 13.
8. Doc. 9/72, Doc. 74/72, and Doc. 106/73.

9. OJ No. C 46, 9.5.1972, p. 10.
10. OJ No. C 82, 26.7.1972, p. 42.
11. OJ No. C 62, 31.7.1973, p. 16.
12. Doc. 26/72.
13. OJ No. C 112, 20.12.1973.
14. Doc. 280/73.
15. OJ No. C 2, 9.1.1974, p. 59.
16. Doc. 284/73.
17. OJ No. C 76, 7.4.1975, p. 34.
18. Doc. 516/74.
19. Doc. 471/74.
20. Doc. 350/73.
21. Doc. 87/74.
22. OJ No. C 62, 30.5.1974, p. 7.
23. Doc. 334/74.
24. Doc. 393/74.
25. OJ No. C 5, 8.1.1975, p. 62.
26. Doc. 507/74.
27. Doc. 53/75.
28. OJ No. C 128, 9.6.1975, p. 13.
29. Doc. 116/75.
30. OJ No. C 157, 14.7.1975, p. 91.
31. OJ No. C 28, 9.2.1976, p. 12.
32. Doc. 392/75.
33. Doc. 213/75.
34. Doc. 457/75.
35. OJ No. C 28, 9.2.1976, p. 16.
36. Doc. 225/75.
37. OJ No. C 28, 9.2.1976, p. 27.
38. Doc. 418/75.
39. See Bulletin of the European Parliament No. 10/74.
40. Doc. 386/74.
41. OJ No. C 76, 7.4.1975, p. 7.
42. Doc. 51/76.
43. PE 44.545/res. and PE 44.545/Part B.

III. ENVIRONMENT POLICY COUNTER-REPORT

European Policy of Protection of Rivers and Water against Pollution

by *C. A. Colliard*

We shall discuss here the activity of the European Community in the field of the fight against the pollution of rivers and water. This activity must be seen in the context of the action programme of the European Communities in questions of environment adopted by the Council on 22 November 1973.

It must be recognized that the Commission had expressed its interest in the problems of the environment long before that. Already in July 1971, the Commission noted the importance of such problems as the purification of streams and rivers like the Rhine and its tributaries which cross the territories of several Member States, or the fight against the pollution of seas such as the Mediterranean or the North Sea, which it considered as "forming a common capital for all the Member States". Again, in March 1972, the Commission sketched the broad lines of an action programme with the purpose of establishing common standards of health and of defining the common qualitative objectives.

This study will concentrate on the different actions taken by the Commission, which is the moving spirit of the Community.

But a word must be said about the actions which we shall examine. In a document entitled "Communication of the Commission to the Council on the progress of the action-programme of the European Communities in matters of environment", a programme to 15 November 1976, three themes are put forward. The first is the "fight against pollution". The second "the improvement of the environment". The third deals with the action of the European Communities and of the Member States, within international organizations, conferences and conventions. The present report is limited to the question of the fight against pollution and within it, the pollution of rivers and water.

A preliminary remark must be made here. The fight against pollution is carried on separately by the Member States themselves and by the European Communities. While in the Communities the main action is that carried out by the Commission, the Member States themselves use their own legislative and administrative powers and participate in the different international actions against pollution. In our study we shall draw a distinction between two large areas of the environment policy of the Communities. The first is the area of the fight against pollution at the internal level of each Member State as well as at the Community level. The second is that of the fight against pollution at the international level. In both cases the national and the Community action are interwoven, but the ways in which the Community and the Member States co-operate are different.

COMMUNITY POLICY AT THE INTERNAL COMMUNITY LEVEL

Here we must distinguish between the action undertaken by the Member States with the knowledge of the Community, and the Community action which provides a general framework for action.

INFORMATION AND KNOWLEDGE OF THE COMMUNITY

On 5 March 1973, an "agreement of the representatives of the Member States" was concluded, for the future harmonization within the Community of measures concerning the protection of the environment. The principal provision of this text is the one which allows the Commission which has been informed of the legislative, procedural and administrative measures which a Member State is proposing to take in matters of the protection of the environment and which might have a bearing on the functioning of the Common Market, to announce within two months to all the Member States its intention to make proposals at Community level. The situation thus created is that of the subordination of the national to the Community interest, with the exception of urgent cases for grave health or security reasons.

The procedure established by the 5 March 1973 agreement completed and improved by a similar agreement of 15 July 1974 has worked satisfactorily as far as the information to be provided by the Member States is concerned. Thus, for all the measures of protection of the environment the Commission had received by 1 July 1976 a total of 147 notifications as follows:

TABLE 1

Member States	Projects of Provisions	Provisions in force	International Agreements	Various	Total
Belgium	1	3	1	—	5
Denmark	1	24	4	—	29
Germany	28	2	2	2	34
France	26	6	3	6	41
Eire	2	—	—	—	2
Italy	4	—	2	—	6
The Netherlands	6	17	—	—	23
Luxembourg	1	—	—	—	1
United Kingdom	6	—	—	—	6
Total	75	52	12	8	147

The question of pollution of water and rivers formed the most important part of this total with 44 texts. At the end of 1976 more than 160 texts had been communicated. Out of these, 40 notifications were made by the Member States. It can be seen that the information side of the March 1973 and July 1974 agreements worked well.

But the Commission withheld only one national text as prescribed in Articles 2 and 3 of the 1973 Agreement, and this was with regard to aircraft noise. The fact that the Commission did not more often use its right to replace a national action by a Community action, is partly explained by the circumstance that the notification takes place at a moment when the proceedings at the national level are already very advanced, if not finalized. At that moment, the Commission does not find it possible or useful to ask the Member State to withhold measures which it has already taken, and to start new proceedings at the Community level. This is important to bear in mind, especially, as we shall see later, the texts adopted or even proposed at the Community level are obviously fewer than the total number of national texts.

THE COMMUNITY ACTION

The Community action is generally organized along the following lines. The Commission singles out one of the problems in the fight against the pollution of water and rivers. Then the Commission directs a group of experts to study it, with a view to proposing a solution to the problem.

Once the solution is proposed, the official way by which the Community action is normally taken, for the formulation of rules, is the directive. The directive, and its procedure, allow the Community to announce its objectives and to put forward a well-defined Community point of view, while leaving the Member States free to choose the way in which they will intervene.

Only exceptionally is a decision taken, therefore replacing the usual directive; and the procedure of regulations is not used in matters of pollution.

By directives we mean the directives of the Council. They are drawn up in a procedure with several stages. At the beginning of the procedure, there is a proposal of directive made by the Commission to the Council. Once the directive is proposed, then the consultative procedure starts, the Council asking for the opinion of the European Assembly and of the Economic and Social Committee. When it has received these opinions, the Council formally adopts the text of the directive. The initial proposals are published in the Official Journal of the European Communities in the part "Communications and Information" while the directive is published in the part "Legislation". The Community action can be analysed by following the different stages.

The work of the organs of the community

In the commission
Among the different problems which the Commission itself is considering, either at the stage of the meetings of experts or at the later stages of the formulation of a draft proposal, one should note:
1. in the matter of qualitative objectives:
– the quality of water for agricultural use;
– the protection of aquatic life in general;
– the quality of industrial water;

– the methods of measurement and frequent sampling of the surface water for the abstraction of drinking water;

2. in the matter of reducing the pollution by dangerous substances discharged into water:

– the protection of ground water from dangerous substances;
– the fixing of restricted values and qualitative objectives; for substances on the "black list" regarding discharge into the aquatic element.

3. in the matter of actions peculiar to some industries:

– the reduction of the pollution of water by the steel industry;
– by the petro-chemical industry;
– by tanning.

The draft directives presented by the commission
It is interesting to specify the exact state of progress of the procedure for each text.

1. In the matter of qualitative objectives:

– three texts of proposals have been presented by the Commission to the Council. The first proposal regards the quality of drinking water. The text was presented by the Commission to the Council on 31 July 1975. The European Parliament gave its opinion in a resolution of 15 January 1976, published in the OJ "Communications C 28/27 of 9 February 1976". The Parliament made a number of changes in five articles out of thirteen and asked its own special Commission *carefully* to see that the Commission had modified its texts accordingly and to report back to it on this subject. The Economic and Social Council was asked by the Council for its opinion on 11 August 1975. The opinion was given on 25–26 February 1976 and was published in the OJ Communications No. C/131 of 12 June 1976.

The definitive text has not yet been adopted although the initial proposal is dated 31 July 1975.

– A second draft directive concerning the quality of fresh water suitable for fish life was presented to the Council by the Commission on 2 August 1976. The European Parliament gave its opinion on it in a resolution of 14 January 1977, published in the OJ Communication C/30 of 7 February 1977 which expresses its agreement in general. The Economic and Social Committee expressed its opinion on 23–24 February 1977. The text published in the OJC of 30 March 1977 gives a favourable opinion, adopted by a remarkably large majority. Here again the Council had not yet adopted a final position.

– A third text must be mentioned. It concerns the common procedure of exchange of information with regard to the quality of surface fresh water in the Community. It is a draft decision and not a draft directive. The text was presented by the Commission to the Council on 4 May 1976. On 8 July 1976 the European Parliament (OJC 178 2 August 1976) gave its opinion with a few changes to be made. On 12 May 1976, the Council sent it to the Economic and Social Committee which gave a unanimous opinion on 29–30 September 1976. Although the procedure in the consultative phase was particularly rapid, the Council however has not yet adopted a final decision.

2. In matters of the reduction of pollution by dangerous substances discharged in water, the Commission has not sent to the Council proposals concerning fresh water. But it has sent to the Council a draft directive

416

concerning the dumping of waste into the sea. It was sent to the Council on 12 January 1976, approved by the European Parliament on 19 November 1976 and was published in the OJC 239 of 13 December 1976. The approval of the Parliament contains some modifications of Appendices 1 and 2, the object of which is that the list of products which should be discharged under given conditions, should closely coincide with the similar provisions of the international conventions in force. The Council decided on 21 January 1976 to consult the Economic and Social Committee, which gave its unanimous opinion on 25–26 May 1976, published in the OJC 197 of 23 August 1976. Although over a year has elapsed since the Commission made its proposals the Council has not yet formally adopted the directive. It must be noticed that the problem of the discharge of waste into the sea, can be solved only by taking into consideration the different international conventions which have been signed by the Member States of the European Community and which are now being ratified. A draft proposal on the quality necessary for water in which shellfish are raised was presented by the Commission to the Council on 5 November 1976 OJC 283 of 30 November 1976. No information is available on the progress of the consultative procedure of this proposal.

3. In matters of actions specific to certain industrial branches:
– two particularly important proposals have been sent by the Commission to the Council. The first with regard to the reduction of the pollution of water by paper-pulp factories in the Member States was presented on 20 January 1975. The European Parliament gave its opinion on 12 May 1975, published in the OJC No. C 111 of 20 May 1975. The opinion was favourable and, moreover, expressed a certain regret because of the delays caused by the Commission in the execution of the action programme. The Social and Economic Committee informed on 28 January 1975 gave its opinion on 23–24 April 1975. The text of this proposal is important. Yet it has not been transformed into a final directive by the Council.

The second proposal concerns the waste produced by the titanium dioxide industry. It was sent to the Council on 18 July 1975. The European Parliament gave its opinion on 13 January 1976, with only two requests for changes in all thirteen articles and two appendices. But the changes asked for by the Parliament are important, especially those with reference to Article 4, insofar as the Parliament would prefer the Commission to give the authorization for discharge after consultation with the authorities of the Member States and not to entrust, as the draft directive suggested, the national authorities with the final approval. It is also significant that the Parliament asked its own appropriate commission to see that the Commission had made the changes which it demanded. The Economic and Social Committee, informed on 29 July 1975, gave its unanimous opinion on 25–26 February 1976. The opinion expressed, however, some anxiety regarding the risk of reducing the international conpetitiveness of the enterprises within the Community, if a general international action were not undertaken at the same time. Although the Council has had this opinion for over a year, it has not yet taken a final decision.

The directives in force
Three directives are presently in force. Two deal with qualitative objectives

417

and the third with the reduction of waste pollution by the dangerous substances.

Qualitative objectives

A directive regarding the quality of surface water for the abstraction of drinking water in the Member States was presented by the Commission to the Council on 21 January 1974. The European Parliament issued a Resolution on 13 May 1974, published in the OJC 62 of 30 May 1974. The observations tend to make it stricter, especially so far as radioactive pollution is concerned. But, otherwise, the Resolution is favourable to the directive. The Economic and Social Committee, informed by the Council on 28 January 1974, gave its opinion on 29–30 May 1974. The Committee's opinion was adopted by a vote of hands and unanimously by the Parliament, which made only a few observations. The opinion was published in the OJC No. 109 of 19 September 1974 and the final Directive of the Council, issued on 16 June 1975 was published in the OJL No. 194 of 25 July 1975. It is to be noticed that the title of the final directive is slightly different. Whereas the proposal of the Commission concerned the quality of surface water for the abstraction of drinking water in the Member States, the 16 June 1975 Directive spoke of the quality required for surface water for the abstraction of water for human consumption in the Member States.

Another directive with regard to the pollution of the sea and fresh water for bathing (qualitative objective) was sent by the Commission to the Council on 7 February 1975 (OJC 67 of 22 March 1975). It was embodied in a Resolution containing the opinion of the European Parliament on 13 May 1975, published in the OJC 128 of 8 June 1975. The Parliament approved the action thus undertaken and only expressed regret for the fact that the Resolution did not cover sufficiently the problem of bathing in swimming pools. The Council informed the Economic and Social Committee on 17 February 1975 which gave its unanimous opinion on 24–25 September 1975, which was published in the OJC No. 286 of 15 September 1975. The Council's Directive was issued on 8 December 1975 and was published in the OJL No. 31 of 5 February 1976. Here, too, there is a slight change in the title, because the Directive is said to concern the quality of bathing water.

Reduction of the pollution

The problem of the reduction of the pollution caused by dangerous substances discharged into the Community water was dealt with in a draft decision of the Commission presented to the Council on 22 October 1974 and published in the OJC No. 12 of 17 January 1975. By a Resolution of 13 December 1974, published in the OJC of 8 January 1975, the European Parliament approved the draft decision stressing favourably the fact that it co-ordinated the provisions of a great number of conventions concerning the use of water.

The Economic and Social Committee was consulted, following a Decision of the Council of 31 October 1974 and gave its opinion on 26–27 February 1975. The opinion unanimously approved the draft directive, but with some reservations. It must be noticed that the text initially presented by the Commission was a draft *decision* and that the European Parliament gave its opinion on a *decision*. But the Social and Economic Committee showed a certain hesitation in its opinion. It approved a draft *directive*, but then discussed the purposes of a *decision* in this matter. A more careful examination of the opinion as a whole leads to the conclusion that the Committee thought that the observations which it made referred to a text which should take the form of a directive. The text finally adopted by the Council on 4 May 1976 and published in the OJL 129 of 18 May 1976 is entitled *directive*. This is a text of particular importance.

Considerations on the procedure of community actions

The procedure of the actions of the Community can be examined from the point of view of its effectiveness, as well as from that of the time taken by the procedure required for the adoption of a text.

The effectiveness of the procedure

The procedure of the adoption of a text starts with the draft of the Commission and ends with the adoption of the text by the Council. Between these initial and these final phases there is also a consultative phase, which is twofold insofar as both the European Parliament and the Economic and Social Committee must be consulted. The opinions of these two organs are published in the Official Journal ("Communications and Information", as is the text initially submitted by the Commission). There is a considerable interval between the presentation by the Commission of a text to the Council and the publication in the OJC of the same text. The ten texts, which we have looked into, show variations of delays in publication of between a minimum of twenty days and a maximum of more than two months.

But more interesting than the delays in publication, which may be due to the accumulation of material at the OJ, is the measurement of the interval between the different stages of the procedure itself.

A first interval occurs between the moment when the Commission's proposal arrives at the Council and the moment when the Council asks the consultative organs for their opinion. It is difficult to know the exact date when the European Parliament is asked by the President of the Council to give an opinion, because that date does not appear in the Journal. What appears in each of the reports is the date when they were presented to Parliament. It is easier to measure the time-lags in the work of the Economic and Social Committee, because it includes in its texts in the OJ the date when it was consulted. This time-lag is generally very short, at the most some ten days.

Once the consultative organs have been informed, there starts the internal procedure of either the Parliament or the Economic and Social Committee. Normally this procedure begins by sending the proposal to a competent Commission. Both the Parliament and the Economic and Social Committee have commissions for the environment, public health and the protection of consumers. In the Parliament, the legal commission is also concomitantly consulted. Each of these commissions appoints a rapporteur. After a few partial deliberations, the general deliberation on the basis of the report by the rapporteur takes place.

419

The intervals between the date when the consultative organ was informed and the date when it issues its opinion is between four and six months. The variations are due sometimes to the importance of the question but also to the amount of work that each of these two organs have on hand. Once the text is adopted, it is published in the OJC with some delay in publication. The data contained in Table 2 shows in general these variations in delays.

Once the consultative procedure is closed, there starts the final phase during which the Council adopts the text. This text takes usually the form of a directive and sometimes of a decision and is published in the OJ in the part Legislation. Two major delays can be noticed.

One is the interval between the issuing of the opinion by the competent organ and the adoption of the final text by the Council. This kind of delay is very variable as can be seen from the Table. More delays occur when the text of the opinion shows that there was a division in the votes or that reservations or even criticisms of the text were made. In these cases the Council will be more circumspect. Sometimes the opinion may even contain proposals for changes and very firm invitations to the Commission to observe the changes as we have seen in many of the opinions of the European Parliament. It is obvious that in these conditions the Council will wait for the changes to be incorporated before it adopts the final version.

But one should also measure the lapse of time between the initial proposal of the Commission and the final text. This is more difficult, because, as we have seen, only in three of the ten cases examined was the procedure actually brought to fruition. The delays are very variable. The shortest delay was that with regard to bathing water and the definition of qualitative objectives which lasted from 7 February 1975 (proposal of the Commission) to 8 December (directive of the Council), that is some ten months. In the other two cases the delays were of 17 months and 18 months respectively. If one compares the procedure of the drawing up of a Community decision with that of the same procedure in the legislative processes of a Member State, one must recognize that the processes of the Community are particularly slow.

The course of the procedure
Here we shall examine the legal basis of the consultation of the Parliament and of the Committee, then the voting procedures and finally the contents of the opinion.

The legal basis
Three texts: Articles 100, 198 and 235 of the Treaty of Rome are usually invoked.

Article 235 has been invoked in the draft directive on the following subjects: discharge of dangerous substances into water, surface water destined to the abstraction of water for human consumption, pollution of bathing water (qualitative objective) and quality of the surface fresh water.

Once Parliament was consulted on the basis of Articles 100 and 235, when the subject was the fresh water suitable for fish life.

Otherwise, Article 100 has been invoked in the following draft directives: waste from the titanium dioxide industry, reduction of the pollution of water by the paper-pulp industry, quality of water for human consumption and discharge of waste into the sea.

As far as the Economic and Social Committee is concerned, Article 198 was invoked for: surface water, this time for human consumption, discharge of dangerous substances into water and quality of the fresh surface water. For the other seven cases, Article 100 was invoked.

Voting procedures

The voting procedures for the Resolution in the Parliament are not very precise. The texts published in the OJ mention the fact that the opinion has been adopted, without giving any details about the voting procedures. What is mentioned is whether modifications have been proposed or not.

More details are given about the proceedings of the Economic and Social Committee. Thus, it is known that the following opinions have been adopted unanimously: discharge of dangerous substances into water, pollution of water for bathing, waste from the titanium dioxide industry, discharge of waste into the sea and quality of fresh surface water. In the other three cases, the opinion was given on a majority vote, the most argued of which was that of the quality of water for human consumption, which obtained forty votes for, eight against and three abstentions.

In conclusion, as far as the Community action at the internal Community level is concerned, we see that since the Community adopted an Environmental policy in November 1973, more than 10 draft directives have been produced by the Commission.

The Commission's initiative in this question must be fully acknowledged. Everything that the Commission did as far as the protection of rivers and water is concerned, was not based on national initiatives.

But on the other hand it must be said, first, that the action of the Commission, praiseworthy as it may be, remains, from a numerical point of view, very limited when compared with the total number of national actions. Then it must be noticed that only three directives have been adopted by the Council or that, in other words, only one-third of the proposals have reached the stage of a final formulation in Community law.

Thirdly, the time-lag between the proposal made by the Commission and the issuing of the directive being, as seen, of between one year and nineteen months—this is obviously a very slow procedure.

In the appended table it can be seen very clearly that while the consultative procedure is effected in a normal time the cause of the major delays lies with the Council. Besides, it is hard to distinguish the delay from what is, at the end, either a silent refusal or the lack of a final decision. In most of the cases that were surveyed here, more than two years have lapsed since the final opinion was issued and yet no final decision has been reached.

These examples are very significant. The Council which is a political organ blocks the solution of all problems which are particularly sensitive and to which some of the Member States attach a particular importance. What is more, because the Council does not even possess specialized commissions in this field, it is difficult to assess its method of work. Such commissions should be created.

As far as the consultative organs, the European Assembly and the Social and Economic Committee are concerned, it was seen and the appended table confirms that their proceedings are rather satisfactory. It can, however, be remarked that the intervention of the Economic and Social Committee is more suited to these requirements than that of the Assembly. The reports are better organized and the texts as published in the OJ are much more precise. The publication of the opinions of the Assembly give hardly any details. The way of publicizing the opinions of the Assembly could certainly be improved.

But also when it comes to the substance, it must be noticed that the opinions of the Committee are more solid and better argued than those of the Assembly. It is true that, on the other hand, the Assembly seems to be much more favourably inclined towards the defence of the environment than the Committee which is, often, for obvious reasons, more sensitive to the economic considerations and especially to the problem of the international competitiveness of the industries of the Member States.

One could wish that the Assembly would choose better rapporteurs, who would know in greater depth the problems of the environment. This will be even more necessary in a Parliament directly elected by universal suffrage, for it must recognize that one cannot expect too much from the current members of the Assembly whose essential interests are still linked with the national parliaments.

COMMUNITY POLICY IN MATTERS OF THE FIGHT AGAINST POLLUTION AT THE INTERNATIONAL LEVEL

The Community action at the international level was laid down in the first programme in matters of environment, adopted in November 1973. In the first part, concerning the actions aiming at reducing pollution and nuisance, the programme is concerned with the pollution of the sea and with the participation of the Community in the conference on land-based pollution which was held in September 1973.

The programme was concerned also with the participation of the Com-

TABLE 2. *Draft Proposals and Decisions of the Commission in Matters of Pollution c*

Object	Date of presentation	Publication O.J.C.	Information European Parliament	Opinio European Parliame
Potable water	21 Jan. 74	Nr. 44: 19 Apr. 74	29 Jan. 74	13 May
Discharge of dangerous substances into water	22 Oct. 74	Nr. 12: 17 Jan. 75	4 Nov. 74	13 Dec.
Pollution of water by paper-pulp industry	20 Jan. 75	Nr. 99: 2 May 75	29 Jan. 75	12 May
Bathing water	7 Feb. 75	Nr. 67: 22 Mar. 75	18 Feb. 75	13 May
Dioxide of titanium	18 July 75	Nr. 222: 29 Sept. 75	30 July 75	13 Jan.
Water for human consumption	31 July 75	Nr. 214: 18 Sept. 75	11 Aug. 75	15 Jan.
Discharge of waste in the sea	12 Jan. 76	Nr. 40: 20 Feb. 76	22 Jan. 76	19 Nov.
Quality of fresh surface water	4 May 76	Nr. 133: 14 June 76	13 May 75	8 July 7
Fresh water suitable for fish life	2 Apr. 76	Nr. 202: 28 Apr. 76	12 Aug. 76	14 Jan.
Quality of conchylicolisal water	5 Nov. 76	Nr. 283: 30 Nov.76		

munity in the fight against the pollution of the Rhine. But the third part of the programme also shows the intention of the Community to give a broader dimension to its action by adopting an international role, whereby it could be associated with the action of the different international organizations or whereby it could be made to co-operate with the Member States. This international action is particularly interesting, but it does present some difficulties. One of these difficulties derives from the fact that the Community action started only in 1973 and became noticeable only much later. But then the great international conventions against the pollution of the sea were concluded before 1973, with the exception of the London Conference of November 1973. The Community did not take a part in the drawing up of the Oslo (February 1972) and of the London (December 1972) Conventions.

The Community action was therefore effective only in conventions which have been signed after the end of 1973. This observation must be qualified in the sense that it applies especially to the pollution of the sea because for river pollution, and notably to the case of the Rhine, the Community action had a somehow retroactive character insofar as the Commission proposed and obtained the adherence of the Community to a text which had been concluded long before. The Community policy can be looked at as, on the one hand, a presence and, on the other, as a participation in international actions. This takes different forms. One is the participation in international negotiations resulting in the conclusion of a treaty. Another is the adherence to a treaty previously concluded. Yet a third is the participation in the activity of international institutions created by a treaty.

Insofar as all these characteristics appear together and are interlocked, the best way to study them is by looking at each treaty separately and to see how the Community action made itself felt. But a further remark must be made here. This is that the Commission has not participated in the drawing up of the treaties of the first conventions concerning the accidental pollution of the sea (Oslo and London 1972) and that the requirements laid down at the time

ter and Rivers

Publication of Opinion	Information Economic and Social Committee	Opinion Committee	Publication O.J.C.	Directive Council	Publication O.J.L.
52: 30 May 74	28 Jan. 74	29–30 May 74	Nr. 109: 19 Sept. 74	16 June 75	Nr. 194: 25 July 75
5: 8 Jan. 75	31 Oct. 74	26–27 Feb. 75	Nr. 108: 15 May 75	4 May 76	L 129: 18 May 76
11: 20 May 75	28 Jan. 75	23–24 Apr. 75	Nr. 248: 29 Oct. 75		
28: 9 June 75	17 Feb. 75	24–25 Sept. 75	Nr. 286: 15 Dec. 75	8 Dec. 75	Nr. 31: 5 Feb. 76
28: 9 Feb. 76	29 July 75	25–26 Feb. 76	Nr. 131: 12 June 76		
8: 9 Feb. 76	11 Apr. 75	25–26 Feb. 76	Nr. 131: 12 June 76		
293: 13 Dec. 76	21 Jan. 76	25–26 May 76	Nr. 197: 23 Oct. 76		
78: 2 Oct. 76	12 May 76	29–30 Sept. 76	Nr. 285: 2 Dec. 76		
0: 7 Feb. 77	11 Aug. 76	23–24 Feb. 77	Nr. 77: 30 Mar. 77		

by the European Parliament in this matter have had no follow up. But there are other examples of international conventions or systems for the protection of the environment on which the Community action had a greater impact.

Examples of community action

One must distinguish between the Community action against sea pollution and against river pollution.

Sea pollution
Three fields of action of the Community can be considered here. The first concerns land-based pollution and has a general character. The other two are geographically defined and limited: the Mediterranean and the Baltic Sea. A few remarks will be made about the conference on the law of the sea in the framework of the United Nations.
Land-based pollution. The pollution of the sea by the direct discharge from the shore, by rivers and by estuaries was not dealt with by the London and Oslo Conventions of 1972.

The participation of the Community at a conference called to conclude a treaty for protection against land-based pollution originated in an invitation sent to the Commission at a meeting of the Council of 19 July 1973, when the environment action programme of the Community was adopted. The invitation was sent by the French Minister for the Environment. The object was a diplomatic conference called by the French Government and which was held in Paris from 17–23 September 1973, with most European countries taking part, The Commission took part in the conference as an observer, as did the Council of Europe and the United Nations Organization. During this first session the Netherlands presented a draft article which proposed that the convention should be opened also to the signature of the Community. But no decision was taken at the time.

On 12 November 1973, the Commission submitted to the Council a draft decision concerning the participation of the European Communities in the negotiations for that particular convention. The Council accepted the proposal. It authorized the Commission to join the conference together with the Member States. It asked the latter to adopt a common attitude and to work with the Commission and it invited the Commission to inform the third countries of its role in the negotiations. The conference ended on 22 February 1974 by adopting a "convention for the prevention of land-based sea pollution".

Article 22 stated that the convention was open from 4 June 1974 to 30 June 1975 to the signature of the states which had been invited to the Paris Conference *as well as to the signature of the European Economic Community*. The convention also stated in its Article 19 that "in the fields where it is competent, the EEC has a right to vote with a number of votes equal to the number of its Member States who are parties to the present convention". The second paragraph of Article 19 stated that the EEC could not use this right to vote in the cases in which the Member States used their right to vote, and vice versa. Thus, the convention recognized the Community in its own right.

424

The Council decided on 3 March 1975 that the convention should be concluded by the European Community and that its President would appoint the persons authorized to sign the convention and give them the powers to commit the Community. The same text shows that the Community is represented by the Commission, within the commission formed by Article 15 of the Paris Convention and that the Commission will put forward the point of view of the Community in accordance with the directives which it will receive from the Council. The signature by the Community took place on 23 June 1975. The Member States, with the exception of Italy had already signed it. It must also be mentioned that the decision of 3 March 1975 had been taken by the Council on the basis of Article 235 which requires the opinion of the European Assembly but not that of the Economic and Social Committee. Article 235 is the operative text for the intervention of the European Assembly.

The protection of the Mediterranean. The problem of the protection of the Mediterranean from pollution was discussed in an intergovernmental conference which was held in Barcelona from 28 January–4 February 1975 in the framework of the programme of the United Nations for Environment. This was followed by a meeting of legal experts held in Geneva in April 1975 for the preparation of a draft convention.

The Commission of the European Community expressed its belief that the Community should take part in its own right, together with two of her Member States, France and Italy, in the intergovernmental meeting in Barcelona in February 1976, and that for reasons similar to those which made it participate in the Paris Convention, it should take part in this new convention as well. Moreover, it pointed out that both conventions were concerned with the problem of land-based pollution. On 28 May 1975, the Commission sent to the Council a draft decision to authorize this participation. The Council gave a decision on 8 December 1975 to this effect. This enabled the Commission to send to the two Member States who were to go to the Barcelona Conference a recommendation dated 19 December 1975. It recommended that in the case in which the negotiations would lead to the conclusion of a protocol concerning the prevention in the Mediterranean of land-based pollution of the sea of origin, its clauses should be inspired *mutatis mutandis* by those of the Paris Convention.

The motivations of the action of the Community are easy to understand. One is the need for recognition of the competence of the Community and the other of the need for a coherent and co-ordinated action.

Articles 20 and 24 of the Barcelona Convention of 16 February 1976 refer, among others, to the European Community. But they are rather different from those of the Paris Convention. Thus, Article 24 states that the convention itself and two additional protocols could be signed by the States which took part in the conference, but also by the European Community as well as by "any other similar regional economic group", of which at least one of the members is a Mediterranean riparian State and which has competence in the fields covered by the convention. Therefore, whereas in the Paris Convention, the European Community was alone in the company of the States, the Barcelona Convention evokes the possibility of the presence of another international body. The term a "similar regional economic group" is obviously very vague. And it is inaccurate, if as is manifestly the case, it refs to the League of Arab States, because the League is not an economic grouping nor is it similar.

Article 19 of the convention which deals with the right to vote is almost identical to Article 19 of the Paris Convention. Like the latter, it stipulates that the European Community and any other regional economic group will have a number of votes equal to that of its Member States, which are part of the convention. It also states that the Community will not use its right to vote, when the Member States do and vice versa. Of course, it should be noted that the great difference between the two conventions is that whereas in the Paris Convention all the Member States of the Community, with the exception of Italy took part, only two Member States were members of the Barcelona Convention.

The Commission asked the Council on 6 May 1976 to take a decision for the conclusion of the convention and of a protocol concerning the prevention of pollution in the Mediterranean by shipping and aircraft. The convention and the protocol were signed on 13 September 1976.

Protection of the aquatic environment in the area of the Baltic Sea. On 22 March 1974 Denmark, Finland, the DGR, the GFR, Poland, Sweden and the USSR, all Baltic riparian states, signed at Helsinki a convention on the protection of the aquatic environment in the area of the Baltic.

The European Community had not been invited but neither had it asked to take part, as it had done for the Barcelona Conference.

Nevertheless recently the Commission started a procedure aiming at the participation of the Community in the Helsinki Convention. On 1 October 1976 it sent to this effect a letter to the governments of Denmark and of the Federal German Republic and in March 1977 it sent to the Council a draft decision.

In the letter of 1 October 1976, the Commission reminded the two governments that the Community had adopted several directives concerning the protection of water and in particular the directive on 4 May 1976 concerning the discharge of dangerous substances into the sea. It stressed that the measures adopted at Community level have given to the Community competences which had been withdrawn from the Member States and that the latter could no longer therefore take commitments towards third countries within international conventions concerning the fight against pollution. In consequence, the Community asserted that it should be a party to such conventions because it is incumbent upon it to take this kind of commitment. Moreover, the Commission asked the two Member States not to ratify the convention unless and until the participation of the Community in the convention had been accepted. As a sequel to this, the Commission asked the Council to authorize it to open negotiations with the third countries, parties to the convention of 22 March 1974 with a view to allowing the Community to adhere to that convention. This could entail some modifications of the convention.

Insofar as this proposal was made only on 10 March 1977, it is obviously too early to know what will be the outcome. The reasoning of the Commission is that the Community should be given at the international level the competences which it has at Community level. This is of course a well-known principle in the legal technique of federalism which requires that the international competences should correspond to the competences at the internal federal level. But it is also known that from the legal point of view this technique is both argued and arguable.

Besides it must be recognized that in this case the Commission was quite bold. It asked to start negotiations for the modification of the convention which was not yet in force because only Finland and Sweden had ratified it. But apart from the difficulty of changing a pre-established text, there was the further difficulty that these negotiations had to be carried out with Baltic riparian States, three of which are Socialist states which until now do not officially recognize the Community. It might be argued that the more positive intentions for negotiations shown by the Council for Mutual Economic Assistance as well as the problems of the fishing zones of the Community offer a new ground for negotiations and the possibility of some bargaining. But can one be sure of this?

The conference on the law of the sea. The question of the European Community's participation in the conference of the law of the sea since the meeting in New York in December 1973 goes beyond the scope of the present study.

It must be remembered however that on 20 March 1974 the Commission had drawn the attention of the Council to the need to adopt a common attitude on all matters which are of the competence of the Community or which are of special interest to it. The Council decided on 4 June 1974 to adopt a procedure of co-ordination along the usual lines. The Community took part in the conference as an observer and a delegation formed by representatives of its different services took part in the work of the conference.

On 2 June 1976 the Commission sent to the Council a communication with regard to the conference and to the attitude of the Community in matters of environment. Two points were of greater impact. One was adoption of a common position towards provisions concerning the pollution by shipping and the second, the adoption of common positions which could link in a coherent way the commitments to be taken in the future convention and the commitments already taken by the Member States in accordance with the Environment programme of the Community. The Commission stressed that in particular in matters concerning the preservation of the aquatic element, certain directives, and notably that of 4 May 1976, gave to the Community competences equal to those given to the States by the unique text of the negotiations.

Pollution of rivers

The action of the Community concerning the pollution of rivers took two different courses: one concerning the Rhine and the water of the Rhine basin and the other the fresh waters of Europe.

The protection of the Rhine. The Rhine forms an important link for the Community even if this feature outstanding for the Community of Six has been a little attenuated by the fact that the Community has now nine members. The Rhine is also a particularly polluted river and therefore requires a common action of protection. It is therefore not surprising to see that the problem of the Rhine was evoked long before the adoption of a Community programme in matters of environment. In a Resolution of November 1970, the European Assembly, showing that the aggravation of the pollution of the Rhine is becoming a serious danger for the population living in the Rhine basin and that it also causes grave economic damage, asked the riparian States to undertake a common action and invited the Commission to take a series of actions to harmonize the measures of this action. It also must be noticed that when the European Assembly took this step in 1970 the problem of the protection of the Rhine against pollution had already been the object of an international convention signed in Berne on 29 April 1963 by all the riparian States of the Rhine. The text sets up a system of international co-operation between the riparian States and around the new institution of an International Commission for the protection of the Rhine against pollution.

But apart from the activity of this Commission, the States which signed the Berne Convention frequently met in Ministerial conferences in order to give a greater impetus to the fight against the pollution of the Rhine. Thus a first conference was held on 25–26 October 1972 in the Hague at the initiative of the Dutch government. The European Community took part in that conference as well as in the second such conference on 4–5 December 1973. At that conference the Commission, which had already adopted its Community programme for the environment on 22 November 1973 asked that the conference accept that the work carried out by the European Community within that programme should be taken into consideration. Later on, when on the initiative of the International Commission negotiations for a project of a convention for the protection of the Rhine against chemical pollution, were begun, the European Commission pointed out the analogy between some of the measures proposed with the measures already contained in the Community programme.

The European Commission asked the Council on 10 June 1975 to participate together with the respective states in the negotiations of this convention so that the latter could be concluded by the Community. On 10 January 1976, the Commission received from the Council the mandate to negotiate. The negotiations led after a third Ministerial conference in April 1976 to the approval of a draft convention against the chemical pollution of the Rhine. On 17 September 1976 the Commission asked the Council to authorize the Community to sign both the convention and an agreement additional to the Berne Convention of 1963. The Council gave its authorization.

On 3 December 1976 two separate agreements were concluded in Bonn. One is the convention for the protection of the Rhine against chemical pollution. It has six signatories. Five are the riparian States of which four are Member States of the Community and the sixth the Community itself.

The other text is the agreement additional to the Berne agreement which is signed by the same parties and which states that the Community becomes a party in its own right of the 1963 agreement of Berne. Insofar as Article 12 of the 1963 agreement had decided on a division of the cost of the work of the Commission between the five signatories this apportioning was modified by the new agreement and the percentages of the initial members were reduced. The Community assumed 13%, the three large Member States each 24.5%, Switzerland 12% and Luxembourg 1.5% of the cost. This financial participation underlines the difference between the participation of the States and the participation of the Community.

Moreover, Article 6 of the initial agreement is modified so as to allow the Community to use, in the field of its competence, its right of vote with a number of votes equal to that of the Member States, parties to the agreement.

The convention on the protection of the Rhine is rather technical and therefore does not have a great significance from the point of view of Community policy, apart from the fact that the preamble acknowledges the Community action, as described in the Council's directive of 4 May 1976.

The draft European convention for the protection of international rivers from pollution

Already the draft conventions for the protection of international rivers from pollution had posed the problem of the collaboration between the European Community and the Council of Europe.

On 12 May 1969 the consultative assembly of the Council of Europe had asked the Committee of Ministers, through the Recommendation 555, to appoint a committee of governmental experts which would prepare a draft convention for the fight against fresh water pollution, and taking as its basis a draft prepared by the Assembly. This draft showed a certain boldness insofar as it comprised the fresh water both surface and ground and that it introduced the idea of a basin for international drainage.

But the work took much longer than was expected. The Commission duly invited took part in the last meeting of the *ad hoc* committee from 5–8 February 1974.

A new draft was submitted on 13 March 1974 which differed greatly from the initial one because it dropped the idea of fresh water in general and especially that of the drainage basin. But nor was this text adopted by the Committee of Ministers of the Council of Europe.

In November 1974 the Council asked the Commission to authorize the formal participation of the Community in the preparation of the convention, but no final decision has yet been taken. However, the principle of correlating the action of the Council of Europe with the more dynamic action of the European Community has been accepted.

Impact and value of the community action at the international level

The Community action at the international level started in earnest after the adoption by the Council and by the Member States of the declaration of 22 November 1973 for an action programme of the European Communities in environmental matters. As has been seen, the Community concluded the Paris Convention of 1974 and the Barcelona Convention of 1976. In both cases, it appeared as a *signatory* of a convention in the preparation of which it had participated. The same is true for the 3 December 1976 convention for the protection of the Rhine. But this amounted to an extension of the Community action insofar as, here, the Community adhered to conventions made before and without its participation. Insofar as the Baltic zone is concerned, the Commission has asked the Council for the authorization to open negotiations with the participants in that convention, but the Council had not yet decided.

Two aspects can therefore be noticed. One is that of the participation of the Community in its own right in the preparation of international conventions, a participation which is sometimes direct and sometimes made retroactive by the mechanism of adherence. The other aspect is the Community's participation through the Commission in the institutions set up by the conventions for protection, as for instance in those of the Paris Convention against land-based pollution and in the international commission for the protection of the Rhine. This kind of action needs to be qualified in two respects. First, some of these treaties set up special institutions with attributions of management, for instance in the case of the Mediterranean, the programme of the United Nations on the environment is used. In such a case, the participation of the Commission takes a particularly limited form.

Second, when both the Community and the Member States take part in the managing Commission, some special rules have to be drawn up in the voting procedures. As has been seen, the Community may be given all the votes resulting from the addition of the votes of the Member States. But as in such cases, the Member States do not vote there are alternative votes, some emanating from the Community and some from the Member States. Further difficulties from this point of view arise from the fact that the Commission's intervention is generally circumscribed to "fields in its competence". This requires a distinction to be drawn between Community and national competences. Sometimes this does not prove to be easy. The Commission assesses the international competence of the Community and more often than not its own participation as a Community organ, on the basis of the internal competences within the Community. As mentioned above, this is the technique of the federal states, whereby the Member States claim that the internal distribution of competences should be extended to the international competence. It would seem that here the technique is the same, but actually it is the other way round, for it is obvious that the Community can have only competences of attribution. What is being claimed is that the Community should be given at the international level, competences which amount to the extension of the competences it has at the internal Community level.

It is inevitable that in all these activities the Community will clash with the states. It will clash with the Member States, which are in general reluctant to abdicate their rights in favour of the Community. It will clash also with the third states which, when the Community has not taken part in the preparation of a convention, would have reservations about its adherence to the convention—as we have seen in the case of the Helsinki Convention.

Finally, it must be recognized that in certain cases, the policy of the Community, and especially that of the Commission, is quite bold. These are the cases when only a few Member States of the Community are members of a convention. There are many reasons for which in the case of the Mediterranean, France and Italy would not allow the Community to speak and act on their behalf. And there are many reasons for which, if the Community were in the future to take part in the Helsinki agreement, Denmark and the German Federal Republic would show the same reluctance.

When all the Member States are concerned, the Community action is more understandable. But nevertheless even this kind of action at Community level is justified above all by the need to ensure at the Community level the harmony and the coherence of international policies, which are no longer within the exclusive competence of national organs.

IV. CONCLUSIONS

European Policy of Protection Against River and Water Pollution

by *Pierre Gerbet*

Environmental policy, in particular on water pollution, is not included in the treaties except in certain very sectorial cases concerning the ECSC and Euratom. It is not mentioned in the Treaty of Rome.

This policy was worked out between 1971 and 1973 and was initiated by the Commission in response to pressure from the public and European Parliament. By the end of 1973, the Community had drawn up a complete plan of action. This programme sets out the aims and principles for action by the Community. One main principle is to determine what level of action best suits the type of pollution concerned as well as the geographical zone to be protected. Was there a European alternative or not? But this is not the real question. There was no other possible policy than that which was adopted.

One vital element of this policy was water protection, both in the interests of the population and of the economy. Efforts in this area were clearly essential.

Community action has proceeded along two paths; on the Community level, and on that of international cooperation in a wider framework.

On the international level in its wider sense, community policy is combined with either that of Member States or of third countries depending on the situation. There are three possible procedures.

a. According to procedure No. 1, the Community as such is represented at the stage of international negotiations and signs international agreements. As this can be justified on the grounds of defense of the environment, Community water protection policy can also be regarded as a manifestation of a wider Community policy in the general context of international negotiations. Thus the Barcelona negotiations were an integral part of the Community's Mediterranean policy.

After the convention had been drawn up, the Community, represented by the Commission in the institutions set up by the Convention, took part in the management of the international system which had been established. The Commission had thus found an opportunity to coordinate its own work with that carried out on an international level.

b. Procedure No. 2 is similar to that described above. The Commission, faced with an established treaty drawn up after negotiations in which it has taken no part asks for membership of this treaty and for representation in its institutions. The Rhine Conventions of December 1976 provide a good example of such a procedure.

c. Procedure No. 3 envisages a more limited participation. The Community has not signed the treaty but the Commission takes part as observer in the work carried out under this treaty. This procedure can be seen in the case of the conventions against maritime pollution like those of Oslo or London, and more generally those concluded and implemented by IMCO.

It is worth noting that the Commission has succeeded in promoting co-ordination between the Member States when they take action on the general international level, for instance at the ONU.

In the Community itself, the battle against water pollution has been character-ized by a major debate in which those supporting an optimal approach over quality objectives have been opposed to those supporting the more direct approach over emission criteria. In practice, there were really no alternatives when on 4 May 1976 the Community adopted a most important directive on the discharge of dangerous substances in the aquatic environment and combined the two approaches.

Since this programme was adopted, the Commission has undertaken to prepare twenty or so directives; amendments have been proposed for about half of these and about three have been adopted by the Council.

The way in which these texts have been adopted has brought into play, in a consultative capacity, the Economic and Social Committee of the European Parliament, whose findings have generally been favourable to the Com-mission. As far as the European Parliament is concerned, it is to be hoped that its opinions could be reached by some more sophisticated method and its debates so organized that they would make a greater impact on the public opinion and on national parliaments.

In concluding these discussions, the group considered that:
1.   Community policy over the protection of water represents an essential aspect of Community policy. In fact, one notes that this policy has had its effect on the international scene (thus, the change in the Rhine regulations was the result of the directives of 4 May 1976).
2.   The adoption of a Community policy for the environment came about in difficult circumstances. Politically, the enlargement of the Community posed several problems and slowed down the implementation of the common policies, while it accentuated the administrative disparities between the different Member States. Economically, the energy crisis and the economic recession coincided with the adoption of the programme.
3.   Even if the Commission's initiatives appeared satisfactory, one can but regret that the Council has only adopted these decisions in a limited number of cases. This holding up of progress which can be observed also in other fields, seems to be the result of procedures which slow down the rhythm of work. The group was worried about the growing number of proposals which have piled up on the Council tables.

Despite all these difficulties, it must be admitted that a Community policy on water pollution does exist notwithstanding the lack of formal clauses in the Treaty; and this should be an encouragement when one considers that certain policies which are formally envisaged under the Treaty have never been implemented.

European public opinion ought to be more closely associated and would act as a stimulant. The European Parliament, in giving more attention to the matter in its debates, could play an important role.

In the future, environmental policy should be more closely associated with regional and competition policy, which are the most essential activities for the construction of the Community.

Finally it is to be hoped that the debates in the Council do not introduce an excessive number of technical details; they should rather be distinguished by a political desire to reach some conclusion. The formula of directives generally used in the case of this policy of the battle against water pollution seems to give the Member States adequate guarantees.

ECONOMIC AND MONETARY POLICY

I. ECONOMIC AND MONETARY UNION POLICY

The Resolution of the Council of Ministers of 22 March 1971

by *H. Etienne* and *G. Ciavarini-Azzi*

In accordance with the aim of the research project, this report is designed to enable the policy pursued by the Commission to be compared with that eventually adopted by the Council in the field of economic and monetary union. It brings out the circumstances under which the various measures and decisions have been adopted. The feasibility and merits of Community initiative in this field should be assessed in the light of these circumstances. Since the report is designed to provide a political assessment of the measures taken relating to economic and monetary union, the authors have not referred to economic and monetary analyses.

The authors have thus avoided covering the same ground as that covered in detailed reports on the problem of economic and monetary union, particularly the report of the Study Group chaired by Mr. Robert Marjolin on the subject "Economic and Monetary Union 1980" (April 1976), the passages relating to economic and monetary union in the Spierenburg report on "European Union" (May 1975) and the ideas developed by the Commission itself in its report on "European Union". These reports deal with the fundamental question of what economic and monetary union should comprise and of how it should be achieved.

They have also avoided duplication of the excellent analysis contained in the relevant parts of "Droit de la Communauté économique européenne" (European Economic Community Law), published by the Free University of Brussels.

The authors' aim has been to enable those concerned with policy to decide whether, in view of the circumstances, an alternative policy would have been possible and what chances of success it would have had.

An attempt will be made to distinguish between the various stages in the Communities' development to which the different approaches to the problem of economic and monetary union have corresponded.

The discussions ("for and against") which took place concerning the major decisions taken at any given time will also be reviewed.

Finally, an assessment of the political merits of the measures taken will be attempted.

INTRODUCTION

What is meant by economic and monetary union?

The term "economic and monetary union" was given official recognition at the Summit meeting in The Hague on 1–2 December 1969, when the

Council was asked to prepare during 1970, in close collaboration with the Commission, a plan aimed at creating by stages an economic and monetary union. The Communiqué issued in The Hague referred to the Commission's memorandum to the Council on the coordination of economic policies and monetary cooperation within the Community of 12 February 1969, this memorandum having been based on an earlier one dated 5 December 1968. The actual content of the economic and monetary union was to be the subject of at least as much discussion as the methods to achieve it. Rather than attempt to define economic and monetary union, it would seem preferable here to indicate the area within which, by discussion and argument, the problems which have arisen since the Treaty was signed will have to be solved.

Economic and monetary union constitutes the response to problems unsolved, since the signing of the Treaty of Rome, because of the need to overcome the contradictions between:

a. rigid rules and an effective decision-making procedure as regards measures to liberalize trade and the absence of specific rules and Community decision-making powers as regards economic and monetary policies;

b. the maximization of resources through free competition arising from the dismantlement of obstacles to trade and the Member States' ultimate freedom as regards exchange rates and monetary policy; and

c. the maintenance of fixed currency parities and the absence of an economic and monetary policy.

The fact that the Treaty has relatively little to say about the joint conduct of economic and monetary policies may be due, at least in part, to the concern of the monetary authorities, as broadly defined, to keep the degree of autonomy desired or already enjoyed in the Member States in the Community as well. The strain between the Community and Member States as regards the influence exercised over economic and monetary policy will continue to be affected by the transposition, to Community level, of the unresolved conflict concerning the location of monetary and financial authority in Member States.

In terms of sovereignty, it is undeniable that those founding Member States which were most concerned about their ability to keep up with the integration movement intended to retain full freedom as regards exchange rates. This attitude was tolerated all the more easily at the time since all countries considered themselves bound to a system of fixed parities, and the exercise of a sovereign right to change parity or even float apparently had theoretical rather than practical implications. It was only later, in the 1970's, that the problem of sovereignty assumed a new meaning, when trade union leaders in some countries called on their Governments to preserve at all costs the freedom to pursue an economic policy consistent with their social requirements—a demand which excluded any formal link in the field of monetary policy.

THE EARLY YEARS: IN SEARCH OF A STANDARD

The first ten years of the Common Market were devoted mainly to the organization of trade and to liberalization measures. This stage was completed on 1 July 1968 with the disappearance of the last tariffs and the introduction

of a common price for the principal agricultural products. During this stage—
one in which currencies were convertible, at any rate indirectly, into gold—
calm generally prevailed on the foreign exchange markets. The Community
experienced a single currency realignment in 1961, when the mark and guilder
were revalued by 5%. The preservation of fixed parities was the basic doctrine
underpinning the Common Market and the economies of the West. The main
concern was therefore to give this system of fixed parities a definitive economic
basis and an unassailable legal form (thereby amplifying the Treaty, which,
in Article 107, states only that "each Member State shall treat its policy with
regard to rates of exchange as a matter of common concern").

The fixing of a common price for cereals—a fundamental aspect of the
Community's work—in units of account (defined directly in terms of gold
as containing 0.88867088 grammes of fine gold) provided the legal and
economic basis for a common standard. When, during the night of 22
December 1964, the Council adopted this common price for cereals—to be
applied until 1 July 1968—the President of the Commission, Mr. Walter
Hallstein, summarized at his press conference what had taken place by
simply declaring that the European currency had been born.

Council Regulation No. 129 of 1 November 1962 (OJ No. 2553/62) does
not specifically provide for changes to parities declared by the Member
States. The Regulation does state, however, that it is for the Council or the
Commission, acting within their powers, to take measures derogating from
the Regulation on the unit of account where monetary practices of an exceptional nature are liable to jeopardize the implementation of Community
instruments.

Even before the common price for cereals was fixed, a statement was
issued on 3 May 1964 by the representatives of the Government of the
Member States of the EEC, meeting within the Council, concerning the organization of prior consultations between Member States in the event of changes
in the exchange parities of their currencies (64/306/EEC, OJ No. 1226/64).

In Regulation (EEC) No. 653/68 of 30 May 1968, the Council specified how
the value of the unit of account used for the common agricultural policy
could be changed (OJ L 123/4).

It should be pointed out that the Council at this time simply noted the
possibility, in the event of changes in parities, of altering the value of the unit
of account. Against the advice of the Commission, the Council also decided
that alterations to agricultural prices could be adopted by the Council on the
same occasion. However, these alterations had to be common. On the other
hand, it appeared that Member States could not avoid reflecting in their
national prices (expressed in national currency) parity changes where the
value of the unit of account was maintained. The prospect of having to reduce
domestic prices as expressed in national currency was considered by the
Commission an adequate deterrent against possible revaluations, while the
prospect of having immediately to increase agricultural prices in national
currency in the event of a devaluation was rejected from the outset by Member
States. Even if the legal constraint through the agricultural unit of account
should fail, fixed parities were still bound to be respected because of the
economic, political and social constraints of the system. The Member States
had burnt their boats and had condemned themselves to a policy which ruled
out exchange rate movements.

The system was first put to the test with the 11.11% devaluation of the French franc on 8 August 1969. The French authorities pointed out, with some justification, that the devaluation would fail if it were automatically accompanied by a corresponding increase in agricultural prices in France. The Commission had no option but to defer to these arguments and to accept the partial maintenance of French prices—the unit of account remaining unchanged—by means of a system of subsidies and export levies. This system was self-correcting on an economic level (import subsidies, export levies) and, partially, on a financial level (the import subsidies were paid by the French Treasury). The gradual process of adjusting common prices as expressed in French francs was completed by 1 August 1971.

On the occasion of the 9.29% "Schiller" revaluation of the mark on 27 October 1969, Germany refused—the value of the unit of account remaining unchanged—to lower its prices expressed in marks. The prices had to be maintained partly by introducing compensatory measures at the borders— this time in the form of import levies and export refunds. The nature of the German system and Germany's agricultural balance were such that no scope was available for discussion and there was no self-correction. When, on 15 May 1971, the mark was allowed to float freely, the system was adapted (whereas the Netherlands rejected facile solutions by introducing a system of limited fluctuation, thus avoiding the need for border compensation measures). On principle, the Netherlands was fully prepared to take account of fluctuations in its exchange parity in relation to the agricultural unit of account, if necessary by reducing national prices. The subsequent lowering of German prices was offset by direct aid to German farmers borne by the Community.

It has been suggested that the technical skill with which the Commission developed these adaptation measures itself dealt a mortal blow to the agricultural unit of account: some at least of the implications of the common price system could be disregarded after all—so much for the Community standard.

The problems are, in fact, more complex than this. Farmers exert continual pressure on countries whose currencies have depreciated with a view to bringing about a realignment of domestic prices, while countries which have revalued are subjected to very strong pressures from their partner countries to abolish compensatory measures at frontiers. The agricultural unit of account system therefore continues to help towards a convergence of monetary policies. On the other hand, its influence has not penetrated the economic policies of Member States, nor has it been possible to get Member States to accept all its domestic consequences.

But is it fair to criticize the Commission for basing its strategy in the 1960's on the agricultural unit of account?

There was in fact little criticism, at the time, of the decisions taken. In the context of the 1960's, the formula adopted was workable; this would probably no longer be the case now, when the problems of convergence have assumed a formidable scale. It cannot be said that the Commission failed at that time to recommend the convergence of the economic policies of Member States and common measures to combat external speculation: is it fair to blame the Commission for failing to foresee the refusal of Member States to follow its recommendations? The integration technique consisted in forcing breakthroughs wherever possible, with a subsequent realignment of the front towards the most advanced point. Finally, we should not underestimate the effects of the events of May–June 1968, which almost lead to the disintegration of the foundation on which the Common Market was built. Nonetheless, the problem of establishing fixed parities between the currencies of Member States is now more acute than ever.

ENLARGEMENT AND THE PLAN TO ACHIEVE ECONOMIC AND MONETARY UNION BY STAGES

Like any other political initiative, the plan for economic and monetary union was the outcome of a number of circumstances and policy considerations. Although we should not underestimate the Commission's insistence on the need for greater convergence of economic policies and better monetary cohesion, it was in fact the prospect of the United Kingdom's accession to the Community which first caused the Community to renew its efforts towards improved cohesion.

Internal events subsequently occurred which shaped attitudes, the two factors finally blending together.

When, on 2 May 1967, Mr. Wilson officially expressed the United Kingdom's desire for negotiations on its accession to the Community to be reopened, the Six were deeply divided on this subject. France's basic view was that the United Kingdom was not equipped to adapt to the integration process. The French believed that the Community should first be "completed" (i.e., through the definitive financing of agriculture and the introduction of own resources), whereas the Commission felt at the outset that the problems raised by the United Kingdom's accession—problems which would be made clear during the course of negotiations—could be dealt with properly only if its decision-making powers were first extended.

In its opinion of September 1967, in which it came out in favour of opening negotiations, one of the Commission's conclusions was as follows: "To sum up, the new membership applications are impelling the Community to tackle at one and the same time the problems involved in its development and those involved in its enlargement".

The Commission dealt at length with the problem of sterling and expressed serious doubts as to the prospects, given the present circumstances, of the United Kingdom participating in the Common Market in compliance with its rules. The Commission also pointed out that, after enlargement, sterling could not continue to enjoy a place in the international monetary system different from that occupied by the currencies of other Member States. "If the enlargement of the Community is to be given every chance of success, steps must be taken to achieve a closer coordination of the economic, monetary and financial policies of the (present) members of the Community." In its supplementary Opinion of 2 April 1968, the Commission put on the same level the preparatory phase for enlargement and the introduction of a programme containing a rough outline of the planned economic and monetary union:

443

"As pointed out above, the Commission hopes that the Council will also examine the measures which the Community should take in order to prepare itself for enlargement by strengthening its structure, applying common policies and completing its economic unity.

The Commission reaffirms the growing and increasingly urgent need to coordinate the economic and monetary policies between the six Member States. Furthermore, of the objects it would be important to reach within the next two to four years, the following appear to be of particular note:
– Fulfilment of the conditions required to eliminate frontier controls on the movement of goods within the Community;
– . . .
– Establishment of a European financial market comprising the free movement of capital where the investment of funds and the granting of credits are concerned.

These steps are mainly required in order that the economy of the Community should benefit more fully from the establishment of the customs union which is now practically complete; they are also desirable for the purpose of making the Community better prepared to enjoy the advantages of extension."

Concluding, the Commission declared its readiness to submit more detailed proposals for the strengthening and development of the Community with a view to the accession of the new members.

In fact, the Commission had already advised the Governments of its views in a memorandum submitted in February 1968 to the meeting of the Finance Ministers in Rome, the capital of the Member State whose turn it was to provide the Presidency of the Council.[1] The "Memorandum on Community Action in the Monetary Field" was treated with great discretion. Complying with the custom with regard to the way in which monetary affairs were conducted in the Community, the Commission "suggested" that the Committee of Governors of the Central Banks and the Monetary Committee should carry out "studies" on the following topics:
  i. parity changes only by joint agreement,
 ii. elimination of the fluctuation bands between the currencies of the Member States, and application of the same fluctuation bands vis-à-vis non-Member States,
iii. establishment of a mutual assistance arrangement on the basis of Articles 108 and 109 of the Treaty,
 iv. definition of a European unit of account to be used for joint action.

The Commission also expressed the wish that the Member States should confirm their support for the international monetary system (fixed parities defined by reference to gold). This was in fact a thinly disguised attack on certain ideas which were being ventilated in the Federal Republic in favour of floating currencies, even between the Member States.

The Memorandum considered only the monetary aspects of the problems arising. But the mandate for studies requested by the Commission was not given until the Conference of Ministers of Financial Affairs held in September 1969.

It is probably fair to say that five Member States were not willing to proceed to any far-reaching change in the profile of the Community in view of its enlargement, while the sixth was essentially concerned with obtaining assurances prior on the principal points of concern to it.

But the events of May/June 1968 and their immediate fall-out in the form

444

of the first restrictive measures introduced in France in August 1968, and the disturbances of November 1968, had served to heighten awareness of current economic and monetary problems. The Commission referred to the Council in early September 1968 a memorandum on the policy needed in the Community to cope with current economic and monetary problems. In this paper, the Commission specified in precise terms, for each Member State, the economic, monetary and budgetary policy measures needed. The Commission's conclusion was the absolute need for better coordination of policies, felt to be indispensable "if exchange parity stability between the currencies is not to be directly threatened".

The Monetary Committee handed down on 15 January 1969 the opinion requested by the Ministers in September. The opinion was very encouraging with regard to the suggestions made by the Commission, while emphasizing the need for coordination of economic policies.

The Commission, spurred on by events, and strongly encouraged by the Monetary Committee, laid before the Council in February 1969 a document which has been called the "Barre Plan" (Commission Memorandum to the Council on Coordination of Economic Policies and Monetary Cooperation within the Community).

In contrast with the document of February 1968, the Commission now emphasized the need for coordination of economic policies to be achieved through intensive consultation within the three Committees involved (the Monetary Committee, the Short-term Economic Policy Committee, the Budgetary Policy Committee) and through fuller utilization of medium-term programmes. The Commission recommended the introduction, before the end of the transitional period (31 December 1969) of the Community monetary cooperation mechanism. For the Commission, short-term support was to consist in the placing at the disposal of an "agent" (in fact, the BIS in Basle), by the Member States, of resources not exceeding a certain ceiling. The benefit of such support would have been relatively automatic, whilst medium-term assistance would be the subject of Council decisions to which conditions could be attached. The Commission stressed that this mechanism was not to supersede existing international machinery, but that it was to be used on a priority basis. Lastly, the Commission noted that mechanism proposed, far from making the enlargement more difficult, could be regarded as an appropriate arrangement favouring accession.

It will have been noted that the "Barre Plan" left out the idea of the need for joint agreement for parity changes, and also the idea of elimination of fluctuation bands as a priority objective. The Plan in fact tended to take these points for granted, as necessary consequences, provided that the economic policies were coordinated and that auxiliary mechanisms were introduced. The Plan took an extremely sober view of the more remote outlook and of institutional developments. In an effort to be practical and effective its authors avoided the danger of the introduction of "clauses deprudence" which any more ambitious plan, of definitive character, would almost inevitably have entailed.

As long as differences of views persisted on the principle of opening negotiations—a first glimpse of the decision actually to be taken was not obtained until The Hague Summit—there could be no question of introducing internal development mechanisms of any substance, while the prospects of enlargement, once plainly visible, led the Council to adopt a "wait-and-see" attitude, pending the major qualitative change which was to be the start-up of the enlarged Community.

But the prospect of an enlarged Community was a generous incentive to the establishment of comprehensive blueprints opening new horizons to the old Member States as well as the new ones. It would be hard to exaggerate the difficult situation of Georges Pompidou and Mr. Chaban Delmas's government with regard to that part of French public opinion which had, over the years, got used to regarding enlargement as synonymous with a weaker Community: it was therefore vital that the Six and the new members should agree on a future outlook, this to include solutions for the problems—which had never been out of the limelight—with which the United Kingdom specifically had to contend. Thus, at The Hague Summit the idea was born of a phased plan designed to lead to economic and monetary union. A need for firm guidance as to the future was felt all the more strongly among the public because the six-member Community had been jolted in August by the devaluation of the French franc and because, a few days before The Hague meeting, the Federal Republic of Germany had carried out its "Schiller revaluation" (9.29%); here observers would have welcomed a practical demonstration of the maintenance of the unity of the Common Market in difficult circumstances; failing this, it was natural that they should look to the future for the developments that would ensure the preservation of Community momentum.

On 4 March 1970 the Commission sent to the Council its Communication regarding the formulation of a phased plan with a view to the creation of economic and monetary union. In accordance with the Commission's consistent approach, the Communication—the Commission had reserved the right to make proposals—was somewhat cautious in tone. It is true that the Commission drew heavily on the capital which was provided by Point 8 of The Hague Communiqué, but was careful not to go beyond it by calling on the Member States to take decisions which they were not ready to take or which they could not in fact have implemented. This said, the Commission, responding to the invitation made to it at the Summit, used the device of timetables—which is one used in the Treaties—without making a fetish of this idea: "Adoption of a timetable does have the advantage of not leaving room for undue uncertainty as to how long each stage will take, and of making it an obligation to achieve, within a reasonable space of time, the ends laid down for the Community by the Heads of State and Government. Nevertheless, the timetable must be kept sufficiently flexible to allow for effective adjustment to operation requirements".

The Commission's plan emphasized the practical measures to be adopted over three stages to achieve economic and monetary union, an objective defined with great restraint: an area in which freedom of movement is ensured and which must be seen from the outside as an individualized economic and monetary whole. The mutual consistency of the various policies, the handling of exchange rate policy and the cohesion of monetary policies were regarded as contributing on a subsidiary basis to the general objective. The whole should have been established within eight years (1970–

78), it being understood that a sort of prior stocktaking would be made before moving on to the final stage. From the Commission's point of view, the first two stages should have involved a number of specific technical decisions.

The most significant decisions—particularly those concerning the assignment to the institutions of the necessary powers—were to be adopted once this first barrier had been overcome. The Commission was careful not to raise the question of the need for, or the possibility of, amending the Treaties. It would be at that time that the decisions on the establishment of a European reserve fund, the elimination by stages of fluctuation bands, and the irrevocable fixing of parities were to be taken.

The Council saw the Commission's Memorandum for the first time on 6 March 1970 and asked a group of experts under the Chairmanship of Mr. Pierre Werner, Luxembourg Prime Minister and Minister for Financial Affairs, to make an interim report to the Council meeting scheduled for 20 May. Considerations of national pride and susceptibility often intrude on the adoption of Community decisions and the present case was no exception. To make sure that some of the governments were not forgotten, the Council drew up the mandate "noting suggestions formulated by the Governments and the communication from the Commission". The establishment of the group was an institutional innovation, in that the report was not requested from the Permanent Representatives Committee, but from a group made up of the chairmen of the Monetary Committee, of the Committee of Governors of the Central Banks, of the Medium-term Economic Policy Committee, of the Short-term Economic Policy Committee and of the Budgetary Policy Committee and by the Commission Representative. The membership of the group was bound to influence the impact of the report: it was to be the work of the most responsible people in the Member States concerned on the questions dealt with.

In the meantime, the Council reached final agreement on the "own resources" of the Community and the strengthening of the budgetary powers of the European Parliament (20 April 1970), so that there was no further obstacle to the opening of the accession negotiations. The latter were to be carried out on the basis of new Member States acceptance of everything the Community had achieved so far, the so-called "acquis communautaire" which, community negotiators declared, could include resolutions or statements of intention on the future of the enlarged comments.

France was the country which felt most strongly that the essential points with regard to the establishment of the economic and monetary union, i.e., the future of the Community, should be "acquis" among the Six to constitute a "guarantee" as to the future of the enlarged Community.

Mr. Werner laid his interim report before the Council meeting of 8 and 9 June, which "endorsed" the common conclusions emerging from the group's work.[2]

In contrast with the Commission's approach, which was rather functionalist and "low profile", the group had bent to its task with more ambitious political perspectives. The key sentences were the following: "Economic and monetary union means that the main economic policy decisions will be taken at Community level and therefore that the necessary powers will be transferred from the countries to the Community. The ultimate goal could be the adoption of a single currency, which would ensure that there was no going back on decisions taken." . . . "Some measures entail amendment of the Treaty of Rome, and preparations for this should be completed during the first stage. Nonetheless, the clauses as they now stand already allow for substantial progress."

In France, these passages proved highly controversial and resulted, like the December 1964 Agreements on the common cereals price, in a rekindling of the debate delaying for several months the adoption of the plan by stages for monetary union. The main consequence was the scrapping of the "political perspectives" approach, although this approach was in itself perfectly feasible and was supported by the Netherlands with the proviso that the Parliament's rights of control should be endorsed.

But the members of the group, in a practical spirit, urged the completion of the measures recommended in the Commission's Memorandum of February 1969. In particular, the Council was to take a decision before the end of the year on the definition of medium-term quantitative guidelines[3] and on the institution of medium-term financial assistance.

The Werner group felt that the objective of economic and monetary union could be achieved within the decade "provided it has permanent support from the governments".

The group was asked to complete its report, which was then submitted to the Council on 8 October.

In the meantime—on 30 June—the negotiations with a view to the enlargement of the Community were formally opened. It had been agreed that monetary questions would be left to the end of the negotiations.

The Werner group had no power to commit the governments—as the Permanent Representatives Committee could have done.

Mr. Werner was careful, however, to state that "the present report does not reflect the individual preferences of the members of the group but formulates replies in common. The ideas expressed are given on the personal responsibility of the members of the group".

In contrast with the remarkable haste with which the Werner group had to work and the speed the Council had shown in adopting the first conclusions on 8 and 9 June, the Council then showed little sense of urgency in considering the final report.

The Commission handed in its Communication and the proposals relating to the institution by stages of the economic and monetary union on 15 Nov. 1970.

The European Parliament adopted on 3 December 1970 a resolution approving the final report and the Communication and proposals from the Commission.

There was a clear impression in the Council held on 15 and 16 December that all the policy decisions had not yet been taken in Paris. It is true that the French Delegation was able to agree that the decisions of the Council of 8 and 9 June should be incorporated in full in the preamble and it accepted the idea of a Community central bank system with a view to the creation of a common currency. But it was not in a position to give its agreement to the passages in the draft resolution concerning the transfer of powers from the national level to the Community level. While the principle of the "subsidiarity" of Community power was acceptable, the Council was unable to overcome the basic problem of the definition of these powers and of the allocation of responsibilities between the institutions.

The Communication from the Commission was essentially a return to the functional and practical approach adopted in the document submitted in March. The Commission's main concern was to present a text that could be agreed to by all the Member States. The Commission therefore refrained from restating the principle of the transfer of responsibilities and made no mention of the unavoidable amendment of the Treaties from the beginning of the second stage.

The Commission maintained its idea that when the Community moved on to the second stage the measures leading to the full economic and monetary union would have to be adopted, if necessary on the basis of Article 235 or Article 236 of the Treaty. No reference was made to the creation of a political union, and emphasis on the creation of a European currency was also avoided. Above all, the Commission left out the Werner group's idea of creating a "European decision centre" having economic responsibilities (the Community central bank system on the lines of the Federal Reserve System).

On the other aspects, there was a very broad consensus in the report of the Commission's working party. However, the Commission insisted that in the first stage the Council should adopt a number of supporting decisions, particularly in the taxation field and with regard to the free movement of capital.

Discussion in the Council on 8 and 9 February 1971

This discussion led to the Resolution of the Council and the Representatives of the Governments of the Member States of 22 March 1971 on the achievement by stages of economic and monetary union in the Community.[4]

The Council was attended by the Ministers for Foreign Affairs and Ministers for Economic Affairs and Financial Affairs of the Member States. The Chairmen of the five committees (Governors of the Central Bank, the Monetary Committee, the Short-term Economic Policy Committee, the Medium-term Economic Policy Committee and the Budgetary Policy Committee) also attended.

Preparatory work previous to the meeting had yielded a consensus on fundamental parts of the draft.

In particular, it had been agreed to limit the scope of the first stage to an experimental phase. As a result, this phase entailed no real constraints with regard to the coordination of the economic policies and, by the same token, it allocated no increased powers to the institutions.[5] In the monetary field, too, the emphasis was on intensifying consultation and on action by consent[6] (thus, the Community was to adopt "progressively" common positions in relations with non-member countries and international organizations). The powers assigned to the large number of existing committees were respected.

The Central Banks were invited, again on an experimental basis, to maintain until the beginning of the second stage the fluctuations of exchange rates between the currencies of the Member States within bands narrower than those respected vis-à-vis the US dollar, this to be achieved through concerted action in respect of the dollar.

The decision to treat the first stage as experimental in nature was not only a matter of healthy empiricism and of a natural desire to avoid measures not properly thought out. And there was not only the feeling that it was proper that the decisive step should be taken only in an enlarged Community. The fact is that the French Delegation, which, during the discussions, pressed for compulsory arrangements committing the parties—for reasons of internal policy with a view to the enlargement—was at the same time unable to accept there and then the institutional implications inherent in any allocation of powers to the Community, to accept from the outset that the economic and monetary union would involve the assignment of new powers to the Community and could require amendment of the Treaty, or at least recourse to Article 235 of the Treaty. In some respects, the limits within which the French Delegation was held were really very narrow. For example, it had to demand that the consultation which the Commission was to have with the "social partners" with a view to the preparation of its proposals on the main lines of economic policy had to be held within the Economic and Social Committee. It seemed to be feared in Paris that an increased margin given to the Commission to make contacts with the "social partners" could have so strengthened the Commission that things might have got out of hand. In view of the fact that in the eyes of the German Delegation coordination of economic policies had to necessarily obtain the consensus of the social partners on the basis of "concerted action", the French position—based on purely institutional considerations—could be interpreted as a reservation with regard to the coordination of the economic policies.

The political compromise obtained at the time consisted in retaining in the preamble of the Resolution the Council's conclusions of 8–9 June 1970 defining ambitiously the content of the union—including the principle of transfers of sovereignty—and in going no further than defining in the body of the Resolution the areas to which the "functional" compromise agreed would apply (when the Community was to move on to the second stage, a decision would be taken as to whether the measures entailed would involve amendment of the Treaty or not). But even this field of future application was in some respects defined restrictively: the German Delegation declined to include for example which financial aid to non-member countries should, it felt, remain in the hands of Member States.

In the field of regional policy, the principle of transfer of resources and of the creation of new instruments was not endorsed. It should be noted that the Italian Delegation, in contrast with the attitude of the British Conservative Government later, did not make an issue out of this question.

Reservations with regard to the institutional implications of the union served, at all events, as a protective screen for the German Delegation and the Netherlands Delegation, which were thus never compelled to show the cards indicating what step they could really accept.

However this may be, the German Delegation's insistence on the insertion of a "clause de prudence"—though supported by Professor Schiller as necessary because of the inadequate commitment to the coordination of economic policies—was felt by many to indicate an attitude of cautiousness and mistrust with regard to the forces of momentum inherent in any solemn undertaking of the Community. The inhibiting impact of the request for a "clause de prudence" (Point II, paragraph 9 of the Resolution) was all the greater in that the measures, thus formally robbed of their vigour and bite, were as a consequence experimental and limited in time from the outset.

Seen five years afterwards, the Resolution may be judged as a "feasible" compromise, given the positions adopted by the delegations at the beginning, but not one involving fundamental political commitments or strong enough to withstand future vicissitudes. The Community seemed to be placing its faith in the future and in the maintenance, in the economic and monetary field, of the automatic mechanisms which had proved their worth during the process of eliminating obstacles to trade. The need for coordination of economic policies did not seem to be disputed. On the other hand, there seemed to be fundamental disagreement on methods of achieving this coordination. The German and Netherlands Delegations felt that coordination should be achieved under the aegis of a Community in a position to impose its views with regard to stability and harmonious growth, whilst other delegations, including the French, felt that coordination should be the result of monetary disciplines (although these were the subject of numerous limitations). The Press, on the whole, was more interested in the fact that an agreement had been achieved at all than in the reservations and hesitations surrounding it. All in all, European opinion assigned the same credibility to this step as to other political resolutions.

The British Press was well aware that so far nothing had been formally decided. *The Times* noted with satisfaction, from the British point of view, that with regard to future developments, all possibilities still remained open.

In the German Press, there was, however, a discordant voice: "Is it believed that the stage-by-stage plan will be enough by itself to make our EEC partners apostles of stability?" "There is reason to fear that reality will bring us to the opposite of stability" ... "They (Member States not pursuing a stability policy) will be free in the future to draw on the 2,000 million of foreign exchange compensation funds most of which will be provided by the Federal Republic".

Several newspapers regretted that the Ministers had not confirmed that the European Parliament's powers would be strengthened, but by and large the Press avoided any extensive analysis of the problem of the institutional implications of the final establishment of an economic and monetary union.

The European Parliament welcomed the agreements without reserve.

In short, the Resolution on economic and monetary union was an act of confidence in the future, which, it was hoped, would not be unduly troubled. Conceived as the future mould for an enlarged Community, it was in fact only a procedural framework with a somewhat thin content. With regard to European opinion, the authors of the decision could not do other than present the Resolution as the route to be followed for the second generation of Community development. This presentation was supposed to constitute an element of pressure on the institutions and the Member States to ensure that the behaviour of both the former and the latter would be in line with the wishes expressed.

In fact, the Council was not in a position to give a precise content to a Community policy of balanced development, or to agree on a common monetary policy with regard to the outside world.

Such a "leap forward" would have required, as balancing factors, fundamental political commitments—commitments which had not been entered into.

THE MARK AND THE GUILDER FLOAT SEPARATELY

Less than three months after the acceptance of the Resolution on economic and monetary union, the Community (Council meeting of 8–9 May 1971) faced a German request for a joint currency float. The problem had not been tackled under the Resolution, but it must be acknowledged that the Community had been based on the premise of fixed currency parities and that one of the specific objectives of economic and monetary union was the narrowing of the bands of fluctuation between currencies; the floating of currencies between Member States was hardly reconcilable with this objective.

The German Government followed to the letter the rules of procedure laid down in the Decision of 17 July 1969 on coordination of short-term economic policies and consulted the Council on its intention to discontinue buying in dollars to hold down the mark. It should also be remembered that Mr. Willy Brandt's Government, with Professor Schiller as its spokesman, formally proposed the joint floating of the currencies of the Member States and made it known that Germany was willing to assume its responsibilities for ensuring the proper working of the joint float. This offer was turned down by France and Italy, both countries feeling that the origin of the German problem was an artificial inflow of capital which should have been tamed by appropriate measures and that there was no genuine overvaluation of the European currencies.[7] The Commission was very doubtful at the time as to the wisdom of a joint float of the European currencies, it being felt that the Community would thus compromise the established currency exchange system. Given the competitive positions of France and Italy, the Commission felt it could hardly ask these countries to raise the cost of their exports. In terms of bargaining psychology, an important factor was the polarization of discussion on the issue of the control of capital flows.

Most of the Member States felt that this problem was at the heart of the debate, but Professor Schiller refused to make the slightest concession in this area. In addition there is no escaping the impression that the French and Italian Governments seemed to welcome any suggestion likely to facilitate exports and that in view of this dominant consideration, the warnings of the Commission—especially those of Mr. Mansholt—with regard to the disruption which the separate floating of individual currencies would entail in the long run had little impact. In any event, the announcement in advance by the German Government of its intention to introduce border compensatory measures prompted no fundamental objection from the French Delegation.

The Council was not disposed to recognize that what had happened was a threat to the dynamics of the economic and monetary union. It took the precaution of arranging that the isolated floating of certain currencies would take place for a limited period (the German Delegation was opposed to the fixing of any period in advance).

Was it a lack of insight on the Commission's part at the time not to recommend the joint floating of the Community currencies, as urged implicitly by the European Parliament in its Resolution of 17 May 1971?

MONETARY QUESTIONS IN THE FINAL PHASE OF THE ENLARGEMENT NEGOTIATIONS

At the sixth Ministerial Meeting of 7 June 1971, the United Kingdom's Delegation surprised the Commission with a statement concerning the sterling balances problem. It recalled the positions already adopted by the Government in the House of Commons to the effect that the role of sterling as a reserve currency had already declined and that this process would continue, and that any change in the current situation would also entail approval of the owners of the sterling balances.

The United Kingdom's Delegation did not rule out, however, a phased elimination of the role of sterling as a reserve currency, its place being taken by another instrument, provided that the result was not an unacceptable burden for the United Kingdom and that the arrangement made should benefit the international monetary system and satisfy the creditors. The ball was back in the Community court.

The Community Delegation noted this statement and the British dossier was closed.

It must be said that the Commission had seen the matter differently. It had asked the United Kingdom to accept a separate protocol concerning the future conduct of its monetary policy with:

   i. an obligation to phase out sterling as a reserve currency, under the Resolution on economic and monetary union;

  ii. an obligation to ensure that the consequences of any defence of a reserve currency should not run counter to efforts to coordinate and harmonize economic policies in the Community;

 iii. stabilization of the amount of the sterling balances and negotiations with a view to disposing of them;

 iv. efforts to seek solutions in a framework wider than that of the Community.

This brought the parties concerned to the final phase of the negotiations, which ended in Luxembourg on 29–30 June. Mr. Heath had visited President Pompidou and there is every reason to believe that the two men had reached agreement to complete the negotiations on the basis of maintenance of everything the Community had achieved so far (the "acquis communautaire"), and that there was all the less reason to ask the United Kingdom to enter into further commitments—which the British public would be unlikely to welcome—in that the immediate problem had shifted as a result of the separate floating of the mark.

Thus in the middle of 1971, the Commission had abandoned its efforts to define what should be the profile of the future enlarged Community, and this meant that the final conditions governing the construction of the economic and monetary union remained almost entirely open, and that it was going to be up to the enlarged Community to reconsider the entire question.

NOTES

1. Until the February 1974 decision providing for a monthly meeting of the Ministers of Economic and Financial Affairs in the "Council", the Ministers of Financial Affairs met every month among themselves, the meeting being attended by the Vice-President of the Commission responsible for Economic and Financial Affairs; simplified secretariat arrangements for the meetings were made by the relevant Directorate-General of the Commission.

2. The Council's draft decision sheet prepared by the Council Secretariat stated that the Council had "noted" the conclusions. (This is also what the authors of this present paper remember of the discussion.) The change was made at the insistence of the French Delegation.

3. This marked the disappearance of one of the taboos of German economic policy, which, in Professor Erhard's time, had been hostile to any efforts to quantify policy.

4. OJ of the European Communities, No. C 28 of 27 March 1971.

5. Cf. Council Decision of 22 March 1971 setting up machinery for medium-financial assistance (OJ of the European Communities, No. L 73, 27 March 1971).

6. Council Decision of 22 March 1971 on the strengthening of cooperation between the Central Banks of the Member States of the European Economic Community (OJ of the European Communities, No. L 73, 27 March 1971).

7. In addition, the French and Italian Governments were unwilling to participate in a joint currency float because they believed that the DM was undervalued: in a joint float their own currencies would have been artificially overvalued, at least as long as Germany did not revalue the DM.

II. ECONOMIC AND MONETARY UNION POLICY

The Resolution of the Council of Ministers of 22 March 1971

by *Antonio Papisca*

THE DIFFERENT CONCEPTIONS OF THE EMU

The few measures which have been initiated in the name of economic and monetary union, beginning with the Resolution of 22 March 1971, are like the scattered tiles in a mosaic. The further away one goes from the time when EMU was officially "defined", the more clearly one sees how necessary it is but also how difficult it will be to bring about.

Economic and monetary union is the essential condition for the European Community's existence as well as of its development. This is why the political analysis of the failure of EMU is at the same time the analysis of the reasons why European integration as such has not progressed.

In the past, an attempt was made to distinguish between the image of the whole, or teleological image, of EMU and a range of recommendations, spaced out in time;—between what was politically desirable and what was politically feasible. The official image of EMU, as it was transmitted to us by the Resolution of the Council of March 1971 is really the result of a compromise between the two images, but which leaves open the many dichotomies which cut across the idea-project of EMU. These were the dichotomies between conjuncture and structure, economy and currency, political will and technical feasibility, economic union and political union, system of European integration and international monetary system, proposal and decision, action and institution.

Today, in the light of the overall picture of the interdependence of the problems and of the ineffectiveness of the measures taken, the dichotomies reappear as they were from the beginning: the same relations of inter-dependence and of simultaneity between equally important variables.

The initial approach to greater economic and monetary integration between the Member States of the European Community was the expression of an idea, or rather of an illusion, which is essentially "functionalist" and which in order to preserve the "acquis communautaire" treated differently economy (and technique) on the one hand, and policy, on the other, and took different attitudes towards *low politics* and *high politics*.

In 1962, the Commission pointed out the need for a closer coordination between the economic policies of the Member States and of active monetary cooperation. This was interpreted as an extension of the obligations in matters of reciprocal financial assistance on the basis of the Treaty of Rome.[1] In practice, however, this merely resulted in the creation of a series of "committees", and never passed beyond the consultative stage.

The undisturbed state of the international monetary system, and the internal economic stability of the Member States at the time, as well as the opposition of General de Gaulle to any form of supranationality prevented any advance towards economic and monetary union until 1968. It was from this year onwards that the pressure of a triple series of internal and external variables within the European system of the European Community gave the subject importance. These variables were:

1. the acceleration of infra-community trade and the putting into practice of common agricultural policy—which gave rise among the Member States to increased interdependence and a greater reciprocal sensitivity in the respective economic systems, and had an immediate effect upon the balance of payments;
2. the growth of social conflict as well as the increasing economic difficulties within certain countries, particularly France and Italy;
3. the haphazard behaviour of the international monetary system (and the fundamentally hegemonic nature of the American monetary and commercial system).[2]

The importance of this last variable in spite of its effect upon the balance of payments of the European countries was not fully realized by the European political leaders.

In the Barre report of February 1969, it was clearly stated that a "plurinational" Community (the word "supranational" was still banned) cannot be based solely upon a customs union for industrial products, nor on a common agricultural policy nor on a few fiscal "harmonizations"; what might have been useful in the 19th century—the report states—is no longer useful when, like nowadays, the economies are influenced and managed by the governments, and by the great private economic concerns, each acting according to its own particular strategy.

Coming more specifically to the common agricultural policy, the Barre report stressed that the implications of such a policy go beyond its particular framework. They affect the general level of prices, public finances as well as the monetary relations of the Member States. Serious incompatibilities, not only of a conjunctural type, which exist between the economic and social situations in the different countries demand that greater attention be paid, from the operational point of view, to what the Barre report called the "reference to the communitarian phenomenon itself". Although allusions to the pressures and the needs of the international system are not lacking in the report, the "coordination" of the economic policies and the monetary "cooperation" which it proposed depended essentially on a pragmatic logic from within the system of European integration.

Adopting the functionalist approach, the Barre report prescribed for the new phase of infracommunity relations a series of "procedures", and neither a set of "institutions" nor a "status" of integration (it must be remembered that the label "economic and monetary union" had not yet been used. It was the Summit Meeting in The Hague of 1–2 December 1969 which launched it officially).

The first model of economic and monetary union which emerged from the reflection of the Commission, was therefore a pragmatic and evolving scheme of "procedural" integration. It was composed of three essential elements:

1. the convergence of national lines of medium-term economic policy to be reached by the definition in common of fundamental objectives, such as the rate of growth of production and of employment, and the overall balance of payments;

2. the coordination of short-term economic policies in order to prevent possible imbalances;
3. a mechanism of monetary cooperation functioning within the framework of medium- and short-term objectives of economic policy and itself destined to prevent imbalances by means of short-term monetary support and medium-term financial support.

It is noticeable that in the Barre report (which was to be taken up again and polished in another memorandum of the Commission in March 1970) the specific sector of exchange rates is somewhat neglected. In this respect, the report merely acknowledges the technical difficulties which could result from the elimination of margins of fluctuation as well as the fact that it would restrict the autonomy of states to deal with their respective monetary policies. It nevertheless affirms that in order to respond to the demands, either of the common agricultural policy or of the gradual unification of the markets, it is necessary to proceed to the gradual narrowing of the rates of exchange, and at the same time to proceed to the coordination of economic and monetary policy within the framework of the Community. Thus a principle was affirmed—that of rigid exchanges—in which the Commission had always firmly believed and which had already been the subject of an *ad hoc* memorandum sent by the Commission to the governments in February 1968.

As for the international environment, the Barre report, inspired as it was by its internal communitarian view, preferred to take an attitude of *quieta non movere* rather than to propose the creation, for the Community, of an international monetary individuality.

This first conception of economic and monetary union is thus a politically and technically "soft" conception (as opposed to that of the Werner report which is a politically "hard" conception). According to the Barre report, greater economic and monetary union will be only the natural and necessary development of an already existing entity, namely the European Community as defined by the Treaty of Rome.

It was during The Hague Summit Meeting, that the conception of the EMU was situated within the political framework which characterizes it—and which will condition the way in which it might be reached in the future. The Communiqué of the Summit began by restating some great values (faith in the political objectives of the Community; objectives of stability and of economic expansion for the future of the Community) and announced a plan for the creation of an economic and monetary union founded on the famous principle of "parallelism" (the basis of the action designed to develop cooperation in the monetary field should be the harmonization of economic policies). The possibility of creating a European reserve fund was also envisaged as the result of a common economic and monetary policy (see paragraph 8 of the final communiqué of the Summit).

The idea of the EMU had now an official progenitor (the Summit) which would supervise the planning of this idea by making great statements of intent. In practice, the Commission was expropriated of its own project in favour of the Council of Ministers which was charged by the Summit with drawing up a plan by stages; a group of independent experts were to be entrusted by the Council with the final assessment.

In passing from the Commission to the Council and the Werner group, the conception of the EMU was transformed into a "hard" conception. The pursuit of the objectives of a deeper integration in the economic and monetary field was directly related to the institutional strengthening of the framework of the Community. One can say that in this phase, which was as short as it was intense (it was the period running from The Hague Summit to the final presentation of the Werner report, a period in which the decisions of the Council also adopted the interim conclusions of the Werner group), the conception of the EMU became that of an "economic and monetary entity". A sort of personalization of EMU was achieved which in the eyes of the Commission should never have been made. It was now inspired by a decidedly prescriptive approach, whereas the Barre outlook had been more diagnostic. As for the diagnosis of the infra-Communitarian situation, the Werner report referred back explicitly to the Barre report. As far as the international situation was concerned, it merely remarked on the dangerous phenomenon of the enlargement of the market of Eurocurrencies as well as on the speculative movements of capital. Although the Werner report states that the group was not trying to draw up an ideal system in the abstract, but rather to define the elements indispensable to the existence of a complete economic and monetary union, the final result was exactly the opposite. The insistence which the short-term arrangements were linked to those of the final phase is an example of this contradiction.

The spirit of the Werner report is a teleological, theoretical and sometimes academic spirit (see, for instance, the influence of the theory of optimal monetary zones)[3] while that of the Barre report is a practical and managerial one. Werner's vision of the EMU is that of an extraordinary, almost traumatic realization, whereas that of Barre is that of a fact of ordinary administration, although it is visualized as a process moderately evolutionary. To be sure, the EMU of Werner presupposes that of Barre but only in order to overtake it as quickly as possible. This is explicitly stated in the group's reports: "The implementation of the actions foreseen in the memorandum of the Commission to the Council of 17 February 1969 could give a new impetus to the efforts to coordinate and to harmonize economic and monetary policies. But this is only a starting point for the economic and monetary union which should be rapidly achieved". The EMU of Werner is a genuinely supranational political system. Among its provisions it was stated that currencies of the Member States are guaranteed a total and irreversible reciprocal convertibility, without exchange fluctuations and with relations of immutable parity or, even better that the individual national currencies should be replaced by a single European currency. It was stated also that liquidity should be created throughout the area and that the monetary policy and credit should be centralized, that the external monetary policy is the responsibility of the Community, that the policies of the Member States towards the markets of capital should be unified. It was also agreed that the basic provisions of the public budgets and in particular the variations of their volumes, as well as the way they would be financed and used should be decided at Community level; and finally, that the regional and structural policies would no longer be the exclusive province of the Member States and that a systematic consultation of the social partners should be observed at the Community level.

From an institutional point of view, the Werner report foresaw the transfer of power at the national level to that of the Community, the modification of the Treaties, the creation of a decision-making centre for economic policy which would be able to influence the national budgets and a European system of central banks, as well as the strengthening of the role of the European Parliament.

Compared with the Barre report which was simply based on a mechanism of voluntary coordination and on a mechanism of reciprocal aid—the whole contained within the clauses of the Treaties of the Community—the Werner report represented a "qualitative jump". The Council of Ministers, as I have already indicated, underwrote by the decisions of June 1970 the implications of the political-institutional order contained in the interim report of the Werner group to the effect that "the economic and monetary union implies that the principal decisions of economic policy will be taken at Community level and that all necessary power will be transferred from the national to the Community plane". At that moment the project of the EMU reached its maximum political "swelling". Later, once the Commission had taken back to the Council the proposal in order to formulate the official directive to the Council,[4] the whole project was to be reoriented towards a "soft" approach.

After the final "treatment" by the Commission, the technical conditions indispensable to the existence of an economic and monetary union, as well as its economic consequences, but not the political ones envisaged by the Werner report, were reaffirmed by the Commission (in accordance with what had already been proposed in the second Barre report). The Commission insisted especially on the theme of the coordination of economic policies and pointed out the need to pay more attention—even in the first phase of the carrying into effect of the EMU—to the structural and regional actions in order not to endanger the achievement in good time of the Union.

From the point of view of the technical measures, the reshaping effected by the Commission, rather amounted to a supplement of the Werner report. But, from the institutional point of view, the conception of EMU as visualized by the group Werner was subjected to a reversal in the opposite, "soft" direction. After having noted the general views of the Werner report with regard to the centre of decision for economic policy as well as to the communitarian system of central banks, the Commission tried to make clear (without success) that the transfer of powers from the Member States to communitarian level "should be restricted to what is necessary for the cohesion of the Union and for the effectiveness of communitarian action", and that the adaptations (not the modifications) of the Treaty of Rome should be defined in accordance with "the progress to be achieved".

This reshaping was to remain final because the formula proposed by the Commission was retained integrally by the Council of Ministers and by the representatives of the governments of the Member States in the resolution of 22 March 1971, concerning the gradual achievement of economic and monetary union in the Community.

It is in this resolution, which has the solemnity and the breadth of a true international treaty that the definitive well-known image of EMU is enshrined. Yet, in fact, it is not a concrete commitment but rather a theoretical compromise between the political approach of the Werner plan, relegated to a long preamble, and the functionalist approach of the Commission and of the Barre report, retained in the body of the resolution. By this act, the governments declared themselves aware of the profound political meaning of economic and monetary union as well as the consequences of economic policy which would flow from it. But they did not accept the institutional implications.

The system of EMU defined by the resolution contains:
1. a monetary area within which the margins of European currency fluctuation between themselves are more restricted than in relation to the dollar;
2. a mechanism of financial aid in the medium term to be managed by a European Fund of monetary cooperation;
3. a mechanism of coordination (having an essentially consultative character) of the national economic policies;
4. the provision of a common discipline of the markets of capital;
5. the provision of intervention at the regional and structural level.

More specific commitments would be taken by other decisions and notably by the resolution of the Council of 21 March 1972 which sets down in detail the mechanisms of coordination for economic policies, outlines the first (and modest) steps to be taken in the direction of a structural policy and fixes the margins of variation of the exchange rates of European currencies between themselves (2.25% above and below parity: in practice the margin of fluctuation permitted by the Smithsonian agreement of December 1971 is reduced to half as regards the relations between currencies other than the dollar but in every case it is a far wider margin than the one set the previous year by the European governments).

THE "REALITY" AND THE "CULTURE" OF EMU

What is the practical objection to the claims of EMU? What is the consistency of the scattered tiles of the great mosaic?

A short description of the real situation is needed in order to select the dependent variable of this analysis and above all to verify how much applicability and how much ritualism were contained in the 1971 resolution. In fact, rather than being decided the Economic and Monetary Union was "proclaimed": the discretionary clause of Paragraph 9 shows that the differences which exist between the governments have not been overcome and that the "political will" affirmed in the resolution is simply "confidence in the political will" of the future.

Very briefly, what we see today as the fragments of the initial stage of EMU can be described under four headings:
1. In the monetary field there was established a system of joint fluctuation of several European currencies (communitarian and also extra-communitarian) which in its present version forms a veritable international monetary sub-zone around the DM. (It is the "snake" out of the "tunnel"). There was also established a system of medium-term financial aid, managed by the Council of Ministers of the Community; the countries which want to benefit from it must undertake certain obligations in economic policy on the basis of the indications made by the Council. Lastly, there was also created a rather

unimportant mechanism of short-term and very short-term currency support. A European Fund of monetary cooperation has been created to ensure the coordination necessary for the smooth working of the exchange system in the Community.

2. For the coordination of the economic policies, there has been set up first of all a Committee of economic policy which has taken over the powers of the three former Committees (respectively for the conjuncture policy, for the budgetary policy, and for the medium-term economic policy). The main function of this Committee is to prepare, on the basis of all available information, the preliminary plan for the medium-term economic policy which the Council of Ministers adopts for not longer than five years, in order to facilitate and to guide the envisaged structural changes—sectoral, regional and social— as well as to ensure the convergence of overall economic policies. The system of coordination is based upon a mechanism of permanent consultation between the governments either in the sector of general economic policy or in that of the monetary policies of the central banks. A coordination group, which meets at least once a month, was created within the Council of Ministers. This group collaborates with the Committee of Permanent Representatives to prepare the three annual coordination meetings of the Council. The system of coordination in addition to the graduated programmes of medium-term economic policy is based on the annual report of the Council with regard to the economic situation of the Community and the guidelines of economic policy which each Member State ought to follow for the following year. The annual report is transmitted to the governments and parliaments so that they can take it into account in the preparation and debates on the national budgets. In the case in which a government decides to take a different line a meeting of the coordinating group is called.

3. As far as the capital market is concerned, the Council has drawn up directives designed to regulate international liquidity and to discourage hot money as well as to suppress the restrictions against the free circulation of infra-communitarian capital, introduced by the Member States themselves after the resolutions of March 1971 and March 1972.

4. In the field of interventions with a structural purpose mention must be made of the beginning of the Community's aid policy to the developing regional development, with its well-known limitations of funds and its provisional character.

From this brief description it can be fairly easily seen that all the measures adopted—with the exception of the "snake"—are more in line with the spirit of the Barre report than with that of the Werner report: that is, what remains is precisely the "soft" and limited set-up which the Werner report considered only as a preliminary phase to be quickly passed through.

Was the Barre plan then far more realistic? Clearly yes, although this does not imply a judgement on the effectiveness of the measures adopted, especially if they are compared with the fundamental objectives of EMU, namely the equilibrium of the balance of payments, the stability of prices and full employment. In fact, faced with inflation in double figures, with the energy crisis, the upsetting of the Bretton Woods system, and the widespread unemployment, the system of consultative coordination and mutual aid has been proved completely derisory.

On the contrary, some of the results of this system are rather paradoxical. The frequent consultations, increasing the volume and the speed of information between the governments and between their respective bureaucracies have to some extent helped governments to direct more autonomously their economic policies; this has accentuated the different trends of inflation. A positive aspect of this system, at least in perspective, is the growth of the sensitiveness of social and economic circles to the political aspects of the problem of economic and monetary integration.

In fact there developed a kind of "culture" of EMU based on the recognition of the principle of the globalization of the European problems and of the "primacy of politics" over economics. A curious aspect is the fact that while the Werner report is still criticized together, naturally, with the resolution of 22 March 1971 because they are thought to be too ambitious from the institutional point of view, the same critics prescribe new sets of rules which arise directly from the political institutional logic of the Werner project. For example, the authors of the report of the EMU study group, entitled "European economic integration and monetary union" (October 1973), after remarking that "the final motivation of European integration is political" stated that "the stress should be moved from market integration to institutional integration", in order to create "the necessary organization, that is the expression of a common political responsibility for achieving the objectives and the policies which are the heart of the EMU".[5]

The need to set up solid common institutions is still further stressed in the report of the study group *Economic and Monetary Union 1980*, "the Marjolin group" (March 1975). This report strongly criticized first all those who directed the study of Economic and Monetary integration in the sixties: "in 1969 it was decided that Economic and Monetary Union should be used during the next ten years without any clear idea of what was being undertaken. At governmental level, there had not even been an approximate analysis of the conditions which must be fulfilled. Everything was done as if the governments were acting in the naive belief that all they had to do was to decree the formation of the Economic and Monetary Union and this would be formed after a few years without any real effort and painful economic and political changes".[6]

At the institutional level, the prescription of the Marjolin report is that of a strong and binding community political framework, implying a European political power, a substantial Community budget and an integrated system of central banks. It is clearly indicated that what the Economic and Monetary Union requires is a common monetary policy, a common economic policy, a common social policy—as well as the following institutions: a common central bank or a system of regional central banks in charge of the European monetary policy; a decision-making centre for the economic and social policies able to act on the basis of a Community budget and a European Parliament elected by universal suffrage with genuinely legislative powers.

Clearly this is a reformulation, but more explicit and advanced from the point of view of the compulsory character of organization than that envisaged by the Werner report. What the Marjolin group proposed in the institutional field is perfectly consistent with the structural dimension and direction which it assigns to the EMU since the criteria characterizing the whole undertaking will be, *inter alia*, based on the social consensus of large sectors of the European peoples, and on a centre of decision in which the three classic powers should be represented: legislative, executive and judiciary.[7]

An analysis which can be seen as a sort of "authentic interpretation" of the Werner plan in the light of the failure of EMU is that made by two protagonists of the Werner group, Messrs. B. Clappier and G. Brouwers in a report dated April 1974.[8] The authors distinguish between the secondary and the major causes of what they call the relative failure of EMU. The secondary causes are the changes in the international environment, the enlargement of the Community, the disparity between the economies of the Member States, the failings in the infra-communitarian trade. The major causes are the absence of a Community authority responsible for the management of the system of European exchange, and of the institutional possibility to harmonize progressively the economic policies (the report remarks on the inefficiency of the "intensive" consultation alone) as well as the lack of financial solidarity at the European level. The authors' concluding remark is again inspired by the political approach. They criticize the approach, which consists of setting the technical objectives of integration, without being willing to admit that, from the first stages, their achievement depends on political priorities.[9]

The constant remembrance of the "political will' and of "the institution" is the meaningful change which has taken place in the study of European integration. It marks in particular the passing of the functionalist theories which have inspired the conduct of most of those who were engaged in the preparation of the EMU. What is now questioned—as stated, for instance, in the Marjolin report—is the very idea which for twenty years has been the basic thought of innumerable Europeans, namely that a European political union, especially in economic and monetary matters, would come about almost imperceptibly. This was the Europe of "little by little". Nothing that has happened until now lends credence to this idea. It can be asked today whether what is needed to create the conditions for EMU is not a profound and almost instantaneous transformation, which would take place of course after lengthy discussions, but a transformation which would at a given time, create the European political institutions.[10] The same political approach is to be found again in another important document, the Spierenburg report.

On the other hand, this new tendency can also be interpreted as an attempt by economists and some technocrats to blame the political leadership for the uncertainty of the different technical prescriptions on which EMU could be founded; or in other words a sort of transfer of risks in the application of their plans and even an attempt to cast a serious doubt on the scientific status of the macroeconomy. Of course, it is not true to speak of a corporative bluff by the macroeconomists, given that they themselves explicitly recognize, as in the authoritative Marjolin report, the provisional and experimental character of their own prescriptions. Moreover, they claim for the European institutions which will be entrusted with the management of the economic and monetary policy at community level, a "*discretionary* power similar to that which the national governments now possess in order to deal with unforeseen events".

In short, a plan to create an Economic and Monetary Union, however correct it may be from the strictly technical point of view, is not an infallible recipe. Rather it should be seen as a network of potentialities which depend on the existence of a discretionary dimension of power which should manage them. But is not this type of power representative of all the political power, that is the power of powers?

Would this be an almost paralysing perspective for national governments called on from the first to be responsible for an operation of intense "de-sovereignization" as well as for the onus and the risks associated with the experimental character of the economic and monetary measures? Be that as it may, no viable and valid alternative seems to exist for the Member States, given the very high degree of penetration already effected between their respective economies and social systems. These same economists tell us that an alternative to the supranational management of the economic and the money supply could in our particular case be far more expensive than that of "desovereignization".[11]

THE REASONS FOR FAILURE

This being said, we shall pass now to a more detailed analysis of the decisional process concerning EMU as well as the contents of the resolutions of the Council of Ministers with a view to analysing the specificity and feasibility of the undertaking as well as the consistency of political will deployed towards it.

Rather than as a single community policy the EMU should be seen as an ensemble of policies, which is itself a political system. From the point of view of operative instruments it does not add to the policies of the Member States but quite simply or gradually absorbs them; the specific character here is that of a *substitution*.

From the point of view of objectives, they fit in with the ultimate ends of the states in the economic, monetary and sometimes social field, for through the EMU they can be assured of a satisfactory expansion of the economy, full employment and stability within the Community; to redress the structural and regional imbalances from within the Community and to strengthen its contribution to international economic and monetary cooperation so as to obtain a stable and developing Community. (Resolution of 22 March 1971.) In this context the specific character is the *diffusion*.

The idea of the EMU contained in the Werner report presents the maximum of specificity from this twofold point of view for it is an essentially supranational system. In the Barre plan, there is no intention to substitute any mechanisms which are envisaged as complementary to those of the Member States. Only the part relating to mutual aid presents characteristics of specificity, although it is not a completely new practice at the level of international economic relations.

In the resolution of March 1971 the idea of substitution of EMU is to be found only in the preamble. Thus, one can speak only of a specificity in perspective. The contents of the outline are "soft" in character. There is no specific idea in the field of coordination of economic policies. There is a modest degree of specificity in the measures with regard to the rates of exchange and financial aid. The sphere of competencies and powers of the

464

Member States remains intact; even taking into account the "technical" measures which have been mentioned nothing has been added, from the point of view of substance to the load of obligations to which the Member States were already subject by virtue of international cooperation (for example within the IMF). In reality rather than taking concrete *actions* certain *principles* were confirmed which were themselves current in international practice (in any case they are being overtaken by events).

Given the low degree of specificity as well as the lack of any genuine constraint in the technical measures (as the adoption of the discretionary clause of paragraph 9 proves) the problem of compatibility with the policies of the Member States arises only in connection with the measures concerning the narrowing of the fluctuation margins of the European currencies between themselves. In fact, this measure was not objectively convenient as such for any of the Member States; not to Germany, whose government wanted to recover for the DM its "fair" parity, above all in relation to the dollar in the framework of the dynamics of real economic phenomena. But the neo-liberal attitude of the German government was also reinforced by the political and military need not to annoy the United States, which refused officially to devalue the dollar and which supported the revaluation of European currencies (and of the yen). Neither did the narrowing of the fluctuation margins suit France (notwithstanding the last ditch defence of the principle made by the French authorities) because it would have deprived the French policy-makers of an important means of action, precisely that of the exchange rates policy so useful for a government which is far more sensitive to the problems of employment and of growth than to those of stability. Nor did this measure suit Italy. In reality what was fairly specific showed itself incompatible with the real national interests and thus was not feasible.

The problem of the feasibility of the EMU itself should be examined in relation to the whole project or to the particular measures taken in 1971. Neither the one nor the other, as they were conceived, were really feasible at that time. First of all, because the structure of the European Community system was by its very nature alien to the macroeconomic logic and to the political portent of the EMU; for, the working of EMU as a system of economic management would have implied first of all a confrontation and a discussion of the basic orientations of the national economic systems in a phase of rapid differentiation. (Even the functional treaties like those of Rome would not have been signed in 1971!) The discussion of the basic values of the different regimes was in effect incompatible with the functionalist, technocratic and summit-like logic which had been strengthened by the compromise of Luxembourg of January 1966 and which continued to be the cornerstone of the Community. Such a confrontation, precisely because of its political and social implications, would not have been possible without a significant (and not purely symbolic) support of one of the main layers of the social European body, that is of the political parties and trade union forces which remain structurally excluded from the vertical and fundamentally corporatist dynamism of the Community system.

I mean by that that a political prerequisite is indispensable to the achievement of a true economic and monetary union in the Community. The Union requires a certain type of "political development" of the Community.[12]

The Werner plan expressed clearly the need for a qualitative transformation of the Community system. The error, let us call it theoretical, of the Werner group was to consider such a transformation as a dependent variable of its project and not as an independent one. This would have delayed its execution but would have forced the political will of the countries to accept measures which were politically limited but technically correct and effective. What I have just said will be better understood when we have examined the situations which existed outside and inside the Community at the time of the EMU debate. On the international plane, the monetary order created at Bretton Woods was already in a state of crisis and there was some awareness of this crisis, even though the milieux of European central banks were officially silent on the subject. The exchange rates between the European currencies and the dollar had altered greatly. The speculative movements (hot money) on the stronger currencies succeeded one another either (directly) by the initiative of private individuals or (indirectly) by the will of the American government, which pushed for a revaluation of European currencies, especially the DM. The tension on the exchanges was consequently continuous and insupportable for the European reserves, being obliged to intervene more and more heavily on the rates of the dollar.

In the meantime, the negotiations for the entry of the United Kingdom, Denmark, Ireland and Norway were officially opened on 30 June 1970. Two problems arose directly out of this in relation to the pursuit of the plan for EMU; that of the sterling balances and that of the international role of the British currency and that of the link between the enlargement and the reinforcement of the Community by creating a strong common framework. "No enlargement without reinforcement," was the pervading principle at the time. As for the behaviour of the international system, it must be said that there were cogent enough reasons for the Europeans to press for the construction of a more integrated economic and monetary system within the Community. They needed to defend themselves against:

1. the importation of the inflation in dollars resulting from the deficit in the American balance of payments
2. the speculative movements of short-term capital facilitated by the inclusion within the structures themselves of the Community's economy of the multinational American corporations (a sort of long arm) and by the availability on the spot of liquidity in Eurodollars
3. the legitimate claims of the United Kingdom to negotiate its entry into the Community at as low a price as possible for its balance of payments as well as for its international prestige.

But the "urge to act", the reasons for acting to be found in the international situation were not fully recognized and weighed by the European political leaders, whose internal divisions proved to be far stronger than the pressure from outside and prevented a unified and effective reaction.

An official response on the part of the European governments either to the behaviour of the international system or to the authentic needs of the process of integration was given. But it was a false reply from the political point of view and an incorrect solution from the technical point of view. The international system reacted in a completely negative and dominant way by neutralizing the first practical step taken by the Council in the field of exchanges.

Politically the response was false because the Member States did not follow up at all their pledge to proceed with the second stage of EMU.

Within the Community there existed therefore a complicated situation regarding the objective economic conditions in the different countries and above all regarding the way in which such situations were interpreted by the governments and handled outside in the name of the national interest.

As far as the system of integration as such was concerned, one can say that there was an objective, even functional, need to adopt the new measures which were required, if integration was to progress and the "acquis communautaire" to work well. In particular, the common agricultural policy which had been endangered since the coming into force of the system of unitary prices by the instability of the exchange rates (especially the French franc and the DM) and thus by the different purchasing power of the European currencies had required for a long time a system of fixed parities and rigid exchanges instead of the very complicated mechanism of compensations and restitutions instituted at the request of France and Germany in 1969.

Furthermore, the complete achievement of customs union which coincided with the end of the Gaullist era had created the need—perhaps more psychological than technical—to right the wrongs inflicted on the Community and to be more committed to integration.

Lastly, there was another demand, undoubtedly more urgent than the above-mentioned, even if the political leadership as a whole and public opinion was not so aware of it; that of creating a set of monetary and financial instruments directly and autonomously managed by the European Community as such which would correspond to the volume and speed of infra-communitarian trade.

Different from these needs, which constituted the Community's real interest, were the particular interests and attitudes of the Member States.

In France and Italy, after the events in the spring and autumn of 1968, the political and social situation changed rapidly; the social conflict and the pressure of wages increased while public expenditure expanded especially in Italy. Thus we saw attitudes which were definitely anti-economic from the point of view of the neo-liberal (and German) rationality, as, for example, the increase in wages at the same time as opposition to devaluation in France in 1968.

By contrast, stability in Germany was very seriously threatened by the flood of short-term capital which forced the Bundesbank to intervene massively in dollars.

Inflation trends in the various countries towards the end of the 1960's began to show marked differences, not so much at first in monetary terms (the rates of inflation varied from 3 to 5% in 1969–1971), as in real terms (rates of productivity) and political choice (inflationary or deflationary policies). In France and Italy, the governments' priorities were full employment and growth, whereas the German government thought that Europe should be "an area of stability".

The different curve of the inflation clearly implied that there was a different assessment of the economic problems and of the role of the monetary and financial instruments; in any case it accentuated in a macro-economic and structural, and therefore political direction, the problems of EMU. This was translated into divergent attitudes towards the nature and the pursuit of the interest of the Community.

467

Negotiations between governments at Community level was prevented by the structural impossibility of effective participation at the same level of the social and political forces which conditioned the governments inside the respective countries. The strength of the objective demands of the European Community was far less than that of the governmental interests of the Member States. The "proclamation" of EMU could only be a symbolic compromise. Even the technical principles inserted into the resolution of March 1971 were only an abstract theoretical warning.

Given the practical impossibility of starting an efficient and compulsory harmonization of the national economic policies, the first concrete step could only have been monetary measures; and this is exactly what was done, but on the basis of a principle which was not suitable at the time, namely the rigidity of exchanges.

It must be mentioned here that a long time before the 1969 currency crisis, it was considered as very useful, if not indispensable to ensure a wider flexibility of the margins of fluctuation. For the flexibility and not the rigidity of rates of exchange linked with parities as well as the possibility of proceeding automatically to slight but constant adjustments of the parities themselves (crawling peg)[13] would have given to this adjustment of the currencies a permanent and real character in relation to the various trends in the national economies. But on the contrary the solution of the gradual narrowing of the margin of fluctuation was adopted. This went against both the real interest of the individual countries and against the main trends of the international system as such.

In summary, the project of Economic and Monetary Union even and especially in the compromise obtained through the Resolution of March 1971 was not feasible, if one takes into consideration the following fundamental reasons:

1. the growing difference between the economic and social systems of the main Member States of the Community
2. the absence of a Community framework structurally able to initiate a "European Social Pact", which alone would have "legitimized" the harmonization of the different policies
3. the anachronism of the principles of fixed parities and of rigid rates of exchange
4. the incompatibility between the aim of the supranational strengthening of the institutions and the aim of the entry of the United Kingdom into the Community.

To be sure, even if they had not fulfilled the major objective of the Werner plan, the governments could have taken important decisions had they been convinced that the cost of the failure (and of the bluff) of the EMU would be higher than that of a reasonable success. But for that they should have held a common view of the international reality as well as of the future of the Community. This is precisely what was lacking at the time of the negotiations.

Above all, what was missing was a really political approach—namely, the approach of political utility. For the principle reasons for achieving an undertaking like that of the EMU, with its profound interdependence between the Member States, should be founded on political or ideological grounds before they are founded on the grounds of strictly economic or technical interests.[14] From this point of view, it was correctly remarked that "a serious coordination of the economic policies cannot create the will for political integration, but on the contrary assumes that it already exists".[15]

The central problem of this undertaking, that is the problem of the cost of adjustment in the weaker countries, cannot be solved by looking at it from the viewpoint of economic utility. It is difficult to understand, in any case, why richer countries should take it upon themselves to transfer a part of their wealth to poorer countries or to countries in difficulties. The principle of active solidarity when it is applied to States and not to individuals is not based on ethics, but on political convictions (and calculations). The utility of the principle of active solidarity for rich and poor countries alike must be perceived in the political perspective and especially for the reason that *political instability is as contagious as monetary inflation*, especially between countries which are "open" and linked by a network of communications of all kinds.[16] Nevertheless, the analysis of the special interests of the different European states, and even more of their actual behaviour shows that the approach of political utility was not shared even by those countries which officially adopted the political approach in general.

In order to analyse the behaviour of the governments in the case of the EMU, it could be useful to draw a distinction between the internal and the external actors: on the one hand, the Six, and on the other the United States and the United Kingdom.

It must be remembered that within the Community itself the thinking on and the negotiation for the EMU had been actually a bilateral activity between Germany and France. They were the two protagonists in the group of the internal actors. The role of the Commission, because of its almost continual endorsement of the French proposals, appears as somehow secondary, at least until the moment of the formulation of the final proposals to the Council. The other Member States of the Community shared, according to their respective interests and objectives, the attitudes of one or the other European Power. As a matter of principle, the countries of Benelux and Italy were in favour of the so-called political approach. Generally speaking, there was therefore a great coalition: how then to explain the failure of the EMU?

From outside the Community two powerful actors were at work: one, the United States in an official position of "benign neglect" (at least until President Nixon's statement of 15 August 1971); the other, the United Kingdom, as an active participant in the negotiations for adhesion and therefore playing a quasi-Community role.

Now let us look at the positions of the major actors.

France. What purposes did she want to achieve by an Economic and Monetary Union? Her fundamental purposes were:
1. to save the Common Agricultural Policy, threatened by the instability of the rates of exchanges and therefore of prices;
2. to receive Great Britain within a strong Community framework, and
3. to find a counterpoise, through the means of a European monetary unit, for the hegemony of the dollar and for the American policy at the level of international transactions.

The requirements of the Common Agricultural Policy being interpreted almost exclusively through the system of unitary prices the optic could only be monetaristic, namely towards the narrowing of the margins of fluctuation. France was decidedly opposed to the German thesis of the subordination of the financial and monetary measures to the prior coordination of the economic policies. France's interest was here to conserve her own autonomy in the field of conjunctural policies. Belgium, Luxembourg and even Italy had also taken the monetaristic position of France. (But the monetary option of Italy was no doubt weaker than that of the others.)

As far as the interest of preparing a constraining Community framework, in view of the United Kingdom's entry, this also revealed a deep contradiction in the French position. Objectively, it would have been logical that the actual strengthening of the Community framework should have consisted of an increase of the powers of the European institutions, rather than of the formalization of a system of intensive consultations. But France was content with the agreement of 22 April 1970 on the Community regime of "ressources propres" and the budgetary powers of the European Parliament. The French Parliament was the first to ratify that agreement on 23 June 1970. The other countries followed suit at the end of the year. This hurry could be explained on the one hand by the interest of France to finalize completely the system of the Common Agricultural Policy (the agreement of 22 April was the last promulgation) and on the other hand, by her will to possess a greater power of negotiation when coming to the meeting with the United Kingdom. The suspicion that the behaviour of France was in reality a game of role-playing is confirmed by the agreement which was afterwards concluded with the United Kingdom at the Heath–Pompidou meeting of 20 and 21 May in Paris, where the two leaders stated, "the convergence of their conceptions of the European structure".[17]

The attitude of France towards the United States is perfectly consonant with a line of foreign policy inaugurated since the early sixties. Among other conditions, there was the demand that the price of gold should be raised, which would have been tantamount to the practical devaluation of the international currency. The interest of France was therefore completely opposed to that of the American government.

Germany. The objectives of Germany were entirely different. The principal task assumed by the German government since the end of the war was that of achieving economic stability at the European level as well, through the effective coordination of the national economic policies (the German government was convinced that the cause of inflation was not to be found in the behaviour of the market, but rather in the bad policies of the governments). As for the problem of exchange rates, the position of Germany was favourable to a system of fluctuations. Its interest was, above all, to give back its parity to the DM, without violating the rules of the market. From the institutional point of view, Germany remained faithful to its macro-economic approach and maintained the thesis of the need for an economic and monetary policy managed by the institutions of the Community—or in other words in complete agreement with the "political" thesis of the Werner group.

The Netherlands. The Netherlands shared the German macro-economic position and were even more explicit in stressing the need for a system of concerted fluctuation. But in the specifically institutional question, the Netherlands were rather inclined to postpone all important decisions until after the United Kingdom's entry into the Community.

The German attitude towards the EMU looks in retrospect to be the most coherent. This is because it was the outcome of a long reflection and of undeniable technical competence (as well as of a healthy internal economic situation). It was not surprising to see Chancellor Brandt arriving at The Hague Summit with a plan of monetary and economic union, with the provision of a Reserve Fund, already prepared and with a timetable for its preparation in stages.

Coming now to the external actors, the United States had real interests which, beyond the official position of "benign neglect", were completely contrary to the creation of the EMU. The American government subordinated any attempt of monetary regionalization to the reform of the international monetary system. One of the immediate interests of the United States was to make Europe absorb a part of the liquidity in dollars, therefore passing on to others the effects of its own inflation. Another interest was to oppose by every possible means the Community's common agricultural policy. In the meantime, private operators were causing a strong outflow of dollars in Europe as well as in Japan either for the purpose of getting higher interest on the Eurodollar market or with a view to profiting from any possible revaluation of the European currency.

The United Kingdom, in turn, seemed to be more preoccupied in the negotiations with the Six by the commercial and tariff aspects—aspects which were not immediately important for the specific purposes of the EMU—rather than by the international role of its currency which was, on the contrary, France's great concern.

The jigsaw puzzle of the special interests of the Member States and other states is therefore rather complicated.

It is difficult to single out anyone who represented the interests of the Community, *qua* Community, in achieving the EMU. It is easier to find it in the documents than in the organs. The long-term interest of the Community, which is tantamount to the institutional strengthening of the Community, can be found in the Werner plan. The short-term interest of the Community is, on the contrary, to be found in the Barre report: to defend the "acquis communautaire" meant above all, as has already been seen, to make the system of unitary prices function within the framework of the CAP. This could have been obtained through the system of the free coordination of the economic policies, through the narrowing of the margins of fluctuation and through the mutual financial aid.

In practice, the organ which officially embodied the interest of the Community, the Commission, took upon itself this second kind of interest, concerned as it was not to politicize, and consequently, debilitate the foundation of the Community as it then was. Any modification of the Treaty was exorcized. The view of the Commission was fundamentally "internal", hence its determination not to upset the external interests of the Member States (the realm of "high politics") and therefore to defend the official principles of the international monetary system. This view suffered from an obvious narrowness of vision.

The Commission therefore can be reproached for first of all having committed the fundamental error of not keeping open the problem of the exchange rates. We have already noticed that the first Barre report showed a certain perplexity on this particular point. But the Commission, having received the technical support of the Committee of Governors of the Central Bank, reasserted its traditional monetaristic line in the Memorandum of 1970 (point D). The option in favour of the rigidity of exchange rates is a permanent attitude of the Commission.

Another mistake by the Commission was not to have insisted on a more compulsory system of the coordination of economic policies, not even when all the empirical evidence had proven the futility of the system of consultation. Two examples are highly significant from this point of view. The "preliminary" consultation of the Monetary Committee on the devaluation of the French franc in 1969 took place on 10 August, which is two days after the devaluation had taken place. The consultation on the revaluation of the DM took place on 29 September, that is the very day when the German government had already taken the decision.[18]

To be sure, the low profile policy of the Commission towards the EMU had its own reasons. But it cannot be entirely justified, given all the facts which would have objectively motivated a "raising" of the profile in the Community's interest of both short and long term. Among these facts, one must recall the agreement of 22 April on the Community resources and powers of the European Parliament; the decisions of the Council of 8–9 June 1970 which, as has already been seen, look in retrospect like the political highlights in the history of the EMU; the fact that some French Cabinet Ministers had at the time begun to have doubts about the validity of the principle of the rigidity of exchanges; and especially the fact that some members of the Werner group, as for example the Germans, had worked "very close to the sources of power". The Commission made the mistake—blameworthy from the point of view of Community ethics—of minimizing the Werner plan in its communication to the Council in October 1969.

The Commission should have used this last moment of politization to stress the general interest of the Community as against the individual interests of the Member States. On the contrary, the Commission did what could have been done by the Council. Instead of putting forward, on behalf of the Community, a synthesis of the different national interests at the highest possible common denominator, the Commission undertook a kind of reductive diplomatic mediation at the lowest common denominator.

A greater political determination by the Commission would certainly not have been sufficient by itself, to bring into being the EMU of the Werner plan. But at least it would have slowed down the dissolution of the project of the Economic and Monetary Union in the Council.

The conduct of the Commission can be explained by the fact that it had become increasingly cautious because of the frustration it had suffered in recent years. But its composition at the time and the attitude of some of its influential members might have also influenced its conduct. The Commission at the time seems to have been somehow susceptible to the French point of view. It also showed a certain irritation (or even jealousy) towards the Werner group which it somehow considered as the usurper of its institutional functions. The paradox of the whole thing is that the "usurper" appointed by the Council and therefore by an organ less Community-minded than the Commission proved to be more Community-minded than the Commission.

From the institutional point of view the Werner group must be considered as a sort of hybrid: while appointed by the Council, it did not have either an inter-governmental or a strictly technical nature. It was formed by Community personalities, namely the presidents of five technical committees, the General-Director for Economic Affairs (and another functionary of the Commission as the Secretary). Yet it acquired a real political representativeness when M. Werner, Prime Minister of Luxembourg (the only country which did not have a representative in the group), was appointed its president. Notwithstanding its official character as a group of experts, the origin of the group's mandate, its geographical representativeness as well as a presidency which was uninhibitedly political, gave a definite political character to its structure and to its action. From the outset, its basic approach was political as is proven by the fact that in its interim report to the Council the group intended to provide a sort of political institutional projection of the EMU rather than to give precise indications on the technical ground. It is also known that the group worked very concentratedly and in a very optimistic atmosphere. Within the group the members behaved as if they were committed not only in their personal capacity as experts but also as the spokesmen of their respective countries. Yet the discussions within the group were very lively especially in the second phase of the work, namely after the moment when the technical aspects were submitted to the governors of the central banks and the latter dealt only with the monetary measures. This provoked a clash between the economists and the monetarists, rather than between the functionalists and the politicians. The group concluded its work with the conviction, which was particularly strong within the German delegation that everything that the group had proposed was binding and could not be the object of any kind of reduction by the Council, still less by the Commission.

Within the Council of Ministers the representatives of the governments, divided from the beginning between the economists and the monetarists and even more between the politicians and the functionalists, could not agree to find in the proposals the basis of a real synthesis of the different interests. But it must be recognized that at the moment of the final decision about the EMU, of the EMU which had been proposed, the will for action was already very weak because of the two external factors; the progress of the negotiations with the United Kingdom and the uncertainties of the behaviour of the international system (and of the government of the United States in particular).

The greatest absentee of all was, in the case of the EMU, public opinion. Apart from a few professional associations, there were no important reactions from the social sectors. This lack of participation must be explained apart from the technical and therefore difficult aspects of the EMU by the fact that effects of inflation were not yet felt in the national family budgets. It is only from that moment (1973–1974, but which occurred after the failure of the EMU) that the fight against inflation became the main concern of public opinion, as is clearly shown in the opinion polls published by *Euro-barometre*.

473

The same polls assert that the creation of a European currency was only the last or next to last interest of the public. Should we interpret that as a clear tendency of public opinion in favour of the *economists'* point of view?

(The author would like to thank the officials of the Commission of the European Communities and in particular MM. Henri Etienne and Giuseppe Ciavarini-Azzi of the General Secretariat for their help during the preparation of this report. Their report on the same subject was a fundamental source for the present research; the Office of the Communities for Italy; the many Italian colleagues who took part in an *ad hoc* round table organized in Rome by the "Movimento per l'integrazione universitaria europea" (MIUE).

The author expresses his profound gratitude to M. Pierre Werner who accorded him a very rewarding interview in Luxembourg.

The opinions expressed in the text are the sole reponsibility of the author.)

NOTES

1. *Memorandum of the Commission on the Action Programme of the Community in the second stage*, 24 October 1962.
2. For an analysis of this period, see, among others, L. B. Krause—W. S. Salant, eds., "European Monetary Unification and its Meaning for the United States", Washington, The Brookings Institution, 1973. See also L. W. Ross, "The Washington Monetary Agreement, 1971", in "The Yearbook of World Affairs", Vol. 26, 1972, p. 203 f.
3. See, among others, R. A. Mundell, "A theory of Optimum Currency Areas", in M. B. Krauss, ed., "The Economics of Integration", London, Allen and Unwin, 1973, p. 177 f; and also J. E. Meade, "The Balance-of-Payments Problems of a European Free-Trade Area", Ibid., p. 155 f.
4. See *Communication and Proposals of the Commission to the Council referring to the institution by stages of the Economic and Monetary Union*, 31 October 1970.
5. "European economic integration and monetary union", p. 52.
6. *Ibid.*, p. 4.
7. *Ibid.*, p. 27.
8. *Analyse critique de la première étape de l'Union économique et monétaire européenne*, Bruxelles, Avril 1974.
9. *Ibid.*, p. 12.
10. Marjolin Report, p. 5., March 1975.
11. See J. Pinder, "Il nuovo disordine economico internazionale e le sue conseguenze per l'Italia", in "La politica estera italiana: Autonomia, interdipendenza, integrazione e sicurezza", Milano. Ed. Comunita, 1977, p. 124 f.
12. On the theory and problem of "the political development of the Community", see, among others, A. Papisca, "Europa" 80: dalla Comunità all "Unione europea", Roma, Bulzoni, 1975: IDEM, "Comunità europea: dal consenso permissivo alla partecipazione politica", in "Rivista Italiana di Scienza Politica", 1976, No. 2, p. 289 f.
13. On this subject, see, among others, G. Carli, "The Monetary Aspects of British Entry into the Common Market", in "Problems of British Entry into the EEC", Reports to the Action Committee for the United States of Europe, European Series No. 11 (London, Chatham House and Political and Economic Planning, PEP, 1969, p. 47; B. Balassa, "Monetary Integration in the European Common Market" (paper). Conference on Europe and the Evolution of the

International Monetary System, Geneva, Graduate Institute of International Studies, 1972.

14. Cf. W. M. Corden, "The Adjustment Problem", in L. B. Krause—W. S. Salant, "European Monetary Unification and its meaning for the United States", p. 179.

15. W. Neubauer, "La politique actuelle d'Intégration européenne: solutions de rechange au plan Werner", in Rapport du Groupe de réfléxion "Union économique et monétaire", Bruxelles, Octobre 1973, p. 141.

16. Cf. J. Pinder, *op. cit.*, p. 130.

17. Cf. P. Gerbet, "Les Communautés Européennes en 1971: Elargissement sans reforcement", in "Conflicts et coopération entre les Etats, 1971: Prélude à un nouvel ordre international?", Paris, Colin, 1973, p. 211 f.

18. A. I. Bloomfield, "The Historical Setting", in L. B. Krause—W. S. Salant, *op. cit.*, p. 9.

III. ECONOMIC AND MONETARY UNION POLICY

The Need for a Medium-term Goal

by *John Pinder* and *Loukas Tsoukalis*

The decisions of the Council of Ministers in March 1971, which launched the project for economic and monetary union, already disappointed the hopes that had been raised by the summit of December 1969. Three years later, after the end of the first stage, little of what was planned had been achieved. Five of the Community currencies were floating jointly and the other four separately; the liberalization of capital movements was less than in the 1960's; the Council's common guidelines for policy, when they were more than very general recommendations, were honoured only in the breach; and the European Fund for Monetary Cooperation was not much more than a brass plate on a door in Luxembourg. Up to now, three years later again, there has been little if any further progress. Why, after such high hopes, has the performance been so low?

Economic misfortune, in the form of turbulence rougher and more durable than expected, is one explanation. Lack of political will on the part of Member States or of prudence in the presentation of the project are others. These explanations doubtless have some validity. But they could lead one to conclude that the obstacles lay in the economic or political conjuncture: that when the conjuncture improves, the same formula should be tried again. There are grounds to believe that such a conclusion would lead only to renewed disappointment.

This paper argues that there were, on the contrary, some profound structural reasons for the failure of the project, so that a different strategy must be followed if another major initiative is to succeed. The project was, it is suggested, unsuited to the contemporary economy; and although the admirably lucid paper presented to this conference by representatives of the Commission, L'Union Economique et Monétaire, refrains from discussing the issues of economic substance, we cannot follow their example because the question of economic feasibility is central to our argument. Politically, the contention of this paper is that the proposals considered by the Council were all, in varying degrees, unsuited to the character of contemporary Member States or to the requirements of effective integration in terms of institutions or, more precisely, instruments.

AN ECONOMIC STRATEGY UNSUITED TO THE MODERN ECONOMY

After the French devaluation in 1957 and the Dutch and German revaluations in 1961, there were no further changes of parity among the Six until

1969. Because people tend to look at the future through the lenses of the recent past, it became widely assumed that a *de facto* monetary union, at least as far as exchange rates were concerned, had already been achieved.[1] These were the circumstances in which agreement on common cereal prices was believed to have forced member governments into the permanent locking of parities; and although the will of governments to ride over the economic dislocations that maladjusted parities could cause was doubtless exaggerated, the potential significance of such maladjustments was grossly underestimated too. The neo-functionalists, in expecting the agricultural tail to wag the economic dog, reflected the prevalent view in the Community that the economic dog could be readily trained to do any necessary tricks.

The stability of the six in the sixties was the exception, not the rule

It was too easily forgotten how exceptional was the experience of the Six in that decade. Among major industrialized areas in the previous half century, only the United States in the 1950's had known a decade of similar strength and stability. As the expression "island of stability", much used in Community literature, implied, this set the Six apart from the international economy during that period, when Britain and the United States were suffering repeated currency crises. The feeling grew that the Six were not as other countries were (nor, indeed, as they themselves had been in the quite recent past). General de Gaulle, in his press conference in November 1967, explaining why Britain could not be allowed to join the Community, drew attention to the recent devaluation of sterling to illustrate why Britain could not "be part of the solid, interdependent and assured society in which the Franc, the Mark, the Lira, the Belgian Franc and the Florin are brought together".

Six months later the events in Paris led to wage increases which led in turn to the devaluation of the franc in August 1969. Against the background of mounting dollar crises, this was followed in October by a revaluation of the mark. So the summit of December 1969, at which it was agreed that a plan for economic and monetary union should be drawn up, took place when the Community's brief golden age of stability was already past. It was assumed, however, that these were temporary aberrations,[2] and the Council took its decisions to launch the economic and monetary union in February and March 1971, based on the hope that the future "ne fut pas trop agité".[3]

This hope was not justified. Three months later, in May 1971, the mark was floated and in August with the floating of the dollar the Bretton Woods system came to an end. It may well be argued that if awareness that this system was breaking up had been more widespread, the German offer of a joint Community float would then have been accepted; and this might indeed have strengthened the monetary identity of the Community. But stable parity relationships among the Community currencies would not have lasted much beyond 1973.

For in 1973, responding to the synchronized boom in the major industrial areas, the violent inflation of commodity prices was followed by OPEC's quintupling of the price of oil. This injected a massive volume of both deflation and cost-push inflation into the world economy in general and the

Community in particular, which raised the question whether the old assumptions about the type of economic and monetary management suitable for the modern economy were any longer valid, not only for the international economy but also domestically, for the Member States of the Community as well.

This storm did not come suddenly out of a clear sky. Since 1968, the trend in the industrialized countries had been for both inflation and unemployment to increase. But this trend was suddenly and sharply magnified. Inflation in the Community countries was lifted to a range of between 7 and 25% and balance-of-payments disequilibria to a range of between $-\$7$ billion and $+\$8$ billion. Unemployment converged on rates of 5% and more. Attention has focused on the problems of Britain and Italy, and latterly France, where social and political weaknesses have made it difficult to get a grip on inflation; and this may lead people to suppose that the trouble lies in particular deficiencies of these countries and not in a general weakness of the system. Particular weaknesses there certainly are, but it is important to realize how bad the best performance in the Community still is, by any standards that were recently regarded as normal. With unemployment at 5%, investment stagnating and growth averaging 2% a year in the 1970's, the record even in Germany is highly unsatisfactory; and the strength of cost-push inflationary pressure is reflected in the official fear of reflation despite such high unemployment.

If this is a conjunctural agitation in the Community economy, which can be remedied by the conventional global demand management on which the project for economic and monetary union depended, the process is taking so long that the project would need to be redesigned to deal with any further such aberrations in the future. But it seems more likely that the scale and nature of the difficulties reflect structural changes in the economy which call for new methods of economic management.

Structural changes call for new methods of economic management

There seems to have been no doubt among the actors in the decisions that led to the launching of economic and monetary union that global demand management could maintain equilibrium among the economies of the Member States in an acceptable way. Notwithstanding the differences between "economists" and "monetarists" about the relationship between economic policy coordination and monetary integration, both sides of the argument were agreed that parities could be permanently locked within ten years and equilibrium could be achieved by harmonizing the policy preferences of the Member States in their management of global demand.

The Werner report recognized that global demand management is not enough. "In the framework of an economic and monetary union . . . it will also be necessary to envisage measures bearing on structural problems the essence of which will be profoundly modified by the realization of this process".[4] But there was no detail on the nature of these problems and no concrete measures were proposed. The Commission proposed measures of "accompagnement" for the first stage of the project, but the thrust of these was towards the further removal of barriers and distortions to competition (liberalization of capital movements and fiscal harmonization),[5] not towards

479

measures of positive integration to deal with the Community's structural problems. The Council dropped a proposal for a regional fund and did not adopt any others outside the field of monetary and general economic policy.

There is an important school of economists who would still agree with this approach; and despite the great expansion of policy activity beyond the conventional management of demand, governments still lack a conceptual framework for their new methods of economic management, which could offer the basis for a revised concept of economic and monetary union itself. But it seems rash not to allow for the strong possibility that the turbulence of the 1970's reflects changes in the structure of the modern economy which have rendered the management of global demand ineffective unless accompanied by forms of economic management relating to particular markets as well, so that reliance, as in the economic and monetary union project, on the coordination of general economic policies could produce equilibrium only by intensifying unemployment and provoking economic decline.

These changes of economic structure include the growth of specialization and interdependence, and of skill and capital intensity. To change people or capital equipment from one function to another in response to market forces may be costly, slow or even impossible. These rigidities also manifest themselves in inelasticities of supply and demand which provide a powerful basis for the administration of markets by suppliers of labour or of products: that is to say, for cost push and price push. It follows that a squeeze of global demand can cause unemployment and stagnation in many of the particular labour and product markets without controlling inflation in those that are more strongly placed. If this is so, stagnation is inherent in the modern economy unless the adjustments in the particular markets are helped by manpower and industrial policies, and the cost push and price push are controlled by price and income policies.

These new problems are superimposed on older ones such as the chronic underdevelopment of some regions and much intensified by a new level of social demands, articulated through social organizations and political democracy, which resist the imposition of hardship resulting from economic change.

The result is that price stability and economic growth depend, not just on policy preferences in relation to global demand, but on the behaviour of individuals and groups and on rigidities of economic structure which can be managed and adjusted only by intervention of a more detailed kind. Until these methods of intervention have become successful enough, our economies are likely to continue to converge on high unemployment, which depends on the similar structures of their capital and labour stocks, and to diverge in their inflation rates, which depend on the differing behaviour of their individuals and groups.

The governments of West European countries have already gone a long way in developing the new policies that are needed. Sweden and Germany have gone farthest with manpower (or labour market) policies. Sweden's industrial policies have had good results, with industrial investment strongly supported during the world recession, and unemployment, helped also by the manpower policy, at not more than 2%. Germany's voluntary incomes restraint, based on the *Konzertierte Aktion*, has been the best example of an incomes policy, though not successful enough to allow the reflation of an under-employed economy. But although all of our governments have done much in an *ad hoc* sort of way, none has yet developed a set of policies powerful enough to ensure stable prices with full employment; and the implications of these new policies for economic management at the Community or wider international level have as yet scarcely been thought about.

Yet if these arguments are in the main justified, there are some profound consequences for the Community. Divergence among the Member States' rates of inflation is likely to remain until the social and technical problems inhibiting effective income policies have been resolved or the degree of economic interdependence is such that prices and wages cannot diverge as much as they do now; and the permanent locking of parities must wait until then. The common market will increasingly be affected by the Member States' industrial and manpower policies; and the Community must have much more ample industrial and manpower policies if it is, as a minimum, to retain meaning for the common market and, preferably, to promote the Member States' many common interests in these fields. "Measures bearing on structural problems" have become more urgently necessary, and in different ways, than was expected at the time of writing of the Werner report.

Whether more of this should have been anticipated at the time is no longer a practical question. Certainly nobody foresaw the full force with which the changes in the structure of the modern economy were to be revealed by the events following 1973. The need now is to recognize that the changes have taken place, and that the concept of economic and monetary union must consequently be redesigned; at least to allow, by a suitable combination of credit and adjustment policies an adequate response to large and long-lasting conjunctural fluctuations without causing needless suffering to the peoples of the Member States; and probably also to include a common approach to deep structural problems which require that a new form of economic management be grafted onto the old.

AN UNFEASIBLE POLITICAL STRATEGY

Through most of the 1960's divergence between France and Germany in their attitudes towards the United States and Britain and their political and economic philosophies stood in the way of the formation of a separate monetary identity for the Community. By the time of the summit in December 1969, however, these obstacles seemed on the way to being removed. With the growing importance of Community markets for German exports and the realization that the Bretton Woods system could no longer provide a framework for stability, German policy-makers had become more ready to accept the idea of a regional monetary system. Meanwhile, the French had realized that neither the strength of their economy and balance of payments nor fixed intra-Community exchange rates were any longer guaranteed. As a consequence, there was an increased interest in laying the foundations for a European monetary union.

Germany's need for a Westpolitik based on the Community was balanced by a new French willingness to accept British entry and a less anti-American policy. German readiness to give economic support to European integration if the Community institutions were reinforced had its counterpart in a French desire to strengthen the Community in advance of British entry. Monetary instability threatened both the common agricultural policy and the customs union, on which France and Germany respectively relied. All actors in the Community accepted the feasibility of a permanent locking of parities ensured by an appropriate management of global demand. The difference between "economists" and "monetarists" was not so fundamental as it appeared at the time since both agreed on the feasibility of the final goal and the controversy was only about the strategy to be adopted during the transitional period.

Yet this convergence of different interests did not last for long. An important turning point was the abortive meeting of the Council of Ministers in December 1970, when it became clear that at least one country, namely France, was not prepared to accept the political and institutional implications of the Werner report. From then on, EMU became increasingly identified with short-term political and economic considerations.

Were the differences between France and the other countries so incompatible that no substantial project could have succeeded? Or did the failure lie in the presentation and timing of the plan that was put to the Council? We will argue that neither of these explanations is satisfactory: that the permanent locking of parities, or a common currency, was itself politically unsuitable as the central aim, and that the methods proposed to implement it were inappropriate to both the politics of Member States and the integration process.

Could a commitment to federation have been accepted?

Economic and monetary union, as defined in the Werner report, meant that "the principal decisions of economic policy will be taken at the Community level and therefore that the necessary powers will be transferred from the national plane to the Community plane".[6] This, as the report said, "raises a certain number of political problems",[7] which was surely putting it mildly. If the powers to take the principal decisions of economic policy are transferred from the national to the Community plane, we have a federation. It is not enough to say that the process implies "the progressive development of political cooperation", or that economic and monetary union "appears as a leaven for the development of political union, which in the long run it cannot do without".[8] Monetary union defined in this way is transferring what are arguably their most important functions from the Member States to the Community, and if the Community does not by then have solid federal institutions, disaster will soon follow. The report was near the mark when it affirmed the need for a centre of decision of economic policy which "will be politically responsible to a European Parliament".[9]

Given the euphoria of the 1960's about the stability of exchange rates, could the group have underestimated the political magnitude of the change proposed? Was there an element of Friedmanite belief that money could be kept out of politics, or of neo-functionalist confidence in the safe hands of the technocrats and the "automatismes qui avaient fait leur preuve dans la suppression des obstacles aux échanges"?[10] Although such ideas were behind the "monetarist" approach, the Werner group did not in the end follow such a line. The need was expressed for the Community centre of decision, for its responsibility to the European Parliament, and for Community control over the main decisions on Member States' budgets. Yet in delivering their report to the Council, and thus in effect presenting the member governments with a proposal to commit themselves to federation, the Group avoided discussion of the immense institutional implications for the Community and the Member States. Nor did they seem aware of the need for intense political preparation for such a fundamental step. They said only that "a deeper study of the institutional problems thus raised is outside the framework of the mission of the Group";[11] and they limited their concrete proposals to the convocation of an intergovernmental conference during the first stage—that is to say after the decision to establish the federation was to have been taken— to consider proposals for amendments to the Treaty of Rome.[12]

This was done in the hope that the member governments would accept. Statements already made by President Pompidou in favour of an EMU, together with the presence of M. Clappier, Deputy Governor of the Banque de France, in the Werner group and his endorsement of the final report, must have given the group the impression that Gaullist continuity had been abandoned to the point where the French government would commit itself to a federal Community, implicitly perhaps at first but explicitly within two or three years. But the group was mistaken about the balance of political forces prevailing in France at the time. The strong Gaullist reaction to the Werner report and the reversal of official French attitudes made it clear that France was interested in monetary measures without being ready to accept the institutional consequences inherent in the attribution of competences to the Community.[13] France, that is to say, was far from willing to accept a commitment to federation.

Perhaps it was thought that the desire for monetary measures must imply an acceptance of such institutional consequences. It certainly seems unrealistic to suppose that governments will, in a context of purely intergovernmental cooperation, make all the hard choices that will be required if balance-of-payments equilibrium is to be maintained with exchange rates permanently fixed and trade permanently free within the Community. Even with its commitment to the common agricultural policy, and even with the constraint of the existing Community institutions, it was France that had secured derogations from the common agricultural price levels after devaluing in 1969; and fixed exchange rates could impose much greater strains than that, involving for example hundreds of thousands of unemployed. But in order to square its desire for the locking of parities with its rejection of a supranational Community, the French government had to believe that national governments would impose on their countries whatever monetary discipline might be needed to operate a Community system which would bear close resemblance to the gold standard and laissez-faire, although this was in contradiction with their own internal economic policies and their past experience.

This belief of the French government was not credible to Germany and other Community partners, who were not willing to take more than small and tentative steps towards the permanent locking of parities without agreement to transfer powers to Community institutions. The paper on *L'Union Economique et Monétaire*, on pages 12 and 16, suggests that the Commission's low-profile, functional and practical approach would have been more likely to secure agreement. But so long as permanent parity-locking was at the centre of the project, Germany and others would have insisted on the need for institutional arrangements which France refused to accept. Quite apart from the question of what would happen somewhat later when the issue of institutions would have to be raised, the Commission's proposals following the Werner report succeeded in avoiding French opposition only at the expense of causing irritation and disappointment in the other Community countries and particularly in Germany and the Netherlands.

Were the two positions on institutions, then, unavoidably incompatible? Only, it may be argued, in relation to the ultimate goal of permanently locked parities, which France's partners held, in one way or another, to imply the conversion of the Community into a federation. The French government had recently agreed to the grant of budgetary powers to the European Parliament in return for its partners' agreement to give the Community its own fiscal resources; and the European reserve fund, proposed by France, itself implied some sacrifice of sovereignty which France had hitherto been unwilling to concede. It follows that French policy had evolved to the point of accepting measures with significant implications for sovereignty, but not so far as to accept the loss of control over the commanding heights of economic policy.

Would the Member States now agree to federate?

If this French position had been associated only with the person of General de Gaulle and the immediate aftermath of his regime, it would now be of no more than historic interest. But there is reason to believe that it was more structural: that changes since the 1950's in the character of Member States have caused not only France, now joined by Britain as the principal resisters to supranationality, but also other Community countries to view political integration in a different perspective from that of the 1950's.

These changes may be obscured by the use of a general concept of political will towards unity. The Member States of the Community are, for the most part, much more strongly entrenched than they were soon after the war, and the desire to merge their identity in a federation consequently lacks its former pervasive force. They have many goals and interests to satisfy, and European unification has to take its place among them. If it seems to reinforce the other interests, it is desirable; if it prejudices them, it is not desired. If the proposed form of unity fits the government's conceptions, unification is acceptable; otherwise not.

Among the interests of Member States, in the rough world of the 1970's, the control of economic forces which are causing so much inflation and un-employment stands very high. This is in theory a plus for the Community, because some of these forces are international and beyond the scope of national governments to control. But the normal reaction in times of stress is to rely on the familiar, established and probably stronger institutions, in this case the national governments. It is only in a shattering crisis, which may of course come and for which we should be prepared, that enough of the Community's peoples and governments would be likely to accept willingly the irrevocable transfer of predominant economic power to the Community. Otherwise, it seems more plausible that they would agree to enable the Community to take substantial action in the common interest, without an irreversible commitment to federation: if not continuous creation, then at most a series of small or middle-sized bangs, rather than one big bang of a decision to create this political universe.

Even if the logic of the federalist position is accepted, the force of this line of argument must be recognized. For the burden of responsibility for economic policy in the circumstances of the 1970's is very great, and newly responsible federal institutions might well be crushed by it, since the people would tend to blame them for problems such as inflation and unemployment (as the British, whose entry into the Community coincided with the new time of economic troubles, tend to do), even if the problems would have been worse under the responsibility of the national governments. If a middle point can be found, where the Community would have substantially more responsibility than it does now without carrying sole responsibility for the "principal decisions of economic policy", the capacity of the institutions to go on to take the principal decisions could be more confidently judged. Perhaps such a middle-point solution is as much as the Member States would now accept as a binding commitment, even if they maintain the perspective of an eventual transition to full economic and monetary union, subject to a later decision to proceed with it.

Can Community policies be implemented through national instruments?

The validity of the French insistence on the sole responsibility of national governments, constrained only by the discipline of fixed exchange rates, for economic policy in a monetary union was rejected by other governments of Community countries and by the Werner group, who put their faith in the coordination of economic policies. But as the term implies, the emphasis was on the coordination of national policies undertaken with national instruments, not on the execution of common policies by means of common instruments. There is reason to doubt whether such a system of intergovernmental execution would be much more effective than the intergovernmental decision-taking preferred by the French authorities; and if it were to be effective, the question arises whether Community control over national budgets would not needlessly emasculate the national political systems, and thus be less acceptable than a normal federal system in which there would be Community control over a substantial Community budget while leaving national budgets under the control of national governments.

The Werner report sought control over the budgets of member governments because the "economic significance" of the Community budget would "still be weak compared to that of the national budgets, the harmonized management of which will be an essential feature of cohesion in the union".[14] Control in some detail was envisaged: "The margins within which the main budget aggregates must be held will be decided at the Community level";

this would include determination of variations in the volume of budgets, with quantitative guidelines on "global receipts and consumption, and the direction and amount of the balance"; "searching comparisons will be made of the budgets of the Member States from both quantitative and qualitative points of view. From the quantitative point of view the comparison will embrace the total of the public budgets, including local authorities and social security".[15] The Community would decide not just the size of the member governments' budget balances, but whether their public expenditure should be raised or lowered and whether they should spend more or less on investment or public consumption.

On the monetary side, there would be, either *de facto* or *de jure*, a common Community currency after parities had been permanently locked at the end of the final stage, and this would be a most powerful Community instrument. But there seemed to be no hurry to establish Community instruments meanwhile, during the stages when the coordination of policies was to be consolidated. The European Fund for Monetary Cooperation should be set up as soon as possible "in order to prepare for the final stage in good time", but this could be done during the first stage only if sufficient harmonization in economic policies had already been achieved.[16] If effective harmonization depends on the existence of adequate common instruments, the results required for progress towards the final stage would never be achieved.

The concept of harmonization through Community control over national instruments seems to be less acceptable, politically, than the Community use of common instruments, at least in the form of control the Werner group proposed for national budgets. It is hardly conceivable that the American states or the Swiss cantons would accept such intervention by the federal authorities in matters so central to their social responsibilities. It is the essence of a federal system that the states should be free to order their own affairs; and the size and distribution of expenditure in the budget is surely central to these.

It may also be asked whether such detailed control over budgets would really be necessary for Community demand management. The effect on global demand would come mainly from the surplus or deficit, and a case can be made for Community influence over these, if so much importance and trust are attached to attempts to adjust global demand. But to go further is surely to incur heavy political costs in the pursuit of a theoretical perfection in what is in practice an extremely imperfect art.

But the principal argument against Community rule through national instruments is not that it will, if effective, give the Community unnecessary power over the national systems, but that it will be ineffective and thus leave the Community as powerless as before. It was not for nothing that the Commission and the French government fought so hard for the Community's own fiscal resources, in the belief that national contributions would be less reliable. Uncomfortable monetary instructions to a member government from a Community without monetary resources might well prompt the question: "how many SDRs has the Commission?"

The use of the main instruments of economic policy is a product of the highly articulated political systems of the Member States. These have a strong momentum and an inner logic which are very hard to shift. They would resist with all their formidable strength Community instructions that appear to imply higher unemployment, lower social spending or more inflation for a Member State than it would choose of its own accord—and major decisions of economic policy tend to do such things. The result would be, since at least until federation is achieved the member governments will have a powerful role in Community decision-making, that Community decisions would in fact ratify the existing policies of member governments; and this has indeed been the normal content of economic policy coordination up to now. If decisions are nevertheless taken which go against the grain of a member government, it is most questionable whether they will be enforced, because it is so hard to know, in ever-changing circumstances, whether a failure to meet the targets is due to objective factors or to a lack of determination to comply.

For such reasons it seems unlikely that Community competences to decide in matters of economic and monetary union can be adequate, without Community instruments with which to execute the decisions, or to influence member governments to change their own policies, for example by offering or withholding credits or matching grants.

This analysis has focused on the Werner report, because it gave the fullest exposition of how economic policies could be coordinated. But without commitment to all the detail of the report, the German government supported its general approach. Naturally, being the principal creditor among the Member States and likely for some time to remain so, Germany wanted to ensure that there was some control over the use to which its money would be put. Where this was to comprise Community control over resources embodied in Community financial or budgetary instruments, the German demand was incontrovertible. But before the Community instruments (fund for monetary cooperation, reserve fund, bigger Community budget) were established, Community control based on the provision of German national resources would look like, and would probably in fact be, a guise for German control. Added to the Werner proposals for detailed control over national budgets, this presented genuine difficulties to France.

It is difficult, and now a matter of historical interest, to apportion shares of the blame for the institutional impasse which so much reduced the project for economic and monetary union by the time the Ministers took their decisions in February and March 1971. But it does seem in principle necessary that the countries which are in a stronger financial position should be ready to put their share of money into Community budgetary and financial instruments from the outset of any project to enhance the Community's role in economic management. Otherwise that role is not likely to be enhanced, since action with the Community's own instruments will be impossible and influence over the member governments' instruments is likely to be more apparent than real.

The need for a medium-term goal

The Werner report recommended the goal of complete and tightly defined monetary union with some immediate monetary steps towards that end and the coordination of economic policies. The monetary steps would be small so long as Member States could adjust their parities out of the snake and into it again, and enormous once that instrument of national policy lapsed.[17] The policy coordination, particularly with respect to national budgets, would be relatively unimportant if the above argument is correct, and enormously important if it is not. Although it could be argued that the Community should move incrementally from the adjustable snake to the lapsing of such adjustment, and from a gentle application of economic policy coordination to a firm and decisive one, there was no indication as to how this incremental progress would take place, nor indeed any clear medium-term objective between the snake as a technical device for reducing margins of fluctuation and the permanent locking of parities which would amount to a common currency. Between the very small step and the very big goal, the middle ground was left vague. Since the economic and monetary unification to achieve the final objective that had been established "with clarity and precision" was to be "an irreversible process which must be approached with the firm intention to pursue it to its conclusion",[18] it may have been thought that a major medium-term objective would only distract attention from the final aim.

In view of the incompatibility of the views of the French and the other governments about the institutional implications of the final aim, the Commission tried to avoid trouble by being less precise about the end and more reticent about the institutions.[19] But the final aim of economic and monetary union still seems to have loomed large enough in the Commission's plans to have caused at least the Germans to raise the issue of institutional implications; and the Commission's thinking about the foreground, being concentrated on relatively modest amounts of automatic short-term credits and conditional medium-term credits, was on sound lines but insufficiently ambitious to canalize all the political will for economic and monetary unity that had been evident at the time of the summit in December 1969.

Given the impasse on the institutional implications of complete monetary union, this political will could have been canalized only by detaching it from the precise final aim (which the Commission intended to do) and attaching it to an intermediate goal of really substantial importance (from which the Commission's concrete proposals fell too far short). The final aim would have remained as a perspective and a commitment of principle, which the member governments could convert into a firm commitment once the interim objective had been satisfactorily achieved. But the medium-term goal would have to be valid, useful and important enough in its own right to be worth achieving even if the member governments then found that they did not want to go farther. It will be argued, in the concluding section, that such a strategy could be designed, especially if substantial elements of the new policies for dealing with structural problems are included.

A NEW STRATEGY FOR ECONOMIC AND MONETARY UNION

Since the disappointments of the first stage of the project for economic and monetary union, the Community has not lacked proposals for useful activities in the economic and monetary field. The Regional Fund has been established and the Social Fund expanded. The Marjolin report,[20] the Commission's report on European union[21] and now the MacDougall report[22] have considered many useful ideas, including the pooling of a proportion of Member States' reserves, the creation of a parallel currency that could replace the dollar in some of its international functions and the expansion of the Community budget to $2\frac{1}{2}\%$ of Gross Community Product, which would make possible much more powerful employment, industrial and regional policies. The Tindemans report[23] included a number of these proposals but, unlike the other reports, reverted to the role of the snake as a *force motrice*. The problem is how to weld such heteregeneous proposals into a strategy that could canalize the member governments' political will when it is next available, and thus help our countries to regain, through the Community, some of the control over economic forces which have escaped the influence of national governments, partly as a result of the postwar international liberalization and the very successful liberalization of the Community's own internal market.

Many of the measures proposed imply substantial policy instruments for the Community. Some of these are financial, such as the reserve fund and parallel currency. Others are budgetary, such as the Community expenditure implied in many suggestions for manpower and industrial policies. Others are legal, such as the European company statute. Taken together, such instruments would enable the Community both to act directly on its economic problems and to influence the actions of the member governments. The Community would, like its Member States, have a substantial capacity for management of a mixed economy and a number of the attributes of a welfare state. But the Community would not remove from the member governments their power to control their own economic policies, although its financial and budgetary weight could make its influence a fairly powerful one. Exchange rates would remain adjustable by the Member States, although real substance would be attached to the recognition that exchange rates are a matter of common interest, through the Community's use of its own financial resources in support of its exchange rate policy. Agreement for better coordination of the relevant economic policies, while less ambitious in theory than before, would be more effective because the Community's resources would lie behind it.

These proposals do not, in themselves, depend on the convergence of the Member States' economies. Thus the reduction of surplus shipyard capacity, modernization of the remaining yards and retraining of workers are a common interest, even if the Member States' rates of inflation differ. In such a context, the enlargement of the Community to the south presents a less formidable problem, because the new members could participate in a broad range of the Community's policies, and any differing treatment with respect to exchange rates, for example, would not appear such a striking anomaly.

The differential political attitudes of member governments towards the concept of federation could also be more readily accommodated within such a project. The project could, indeed, be said to be extranational rather than supranational, because the Community would act outside the authority of the separate member governments but not above them.[24] Having become accustomed to the activity of such a substantial extranational Community and found it of value, even the more sceptical governments might then look more favourably on proposals for a further advance to federation.

489

To wait for economic convergence before any major new Community initiative may be, in contemporary economic circumstances, to wait for a long time. Meanwhile, the many Community policies that could be of benefit to the Member States, a number of which are the subject of other papers for this conference, would languish for lack of political interest in the Community. To repeat the EMU formula much as before, as Mr. Tindemans and others have recently appeared to suggest, would only risk a repetition of the previous failure, in the face of similar obstacles, both economic and political. The passage between this Scylla and Charybdis could be towards the medium-term goal of a major endowment of financial, budgetary and legal instruments to the Community, to enable it both to influence the economic conjuncture and help solve the new structural problems, combined with a commitment to closer economic cooperation by the member governments but without removing their control over their own instruments of economic and social policy.

NOTES

1. The origins and development of the Community's policies relating to economic and monetary union are analysed in Loukas Tsoukalis, *The Politics and Economics of European Monetary Integration*, George Allen and Unwin, London, 1977, in which the original sources of information used in this paper are fully documented.

2. The devaluation was described as "signifiant le réglement pour solde de tout compte des séquelles des événements de mai–juin 1968". *L'Union Economique et Monétaire*, p. 15.

3. *Ibid.*, p. 21.

4. *Report to the Council and the Commission on the realization by stages of Economic and Monetary Union in the Community: "Werner Report"*, Supplement to Bulletin 11–1970 of the European Communities, Luxembourg, 1970, p. 25.

5. *L'Union Economique et Monétaire*, p. 17.

6. Werner report, p. 26.

7. *Ibid.*, p. 13.

8. *Ibid.*, p. 12.

9. *Ibid.*, p. 13.

10. *L'Union Economique et Monétaire*, p. 20.

11. Werner report, p. 13.

12. *Ibid.*, p. 24.

13. *L'Union Economique et Monétaire*, p. 18.

14. *Op. cit.*, pp. 10, 11.

15. *Ibid.*, p. 25.

16. *Ibid.*, p. 25.

17. The Werner report expected that this should happen in the second stage. *Op. cit.*, p. 25.

18. *Ibid.*, p. 14.

19. *L'Union Economique et Monétaire*, pp. 12, 13, 16.

20. Commission of the European Communities, EMU/63, March 1975.

21. Commission of the European Communities, *Report on European Union*, COM(75) 400, 1975.

22. *Report of the Study Group on the Role of Public Finance in European Integration*, Commission of the European Communities, April, 1977.

23. European Union, *Supplement to the Bulletin of the European Communities*, No. 1/76.

24. These ideas have been more fully developed in J. Pinder, Europe as a Tenth Member of the Community, *Government and Opposition*, Autumn 1975, and Das Extranationale Europa, *Integration*, Bonn, 1/78.

IV. ECONOMIC AND MONETARY UNION POLICY

Some Political Problems of European Monetary Integration

by *Karl W. Deutsch*

Those who wish to restrict the interference of governments to a minimum are nowadays monetarists and they still prefer the least degree of public control of monetary matters. But control of money means the levels of employment or unemployment. It means the levels of prices and therefore their rate of inflation. It means to a large degree the rate of economic growth in real terms as well as in nominal terms. We do not have, even on the national level, a sufficient understanding of economics to know precisely how one manages these instruments of control. And my colleague, when I was at M.I.T., Paul Samuelson, wrote about 1950 that luckily now, at long last the problems of economic freedom and planning had been solved. Thanks to Keynes, he wrote in 1950, we now understand how to have full employment, stable prices and steady economic growth. Twenty-seven years later Paul Samuelson no longer thinks so. In the meantime, having become older and more sceptical, he has earned a Nobel Prize in economics. Perhaps, precisely, because he has become more sceptical.

The first problem that arises in regard to European monetary integration seems to me to be to what extent can ignorance be diminished by writing it large? If one does not know how to steer a lifeboat, does it follow that one knows how to steer the Titanic? One could possibly argue that a political–economic unit that is bigger has greater reserves and can therefore afford more errors and mistakes. It is possible that a united Europe could afford more ignorance than can single national states. But it is also possible that the errors of a larger united political community could be more fateful than the scattered and divergent errors of constituent nation states.

Monetary unions were tried several times in the nineteenth century. There are still French francs, Belgian francs and Swiss francs to remind us that once there was a Latin Monetary Union. There are kronors in Scandinavia to remind us that Sweden, Norway and Denmark once had a common currency which they only gave up in 1912. How much have we learned, how much more competence do we have now, so that there are good reasons to expect that a monetary union of the European Community will do better than its smaller predecessors did?

Here we are confronting a key issue. Money is the key instrument of economic guidance and control. If that instrument can be merged or integrated, almost everything else can be integrated. On the other hand, it has been said at this conference and elsewhere that one should not overlook the national diversities.

As a political scientist, I must suggest that we should make more precise what diversity might imply in social and political terms. Between Northern

493

and Southern Europe it might imply a high diversity in the rates of infant mortality, a high diversity in life expectancies, a high diversity in the number of Communist votes, a high diversity in political stability. The most diverse political systems at the beginning of the century were, on the one hand, Tsarist Russia, and on the other hand, the Austrian–Hungarian monarchy, and we know what happened to them. The Western European idea of having a high degree of intervention by welfare officials and an interventionist state has its difficulties. But in the Mediterranean countries we have had less interventions by social workers and more interventions by colonels and generals.

A European Community now seems politically more feasible with a Europe of 12, because the Mediterranean countries, at the moment, are luckily all in a phase of either constitutional government or, as in the case of Spain, of a cautious approach toward constitutional government. Unless we get a degree of European solidarity, a degree of a European welfare state, a degree of social adjustment on a European level, it does not seem very likely that this period of constitutionalism in the northern Mediterranean will last indefinitely; and the political difficulties of creating a Europe half constitutional and half dictatorial would be formidable. In fact the European governments have quite consistently refused to accept Spain in her days under Franco into the European Community.

I would like here to draw attention to two notions which perhaps are much more the pre-occupation of political scientists, the pre-occupation with quantitative data. One speaks of the welfare state. Another speaks of prohibitive costs. How much would even a modest European welfare policy cost? Who has tried to work it out? After all the European Commission has considerable research resources. In addition, many basic facts are known. We know roughly how many people there are. We know what the income figures are. We know the unemployment figures. We could have some ideas of what would have to be done.

Moreover, we have some relevant experiences from particular countries. How large a proportion of the gross national product of the German Federal Republic went into the equalization or burdens, both among regions and between the category of one-fifth of the population, who were expellees and had come penniless into Germany, and the four-fifths who already had been settled there. In other words, Western Germany had more formidable problems of equalizing disparities in income with one-fifth or one-fourth of its population who were refugees or expellees from Eastern Europe. And West Germany succeeded. How much did this *Lastenausgleich* cost? I am sure the orderly German Federal Republic has all the necessary statistics, and these could help you estimate what a European social policy would cost.

There is a second point which is slightly related to the first. If one unifies currencies one gets conflicts of adjustment which economists call *friction*. And here a very strange thing occurs. Theoretical physicists sometimes treat friction as almost negligible. But engineers measure friction very carefully; they say how much of it there will be and how long it will last.

Economists usually speak about friction, but at least in their text books they dismiss it. We would want to know how much, how long, what would be the costs, what are the orders of magnitude we are dealing with? I think on this point the discussions highlight a serious qualitative concern with the important intellectual and political alternatives, such as the functionalist alternative, the federalist, and the solidarist options. What we do not have yet is enough information to fill the quantitative knowledge gap. We have a knowledge gap as to what would be involved in these matters on a European scale. The quantitative filling up of these alternatives in terms of time and cost would help us a great deal, and the discussion could go one step forward if we had these estimates and data. Another point made was that Europe was shattered by the shock of 1973, or at least that European monetary union was greatly set back by it. There is truth in that. We remember also that in 1933 the great depression pushed states apart. But within a large continent, in the United States, the American response to the depression was an increase both in federalism and in solidarism. The depression brought about the social security laws, a federal minimum wage, a federally-set interest rate on loans by the Reconstruction Finance Corporation and all the other measures that reduced disparities among the states of the union. Since we are thinking of a federation, this American experience is not wholly irrelevant.

I have another point to raise before this group. When European agricultural prices were put together, there was not only some institutional machinery provided, but there was a considerable provision of at least in part unrequited transfers. That is to say, some subsidies were paid to agricultural producers in different fields, and some of these subsidies were raised in some parts of the Community and disbursed in other parts of the Community, leaving some countries and regions without an immediate return flow of payments.

The economist Kenneth Boulding has argued that one of the tests of the integration of a group is the willingness of its members to accept some degree of unrequited transfers. Now one cannot run an entire economy on unrequited transfers, but if everything has to be exchanged against countervalues this balancing of accounts each way for every unit will rarely result in full integration.

What strikes me in the papers and in the discussion so far both in the Commission report and in the university papers, is that nobody seemed to think very much of the possible need for such unrequited transfers, just as one is transferring now some economic resources to support the prices which farmers can expect for their produce. There was no discussion for any equalization of burdens or any transfers to help stabilize employment in those parts of Europe either in national states or regions most in need.

Within the nation states such transfers are made quite often, though to a limited extent. In the United States, which we often mention as a kind of model of an integrated continent with its fifty states, the citizens of Connecticut get one dollar from the national government for every two dollars they pay in taxes. The citizens of Montana get two dollars federal subsidies for every dollar they pay in taxes. The net result is therefore that Connecticut, to some degree, subsidizes Montana in the not unjustified hope that a general circulation and generation of wealth in the United States, as a whole, will also result in financial benefit to the citizens of Connecticut. Here in Europe we find, so to speak, a political and economic non-event. Nobody discusses the question whether any parts of Europe might need some equalization of burdens but the European countries may need to consider explicitly this possibility, if they wish to develop and use their relationships so that Europe will begin to look more like one country. In the German Federal Republic for instance, there have been very major efforts to equalize the living standards, the per capita incomes and the levels of employment among the ten Länder which constitute between them the German Republic. Our Italian colleagues know certainly much better than I can the efforts Italy has made for years, dealing with the Mezzogiorno and in general reducing the sectoral differences and regional differences within the nation. But whereas on the national level or even on the continent-wide level of the United States measures for reducing disparities are part and parcel of the discussion of a common economic policy and a monetary policy, a reduction of intra-European disparities seems to be discussed in a different context and not in connection with economic and monetary measures to reduce intra-European disparities, particularly between Northwestern Europe, on the one hand, and Mediterranean Europe, on the other. Is it a good idea to keep monetary unification in one field and matters of social policy and social integration, such as a reduction of disparities or equalization of burdens or stabilization of employment, entirely in another?

V. CONCLUSIONS

Problems of Economic and Monetary Union

by *Karl W. Deutsch*

The following points of agreement emerged during the discussions.

1. The idea of European integration still implies as an objective the joint management of the economy, perhaps going as far as a common currency; this objective may be described as economic and monetary union.

2. The resolution of 22 March 1971 was a failure for the reasons given by the rapporteurs:

a. the differences between the structures of, and economic and social systems in, the different Member States, and the absence of Community action in this context;

b. political differences, and no political system which might resolve them (through consensus or majority);

c. contradictions within the resolution itself, which were not suited to the situation;

d. the external environment.

In brief, the functional approach had not worked. A new type of federal approach should be sought, based on social and political solidarity.

3. Monetary union, if it comes about, will have to be accompanied by an adequate Community welfare policy for all those living in the Community; this does not mean that social situations and consumption patterns must become identical, but that inequalities must be reduced to a tolerable range politically. In this sense vertical integration should give way to horizontal integration.

4. If Europe is to achieve an adequate welfare policy, and impose the necessary balance between consumption and investment, it must take the path of democracy.

5. These problems will take on added dimensions with a further enlargement of the Communities.

6. The cost of this "welfare democracy" will have to be calculated. The Commission should do this. The effort required is within the Community's capabilities, witness the Federal Republic's achievements in the equalization of burdens. It appears that this basic point has never been properly studied, but the principle of solidarity with the poorer countries where welfare is concerned seems to be closely linked with Community solidarity in other fields, including the monetary field and such fields as external relations.

7. Integration will imply economic adjustments, and the extent of the "friction"—that is, the delays and social and economic costs—these adjustments will involve should be calculated.

8. The Community responds to international events. In 1973 crisis, the

Community was divided. In 1933, Europe broke up while the United States reinforced its Federal system and intervention at Federal level.

9. The Community should have strong leadership. It is essential that agreement be reached on the Community's aims and on the main economic and social choices.

10. In any case, to attain the harmonization of structures essential to EMU, the Community must have:

a. a budget significant enough to be an instrument of solidarity;

b. a reserve fund, and perhaps a reserve currency.

11. These aims would be difficult to achieve without an elected Parliament, and without effective participation mechanisms for the two sides of industry at the European level.

GENERAL CONCLUSIONS

Ideas in the Making of Europe

by *Ghita Ionescu*

> "If the ideas are correct, it would be a mistake, I predict, to dispute their potency over a period of time. At the present moment people are unusually expectant of a more fundamental diagnosis; more particularly ready to receive it; eager to try it out if it should be even plausible . . . I am sure that the power of vested interests is vastly exaggerated compared with the gradual encroachment of ideas. Soon or late it is ideas, not vested interests, which are dangerous for good or evil."
>
> John Maynard Keynes,
> *The General Theory*, pp. 383–384

The purpose of the study, and of the intensive research, lasting almost two years, which preceded it, was to examine the specific character and the feasibility of the policies of the European Community. We surmised that the best means of studying the specificity of these policies was to contrast them with the same type of policies being carried out, at the national level, by the Member States of the Community. We surmised that if one were to contrast these two kinds of policies in this way, one could, with a fair amount of scientific accuracy, discern the specifically European characteristics of, say, the Environment or the Energy policies proposed by the Community, their advantages, or disadvantages, when compared with the Environment or the Energy policies pursued by each of the individual Member States. In other words, why and how can the policies of the Community be considered as the "right alternatives" to the national policies?

But, at the same time, the study of the European policies also entailed a critical assessment of the feasibility of the policies proposed. If these policies were to be implemented, how practicable, realistic, effective and acceptable to public opinion at large would they be? And how well have those policies of the European Community which have already been implemented in the Member States been prepared and presented to the citizens of the European Community?

These are the two questions which the Research Project, the Conference and now the book, endeavoured to answer, by submitting the reports of the experts of the European Commission to the critical analysis of the counter-reports of the eleven European Universities engaged in the research—and finally to the common discussion of the Conference.

However, the reports and counter-reports on each of the area alternatives discussed, together with the conclusions which the groups drew from their case-studies, need to be interconnected. The disparity of the separate findings and the fact that together they covered only part of the political output of the Community[1] are two important difficulties to be reckoned with when one attempts to draw more general conclusions. But in most of the texts, and even more so in the discussions of the group and the plenary meetings, themes of a more general character were heard with significant frequency. Both the research and the Conference referred constantly to the mutations already effected in the policies of the Member States by the importation of the "European dimension"; to the specific differences between Communitarian and national solutions for the same political problems; to the transformations or deformations suffered by these solutions when and if applied; to the need for a new European legitimacy; to the contact or lack of contact between European policy-makers and the European public.

In order to give to these and other themes a greater coherence these conclusions have been grouped into four parts: the mutations in European policy-making; the intrinsic differences in processes of policy-making; the coherence and validity of the policies of the European Community; and the dialectics of the European alternatives.

THE MUTATIONS IN EUROPEAN POLICY-MAKING

In attempting the study of national and of European policies, we have been using as the standard of value judgment the European point of view, the general as against the particular. This does not preclude using the national point of view in assessing the value of national policies. But the former approach is justifiable, indeed legitimate, insofar as, since the entry of each of the nine Member States in the Community, an essential mutation has been continuously taking place in its national policy-making processes. The rationale of the national policies is, by the very fact of the nation's accession, being superseded by the Community policies. The particular logic of their previous policy-making processes is being gradually contrasted with the general logic which will eventually embrace the component national logics.

There is nothing new in this "mutation"—it is the characteristic federalist mutation. But can this federalist mutation operate also in the case of the European Community—which is not a federation, but only a process of integration? The answer is yes, in spite of current disappointments.

To be sure the process of integration has been slowed down, in the sense that it has not yet entered the phase of positive, structural integration for which further institutional changes or qualitative jumps are required. For the last decade or so integration has been submitted to the hesitating decisions of the Council of Ministers, an essentially ambivalent institution of the Community as it turns one face toward the European problems as a whole, and another face to the separate national problems of the Member States. But neither can we speak of disintegration. The typical symptom of disintegration which is the withdrawal of one or more Member States from the Community, is missing. Conversely, as long as all Member States remain in the Community and work within its present structures, weak and flexible though they may be, the slow mutation of the national policies towards Communitarian policies will continue to take place.

Three factors confirm this continuation of the mutation. One is the increased tendency of national governments to "hive-off" national problems to the Community. The two others are *l'acquis communautaire* and *le fait communautaire*.

500

It is becoming increasingly clear that the national governments are inclined to "hive-off" more of their previous national political responsibilities on to the European Community. One of the latest examples can be found in the reiterated statements by the President of the French Republic and by the Prime Minister of the United Kingdom, two statesmen particularly proud of their country's national sovereignty, to the effect that unemployment is no longer a problem which can be solved by any European Member State within its own borders and that it ought to be solved by the European Community for all the Member States. This might be seen as just a political manoeuvre, a way of "passing the buck" of one of the most arduous problems to somebody else. But, whether sincere or not, these statements do represent, beyond the intentions of those who made them, the reality of the increasing inability of Member States to solve their own problems with their own means. The corollary to this growing realization is the need to act together within the Community framework. And the corollary to this is, inescapably, the need for further, positive, integration. This conclusion however is not yet accepted by the majority of the Member States. For these governments, inclined though they may be to consider the European Community as a *deus ex machina* for solving their insoluble problems, are consistently disinclined to provide the Community with the institutional framework and the instruments which would give it better facilities to solve these problems.

The pressure exercised by the Member States on the Community to assume responsibilities and find general solutions on such acute collective problems as unemployment, and the continuous decline of the dollar in the stock exchanges of the world, were among the causes for the sudden revival of the project of Economic and Monetary Union since December 1977. As the reader has seen, the study group which reported in this book on the Economic and Monetary Union, treated it as one of the "lost opportunities" of recent European history. Yet, as early as December 1977, the new President of the European Community, Mr. Roy Jenkins, was able to put forward again some immediate plans related to, and leading to, the ultimate project of a European and Monetary Union. To be sure, the first steps to be taken would be toward the further coordination of the currencies of the Community so as to protect them together against the threat of the instability of other non-European currencies. But action only in the monetary sphere would be precariously insufficient. Monetary arrangements will have to be sustained by a general European economic policy. This was in a sense also the implicit reply of the Community to the request of the Member States that the Community should find European solutions to the problems of unemployment in all Member States. Unemployment, and employment policy, are only by-products of the general economic policies. As such, they could not be examined, at the European level, without having the economic policies also examined at the same level and from the same point of view. The interdependence of their economies and the interdisciplinarity of the economic, monetary and social problems, cannot but gradually convince the public opinions of the Member States of the ultimate logic of long-term integration.

Another factor to be reckoned with is what has been called *l'acquis communautaire*, i.e., the sectors or policies already integrated, of previously separate national sectors or policies. The agricultural policies of the Member

States, for instance, are now superseded by, and subordinated to the Common Agricultural Policy. As explained in the corresponding chapter of this book, it is a policy which could and should be reformed; but it cannot be evaded or rejected by any of the Member States as long as it remains a member. The External Relations of the nine Member States have also been integrated in many directions and areas. Moreover here the phenomenon of integration is significantly confirmed and amplified by the fact that the outside world and in particular the Asian and African and now the East European countries too have rapidly come to consider the Community as one large unit, and no longer regard it as nine separate states or powers. This is, as it were, a dual perception of European integration, from without and from within.

Finally one has to reckon with what is called the European dimension or *le fait communautaire* in the current processes of policy-making of the nine Member States. What this means is that those processes and the policies which result from them are already strongly influenced by, and moulded on, the general European orientation and guidance. Many of the national policies—the environment-policy is one example which comes to mind—are progressively aligned toward a common or Communitarian orientation. Moreover, in most of the case-studies contained in this book the authors have found that even where there is no agreed Community-policy, and *a fortiori* where there is, a gradual permeation of thinking between the national administrations and the national groups on the one hand and the Community, on the other, is taking place. The Management Committees of the Common Agricultural Policy are a good example of this permeation.

The mutation toward the Communitarian rationale in the national policy-making processes is not yet sufficiently acknowledged by the national opinions. One important reason for this ignorance is that national political circles try to conceal this mutation. This problem has been well described recently by a former European Commissioner, Sir Christopher Soames when he said that "the present malaise in the Community did not arise so much from its economic crisis as from the fact that member governments, especially those of the larger countries, refused to give it its due. These governments do not take into account the European dimension and tend to attribute all that is positive in it to their own action, and all that is negative to the Commission."[2] The case-studies, published here, on oil policy, agricultural policy, air policy, environment policy among others provide good examples of how serious misunderstandings between national opinions and the European Community have been caused by the conscious and subconscious omissions in the national information. Conscious because the government and their advisers are naturally anxious to maximize in the eyes of their public opinons, and specially of their electorates, the part which they think that they have played in a successful Communitarian action and conversely to use the Community as a scapegoat for many of their difficulties, or mistakes at home. Subconscious in the case of the national media, because both the national Press and radio-television are still professionally accustomed to the techniques of the popularization of the political issues by linking them with national Political leaders and personalities; and also because the media and specially the popular Press still think that large sectors of their audience respond favourably to facile criticisms of, and sarcasms toward, the Community. Examples of this kind of gratuitous and almost sublimal castigations of the Community by the popular Press are to be found everywhere, everyday.[3]

INTRINSIC DIFFERENCES BETWEEN THE POLICY-MAKING PROCESSES

> "Le gouvernement fédéral est plus juste et plus modéré dans sa marche que celui des Etats. Il y a plus de sagesse dans ses vues, plus de durée et de combinaison savante dans ses projets, plus d'habileté, de suite et de fermeté dans l'éxécution de ses mesures."
>
> Alexis de Tocqueville,
> *De la Démocratie en Amérique*, Vol. I, p. 222

Tocqueville's opinion that the Federalistic manner of governing (for this is how "la marche du gouvernement" should be translated in this context) is intrinsically superior to the manner of governing of the States, Republics, or *Länder* which form that Federation, is relevant *mutatis mutandis*, also for the comparison between the Community and the Member States. The same question asked in both cases is, that once a historical evolution has determined formerly separate states to join into one form or another of integrative Community, which of the two kinds of distinct ways of governing, the communitarian or the national, the comprehensive or the separate, the global or the particular alternatives, is likely to produce the more adequate solutions for everybody concerned?

In the case of the United States, Tocqueville, who incidentally was not a Federalist and who, on the contrary, had strong reservations against the political principles of Federalism, comes down in favour of the Federal way of governing. Particularly relevant to his ultimate judgement is that sentence in the text where he says that "the views of the Federal Government are wiser and its projects are more durable" than those of the States of the Union. This is an abstract judgement based on the intrinsic advantages of one higher vantage-point when compared with several lower ones, of one comprehensive perspective instead of several inner-oriented ones, of one long-term approach instead of several short-term ones.

In our case too, the general view of the study-groups expressed was that the higher vantage-point, the global aim and the long-term approach of the Community is, in the world of today, more conducive to the adequate solutions than the national ones. Indeed, a different concern was frequently expressed, namely, whether by now the West European vantage-point was still sufficiently comprehensive to provide the right solutions for contemporary transnational problems.

The two principal arguments in favour of the "European alternative" were the *potential effectiveness* of a European solution, and the *comprehensiveness of the assessment* of the European policy-makers as against the national ones.

The arguments for potential effectiveness (greater pool of common resources to draw from, larger market to act on, unified strength to oppose to competitive and rival forces, etc.) are too frequently repeated in all nine conclusions to need recapitulation here. But the word *potential* is operative insofar as, in most cases, it seemed that the European advantages had not been used.

It was generally agreed that in those cases in which the same issue affected the interests of all nine Member States more or less in the same way (though bearing in mind inevitable differences), and affected even more directly the interests of the Community as a whole, the initial assessment produced from the Communitarian point of view was both more far-reaching and more comprehensive. The proposals emanating from the Community, which could count, for their implementation on the more powerful means of action at its disposal, made more sense in the long term. They may at times have appeared somewhat Utopian, but even Utopian solutions are better than the limited, or sometimes contradictory solutions emerging from the national levels of assessment. In several cases, the study-groups which discussed the Communitarian and national policies expressed their regret that an initial Communitarian solution was watered down and modified in order to make it more acceptable to one or more of the Member States, and lost, thereby, much of its original Communitarian logic and purpose.[4]

For, the more the solutions proposed by the Community were to conserve their audacious European originality, the more could they appeal to the citizens of the Member States. These citizens have grown weary of the indecisiveness and of the repetitive banality in which their national politics have been stagnating since at least the end of the Second World War. Since then Western Europe as a whole and most of the European states in part have grown relatively weaker in the new international world. In consequence, their policy-making processes have been crippled by a decline of confidence in their own power—a phenomenon well known to Machiavelli. "Irresolute states" he writes in the *Discourses* "never choose the *right alternative* unless they are driven to it, because their weakness does not allow them to arrive at any decision where there is any doubt".[5]

The difficulty of making and applying a solution at the national level arises also from the fact that the policy-making processes of the government in modern industrial democracies are concerned mainly with short-term problems which require immediate solutions of the crisis management type; or, if they are concerned with national long-term courses of action, they are conditioned by and framed within sacrosanct traditional ways of thinking, precisely because they are national, and often severely restricted by national boundaries. Communitarian policy is, in contrast, long-term oriented and therefore more prepared to consider new and unrehearsed solutions.

Finally, there is a more practical and at the same time more fundamental question which is related to this incompatibility in principle, but not always in practice, between the predominantly long-term trend of European Community policy-making as distinct from the predominantly short-term trend of the policy-making of the nine national governments. This is the question whether intergovernmental consultations, or transnational "concertations" or "political cooperation", useful as they undoubtedly are for the management of Community affairs, can give birth to new European policies, or, in other words, to genuine alternatives to the national policies? Taking into consideration the fact that, for objective or subjective reasons, such intergovernmental consultations have shown how difficult it is to reconcile some of the national policies, and the fact that when agreement is reached it is more often reached on a compromise representing the lowest common denominator—the answer must be in the negative. This only confirms the wisdom of the Treaty of Rome which assigned the (European) policy-initiating function to the supranational institutions of the Community: the Commission at present and the directly elected European Parliament in the future.

COHERENCE AND VALIDITY OF THE POLICIES OF THE COMMUNITY

The studies here presented have concentrated on those policies recognized as of direct Communitarian origin and significance, regardless of whether they have been fully, or only partly, carried out, and even of whether, though still feasible, they were never applied, and thus belong to the genus "lost opportunities". For what really mattered from the point of view of this research was how original (and therefore different from the national policies) were the policies studied? How specifically Communitarian were they (and therefore designed for the general interests of the Community as a whole, and not for the national interests of one or more national states)? How feasible were they (i.e., how well prepared and presented, with how much consultation)? And how coherent were they as a political programme?

This being said, one still has to qualify these statements by distinguishing between the different kinds of Community policies, or alternatives, which were examined during the research. The first kind, namely the policies of the European Community which are already being implemented, is illustrated by the common agricultural policy. Here, as argued by the Rapporteur of the study-groups which discussed it, the alternative would be to abandon the policy already being applied, and either to modify it, or to fall back on nine, separate and conflicting, national policies. This was very difficult to envisage insofar as the integration which has already taken place in the last twenty odd years has essentially modified the previous national structures of at least six agricultures. One could not de-Europeanize and "renationalize" them now without running the risk of inflicting very serious mutual damage. Moreover, the study-group also agreed that the national agricultural policies, supposing that they could be reimplemented, would again reveal their initial disadvantages when compared with a common agricultural policy, even if modified.

The second kind of policy discussed can be defined as the "ideal-type" Community policy. These are policies proposed by the Commission, but which as in the case of the coal, textile, air and other policies, have not yet been decided upon by the Council of Ministers, or as in the case of the Energy policy before the Yom Kippur War, or the Economic and Monetary Union, have been rejected by the Council of Ministers—the "lost opportunities".

Among the "ideal-type" policies one finds also policies which have only recently been inaugurated by the Community although the Treaty of Rome had not foreseen them. The Treaty of Rome had not laid down a policy for Food Aid or for Raw Materials, or the Environment. (One might add that though the Treaty of Rome had foreseen a Common Commercial Policy, nevertheless the Community now conducts a wide ranging External Relations policy which goes well beyond the scope laid down by the Treaty for the Common Commercial Policy.)

The group which discussed the Raw Materials Policy was faced with the difficulty of deciding whether one could already speak of a fully fledged Communitarian policy, or whether it would be more accurate to speak merely of an attempt to formulate, or to prepare one. But its conclusions stressed the common position of all nine Member States, all of which are massive importers of raw materials from either developed (USA, Canada, etc.,) or underdeveloped (Third World) countries. Similarly, it was recognized that a Community Food Aid Policy had now been formulated even if it was still an "ideal-type" policy. Moreover, this policy was clearly different from the Food Aid policies of the Member States, especially in its motivations. But the present financial restrictions on Community Food Aid Policy meant that it could only be regarded as parallel and complementary to the national policies.

In the case of the Environment Policy, it was evident that, at least as far as the pollution of rivers and other waterways was concerned, the environment policies of the Member States had preceded that of the Community. Nevertheless, it was also evident that, for obvious reasons of transnational coordination, the Community Environment Policy, like the Food Aid Policy and the Raw Materials Policy could one day bring together the national policies into comprehensive Community policies with ampler aims, more powerful means and a greater intrinsic feasibility.

Looking first at all the policies examined in the case studies as a whole, i.e., from the point of view of their interrelatedness and common principles, the impression is that they could form together with the other policies, not analysed here, a European programme. When the individual policies themselves are examined together, they could provide a logical ensemble for a general European action of the future. Their common dual purpose can be said to be to preserve political freedom in Europe while at the same time devising new instruments and institutions to cope with the new European economic and social problems. This dual concern of any modern welfare state was bound to become a concern of the European Community, which, at its foundation, consisted of a relatively homogeneous group of advanced industrial states. Each of these states is imbued with the political principles of democracy, the social principle of the welfare state and the economic principles of the mixed economy. The ensemble of Community policies projects these principles at the broader European level and endows them with the vision, the scope and the power of the European rationale.

What seemed to many participants in the Conference to be a greater danger to the coherence of the Community policies was the growing disparity in the structural conditions both within the present group of Member States where for instance Ireland stands out, and, even more so, between the present mostly highly industrial states and the possible future Member States like Greece, Portugal and Spain. This increasing differentiation in the situation of the individual Member States was brought out and accentuated by the economic recession, with its characteristic symptoms of stagflation, which has for the last decade or so affected most industrial societies. This recession precipitated the differentiation within the Community of the Nine between the strong states, which grew stronger, and the weak states, which grew weaker, because of the crisis.

The entire feasibility of the programme, and of the policy-making process of the Community, is ultimately based on the readiness of the Member States to align themselves on a new joint action, from which further progress towards the integration of the previous national structures will result. In order to win this readiness it is necessary to reckon with a certain identity of structure and interest if not of all, at least of the majority of the Member States. To embark on further operations of integration involving states separated by yawning differences in economic and other kinds of development would be, from many points of view, counter-productive. First, the sharing of burdens would become intolerably unequal. Then the slow rhythm to be observed in the less developed and/or weaker states would deprive such operations of the speed which is essential to them, and would render their cost-effectiveness highly questionable. Thirdly, and perhaps above all, the tergiversations and procrastination which would accompany the operation of reconciling the opposing objective interests would probably result once again in the shelving of the entire project. This, alas, has already happened in the case of most of the "ideal-type" policies which were proposed by the Commission, but which the Council and the Member States have still not finally decided upon.

There is undoubtedly a causal relation between further territorial enlargement and the coherence, or conversely, the dilution of the integrative policies of the Community. The coherence of the policies reflects the consensual similarity of interests. Even if the ultimate interest of all Member States is to achieve integration in the future, regardless of the present differences and of the mutual sacrifices which this might entail, there are objective differences of structure which could render impossible agreement on some individual policies. The Community has learnt to accept such structural incompatibilities.

These new and growing difficulties in the policy-making process of the Community, led several participants in the Conference to wonder whether the history of the Community has now reached a turning point, namely, the moment when it is being constrained to abandon its basic neofunctional philosophy, with its belief in a spill-over from peripheral actions of economic integration to political and institutional decisions. Most reports concluded by expressing the hope that the directly elected European Parliament might revive the policy which they had analysed. Can this be interpreted also as a change from the neo-functionalist, ideological, approach to a new quest for political legitimacy and voluntarism?

This leads on to two observations—one of general import and the other narrower and more specific—on the policy-making processes of the Community.

The most important and general observation is that because the institutional framework of the European Community is still unfinished, its policy-making process does not have a European legitimacy and/or a European public accountability. The Member States draw their legitimacy from, and are accountable to, their national representative institutions, which, in turn, make the Council of Ministers, ultimately responsible to the same institutions.

The Commission of the European Community does not have either an institutional controller of European legitimacy or an institutional European interlocutor. This institutional imbalance explains the propensity of the Council of Ministers to procrastinate. On the other hand, the Commission, which is asked to assume responsibilities without being given the institutional power to carry them through, might, because of this institutional imbalance, have a tendency to escape into "great designs" only indirectly related to the pressing problems of the day; it might also have insufficient contact with the citizens and obtain insufficient information from them on their needs and sentiments. This problem, which was noticed in each of the case-studies, is discussed at greater length in a later section of these Conclusions. But the common observation which links together all these findings is that only direct elections to a European Parliament and, consequently, the legitimate supervision by a directly elected European Parliament of the political activities of the Community will bring into these activities the sense of participation of, and inspiration by, the public opinion which is now so needed in the policy-making processes of the Community.

From the narrower and more direct point of view of coherence in the preparations of the policies it was noted that because of the initial vertical structure of the Commission, divided in general Directorates with exclusive and limited competences, the individual policies or draft policies were insufficiently correlated with each other. This sometimes led to overlapping, sometimes to conflicts of attribution and sometimes to discrepancies of attitudes. Of late, the situation has improved. The policy-making processes of the Community, and of the Commission especially, have been gradually revised to allow for closer internal consultation and correlation. But still more needs to be done in this direction. Cases of the left hand not knowing what the right hand was doing, are still frequent. Several study-groups at the Conference reported that the policies which they had studied would benefit from more overall coordination.

Validity of the European alternatives

Most of the policies of the Community which were studied by the study-groups and afterwards discussed by the whole Conference, were recognized by the latter as *European Alternatives*, i.e., as specifically supranational solutions to problems which have become increasingly difficult to solve at the national level.

The studies found that the policies or draft policies prepared by the Commission (with the exception of the Raw Materials Policy which is still in gestation) provide clear definitions of valid courses of action for the European Community as a whole, which are different from, and offer European Alternatives, to the national policies in the same fields. The Commission has the merit of having provided the Council and the Parliament with a set of interrelated projected European policies which, when put together, might form a viable European programme of government. The approach of the Commission has been authentically European, the policies it has proposed reflect, in general, a global European inspiration and logic. They do not imitate the national policies, but look at the problems from points of view inaccessible to the national policy-makers. It was also significant to note that, more often than not, the European Parliament and the Economic and Social Committee have shared in the global European rationale of the policies proposed by the Commission, as against the national, or nationalistic logic of the Member States.

Nevertheless, this does not mean that all and each of the nine policies analysed displayed the same qualities and had equal merits. First of all, it was, of course, impossible to compare satisfactorily a policy which had already been tested and experimented with, like the Common Agricultural Policy, with a policy which was not even completely formulated as yet, like the Raw Materials Policy.

Then some policies are more distinctively European and argued in more characteristically European terms, than others, according to the problems which they pose. The problems of the European textile industry for instance, affect that industry in all highly industrialized countries. This is a universal phenomenon, precipitated by the fact that some underdeveloped countries seem to have a net advantage in the field of textile industry over highly industrial countries. The solution of this problem lies mostly in the common attitude of the latter as a whole, with the European Community proposing merely European variations on the major themes. Yet, since the study-group finished its report it became evident that the European Community has played a direct and most effective part in the realignment of the textile industry in all the Member States towards the new positions required by these world-problems.

Finally, not all nine policies which were analysed have had an equally felicitous preparation, i.e., prior assessment of their feasibility, institutional support and modalities of launching. Some, like the agricultural and coal policies, were based on a long consultation with European economic and political circles. They were provided from their very inception with adequate institutional frameworks and with effective instruments. But an important policy, like the Economic and Monetary Union, was announced in 1972 by the Council and the Summit as already in the making, without sufficient consultations with the economic and social interests and before the institutional framework, the instruments, and the technical means had been properly envisaged, let alone set up.

All in all the following questions were raised most frequently with regard to the approaches of the Commission.

Laissez faire and dirigisme

Many reports referred to the "ideological" differences within the Commission and wondered whether such differences were sometimes one of the reasons for the hesitating action of the Commission. It is known that some Member States, notably France, are nearer to the planning school of thought, whereas the Federal Republic of Germany is an outstanding representative of the neo-liberal school of thought. But these differences in schools of thought also cut across the top personnel of the Commission, the history of which abounds in instances of ideological arguments between Commissioners. The main bone of contention is whether to adopt a dirigist method of work and therefore to see the role of the Community as intervening in the economic activities as practically all welfare states' governments do now at the national level, or whether to let the market, in this case the "common market", work by itself while the Community limits its action to the creation of favourable financial and legal conditions for the functioning of the enterprises within the territory of the Community. But things are not so simple and clear cut. The Community is an association of welfare states and in these states intervention and control by the state in some sectors of industry is increasing rather than diminishing. And some policies of the Community, notably, the Common Agricultural Policy have, by necessity, many interventionist aspects.

It might be to the point to examine these apparently everlasting "ideological" differences from a more historical perspective and to ask whether they have not been more acutely felt when the Community was passing from what John Pinder has felicitously called the phase of "negative integration" (customs union and removal of non-tariff discrimination) to the phase of "positive integration", which requires major structural policies at Community level and the coordination of the monetary, budgeting and incomes policies of the Member States. In other words, would the laissez faire attitude be more suitable for the past phase—and should, on the contrary, any long- or medium-term economic policy be necessarily more "dirigist"?

Eurocentrism

The policies of the Community seemed sometimes to be concentrating too much on the exclusively European interest, the exclusively European aims and the exclusively European means. Yet in many of the policies analysed it is difficult to distinguish the exclusively European interests from the more general Western, or Atlantic interests, or from those of developed or industrial countries. Similarly, it was difficult to see how exclusively European means could suffice for the implementation of exclusively European aims. The discussion in the study-groups on Energy Policy and on the Aerospace Policy highlighted this very difficult problem. It was argued that in the first case the European policy should not be counted as self-contained and independent, but rather as a special European stand within the attitude of a community of interests of industrial countries larger than the European Community; in the second case it was argued that it should be recognized that the organized collaboration of the principal European air industries, backed and coordinated by the Community, with the American air industry, might probably be a more realistic objective.

Producers' bias

The policies proposed by the Commission seem to be concerned more often than not with the producers. This came out emphatically in the discussion of the Common Agricultural Policy—which has given birth, of late, to a transnational clash of views between the producers and the consumers in the nine

510

countries, while continuing as before, to give rise to a conflict between some of the nine countries. Politically, though, this has led, at any rate in some countries, to an increasing antipathy to the Community which is blamed by consumers for the rise in prices of basic food products. But in general and for two main reasons, all policies of the Community reflect a greater concern with the interest of producers, employers and, to a certain extent, labour than with those of the consumer. The first reason is that as an Economic Community it was and is naturally concerned with growth and with the conditions of production. The second reason is that the Council of Ministers, and especially some Member States, isolated the Commission in the sphere of economic administration, and took upon themselves exclusively all political and social tasks, including those of consultation with the social interests, which the national governments do consult at the national level for their own policy-making. A Consumers Consultative Committee of the Commission was set up only in 1975.

THE DIALECTICS OF THE EUROPEAN ALTERNATIVES

The plausibility of a political idea is in reality a dialectical process. The more plausible it is, the more support it gathers and the more support it gathers, the more plausible it becomes.

This proposition fully applies also to the European ideas or alternatives which we have examined. In the preceding sections we have concentrated especially on the intrinsic plausibility or adequacy of the nine ideas or alternatives. But, as evident from the chapters dealing with each of them, the study groups have been at the same time rather critical of the ways in which the Community has effected the second part of this dialectic operation, of how, in other words, it has tried to inform European opinion about the proposed policies and to gather support for them.

Of the three principal political institutions of the Community the Council of Ministers cannot be directly criticized for not publicizing the Communitarian ideas. This is so for the simple reason that it is not the Council which initiates the European ideas. In its capacity as the executive body, the Council is situated at the receiving end of the processes of policy-making of the Community. The Commission is the initiator and the proposer of the European policies.

Of course, the Council of Ministers (or the Summits, or now the European Council), takes initiatives, propose ideas, or appropriates for itself and modifies the initial projects of the Commission. To take a current example, the Council of Ministers and the European Council now advocate more openly than the Commission the further enlargement of the Community to include also Spain, Portugal and Greece. The Commission is now more concerned with the possible disintegrative effects which this further enlargement might have on the Community. Or, to take a past example, extensively examined in the relevant case-study in this book, it was the Council, and the Summit, which amplified the more cautious proposals of the Commission towards a Monetary and Economic Union; and it was the same bodies which speeded up its timing so that in 1972 it was announced, through the endorsement of the Werner Plan, that the Economic and Monetary Union would be put into effect within a few years. Yet neither European opinion at large, nor the European economic interests had been adequately consulted beforehand. The failure of the "Plan" was therefore to be expected. But this ill-prepared and ill-timed idea made the Community lose a great deal of credibility in the eyes of public opinion.

But the trouble with the Council of Ministers was that, for one reason or another, it has failed in its role of decision-maker. Almost unanimously, the reports of the nine study-groups found that the principal cause of this failure was the recurrent inability of the Council of Ministers to agree on the decisions to be taken.

Caught between its role as the supreme decision-making body of the Community and its composition as the grouping of the Ministers of the nine national governments, the Council of Ministers was often unable to adopt the policies proposed by the Commission. The causes of this inability arise in part from the divergences between Member States, based very often on the objective irreconcilability of interests and structures as analysed in a previous section of these conclusions. (See above; "Coherence of the European Alternatives").

On the other hand, it cannot be denied that a permanent obstacle lies in the fundamental reservations harboured by practically all national governments, for overriding reasons of national sovereignty, against committing themselves to the adoption of courses of action necessary to coherent and sustained communitarian policies. Frequently concerned with national political problems, which are sometimes merely party or electoral problems, the national governments, although agreeing in principle, and sometimes even having in the past used the "Summits" to make impressive pledges of future communitarian action, have, with few exceptions, delayed or emasculated or sometimes even rejected, many of the policies proposed by the Commission. Given the interrelatedness of these policies, if one of them was cancelled several other policies could not make further progress.

To be sure this has arisen mostly because of the clash of objective interests and structures. When a group of national governments gave its approval, for national reasons, to one or another policy proposed, the rest, for their own national reasons, opposed it—thus creating in almost every case a decisional deadlock.

The European Parliament cannot be blamed either for not having won public support for the European ideas, for the very reason that it was not directly elected and that it therefore lacked public credibility. Most of the study-groups expressed openly the hope that direct elections to the European Parliament and the directly elected Parliament itself would enable the Community to change and improve its processes of decision-making. Apart from leading to the birth of a new, fully fledged Parliament, the elections were regarded as an important exercise in the education and information of the citizens of Europe.

Regardless of the relations which will be created between the European Parliament and the national parliaments, and which will no doubt go through several phases and crises, the former will be the source of the legitimacy of the new decisions to be taken by the Community as a whole. The anti-Community forces in the Member States have successfully used their distrust of the "faceless Eurocrats", and have cast doubt over most of the initiatives of the Commission by accusing it of being unrepresentative and bureaucratic. The Council of Ministers and the national governments have often held in check the progress of integration, concerned as they have been with the objective differences between the interests of the nine countries, but also with the party-political and electoral impact which the steps taken by the Community might have in their respective countries. As long as representativeness was only by delegation from the national electorates, it was very difficult to visualize, for reasons already discussed in these conclusions, how a great, innovatory, progress could be made in European integration.

From the moment the European Parliament is elected, although its powers will naturally be limited by the power of the national parliaments, the Community decision-making processes will acquire a supranational legitimacy which they did not possess before. This does not mean that the two supranational institutions, the Commission and the Parliament, will always see eye to eye in all respects. But the experience of the present European Assembly, though it is comprised of national delegations, shows convincingly that the Assembly has more often than not expressed the Communitarian point of view of the Commission as against the multi-national objections of the Council of Ministers or of the Member States.

With this we come to the principal problem of the European dialectics— the problem of the present relationship of the institutions of the Community with European public opinion in general on the one hand, and on the other hand with the groups, or interests, of European society, in particular.

Several of the study-groups found that in the past, as in the present, the representatives of the European interests, which have by now formed European associations in most fields, have not participated in the policy-making of the Commission as much as they should or could. This gap in communication between the European institutions and the European interest groups with a common European viewpoint (not infrequently the points of view of the European interests and especially of the European consumers differ from those of the national interests with which the national governments "concert") has deprived some of the initiatives of the Commission of a natural support.

The European interest groups could buttress the initial proposals of the Commission with their own ideas and opinions as well as with the public support which they could mobilize. Yet the Commission has not addressed itself openly, and above the heads of the Member States, to these groups. Instead the Commission, pre-occupied by the institutional procedures of the Community, has in some cases watered down its own initial proposals so as to meet halfway, first the Committee of Permanent Representatives and then, the Council of Ministers. The result has been that, in some cases, the European Parliament, the Economic and Social Committee and the European interest groups have been shown hybrid proposals which, though they had lost some of their initial coherence, were still not acceptable to the Council. Several rapporteurs of the Conference were inclined to think that it would have been better in such cases to stick to the policy initially proposed by the Commission, and to consult more intensely with the other European institutions, European interest groups and with European Public Opinion at large.

These interest groups are more likely to participate in issues in which they are directly, socially and professionally, involved, rather than in the, to them, abstract, institutional or ideological, issues which appeal more to the political elements of public opinion at large. Many members of the Conference shared the point of view expressed by Professor Karl Deutsch, that after the failure of the attempt to construct an Economic and Monetary Union, the Community should now look in greater depth at the social problems which lie behind the economic problems, which in turn lie behind the monetary problems of the European Community. Professor Deutsch referred specifically to the fact that Monetary Union, if it ever comes about, will have to be accompanied by an adequate Community welfare policy—for all those living in the Community.

Indeed, seen in retrospect, perhaps the deepest, and most widespread criticism of the Commission put forward by the study-groups was that it had not succeeded in arousing the European interest groups at the European level to an awareness of the alternative European solutions to their specific problems. Whereas the Member States are directly influenced by, and actively consulting with, the national interests, the Community has not yet established a corresponding relation with the European interests, animated by the larger and newer European perspectives. In this respect the Community lags behind most of its Member States, which, each and all, use a variety of processes of "concertation" or of "social contracts" as indispensable methods for socio-economic policy-making. The Commission, in its most important role as the initiator of Communitarian policies, has not yet animated the still latent European social groups with ideas (like for instance "Community Welfare" or a Community-wide National Health Service) which could interest them, especially *qua* social groups, in this case *qua* European social groups.

Yet, it must be repeated here, these ideas are parallel to, but also different from, the major political ideas, like the European Union Integration or Federation, which are of general interest for European citizens, political parties and political circles at large. European social groups, that multitude of vertical and horizontal, latent and manifest, interest or value groups, which make up European (industrial) society, should be made aware of the range of those European policies which concern each of them directly and which can be rightly considered as useful alternatives to the exhausted national policies. These groups could also be stimulated by new approaches to the socio-economic problems in which they are professionally engaged, and which they now face daily, at the national level, in the guise of economic crises, social unrest and widespread violence.[6]

The new exchanges

European integration, is now immobilized between the stage, since long past, of the full sovereignty of its Member States, and the stage, not yet in sight, of a European Union. It needs ideas above all to get it moving again. These ideas should offer adequate and plausible alternatives to the doubly obsolete national solutions: obsolete, first, because the national problems have long

514

since been transformed into vast transnational problems, and obsolete again because in the meantime these states have joined the Community and must therefore henceforth devise their policies within the Communitarian framework. But the alternative European solutions, once they have been pinpointed, should also be made known to the only forces which could bring them into fruition, namely European public opinion where the general European political issues are concerned and European·interest groups where the separate European policies are concerned.

The joint research undertaken for this book has enabled Western European academics for the first time to examine more closely nine European policies, as alternatives to the national policies. The conclusion drawn from these discussions is that these policies have helped when applied and could have helped if applied, by all Member States, to problems which otherwise are or would still be unsolved at the national levels. But, at the same time, it appeared that the European policies suffer from the indifference in which they are regarded by those who should be most aware of them: European public opinion and the European interests. The failure of the European policies was, in almost every case, due to the breakdown in communication. Insofar as "politics is communication", that breakdown goes a long way to explain why a breakdown in European politics also occurred.

This book, to be published on the eve of the first direct elections to the European Parliament, is perhaps best viewed as an example of efforts which will henceforth be made to bridge the gap between the proposers of the new European policies and independent opinion in Europe. It is hoped that the new ground which it has helped to break will be, from now on, more intensively explored.

Undoubtedly after the directly elected European Parliament begins to make its formidable impact felt, European policy-makers and European opinion and interests will be able to join in a new form of direct exchanges of views. Those which have taken place, admittedly, only on an academic ground, between the practitioners of the European institution and the experts of the Universities for the preparation of this book have fully confirmed the benefits both sides could draw from this kind of mutual information.

I cannot put down my pen without thanking all the authors from both sides, as well as Mr. Lyng, the indefatigable editor at Sÿthoff, the publishers, for the effort they have made to bring this novel form of collaboration to a successful outcome.

NOTES

1. There were three reasons why these policies, or only nine policies were selected for the study on "European Alternatives": a) because these were precise community policies: there are fields of policy-making, like for instance social policy, where it would be more difficult to assess the specificity of the attitude of the community; b) because the choice had to be impartial and avoid selecting the most dynamic Community policies, like for instance External Relations and c) because of the availability or lack of availability for one reason or another, of data and documentation.

515

2. *The Times*, 10 November 1977.

3. My eyes fell, as I was writing, on the following extract from the travel-column (an essentially neutral part of a newspaper) of the London *Evening News* (an essentially neutral and popular tabloid) of 15 November 1977. "There is much more to Brussels than its army of faceless EEC bureaucrats building butter mountains and draining wine lakes behind the equally faceless façades of their modern offices. And although they have helped to make it the most expensive city in Europe . . . there is still plenty to do and to eat . . ."

4. See below, pp. 513–4.

5. *Discourses*, I, 38 (my italics).

6. See also my "Centripetal politics", London, Hart-Davis, MacGibbon, 1975.

SELECTED BIBLIOGRAPHY

Agricultural policy

Agence Europe 2176 and 2205.

Assilec, *Assilec Editorial*; J. G. Becue, Bill 1/10/76 No. 368; Bill 1/10/76 No. 372; Bill 1/10/76 No. 375; Bill 1/10/76 No. 377.

Barton, A. P., Young, S. "The structure of the dairy industry in the EEC." *Oxford Agrarian Studies* (1975) 2: 181–200.

Baudin, J. "The common agricultural policy: an appraisal of the balance sheet." *Common Market Law Review* (March 1976).

B.E.U.C. (European Bureau of Consumers Unions). *Comments of consumers on the proposals for fixing agricultural prices for the period 1977/78*, submitted during hearing by the Agricultural Committee of the European Parliament at Luxembourg on 15 March 1977.

B.E.U.C. "B.E.U.C. contribution to preparation of opinions of the Consumers Contact Committee on agricultural matters." *CIRC* No. 24 (1976) (based on questionnaire CCC/46/76).

B.E.U.C. "*Who are we?*" (31 December 1976), Brussels.

Broders, M. "La crise du marché de la viande bovine, origines et perspectives d'avenir." *Revue du Marché Commun* (1975) 185: 203–220.

Bublot, G. *Equilibrium of the milk and beef markets in EEC. General problematic. Report presented to the Committee for research into European unification* (June 1977), Brussels.

Commission of the European Communities:

- *Fifth financial report on the European Fund for Agricultural Orientation and Guarantees, year 1975* (25 October 1976) COM (76) 533 final, Brussels.
- *Financial consequences of proposals for agricultural prices and related measures 1977/78* (Communication of the Commission to the Council) COM (77) 150 final (11 February 1977), Brussels.
- *European Documentation*: "The agricultural policy of the European Community." (1976/5), Brussels.
- *European Documentation*: "The professional agricultural organisations and EEC." (1969).
- *News of the common agricultural policy*: "The common agricultural policy operating on behalf of the farmers and consumers during a period of economic instability." (June 1975), Brussels.
- *The situation of agriculture in the Community* (1976 Report) (January 1977), Brussels, Luxembourg.
- *Action Programme for 1977/1980 aimed at progressive stabilization of the milk market* (Presented by the Commission to the Council) COM (76) 300 final (6 July 1976), Luxembourg.
- *Proposals of the Commission regarding fixing of prices for certain agricultural*

products and certain related measures 1–2, COM (77) 100 final (February 1977), Brussels.

– Council of the European Communities *Press Communiqué* (25 and 26 April).

Committee of Professional Agricultural Organizations of the European Community (COPA). *Comments of COPA and COGECA on the proposals contained in the draft regulations and decisions drawn up by the Commission for implementation of its "Action Programme for 1977/1980 aimed at progressive stabilization of the milk market"* Pr (76) 19, CP (76) 6 (5 November 1976), Brussels.

Committee of Professional Agricultural Organizations of the European Community (COPA). *First reactions of COPA to the proposals of the Commission regarding agricultural prices for the 1977/1978 season, and certain related measures* (COM/77 100 final) Pr (77) 5 (24 February 1977), Brussels.

Consumers Contact Committee. *Consumers Committee for contact with the European Community*, Euroform "Europe from day to day" (4 January 1977), Brussels.

Consumers Contact Committee. *Draft CC opinion on the CAP* CCC 126 (1976).

Consumers Contact Committee. *Proposals for CCC views on Common Agricultural Policy* CCC 127 (1976) (7 October 1976), Brussels.

"Dossiers (Les) d'Economie Agricole: Le Lait." *Economie Agricole* (1977) 2: 7–31.

Economic and Social Committee (C.E.S.): opinions of C.E.S. on:

– *Proposed regulations by the Council setting up a system of premiums for non-marketing of milk and dairy products, and conversion of herds of beef cattle for dairy products* (30 September 1976), Brussels.

– *Proposed regulations by the Council regarding a co-responsibility levy and measures intended to expand the markets in the milk and dairy products* (24 November 1976), Brussels.

– *The proposed Council (EEC) regulations temporarily suspending certain national and Community aid in the milk and dairy products sector* (24 November 1976), Brussels.

– *Proposed regulations by the Council regarding a tax on certain fats* (24 November 1977), Brussels.

– *Commission's proposal to the Council regarding fixing of prices for certain agricultural products, and certain related measures* (24 February 1977), Brussels.

– *Balance-sheet of Common Agricultural Policy* (17 July 1975), Brussels.

– *Action Programme for 1977/1980 aimed at progressive stabilization of the milk market* (Submitted by the Commission to the Council) (30 September 1976), Brussels.

– *The Common Agricultural Policy in the international context—consequences and arrangements which may arise therefrom* (27 January 1977), Brussels.

"Evolution récente du marché mondial de la viande bovine." Banque Française et Italienne pour l'Amerique du Sud. *Etudes Economiques* (1976) 8: 1–23.

Giraudy, J-L. "The impact of the lobbies." *Common Market Review* (1976): 233–236.

"Lait écrémé en poudre: situation et perspectives." *Bulletin Mensuel Economie et Statistique* 25 (1976) 7–8: 29–34.

Marché Communitaire Nos. 396, 397, 399, Brussels.

Meynaud, J., Sidjanski, D. *The pressure-groups in the European Community 1958–1968* (Publications of the Institute of Sociology) (1971), Brussels.

Muller, F. *The agricultural policy. The surpluses of agricultural products in the Community as regards beef and dairy products. Report presented to the Committee for research into European unity* (November 1976), La Panne.

National Federation of the Dairy Industry. *Rapport Moral* presented by Francis Lepatre, Chairman, to the 1976 ordinary annual general meeting, Paris.

"Produits laitiers: un marché malade de ses trop bons rendements." *Europolitique* (1976) 371: 11.

"Recent Developments and prospects on world beef market. Expansion in world meat trade forecast." *Agra Europe* (1977) 721: M3–M7.
Sidjanski, D., in collaboration with T.H. Ballmer-Cao. *The trades unions and the French pressure-groups as they face European integration, in France and the EEC countries* (J. Rideau, ed.) L.G.D.J. (1975), Paris.

Energy policy

Agence de l'O.C.D.E. pour l'énergie nucléaire. *Uranium. Ressources, production et demande comprenant d'autre données relatives au cycle de combustible nucléaire* (drawn up in co-operation with l'Agence Internationale de l'Energie Atomique) O.C.D.E. (1976), Paris.
Alting von Geusau, F.A.M. (ed.). *Energy in the European Communities* (1975), Leyden.
Bailey, R. *The European Community in the World* (1973), London.
F. Ebert Stiftung. *Zukunftsorientierte Energie- und Rohstoffpolitik* (Internationaler Fachkongress, Bonn, 13–14 Oktober 1975) (1976), Bonn–Bad Godesberg.
Energy Policy (European Communities Secondary Legislation. Part 7) (1972), London.
Mauksch, M. *Energy and Europe. EEC energy policy and economy in the context of the world energy crisis* (1975), Brussels.
Mulfinger, A. *Auf dem Weg zur gemeinsamen Mineralölpolitik. Die Interventionen der öffentlichen Hand auf dem Gebiet der Mineralölindustrie in Hinblick auf den gemeinschaftlichen Mineralölmarkt* (1972), Berlin.
Organisation de Cooperation et de Developpement Economiques. *Perspectives énergétiques jusqu'en 1985. Evaluation des problèmes et des politiques énergétiques à long terme: un rapport du secrétaire général* (1974) O.C.D.E., Paris.
Organisation de Cooperation et de Developpment Economiques. *Perspectives énergétiques mondiales. Réévaluation des évolutions à long terme et des politiques dans le domaine énergétique. Rapport du Secrétaire général* (1977) O.C.D.E., Paris.
Ray, G. F. *Western Europe and the energy crisis* (1975), London.
Uranium Institute. *Uranium supply and demand. Proceedings of an international symposium, London, 15–17 June 1976* (Michael J. Spriggs, ed.) (1976), London.
Workshop on Alternative Energy Strategies. *Energy: global prospects 1985–2000* (1977), New York.

Coal policy

"C.E.E.: situation du charbon en 1975." *Europe-Energie* (1976) 24, Brussels.
Communautés Européennes. Commission. *Orientations à moyen terme pour le charbon 1975–1985* J.O. des Communautés Européennes No. C 22 (1975).
Institution of Electrical Engineers. *International conference on Energy, Europe and the 1980s. 6–9 May 1974* (1974), London.
Parlement Européen. Commission de l'Energie, de la Recherche et de la Technologie. *Rapport sur la proposition de la Commission des Communautés européennes sur "les orientations à moyen terme pour le charbon 1975–1985"*, Doc. P.E. 147/75 (1975), Luxembourg.
Pire, E. "Le prospettive del carbone nella CEE" (estratto da "Revue dela Societe d'Etudes et d'Expansion") *Mercurio* 19 (1976) 7: 13–19.
Reichert, K. "Eine Kohlenwirtschaftspolitik für die Europäische Gemeinschaft." *Glückauf*, (1975) 3: 123–130.

Commodities and raw materials

Agence Européenne d'Informations. *Le Dossier des matières premières* (1975), Brussels.
Bouvier-Ajam, M. *Matières premières et coopération internationale* (1976), Paris.
Brookings Institution. *Trade in primary commodities: conflict or cooperation? A tripartite report by fifteen economists from Japan, the European Community and North America* (1974), Washington.
Callot, F. *Die Mineralrohstoffe der Welt. Produktion und Verbrauch* (1976), Essen.
Charnley, A. H. *The EEC. A Study in applied economics* (1973): 96–128, London.
Connelly, P., Perlman, R. *The Politics of scarcity. Resource conflicts in international relations* (1975), London.
Conseil Economique et Social (France). *Les Ressources mondiales et l'économie française.* Avis adopté par le 15 Janvier 1975 (1975), Paris.
Corbet, H. *Raw materials. Beyond the rhetoric of commodity power* (1975), London.
"Cuivre: Les résultats de la conférence de Lima constituent une évolution statisfaisante pour producteurs et consommateurs de cuivre." *Telex-Afrique* 3 (1975) 46: B1–B3.
Hager, W. *Europe's economic security. Non-energy issues in the international political economy* (1976), Paris.
Harris, S. *The World commodity scene and the Common Agricultural Policy* (1975), Ashford, Kent.
Houthakker, H. S. *Les Ressources globales dans un monde interdépendant* (1976), Lausanne.
Michaelis, H. *Europäische Rohstoffpolitik* (1976), Essen.
Redman, C. "Cuivre: un cas test pour les relations Nord-Sud." *Europolitique* (1976) 361.

Food aid policy

"Aide (L') alimentaire de la C.E.E." *Problèmes Economiques* (1975) 1.405: 18–20.
Bauer, H. "Agrarwirtschaftliche Auswirkungen der Nahrungshilfe an Entwicklungsländer. Evaluerungen in Bangla Desh, Indonesien, Pakistan und Sri Lanka." *Ernährungsumschau* 22 (1975) 9: 270–275.
Dreesmann, B. "Zur Arbeit der Freedom from Hunger Campaign und der deutschen Welthungerhilfe." *Zeitschrift für ausländische Landwirtschaft* 15 (1976) 3: 381–390.
"Europe and the world without. Policies and programmes of the European Community and their impact on world poverty." *OXFAM Public Affairs Report* (1977) 3.
"Face à la crise alimentaire." Dossier. (Par) A. H. Boerma (e.a.) *Courrier de l'Association* (1974) 27: 14–51.
"Food Aid: The Commission's three year programme." *Bulletin of the European Communities* (1976) 9, paras. 1404–1406: 18–21.
Isenman, P. J., Singer, H. W. "Food aid: disincentive effects and their policy implications." *Economic Development and Cultural Change* 25 (1977) 2: 205–237.
Jones, D. "Food interdependence." *ODI Review* (1975) 2: 25–37.
Kitzinger, U. *Europe's wider horizons* (1975), London.
Koffsky, N., Skellie, D., Kotamraju, P., Bachman, K., Nweke F., Rao, M. S., Gavan, J. *Meeting food needs in the developing world; the location and magnitude of the task in the next decade* (Research Report, International Food Policy Institute, USA) (1976) No. 1.
Mellor, J. W. "Food aid and long-run world food population balances." *Columbia Journal of World Business* (1975) 3: 29–35.

"Nahrungsmittelhilfe der Europäischen Gemeinschaft. Alibi für Uberschuss-produktion?" *DIW Wochenbericht* 42 (1975) 51–52: 421–424.
"Nouvel accord international sur le blé et aide alimentaire communautaire." *Union Agriculture* (1971) 324: 31–36.
Singh, M. *Problems of hunger and malnutrition in developing countries* (1975), Vancouver.
Soper, T. "The E.E.C. and aid to Africa." *International Affairs* (1975) 3: 463–477.
United Kingdom. Ministry of Overseas Development. "British Aid and the relief of malnutrition. Report on the ODA advisory committee on protein." *Overseas Development Paper* (1975) 2.
Weiss, T. G., Jordan, R. S. *The world food conference and global problem solving* (1976), New York.
Witt, M. "Die Konvention von Lomé—eine ernährungspolitische Verplichtung der EG." *Ernährungsumschau* 22 (1975) 8: 227–234.
"The World Food Problem: A dossier." *Courier* (1976) 35: 28–50.
"The World Food Program. Multilateral food aid—a progress report." *Agriculture Abroad* 32 (1977) 1 (suppl.).

Air industry policy

"Aéronautique en Europe, espoirs et blocages d'une industrie essentielle." *Vision* (1976) 70: 44–55.
Forestier, J. "Une industrie aéronautique indépendante: un luxe pour l'Europe de demain?" *Transports* (1976) 210: 79–86.
"Industrie aéronautique et Europe." *Etudes* (1975): 497–518.
"Politique industrielle dans le domaine aéronautique." *Europe Documents* (1977) 935.
"Programme d'action pour l'aéronautique européenne." *Les Annales du Marché Commun* 18 (1975) 5–6: 13–20.
"Programme d'action pour l'industrie aéronautique européenne." *Europe Documents* (1975) 865: 1–7.

Textile policy

Comité de coordination des industries textiles de la Communauté Economique Européenne. "L'Industrie textile de la C.E.E. et l'économie mondiale—E.E.C. textile industry and world economy." *Comitextil* (1972), Brussels.
"The European Textile Industry." *European Trends* (1976) 48: 14–27.
Gesamtverband der Textilindustrie in der Bundesrepublik Deutschland. *Auf dem Weg zu einer europäischen Textilpolitik. Vorträge und Diskussionen anlässlich der Jahreshauptversammlung Gesamttextil vom 2. und 3. Dezember 1971 in Bonn* (1971), Frankfurt.
Spinelli, A. "La politique sectorielle textile de la C.E.E. et ses développements face à l'élargissement du Marché Commun—The textile sector of the E.E.C. and its development resulting from the enlargement of the Community." *Comitextil Information* 73/1 (1973).
Telex Afrique. *Textiles: la politique extérieure de la Communauté Européenne. Etude réalisée par Télex Afrique et Télex Meditéranée s.1. direction de Laurence Talichet.*" (1976), Brussels.
Warnecke, S. J., Suleiman, E. N. (eds.) *Industrial policies in Western Europe* (1975), New York.

Environment policy

Amaducci, S. "Fresh and sea waters of the EEC: Common Solutions?" *Sedit. Diritto Comunitario e degli Scambi Internazionali* (1975) 4: 513–539.
Bungarten, H. H. "Umweltpolitische Aspekte einer europäischen Integration." *Verteilung der wirtschaftlichen Kräfte im Raum. Bericht der Facharbeitsgruppe* (1976): 165–198, Baden-Baden.
Bungarten, H. H. "Zur Praxis der Abwasserabgabe und ergänzender Instrumente in der Europäischen Gemeinschaft." *Informationen zur Raumentwicklung* (1976) 8: 391–403.
Communautés Européennes. Commission. *L'Etat de l'environnement* (1977), Luxembourg.
Communautés Européennes. Commission. *Programme d'action des Communautés européennes en matière d'environnement (1977–1981)* (1976), Luxembourg.
Communautés Européennes. Conseil. *Résolution . . . et des représentants des gouvernements des Etats membres, réunis au sein du Conseil, du 17 mai 1977, concernant la poursuite et la réalisation d'une politique et d'un programme d'actione des Communautés européennes en matière d'environnement* (1977), Luxembourg.
Douwes, B. J. "Water als object van milieubeleid in de Europese Gemeenschappen." *S.E.W., Tijdschrift voor Europees en Economisch Recht* (1975) 5: 308–330.
Environmental pollution control. Technical, economic and legal aspects. Ed. by Allan D. Mcknight, Pauline K. Marstrand, T. Craig Sinclair (1974), London.
McLoughlin, J. *The Law and practice relating to pollution control in the member states of the European Communities: a comparative survey* (1976), London.
Riegel, R. "Um weltschutzaktivitäten der Europäischen Gemeinschaften auf dem Gebiete des Wasserrechts und deren Bedeutung für das innerstaatliche Recht." *Deutsches Verwaltungsblatt* 92 (1977) 2/3: 82–89.

Economic and monetary union

Dahmen, E. "European Monetary Union—A look at the possible consequences." *Skandinaviska Enskilda Banken Quarterly Review* (1973) 1: 13–19.
Denton, G. (ed.) *Economic and Monetary union in Europe* (1974), London.
Hellmann, R. *Europäische Wirtschafts- und Währungsunion. Eine Dokumentation* (1972), Baden-Baden.
Hellmann, R., Molitor, B. *Textsammlung zur Wirtschaft und Währungsunion der E.G.* (1973), Baden-Baden.
Kapteyn, P. J. G. (ed.) *The Economic law of the member states in an economic and monetary union* [repr. *C.M.L.R.* 13 (1976): 145–227] (1976), Leyden.
Krause, L. B., Salant, W. S. (eds.) *European monetary unification and its meaning for the United States* (1973) Washington D.C.
Magnifico, G. *European monetary unification* (1973), London.
Readman, P. (e.a.) *The European Money Puzzle* (1973), London.
Willgerodt, H. (e.a.) *Wege und Irrwege zur europäischen Währungsunion* (1972), Freiburg.